Clinical Mental Health Counseling
FUNDAMENTALS OF APPLIED PRACTICE

Donna S. Sheperis
Walden University

Carl J. Sheperis
Lamar University

Boston   Columbus   Indianapolis   New York   San Francisco   Upper Saddle River
Amsterdam   Cape Town   Dubai   London   Madrid   Milan   Munich   Paris   Montréal   Toronto
Delhi   Mexico City   São Paulo   Sydney   Hong Kong   Seoul   Singapore   Taipei   Tokyo

Vice President and Editorial Director: Jeffery W. Johnston
Senior Acquisitions Editor: Meredith Fossel
Editorial Assistant: Janelle Criner
Vice President, Director of Marketing: Margaret Waples
Senior Marketing Manager: Darcy Betts Prybella
Production Project Manager: Jennifer Gessner
Development Project Management: Aptara®, Inc.
Manufacturing Buyer: Pat Tonneman
Senior Art Director: Jayne Conte
Cover Designer: Karen Noferi
Cover Photo: © johnny-ka, Fotolia
Media Project Manager: Noelle Chun
Full-Service Project Management: Aptara®, Inc.
Composition: Aptara®, Inc.
Printer/Binder: LSC Communications
Cover Printer: LSC Communications
Text Font: ITC Garamond Std 10/12

Credits and acknowledgments for material borrowed from other sources and reproduced, with permission, in this textbook appear on the appropriate page within the text.

Every effort has been made to provide accurate and current Internet information in this book. However, the Internet and information posted on it are constantly changing, so it is inevitable that some of the Internet addresses listed in this textbook will change.

Library of Congress Cataloging-in-Publication Data

Clinical mental health counseling : fundamentals of applied practice/
[edited by] Donna S. Sheperis, Carl J. Sheperis.—1e.
    p.; cm.
Includes bibliographical references.
ISBN-13: 978-0-13-708370-1
ISBN-10: 0-13-708370-X
  I. Sheperis, Donna, editor of compilation.   II. Sheperis, Carl, editor
of compilation.
  [DNLM: 1. Counseling. 2. Mental Health. 3. Models, Psychological.
WM 55]
  RC467 2015
  616.89—dc23
                       2013042183

ISBN 10:   0-13-708370-X
ISBN 13: 978-013-708370-1

This text is dedicated to my partner, husband, and the coauthor of our lives, Dr. Carl Sheperis. Thanks for trudging the road with me.

—DONNA S. SHEPERIS

To my sun, moon, and stars. Thanks for lighting my way.

—CARL J. SHEPERIS

ABOUT THE EDITORS

Donna S. Sheperis earned her PhD in Counselor Education from the University of Mississippi. A core faculty member in the Mental Health Counseling Program of Walden University, Dr. Sheperis is a Licensed Professional Counselor, National Certified Counselor, Certified Clinical Mental Health Counselor, and Approved Clinical Supervisor with over 20 years of experience in clinical mental health counseling settings. She has served as cochair of the ACA Ethics Committee and is involved with the Association for Assessment and Research in Counseling, the Association for Humanistic Counseling, and the Association for Counselor Education and Supervision. Dr. Sheperis has authored numerous articles in peer-reviewed journals in addition to publishing chapters in edited texts. Dr. Sheperis presents regularly on topics related to clinical mental health counseling and has received several awards for her teaching, scholarship, and research. Her primary areas of interest include clinical mental health counselor development, assessment of mental health and coping, counseling ethics, and supervision.

Carl J. Sheperis is the chair of Counseling and Special Populations at Lamar University. He has over 20 years of clinical experience in the assessment and treatment of behavioral disorders and psychopathology in infancy and childhood. Aside from being a university administrator, Dr. Sheperis teaches master's-level courses in mental health counseling, assessment, and research. He is the lead editor of *Counseling Research: Quantitative, Qualitative, and Mixed Method Designs* for Pearson. Dr. Sheperis is a member of the board of directors of the National Board for Certified Counselors. He has received the ACA Counselor Educator Advocacy Award, the Outstanding Counselor Educator Pre-tenure Award from the Southern Association for Counselor Education and Supervision, and the Donald Hood Research Award from the Association for Assessment and Research in Counseling. Dr. Sheperis has authored over 100 articles, book chapters, encyclopedia entries, and books. He presents regularly on topics related to clinical mental health counseling.

ABOUT THE AUTHORS

Mary L. Bartlett

Mary L. Bartlett earned her doctorate in Counselor Education from Auburn University and is an independent behavioral health consultant, suicidologist, and international speaker. She formerly served as suicide prevention and risk consultant to a national treatment center for eating disorders and has been an assistant professor. With 15 years of clinical and teaching experience, she is an authorized trainer for the American Association of Suicidology and the Suicide Prevention Resource Center, and is a qualified master resilience trainer. Her professional credentials include certification as a National Certified Counselor, a Licensed Professional Counselor, a certified state counseling supervisor, a certified family life educator, and a military family life consultant. Dr. Bartlett has authored numerous articles in peer-reviewed journals in addition to publishing chapters in edited texts; has received awards for her teaching, scholarship, and research; and presently serves Department of Defense leadership on suicide- and resilience-related matters.

Ioana Boie

Ioana Boie earned her PhD in Counselor Education from the University of Texas at San Antonio. She is a core faculty member in the Clinical Mental Health Counseling program and Counselor Education and Supervision with Marymount University, and is also a Licensed Professional Counselor (Texas) and a National Certified Counselor. She has served as secretary for the Texas Counselors for Social Justice and is involved with the National Eating Disorders Association, Association for Creativity in Counseling, Texas Counseling Association, and Association for Counselor Education and Supervision. Dr. Boie has published several articles in peer-reviewed journals and presented at numerous professional conferences on topics related to diversity of eating disorders and body image, clinical supervision, immigration issues, and equine-facilitated therapy.

Caroline S. Booth

Caroline S. Booth is an associate professor at North Carolina A&T State University. A marriage and family counselor by training, she now teaches and supervises in the Mental Health Counseling (Clinical) program. Dr. Booth graduated from The University of North Carolina at Greensboro where she earned her MS in Community Counseling, EdS in Marriage and Family Counseling, and PhD in Counseling and Counselor Education. Currently, Dr. Booth is a National Certified Counselor, Licensed Professional Counselor in North Carolina, Distance Credentialed Counselor, and Approved Clinical Supervisor. She is the author of numerous publications and professional presentations relating to her research interests in wellness across the life span, gender issues, family counseling, and the effective use of technology in counseling.

Matthew R. Buckley

Matthew R. Buckley earned his master's in Community Counseling and EdD in Counselor Education from Idaho State University. He served as the former program director for the Master of Science in Mental Health Counseling program for Walden University and is currently a core faculty member for the program. Dr. Buckley is a Licensed Clinical Mental Health Counselor, Licensed Professional Counselor, National Certified Counselor, Approved Clinical Supervisor, and a Distance Credentialed Counselor with over 20 years of experience in clinical mental health counseling settings. He serves as an exam committee member for the National Clinical Mental Health Counseling Examination (NCMHCE) for the National Board for Certified Counselors and has worked extensively with licensure and credentialing issues through most of his career. Dr. Buckley's primary areas of interest include counselor development, group counseling, licensure and credentialing, and clinical supervision.

Melanie Bullock

Melanie Bullock is an assistant professor in the Counseling and Development program at Lamar University. Her clinical experience includes working with adjudicated youth through the Texas Youth Commission, with victims and perpetrators of relationship violence, and in the clinics at the University of North Texas. Dr. Bullock's research interests include working with at-risk youth and technology in counseling. She has served as president of the Texas Association for Counselor Education and Supervision and has held board positions with the American College Counseling Association, Texas College Counseling Association, and Chi Sigma Iota. Dr. Bullock has presented on various counseling-related topics at state, national, and international conferences.

Catherine Y. Chang

Catherine Y. Chang, PhD, LPC, NCC, is a professor at Georgia State University and program coordinator for its Counselor Education and Practice doctoral program. She has published and presented in the areas of social justice and advocacy, multicultural counseling competence, privilege and oppression issues, and supervision. Additionally, she was the lead editor for the book *Professional Counseling Excellence Through Leadership and Advocacy* and the lead editor for the special issue on social justice of the *Counselor Education and Supervision* journal. She has held several leadership positions, including president of Chi Sigma Iota (2009–2010) and vice president for the Asian and Pacific Islander American concerns of the Association for Multicultural Counseling and Development (2010–2013). She is the recipient of the American Counseling Association (ACA) Research Award, the ACA Counselor Educator Advocacy Award, the Association for Assessment in Counseling and Education (AACE) MECD Research Award, the Pretenure Counselor Educator Award from the Southern Association for Counselor Education and Supervision, and the Alumni Excellence Award from the Department of Counseling and Educational Development at The University of North Carolina at Greensboro. She serves on the editorial boards of the journals *Counselor Education and Supervision*, *Measurement and Evaluation in Counseling and Development*, and *Counseling Outcome Research and Evaluation*.

R. J. Davis

R. J. Davis, PhD, LPC-Intern, is an assistant professor at Lamar University. Dr. Davis's teaching career began in secondary education with a decade of experience working with, and teaching multiple subjects to, diverse populations. His experience as a counselor comes from his service as a university career counselor and later as a director of a counseling and training clinic. Dr. Davis is active in service to the profession in his current role as president of Texas Career Development Association and president elect of Texas Counselors for Social Justice. He is also an active member of state and national counseling associations and has presented at state and national level conferences, including the Texas Counseling Association, Texas School Counselor Association, Texas College Counseling Association, American Counseling Association, Association for Counselor Education and Supervision, and Association for Assessment and Research in Counseling.

Laura R. Haddock

Laura R. Haddock received her PhD in Counselor Education from the University of Mississippi. Dr. Haddock has been a counselor educator since 2005, supported by more than 20 years as a mental health counselor. She serves as core faculty for the Counselor Education and Supervision program at Walden University and is a Licensed Professional Counselor, National Certified Counselor, and Approved Clinical Supervisor. Dr. Haddock is an active counseling professional and has served on the Mississippi State Board of Examiners for Licensed Professional Counselors and the executive boards for the Mississippi Counseling Association and Mississippi Licensed Professional Counselors Association. Dr. Haddock routinely presents research at the state, national, and international levels and publishes scholarly writings for professional counseling journals and textbooks. She serves as an editorial board member for the *Journal of Counseling Research and Practice* and the *Tennessee Counseling Association Journal* and has won awards for her teaching and research. Her research interests include counselor wellness and secondary trauma, spirituality, crisis response, cultural diversity, and supervision.

Stacy Henning

Stacy Henning is assistant professor in the Professional Counseling Department at Webster University. She holds a PhD in Counselor Education from CACREP-accredited doctoral and master's programs and is a Licensed Professional Counselor and an Approved Clinical Supervisor through NBCC. Dr. Henning is an active member of ACA committees, a site team chair for the Council for Accreditation of Counseling and Related Educational Programs (CACREP), and a practicing professional counselor in St. Louis. Current research includes ethics in counselor education, diversity and religion and spirituality in counseling, women in life transition, teaching efficacy in counselor education, and neurobiology and counseling efficacy.

K. Dayle Jones

K. Dayle Jones is associate professor and coordinator of the Mental Health Counseling program at the University of Central Florida. Dr. Jones has been in the counseling field for 22 years and is a Florida Licensed Mental Health Counselor (LMHC). She earned her master's in Education and Human Development from Rollins College and her PhD in Counselor Education from the University of South Carolina. Dr. Jones is very active in the areas of scholarship, research, and professional service. She has published two textbooks: *Introduction to the Profession of Counseling* and *Assessment Procedures for Counselors and Helping Professionals*. Dr. Jones's research interests include assessment, diagnosis, and treatment of mental disorders. She served as chair of the American Counseling

Association's DSM-5 Proposed Revisions Task Force and is column editor for *Counseling Today*'s "Inside the DSM-5."

Monica Leppma

Monica Leppma is a core faculty member in the counseling program (community and school tracks) at West Virginia University. She earned her PhD in Counselor Education from the University of Central Florida. Dr. Leppma is a Licensed Mental Health Counselor and a National Certified Counselor with over 10 years of experience in clinical mental health counseling and three years as a supervisor. She is involved with the Association for Spiritual, Ethical, and Religious Values in Counseling as well as the Association for Counselor Education and Supervision. Dr. Leppma has authored several peer-reviewed articles and serves on the editorial board for *Counseling and Values*. She presents regularly at the state and national levels on topics related to mental health and school counseling. Her primary areas of interest include counselor development and competency, as well as issues affecting children.

Todd F. Lewis

Todd F. Lewis, PhD, is an associate professor of counseling and counselor education at The University of North Carolina at Greensboro. He earned his doctorate in Counseling and Counselor Education and Supervision at Kent State University. He is a Licensed Professional Counselor in North Carolina and a National Certified Counselor. Dr. Lewis is past treasurer and president of the International Association of Addictions and Offenders Counseling (IAAOC), a subdivision of the American Counseling Association. Throughout his career, he has taught graduate-level students in substance abuse counseling, assessment, diagnosis, and treatment planning. Dr. Lewis has published numerous research articles related to substance abuse, collegiate drinking, and theoretical approaches to addictions treatment. He has presented on these topics at numerous local, state, national, and international venues. Dr. Lewis is currently a member of the Motivational Interviewing Network of Trainers (MINT). In addition to his full-time faculty work, Dr. Lewis practices clinically part time at Presbyterian Counseling Center in Greensboro, NC, where he helps coordinate substance abuse clinical research and treatment services with clients struggling with a range of substance abuse issues.

Ruth Ouzts Moore

Ruth Ouzts Moore is a core faculty member for the Masters of Mental Health Counseling program at Walden University. She is a Licensed Professional Counselor and National Certified Counselor with 18 years of experience in mental health counseling. Her area of specialty is counseling children and adolescents, particularly those who have experienced abuse and trauma. She is a graduate of the Association for Play Therapy Leadership Academy and is a frequent presenter at the state, national, and international levels on topics including parental alienation and high-conflict divorce, abuse/trauma, play therapy, courtroom testimony, creative counseling techniques, and legal and ethical issues. Dr. Moore has published in peer-reviewed journals and professional literature. She is called regularly to serve as an expert witness in criminal, chancery, circuit, and family court for her involvement in cases with children who have experienced physical and sexual abuse, parental alienation, and custody and visitation issues.

Jason Patton

Jason Patton, PhD, LPC-S (TX), is core faculty in the Mental Health Counseling program at Walden University. He is currently cochair for the ALGBTIC Transgender Committee and serves on the ACA's DSM-5 Task Force; he has also been cochair for the SACES Online Education Interest Network. Dr. Patton is a journal reviewer for the *Electronic Journal of Human Sexuality*. His clinical expertise includes providing counseling to LGBT persons, survivors of abuse and unaccepting families, PTSD, religious or spiritual crisis, and psychopharmacologically focused collaboration; his theoretical orientation is relational cultural theory, but he employs EMDR and REBT in his work as well. His research interests include gender and sexual diversity, counselor training and competencies, bullying, resilience, and abuse survival. He is currently collaborating on an ethnography exploring resilience developed by drag performance for both the performers and the LGBT community at large.

Michelle Perepiczka

Michelle Perepiczka, PhD, LMHC, CSC, RPTS, NCC, is core faculty in the Mental Health Counseling program at Walden University. She is a past president of the Association for Humanistic Counseling (AHC) and an active member in the Association for Assessment and Research in Counseling (AARC). Dr. Perepiczka is a journal reviewer for the *Journal of Humanistic Counseling* and the *Journal of Counseling & Development*. She also received the Outstanding Humanistic Educator and Supervisor Award from the Association for Humanistic Counseling. Her clinical experiences include providing counseling and play therapy services in agency and school settings to children who experienced various forms of abuse and their families. Her research interests include wellness, humanism in counseling, and impact of counseling education techniques on student learning.

L. Marinn Pierce

L. Marinn Pierce received her PhD in Counselor Education from the University of Tennessee (CACREP accredited). Currently a faculty member in the Counselor Education program at California State University, Fresno, Dr. Pierce's clinical experience includes work with a variety of populations across multiple settings. Although her primary area of emphasis is children and youth and their families, she has worked with adolescents in residential treatment, individuals with diverse counseling needs in community outpatient settings, children and adolescents in intensive outpatient and partial hospitalization, and child and adolescent victims of sexual trauma. Her research interests include counselor professional identity development, wellness, and the integration of spirituality into the counseling process.

Stacee Reicherzer

Stacee Reicherzer is a Licensed Professional Counselor-Supervisor in Austin, Texas. She has extensive clinical and research experience in complex trauma and grief for LGBT persons and has presented and published in the United States and internationally on the topic for the past 10 years. Dr. Reicherzer is currently developing a new web series, "Ask Dr. Stacee," which will serve as a medium for answering questions she frequently receives at her Web site, www.drstacee.com about sexuality, gender, trauma, and a variety of other mental health topics that are the subjects of her weekly blog. In addition, she is engaged in ethnographic research to study a drag queen community's resilience. Dr. Reicherzer's consulting and supervision practice leverages her knowledge of counseling services to the transgender community, and she is a frequent guest speaker at training events and conferences.

Tiffany Rush-Wilson

Tiffany Rush-Wilson received her PhD in Counseling from the University of Akron in 2003. She currently serves as the Skill Development Coordinator for the Master of Science in Mental Health Counseling program at Walden University with a focus on both the online classrooms and in-person residencies. She has taught a variety of courses in the Mental Health Counseling and Psychology programs. Professionally, Dr. Rush-Wilson is independently, and dually, licensed and certified as a counselor in the United States and Canada. She has worked in community mental health, children's services, and extensively in private practice. She is a member of both American and Canadian Counseling Associations, has participated in community outreach, and presented on women's issues, scope of practice, and eating disorders at local, national, and international venues.

Jayne Smith

Jayne Smith completed her doctoral work at Old Dominion University. She is a National Certified Counselor, license eligible for the California LPCC, and certified to administer the Strong Interest Inventory. She has worked in mental health agency, private practice, and higher education settings since 2001. During this time, she developed and implemented countless programs geared toward empowerment and leadership for young adults. Additionally, Dr. Smith has clinically supervised mental health and school counselor trainees with an emphasis on developing advocacy and multicultural competencies. Dr. Smith has taught courses in counseling and human services programs. She designed and implemented a training series in psychopharmacology for mental health counselor trainees. Dr. Smith is interested in program evaluation, qualitative research, social justice counseling and supervision, and high school dropout prevention.

Shawn L. Spurgeon

Shawn L. Spurgeon is an associate professor of counselor education at the University of Tennessee at Knoxville, teaching in the Mental Health Counseling program. He received his PhD in Counseling and Counselor Education in 2002 from The University of North Carolina at Greensboro. Dr. Spurgeon is currently a member of the American Counseling Association's 2014 Ethics Revision Task Force and serves on the editorial board of the *Journal of Counseling Research and Practice* and *The Professional Counselor*. He currently serves as president elect for the Association for Assessment and Research in Counseling (AARC). Dr. Spurgeon has previously worked as a mental health counselor in a family services agency, private practice, and community mental health center. His work has included couples, families, and adolescents with emotional and behavioral problems. He is currently licensed as a professional counselor in North Carolina and Tennessee.

Heather C. Trepal

Heather Trepal earned her PhD in Counseling and Human Development Services from Kent State University. A faculty member in the Department of Counseling at the University of Texas at San Antonio, Dr. Trepal is a Licensed Professional Counselor and board approved supervisor (Texas) with over 17 years of experience in clinical mental health counseling settings. She has served as president of the Association for Creativity in Counseling, past chair of the ACA Graduate Student Committee, and president of the Southern Association for Counselor Education and Supervision. She is also involved with the Texas Counseling Association and the Association for Counselor Education and Supervision. Dr. Trepal publishes and presents regularly on topics related to clinical mental health counseling. Her primary areas of interest include self-harm (nonsuicidal self-injury and eating disorders), relationships/relational competencies and development (relational-cultural theory), supervision, gender issues in counseling, and counselor development.

Robyn Trippany-Simmons

Robyn Trippany-Simmons received her EdD in Counselor Education from the University of Alabama. She serves as residency coordinator and core faculty in the Master of Science in Counseling program at Walden University. Dr. Trippany-Simmons's research and clinical interests include sexual trauma, vicarious trauma, play therapy, spirituality in counseling, and professional identity issues. She serves on the editorial review board for the *Journal of Mental Health Counseling*, *Play Therapy* magazine, and *Tennessee Counseling Association Journal*. Dr. Trippany-Simmons is a Licensed Professional Counselor in Alabama and a Registered Play Therapist. She also maintains a small counseling practice, where she works with individuals and couples in a faith-based counseling setting.

Maggie E. Walsh

Maggie E. Walsh earned her PhD in Counselor Education and Practice from Georgia State University. Dr. Walsh is a Licensed Professional Counselor, a Registered Play Therapist, and a National Certified Counselor. She specializes in working with children, adolescents, and families and has clinical experience in community, private practice, and school settings. Dr. Walsh has presented at numerous professional conferences and provided community trainings on mental health topics. Dr. Walsh currently practices in both community and private practice settings as well as teaches counseling courses and provides clinical supervision at Georgia State University.

PREFACE

Clinical mental health counseling is a relatively new profession that is evolving to meet the needs of today's society. Clinical mental health counselors provide services to a broad array of clients presenting with various issues and diagnoses. In the past, counselors were generally relegated to working in community agencies, but with the passage of state counseling laws and the development of national certifications, clinical mental health counselors now work in private practice, hospital settings, the Department of Veterans Affairs, community agencies, and other related facilities. The outlook is bright for the future of clinical mental health counseling.

In this text, we offer a broad-based introduction to the theories and practices related to clinical mental health counseling. Our goal is to provide you the fundamental information required to begin the journey toward becoming a licensed or certified clinical mental health counselor. Of course, this text will be only one part of your journey, but it is designed to continue to be a resource for you throughout your professional development.

The materials in *Clinical Mental Health Counseling: Fundamentals of Applied Practice* are organized in order to match your developmental understanding of the profession. The text is divided into three parts: Introduction to the Profession of Clinical Mental Health Counseling, The Practice of Clinical Mental Health Counseling, and Contemporary Trends in Clinical Mental Health Counseling. Each chapter is designed to meet learning outcomes associated with the 2009 accreditation standards established by the Council for Accreditation of Counseling and Related Educational Programs (CACREP). The learning outcomes are based on general core areas of the CACREP standards and those related to the specialization of clinical mental health counseling.

In Part 1 of the text, we provide an introduction to clinical mental health counseling. This part focuses on the history of mental health counseling and professional development. The chapters in the first part cover

- The development of clinical mental health counseling as a profession
- Ethical and legal issues in clinical mental health counseling
- Education and credentialing
- Employment settings

Part 2 of the text is dedicated to the practice aspects of the profession. The general focus is on developing both an understanding of client issues and approaches for addressing those issues. The chapters in this part cover

- Advocacy
- Assessment and diagnosis
- Case conceptualization and treatment planning
- Managed care
- Consultation
- Prevention and crisis intervention

Part 3 of the text is designed to address the major trends and changes occurring in the clinical mental health counseling profession. We review many of the emerging practice areas and provide an overview of essential knowledge related to the following areas:

- Psychopharmacology
- Forensic mental health
- Addictions
- Clinical supervision
- Internet-based counseling

The underlying emphasis of this text is that clinical mental health counseling is a specialized helping profession. Further, the consistent theme is that mental health counselors are well prepared to provide quality services in a variety of settings. Although many different professions provide mental health services, clinical mental health counselors have the training, knowledge, and expertise necessary to treat a broad range of mental health issues.

Our text is a collaborative effort based on our experiences as clinical mental health counselors and counselor educators. As editors, we have more than 40 years of combined experience in the mental health field and have seen thousands of clients. We have also had the privilege of training hundreds of students. Our colleagues who have contributed to this effort have vast experience as well, and we have learned from their contributions. The pages of this text are a result of all our combined efforts.

 ### Video Icon

A series of online videos, developed specifically for this book, are available in the e-text edition of this text. If you are viewing the e-text edition, please click the Video Icon in each chapter. Icons appear throughout the text.

ACKNOWLEDGMENTS

A text of this scope could not have been possible without the help of our wonderful colleagues in the field of clinical mental health counseling. We are indebted to both the chapter authors and the practitioners who contributed their Voices from the Field. It is because of the work of these professionals that we are able to assure readers they are getting the most current and relevant information available.

We are also grateful for the input of our editor, Meredith Fossel, who has been a steadfast supporter of this project since its inception. Her tireless enthusiasm and willingness to mentor this project will not be forgotten. We are fortunate to have been one of her last book projects in counseling before moving upward and onward in her profession.

We want to thank Jenny Gessner, our project manager from Pearson, for keeping our project moving forward. We would also like to thank some of the people who mentored us individually along the way: David Capuzzi, Harry Daniels, Larry Loesch, and Joe Wittmer. In addition, we would like to thank some colleagues who sparked our passion for mental health counseling: Mike Whelan, Bob Wilson, Nick Hanna, Max Parker, and many others.

We are grateful for the input from the reviewers of this manuscript: Richard Deaner, Georgia Regents University; Dilani Perera-Diltz, Cleveland State University; and Cirecie

West-Olatunji, University of Cincinnati. Your contributions helped to shape this into a valuable text for clinical mental health professionals.

Finally, we are forever grateful to our friends and family who not only supported this project but also supported us along the way. Our children Ellis, Jake, Joe Lee, Emily, and Laura Beth are a constant source of inspiration and motivation. Our friends around the world and closer to home, including Mississippi, Jacksonville, and Beaumont, provide us with the foundation we need to serve others in this profession and beyond.

BRIEF CONTENTS

CONTENTS

PART 2 The Practice of Clinical Mental Health Counseling   81

PART 3 Contemporary Trends in Clinical Mental Health Counseling 241

PART 1

Introduction to the Profession of Clinical Mental Health Counseling

1

What Is Clinical Mental Health Counseling?

Donna S. Sheperis

CHAPTER OVERVIEW

This chapter covers the differentiation between clinical mental health counseling and other forms of professional counseling. We first discuss the history of clinical mental health counseling and its relationship to the medical model of treatment. Then, we address the unique professional identity of clinical mental health counselors. In addition, we discuss the complexities of the professional licensure process. This chapter concludes with the various additional certifications available to clinical mental health counselors.

LEARNING OBJECTIVES

The learning objectives for this chapter are designed to be consistent with the 2009 Council for Accreditation of Counseling and Related Educational Programs Standards (CACREP, 2009). As such, upon completion of this chapter, the student will have knowledge of the following clinical mental health counseling standards:

1. Understands the history, philosophy, and trends in clinical mental health counseling. (A.1)
2. Is aware of professional issues that affect clinical mental health counselors (e.g., core provider status, expert witness status, access to and practice privileges within managed care systems). (A.7)
3. Understands professional issues relevant to the practice of clinical mental health counseling. (C.9)

Additionally, students will have knowledge of the following core entry-level standard:

1. History and philosophy of the counseling profession. (G.1.a)

INTRODUCTION

Welcome to your introduction to clinical mental health counseling. As a student, you are poised to enter the profession of counseling. You may have heard others saying the "field of counseling" but you are truly entering a profession. What you will learn as you pursue your studies is that counseling is a distinct profession because it is governed by a code of ethics and each state has enacted laws that define a scope of practice. Clinical mental health counseling is a specialized area of the counseling profession that involves unique training, education, and clinical work. Among the various counseling areas, clinical mental health counseling is the primary specialization for the prevention, assessment, and intervention of issues associated with mental health (AMHCA, 2012).

The profession of counseling is relatively young within the field of helping professions. Emerging formally on the scene in the late 1800s, the counseling profession has transformed from mere vocational guidance to myriad counseling specialties and occupations.

 ## HISTORICAL OVERVIEW OF CLINICAL MENTAL HEALTH COUNSELING

One way to fully appreciate the profession is to explore the history of counseling and, more specifically, the history of clinical mental health counseling (CMHC). In the seminal article by Aubrey (1977), counseling is described as a profession that arose in response to societal changes of the late 19th century. Movement from a primarily farm-based society to a society dependent on manufacturing and transportation created opportunities for vocational guidance in industrial and education settings. This movement was spearheaded by Frank Parsons, commonly referred to as the "father of vocational guidance" (Aubrey, 1977). His posthumous book, *Choosing a Vocation,* became a manual for counselors working in vocational settings (Briddick, 2008). The strength of Parsons's approach lay in finding the best way to place the best people in the work environments that would make them, and the companies they worked for, successful. As commonplace as that seems today, it was absolutely revolutionary at the time!

By the mid-20th century, counseling had begun to shift from the assessment of skills for employment to a focus on the client's needs and well-being. This shift was a direct result of the impact of Carl Rogers and his person-centered approach on the provision of counseling services (Aubrey, 1977). Of course with this focus on the client, the issues and concerns of the client began to come to the forefront. By the 1970s, it was clear that counselors were providing services that we would now call clinical mental health counseling. However, at that time, mental health counselors were not organized and had no professional identity distinct from that of guidance counselors (Colangelo, 2009).

CMHC developed within the larger profession of counseling when master's-level practitioners working in agencies, hospitals, and private practice found they lacked a professional home because psychologists practiced at the doctoral level whereas social workers practiced at the bachelor's level. These disenfranchised counselors found that, because they were not eligible for licensure in other helping fields such as psychology, they needed to band together to form an identity unique to clinical mental health counseling. These efforts helped to distinguish CMHC from the larger profession of counseling and other disciplines such as social work and psychology. With the formation of the American Mental Health Counselors Association (AMHCA) and the advent of professional licensure, clinical mental health counselors finally had a professional voice. But what is their professional identity?

A critical concept to be discussed in relation to the history of mental health counseling, as well as ongoing professional challenges, is that of professional identity. In other words, what sets clinical mental health counselors apart from other helping professionals? There are many similarities to the various helping professions, which results in significant confusion to the public that the profession serves. Psychologists, with their traditional role as assessors and diagnosticians, are qualified and licensed at the doctoral level. Psychiatrists, who hold prescribing privileges (as do some psychologists but that is beyond the scope of this distinction), are qualified and licensed as medical doctors. Social workers, with their emphasis on case management, are qualified and licensed at the bachelor's level (although some do pursue master's clinical degrees). Clinical mental health counselors, however, are the only helping professionals qualified and licensed at the master's level. In addition, their primary role is to counsel. Although other helping professions may employ some aspects of counseling, just as clinical mental health counseling employs diagnostic, assessment, and case management practices, CMHC is the only profession whose primary purpose is counseling.

What does this mean? When clients decide to see a counselor, they may or may not seek a clinical mental health counselor. They often see those in the disciplines of psychology, psychiatry, and social work as equivalent. The rich history of clinical mental health counselors as providers of counseling services sets the profession apart philosophically, if not practically, in the public eye. One such distinction is in the profession's use of the wellness model as opposed to the medical model. Additionally, counselor preparation programs, which are master's-level graduate programs, separate CMHC from the other helping professions.

The Medical Model and the Wellness Model

The term *medical model* is often used in the discussion of the helping professions, but what does it mean? The medical model is an approach to how clients are best helped and begins with the identification of a problem from a pathology perspective. The medical model is grounded in the belief that mental illness is like any other illness and treatment practices borrowed from medicine will be effective in addressing mental health concerns (Wampold, 2001).

It is not unreasonable to make such assertions. Clinical mental health counseling's history of helping is grounded in experimental approaches to the treatment of mental health concerns. Early societies viewed mental illness as requiring treatment by the tribal elders. Individuals with psychiatric problems were often sidelined from society, subjected to what are now considered to be inhumane treatments, such as the use of hallucinogens, bloodletting, starvation, and beatings. Any "success" with such methods resulted in their increased use. Of course, it is now known that such methods are not the most desirable forms of treatment.

Psychologists and behaviorists of the time scientifically approached mental illness and adopted the early medical principles that continue to influence the helping professions. Mental illness was treated primarily in hospitals, if at all, requiring a medical approach. Emil Kraepelin (1856–1926) is credited with developing the first system of organizing mental health concerns when he published a compendium of psychiatry asserting that psychiatry was a branch of medical science worthy of scientific investigation (Hippius & Müller, 2008). Kraepelin's work served as the foundation for both the *International Statistical Classification of Diseases and Related Health Problems* (commonly known as the ICD), which classifies physical illnesses, and the *Diagnostic and Statistical Manual of Mental Disorders* (DSM), which classifies mental illnesses.

The medical model serves as one lens through which to view the development and treatment of client problems. However, counseling differs from psychology and psychiatry in that it takes a wellness and strength–based approach to the treatment of mental health concerns. The profession of counseling is unique in the mental health field in its use of the *wellness model* as opposed to the medical model. Whereas other mental health professionals such as psychologists and psychiatrists view mental or emotional concerns as illnesses from the diagnostic perspective, mental health counselors view these concerns as a part of normal development. Clinical mental health counselors operate from this wellness perspective and receive additional training in the medical model and pathology. In addition, mental health concerns are viewed through a developmental lens, and mental health counselors take into account life stages. In other words, one's mental health is assessed based on a developmental continuum, because some forms of mental illness are not exclusive to one stage of development. The mental health counselor works with all clients to improve their quality of life. However, as emerging clinical mental health counselors, you need to be well versed in the responsibilities of using the medical model, particularly in a managed care atmosphere, as discussed in Chapter 8 of this text.

Because much of the treatment of mental illness came from a medical model perspective, this work occurred in hospitals and institutions where medical doctors could work. Generally known as lunatic asylums, institutions were built to contain and restrain the mentally ill, who were often viewed as demon possessed and treated as inmates. In the mid-1800s, Dorothea Dix championed for an increase in the number of asylums from 8 to 32 in the United States. The US census began counting and categorizing those with mental illness and mental retardation through the inclusion of the category "Insane and Idiotic." Although the number of asylums grew, the treatment was not improving from earlier barbaric times. In the early 1900s, American treatment of mental illness included rampant physical abuse, which was highlighted by Clifford Beers in his 1908 book *A Mind That Found Itself.*

Beers, a Yale graduate and intelligent businessman, suffered from mental illness including an intense depression following the death of his brother. Following a suicide attempt, Beers was hospitalized for treatment in a private institution where he was confined, beaten, and subjected to unhygienic and unsafe conditions. He endured multiple institutionalizations prior to writing his book, in which he exposed the living and treatment conditions of the helpless mentally ill and thereby changed the face of hospitalization for mental illness.

Beers's work became the foundation of the Connecticut Society for Mental Hygiene, which then became a national organization and is still in existence under the title Mental Health America (MHA). For decades MHA has been at the forefront of educational and legislative initiatives to advocate for the right to fair treatment of mental illness (2011). The development of this national awareness caused hospital conditions to become more humane and the treatment of mental illness to receive national focus. While hospital conditions improved, the number of those in need began to increase beyond the institutions' ability to serve them. A congressional Joint Commission on Mental Illness and Mental Health was formed in the 1950s to educate the public and promote mental health awareness. Although this was a laudable goal, it did not address the increase in inpatient needs and the limitations of our nation's hospital systems. This disparity was addressed when President John F. Kennedy introduced the Community Mental Health Act of 1963, also known as the Mental Retardation and Community Mental Health Centers Construction Act.

Community Mental Health Act of 1963

Early mental health treatment was provided using the best resources and research available. Although they were not ideal, treatment options certainly improved throughout the early 20th century. Prior to the mid-1960s, virtually all mental health treatment was provided on an inpatient basis in hospitals and institutions. Many hospitals were state run, and typically in the larger population centers of each state. Few could afford private care, and state-funded care would be considered substandard, at best.

Using the medical model previously discussed, psychologists, psychiatrists, and physicians worked diligently to keep patients safe and provide treatment for their mental health needs. Upon discharge from the hospitals, patients were returned to their home communities where they often did not receive appropriate follow-up care. This resulted in a return of symptoms and, ultimately, a return to the hospital. However, the institutions in which these patients were placed were becoming increasingly overcrowded.

During this time research being conducted suggested that patients who improve while institutionalized would remain stable longer if they received ongoing care in their communities. Yet community-based mental health care was unheard of during this time. President John F. Kennedy endorsed a proposal that mental health patients would benefit from staying in their home communities with familial support and community-based treatment. This proposal resulted in the Community Mental Health Act of 1963.

The Community Mental Health Act of 1963 proved to be the first time that the US government became involved in mental health care. The act's primary focus was deinstitutionalization, with community mental health centers taking on treatment of the previously hospitalized patients. President Kennedy hoped for a reduction in hospitalizations of 50%, and the National Institute of Mental Health (NIMH) was created to serve as an oversight for community centers (Feldman, 2003). Federal grants were provided and community centers sprang up all over the United States. Some states used this as an opportunity to close state-run hospitals, which did not ultimately help with overcrowding. However, the creation of the community-based treatment facilities increased the jobs available to counselors, and the profession of clinical mental health counseling grew out of this act.

The placement of care in communities, rather than in centralized hospitals and institutions, truly embodied the community mental health model. Many of the existing counselors had been trained in colleges of education and did not have the strength of a professional identity. These new professionals, functioning as clinical mental health counselors, banded together to form the American Mental Health Counselors Association (AMHCA) in the late 1970s to increase the professional identity. With this increase in CMHC positions for counselors came a need for standardized training programs. Licensure and certification for counselors also came under scrutiny in order to improve opportunities for counselors wishing to work in CMHC positions. See Chapter 3, Education, Credentialing, and Professional Development, for more information about advances in education, licensure, and certification for clinical mental health counselors. A brief exploration follows.

DEVELOPING A PROFESSIONAL IDENTITY

We have just learned how clinical mental health counselors came to exist. However, what is the professional identity of counselors? The answer may seem obvious. They are, after all, counselors, right? As you have been reading, however, the identity of counselors is not always clear. Let's consider what it means to be a professional clinical mental health counselor.

As already mentioned, counseling is a profession, not a field. Professional counseling is built on a strong foundation rooted in a code of ethics, established through defined theories, and maintained through licensure, credentialing, and professional organizations. Professional mental health counseling was defined in the late 1970s as "an interdisciplinary multifaceted, holistic process of (1) the promotion of healthy life-styles, (2) identification of individual stressors and personal levels of functioning, and (3) preservation or restoration of mental health" (Seiler & Messina, 1979, p. 6). In other words, mental health counselors have always identified with the wellness and prevention-based approach. They assess stressors and strengths, develop an understanding of the etiology or cause of the concern, and generate interventions and preventions to fit the needs of the individual client.

As clear as this may seem, being a professional counselor is not without controversy. Relationships with the sister disciplines of psychology, psychiatry, social work, and marriage and family therapy have not always been harmonious, which brings us to a discussion of scope of practice.

Scope of Practice

Scope of practice is a term commonly used by national and state licensure boards to describe the rights and limitations of the practice of any particular profession. Usually, scope of practice embodies the procedures, processes, and clientele served by a particular profession. Within the counseling profession, scope of practice is determined by state licensure boards and written into state law. As such, scope of practice for professional counselors varies from state to state.

In most states, clinical mental health counselors are granted, through their scope of practice, the ability to provide intake assessment, diagnostic evaluation, and treatment of individuals, families, and groups. The terms *psychotherapy* and *psychoanalysis* are examples of terms that might be protected due to scope of practice limitations. In many states, clinical mental health counselors can provide psychotherapy but rarely, if ever, are they allowed to call themselves psychoanalysts. That title is typically reserved for professionals with an MD (doctor of medicine), PhD (doctor of philosophy), or PsyD (doctor of psychology) degree and additional training in psychoanalysis.

Because the profession of counseling is regulated on a state-by-state basis, these distinctions can become very complicated for counseling students. It is essential to research your state law and understand the title designated to professional counselors in your state, scope of practice limitations, and licensure requirements. This is further explored in Chapter 3.

Professional Training

As already mentioned, when professional counselors emerged on the scene, there was a need to standardize their professional training. Because a strong professional identity was missing in the field of counseling, initiatives began to ensure that those who call themselves professional counselors have received adequate training to provide clinical mental health counseling services. To meet this need, a division of the American Counseling Association (ACA) became involved in the standardization of training. The Association for

Counselor Education and Supervision (ACES) developed some initial standards that would allow counselor preparation programs to seek voluntary accreditation. From this initiative, the Council for Accreditation of Counseling and Related Educational Programs (CACREP) was born.

Beginning in the early 1980s, CACREP offered voluntary accreditation to counselor preparation programs. The purpose of accreditation is to create a unified set of training standards that, in turn, strengthen the professional practice of counseling (CACREP, 2013a). CACREP accredits close to 600 programs at universities across the United States in the following specialty areas:

- Addiction Counseling
- Career Counseling
- Clinical Mental Health Counseling
- Marriage, Couple, and Family Counseling
- School Counseling
- Student Affairs and College Counseling
- Counselor Education and Supervision

Of specific interest to this text is the clinical mental health counseling specialty. This program's accreditation is one of the newest offered by CACREP and represents a movement away from the separate programs of community counseling and mental health counseling. The clinical mental health counseling specialty was introduced in 2009 and is defined in the following section.

Clinical Mental Health Counseling

Clinical mental health counseling programs prepare graduates to work with clients across a spectrum of mental and emotional disorders, as well as to promote mental health and wellness. Clients may be seen individually, as couples, in families, or in group settings. Clinical mental health counselors are knowledgeable in the principles and practices of diagnosis, treatment, referral, and prevention and often work in interdisciplinary teams with other health professionals (e.g., psychiatrists, social workers, MDs). Employment opportunities may include private practice, community-based mental health centers, hospitals, and other treatment settings (CACREP, 2013b).

Students who pursue a master's degree in a CACREP-accredited clinical mental health counseling program take courses that meet a multitude of requirements in these areas:

- Foundations of Counseling
- Counseling, Prevention, and Intervention
- Diversity and Advocacy
- Assessment
- Research and Evaluation
- Diagnosis

Central to the CACREP philosophy is that students are assessed on both knowledge and skills in relation to these topic areas. Because of this, CACREP graduates are afforded a number of additional opportunities in employment, certification, and licensure. Let's hear from one such graduate and how she has found her place in the profession of counseling.

VOICE FROM THE FIELD 1.1

I have a passion for counseling and helping others reach their full potential. Helping clients and students discover coping mechanisms they did not know they possessed and identifying alternative ways of approaching everyday problems is what I enjoy the most. I like the fact that counseling serves as a stronger, more realistic link between education and work. This is one of the main reasons the profession is growing so fast. Some factors that have influenced me the most would be the opportunity to teach counselors in training, embrace diversity and community, and foster change within my clients and in my community. I received my master's from a CACREP program at Delta State University and now am a PhD student in the Counselor Education and Supervision program at Walden University. My educational experiences have afforded me the opportunity to act as a social change agent and contribute not just to my profession but to my community as well.

The flexibility, objectivity, and the nonjudgmental approach of counselors is what, I think, separates counseling from other disciplines. This is not to say that any of the other human service professions (social work or psychology) do not provide this same opportunity, but only that, for me, the counseling profession seemed to go beyond the basics and provided insight that is more beneficial in order to help clients be able to help themselves. In many ways it has to do with who I am and where I believe my strengths and skills will have the greatest impact.

As director of student support services for the Robert E. Smith School of Nursing at Delta State University, I have been able to apply concepts and counseling approaches that I learned from my master's counseling program, in order to benefit and support a population of at-risk students, many of whom had not been exposed to counseling before. Currently I serve as president of the Mississippi Counseling Association, and this experience has only served as verification that I am pursuing the correct profession. The ideas, standards, activities, and functions within the association fit my beliefs of the importance of counseling as well as provide me with an opportunity to advocate for my profession. Having the opportunity to serve as president of a state association has given me a great sense of pride and accomplishment, not just for my profession but for who I have become as a result of being a counselor and a person.

DEIDRA M. BYAS, MED
Director of Student Services, Delta State University, Robert E. Smith School of Nursing

---

LICENSURE AND CERTIFICATION

In the field of clinical mental health counseling, certification is offered by a host of providers whereas licensure is offered by states only. Both topics are briefly covered here. For a deeper discussion, please see Chapter 3.

Licensure

As already mentioned, CACREP is an accrediting body that sanctions the training process of counselors. Accreditation is one way that the profession shows accountability to standards. However, CACREP addresses graduate training only, and although it provides an excellent foundation for the licensure process, simply graduating from a CACREP program does not guarantee licensure. Licensure is government-sanctioned regulation of the practice of counseling that occurs at the state level.

Licensure as a professional counselor is defined by the regulatory power of each state. In other words, every state is charged with both the right and the requirement to pass licensure laws, develop state regulatory agencies, and engage in all necessary activities deemed appropriate to protect the public (ACA, 2012). In most states, it is illegal to practice counseling without a license. However, because state laws differ, it is possible that your state does not require a license for all types of employment as a counselor. As counselors in training, it is imperative that you become extremely familiar with your state's licensure law and state regulations for acquiring and maintaining your license. You will also want to investigate the type of license: will you be licensed as a Licensed Professional Counselor (LPC), or a Licensed Mental Health Counselor (LMHC), or does your state use another title?

From state to state, these licenses do not have automatic reciprocity; that is, simply because you hold a license in one state does not mean you will automatically receive a license in another state. Each state holds the responsibility to establish standards toward licensure and moderate its practice in the state. There are substantial differences in training requirements, supervision requirements, and state-specific continuing education requirements between states. For example, most states recognize CACREP as the minimum standard for training. For students graduating from non-CACREP-accredited programs, states may require copies of syllabi or course descriptions to determine CACREP equivalency. In addition, the state may require added coursework that your graduate program did not require. In Florida, the license is LMHC (Licensed Mental Health Counselor). Students who graduate from a CACREP Clinical Mental Health program have their training automatically counted toward licensure. As someone who graduated from a CACREP Community Counseling program, I had to provide evidence that I had taken courses in substance abuse and sexuality counseling to qualify for consideration for licensure. In addition, I am required to take continuing education courses in the prevention of medical errors, Florida laws and rules, HIV/AIDS, and domestic violence in order to complete requirements for licensure. Of course, ongoing specified continuing education is required to maintain the license once it is granted.

In recent years, all 50 states have established laws to regulate the profession of counseling. Although an in-depth discussion of all of the states is beyond the scope of this chapter, there are some basic commonalities and areas of difference for counselors in training to be aware of. In all 50 states, a master's degree is required for a license as a professional counselor or a professional mental health counselor. Most states require that the degree be in counseling, although some states allow for related degrees. Counseling psychology is also accepted in many states. Master's degrees in psychology or social work are rarely accepted for initial licenses in counseling, but they may be accepted in situations of reciprocity or endorsement of a license from another state. In other words, someone who was licensed decades ago based on his or her master's in social work might be eligible for a license in another state that would not currently accept a master's in social work candidate. The endorsement of the previous license is based on the fact that at the time the person was initially licensed, he or she met all qualifications required by that state. Because state laws change so often, it is important to keep up with licensure regulations of your current state as well as any states you may consider moving to.

Aside from the type of graduate program required, the number of supervised clinical hours post-master's is also a subject of discrepancy among states. Some states require 1,000 hours post-master's, whereas others may require up to 3,500 hours but allow the hours you accrued during your degree program to count toward that total. Certain states require that the supervisor be another licensed helping professional from any discipline, whereas others require that the supervised hours be provided by a board-qualified supervisor in the same profession. When investigating the number of supervised clinical hours needed for your state, be sure to inquire about the type of supervisor needed, the number of hours needed, and whether or not any hours from your master's program will count toward the total.

Once you are licensed, you will be required to maintain your license by completing a specified number of continuing education units on a regular basis. Some states have annual renewals, whereas others renew every two years. Many states require that your continuing education be in specified topic areas such as ethics or medical errors. Again, this is information you will need to verify as you begin your career as a licensed counselor in your state.

The role of the state licensure board is to protect the public. One of the ways the board does this is through adjudication of complaints. Serving as the ultimate authority over a counselor's license, state boards can grant, suspend, or revoke licensure for cause. Although this is a rarity, it does happen. If a complaint is made to the board, an investigation occurs. The counselor is not charged with proving innocence, but in some cases the complainant is able to prove guilt.

The idea of an ethical complaint is frightening to most counseling students—with good reason. They enter into this profession with the desire to help people. They cannot imagine a time when their practice may be considered unethical. The reality is that counselors do not practice without risk. They carry liability insurance, attend risk management seminars, and complete continuing education units in counseling ethics in order to protect themselves, their clients, and their license. Although the number of inquiries about ethical practice is on the rise (ACA, 2013), the actual number of filed complaints is still very small compared to the number of practicing counselors.

Certification

Whereas a license is established and governed by the state, certification is available to counselors through various other entities such as the National Board for Certified Counselors (NBCC), which offers the National Certified Counselor (NCC) credential. It is often difficult for people outside the counseling profession to understand why state licensure is more important than certification through a national body such as NBCC. As an example, most people go to a hairdresser or barber to get their hair done or cut. This person may be extremely skilled and have graduated from a great program (that is, similar to the counselor's CACREP). She or he may have gone for advanced training at a specialty school in another state and become certified in a particular color or cut method; this certification is similar to certification as a National Certified Counselor (NCC), for example. However well prepared (degree program) and trained (certificate) that hairdresser or barber is, she or he cannot touch someone's hair without having a state license.

So, outside of becoming an NCC, what types of certifications are available for clinical mental health counselors? Some certifications are natural extensions of counselors' areas of interest, whereas others support the type of work environment in which they practice. This section continues with two certifications offered by the National Board for Certified Counselors and two offered by alternate professional entities. Be sure to explore these and other certifications to determine your best fit.

CERTIFIED CLINICAL MENTAL HEALTH COUNSELOR   The dominant certification for clinical mental health counselors is the Certified Clinical Mental Health Counselor (CCMHC) designation through NBCC. The CCMHC is earned after successfully taking and passing the Clinical Mental Health Counseling exam. This exam is used in a number of states for licensure as an LMHC. At the national level, the exam is required for certification as a CCMHC. In addition to the exam, the counselor must also hold the NCC and show proof of requisite training and experience. For further information about becoming a CCMHC, visit the NBCC Web site at www.nbcc.org/Specialties/CCMHC.

MASTER ADDICTIONS COUNSELOR   The Master Addictions Counselor (MAC) designation was developed as a joint venture between NBCC and the International Association of Addictions and Offender Counseling (IAAOC), which is a division of ACA. The MAC certification shows evidence of a specialty in addictions counseling and allows those credentialed to seek employment with the US Department of Transportation as a substance abuse professional. Candidates for the MAC must successfully take and pass the Examination for Master Addictions Counselors (EMAC) and show proof of graduate or continuing education in addictions and a substantive work experience in addictions counseling. For further information about becoming a MAC, visit the NBCC Web site at www.nbcc.org/Specialties/MAC.

CLINICALLY CERTIFIED FORENSIC COUNSELOR   The Clinically Certified Forensic Counselor (CCFC) is one of many certifications offered by the National Association of Forensic Counselors (NAFC). CCFC certification indicates competency in working with offenders. Counselors who are licensed in their state and have three years of experience working with offenders or ex-offenders are eligible to take the certification exam. More information about forensic counseling can be found in Chapter 12 of this text. For further information about becoming a CCFC, visit the NAFC Web site at www.nationalafc.com.

REGISTERED PLAY THERAPIST   The Registered Play Therapist (RPT) is a certification offered by the Association for Play Therapy (APT) to state-licensed counselors who have specialty training and experience in play therapy. The RPT designation indicates that the counselor has supervised work experience as a play therapist and has met multiple standards of training competency in play therapy. In addition, certified RPTs can elect to become RPT-Ss, or Registered Play Therapist-Supervisors. For further information about becoming an RPT, visit the APT Web site at www.a4pt.org.

These are but a few examples of the many forms of certification available to mental health counselors as you continue in your career. Work environment, client population, and personal interest will determine the certifications you pursue. By attending continuing education events and professional conferences, reading various journals, and participating in networking with colleagues, you will find the advanced certifications that best complement your licensure. If you think of licensure as the meat and potatoes of your professional credentials, certifications are really the fantastic side dishes and desserts that set you apart from others in your area.

Conclusion

This chapter has served as your introduction into the profession of clinical mental health counseling. As you have learned, clinical mental health coun-selors have specialized training in their graduate programs. CACREP standards dictate the training for accredited programs. The National Counselor

Examination and the National Clinical Mental Health Counseling Examination serve as testing points to provide evidence of academic and clinical competency. Supervised work experience, supervisor endorsement, and state-specific continuing education allow candidates to be licensed at the state level. Certification as an NCC or NCMHC is also available to clinical mental health counselors. Finally, certifications from outside professional organizations provide additional opportunities for mental health counselors to showcase their experience and talents to prospective clients.

References

American Counseling Association (ACA). (2012). *Licensure and certification*. Retrieved from http://www.counseling.org/knowledge-center/licensure-requirements

American Counseling Association (ACA). (2013). *Ethics committee summary—FY 11*. Retrieved from http://www.counseling.org/knowledge-center/ethics

American Mental Health Counselors Association (AMHCA). (2012). *Facts about clinical mental health counselors*. Retrieved from http://www.amhca.org/about/facts.aspx

Aubrey, R. F. (1977). Historical development of guidance and counseling and implications for the future. *The Personnel & Guidance Journal, 55*(6), 288–295.

Beers, C. (1908). *A mind that found itself*. Retrieved from http://www.gutenberg.org/files/11962/11962-h/11962-h.htm

Briddick, W. C. (2008). *Choosing a vocation: Book review*. Retrieved from http://ncda.org/aws/NCDA/pt/sd/news_article/5442/_parent/layout_details/false

Colangelo, J. J. (2009). The American Mental Health Counselors Association: Reflection on 30 historic years. *Journal of Counseling & Development, 87*(2), 234–240.

Council for Accreditation of Counseling and Related Educational Programs (CACREP). (2009). *CACREP accreditation manual: 2009 standards*. Alexandria, VA: Author. Retrieved from http://www.cacrep.org/doc/2009%20Standards%20with%20cover.pdf

Council for Accreditation of Counseling and Related Educational Programs (CACREP). (2013a). *Vision, mission and core values*. Retrieved from http://www.cacrep.org/template/page.cfm?id=40

Council for Accreditation of Counseling and Related Educational Programs (CACREP). (2013b). *For students*. Retrieved from http://67.199.126.156/template/page.cfm?id=5

Feldman, S. (2003). Reflections on the 40th anniversary of the US Community Mental Health Centers Act. *Australian and New Zealand Journal of Psychiatry, 37*(6), 662–667. doi:10.1111/j.1440-1614.2003.01268.x

Hippius, H., & Müller, N. (2008). The work of Emil Kraepelin and his research group in München. *European Archives of Psychiatry & Clinical Neuroscience, 258*, 3–11. doi:10.1007/s00406-008-2001-6

Mental Health America (MHA). (2011). *History of the organization and the movement*. Retrieved from http://www.nmha.org/index.cfm?objectid=da2f000d-1372-4d20-c8882d19a97973aa

Seiler, G., & Messina, J. J. (1979). Toward professional identity: The dimension of mental health counseling in perspective. *American Mental Health Counselors Journal, 1*, 3–8.

Wampold, B. E. (2001). *The great psychotherapy debate: Models, methods, and findings*. Mahwah, NJ: Erlbaum.

2

Ethical and Legal Issues

DONNA S. SHEPERIS

CHAPTER OVERVIEW

Ethics and legal issues are some of the most challenging that practicing counselors will face. This chapter introduces readers to the American Counseling Association (ACA) and the American Mental Health Counselors Association (AMHCA) codes of ethics and how they apply to the practice of counseling. Readers will be exposed to various ethical decision-making models that may be used to guide counselors as they approach ethical dilemmas in practice. Legal issues and concerns that are relevant to clinical mental health practice will be discussed. Finally, specific ethical and legal concerns and their relevant codes will be provided so that readers can begin to learn how to apply the professional codes of ethics to common ethical dilemmas.

LEARNING OBJECTIVES

The learning objectives for this chapter are designed to be consistent with the 2009 Council for Accreditation of Counseling and Related Educational Programs Standards (CACREP, 2009). As such, upon completion of this chapter, the student will have knowledge of the following clinical mental health counseling standards:

1. Understands ethical and legal considerations specifically related to the practice of clinical mental health counseling. (A.2)
2. Is aware of professional issues that affect clinical mental health counselors (e.g., core provider status, expert witness status, access to and practice privileges within managed care systems). (A.7)
3. Demonstrates the ability to apply and adhere to ethical and legal standards in clinical mental health counseling. (B.1)

Additionally, students will have knowledge of the following core entry-level standards:

1. Ethical standards of professional organizations and credentialing bodies, and applications of ethical and legal considerations in professional counseling. (G.1.j.)

INTRODUCTION

A cornerstone to every profession is a code of ethics developed by the profession for the profession. In the case of clinical mental health counselors, there are a number of codes of ethics under which they may fall. Regardless of professional affiliation, the code of ethics developed and adopted by the American Counseling Association often serves as the gold standard in legal complaints. Although you will likely take a separate course in ethics, in this chapter we review the broad principles of ethics that undergird the profession of clinical mental health counseling, consider ethical decision-making models as they apply to the contemporary practice of counseling, address specific codes to which you may adhere, explore legal considerations in the profession, discuss common ethical complaints and sanctions, and evaluate ethical dilemmas through the use of selected case studies.

ETHICS AND CLINICAL MENTAL HEALTH COUNSELING

The discussion of ethics in clinical mental health counseling begins with an overview of general ethical principles. Ethics is "a discipline within philosophy that is concerned with human conduct and moral decision making" and "standards of conduct or actions taken in relation to others" (Remley & Herlihy, 2010, p. 3). In other words, ethics is both a process of decision making and the behavioral outcome. You might wonder why those training to be helping professionals, dedicated to serving the greater good of vulnerable client populations, even have codes of ethics. It seems that the very nature of what counselors do would require an ethical approach. Ideally, that is the case. However, as a profession it is important to develop, publish, and uphold a standard of ethics in order to set minimum professional standards and develop a system of accountability to protect clients and practitioners alike.

Historically, there are references to ethics, morals, and values in virtually all world religions. Philosophers such as Plato have long explored and debated the finer points of ethical decisions. Essentially, ethics provides a moral map but rarely offers explicit answers. In fact, ethics tends to provide us with multiple answers, and then the individual making the decision has to determine which path on that moral map to take. Ethics is one of those arenas in which there may be more than one right answer.

Let's take a look at a brief case example to see how this might be true. Your client, Kevin, is doing well in therapy. During this particular session, he informs you that he has lost his job due to a recent plant closure and will not be able to continue seeing you because of his inability to pay your fees. How might you respond? When I present this scenario to beginning counselors, they often have a host of questions: How long have I been seeing Kevin? What have I been seeing him for? What does it mean that he's been "doing well"? Did he know that the plant was going to close? Granted, this is a brief scenario, but even with this small amount of information some ethical responses can begin to be developed. For example, some counselors decide that they will continue to see Kevin on a pro bono basis. This appears to be ethical in that the client continues to get services and there is no abandonment of the client. However, from a practical perspective, how many pro bono clients can any counselor afford to take? Another take on this case example is to refer Kevin to a clinic that charges according to a sliding scale so that he can afford to continue treatment. Although this is a very different answer, such an action may also be ethical in that the client continues to receive treatment. Others respond that they will continue to see Kevin while allowing him to essentially run up a tab in therapy that he can pay when he is once again gainfully employed. This approach may also be ethical in that the client continues to receive services, and in this case, the counselor has an opportunity to perhaps receive compensation for the services. So here is one ethical dilemma with perhaps three very different but still ethical responses!

Although the case of Kevin provides only a brief example, it demonstrates that ethical decisions can be very complex and can have numerous answers. In this chapter, we look at ethical decision making models that will help you arrive at the conclusion that best fits your values and the needs of your client.

As a clinical mental health counselor, you may have a number of codes to adhere to. You will find that codes have more in common than they do differences. For the purposes of this text, we explore the two primary codes that apply to clinical mental health counselors: the code of the American Counseling Association (found at www.counseling.org /Resources/aca-code-of-ethics.pdf) and the code of the American Mental Health Counselors Association (found at www.amhca.org/assets/news/AMHCA_Code_of_Ethics_2010_w _pagination_cxd_51110.pdf).

American Counseling Association Code of Ethics

Considered the gold standard of counselor ethics, the American Counseling Association code is the umbrella under which all counselors fall. Dating back to the early 1960s, the first code was developed for the organization, formerly known as the American Personnel and Guidance Association (APGA). Donald Super, in his role as president of APGA, called for the first code of ethics. The initial code took eight years to develop. Two years after the code was published, the association began collecting case examples of ethical dilemmas from counselors. By 1965, ACA (operating as APGA) published its first ethical standards casebook. Both the code and the casebook have been revised many times in the history of the organization (Kennedy, 2005).

By 1990, the profession of counseling had changed dramatically. Despite several revisions along the way, an extensive revision of its code was necessary to address emerging trends in contemporary counseling. This time, the revision was a more transparent process with ACA members invited to submit ideas for the code and to comment on the initial draft. A final product was published in 1995, with another comprehensive revision occurring in 2005 (Kennedy, 2005). More recently, the code has gone through yet another comprehensive revision.

Why do the codes need to be revised so often? Shouldn't ethics be like morals and stay the same through the years? In actuality, the code of ethics is a dynamic document that requires practitioners to revisit it regularly to ensure that it meets the needs of their clients and the standards of the profession of counseling. Codes are rewritten to reflect a broadening awareness of multicultural factors, to address social changes, and to ensure applicability to a modern society.

It is essential to take note of the purposes of the code. The ACA Code of Ethics serves five main purposes:

1. The Code enables the association to clarify to current and future members, and to those served by members, the nature of the ethical responsibilities held in common by its members.
2. The Code helps support the mission of the association.
3. The Code establishes principles that define ethical behavior and best practices of association members.
4. The Code serves as an ethical guide designed to assist members in constructing a professional course of action that best serves those utilizing counseling services and best promotes the values of the counseling profession.

5. The Code serves as the basis for processing of ethical complaints and inquiries initiated against members of the association (ACA, 2005, p. 3).

As you can see, the ACA code is instrumental in clarifying the professional responsibilities of all counselors and guides their practice. It also serves to protect clients of all types of counselors.

American Mental Health Counselors Association Code of Ethics

Whereas the ACA Code of Ethics provides primary direction for the work of counselors, most clinical mental health counselors are also governed by the ethical code of the American Mental Health Counselors Association (AMHCA). To better understand this code, it is important to understand AMHCA as an organization.

The American Mental Health Counselors Association was formed in the mid-1970s when it became apparent that the counselors falling under the umbrella of the APGA, the organization which later became ACA, held a multitude of specialties and functioned in a variety of work settings. Mental health counselors discovered a need for a subgroup to focus on mental health counseling concerns and investigated the creation of a new division within APGA. However, APGA had passed a moratorium on the creation of new divisions, so AMHCA developed as a freestanding entity; it later rejoined APGA when the moratorium was lifted. Membership grew rapidly, and this committed group of individuals began to formalize its professional identity through the development of leadership, training standards, and a code of ethics (Colangelo, 2009).

AMHCA and ACA have not always been content as partners. AMHCA membership often felt that ACA was too spread out and unfocused. AMHCA prided itself on truly serving the clinical mental health counselor and promoting associated legislation. Over the 1990s, AMHCA membership continued to grow, ACA membership fell, and ACA moved away from the type of legislative efforts important to AMHCA. As such, the two organizations separated in terms of finances and administrative hierarchy. However, AMHCA continues to maintain its status as an official division of ACA (Colangelo, 2009), and thus its code of ethics falls within that structure.

The AMHCA code was first written in 1976 when the organization formed and was most recently revised in 2010 (www.amhca.org). Its preamble distinguishes the code as being specific to mental health counselors and highlights the commitment mental health counselors have to ongoing education of themselves and about the clients they serve (AMHCA, 2010).

The AMHCA code defines its purposes as

1. To assist members to make sound ethical decisions
2. To define ethical behaviors and best practices for Association members
3. To support the mission of the Association
4. To educate members, students and the public at large regarding the ethical standards of mental health counselors (AMHCA, 2010, p. 1)

From a technical perspective, only AMHCA members are governed by this code. However, taking that technical perspective meets only the letter of the law, not the spirit. All clinical mental health counselors should consider the AMHCA code when faced with ethical conflicts. Why? The AMHCA code not only encompasses all the core values and principles of the ACA code but also provides a section specific to client rights. So although counselors may not fall under both codes, a distinction discussed in the next section, they should consider them both as they formulate ethical decisions.

VOICE FROM THE FIELD 2.1

Being a self-admitted ethics geek, it is hard to pinpoint the exact time in my professional career when I became interested in counseling ethics. During my PhD program, I began to do more research into ethics and ethical practice. Toward the end of my PhD program, I saw that the president of ACA was seeking volunteers to serve on its various committees. One committee option was the ACA Ethics Committee.

I figured it was a long shot, but I submitted my application and was later surprised when the president appointed me to a three-year term on the Ethics Committee. I was both nervous and excited about this professional opportunity. This is when my true passion for ethics came alive. I got to work side by side with the leading ethics experts in our field. We debated issues of ethical practice, and through each dialogue we had, and each ethics hearing we conducted, I learned about the importance of valuing the gray in counseling and ethical decision making. During my time on the ACA Ethics Committee, I was appointed to chair the ACA Code of Ethics revision process. Our task force met for three years as we crafted what is now the 2005 ACA Code of Ethics. If someone were to have told me during my graduate training that someday I would be chairing the task force that would be writing ethics policy and standards that would impact the entire profession, I would have thought he or she were a little . . . well . . . crazy. Helping write the ACA Code of Ethics was one of the highlights of my professional career, an experience I will never forget. It was a privilege to work with such visionaries and scholars in creating ethical standards in a wide range of areas, such as diversity, end-of-life issues, technology, boundaries, and a host of others.

I think our profession has to address the cutting-edge ethical issue of social media, as more and more people are using it; according to some reports, if you were to count all the people in the world that use social media, it would be the third largest country in the world! Because of the vast potential of emerging technology, along with legitimate ethical concerns about it, counselors must further learn about the ways to use it to best serve their clients. I also think that the profession will continue to grapple with traditional ethical issues such as confidentiality, boundaries, and dual relationships, especially in various cultural and rural communities.

When I teach my graduate ethics course to counseling students, I give each student a ribbon on the first day of class. This ribbon has three stripes—one white, one black, and one gray—and is emblematic of what I hope my students will take away from my ethics course. I want them not to study or memorize a bunch of rules or ethics standards to avoid getting into professional trouble, but, more important, to embrace the gray of ethics; to recognize the importance that sometimes ethical dilemmas are multifaceted and complex. Counseling professionals have to become comfortable in their "thinking" about ethics, as well as their "feeling" about ethics and about the gray space in each and every ethical challenge . . . it is what I call the "head" and "heart" process of ethics. I encourage any graduate student and new professional to consider joining a professional ethics committee. Learn all you can about ethics. Share your passion for the gray!

Michael M. Kocet, PhD, LMHC
Associate Professor of Counselor Education, Bridgewater State University

---

Which Code Do I Fall Under?

Which code do you fall under as a clinical mental health counselor? This is a complex question with a deceptively simple answer: it depends. First of all, it depends on an individual's professional affiliations. If counselors are a member of ACA and of AMHCA, they fall under both codes. The ACA code is used when counselors hold no membership; and because ACA is the parent organization and AMHCA a division, it is likely that even counselors with only AMHCA membership are to uphold ACA standards as well. The second consideration is state law. Each state has the independent liberty to elect to adhere to the ACA, AMHCA, or state-specific codes. Many states choose to use the AMHCA code because it encompasses the ACA code and is specific to professional mental health counselors. However, many other states use the ACA code as the "parent" code for all counselors. Ultimately, it is individual counselors' responsibility to understand both their professional memberships and state law.

Be aware that the two codes discussed here are not the only codes under which clinical mental health counselors may fall. Those seeking credentialing as a National Certified Counselor will fall under the National Board for Certified Counselors (NBCC) code. Those electing to obtain additional certification, for example, as a Certified Substance Abuse Counselor, will need to adhere to that code as well. As previously mentioned, the good news is that ethical codes have more in common than they do differences. However, it is each individual's obligation to understand and uphold all of these codes in his or her practice as an ethical counselor. Most licenses and certifications require ongoing continuing education in ethics in order to keep professionals in touch with these guidelines. By complying with those standards of career-long learning, clinical mental health counselors will be able to maintain an understanding of ethical codes and current trends in the profession.

Ethical Decision-Making Models

Identify a time when you had to make a particularly difficult decision in which there was no one right answer. How did you determine what to do? What steps did you take? In counseling the ethical codes are the framework for all ethical decisions; however, they do not tell anyone how to make those decisions. A professional may know that something is wrong, but be unsure about how to make it right. Of great importance to the ethical counselor is the use of ethical decision-making models. The foundation of all ethical decision making is this set of fundamental principles originally conceptualized by Kitchener (1984):

1. *Autonomy*—Counselors believe in the client's right to independence and ability to choose.
2. *Nonmaleficence*—Counselors believe that they have an obligation to do no harm.
3. *Beneficence*—Beyond doing no harm, counselors believe in the obligation to do good and to be of help to the client.
4. *Justice*—Counselors treat clients the same under the same conditions.
5. *Fidelity*—Counselors are loyal, faithful, and trustworthy in order to support the client.

These central principles represent the base on which ethical codes and ethical decision-making models are built. The ultimate goal of these principles is to create a trusting environment that represents the client's best interests. This is crucial to keep in mind in the discussion of how to determine whether an ethical dilemma exists and how best to address it.

Ethical decision-making models are stepwise means to approach an ethical dilemma. In the ACA Code of Ethics purpose statement, counselors are specifically asked to use an ethical decision-making process whenever they face an ethical dilemma (ACA, 2005). Because numerous ethical decision-making models exist, and because counselors differ in their values and expectations related to ethical decision making, they "are expected to be familiar with a credible model of decision making that can bear public scrutiny and its application" (ACA, 2005, p. 3). Using such a model, counselors can then make sound ethical decisions that are in the best interests of the clients and public they serve.

In short, ethical counselors are required to utilize an ethical decision-making model when faced with an ethical quandary. If proof of doing so is requested, the counselor should be able to produce the model and discuss the steps taken, including how the counselor arrived at the outcome and the actions taken as a result.

Because an ethical decision-making model is essential to use, and because no one model is empirically validated above another, this discussion focuses on a number of well-known and often used models in the counseling profession. As you review these, recognize that some of these models fit particular theories, whereas others fit particular types of mental health counseling. It is incumbent on counselors to find and utilize the model that best fits the problem or challenge at hand. And, as always, it is their professional responsibility to document the process.

There are numerous ethical decision-making (EDM) models available for counselors. ACA provides counselors with "A Practitioner's Guide to Ethical Decision Making" (Forester-Miller & Davis, 1996) as a guide in deciding how to make ethical decisions. ACA offers a blended model that incorporates multiple well-known EDMs, and it serves as the basis for discussion in this chapter.

VOICE FROM THE FIELD 2.2

I originally developed an interest in ethics when I noticed the lack of actual ethical decision making (i.e., the use of an ethical decision-making model or systemized plan) occurring among practitioner colleagues, field supervisors, and recent graduates. Instead, it seemed more common practice to "talk one's way out" of a gray area with a client and then document one's actions. Although some in this circle went as far as consultation with other professionals—which is a good thing—following an actual plan when faced with a gray area or ethical dilemma seemed to occur infrequently. Additionally, it appeared that many master's-level students understood the definition of ethical decision-making (EDM) models and had learned about them, yet stopped short of applying this awareness into practice. Frankly, in my 10 years of supervising master's-level field experiences, I cannot recall a field experience supervisor using and/or teaching an actual ethical decision-making model to an intern. This is not to say that these supervisors and others are not doing so, but I never experienced it. This concerned me.

Implementing an ethical decision-making model is listed as number two of the top ten risk management strategies that may lower counselors' risk of liability (Wheeler & Bertram, 2008). So although EDM models seemed not to be common practice, use of them may protect practitioners from legal risk.

Becoming aware of what seemed to be limited use of ethical decision-making approaches made me wonder how ethical decisions were being made by practitioners. I also speculated often about the larger ethical responsibility we have toward each other as practitioners and that counselor educators and supervisors have for counselors in training/students, and counselor educators and practitioners have for the welfare of the general public, one of the foundations of our ethical code (ACA, 2005). I began to consider how I could help in this area of professional counseling, and this led to my considering application to the ACA Ethics Committee.

I would be remiss if I didn't also admit to an odd, but maybe human, fascination with violations of ethical practice in professional counseling. Many of us think of the standard counseling course in ethics as typically tough but nonetheless interesting—and sometimes even exciting—to consider the gray in human behavior that goes astray for what, to the onlooker, seems illogical. At present, the two most common violations of ethical practice are intimate relationships with clients and inadequate informed consent. In our day-to-day practice, we wonder how others can cross professional boundaries and enter into sexual misconduct with those they have a professional obligation to protect and help. And, often we assume informed consent is a sort of "check off the box" procedure; that is, we tell the client how to reach us during a crisis, how we work, when we break confidentiality, and we find out who makes up the client's support system. Often, we don't keep in mind that adequate and appropriate informed consent consists of these elements plus a regular check-in with the client to assess for his or her comprehension. So how is it that others commonly cross professional boundaries and rarely check in with clients for comprehension, when we know the associated risks of both? Seems irrational, doesn't it? This is the personal side of my interest in ethics—an interest in the side of human behavior that involves a paradox of logic and illogic; that is, knowing better but doing it nonetheless.

Being a member of the Ethics Committee enabled me to participate in adjudications that investigated ethical violations of the ACA membership and in delving deeply into the many ethical codes. Reviewing the codes in relation to potential violations, and discussing matters with other committee members, can be fulfilling for those who appreciate complex discussions about gray areas, which also have to follow a particular level of structure. Most of us have a proclivity for a particular area of study or population in which we enjoy being immersed. Ethics is that area for me.

STACY L. HENNING, PhD, LPC, ACS
Assistant Professor/Worldwide Director, Counselor Education, Webster University

KITCHENER   The first EDM addressed is one of the oldest applied to the counseling profession. In 1984, Kitchener wrote a groundbreaking article on the application of moral principles to ethical decision making. In it, she asserted that the five moral principles previously mentioned undergird all ethical concepts (Kitchener, 1984). The moral principles of autonomy, nonmaleficence, beneficence, justice, and fidelity have been widely accepted in the fields of helping professions as crucial to ethical decisions. Kitchener posited that these principles serve as the foundation for understanding the ethical dilemma and thus generating the best solutions. For example, ethical dilemmas about privacy or confidentiality are often impacted by the moral principle of autonomy. When a counselor breaks a client's confidentiality, the counselor is not allowing the client to make the decision about who knows his or her information. Is this always unethical? Of course not! Within autonomy are embedded concepts related to competence. If someone is a minor, mentally compromised, or a threat, that person is not competent to make autonomous decisions. It is in such situations that the various ethical codes may actually seem to contrast with one of the primary principles, such as client autonomy.

In other words, even the principles our ethical codes are built on are not absolute. Rather, when using the Kitchener EDM, we are asked to consider the five moral principles as prima facie binding. This simply means that we are obligated to abide by the concepts outlined within the five moral principles "unless there are special circumstances or conflicting and stronger obligations" (Kitchener, 1984, p. 52). The conditions that overturn these principles must be strong ones, as you can imagine, and may even be dictated by law.

BENEFICENCE MODEL   The concept of beneficence was introduced through Kitchener's model. Later, a model built on that principle emerged and has been effectively used in counseling. Sileo and Kopala's (1993) Beneficence model is composed of an A-B-C-D-E worksheet intended to promote ethical decisions that serve to help the client in the situation; thus the term *beneficence* is applied. The A-B-C-D-E worksheet attempts to make abstract ethical dilemmas concrete and problem solving more practical. Although there are no perfect solutions, and the steps of the worksheet are not ordered sequentially for all dilemmas, this worksheet serves as a handy guide, particularly for the beginning counselor. A brief overview of the model follows:

A. Assessment
1. What is the client's mental state?
   a. What are his/her strengths, support systems, weaknesses?
   b. Is a psychiatric/medical consult necessary?
2. How serious is the client's disclosure? Is someone at risk for physical harm?
3. Are there cultural values and beliefs which should be considered while assessing the client?
4. What are my values, feelings, and reactions to the client's disclosure?

B. Benefit
1. How will the client benefit by my action?
2. How will the therapeutic relationship benefit?
3. How will others benefit?
4. Which action will benefit the most individuals?

C. Consequences and Consultation
1. What will the ethical, legal, emotional, and therapeutic consequences be for:
   a. The client?
   b. The counselor?
   c. Potential clients?
2. Have I consulted with colleagues, supervisors, agency administrators, legal counsel, professional ethics boards, or professional organizations?

D. Duty
1. To whom do I have a duty?
   a. My client?
   b. The client's family?
   c. A significant other?
   d. The counseling profession?
   e. My place of employment?
   f. The legal system?
   g. Society?

E. Education
1. Do I know and understand what the ethical principles and codes say regarding this issue?
2. Have I consulted the ethical casebooks?
3. Have I recently reviewed the laws that govern counseling practice?
4. Am I knowledgeable about the client's culture?
5. Have I been continuing my education through journals, seminars, workshops, conferences, or course work? (Dinger, 1997, p. 37)

Sileo and Kopala (1993) are quick to point out that the worksheet does not provide perfect solutions. There are no formulas for ethical decision making. However, once an ethical dilemma is identified, the worksheet does help counselors evaluate potential courses of action.

FORESTER-MILLER AND DAVIS   The final EDM investigated here is one that is a bit older, but considered seminal in the field: the Forester-Miller and Davis model. This model is derived from earlier seminal works including Kitchener's and is contained in a document housed on the ACA Web site entitled "A Practitioner's Guide to Ethical Decision Making." Forester-Miller and Davis (1996) suggest that the first step in any ethical decision is to determine whether there is a problem. There are numerous challenges in the counseling field but not all of them are unethical. Some behaviors are unethical, some illegal, and others are unprofessional. Can you think of a behavior that a counselor might engage in that is unprofessional but is not illegal or unethical? For example, what if a counselor is routinely 10 minutes late? Or what if a counselor accepts checks but doesn't deposit them for several weeks? Or how about the counselor who decorates her office and herself in all purple, and purple only? These are examples of things that may be unprofessional but are rarely unethical or illegal. Conversely, counselors may engage in illegal behaviors that are not unethical. For example, counselors might speed to an appointment or park illegally when they get there. The point is that when looking at problematic or troubling events, the first step is always to determine whether an ethical problem even exists.

The second step according to Forester-Miller and Davis (1996) is to consult the ACA Code of Ethics. In order for an issue to be an ethical dilemma, it must align with one or more of the codes. Of course, the counselor may also look to AMHCA and other relevant codes to determine how the issue is addressed there. The counselor is then encouraged, in the third step, to "[d]etermine the nature and dimensions of the dilemma" (Forester-Miller & Davis, 1996, p. 3). This simply means that the counselor looks at the moral principles, such as autonomy and beneficence, that were previously discussed. In addition, the counselor is instructed to consult the relevant professional literature that might guide the process. A final part of this step is to consult with other professionals. The act of consultation is critical and shows that the counselor did not act in isolation when making ethical decisions.

The fourth step of the Forester-Miller and Davis model is to generate all possible courses of action. This brainstorming activity is to help the counselor come up with any and all outcomes, even those that might be discarded. It is suggested that the counselor engage the help of a least one colleague in this effort to uncover ideas that he or she may be blind to in the moment. The fifth step involves an actual decision. After brainstorming and consulting, it is time to select and commit to a course of action. The process thus far indicates a willingness to find the best solution prior to acting. Of course, before acting on this decision, the counselor will engage in the sixth step, which is to evaluate this plan of action. Submit the choice to three tests: justice, publicity, and universality. To do so, ask yourself the following:

1. Would I treat other people the same way in a similar situation? (justice)
2. If this action were reported in the news, would I feel OK about my choice? (publicity)
3. Would I recommend this action to another counselor who consulted with me? (universality)

If the counselor can answer positively to all three questions, he or she is ready to engage in the seventh step and actually take the action (Forester-Miller & Davis, 1996).

To review, the model housed on the ACA Web site follows seven steps:

1. Identify the problem.
2. Apply the ACA Code of Ethics.
3. Determine the nature and dimensions of the dilemma.

4. Generate potential courses of action.
5. Consider the potential consequences of all options; choose a course of action.
6. Evaluate the selected course of action.
7. Implement the course of action. (Forester-Miller & Davis, 1996, p. 4)

LEGAL ISSUES IN COUNSELING

Being an ethical counselor means understanding the association and state codes under which the profession falls, developing the ethical sensitivity needed to determine when dilemmas exist, and having an ethical decision-making model to follow to address these dilemmas. Part of the decision-making process involves investigating state or federal laws that may impact the decision. Although many counselors think they generally know what is and is not legal, the vast discrepancies in state laws require serious scrutiny into how ethical counselors practice legally.

First it is important to distinguish between the types of legal concerns that counselors may face. Criminal law would address issues such as felonies. For example, if a counselor were to embezzle from his or her office, that would fall under criminal law. Sex with a minor client would fall under criminal law, as would sex with an adult client in some states. Legal considerations that fall under the criminal heading are usually more obvious to counselors and carry severe penalties. Consequences of breaking laws and being prosecuted in a criminal court are intended to be punishments, such as incarceration. Civil law is different, however. Consequences of civil lawsuits are intended as redress; that is, as a means of compensating the victim for the wrong done to him or her. Civil cases can range from breaking confidentiality to slander to use of improper treatment techniques.

The reality is that anyone can sue anyone for anything. The proliferation of daytime court reality shows provides abundant evidence that we are a litigious society. Counselors do not practice without risk. They carry malpractice or liability insurance to help protect them should they ever need to defend their actions. Most counselors will never need to call upon this insurance policy, but in reality no one is immune to the potential of criminal charges or a lawsuit. It is important to be well prepared. Student counselors who join ACA or AMHCA receive liability insurance free as part of their membership, which will be useful during field placements. Following graduation, a liability policy is considered a necessity in risk management. Of course, the best defense is never to cross a legal boundary when working with clients, but such crossings do occur from time to time. Counselors must be well aware of state and federal laws that impact their work with clients.

Typically, each state will address a number of issues in its legal code. This code may be buried in terms for the medical profession but is likely used with counselors and other helping professionals as well. In other words, all of the laws will not be found under a simple heading "Laws About Counselors" in any state code or the federal code. Student counselors will become aware of the relevant laws during their graduate program, may take a jurisprudence exam about laws in their state prior to licensure, and will constantly seek continuing education to ensure they are aware of changes in the legal structure.

What types of laws impact the practice of counseling? There are many. Laws are on the books related to record keeping and storage, client confidentiality, minor consent and other forms of informed consent, billing and insurance, duty to warn, duty to protect, competency examinations, use of specific assessment instruments, privileged communication, and so on. The specifics of these laws are beyond the scope of this chapter or this text. Individual counselors need to seek out the state laws that impact them and their practice prior to engaging in such practice.

The Counselor in the Courtroom

While on the subject of legal issues, this text would be remiss if it did not also address the counselor in the courtroom. The preceding discussion alluded to the counselor as defendant. That is not a comfortable or desirable place for anyone in the profession to be. However, it may happen. What is also likely to happen is that the counselor will be invited into the courtroom for another purpose: for example, to testify, provide a deposition, produce records, or serve as a competency examiner. Although it is the rare counselor who is sued at the criminal or civil level, virtually every counselor I have ever met has received a subpoena or been involved in a client's court case at some level.

Subpoenas

What is a subpoena and how should a counselor respond? A subpoena is a document requesting one's testimony or records. It can be issued by a court or an attorney (Wheeler & Bertram, 2012). A *subpoena ad testificandum* requests the counselor's testimony and is most likely issued by a court. A *subpoena duces tecum* requests the counselor's records or other documents, and may be issued by a court or an attorney.

Counselors have a number of steps to follow when they receive a subpoena. First, they should accept the subpoena. On television and in movies people often run from the subpoena server. As professionals, counselors are expected to receive this legal document and respond to it. Next, counselors consult with their attorney as well as their supervisor. If a counselor works for an agency, the agency has a right to know that the counselor has received a subpoena, and it probably has a protocol in place about how to respond. Counselors must not ignore a subpoena or they will be held in contempt of court.

Does receiving a subpoena mean the counselor has to produce all and tell all? Absolutely not. It begins the process, but is not the complete definition of the process. For example, I have received a subpoena at the end of a workday to produce records the next day. However, subpoenas must be delivered to allow sufficient time to respond. In this case, I was able to get a delay in order to have adequate time to determine the legal and ethical response. As another example, say that a counselor receives a subpoena to produce records or testimony that his or her client does not want the counselor to share, and the counselor lives in a state where he or she has privileged communication. The counselor may call upon that privilege. Privileged communication is simply any communication that occurs within the context of a legally protected relationship (Remley & Herlihy, 2010). Not all counseling relationships meet this legal standard. For example, I am licensed in a state where privileged communication is offered only to licensed counselors. For those who do not seek licensure or who have not yet earned their license, privileged communication does not exist. An attorney who works with medical and helping professionals will serve as a good guide for a counselor should any legal issues arise.

What about court testimony? As previously mentioned, a counselor may be asked to testify on behalf of a client or because of a subpoena. The profession's ethical code is clear that counselors do not provide forensic testimony about clients they have counseled (see ACA code, E.13.c. Client Evaluation Prohibited; ACA, 2005). On the other hand, if a counselor is hired as an evaluator, then he or she can provide such testimony. However, a counselor cannot be seeing a minor client who is dealing with issues related to his parents' divorce and then offer court testimony related to who should have custody. In this instance, a counselor may have an opinion, but cannot share it.

Finally, counselors are guided by their ethical code to provide only the minimal information needed for any disclosure, even if giving more information is legal. If they receive a request for records, they must ascertain what records are specifically needed. If the client record contains records for a referring source, such as discharge paper from a hospital, counselors are not legally authorized to share that information. In many cases, a summary of the records is acceptable to the court. It is the rare occasion when a court truly wants or needs an entire client record. Generally, counselors will keep their client informed about the subpoena and consult with the client about the appropriate response.

COMMON ETHICAL AND LEGAL DILEMMAS IN CLINICAL MENTAL HEALTH COUNSELING

Now that ethical codes, ethical decision making, and legal issues have been covered, the discussion will move on to those dilemmas that are common in the ethical and legal practice of counseling. This section looks at general areas of ethical and legal concern and is not intended to replace a course in ethics or additional ethical education.

Informed Consent and Confidentiality

Have you ever thought about the level of privacy and confidentiality involved in counseling? You have probably assumed that what is said in counseling stays in counseling. However, this is not always the case. Confidentiality originated when society deemed the individual's right to seek treatment as greater than society's right to know why the individual was seeking treatment. As the helping professions have evolved, the concept of confidentiality has garnered a number of exceptions including duty to warn and protect from harm, court orders, and cases of malpractice.

Limits to confidentiality must be clearly explained to clients in language they can understand (see ACA code A.2.c. Developmental and Cultural Sensitivity; ACA, 2005). Typically, this process is referred to as *informed consent.* Informed consent actually includes a number of elements including risks and benefits of treatment, payment policies, and confidentiality. Informed consent is provided by the treating counselor, not a secretary or administrative person, when counseling is initiated. But informed consent is not a single event; it is actually a process. As such, the counselor is responsible for reminding the client about the limits of confidentiality throughout the treatment process. The ACA Code of Ethics contains an entire section (section B) on the idea of confidentiality and introduces the section with this foundation for understanding the importance of the topic:

> Counselors recognize that trust is a cornerstone of the counseling relationship. Counselors aspire to earn the trust of clients by creating an ongoing partnership, establishing and upholding appropriate boundaries, and maintaining confidentiality. Counselors communicate the parameters of confidentiality in a culturally competent manner. (ACA, 2005, p. 7)

In addition, the AMHCA code contains a section (section I.A.2) dedicated to confidentiality with an emphasis on the need to protect any information about clients whether counselors work with them in clinical practice, research and assessment, or teaching and evaluation (AMHCA, 2010). Although the ACA code addresses the idea of consent, the AMHCA code goes several steps further to discuss types of information that are considered confidential, the storage and disposal of such information, and ethical uses of electronic information. In this section of its code, counselors will also find directions related to confidentiality in specific situations such as when clients have a communicable or life-threatening illness, when a third-party payer requests information for insurance, and when information must be disclosed due to abuse or protection of life.

Competence and Malpractice

Competence and malpractice are not only legal concerns but also ethical concerns. Is the counselor properly trained, certified, and licensed to provide services? Under what governing authority is the counselor granted the ability to work with a specific population or in a specific state? These are some of the ethical questions that must be answered by counselors.

Of course, not every type of counseling requires a specialty credential. Most master's programs in counseling produce graduates who are generalists. In other words, upon graduation these prelicensed counselors have the academic and skill competencies to provide general services. Prior to licensure, counselors in all states acquire numerous hours of practice under the direction of a clinical supervisor who meets the requirements of the state board. During this supervised work experience, beginning counselors may start on a path toward a specialty. When faced with a new client, all counselors should ask themselves, "Am I competent to provide services to this client?"

When competence is an issue or when treatment interventions are poorly chosen, legal and ethical issues may arise. The ACA Code of Ethics (2005) specifically addresses competence and malpractice in several areas:

- Counselors are ethically required to avoid harming clients. (A.4.a)
- Counselors may refer if they are not competent or comfortable with working with clients who have a terminal illness and are making end-of-life decisions. (A.9.b)
- Counselors assess and monitor their effectiveness with clients and work to improve their skills on an ongoing basis. (C.2.d)
- Counselors do not practice when impaired and take steps to avoid burnout. (C.2.g)
- Counselors use interventions that have empirical support or inform their clients that the intervention is not yet proven. (C.6.e)

Even though many components of the Code of Ethics address competence and malpractice, the reality is that no one can measure competence. Counselors can be licensed and certified yet still be of harm to a client if they are not also practicing ethically within their limits. Consulting with colleagues and a supervisor about competence is one means of checking one's own limits.

Boundary Issues

Some of the most difficult challenges professional counselors face are with boundaries. Boundaries are the limits counselors place on their relationships with others. Typical boundary concerns include gift giving, bartering, and multiple relationships.

Many counselors do not consider the ramifications of gift giving as they start their work. However, it is not uncommon for a client to want to commemorate an occasion or holiday with a token of appreciation for his or her counselor. This may sound innocent, but the many facets of such an overture must be looked at. Consider the following:

- A client overhears you telling a coworker how much you enjoy sweets during the holidays. At her next appointment, she brings you a batch of her "famous chocolate chip cookies." Do you accept them?
- You have worked with a client for several months and he has come for his last session. He brings you a card holder that he thinks would look nice on your desk as a way of saying thank you for working with him. Do you accept it?
- You provide services in a children's clinic. One of your regular clients paints a picture for you. Do you accept it?
- One of your adult clients with a developmental disorder sells scarves at a local flea market. She makes one just for you. Do you accept it?
- You have worked for quite some time with a family from another country as family members have faced the acculturation issues of moving to your area. They visit their country of origin over the summer. Upon their return, they bring you a small piece of pottery from their country as a token of their appreciation. Do you accept it?

Some counselors simply make a policy that they do not accept gifts of any kind. This may work in that it provides a hard and fast rule with no exceptions. But is it ethical? The ACA Code of Ethics (2005) includes the following language about gift giving:

A.10.e. Receiving Gifts Counselors understand the challenges of accepting gifts from clients and recognize that in some cultures, small gifts are a token of respect and showing gratitude. When determining whether or not to accept a gift from clients, counselors take into account the therapeutic relationship, the monetary value of the gift, a client's motivation for giving the gift, and the counselor's motivation for wanting or declining the gift.

Similar to gift giving, bartering involves an exchange of goods or services. With bartering, however, the client chooses to exchange goods or services for counseling services. In most instances, bartering involves a professional wishing to perform some skilled labor in exchange for services or someone who has goods worth an identified value that can be exchanged. The addition of bartering to the Code of Ethics came in the 2005 revision; prior codes discouraged bartering under any circumstance.

Counselors tend to fall into one of two camps related to bartering: they either prohibit it completely or see it as a potential solution for clients that is respectful of their culture. Either way, bartering comes with a host of complications. The counselor engaging in bartering should have "the burden of proof to demonstrate that (a) the bartering arrangement is in the best interests of [his/her] client; (b) is reasonable, equitable, and undertaken without undue influence; and (c) does not get in the way of providing quality psychological services to [his/her] client" (Corey, Corey, & Callahan, 2007, p. 282).

Perhaps the most challenging boundary issue counselors face is that of multiple relationships. Formerly known as dual relationships, counselors were advised to avoid these relationships in earlier versions of the ethical code. However, professional organizations such as ACA recognize that being a counselor does not preclude one's right to be a human, shop in local stores, hire local contractors, and the like. By simply going about their lives, counselors may encounter clients living out their lives. Occasional "sightings" of clients are not uncommon and are certainly not unethical. However, ethics is called into question if a counselor takes on a friend or family member as a client. The codes typically prohibit such relationships. However, what if a teller at your bank makes an appointment with you? What if the roofer you hired has an assistant who used to be your client? What if a teacher in your child's school wants you to work with her son?

As you can imagine, multiple relationships can be tricky to navigate. The ACA code (2005) is clear on a few points:

A.5.a. Current Clients Sexual or romantic counselor–client interactions or relationships with current clients, their romantic partners, or their family members are prohibited.

A.5.b. Former Clients Sexual or romantic counselor–client interactions or relationships with former clients, their romantic partners, or their family members are prohibited for a period of 5 years following the last professional contact.

However, the code is less strict about nonromantic relationships.

A.5.c. Nonprofessional Interactions or Relationships (Other Than Sexual or Romantic Interactions or Relationships) Counselor–client nonprofessional relationships with clients, former clients, their romantic partners, or their family members should be avoided, except when the interaction is potentially beneficial to the client.

A.5.d. Potentially Beneficial Interactions When a counselor–client nonprofessional interaction with a client or former client may be potentially beneficial to the client or former client, the counselor must document in case records, prior to the interaction (when feasible), the rationale for such an interaction, the potential benefit, and anticipated consequences for the client or former client and other individuals significantly involved with the client or former client. Such interactions should be initiated with appropriate client consent. Where unintentional harm occurs to the client or former client, or to an individual significantly involved with the client or former client, due to the nonprofessional interaction, the counselor must show evidence of an attempt to remedy such harm. Examples of potentially beneficial interactions include, but are not limited to, attending a formal ceremony (e.g., a wedding/commitment ceremony or graduation); purchasing a service or product provided by a client or former client (excepting unrestricted bartering); hospital visits to an ill family member; mutual membership in a professional association, organization, or community.

Although the ACA code is more specific than it was in the past, there are still a lot of decisions left in the hands of individual counselors and heavily influenced by the specific circumstances involved. There are no cookbook solutions in the Code of Ethics, so this is an area that is full of challenges. To make ethical decisions about multiple relationships, counselors will want to engage in consultation with other professionals, follow an ethical decision-making model, and when possible, involve the client in the decision.

Vulnerable Populations

Counselors are ethically charged with placing client welfare above all. In the ACA code (2005), that mandate is found here:

A.1.a. Primary Responsibility The primary responsibility of counselors is to respect the dignity and to promote the welfare of clients.

However, not all clients are able to make their own decisions regarding their care, and some may not be aware of what is in their best interest. When working with clients who fall into the category of a vulnerable population, counselors have special considerations in the counseling relationship. Clients who are minors, suffering from breaks with reality, or unable to make their own decisions due to illness, injury, age, or other change to cognitive functioning, are considered vulnerable. Vulnerable persons "are unable to avoid risk of harm on their own and are dependent on others to intervene on their behalf" (Remley & Herlihy, 2010, pp. 121–122). Counselors need to recognize their duty to empower their clients to make their own decisions, which is in line with the concept of autonomy. However, autonomy and client safety are not always compatible. Counselors may find that they have to make decisions to protect their clients. These decisions often involve breaches in confidentiality, which have been previously discussed. In terms of vulnerable populations, clinical mental health counselors adhere to legal and ethical standards that protect the client and best meet his or her needs.

ACA ETHICS COMMITTEE

The ACA Ethics Committee was established by the governing body of ACA, known as the ACA Governing Council. Specifically, the ACA Governing Council directs the Ethics Committee to educate ACA members about ethical concerns and the ACA Code of Ethics. In addition, the committee defines the process for adjudication of ethical complaints against members. Information about ethical complaints including the number of inquiries, complaints, and cases adjudicated is published annually by the committee (ACA, 2011).

So how exactly does the ACA Ethics Committee work to meet the directives of the ACA Governing Council? The committee works to educate counselors on the best ethical practices by keeping an up-to-date page on the ACA Web site that contains practitioner guides to understanding and implementing the Code of Ethics. The committee supports the work of the ACA task forces that are established to revise the code on a routine basis. Finally, the committee serves to adjudicate any cases that come before ACA (ACA, 2011).

ACA receives a number of ethical inquiries each year. An inquiry is simply a question posed to ACA as to whether or not something is ethical. These questions are posed to the Ethics Manager, who has a full-time paid position with ACA. If an inquiry has merit, the manager assists the person with the complaint process, which is a time-consuming task with many considerations. First of all, the person the complaint is about must be or have been a member of ACA at the time of the potential ethical violation. If the counselor being accused has never been a member of ACA, the association has no jurisdiction. Second, the complaint must clearly line up with one or more ethical codes. If the issue is not an ethical one, the ACA Ethics Committee has no jurisdiction. Finally, the complainant must be willing to complete all of the necessary paperwork and be willing to break his or her anonymity in order to file the complaint (ACA, 2011).

The ACA Ethics Committee receives and reviews each completed complaint application. Both the complainant and the accused are invited to a hearing and are allowed legal representation, if they like. Because ACA is a national organization, committee members, complainants, and the accused live in various parts of the country. Therefore, the hearings are conducted via conference call. If an ACA member is found guilty of an ethical offense, there may be sanctions or requirements such as completing continuing education hours in ethics. The committee also has the power to revoke ACA membership. Notice that neither of these sanctions directly impacts a counselor's license. The complainant actually has to file a separate case with the state in order for a counselor's license to be suspended or revoked. ACA and state licensure boards work closely together to protect the public from unethical practices by counselors.

Conclusion

Clinical mental health counselors must practice within ethical standards created by the profession as well as according to laws created by society. To do so, counselors stay abreast of changes to ethical codes as well as relevant state and federal laws. Professional counselors employ an ethical decision-making model to address ethical concerns as they arise. In addition, they maintain a network of professionals to consult with in order to ensure compliance with standard professional expectations. Clinical mental health counselors are aware of the roles and function of the ACA Ethics Committee as well as the ethical committees of other organizations and state licensure boards.

Being an ethical counselor sounds easy, but ethical dilemmas are complex. It is important for counselors to continue their education related to ethical matters and legal concerns by attending workshops and reading professional literature about ethical and legal considerations in counseling.

References

American Counseling Association (ACA). (2005). *Code of ethics.* Alexandria, VA: Author.

American Counseling Association (ACA). (2011). *American Counseling Association manual of policies and procedures.* Retrieved from http://www.counseling.org/AboutUs/PDF/Manual_of_Policies_and_Procedures.pdf

American Mental Health Counselors Association (AMHCA). (2010). *2010 AMHCA code of ethics.* Retrieved from https://www.amhca.org/assets/news/AMHCA_Code_of_Ethics_2010_w_pagination_cxd_51110.pdf

Colangelo, J. J. (2009). The American Mental Health Counselors Association: Reflection on 30 historic years. *Journal of Counseling & Development, 87*(2), 234–240.

Corey, G., Corey, M. S., & Callahan, P. (2007). *Issues and ethics in the helping profession* (7th ed.). Belmont, CA: Thompson Brooks/Cole.

Council for Accreditation of Counseling & Related Educational Programs (CACREP). (2009). *CACREP accreditation manual: 2009 standards.* Alexandria, VA: Author. Retrieved from http://www.cacrep.org/doc/2009%20Standards%20with%20cover.pdf

Dinger, T. J. (1997). *The relationship between two ethical decision-making models and counselor trainees'* responses to an ethical discrimination task and their perceptions of ethical therapeutic behavior (Doctoral dissertation). Available from ProQuest Dissertations and Theses database. Retrieved from http://search.proquest.com/docview/304378102?accountid=14872

Forester-Miller, H., & Davis, T. (1996). A practitioner's guide to ethical decision making [White Paper]. Retrieved from http://www.counseling.org/docs/ethics/practitioners_guide.pdf?sfvrsn=2

Kennedy, A. (2005). How the ethics code came to be revised. *Counseling Today, 48*(4), 10, 24.

Kitchener, K. S. (1984). Intuition, critical evaluation and ethical principles: The foundation for ethical decisions in counseling psychology. *Counseling Psychologist, 12*(3), 43–55.

Remley, T. P., Jr., & Herlihy, B. (2010). *Ethical, legal, and professional issues in counseling* (3rd ed.). Upper Saddle River, NJ: Pearson.

Sileo, F. J., & Kopala, M. (1993). An A-B-C-D-E worksheet for promoting beneficence when considering ethical issues. *Counseling and Values, 37*(2), 89–95.

Wheeler, A. M., & Bertram, B. (2012). *The counselor and the law: A guide to legal and ethical practice* (6th ed.). Alexandria, VA: American Counseling Association.

3

Education, Credentialing, and Professional Development

MATTHEW R. BUCKLEY AND STACY HENNING

CHAPTER OVERVIEW

In this chapter, we discuss the importance of professional credentialing in clinical mental health counseling. We first provide an introduction to the process of professional development including differences in types of academic preparation (e.g., programs, levels of training, and specialization areas). Then there is an in-depth discussion of credentialing and licensure. This chapter concludes with recommendations for ongoing preparation/training past the initial licensure and certification stage. Throughout this chapter specific examples help facilitate understanding of the credentialing process.

LEARNING OBJECTIVES

The learning objectives for this chapter are designed to be consistent with the 2009 Council for Accreditation of Counseling and Related Educational Programs Standards (CACREP, 2009). As such, upon completion of this chapter, the student will have knowledge of the following clinical mental health counseling standards:

1. Understands ethical and legal considerations specifically related to the practice of clinical mental health counseling. (A.2)
2. Knows the professional organizations, preparation standards, and credentials relevant to the practice of clinical mental health counseling. (A.4)
3. Is aware of professional issues that affect clinical mental health counselors (e.g., core provider status, expert witness status, access to and practice privileges within managed care systems). (A.7)
4. Understands professional issues relevant to the practice of clinical mental health counseling (C.9)
5. Knows public policies on the local, state, and national levels that affect the quality and accessibility of mental health services. (E.6)

Additionally, students will have knowledge of the following core entry-level standards:

1. Students actively identify with the counseling profession by participating in professional organizations and by participating in seminars, workshops, or other activities that contribute to personal and professional growth. (C)
2. History and philosophy of the counseling profession. (G.1.a)
3. Professional roles, functions, and relationships with other human service providers. . . . (G.1.b)
4. Professional credentialing, including certification, licensure, and accreditation practices and standards, and the effects of public policy on these issues. (G.1.g)
5. Ethical standards of professional organizations and credentialing bodies, and applications of ethical and legal considerations in professional counseling. (G.1.j)

KEY CONSTRUCTS

The following are key constructs necessary for understanding professional development:

Certification: A process through which an organization grants recognition to an individual who meets certain established criteria.

Licensure: The granting of permission by a competent authority to practice a profession.

Reciprocity: An agreement by a state to approve a license based on another state having already granted licensure.

INTRODUCTION

The purpose of this chapter is to introduce the fundamentals of preparing for a career in clinical mental health counseling. The material is presented in such a way as to take you through each step of the process from beginning a counseling program, developing as a professional applying for licensure, preparing for certification and licensure exams, and becoming licensed as a professional counselor while maintaining vibrancy and staying active as a professional.

The path to becoming a clinical mental health counselor begins with enrolling in and successfully persisting through a graduate program in counselor education. Finishing an academic program in counseling includes successful completion of course requirements, demonstrating mastery of academic concepts, skills acquisition, and incorporation of ethical functioning in a culminating field experience (practicum and internship).

Most counseling programs promote lifelong learning through continuing education and professional development as being essential to mastering areas of specialization and keeping current with trends in the counseling profession. Continuing education can include additional coursework, additional training, certification in a particular area of practice, and/ or participation in professional conferences. Continuing education is increasingly becoming a requirement for counseling licensure renewal. State licensure boards require licensees to evidence (or to be prepared to evidence) continued professional development known as continuing education units (CEUs) or continued education (CEs). In addition to continuing education, counseling programs promote the development of professional identity by encouraging students to maintain membership and activity in professional associations.

The decision to engage in formal preparation for any profession is an important one because of the investment of time, energy, and financial resources in acquiring a professional degree. The decision to become a clinical mental health counselor means a multiyear investment that includes application to a counselor education program; successful completion of all facets of the program; post-master's accumulation of clinical counseling hours; and passing a state licensure exam(s). A professional and personal commitment is essential to successfully complete a professional counseling program, obtain appropriate credentialing, and provide "best practice" services.

In addition to academic preparation and professional credentialing, there are some fundamental considerations inherent in developing as a mental health counselor. Consider the following questions as you read through the remainder of this chapter and as you continue your academic preparation:

1. What does it mean to become a professional?
2. How can you be involved in advocacy for the profession of counseling?
3. How will you work on personal and professional wellness?
4. How will you develop multicultural competence?
5. What else do you need to do to develop skills for making ethical decisions and establishing personal and professional boundaries?

These considerations are important in developing a well-rounded and comprehensive approach to becoming a competent counselor.

ACADEMIC PREPARATION REQUIREMENTS

As described in Chapter 1, there are important differences in the preparation of mental health counselors and that of other helping professions. Counselor education has as its foundation the value that entry into the profession requires a master's degree rather than a doctoral degree. There is a basic belief that those with a master's degree in counseling are able to fulfill all essential professional responsibilities and practice independently. Hence, the "terminal" or final degree necessary to practice as a licensed professional counselor is a master's degree in counseling (or related program; e.g., Master of Education with a counseling emphasis). There are no additional licensure levels for those with a doctoral degree in counseling. In comparison, the field of psychology uses the doctorate as the terminal or final degree necessary to practice as a licensed psychologist. The field of social work is similar to counseling in that it requires a master's in social work to practice as a licensed social worker.

It is important to briefly mention the distinction between counseling and counseling psychology. Many entering and some graduating counseling students confuse the two professions for various reasons, so it is important as a counselor to be clear about the differences. Counseling psychology is one of 56 divisions within the American Psychological Association (APA). Its focus includes not only research and practice but also public policy in the field of professional psychology (www.apa.org). One is required to be a graduate of a doctorate in psychology program to hold the title of *counseling psychologist* (although one may have a master's in counseling psychology, the term *psychologist* is reserved for the doctoral degree). This differs from counseling in that to call oneself a counselor one needs a master's in counseling (or like degree in some states). The term *counselor* can be used by the master's- or doctoral-level graduate of a counseling program. Counseling is a profession in and of itself, whereas counseling psychology is a division, or working group, within the APA.

All fields related to mental health counseling (counseling, psychology, and social work) require postgraduate training and study to be licensed. Counseling, psychology, and social work require passing a profession-related national exam. For counseling graduates, the recognized licensure exams are the National Counselor Examination (NCE) and the National Clinical Mental Health Counseling Examination (NCMHCE), and candidates for licensure will take exams as stipulated by the state in which they apply for licensure. In addition to passing the applicable exam(s), the counseling graduate pursuing licensure is required to apply (in the appropriate state) and then complete between 2,000 and 4,000 hours of postgraduate supervised clinical practice (again, dependent on the state in which licensure is sought). In most cases, these postgraduate clinical hours are in the form of a paying job, which is supervised by a licensed professional counselor, or LPC. (Note that the designations for licensure vary from state to state and include some of the following: Licensed Professional Counselor—LPC; Licensed Mental Health Counselor—LMHC; Licensed Professional Mental Health Counselor—LPMHC; Licensed Clinical Professional Counselor—LCPC; and Licensed Clinical Mental Health Counselor—LCMHC.) Some states permit members of other helping professions to supervise counseling graduates as they work toward licensure. Upon completion of the postgraduate supervised clinical hours and passing the NCE and/or NCMHCE, the graduate submits an application for licensure, with evidence of passing the relevant exam(s) and completing the clinical hours. The state licensure board will determine licensure status upon receiving the documentation (ACA, 2012).

State licensure boards may permit reciprocity of licensure once a graduate has attained licensure status. *Reciprocity* is an agreement by a state to approve a license based on another state having already granted licensure. Hence, once you are licensed as an LPC or LMHC, you may be able to receive licensure in another state if the licensure board there determines that the requirements are substantially the same. Each state is different in its limits on reciprocity, so those seeking reciprocity should consult the respective state board for its requirements. (See National Board for Certified Counselors, www.nbcc.org, or American Counseling Association, www.counseling.org, for contact information on state licensure boards to determine policies regarding reciprocity.) Some states specify other states they have reciprocal agreements with, and other state boards note that they review applications and determine the appropriateness of reciprocity on a case-by-case basis.

Forty-Eight Versus 60 Semester Hour Programs

State licensure boards vary in the requirement for total degree semester hours toward professional counseling licensure. The semester hours for licensure have evolved from a total of 24 credit hours originally to a total of 48 to 60 (dependent on the state) credit hours currently required. Because semester hour requirements can change, counselors and counselors in training should stay abreast of changes in their state board's licensure requirements. At the time of this writing, the majority of state licensure boards required the completion of a 60 semester credit hour master's degree in counseling to apply for supervision toward LPC licensure; several states required 48 semester credit hours; one state

(Wisconsin) required 42 semester credit hours; and a few states did not cite a minimum number of required semester hours. Further, several state boards provide two, three, or even four licensure tiers for applicants, with each tier requiring different total degree semester hours. The tiers typically relate to total credit hours completed matched with responsibilities and practices a counselor is permitted to pursue. Hence, counseling licensure (and practice) is dependent upon the total number of degree semester hours. Licensure educational credit hour requirements vary by state and even within state in regard to tiers (ACA, 2012).

Although the number of required credit hours varies, all states require coverage of *core content areas* within the total required credit hours. Sharing core content areas strengthens the portability of licensed counselors when relocating within the United States and provides a common foundation for training. Hence, the 42-hour degree may be similar in core content to the 60-hour degree, but the latter provides the recipient with more content and potentially more specialized training. It is important to note that in professional counseling's quest for licensure portability, the trend appears to be that states are moving toward revising their credit hour requirement to 60 semester hours (90 quarter credit hours) within the next decade or so. Those states that increase credit hour requirements will likely provide a grandfathering period for counselors in the application process.

Academic Preparation

Although not every counselor preparation program is accredited by CACREP, the curriculum model/course content is often tied to state licensure requirements. In every CACREP-accredited program, regardless of emphasis area, curriculum is required to meet CACREP standards in eight core content areas:

1. Professional Orientation and Ethical Practice
2. Social and Cultural Diversity
3. Human Growth and Development
4. Career Development
5. Helping Relationships
6. Group Work
7. Assessment
8. Research and Program Evaluation (CACREP, 2009)

Often, programs actually name course titles after these eight core areas or provide titles that are similar to the eight core areas for ease of identification and to assist licensure boards in determining candidates' acquisition of appropriate content. Each core content area delineates standards that define the content to be covered in the related course. For example, students can expect to learn about "assessment instruments and techniques relevant to career planning and decision making" as denoted under the content area of (and typically taught in the course related to) career development (CACREP, 2009, p. 12). The eight core content areas combine to create the curriculum for becoming a professional counselor and serve as the foundation for a professional identity as a counselor.

The eight core content areas are also used by the National Board for Certified Counselors (NBCC) when developing test items for the National Counselor Examination (NCE). As mentioned previously, all counseling graduates who choose to be licensed as professional counselors are required to pass the NCE or the NCMHCE. Hence, attending a program that teaches the core content areas should provide students with the experience and background necessary to prepare for and pass the appropriate exam to become licensed.

Advanced Training Opportunities

Formal counselor preparation through a graduate program provides a basic foundation for students entering the profession and lays the groundwork for the start of a professional's lifelong education. Furr and Carroll (2003) found that counseling students undergo pivotal experiences within their graduate training that significantly impact their professional development. Busacca and Wester (2006) noted that a significant concern for graduate students is how they might integrate previous experience into their work as counselors and align their values with those of the profession. Students may enter a counseling program immediately upon completion of an undergraduate degree, or they may enter a counselor preparation program after years spent in another career path.

Students within counselor preparation programs have a variety of life experiences that impacts their choices about areas of specialization in the field. Specialization areas constitute working with clients of a particular developmental level, of a certain socio-economic demographic, or in a particular professional context such as mental health, school, or career counseling. A useful strategy in preparing for a career as a professional counselor is for students to remain open to being influenced by the experiences they have in their graduate programs and use them as the basis for advanced training. Some experiences will confirm the choice to pursue a particular specialty or to further research another specialization. These experiences include research of the professional literature, attendance at professional conferences, networking with other professionals, specialized training in the form of workshops or certified trainings, consultations with mentors and supervisors, and field experience. These important experiences plant the seeds of further skill attainment and technical expertise that will shape a personal counseling style, professional identity as a counselor, and career path over the course of a lifetime.

Regarding advanced training opportunities, state licensure boards and certification agencies require professional counselors to practice within the scope of their professional practice (ACA, 2005, 2012). This means that counselors have an ethical obligation to be trained and competent in the specialized areas of their practice. According to the ACA Code of Ethics (2005), "Counselors practice in specialty areas new to them only after appropriate education, training, and supervised experience. While developing skills in new specialty areas, counselors take steps to ensure the competence of their work and to protect others from possible harm" (C.2.b). For example, CACREP-accredited programs prepare counselors to understand career development over the life span, use career assessment instruments, and work with individuals with career concerns. However, a counselor who had taken only an introductory course in career counseling would likely practice unethically by calling herself a career counselor without undergoing additional training in this area of specialization.

Certifications in specialized areas of training typically begin when a new technique or innovative approach is developed and a body of research emerges to build support for the technique or counseling approach. Research informs the refinement of the technique as it is tested through practice in a variety of therapeutic contexts and settings. Research is conducted ranging from the efficacy of a technique or approach to the implications of using a technique with clients of different cultures. As new techniques are developed, recognized experts organize and develop curriculum to train junior practitioners within the discipline. They also develop certifications to signify to consumers of counseling services and to fellow practitioners that practicing counselors have met the highest level of training and that they possess a solid knowledge base and a minimum level of competence through supervised practice.

PROFESSIONAL ORGANIZATION SPECIALIZATIONS To support counselors in the process of continued training, certifications are offered in a number of general specialty areas that enhance professional practice. The NBCC offers certifications in a variety of areas, including School Counseling and Addictions Counseling (www.nbcc.org). The National Career Development Association (NCDA) provides for certification as a Career Development Facilitator (CDF) for professionals seeking advanced training in career counseling (www.ncda.org). These generalized specialization areas also happen to correspond to accreditation standards within the CACREP, which ensures that training programs meet the most rigorous training standards in the preparation of counselors in these general areas.

Professional organizations also offer certifications and trainings to help enhance professional practice and functioning. For example, the Association for Play Therapy (APT) lists a variety of training opportunities and training standards for certification as a Registered Play Therapist (RPT) and a Registered Play Therapist-Supervisor (RPT-S). These certifications require a graduate degree in an acceptable mental health field, a minimum number of courses within the discipline of play therapy, a minimum number of hours of supervised experience from an approved supervisor, and continuing education to maintain the credential (www.a4pt.org).

THEORY-BASED SPECIALIZATIONS Professional organizations built around specific theoretical orientations also provide opportunities for specialized training, such as the use of cognitive behavioral therapy (CBT). A number of organizations offer certification in CBT that will allow practitioners to specialize in this particular approach (see National Association of Cognitive-Behavioral Therapists, www.nacbt.org, or Academy of Cognitive Therapy, www.academyofct.org). Benefits from certification in these types of professional specializations include being a part of a preferred list of practitioners (typically on the Web site), documenting competence in an area of focus, identification with an association, opportunities for service within the organization, professional recognition, and enhanced practice.

Another example of a specialized approach is the emerging specialization in the area of trauma counseling involving the use of eye movement desensitization and reprocessing (EMDR), which involves very specific treatment protocols and techniques to be used, and experienced professional judgment. Competence and eventual expertise in the use of EMDR result from various levels of training (see Eye Movement Desensitization and Reprocessing Institute, www.emdr.com).

Other counseling approaches and techniques require specialized training in order to practice them legally in many states or jurisdictions. Biofeedback, neurofeedback, hypnosis, and progressive muscle relaxation are examples of techniques that also require specialized training and even supervision in order to develop the expertise to use them proficiently and ethically. For example, the Texas law for licensed professional counselors provides for the use of "hypnotherapy which utilizes the principles of hypnosis and post-hypnotic suggestion in the treatment of mental and emotional disorders and addictions" (Texas Administrative Code, Chapter 681.31.13), but also requires that the use of "specific methods, techniques, or modalities within the practice of professional counseling . . . limited to professional counselors appropriately trained and competent in the use of such methods, techniques, or modalities" (Texas State Board of Examiners of Professional Counselors Title 22, 2009). This statute is representative of other state statutes that regulate the practice of professional counseling regarding the specialized use of techniques, interventions, and approaches. Students are well advised to be aware of specific state licensure board statutes as they learn about and explore various techniques they may choose to employ in their professional practice.

RESEARCH SPECIALIZATIONS   In addition to the existing opportunities for advanced training after graduate training is the potential to develop or participate in research within a little-explored field of study. Some master's-level counselors will seek additional training in the form of a doctoral degree within counselor education or a related discipline. As mentioned previously, the doctoral degree prepares students as potential educators and researchers who will eventually become the trainers of future counselors. Training counselors through direct teaching, mentoring, research, and supervision contributes significantly to the growth of the profession and positions professionals to shape and influence the direction of the profession. As with master's-level preparation programs, students are encouraged to research their choice of a doctoral program to ensure that it is accredited and meets the highest training standards.

INTRODUCTION TO THE CREDENTIALING PROCESS

A central aspect and the culminating act of professional training is becoming credentialed as a professional counselor. Although professional credentialing includes obtaining a master's degree within an approved program that will lead to state licensure, there are two main types of credentialing: *certification* and *licensure*. Certification "refers to the process of gaining a credential from a professional organization" (Schweiger, Henderson, Clawson, Collins, & Nuckolls, 2008, p. 4); it results in the recognition from a body of professional peers and the public that a professional has met certain training, experience, and examination standards to practice in a specialized area in the field. Whereas an academic degree signifies training in the profession generally, certification is specialized and demonstrates that recipients have intentionally engaged in a particular field of study that builds on their professional preparation. As mentioned previously, areas of specialized training typically have certifications attached to them that differentiate a professional from her or his peers. The National Board for Certified Counselors (NBCC) is the largest organization that certifies counselors in general and specialized practice. It was incorporated in 1982 from a committee formed by ACA to become an autonomous organization that would credential counselors. Since that time, NBCC has certified over 48,000 counselors who work within the United States and in 40 countries (Schweiger et al., 2008; www .nbcc.org). NBCC's flagship certification is the National Certified Counselor (NCC) credential, which attests that candidates have met the highest training standards in the profession,

TABLE 3.1   Requirements for the NCC Certification

- Completion of an eligible master's degree or higher in counseling. This achievement is documented with a sealed, official transcript showing degree conferral.
- 48 semester hours of graduate-level credit with 2 semester hours or greater in 8 content areas listed below and at least 6 semester hours of field experience.

Content Area Requirements (CACREP areas)

- Human Growth and Development Theories in Counseling
- Social and Cultural Foundations in Counseling
- Helping Relationships in Counseling
- Group Work Counseling Theories and Processes
- Career Counseling and Lifestyle Development
- Appraisal Assessment in Counseling
- Research and Program Evaluation
- Professional Orientation to Counseling
- Counseling Field Experience (in a counseling setting)
- Passing score on the National Counselor Exam (NCE).
- Documentation of postgraduate counseling experience and supervision: 3,000 hours with a minimum of 100 hours of counseling supervision—both over a 24-month post-master's period. Supervisors must hold a master's degree or higher in a mental health field. (Important Note: The post-master's work experience and supervision requirements are waived for graduate students who have completed CACREP-accredited tracks.)

Note: From "Requirements for the NCC Certification," by National Board for Certified Counselors (NBCC). Copyright 2012 by National Board for Certified Counselors. Retrieved from http://www.nbcc.org/nccreqs

whether from CACREP- or non-CACREP-accredited programs (see Table 3.1). Graduates from CACREP-accredited programs have an advantage in being able to apply for national certification while in the advanced phases of their graduate programs (more will be said about this later), and their postgraduate work experience and supervision requirement is waived. Graduates from non-CACREP-accredited programs must document two years of full-time postgraduate counseling experience, which must be overseen by a supervisor approved by the board.

The NCC is required for all subsequent certifications that NBCC offers. These additional certifications are for specialized training in other essential areas of the profession. Current specialized certifications include a Certified Clinical Mental Health Counselor (CCMHC), a National Certified School Counselor (NCSC), and a Master Addictions Counselor (MAC). An affiliate of NBCC is the Center for Credentialing and Education (CCE), which provides other important certifications including an Approved Clinical Supervisor (ACS); this signifies that professionals have met the training and experience requirements necessary to supervise counselors' clinical practice.

State licensure boards review certification requirements in these areas to determine minimal training standards for practice in relevant areas. For example, several states require that candidates for licensure select a supervisor from a list of "approved supervisors" who must hold the ACS credential in order to be recognized as such (ACA, 2012). National certification as a counselor does not equate to licensure, but it helps licensure

TABLE 3.2   Comparison of National Counselor Certification and State Counselor Licensure

	National Certification	State Licensure
Name of Credential	National Certified Counselor (**NCC**)—Issued by NBCC NBCC also offers three specialty certifications for NCCs in addictions, clinical mental health, and school counseling.	Differs from state to state. Most common titles are Licensed Professional Counselor (**LPC**), Licensed Mental Health Counselor (**LMHC**), Licensed Clinical Professional Counselor (**LCPC**), and Licensed Professional Clinical Counselor (**LPCC**). Issued by each state regulatory board.
Purpose	To promote and represent the counseling profession through a national certification program where the standards are set by members of the counseling profession. Compliance with continuing education requirements and the NBCC *Code of Ethics* ensure that NCCs stay current with the profession's best practices.	To protect the public by defining practitioners who can legally use the title of a licensed counselor and/or who can provide counseling services in a particular state. These standards are set by state legislatures.
Examinations	The National Counselor Examination for Licensure and Certification (**NCE**)	**NCE and/or NCMHCE**: State counselor licensure boards contract with NBCC to use one or both of these examinations.
Requirements	• Master's degree in counseling or with a major study in counseling from a regionally accredited institution • 3,000 hours of counseling experience and 100 hours of supervision both over a two-year post-master's time period • Post-master's experience and supervision requirements are waived for graduate students enrolled in or who have completed CACREP-accredited tracks. • Passing score on NCE	Varies from state to state. All require some combination of • Master's degree • Counseling experience and supervision • Passing score on NCE and/or NCMHCE. Some require mental health laws exam of that state.

Note: From "Comparison of National Counselor Certification and State Counselor Licensure," by National Board for Certified Counselors (NBCC). Copyright 2012 by National Board for Certified Counselors. Retrieved from http://www.nbcc.org /Certification-Licensure

board members (who are charged with determining the suitability of candidates for the legal practice of the profession in their state) recognize that an applicant is committed to professional development and competent practice.

The second type of postdegree credentialing is state licensure. Table 3.2 compares the NBCC's national certification with the state licensure of counselors. State licensure is different from certification in that it constitutes the legal permission to practice the profession and/or use the title "professional counselor" within the particular state or jurisdiction. Counselor licensure is categorized into two different types of state law: *practice acts* and *title acts*. Practice acts are more stringent and protective of the public in that they restrict the practice of counseling only to those who are licensed. Title acts restrict the use of the title (i.e., Licensed Professional Counselor) to those who are licensed, while allowing others who may be unlicensed to use the title "counselor" and engage in the practice of counseling (ACA, 2012). Because licensure is the state or jurisdiction's legal permission to practice counseling, it is the level of credentialing for counselors that allows them multiple methods of earning a living through private practice, billing third-party payers (including health insurance companies), and obtaining positions where licensure is a prerequisite for employment and promotion. As mentioned previously, within the licensure process, some states have different levels of licensure (ACA, 2012). These levels of licensure range from required oversight from a senior licensed professional to the ability to practice independently. For example, several states (e.g., Arkansas, Georgia, Florida) license a postgraduate beginning practitioner as a "Licensed Associate Counselor" or "Registered Mental Health Counselor Intern," which generally indicates that an individual is "completing the post-master's supervised clinical experience requirement" (ACA, 2012, p. 25). When considering levels of licensure, students are encouraged to prepare for the highest level of licensure, which ensures their ability to practice independently and includes being able to establish a private practice. There is a variety of important considerations when establishing a private practice, and consulting services are available from capable professionals and/or resources that can assist beginning counselors in establishing their own counseling or consulting practices (Stout & Grand, 2005). Information about credentials based on the NBCC's *Provision of Distance Professional Services* (2012c) is available at the Center for Credentialing & Education (2013).

Unlike professional associations, which have as their central focus the promotion of the counseling profession, licensure boards exist to regulate the practice of the profession within the particular state or jurisdiction, and board members are charged with protecting the public against those who would practice unethically or otherwise harm consumers of counseling services. Licensure board members consist of licensed counselors, counselor educators, licensed professionals from related professions (e.g., social work, marriage and family therapists), and/or public members who are unaffiliated with the profession except through their service to the licensure board. Because states administer their own laws, consumer experiences, institutions of higher learning (which train states' citizens), values of the profession, and practicing professionals within the state significantly influence how state boards regulate the profession (Bloom et al., 1990). Licensure boards incorporate the values of the state in which they regulate and interpret laws pertaining to professional counseling to ensure that licensed professionals practice within the scope of their professional preparation and incorporate best practices in ethical functioning. How the evaluation of licensure candidate applications occurs is a matter of board practice, process, and often tradition. For example, although many states require approved standardized exams to assess competence, some states call for additional activities to assess practice and professional presentation. Arkansas currently requires an oral interview wherein each applicant sits before the board in person and responds to board member questions regarding professional preparation, theoretical orientation, counseling interventions, scope of practice, clinical supervision, ethical functioning, the board's rules and regulations, and state law related to professional counseling. Facilitating oral interviews in this manner may be viewed as a cumbersome process; but it is based on the value that this licensure board wants to examine, in person, every licensure candidate who will work with its citizens and the belief that this activity will help in the assessment of ethical and professional functioning (ACA, 2012).

VOICE FROM THE FIELD 3.1

At 8:30 a.m., I enter the conference room. The board administrator hands me a packet of materials for the meeting. We have a lot to cover, including two hearings, hundreds of applications, next year's budget, and rule revisions. I call the meeting to order, and the vice chair reads the statement of conflict whereby each board member attests to having no known conflict of interest with any matter coming before the board.

The first order of business is approving next year's budget. The board's budget is well over $300,000 per year. I had no idea when I joined the board the costs associated with a licensure board. We manage a staff of five and there always seems to be a need for more administrative support. In the last two years, we have seen a jump in new applications and renewals from 1,500 a year to close to 3,000 per year. Two paid graduate internships are approved in hopes of alleviating some of the administrative strain and as an outreach to the graduate programs in the area.

Next, we discuss the proposed rule changes. The LPC law in our state added two levels of licensure a few years ago, and since then we have encountered a few gaps in the administrative code that need clarification. I guide the board members through our administrative code line by line for an hour. We discuss 12 of the total 31 sections. It is slow going, but the board members are carefully considering questions we have received and lots of "what-if" statements. At the same time, our assistant attorney general is helping ensure that any proposed changes align with the LPC law.

After lunch, we have two hearings. As the chair of the board, I serve as the hearing officer and have to carefully follow legal protocol, such as admitting evidence, ruling on objections, and facilitating the overall process. One case stands out. The petitioner committed murder 20 years ago, and through witness testimony she demonstrates an amazing rehabilitation and dedication to helping others not make the same mistakes she did. There is no way her application alone could have demonstrated what she was able to share with the board; the board unanimously approves her application to move forward.

It's been a long day with lots of hard decisions. Some applicants have been approved; others have not. The meeting adjourns at 6:15 p.m. As an LPC board member, I feel such a great responsibility for protecting the public and serving the counseling community. I never imagined that preparing to be a professional counselor and counselor educator would have provided me with such an opportunity.

NAME WITHHELD
Counseling Licensure Board

American Association of State Counseling Boards

Just as counselors have organizations that promote the profession and offer opportunities to collaborate and network, the umbrella organization focused on supporting state licensure boards is the American Association of State Counseling Boards (AASCB). AASCB was created in 1986 by the American Association of Counseling and Development (now ACA) with the intent to foster communication among state licensure boards and provide a venue for professionals and stakeholders seeking to develop counselor licensure within their own states. Several states sent representatives to the initial meeting in Kansas City, Missouri, where the framework of the organization was developed, bylaws were accepted, and officers were elected (www.aascb.org). Since that time, annual conferences have been held for participating board members and support staff representing their state boards to share current practices, trends within the profession in their states, application processes, licensure testing, board administration, and the training of new board members.

Association members also work on committees relevant to the work of licensure boards and discuss issues pertaining to examination of applicants for licensure; responses to ethical and legal violations; and the monitoring of board actions against culpable licensees, public policy, federal regulations impacting licensure, cyber counseling, and licensure portability. Licensure portability, for example, is an important issue for licensed professionals. Portability refers to the ability of professionals who have relocated to obtain a license in a state or jurisdiction because they have already been licensed in another state. Currently, portability is determined either by the law as an issue of reciprocity or on a case by case basis, which is not guaranteed from state to state. Another important related issue is the maintenance of standardized examination practices, which ensure that applicants successfully passing licensure exams in one state can have those exams recognized in another state or jurisdiction. Through the efforts of AASCB, a model licensure law was developed to help guide the development of licensure processes for each state and jurisdiction, and it is consequently helping to strengthen and legitimize the profession of counseling throughout the nation (Bloom et al., 1990). Because AASCB strongly supports the belief that competent counselors should be licensed or certified by the states in which they practice, it is dedicated to streamlining that process to ensure quality of care to consumers (AASCB, 2013).

Licensure Exams

Even though each state or jurisdiction has its particular licensure laws, they all depend on a standardized method of assessing the competence of those who apply for licensure. Professional competence is in part determined by passing licensure exams, which are based on the "knowledge, skills, and abilities viewed as important for providing effective counseling services" (NBCC, 2012a). Such knowledge, skills, and abilities are embedded in the current practice of the profession, which includes clients served by professional counselors, presenting problems and issues, ethical functioning, practice settings, theoretical orientation and accepted interventions, and multicultural competence.

Inherent in the exam development process are the concepts of *validity* and *reliability* of the instruments used. Validity is determined by an exam measuring what it is designed or intended to measure, and reliability is consistently measuring what is intended over repeated trials. In a way, licensure exams continue to evolve and reflect current practice in the profession. The primary way exams remain valid and reliable is through the use of committees composed of subject matter experts (i.e., seasoned professional counselors and counselor educators) and psychometricians who oversee the maintenance of exams. Exam committees develop specific protocols, follow them, closely monitor how exam items perform, and continually update exam items to ensure they meet the standards of current practice (Shawn O'Brien, personal communication, November 4, 2006). In this way, examinees are ensured to be tested on the knowledge, skills, and abilities related to their professional preparation and current practice in the field. Every five to seven years, each exam committee develops a comprehensive survey of professional practice called a job analysis, which is distributed to thousands of practicing professional counselors throughout the country. The data generated from these job analyses are used to design exam templates from which new exam items are created and existing items are updated.

As previously mentioned, two exams are most commonly used in counselor licensure: the National Counselor Examination (NCE) and the National Clinical Mental Health

Counseling Examination (NCMHCE), which are both owned and administered by NBCC. Each exam is overseen by an exam committee that meets twice a year coincident to exam administrations to review examinee performance data, develop cut scores, discover items that may be problematic, and review new items for consideration.

NATIONAL COUNSELOR EXAMINATION   The National Counselor Examination (NCE) is the most common exam used for state licensure and is also the exam used for national certification. The NCE is designed to test knowledge of general content related to the eight CACREP content areas identified in counselor education programs. These content areas constitute foundational knowledge each counselor should know regardless of specialized practice. Skills and abilities are assessed through work behavior areas, which include professional practice issues, programmatic and clinical interventions, and fundamentals of counseling. The exam consists of 200 multiple-choice items (25 items for each content area). In each content area, five of the 25 items are new items being piloted in the exam for future use; consequently, 160 items are "live" and count toward the passing score, whereas 40 items are being tested for subsequent versions of the exam. Examinees are given four hours in which to complete the exam, which is administered electronically through computer-based testing and in some cases using paper and pencil. In each exam administration, a new edition of the exam is prepared from a bank of test items developed and piloted by the exam committee.

National Certified Counselor for Graduate Students   As mentioned previously, to become a National Certified Counselor (NCC) applicants must document training in an approved master's program, demonstrate mastery of the content through successful passing of the NCE, and obtain approved supervised clinical experience. CACREP- and non-CACREP-accredited counselor preparation programs can apply to the NBCC for approval for students to apply for national certification and take the NCE when well advanced in their academic program (i.e., typically when in the last terms/semesters of their internship). The mechanism for the process of taking the NCE while students are still in their graduate program is through the National Certified Counselor for Graduate Students. Participating programs have an assigned coordinator (typically a faculty member) who is a liaison with NBCC and is charged with informing eligible students about this opportunity. Students complete an application for national certification, which includes the opportunity to sit for the NCE at their institution or at a public site in April and October of each year.

There are a few significant advantages to participating in national certification while still in a graduate program. First, because students are able to take the exam when well advanced in their graduate program, they are tested on material that is still "fresh" and being applied in their internship practice. Some students elect to wait to take the exam after graduation when they apply for licensure. This poses the challenge of relearning the material through review of course textbooks, class notes and papers, and/or commercially produced exam preparation materials. Second, students are able to obtain their first credential (besides their conferred degree) upon graduating from their counselor preparation programs. As part of the application process, program faculty provides written endorsement attesting to the quality of the student's professional preparation. Students are also required to affirm that they will adhere to the NBCC Ethical Code. Then when the degree is conferred, the student requests the degree-granting institution to submit a sealed transcript with the degree posted for the NBCC's review. Third, for students who graduate from CACREP-accredited programs, no postgraduate clinical experience and supervision is required to obtain this important and foundational certification.

NATIONAL CLINICAL MENTAL HEALTH COUNSELING EXAMINATION   The second primary exam utilized by many state boards is the National Clinical Mental Health Counseling Examination (NCMHCE). This exam was originally developed exclusively for licensure but is now used for certification as a Certified Clinical Mental Health Counselor (CCMHC) and for state licensure. Whereas some states (e.g., Florida, New York, and Virginia) require the NCMHCE exclusively for licensure, other states require both the NCE and the NCMHCE for licensure (e.g., Idaho, Kansas, and New Mexico). This two-examination process is based on a model testing process wherein the NCE acts as a postgraduation exam that largely assesses content and concepts related to the counseling profession, and the NCMHCE is a postsupervision exam, which means that students who complete all post-graduate supervision hours as required by their state board are best prepared to success-fully pass the exam. States' adoption of one or both exams is one example of the sovereignty state boards have in determining how to assess candidates' mastery of com-petent professional practice.

The NCMHCE is a very different type of exam from the NCE. It is based on clinical simulations that reflect a thought process and decision-making procedure parallel to what occurs in real practice. Each simulation's brief opening scenario provides the clinical set-ting, a short description of the client and presenting problems (issues), and, in some cases, elements of a brief history. Each simulation also contains five to eight sections that require the examinee to engage in information gathering (IG) or decision making (DM). Content related to gathering information and decision making is contained in three gen-eral domains: *Assessment and Diagnosis,* which involves knowledge and skills in assess-ing including conducting a biopsychosocial assessment or a mental status exam; *Counseling and Psychotherapy,* which targets an examinee's ability to diagnose and develop treatment plans including being able to use the DSM-IV-TR classification system, collaborating with clients, and coordinating treatment within a multidisciplinary treatment team; and *Administration, Consultation, and Supervision,* which is concerned with com-petent and ethical practice of mental health counseling.

In each section of the simulation, choices are available with latent information con-nected to each choice. Once the examinee makes a choice, the latent information will appear, which will be either correct or incorrect. Positive (related to correct choices) or negative (related to incorrect choices) point values ranging from +3 to −3 are related to each selection and are based on "the level of appropriateness for effective client care" (NBCC, 2012b). A correct choice not only will earn positive points but also will provide latent information relevant to subsequent sections in the simulation. Incorrect choices will result in negative points and latent information that is irrelevant in working with the cli-ent. In order to pass the section, the simulation, and ultimately the exam, an examinee must achieve the minimum positive points in each section by understanding which choices, consistent with best and appropriate practice, to make relative to the simulated clients within the exam. Successfully passing the NCMHCE is not based solely on knowl-edge related to the DSM-IV-TR, for example, but also on experience gained through supervised practice. Each administration of the exam includes 10 clinical simulations, and examinees are allowed four hours in which to take the exam. Because the exam is designed to be taken after the examinee has accrued all postgraduate supervised clinical hours, there is no graduate student administration of the NCMHCE.

OTHER EXAMS AND REQUIREMENTS RELATED TO LICENSURE   Two other exams are worth mentioning as accepted by several state licensure boards for licensure. The Certified Rehabilitation Counselor Examination (CRCE), focused on preparation as a rehabilitation counselor, is accepted in several states (i.e., Arizona; Washington, DC; Iowa; Michigan; North Carolina; Oregon; Pennsylvania; West Virginia; and Wisconsin) as an alternate licensure exam (www.crccertification.com). The Examination of Clinical Counseling Practice (ECCP), owned and administered by NBCC, was the original certification exam for clinical mental health counseling; it is accepted as an alternate exam for either the NCE or the NCMHCE in Illinois and Minnesota (ACA, 2012).

A trend within licensure boards is the requirement to have candidates for licensure pass a jurisprudence exam. As of this publication, 10 states require the passing of a jurisprudence exam (i.e., California, Colorado, Maryland, Oklahoma, Oregon, North Carolina, Tennessee, Texas, Utah, and Wisconsin). Some of these state boards have contracted with the NBCC or other testing organizations to develop the jurisprudence exam, whereas other boards have created their own exam. A jurisprudence exam simply assesses examinee knowledge about the state law relative to professional counseling and the board's rules, regulations, and processes (ACA, 2012). Examples of information associated with state law may include limits of client confidentiality in cases of end-of-life decisions, the duty to warn in cases where a client makes a threat to an intended victim's life or safety, and the disclosure of client records when mandated by a judge. Examples of information related to board rules and regulations may include the number of clinical hours required to sit for the licensure exam, the qualifications for an approved supervisor, how the board responds to ethical complaints, and the requirement for a background check for all applicants for licensure. Some states requiring a jurisprudence exam mandate passing the exam as a condition for initial licensure, and other states require passing the exam as a condition for licensure renewal.

Other exam formats used in a few states include an essay exam (New Hampshire); a field review, which is a 30-minute taped counseling session that is reviewed by board members (North Dakota); and an oral interview (Arkansas). Those considering licensure are advised to become familiar with their state board's rules and regulations regarding the jurisprudence and other exams required for licensure.

COUNSELOR EXAM PREPARATION AND PRACTICE OPPORTUNITIES   Preparing for certification and/or licensure exams can be challenging as students often focus on moving through each course successfully within the graduate curriculum with little thought to how concepts or courses link together. CACREP accreditation influences the design of counselor education preparation programs through standards that support the appropriate developmental sequence of content areas, the provision of practice opportunities for skill acquisition and mastery, and the translation of learning into field practice through practicums and internships. This focus is consistent with the mission of encouraging high standards in developing counselor preparation programs (CACREP, 2009). Some counselor preparation programs have developed the practice of comprehensive exams in evaluating the competency of graduate students. Comprehensive exams typically occur at the end of a graduate program and are designed to test knowledge gained through graduate study. The Counselor Preparation Comprehensive Examination (CPCE), administered through the Center for Credentialing & Education (CCE), is used by over 320 counselor preparation graduate programs to assess students' mastery of counseling content (www.cce-global.org/Org/CPCE). It is a 160-item multiple-choice exam that mirrors the NCE in testing the eight core content areas articulated by CACREP. Consultants to CCE develop exam items that are field tested in versions of the CPCE, and there is a strong correlation between the NCE and the CPCE (Shawn O'Brien, personal communication, May 14, 2010); therefore, the CPCE is a good test preparation for the NCE. Counselor graduate programs contract with CCE to provide the CPCE for administration to program students as the sole comprehensive exam or in conjunction with other comprehensive exam components (i.e., an essay exam or oral interview). Among the benefits for counseling programs is the ability to see how students perform to aid in program improvement and to anchor assessment of learning into accepted psychometric standards. The benefits for students include the ability to practice an NCE-like exam and obtain a detailed view of strengths and weaknesses in the core areas of counselor preparation. Graduate programs set their own cut scores (the actual score that determines a pass or no pass of the exam) and work with CCE to provide detailed feedback to students on their exam performance.

Test preparation materials developed commercially are available to students as they prepare to take the NCE and NCMHCE. These preparation programs vary in price and depth of preparation, ranging from a study guide to samples of test items with explanations, audio CDs that provide an overview of relevant content areas, full versions of an NCE, workshops, and preparation consultation. A list of exam preparation materials is available through the NBCC Web site (www.nbcc.org/study) and can be easily accessed through an Internet search of "NCE preparation." Students also utilize a number of strategies to prepare for an examination, ranging from studying independently to meeting together as a group. DiPietro et al. (2010) described one study strategy involving the use of wikis to support the scaffolding of information and providing for the sharing of independent study among exam participants. Focus group findings indicated that this strategy helped students prepare for their comprehensive exams and alleviate the stress and anxiety of taking on the task of exam preparation alone. Regardless of the strategy, it is wise to research exam preparation materials, gain exposure to practice items and exams, and develop a strategy for preparing for and taking the exam. This will help ensure that the investment in a graduate counseling program culminates in the appropriate credentials for professional practice.

Summary of the Steps to Becoming Credentialed as a Licensed Professional Counselor

Although there are various motivations and life experiences that impel individuals into the field of counseling, those who have ambitions to become licensed professional counselors will engage in a very specific process leading to licensure as the ultimate outcome. Even though licensure may not be a decision everyone makes, it is the gateway to independent practice and the marketability of a professional. The following is a summary of the typical steps students take to become licensed professional counselors (Schweiger et al., 2008):

1. ***Successfully complete a bachelor's degree program.*** One of the unique aspects of graduate training in counseling is that students often enter into master's degree programs from a variety of undergraduate disciplines that are legitimate to obtaining

a master's degree in counseling and that bring diversity and variety to professional training and the counseling profession. Bachelor's degrees in English, business, biology, physical education, teacher education, communications, sociology, political science, and a variety of others are legitimate entry points for graduate programs in counseling. Bachelor's degrees highly suited to prepare students for graduate training in counseling include psychology, social work, special education, criminal justice, child development, and family studies.

2. ***Apply and be accepted into a graduate program in counseling.*** Students considering graduate training should research potential programs regarding CACREP accreditation and should make contact with program representatives and ask questions about student satisfaction, program completion, and placement (employment) as a result of being in the program (Schweiger et al., 2008). Individuals mature academically through their bachelor's program; by the time they get to graduate school, they often have a clear idea of what they are committing to when they enter a professional preparation program and are much more serious about this important step. As part of the application process, many programs require interviews (individual and group) with candidates to assess their potential for graduate study, relational skills, problem-solving ability, and emotional stability. Other programs have an open enrollment policy that allows for students to be admitted with a minimum grade point average (GPA) and a bachelor's degree from an accredited institution.

3. ***Complete practicum and internship.*** The capstone of a student's experience in a graduate program is the culmination of learning that manifests itself in the practice of an emerging counseling style and professional mind-set. Launching into field experience is a significant step in one's graduate program, and it helps students break into professional functioning under the supervision of program and field experience site personnel. Students identify practicum and internship as significant milestones in their professional development and as opportunities to try on counseling techniques and interventions as well as professional behaviors. Developing as a professional has many facets, which include a solid work ethic, working successfully with conflict and in ambiguous situations, behaving ethically, achieving a balance between working independently and seeking supervision when necessary, and the successful integration of theory into practice. These activities emerge and are developed within practicum and internship, and continue throughout the course of a professional life span.

4. ***Successfully matriculate through and complete the graduate program.*** Successfully completing a graduate program in counseling even under ideal circumstances is a rigorous process both academically and personally. Students are exposed to a variety of critical experiences that impact decisions they make about themselves and the path of their professional preparation (Furr & Carroll, 2003). Specific coursework, relationships with faculty, interactions with peers, exposure to the professional literature and research, practicum and internship, and professional experiences outside of the academic program include common elements to developing as a professional, but take on significant individual meaning for students in their development. Graduating with a master's degree is a significant accomplishment—the first essential and significant credential for a nascent professional.

5. ***Obtain relevant certifications.*** Commitment to professional growth is manifested through the credentialing process. Certification is an accepted practice that promotes counselors to colleagues and peers, and assures consumers of counseling

services that certified professionals have met accepted training and experience standards. Numerous opportunities exist for professionals to qualify themselves for certification either through the application process or through additional trainings that can enhance practice.

6. ***Complete postdegree supervised clinical hours.*** Clinical supervision not only is essential for students within their training programs but also constitutes an important activity for postgraduate professionals. Postgraduate supervision allows counselors to continue developing their personalized counseling style, test prior assumptions obtained through graduate study beyond the graduate program, and learn more about the real world of practice. Some counselors are able to obtain supervision at their place of employment at little or no cost to them; others must research available board-approved supervisors, interview them, and pay for their supervision services. Counselors aspiring for licensure should be aware of supervision requirements and investigate potential supervisors for goodness-of-fit because supervision represents a significant investment of time and financial resources (Magnuson, Norem, & Wilcoxon, 2002).

7. ***Complete the appropriate licensure/certification exams.*** Passing standardized national exams for either certification or licensure signifies the validation of counselor preparation. Exams take the form of knowledge-based exams (NCE) and applied practice exams (NCMHCE), and they signify to professional credentialing agencies one's competence in professional practice. The NCE and NCMHCE are the accepted standard in all 50 states and jurisdictions across the United States.

8. ***Apply to the state board or jurisdiction for licensure.*** Upon graduation, counselors face at least an additional two years of qualifying postgraduate experience before applying for licensure in their particular state or jurisdiction. The application process is rigorous and includes documentation of graduation preparation, field experience, postgraduation supervised experience, a background check, and passage of required exams. The award of a license to practice ensures a well-prepared, seasoned counselor who will provide competent treatment to consumers of counseling services.

Obtaining relevant credentials including licensure is an individual decision as aspiring professionals consider their career objectives, their values, and their personal resources. Credentialing is an investment in self and builds the basis upon which professional practice rests. It is important for counselors to consider that obtaining relevant credentials will rarely have a negative impact on a professional's career, but instead has the potential to enhance the career and open counselors to a variety of unimagined and unanticipated opportunities. Many of these opportunities emerge from participating in professional organizations and meeting other professionals at professional conferences.

MEMBERSHIP IN PROFESSIONAL ORGANIZATIONS

Professional organizations serve many functions. Students and professionals join professional organizations, also known as professional guilds, in order to network with other counseling professionals; gain access to relative publications such as journals, texts, and media; and participate in continuing education opportunities such as seminars, webinars, and conferences. The American Counseling Association (ACA) is the largest professional counseling guild, supporting approximately 45,000 members.

ACA evolved from the American Personnel and Guidance Association (APGA), established in 1952 to service various types of counseling professionals and to pursue a common purpose. The APGA changed its name to the American Association of Counseling and Development (AACD) in 1983, which changed its name to the American Counseling Association in 1992. ACA has experienced much growth and is the primary professional organization serving professional counselors of all types.

In addition to providing publications, networking, and continuing education, ACA offers many professional opportunities and important services to its membership. ACA represents its membership before Congress and legislatively in regard to legal policies and regulations that govern professional counseling. In these cases, ACA serves as a leader in advocating for members on issues related to professional policy and law such as state and/or national bills that are passed related to the practice of counseling and the education and supervision of counselors. Some recent examples include current legislation that involves reimbursement for mental health services (Department of Defense, TRICARE, and Medicare), participation in providing services to specific segments of the population (the military), and practice limitations (diagnostic privileges and assessment).

ACA also provides its membership with the ACA Code of Ethics (2005) and services of the ACA Ethics Committee. The code stipulates practice guidelines for professional counselors, students, clinical supervisors, and counselor educators. Ethical standards within the code protect the general public by suggesting practice guidelines and protocols related to counseling practice, counselor education, and clinical supervision of professional counselors. By providing practice guidelines, the code provides a sort of standard of practice, which serves to protect those who adhere to the code when questions regarding practice arise. The Code of Ethics is in place to protect the general public and those who adhere to it.

The Ethics Committee works in conjunction with the Code of Ethics (2005). This committee exists to "educate the membership about the ACA *Code of Ethics* (2005), review and recommend changes of the *Code,* receive and process complaints regarding alleged violations of the *Code,* and process requests for interpretations of the *Code*" (www.counseling.org). The Ethics Committee also provides leadership to state chapters of ACA and related ethics committees. It is one of several official committees that are part of ACA and is made up of ACA members, including students.

ACA also includes state chapters, professional divisions, standing committees, and task forces made up of members to further service members. State chapters of ACA began to organize in 1964. They provide professional development through continuing education and support through professional networking on a local basis for members. Lower costs and regional-specific attention are also benefits of local chapter organization.

Professional divisions within ACA also began to form in 1965. There are currently 19 divisions representing unique areas and practices of counseling, which follow:

- Association for Assessment in Counseling and Education (AACE)
- Association for Adult Development and Aging (AADA)
- Association for Creativity in Counseling (ACC)
- American College Counseling Association (ACCA)
- Association for Counselors and Educators in Government (ACEG)
- Association for Counselor Education and Supervision (ACES)—this division has five regional chapters also

- The Association for Humanistic Counseling (AHC)
- Association for Lesbian, Gay, Bisexual and Transgender Issues in Counseling (ALGBTIC)
- Association for Multicultural Counseling and Development (AMCD)
- American Mental Health Counselors Association (AMHCA)
- American Rehabilitation Counseling Association (ARCA)
- American School Counselor Association (ASCA)
- Association for Spiritual, Ethical, and Religious Values in Counseling (ASERVIC)
- Association for Specialists in Group Work (ASGW)
- Counselors for Social Justice (CSJ)
- International Association of Addictions and Offender Counselors (IAAOC)
- International Association of Marriage and Family Counselors (IAMFC)
- National Career Development Association (NCDA)
- National Employment Counseling Association (NECA)

All 19 divisions have organizing committees, sometimes known as executive councils, each guiding the related division. These councils meet regularly in some form to inform the ACA membership of division-related activities, news, and information; and to guide and advance the divisions. Each year, several divisions call for new members to serve on their organizing committee; each committee accepts new serving members each year, with a full turnover occurring approximately every three years for each committee in every division. The ACA divisions are actually those committees that have become large enough, through membership interest, to require a working division.

One of the largest divisions—the American Mental Health Counselors Association (AMHCA) with 6,000 members—functions separately from ACA, although it is still considered a division of ACA. It was organized in 1978 to specifically serve the practitioner population within ACA and has its own membership fees and code of ethics (AMHCA, 2010). Like ACA, AMHCA focuses its efforts on continuing education, affecting public policy, and resources for its members; and it offers a base for state chapters. Unlike ACA, AMHCA specifically targets practitioner-related issues, topics, and concerns, whereas ACA targets practitioners and counselor educators and supervisors. State chapters of AMHCA help new practitioners to get started and provide a referral network of counselors for the general public in addition to its other services of continuing education, public policy, and resources on a local level. When combined with ACA member services, AMHCA and its local chapters are important resources for practicing counselors.

In addition to these practical and essential divisions, there are other working teams of ACA members that have been developed to manage and organize ACA and/or serve the specialized interests of the membership. These teams, known as committees and task forces, are made up of members, including a student member. There are 12 committees that manage the efforts and interests of the ACA membership: Audit Committee, Awards Committee, Branch Development Committee, Bylaws and Policies Committee, Ethics Committee, Financial Affairs Committee, Human Rights Committee, International Committee, Nominations and Elections Committee, Public Policy and Legislation Committee, Publications Committee, and Research and Knowledge Committee. The titles of these committees are descriptive and in most cases inform the reader of their tasks. Membership of these committees is through active nomination and application annually.

Task forces are another type of organizational effort within the ACA membership. They have developed out of a strong interest among members or need within the ACA organization. Other than the Ethics Appeal Panel (which hears appeals from members who disagree with or appeal a decision made by the Ethics Committee regarding a member's particular case), task forces are formed to further inform and educate the ACA membership on particular topics and are open to the participation of ACA members. Organization as a task force typically takes place before a working team is developed into an ACA division. Currently, there are six task forces within ACA; some require volunteer participation and others require elected membership. The current task forces are Crisis and Response Task Force, Cyberspace and Technology Task Force, Ethics Appeal Panel, Graduate Student and Mentor Task Force, New Orleans Community Project Task Force, and Strategic Planning Task Force. Task forces work in conjunction with other professional teams within ACA.

There are also interest networks and listservs that function as communication, information, education, and/or networking tools for interested participants. These networks and listservs are located online, and anyone including the general public may join and receive updated information from the groups on a regular, sometimes daily, basis. Interest networks include sports counseling, trauma, wellness, women's interests, Jewish interests, humor in counseling, grief and bereavement, children, forensics, ethics, and animal-assisted therapy. Public but professional counseling listservs include Diversegrad-L, which discusses multiethnic and cultural issues; COUNSGRADS, established for graduate students in counselor education; and CESNET-L for counselor educators and supervisors. Professional networks and listservs function to maintain currency on a particular topic in which all counselors may not have an interest. In general, they provide information to their readers. The American Counseling Association Web site (www.counseling.org) has detailed descriptions of each division, committee, interest network, and listserv and related links.

PROFESSIONAL NETWORKING

So why should counselors participate in professional organizations? As already mentioned, professional organizations provide resources, public policy representation, and an ethical code from which to gauge practice, supervision, and education. They also serve a wider purpose by contributing to the critical concept of networking. *Networking* is the act of establishing a set of connections or a system within which a student, new graduate, or professional may interact with seasoned professionals in the field; and by networking, seasoned professionals are able to maintain connections to other like professionals for information, education, writing/publishing opportunities, job-seeking purposes, and/or overall engagement. Whether students select the path of becoming a practitioner, an educator, or both, it will be important for them to know others in the field in order to get started and remain on their chosen path. Because counseling is a state-regulated profession, counselors are required to follow certain laws, regulations, and ethical codes in order to maintain the safety of the general public, whom counselors serve. Becoming familiar with states' Web sites helps in building awareness of these particular laws, regulations, and codes. Additionally, students and/or new professionals should remain connected with experienced counselors and educators and supervisors, who can guide them in their professional development. Sometimes this guidance is in the form of an individual providing information and direction through networking and mentoring. At other times, the guidance comes in the form of an organization providing information and guidance, such as the services mentioned earlier in the Membership in Professional Organizations section.

VOICE FROM THE FIELD 3.2

While attending my counselor preparation program in 2010, I entered an essay contest on the convergence of human rights and professional counseling. The prize for the winning essay was an all-expense-paid trip to the 2010 ACA conference in Pittsburgh, Pennsylvania. The judges chose my essay, and I can still remember getting the phone call from my professor when he told me I had won the contest. I was so excited; I cried and had to call or text all of my family members right away.

The trip was filled with meeting many professionals in counseling and exciting events. On the first day of the conference, I met a gracious young couple who shared with me their ups and downs as professional counselors on our walk to the convention hall. I ate breakfast with people from the Dominican Republic who were so friendly that I can still remember the joy they brought to the breakfast table discussing practice and attending college there. Just thinking about our conversations still brings me joy and laughter. Later, I was honored to have lunch with the world wide director of counseling of my university and a few other professors of counseling from our main campus.

The conference sessions were varied and intriguing. I enjoyed the information I heard on how to improve one's professional counseling skills, how to become a better counselor, and methods for introducing faith and yoga into counseling sessions. These sessions encouraged me to continue to strive toward my goal of becoming a licensed professional counselor.

I think my favorite part of the conference was attending the keynote address by Gerald Corey and then later meeting him face-to-face when he signed his books I had bought. He was gracious enough to sign some papers for my friends who were also attending my program of study.

I encourage all graduate counseling students to get involved with their counseling organizations and to attend the annual ACA conference. I am thankful that my essay was chosen and that I was offered this experience. I look forward to staying involved with professional counseling organizations at the state and national level in the future.

CHARLOTTE CREMER
ACA Conference Attendee

VOICE FROM THE FIELD 3.3

I was a little nervous as a master's-level counseling student attending the ACA conference in New Orleans as a first timer. I was going to a new city and did not have any peers going to the conference with me. I made sure to sign up for the first timers' orientation lunch that ACA offers in order to meet new people and feel more at ease in a big city. I was fortunate to run into some of my faculty members at the airport; they helped me get settled in New Orleans and guided me somewhat throughout the trip.

As soon as I walked into the convention center where the ACA conference was being held, I immediately felt at home. It was easy to identify other attendees at the conference because everyone wore a name tag that also emphasized his or her role at the conference, such as first timer, presenter, volunteer, and so forth. I wore the first timer's ribbon on my name tag so people would be able to identify my being new to the conference. I was told others might ask whether I had questions, recommend good places to eat in New Orleans, or suggest different seminars that would be beneficial to attend.

My experience of being surrounded by so many professionals was incredible. I found myself in conversations with professionals from all over the United States, who had varying specialties. For long periods of time, we discussed their line of work, and they also offered words of wisdom for my professional career based on their experiences as professional counselors. As a student, being able to network with such established professionals was humbling for me.

At the conference, I attended many seminars with topics ranging from borderline personality disorder to how to establish a professional identity, substance abuse, and sexual therapy. I chose to attend seminars that covered a variety of different topics that I was interested in. The conference enabled me to network with the presenters of each seminar and exchange e-mails to keep in touch with future questions or to get information. Attending the first timers' orientation luncheon was very beneficial. The ACA president, vice president, and different regional directors of ACA from all over the United States were there and open to answering questions as well as networking with all the newcomers. I met many people whom I now call friends, and we experienced the ACA conference together for the remainder of the trip.

One of the highlights was going to Dr. Judith Beck's presentation on her new book and her experiences in the field. Afterward, having the opportunity to meet her was like meeting a professional celebrity and was such a privilege! The opening party that is free to all registered ACA conference attendees is a must. ACA did a great job of incorporating the essence of New Orleans from the food, music, and parade with a float and band, to the live music. It was so much fun to see all of the professional counselors being able to let loose on the dance floor and have a good time. I also enjoyed being able to spend time with all the people I had met and networked with throughout the conference.

I left the conference feeling more secure that I made the right career choice and having made many networking connections as professionals and as friends. I felt proud to be a part of a profession that is represented by people who strive to help others and are always finding creative, innovative ways to do so. I learned a lot about my professional identity and the areas I now want to specialize in as a professional counselor. I have since utilized some of the networks I made at the conference and have been able to get more involved with ACA and other organizations I am interested in because of those connections.

CAITLIN DUMONTIER
ACA Conference Attendee

There are several ways to network and be mentored in order to learn how to navigate entry into professional counseling. The ACA division AMCHA has streamlined and organized the mentoring process and has encouraged its practice by publishing the *AMCHA Mentor Handbook* (2006) for seasoned counselors at the state chapter level. This handbook provides a format and program evaluation process for those seasoned professionals who have the availability and background to provide mentoring to new professionals. AMCHA offers other formats for professional networking including professional conferences and state chapters.

Many of the professional counseling organizations provide educational conferences, which also serve as networking sites for new and experienced professionals. Professional counseling conferences regularly provide gatherings or receptions for smaller interest groups. Receptions typically revolve around socializing with other professionals for a professional purpose. Hence, receptions are often based at dinners, happy hours, and/or lunches so individuals who are unfamiliar with each other can have the opportunity to meet and chat about a topic without forced engagement. Typically, individuals expecting to network at a professional conference will carry plenty of business cards so they have a way of making contact with professionals who may be helpful to them in the future.

Students often use conferences to network for future employment in addition to the obvious educational benefits. Professional conferences provide one of the broadest opportunities to engage in professional networking.

Opportunities for professional networking also can be found by participating in state chapters, divisions, committees, and listservs of counseling organizations (ACA, AMHCA). As described above, these working groups provide new and experienced professional counselors the opportunity to get to know others and even to work with others who have shared interests and knowledge. Participating not only increases professionals' knowledge but also expands their circle of professional peers. This is critical to an individual with a professional degree, because it provides the opportunity for necessary continuing education and currency in the profession.

Finally, current faculty and/or clinical supervisors are excellent resources for mentoring or networking. Often faculty and supervisors have been connected to the community for several years, possibly even decades. Many faculty members and supervisors consider it their professional responsibility to assist new graduates in getting started in the field, if only from the perspective of mentor and part-time adviser. They are aware of and often have relationships with local counseling agencies, state legislatures, and graduates who have since completed their professional preparation and are now experiencing great success. Thus, faculty and supervisors serve as an important link to the professional counseling community, which is generally a small circle even in the largest of cities.

CONTINUING EDUCATION

The commitment to growing professionally starts with learning what it is like to become a professional. Some activities are so obvious and so much a part of professional training that to violate them would contravene our sense of propriety, such as having a sexual relationship with a client. Other activities are not as obvious or intuitive and therefore require integrating an intentional plan of action in order for counselors to stay vibrant as a professional. One of these activities involves continuing education. Some counselors may believe that once a degree is earned they have "arrived" and know all that is necessary to practice responsibly. They see the importance of continued professional experience, but may devalue continued formal education.

Counselor educators hope that the established requirements for credentialing and licensure are enough to reinforce the need for professionals to keep themselves "sharp" professionally through continuous and lifelong learning. Too often, however, due to counselors' busy and complex lives, continuing education becomes a lower level priority, and therefore it must be integrated into the requirement of certification or licensure renewal. A situation that happens all too frequently is that some professionals get to the date of their certification or licensure renewal only to discover that they have not completed all their required hours for continued certification or licensure. Planning and being intentional about participating in continuing education each year will ensure not only that the spirit of continuing education is met but also that the process will be doable and invigorating.

The minimal requirement to maintain certification as an NCC is 100 hours of continuing education every five years in continued education activities approved by NBCC. State licensure boards also have a similar requirement that ranges from 24 to 45 "contact hours" (synonymous with continuing education hours) every two years or 12 to 24 hours annually, depending on licensure renewal schedules. The majority of licensure boards also require that a portion of continuing education be obtained in professional ethics (typically ranging from two to six hours per renewal cycle), which underscores that licensure boards value their licensees' continually immersing themselves in ethics (ACA, 2012). This is not surprising because the majority of complaints issued against licensed professional counselors involve breaches in ethical functioning (Mascari & Webber, 2006). Two primary issues regarding continuing education are important to consider: selecting the means for continuing education and ensuring that continuing education activities will meet the requirements for continued certification and licensure.

Types of Continuing Education

There are numerous means for obtaining continuing education. They range from the most expensive and intrusive, such as taking a graduate course for credit or attending a multi-day course at an institute for specialized training that leads to certification, to the least expensive and most convenient, such as reading several articles in a professional publication, taking a short exam on the material, and submitting payment for continuing education credits. Following requirements as set forth in licensure board rules and regulations ensures that licensure boards will accept continuing education modalities as legitimate continuing education activities.

NBCC serves as the continuing education clearinghouse for counseling-related continuing education. Individuals, organizations, and corporations desiring to be approved as continuing education providers engage in an application and vetting process with NBCC to have their activities approved and to receive a provider number signifying NBCC's approval. Those sanctioned as providers must adhere to strict guidelines, which include tracking those obtaining continuing education, awarding clock hours, and evaluating presenters, advertising, and the types of continuing education activities offered (NBCC, 2008). Those organizations that are automatically approved as providers include ACA and its state branches and accredited universities that sponsor counselor education programs. Licensure boards accept NBCC-approved providers for continuing education, but may have stipulations about how these continuing education activities are delivered. ACA (2012) has classified the various types of continuing education activities and noted how states are to approve these learning modalities. These continuing education activities include seminars and workshops, conference seminars, home study courses, interactive distance learning, and online distance learning.

Seminars and workshops are activities that professionals participate in a face-to-face environment. They typically are extended educational opportunities lasting from three hours (seminars are usually half a day) to six hours (workshops are typically longer than seminars), with a blend of lecture, discussion, and attendee participation. Seminars and workshops can be scheduled in conjunction with a professional conference, or they may be part of an institute training whereby the expressed purpose is the training itself. As the designation implies, conference seminars coexist with professional conferences and can range broadly from keynote addresses where a special invited speaker addresses all attendees, to breakout sessions where professionals (peers) present research and/or best practices to their peers, to preconference seminars or workshops where a day or half a day is devoted to a specialized training. One of the benefits of professional membership in ACA or AMHCA is being provided with opportunities to participate in such workshops at a discounted fee.

Home study courses involve an independent study of materials or a curriculum sent to participants. After receiving the materials, learners study and typically return an exam that assesses content mastery. Interactive distance learning and online distance learning are closely related activities that allow learners to participate remotely, or not in a face-to-face environment. Interactive learning implies that there is some sort of conferencing either by phone or by video chat in real time (such as Skype technology). Online learning is a type of distance learning that typically involves asynchronous learning, or learning that is not in real time. Distance learning is perhaps the most convenient form of continuing education, but often the most rigorous and demanding because it requires independent effort and initiative to master the material and demonstrate that mastery to continuing education providers.

ACA and NBCC have lists of approved online continuing educational opportunities available for professionals.

Most states accept all forms of continuing education either fully or conditionally. Conditional acceptance means that participants must demonstrate that the continuing education activity is legitimate. As mentioned previously, legitimacy of an activity is determined through the provider being approved by the NBCC or another relevant professional organization. Some states stipulate that only a certain portion of learning in a distance format is acceptable to the board, which translates into professionals having to attend professional conferences and/or seminars. Two states (i.e., Connecticut and New Mexico) currently do not accept any form of distance learning as continuing education for licensure renewal. As previously mentioned, aspiring professionals are advised to become acquainted with their state board's rules and regulations regarding continuing education in order to avoid investing in activities that may not be acceptable to the board.

Documenting Continuing Education

Certification and licensure boards require that some form of documentation be kept on continuing educational activities. Although documentation of learner participation is required from approved continuing education providers, professionals are also required to keep track of their own continuing education activities. Documentation can be as informal as keeping track of what breakout sessions were attended at an annual conference. Most professional conferences make provisions for continuing education credit through a sponsoring institution, which means that the contact hours gained at the conference are translated into university credit. Therefore, it is important to understand the difference between contact hours (real time measured in "hours" spent in a continuing education activity) and continuing education units (CEUs), which are contact hours converted into college credit. Typically, participants are charged an administrative fee to have their hours registered as CEUs and to have a certificate of verification sent to them. This type of verification can then be used to validate continuing educational activities to the certification or licensure board. Other forms of documentation include a signature sheet that may be provided by conference sponsors whereby participants can request presenters to sign their forms as verification of attendance. Typically, in approved seminars and workshops, participants complete a feedback form regarding their experience and an assessment of the content presented, and a certificate of completion is given or sent to them upon completion of the activity.

Continuing education credit obtained through reading professional journals or other publications is a convenient way of meeting continuing educational requirements. Often these publications will provide multiple-choice exams based on their articles, which learners can complete and send back with a fee for verification of completion. Continuing Psychology Education, Inc. (www.texcpe.com) is an example of an organization that markets directly to professionals. It sends all the educational materials for home study directly to professionals (mailing lists are obtained through licensure and certification boards). If learners choose to read and complete the materials by taking the corresponding exams, they simply send in their completed materials along with a fee for review and validation of the activity.

Continuing education may take many forms, but it is always a commitment to professional growth and becoming a lifelong learner. It allows professionals to grow in targeted areas and gain the skills and competencies necessary to further enhance their professional practice.

CASE STUDY 3.1

Emilio was a first-year counseling student who had three years of experience working as a psychiatric technician at a local residential treatment center for adolescents with drug and alcohol addictions. Through his work experience, he enjoyed meeting with the residents in daily group therapy and individual counseling sessions. The clinical staff— composed of mental health counselors, social workers, and family therapists—often consulted with Emilio about his involvement in residents' treatment plans, and he believed he had been able to contribute meaningfully to the treatment outcomes of the residents he worked with. What initially started as a part-time job soon became a potential career option for him. He recently completed his bachelor's degree in journalism and had pursued the idea of becoming a newscaster, but realized that he really liked working with young people, helping them sort out their problems and make positive changes in their lives. He recognized that changing addictive patterns was challenging for the residents he worked with and that persistence and encouragement were important factors in helping them meet their treatment goals. He liked the challenge of helping them even though it was tough work.

Emilio asked a few members of the clinical staff about how they had prepared for their careers as professional "helpers" and what they liked about their professions and what they struggled with. Through this process of inquiry, Emilio determined that mental health counseling was a good choice as a career path because it would offer the most flexibility for his ideas and professional ambitions. He wanted to help youth and their families live in more functional and productive ways, and he liked what he had learned about counseling and its focus on wellness and helping people develop unused strengths. He also appreciated that the counselors he spoke with seemed to be excited about their work, even though it was sometimes discouraging and stressful. These counselors talked about the importance of self-care as a way of coping with the stressors of the work environment and how these strategies were also helpful in their work with residents and their families.

Emilio learned that getting the best educational experience was important as he considered making a significant investment of time and money in his graduate program. He learned from his undergraduate experience that it was important to do as much research as possible before making his decision on a graduate program. He heard about CACREP and checked its Web site about accredited programs in his area. Fortunately, two of the counselors he worked with were graduates of a program that he was interested in, and they had very positive things to say about their experiences in the program. They also said that although they hadn't paid too much attention to CACREP, the program they graduated from was CACREP accredited, and they knew that it was the gold standard of counselor preparation programs. They told Emilio that getting involved in the state counseling organization was important and that there were incentives and discounts for student members. He later learned that as a member of ACA, he would have free liability insurance when he entered his practicum and internship field experiences. He also recognized that before even getting into his graduate program, he had already made his first networking connections with his colleagues at work and that they had provided some important information in helping him get started.

Besides submitting his application materials to the program, Emilio was invited to participate in a half-day individual and group interview with the program faculty and graduate students. He was told that the purpose of the interview was to help faculty determine candidates' potential for strong interpersonal relationships and problem-solving abilities. Emilio knew that this was part of the application process from his consultations with colleagues, so he was well-prepared for what to expect. He was admitted to the program and promptly sent a thank-you card to the faculty committee expressing his excitement about joining the program and commitment to working hard. During his introductory course, he and his classmates were given an assignment to access the state licensed professional counselor board Web site, review the licensure requirements, and mark a checklist of courses in his program of study that would meet those requirements. He also noted that he would have to complete hours beyond his graduate degree to help him prepare for licensure. He would need to successfully pass the National Counselor Exam (NCE) and planned that during his second year in the program he would begin to get ready for the exam by researching exam questions and other preparation materials. Emilio recognized that one of the weak areas in his academic work was test anxiety, so he knew the importance of preparing as much as possible to compensate for this weakness. From this assignment, Emilio understood that licensure would allow him important future opportunities, including being able to work independently in a private practice if he so chose. He liked the idea of being able to work with adolescents out of doors and using recreation as therapy. He had been involved in some outdoor activities with the residents at the residential treatment center and appreciated those experiences. He knew that he would further research these interests and that he would likely have an opportunity to formally explore this in his program coursework.

Emilio understood early on in graduate school that the program faculty was serious about students' professional development and faculty roles as gatekeepers. During the program orientation, faculty members explained that their ethical obligation was to ensure that students who worked with clients (referred to as "vulnerable populations") needed to be skilled, ethical, and emotionally and mentally sound. He remembered his conversations with his colleagues about the importance of self-care and of having a good support system. He communicated with his employers about his graduate work and gained their support of his efforts. He also knew that his family was supportive of his graduate work. He remembered his colleagues telling him that, even under the best of circumstances, graduate school was intense and demanding. Emilio recognized that it would be important to communicate his needs to his family and be very organized with his time in order to meet the demands of family, job, and graduate program. He and his spouse agreed at the end of each week to have a planning session to map out what the following week would bring and to plan their schedules accordingly.

Emilio participated in what he could reasonably do outside of the classroom, but he knew that professional involvement was important. He joined ACA and his state counseling organization and took advantage of student discounts when attending conferences. He was excited to meet students from other programs and begin networking with other faculty and potential employers. Although this was not something he was encouraged to do in his program, Emilio printed business cards to exchange with other professionals he met at conferences. He knew from his undergraduate experiences the importance of marketing himself to others. He was also motivated by the memory of his late father who immigrated and worked hard and smart in using every opportunity to promote himself and learn from senior members of his profession. Emilio applied for scholarships and assistantships when they were made available and was able to work as a graduate assistant for a semester on a special research project for one of his faculty members. He knew that his work to succeed academically as well as his efforts outside of the classroom helped leverage opportunities that came and would come his way.

Conclusion

Becoming a professional mental health counselor consists of many facets that go beyond formal training in a graduate program. Formal education includes graduate training and also the commitment to becoming a lifelong learner through experience in working with clients, colleagues, and professionals from other related disciplines as well as continued education through participation in professional organizations. Formal graduate training establishes the foundation of core knowledge and experience that will help professionals further develop their knowledge, skills, and abilities.

Credentialing is an important process that involves continued focus training to meet standards of the profession and distinguish professionals from their peers as having met and maintained these standards. Certification and licensure are significant events in professional development that allow for the eventual independent practice of mental health counseling services.

Just as the formation of a profession is based on criteria such as an established code of ethics and a body of knowledge and research to support its function, a member belonging to a profession has certain obligations to support and perpetuate the profession in his or her practice. Professional functioning as a mental health counselor requires being active and engaged as a professional on a local, state, regional, and/or national level. A variety of ways to contribute meaningfully to the profession is available. Such activities range from running for an office within an organization to attending professional conferences, to supporting legislative efforts promoting the profession, to working with marginalized client populations and social justice efforts, to simply communicating accurately to the public the unique contributions that counselors make to the mental health of citizens that they serve. Continued professional growth is an individual process, and numerous supports and opportunities are available to assist committed individuals in their development.

References

American Association of State Counseling Boards (AASCB). (2013). *Mission of AASCB*. Retrieved from http://www.aascb.org/aws/AASCB/pt/sp/about

American Counseling Association (ACA). (2005). *Code of ethics*. Alexandria, VA: Author.

American Counseling Association (ACA). (2012). *Licensure requirements for professional counselors*. Alexandria, VA: Author.

American Mental Health Counselors Association (AMHCA). (2006). *AMHCA mentor handbook*. Retrieved from http://www.amhca.org/assets/content/MentorHandbook.pdf

American Mental Health Counselors Association (AMHCA). (2010). *2010 AMHCA code of ethics*. Retrieved from http://www.amhca.org/assets/news/AMHCA_Code_of_Ethics_2010_w_pagination_cxd_51110.pdf

Bloom, J., Gertein, L., Tarvydas, V., Conaster, J., Davis, E., Kater, D., . . . Esposito, R. (1990). Model legislation for licensed professional counselors. *Journal of Counseling & Development, 68,* 511–523.

Busacca, L. A., & Wester, J. L. (2006). Career concerns of master's-level community and school counselor trainees. *Career Development Quarterly, 55,* 179–190.

Center for Credentialing & Education (CCE). (2013). *Distance credentialed counselor*. Retrieved from http://www.cce-global.org/DCC

Council for Accreditation of Counseling and Related Educational Programs (CACREP). (2009). *CACREP accreditation manual: 2009 standards*. Alexandria, VA: Author. Retrieved from http://www.cacrep.org/doc/2009%20Standards%20with%20cover.pdf

DiPietro, J. C., Drexler, W., Kennedy, K., Buraphadeja, V., Liu, F., & Dawson, K. (2010). Using wikis to collaboratively prepare for qualifying examinations: An example of implementation in an advanced graduate program. *Tech Trends, 54*(1), 25–32.

Furr, S. R., & Carroll, J. J. (2003). Critical incidents in student counselor development. *Journal of Counseling & Development, 81*(4), 483–489.

Magnuson, S., Norem, K., & Wilcoxon, S. A. (2002). Clinical supervision for licensure: A consumer's guide. *Journal of Humanistic Counseling, 41*(1), 52–60.

Mascari, J. B., & Webber, J. M. (2006). Salting the slippery slope: What licensing violations tell us about preventing dangerous ethical situations. In G. R. Waltz & R. K. Yep (Eds.), *VISTAS: Compelling perspectives on counseling 2006* (pp. 165–168). Alexandria, VA: American Counseling Association.

National Board for Certified Counselors (NBCC). (2008). *NBCC continuing education policies and procedures*. Retrieved from http://www.nbcc.org/Assets/CEProvider/approvedproviderpolicies.pdf

National Board for Certified Counselors (NBCC). (2012a). *The National Counselor Examination for licensure and certification (NCE)*. Retrieved from http://www.nbcc.org/NCE

National Board for Certified Counselors (NBCC). (2012b). *NCMHCE scoring & results*. Retrieved from http://www.nbcc.org/NCMHCE/Scoring

National Board for Certified Counselors (NBCC). (2012c). *National Board for Certified Counselors (NBCC) policy regarding the provision of distance professional services.* Retrieved from http://www.nbcc.org/Assets/Ethics/NBCC%20Policy%20Regarding%20the%20Practice%20of%20Distance%20Counseling%20-Board%20-%20Adopted%20Version%20-%20July%202012-%20PDF.pdf

Schweiger, W. K., Henderson, D. A., Clawson, T. W., Collins, D. R., & Nuckolls, M. W. (2008). *Counselor preparation programs, faculty, trends* (12th ed.). New York, NY: Routledge.

Stout, C. E., & Grand, L. C. (2005). *Getting started in private practice: The complete guide to building your mental health practice.* Hoboken, NJ: Wiley.

Texas State Board of Examiners of Professional Counselors Title 22. (2009). Texas Administrative Code, Chapter 681. Retrieved from http://www.dshs.state.tx.us/counselor/lpc_rules09/

4

Employment Settings for Clinical Mental Health Counselors

SHAWN L. SPURGEON

CHAPTER OVERVIEW

This chapter is designed to provide mental health counselors in training with an increased understanding and awareness of the different types of careers available for mental health counselors. Information is provided about the different settings in which clinical mental health counselors work. The roles and responsibilities of clinical mental health counselors in each of these settings will be articulated, along with the essential aspects of each position.

LEARNING OBJECTIVES

The learning objectives for this chapter are designed to be consistent with the 2009 Council for Accreditation of Counseling and Related Educational Programs Standards (CACREP, 2009). As such, upon completion of this chapter, the student will have knowledge of the following clinical mental health counseling standards:

1. Understands the roles and functions of clinical mental health counselors in various practice settings and the importance of relationships between counselors and other professionals, including interdisciplinary treatment teams. (A.3)
2. Is aware of professional issues that affect clinical mental health counselors. (A.7)
3. Understands the range of mental health service delivery—such as inpatient, outpatient, partial treatment and aftercare—and the clinical mental health counseling services network. (C.5)
4. Knows public policies on the local, state, and national levels that affect the quality and accessibility of mental health services. (E.6)

INTRODUCTION

According to the US Bureau of Labor Statistics (2012), professional counselors held about 843,250 jobs in 2010. Of all the jobs held by professional counselors, clinical mental health counselors constituted about 13% (115,080) of those jobs and substance abuse counselors constituted about 9% (80,130) of those jobs. Clinical mental health counseling is increasingly becoming an important and relevant career path in the human services realm (Seligman, 2009). Clinical mental health counselors help individuals and families deal with a variety of concerns, including depression, impulse control problems, addictions, and education (Health Careers Center, 2010).

EMPLOYMENT PROSPECTUS

Currently, projected employment for clinical mental health counselors is expected to grow faster than the average for all occupations (US Bureau of Labor Statistics, 2012). Employment opportunities for clinical mental health counselors are favorable due to the increased need for services, flexibility in reimbursement from managed care companies, and increased awareness of the effectiveness of counseling services. Also, the number of job openings has exceeded and will continue to surpass the number of graduates from counseling programs. Given the increased need for mental health services, especially in rural areas, clinical mental health counselors have an opportunity to expand their services and to apply their skills to a number of employment areas. They are able to provide a wide range of services, including direct and indirect clinical services to the community.

EMPLOYMENT SETTINGS

Clinical mental health counselors work in a variety of settings, and their opportunities for employment have expanded significantly since the passage of the Community Mental Health Act of 1963 (Gladding & Newsome, 2010). Before this act, they were restricted to school and career counseling settings. Currently, clinical mental health counselors work in diverse community settings designed to provide a wide range of wellness activities, including rehabilitation, support services, and counseling (US Bureau of Labor Statistics, 2012). Their duties will vary according to the specialization of the setting, the scope of practice, and the population under consideration for services. Professionals in these settings understand that the key to effective treatment and utilization of services by individuals is counselors' ability to recognize and accurately assess clients' core issues.

Community Mental Health

Prior to the Community Mental Health Act of 1963, individuals who had mental problems were housed in state institutions (Gladding & Newsome, 2010). This act removed individuals from these institutions with the intent of providing them with effective and quality care within their own communities. MacCluskie and Ingersoll (2001) state that this act allowed the federal government to provide funds for the construction of community-based mental health centers. These centers were established with the idea that funding for services would be provided by state and local organizations, using block grants that were designed to be provided by the state as the need for services arose. Although the federal government still remains involved with funding through Medicaid, Medicare, and federally funded programs, the burden for funding mainly exists within state and local governments.

Community mental health centers are designed to provide a broad range of services and community care to individuals. The main goal is to provide a comprehensive, systemic approach to service delivery within a network of service providers, payers, and community advocates (James & Greenwalt, 2001). Services offered by these centers include outpatient counseling, day treatment programs, crisis services, substance abuse services, and case management (Gladding & Newsome, 2010). Lewis, Lewis, Daniels, and D'Andrea (2003) characterize the services offered by clinical mental health counselors as direct and indirect services. Direct services include counseling, outreach programs, and educational programs for the community; indirect services include advocacy, consultation, and community organizational activities. The important role that clinical mental health counselors play in these agencies cannot be overstated.

Private Practice

The development of community mental health centers in the 1960s and 1970s provided opportunities for clinical mental health counselors to expand their work; this development, along with an increased public awareness of the importance of professional counseling, enabled clinical mental health counselors to expand into private practice (Mental Health Counseling, 2004). Private practice counselors typically are licensed; most states will not allow an individual to work in private practice without a license (Gladding & Newsome, 2010). Clinical mental health counselors in private practice typically work in an individual or group practice and specialize in a distinct area of mental health treatment. They work with clients at developmental levels throughout the spectrum (from children to the elderly) and tend to use a wellness-based approach to treating their clients, despite the limitations and challenges of dealing with the managed care system (Gladding & Newsome, 2010).

Another major challenge that private practitioners face is the need to balance counseling skills with business skills. Whereas clinical mental health counselors are well-trained clinicians, they often lack the managerial and business strategies necessary to develop, fund, and market a private practice. Therefore, many private practitioners elect to hire a business partner whose sole purpose is to maintain the business side of the practice (Gladding & Newsome, 2010). This person likely handles the office and phones, sets and confirms appointments, manages medical records, and bills insurance and other third-party payers.

Another challenge that clinical mental health counselors in private practice face, whether or not they have a business manager, is that of dealing with insurance companies and varying reimbursement rates and schedules. In order to receive reimbursements, counselors must belong to the insurance company panels that their clients use. First, each insurance panel must be applied to, and often this requires annual renewal on the part of the counselor. Then, insurance plans vary widely with disparate co-pays and reimbursement rates. A session that might typically be billed for $125 to a private pay client may only be reimbursed at $35 to $50 by insurance and supplemented by a $20 to $25 co-pay on the part of the insured. If clients elect to use insurance benefits, their diagnosis and treatment become part of their overall medical record. Because of this, the clientele of clinical mental health counselors in private practice usually consists of middle- to upper-class individuals who do not want to deal with their insurance companies and can afford not to (Mental Health Counseling, 2004).

One last challenge of private practice has to do with the work climate. Some practitioners talk about the isolation they experience as well as the challenge to maintain their ethical responsibilities by providing donated or reduced services to their clients. Though these challenges exist, private practice is a thriving setting for clinical mental health counselors. If you are interested in exploring this work setting further, the American Counseling Association has published a guide for the effective development and establishment of a private practice, as well as tips on how to deal with the challenges related to maintaining a private practice (ACA, 2010).

Hospital Settings

The need for clinical mental health counselors to provide services in hospitals and other health care facilities has increased steadily and continues to grow as these facilities begin to understand the importance of wellness-based thinking to physical healing (Hsiao et al., 2006; Mayerhoff, Smith, & Schleifer, 2008). There are two types of hospital settings available to clinical mental health counselors: inpatient psychiatric facilities, where the client is diagnosed primarily with a mental health disorder, and full-service medical facilities, where the client has a need for medical treatment and also has a mental health condition. In this section, we will discuss the latter, with inpatient psychiatric hospitals covered later in a section called Inpatient Services. Medical facilities that employ clinical mental health counselors can be either public or private facilities and often provide counseling services through support programs, such as cancer patient support or hospice (Gladding & Newsome, 2010). Hospitals serve as a very important part of the comprehensive community mental health system (Browers, 2005) and allow the clinical mental health counselor an opportunity to connect and collaborate with other human service providers.

Clinical mental health counselors typically work in the inpatient services section of hospitals, which is designed to provide treatment for individuals who have both a medical condition and a mental health disorder (Gladding & Newsome, 2010). One of the major challenges clinical mental health counselors will face is adjusting to the clinical approach to working with individuals in hospital settings. For example, individuals who are receiving care in hospitals are referred to as *patients* instead of *clients*. Also, multifaceted treatment teams can include medical personnel, psychiatrists, occupational therapists, and other health professionals. Barker (2001) recommends that clinical mental health counselors learn the terminology specific health professionals use and their roles in treating individuals as a way to strengthen the relationship with other professionals and bridge any communication gap.

Substance Abuse Treatment Centers

Substance abuse treatment centers represent one of the fastest growing areas of employment opportunities for clinical mental health counselors (Health Careers Center, 2010). Substance abuse and problems related to it continue to be the most common mental health concern among individuals in the human services field (Vuchinich, 2002). The challenge that clinical mental health counselors face in dealing with this problem is that often other psychological disorders are connected with substance abuse, so it can be difficult to treat the problem itself (Bauman, 2008). This is known as dual diagnosis; when both mental health and substance abuse disorders exist in the client, the ability to treat one disorder is impacted by the presence of the other. Thus, comprehensive treatment plans for both conditions are needed. As society's understanding and awareness of addiction increases, more individuals are seeking treatment for these dual disorders (US Bureau of Labor Statistics, 2012).

Clinical mental health counselors have a variety of options to choose from in terms of treating substance abuse problems due to the large volume of research available and the commitment from treatment programs to follow evidence-based treatment protocols (Bauman, 2008). When individuals enter into treatment, they are often in denial about their problem, and so a major challenge for clinical mental health counselors is helping their clients try to find some motivation to stop using and abusing drugs. One such approach that has shown significant effectiveness is motivational interviewing, which helps the client examine the root cause of his or her use (Stevens & Smith, 2012). Once the barriers have been removed, effective treatment can begin, and clinical mental health counselors have a defined method for treating addiction.

Detoxification represents the first step in substance abuse treatment and typically requires medical monitoring by a licensed physician (Gladding & Newsome, 2010). It lasts about three to five days, and once the detoxification process has been completed, residential treatment begins. During this time, clinical mental health counselors work with their clients on issues such as skill building, healthy living activities, and general mental health issues. This work is typically done in a group counseling format (Stevens & Smith, 2012), and there are various types of programs in which clients would be involved, including freestanding programs, halfway houses, nonmedical residential facilities, and therapeutic communities. The length of stay in these facilities can range from two weeks to two months.

Clinical mental health counselors typically begin direct clinical work with substance abuse clients when they move from residential treatment to outpatient treatment. In the outpatient treatment setting, clinical mental health counselors work with their clients on a number of treatment issues specifically related to their substance problems (Stevens & Smith, 2012). There are major challenges for clinical mental health counselors during this time, including clients' relapse, high rate of missed appointments, and motivation to continue treatment. Coupled with this is the fact that over time managed care companies have decreased the allowable number of outpatient visits for substance abuse clients (Gladding & Newsome, 2010).

Another consideration for clinical mental health counselors is that substance abuse clients are never cured and are therefore always in recovery (Gladding & Newsome, 2010). Clinical mental health counselors need to develop skills to recognize the different stages of recovery for substance abuse clients so that they can effectively address clients' concerns (Stevens & Smith, 2012). Oftentimes, clinical mental health counselors will employ adjunct services, such as Alcoholics Anonymous and peer support groups, to help clients deal with the daily struggle of addiction. Clinical mental health counselors who work with substance abuse clients recognize the importance of recovery and employ numerous strategies to help their clients effectively deal with their struggles (Gladding & Newsome, 2010).

Correctional Facilities

An emerging and growing body of literature supports the relevance of mental health services in correctional facilities (Diamond, Magaletta, Harzke, & Baxter, 2008; Morgan, Rozycki, & Wilson, 2004). The increased incidences in prisons of suicide, rape, and psychopathology have necessitated the need for clinical mental health counselors to expand their clinical approaches and offer services to this population of individuals. Clinical mental health counselors face a number of challenges when working with inmates; for many, the main difficulty will be working through a system that does not foster development or wellness and that reinforces punishment for negative behavior (Diamond et al., 2008).

One such program is the Knox County Detention Center counseling services program located in Barbourville, Kentucky. This program is designed to provide individual and group counseling to incarcerated men and women (Todd Davis, personal communication, August 24, 2009). There are two components of the program, and clinical mental health counselors are extensively involved in both. The group counseling component consists of an evidence-based program designed to increase the inmates' understanding of drug abuse and its effects on their development. Inmates are required to attend a weekly group counseling session and also to work on previously developed goals related to their sobriety. The individual counseling component consists of a solution-focused approach to understanding life shortcomings and making a change for the better. Clinical mental health counselors work to help the inmates understand the realities of their existence and to take responsibility for their own behavior.

Diamond et al. (2008) believe that inmates will continue to seek services while incarcerated and that many of them will request those services for themselves, as opposed to their being required to participate. Some of these inmates have received services previously and thus understand their value; some use counseling as a way to break the monotony of prison life (Morgan et al., 2004). Whatever the case may be, the need for services will continue to grow as more and more individuals struggle with social norms. Clinical mental health counselors have an excellent opportunity to effect change in a setting that typically has not fostered opportunities to do so.

Nonprofit Organizations

Nonprofit organizations are sponsored by the state, county, or city and typically offer a wide variety of services (Mental Health Counseling, 2004). These services are available to the public and include financial support, shelter, clothing, job skills training, psychoeducation, and counseling. Clinical mental health counselors who work in nonprofit settings are expected to be diverse in their thinking and to take on roles that are not associated typically with mental health counseling (e.g., serving your clients food at the homeless shelter).

Clinical mental health counselors who work in these settings understand the importance of clients' basic needs for food, shelter, and clothing. As such, they are sensitive to making sure these basic needs are met before any type of intervention occurs. The most important aspect of their work is building relationships with clients; the nontraditional roles they take on help to facilitate a stronger connection when clients need counseling services (Browers, 2005). Changes in funding patterns have affected the ability of nonprofit organizations to help individuals, but the role of the clinical mental health counselor in these settings is still an important and relevant one to consider.

School Settings

Historically, school counselors and clinical mental health counselors have worked collaboratively to address child and adolescent development and to address concerns in the school setting (Gladding & Newsome, 2010). Recently, there has been an increased need for clinical mental health counselors to take on a more active role with children in school systems. These professionals are typically referred to as school-based mental health counselors. The main reason for this addition to school-based services is that school counselors cannot effectively provide the mental health services needed by their students due to their extremely large caseloads (Mental Health Counseling, 2004). School counselors are dealing more and more with issues related to crisis and preventive situations, and therefore they are less likely to be able to deal effectively with students' mental health concerns, such as substance abuse and depression.

School-based mental health counselors often provide individual counseling services to clients who struggle with a wide range of emotional issues. They still work collaboratively with school counselors to develop the best possible treatment approaches for working with the students. For example, a school counselor may be facilitating a group with children who are experiencing divorce in their families. There may be an individual within that group who needs more intensive services than can be offered by the group experience. The school counselor would refer the student to the school-based mental health counselor, who would come into the school and have individual or family sessions with the student.

The previously mentioned settings provide clinical mental health counselors with a variety of opportunities to enhance and increase their clinical counseling skills while helping individuals work through their core issues. Clinical mental health counselors work collaboratively within these settings to provide the best possible outcomes for the clients they serve. Their work within these settings demonstrates their commitment to providing the best possible services to their clients. Clinical mental health counselors are expected to understand and increase their awareness of the number of service delivery venues for their clients.

CASE STUDY 4.1

Lynn is a 25-year-old Caucasian female who recently completed her master's degree in mental health counseling. Her first clinical position is working for a human services agency in a grant-funded position. She is required to work within the local school system to identify and provide counseling services for middle school students at risk of dropping out of high school. Currently, she works with one middle school on Mondays and Wednesdays and another middle school on Tuesdays and Thursdays.

Initially, Lynn struggles with her new position. She does not seem to be able to connect with the school counselors at the two schools; although she has tried to work with them through e-mail, they do not respond to her requests. Consequently, she has been unable to build her caseload because the school counselors know the students' schedules and know the best times to pull them from class for a weekly 30-minute counseling session. Lynn is concerned that her agency will not see her as a viable employee if she does not connect with the at-risk students identified by the schools. She reminds both school counselors of the importance of her role and encourages them to ask questions about anything she is doing with the students.

During supervision, she expresses her frustration with the school counselors for their lack of professionalism and lack of cooperation. She wants to find a way to connect with them but has been unable to do so. She feels her next step is to talk with the principals at the two schools and ask them to remind the school counselors about her duties. Her supervisor encourages her to consider other ways in which she could be proactive without seeking out the principals, but Lynn is unable to think of anything. She is at her wit's end and believes she has done all she can at this point. She feels like she is running out of options … fast.

As you read this, consider what may be going on with Lynn that helps her in this situation. What do you think hinders her? In addition, you will want to consider what may be going on with the school counselors that helps or hinders the situation. Finally, it will be helpful to conceptualize what aspects of her training may help Lynn so that you can provide her with some means of reaching her goals.

SERVICE DELIVERY

There are some who would argue that the delivery system by which a client receives services is just as important as, if not more important than, the therapeutic relationship between the counselor and the client (DHHS, 1999; Gladding & Newsome, 2010). It is important for clinical mental health counselors to know about a number of service delivery methods that often serve as the cornerstone for their clients' therapeutic growth and development. The counselor's clinical assessment of the client's core issues serves as the backdrop for determining the most appropriate setting for the client, referred to as the *least restrictive placement* (Stevens & Smith, 2012). The range of services includes inpatient services, partial treatment services, and outpatient services.

VOICE FROM THE FIELD 4.1

I was hired as the program director for a pilot project for a local mental health mental retardation (MHMR) facility to set up a dual diagnosis (DDX) program and network of providers. My first task was to identify all the area treatment facilities and mental health providers. Several of the treatment facilities were in rural locations. It took about a month to develop an intake process with all the complementary paperwork to make up a client record. As is always the case when working on a time-sensitive grant, I had to develop a database to capture the admissions from the mental health side and the treatment centers. I spent a lot of my time on the phone and on the road driving between substance abuse facilities, hospitals, and MHMR offices in three counties. The process was that if a treatment center had an admission of a person that had a mental health history or was currently being treated for a mental health (MH) issue, that person was also admitted to the DDX program, and I would serve as his or her case manager.

Once admitted, the clients would attend a specific group for dual diagnosis once a week while in treatment or once they got out, depending on their location. The group was offered only at the MHMR office, which proved to be inefficient in the long run. On the MHMR side, the intake specialist, psychiatrist, or case manager would first identify a substance abuse issue in a client. The specific professional would then contact me, and I would do what I could to assist in getting that person into treatment. This proved to be the most challenging aspect of the job. Although I had worked in a substance abuse treatment setting before, here I was suddenly faced with the daunting task of finding a person a bed in an already overwhelmed system. Generally, if the MH client was stable, then I would act as advocate for him or her to enter a substance abuse outpatient program at MHMR. Training the providers on the MH side about the illness of addiction and the substance abuse counselors about the MH illness was always part of the job. This consisted of formal training sessions or just being on the phone talking a counselor down from discharging a client simply because of the client's illness and the way it affected others.

Generally, I worked out of my car, at two MHMR locations, and in four main chemical dependency treatment centers. At the treatment centers, I would often find myself outside under a tree conducting an intake session or using any available closet, cafeteria, or office space. There were many times I found myself turning the car around to go back to a treatment facility to assist with a non-med-compliant MH client who was threatening others, himself, or just acting out in general. The days generally were not predictable because they did not go according to the schedule of appointments; I found that flexibility was the name of the game. Having had a case management and treatment center background, I was a bit more prepared than most, I guess, for the fast pace, the crisis situations, and the obstacles of starting something new. In the end, the outcomes were great; the clients received more efficient and comprehensive treatment for their dual issues, and the program was able to receive funding to continue the groups, counseling, and case management.

KIM ARRINGTON, LPC

Inpatient Services

Inpatient services are typically designed for those individuals who have severe and persistent mental illness, who are in danger of hurting themselves or someone else, and who do not have the mental capacity to attend to their basic needs (Stevens & Smith, 2012). These services are collaborative in nature in that there are a number of human services treatment personnel, including social workers, psychiatrists, and counselors. This type of delivery system is most effective when professionals within the system operate as one entity to provide support and care for the client.

An example of such a system is an assertive community treatment team (ACT) (DHHS, 1999). This model, developed in the 1970s, relies heavily on the interdisciplinary approach to helping individuals with severe and persistent mental illness. The team provides 24-hour, 7-day-a-week monitoring of the client, comprehensive treatment planning, and ongoing clinical support, and manages small caseloads for optimal support and development. Because the ACT is individualized and targeted to an individual's specific and unique needs, it represents the most cost-effective approach to helping individuals who have suffered with multiple hospitalizations (DHHS, 1999).

Partial Treatment Services

Partial treatment services are provided for those clients who do not need continual 24-hour monitoring but do need 24-hour supervision (Gladding & Newsome, 2010). Most partial treatment facilities reside in medical hospitals and are staffed by an interdisciplinary team, including social workers, psychiatric nurses, and psychiatrists. Clinical mental health counselors typically are responsible for group and individual counseling as well as psychoeducation for clients' family members.

Partial treatment facilities include day treatment programs and residential programs. Day treatment programs are designed to provide intensive services using a combination of individual and group counseling modalities, recreational therapy, life skills training, and programs designed to help with adjustment to everyday life situations (Gladding & Newsome, 2010). Residential programs operate very similarly to day treatment programs but usually serve a different type of population. Typically, these programs are reserved for populations of individuals who have been discharged from the hospital and are learning to readjust to independent living. These populations include delinquent youths, individuals with developmental disabilities, and individuals who need more intensive treatment for substance abuse problems (Gladding & Newsome, 2010).

Outpatient Services

Clients using outpatient services are exposed to a variety of individual, group, and family modalities to help them work through their core issues. Typically designed to help individuals improve their social and personal functioning, these services address both acute and chronic problems and usually incorporate case management and medication management services as well.

Clients involved in these services are generally individuals who have the ability to live independently. Also, there is an assumption that these individuals have the mental capacity to work through their own concerns without the need for more intensive services. Because outpatient services represent the least restrictive placement for individuals in society, clients typically have a variety of venues through which they can get their needs met (Gladding & Newsome, 2010).

It is important to note that case management and consultation are becoming increasingly important and relevant for clinical mental health professionals. These tasks have typically been assigned to social workers (Remley & Herlihy, 2010); however, due to the changing demographics of individuals in need of care and the financial constraints agencies experience, there is an increasing need for clinical mental health counselors to expand their understanding and role in these types of service delivery methods (Health Career Centers, 2010). Clinical mental health counselors need to understand their roles in these service delivery settings as well as the professional issues that can affect client treatment.

PROFESSIONAL ISSUES

Clinical mental health counselors encounter a number of professional issues that will affect their clinical work. This chapter introduces clinical mental health counselors to two issues that are influential in their work with clients: managed care and online counseling. Managed care has changed the provision of health care and, more specifically, mental health care. Wilcoxon, Magnuson, and Norem (2008) recognize the emergence of managed care companies or health maintenance organizations as an evolutionary offshoot of the multicultural awareness movement in the counseling profession. Similarly, the increased need for communication and the extensive use of the Internet have slowly become an integral part of the clinical mental health counseling profession (Bradley, Hendricks, Lock, Whiting, & Parr, 2011).

Managed Care

Managed care is described by Gladding and Newsome (2010) as a way to administer clinical mental health care services by someone other than the client or the practitioner. It is covered in more detail in Chapter 8. The two general goals of any managed care organization are to manage costs and to ensure service quality. These third-party systems were designed to replace the costly fee-for service systems that were prevalent prior to the 1980s. Up until that point, health insurance costs were spiraling out of control. Managed care companies were developed in the 1940s to address this concern, but it was not until 1965 when the federal government established Medicare and Medicaid programs that they began to grow and affect the clinical mental health counseling field. By 1996, approximately 84% of all Americans had some type of insurance coverage (DHHS, 1999).

Most organizations have some form of third-party reimbursement procedures for their clinicians. There are literally hundreds of managed care companies operating in both the public and private sectors of mental health services (Gladding & Newsome, 2010). These companies contract with local human services agencies to monitor service provision for the community as well as to ensure service quality to the community. Cohen (2003) characterized this monitoring process as a business approach to understanding and evaluating the therapeutic relationship between counselor and client.

The benefits of this type of monitoring include greater access to services for the public, increased referrals for practitioners, and the effective use of quality control procedures for clinicians. The effect that managed care mental health has had on the clinical mental health counseling profession cannot be overstated. Some of the rules and regulations that govern mental health counseling are a direct result of managed care companies. For example, managed care companies require mental health clinicians to be licensed by the state in which they work as well as to have a certain number of years of clinical experience. Therefore, state licensure boards now require individuals who want to work in private practice to be licensed at the highest level of license for the state in which they practice, according to the American Association of State Counseling Boards (AASCB) (2013).

There are some who would disagree with the notion that managed care companies have impacted the clinical mental health counseling field in a positive way. For example, Cohen, Marecek, and Gillham (2006) believe that managed care companies have become a major stumbling block when trying to work within the bounds of a therapeutic relationship with a client. They describe these companies as triangulating in nature and assert that their influence is often a detriment to effective clinical work. Similarly, Cooper and Gottlieb (2006) express concern that the medical model on which these companies are based further pathologizes clients and creates ethical problems for clinicians.

There are a number of procedural obligations that agencies have to agree to abide by in order to maintain reimbursement viability with managed care companies, such as utilization reviews and preadmission screenings. Also, an explanation follows of the major types of managed care plans that counselors will be exposed to during their clinical work.

HEALTH MAINTENANCE ORGANIZATION (HMO) These organizations represent large group practices that initiate medical services on a prepaid, per capita basis. Developed by the Kaiser Foundation, health maintenance organizations (HMOs) were originally designed to provide reimbursement for mental health disorders that were responsive to short-term treatment (DHHS, 1999). The provision of health services is coordinated by a primary physician, who makes all of the decisions regarding treatment options and services (Gladding & Newsome, 2010).

PREFERRED PROVIDER ORGANIZATION (PPO) These managed care plans are designed to provide enrollees with low cost-sharing measures by encouraging their users to select from a network of providers. If a plan member chooses to pursue a provider who is not within the network, the out-of-pocket costs for the plan member are extremely high (DHHS, 1999). The network of providers is contracted by the managed care company and agrees to provide services on a discounted fee-for-service basis.

POINT OF SERVICE (POS) PLAN The point of service (POS) plans represent a combination of the prepaid plan and the fee-for-service plan. Similar to the PPO plan, POS enrollees can choose to use a network provider at a reduced cost. The major difference between the two plans is that the use of in-network services in the POS plan must be approved by a primary care physician. Another difference is that enrollees can use nonnetwork providers but only at a significant out-of-pocket co-payment that is due at the time of service.

CARVE-OUT MANAGED BEHAVIORAL HEALTH CARE This type of plan allows a larger range of services without the increased managed overhead costs. Basically, there are segments of insurance risk that are isolated from the overall insurance plan. These risks are covered in a different plan between the service provider and the enrollee (DHHS, 1999). Management of mental health services is delegated to a specialized vendor known as a managed behavioral health care organization (MBHO). The two general types of carve-out plans are payer plans and health plan subcontracts. The difference between the two plans lies in who takes on the responsibility of carving out a separate plan for mental health services. In payer plans, the enrollee makes the choice; in health plan subcontracts, this responsibility falls to the plan administrator.

Whatever the case may be, counselors need to increase their awareness of the role managed care companies will play in their clinical work. Wilcoxon et al. (2008) encourage clinicians to consider the significance of managed care companies and confront the business paradigm from which they operate.

Gladding and Newsome (2010) highlight a number of ethical issues counselors face when working within a managed care environment and posit necessary steps to take to provide quality care without compromising their ethical and legal obligations to clients.

Online Counseling

The use of online counseling services has emerged as an important and relevant part of the current and future clinical work of mental health counselors (Gladding & Newsome, 2010; Nassar-McMillan & Niles, 2011; Remley & Herlihy, 2010). Online services such as e-mail have been used extensively in the business sector, but online counseling hase gained usage only recently in the human services arena (Bradley et al., 2011). The Pew Charitable Trust (2009) reported that in 2009, 61% of all Americans searched online for health care services, including reading about others' experiences, comparing doctors and facilities, and listening to podcasts about medical issues. This increase in online services has made a significant impact on the mental health counseling community as well.

Remley and Herlihy (2010) point out that counselors need to make sure they understand the difference between e-mail and online counseling. Whereas e-mail has been an important form of communication between counselors and their clients since the advent of the Internet, online distance counseling is a new phenomenon that merits further attention. For example, Centore and Milacci (2008) report that human services organizations such as the American Counseling Association (ACA), the National Board for Certified Counselors (NBCC), and the American Psychological Association (APA) have written ethical statements and codes designed to help service providers understand the ethical and competence issues that come with using the Internet for counseling.

EFFECTIVENESS   There is a dearth of research that supports the effectiveness of online counseling; however, researchers are beginning to explore the relevance of online counseling for mental health professionals. For example, Wells, Mitchell, Finkelhor, and Becker-Blease (2007) report that in a sample of more than 2,000 social workers, psychologists, and counselors only 2% used the Internet for more than client correspondence and appointment setting. Participants highlighted the ethical challenges related to online counseling as a major deterrent for clinical work with clients. Similarly, Trepal, Haberstroh, Duffey, and Evans (2007) reviewed studies that evaluated the effectiveness of online counseling. Though the themes of these studies highlighted the favorable nature of using online counseling, they also pointed out the inherent problems related to online communication.

Centore and Milacci (2008) surveyed 854 mental health professionals to investigate their perceptions and use of counseling via online, telephone, e-mail, and videoconference.

The results of their study showed that these professionals reported using online services in some shape or form. Participants believed that the only advantage gained from using online counseling services was reduced client social stigma. However, the disadvantages included decreased ability to build rapport, ethical challenges, and ineffectively treating mental disorders.

Leibert, Archer, Munson, and York (2006) completed an exploratory study about the advantages and disadvantages of online counseling services and client satisfaction. They compared satisfaction with services between participants who had past experiences with online counseling and those whose past experience had been with face-to-face counseling. Their results showed that clients who received services online were satisfied with them but not as satisfied as those who received face-to-face services.

CHALLENGES   One of the major challenges related to online counseling services is the inability to incorporate nonverbal behavior into the assessment and evaluation of client concerns (Remley & Herlihy, 2010). Another relevant challenge is the lack of relationship building between client and counselor, which is based in part on visual cues between the two. Wells et al. (2007) identified confidentiality, liability issues, and misinformation provided by clients as the three most salient concerns for clinical mental health professionals. They conclude that mental health service providers need to be objective and ethically sound when evaluating the advantages and disadvantages of online mental health services.

Bradley et al. (2011) highlight the cultural challenges related to providing online counseling services. They believe that the effectiveness of online counseling with certain non-White populations is greatly diminished due to the inability of the counselor to attend to the communication style of the minority client. Similarly, Wells et al. (2007) highlight the disadvantage of the absence of the counselor's warm and congruent presence when working with the client online and how this is a major deterrent to client growth and development. Remley and Herlihy (2010) also point out that many individuals experience technical problems when using the Internet, and the lack of immediate technical support could present an ethical dilemma if a counselor were working with a client in crisis.

It is clear that managed care and online counseling present prevalent challenges for mental health professionals. Though there are positives in working with managed care, there are some drawbacks related to creativity and treatment planning that need to be considered. Furthermore, the explosion of the Internet and the convenient services it provides can be both a detriment and a support for mental health professionals. Mental health counselors need to be aware of the inherent challenges when working within these venues and must be willing to seek supervision and consultation when facing these challenges.

PUBLIC POLICY AND ACCESS

Given the challenges faced because of the increasing number of individuals in need of mental health services, several states as well as the federal government have worked to improve access to mental health services by mandating mental health benefits for individuals in society (Markowitz, 2005). There are newly developed mental health parity laws that forbid states and insurance companies from offering mental health plans that are more expensive than physical health plans. These plans are designed to lower the cost of mental health services for individuals in society and to increase public access to mental health services.

A major benefit of these initiatives is that clinical mental health counselors are increasingly able to receive the same recognition as their human services counterparts for the same type of clinical work with individuals in society. Such initiatives have been critical in moving the mental health counseling field forward and in increasing its viability and utility in the helping profession. Examples of specific initiatives include the Department of Veterans Affairs (VA) recognition of licensed professional counselors (LPC) and Army Directive 2011-09, which granted licensed professional counselors independent authority to practice as army substance abuse practitioners, an area that had not been previously reimbursable for LPCs working in VA facilities.

Department of Veterans Affairs

In September 2010 the Department of Veterans Affairs (VA) issued an occupational standard for licensed professional mental health counselors (LPMHCs). This standard granted mental health counselors the same pay grade and responsibilities as social workers (Department of Veterans Affairs, 2010). The VA has provided strict requirements for counselors who want to work as LPMHCs, including graduation from a program accredited by the Council for Accreditation of Counseling and Related Educational Programs (CACREP) and being fully licensed or working toward licensure in one's chosen state of practice. The bill also included language that explicitly recognized licensed professional counselors as mental health specialists within health care programs overseen by the VA.

The benefit of this law is that mental health counselors now have their own category under which they can provide services to individuals. The VA has long employed rehabilitation counselors and clinical mental health counselors to provide readjustment counseling services to veterans; however, these professionals did so with little or no recognition (National Academies Press, 2011). This new law allows the VA to hire licensed mental health counselors at the same level as clinical social workers and enables them to apply for supervisory positions that have been traditionally reserved for clinical social workers. Though this is a major step forward for the mental health counseling field, there are some challenges to the enforcement of this new law. The American Counseling Association, American Mental Health Counselors Association, and NBCC (2010) sent out a legislative alert, asking their members to advocate for the use of the new designation when advertising federal government positions.

Army Directive 2011-09

As previously mentioned, Army Directive 2011-09 authorizes the Army Substance Abuse Program (ASAP) to employ licensed professional counselors and licensed mental health counselors as independent practitioners within a well-defined scope of practice (Secretary of the Army, 2011). Mental health professionals have to meet specific criteria for inclusion in the ASAP program, including holding a master's degree from a CACREP-accredited program (there are some situations in which this requirement can be waived); possessing a state license as a professional counselor or mental health counselor; achieving the highest clinical level offered by the state licensure board; and passing the National

Clinical Mental Health Counseling Examination (NCMHCE). The policy was effective immediately and gave mental health counselors instant access to a population they were once restricted from working with.

The authorization of this new policy has opened a door that was traditionally closed for the mental health counseling profession. One of the major challenges of this new directive is the NCMHCE. Most mental health counselors have not taken this examination because it is not a requirement for licensure in most states (NBCC, 2012). In response to this dilemma, NBCC has increased its advocacy efforts for mental health professionals interested in the ASAP program. In collaboration with state licensure boards, NBCC has developed a registration process for the NCMHCE and is encouraging national certified counselors (NCCs) to use the NBCC Web site to facilitate the registration process (NBCC, 2011).

Conclusion

This chapter describes some of the settings in which clinical mental health counselors are employed. Though this list is not a comprehensive one, it serves as an excellent snapshot of the different opportunities available for counselors to provide services to different populations who are dealing with a variety of challenging issues and concerns. From the structure afforded by community mental health centers to the uncertainty and challenges of private practice, clinical mental health counselors have a variety of available options to pursue counseling services and to make their presence felt in the human services field.

It is incumbent upon mental health counselors to continue to challenge themselves to think globally in providing services to individuals. Clearly, there are populations that do not fit the traditional 50-minute model of service provision. Mental health counselors have an opportunity to reach these populations with a wellness-based model that emphasizes empowerment and growth when facing challenging situations. Also, mental health counselors need to continue to gain the requisite knowledge, skills, and training to address society's changing needs.

References

American Association of State Counseling Boards (AASCB). (2013). *Licensure and portability.* Retrieved from http://www.aascb.org/aws/AASCB/pt/sp/licensure

American Counseling Association (ACA). (2010). *Private practice pointers for ACA members.* Retrieved from https://files.counseling.org/Counselors/TP/PrivatePracticePointersMembers/CT2.aspx

American Mental Health Counselors Association (AMHCA). (2010). *AMHCE/ACA/NBCC update: The Department of Veterans Affairs recognizes licensed professional counselors!* Retrieved from http://www.amhca.org/news/detail.aspx?ArticleId=224

Barker, S. B. (2001). Counseling in medical settings. In D. C. Locke, J. E. Myers, & E. L. Herr (Eds.), *The handbook of counseling* (pp. 373–390). Thousand Oaks, CA: Sage.

Bauman, S. (2008). *Essential topics for the helping professional.* Boston, MA: Longman.

Bradley, L. J., Hendricks, B., Lock, R., Whiting, P. P., & Parr, G. (2011). E-mail communication: Issues for mental health counselors. *Journal of Mental Health Counseling, 33*(1), 67–79.

Browers, R. T. (2005). Counseling in mental health and private practice settings. In D. Cappuzzi & D. R. Gross (Eds.), *Introduction to the counseling profession* (4th ed., pp. 357–380). Needham Heights, MA: Pearson/Allyn & Bacon.

Centore, A. J., & Milacci, F. (2008). A study of mental health counselors' use of and perspectives on distance counseling. *Journal of Mental Health Counseling, 30*(3), 267–282.

Cohen, J. A. (2003). Managed care and the evolving role of the clinical social worker in mental health. *Social Work, 48,* 34–44.

Cohen, J., Marecek, J., & Gillham, J. (2006). Is three a crowd? Clients, clinicians, and managed care. *Journal of Orthopsychiatry, 76,* 251–259.

Cooper, C. C., & Gottlieb, M. C. (2006). Ethical issues with managed care: Challenges facing counseling psychology. *The Counseling Psychologist, 28,* 179–236.

Council for Accreditation of Counseling and Related Educational Programs (CACREP). (2009). *2009 standards.* Retrieved from http://www.cacrep.org /doc/2009%20Standards%20with%20cover.pdf

Davis, S. R., & Meier, S. T. (2001). *The elements of managed care.* Belmont, CA: Wadsworth.

Department of Veterans Affairs. (2010). *VA handbook 5005/42.* Retrieved from http://www.va.gov /vapubs/viewPublication.asp?Pub_ID=507&FType=2

Diamond, P. M., Magaletta, P. R., Harzke, A. J., & Baxter, J. (2008). Who requests psychological services upon admission to prison? *Psychological Services, 5*(2), 97–107.

Gladding, S. T., & Newsome, D. W. (2010). *Clinical mental health counseling in community and agency settings* (3rd ed.). Upper Saddle River, NJ: Pearson Education.

Health Careers Center. (2010). *Mental health counselor.* Retrieved from http://www.mshealthcareers.com /careers/mentalhealthcounselor.htm

Hsiao, A. F., Ryan, G. W., Hays, R. D., Coulter, I. D., Andersen, R. M., & Wenger, N. S. (2006). Variations in provider conceptions of integrative medicine. *Social Science & Medicine, 62*(12), 2973–2987.

James, S. H., & Greenwalt, B. C. (2001). Documenting success and achievement: Presentation and working portfolios for counselors. *Journal of Mental Health Counseling, 79,* 161–165.

Leibert, T., Archer, J., Munson, J., & York, G. (2006). An exploratory study of client perceptions of Internet counseling and the therapeutic alliance. *Journal of Mental Health Counseling, 28,* 69–83.

Lewis, J. A., Lewis, M. D., Daniels, J. A., & D'Andrea, M. J. (2003). *Community counseling: Empowering strategies for a diverse society* (3rd ed.). Pacific Grove, CA: Brooks/Cole.

MacCluskie, K. C., & Ingersoll, R. E. (2001). *Becoming a 21st century agency counselor: Personal and professional explorations.* Belmont, CA: Wadsworth.

Markowitz, S. (2005). *Mental health and public policy.* Retrieved from http://www.nber.org/reporter /spring05/markowitz.html

Mayerhoff, D. I., Smith, R., & Schleifer, S. J. (2008). Academic–state hospital collaboration for a rehabilitative model of care. *Psychiatric Services, 59*(12), 1474–1475.

Mental Health Counseling. (2004). *Counseling in mental health and private practice settings.* Retrieved from http://www.ablongman.com/helpingprofessions /coun/ppt/other/counselinginmental.ppt

Morgan, R. D., Rozycki, A. T., & Wilson, S. (2004). Inmate perceptions of mental health services. *Professional Psychology: Research and Practice, 35,* 389–396.

Nassar-McMillan, S., & Niles, S. G. (2011). *Developing your identity as a professional counselor.* Belmont, CA: Brooks/Cole.

National Academies Press. (2010). *Provision of mental health counseling services under TRICARE.* Retrieved from http://www.nap.edu/openbook.php?record _id=12813&page=151

National Board for Certified Counselors (NBCC). (2011). Army directive grants counselors independent practice authority. *The National Certified Counselor, 27,* 1, 3.

National Board for Certified Counselors (NBCC). (2012). *National clinical mental health counseling examination (NCMHCE).* Retrieved from http:// www.nbcc.org/NCMHCE

The Pew Charitable Trust. (2009). *61% of American adults look online for health information.* Retrieved from http://www.pewtrusts.org/news_room_detail .aspx?id=53352

Remley, T. P., Jr., & Herlihy, B. (2010). *Ethical, legal, and professional issues in counseling* (3rd ed.). Upper Saddle River, NJ: Pearson Education.

Secretary of the Army. (2011). *Army Directive 2011-09.* Retrieved from http://www.apd.army.mil/pdffiles /ad2011_09.pdf

Seligman, L. (2009). *Fundamental skills for mental health professionals.* Upper Saddle River, NJ: Pearson Education.

Stevens, P., & Smith, R. L. (2012). *Substance abuse counseling: Theory and practice* (5th ed.). Upper Saddle River, NJ: Pearson Education.

Trepal, H., Haberstroh, S., Duffey, T., & Evans, M. (2007). Considerations and strategies for teaching online counseling skills: Establishing relationship in cyberspace. *Counselor Education and Supervision, 46,* 266–279.

US Bureau of Labor Statistics. (2012). *Occupational outlook handbook, 2012–13 edition*. Retrieved from http://www.bls.gov/ooh/

Vuchinich, R. E. (2002). President's column. *Addictions Newsletter, 10*(1), 1, 5.

US Department of Health and Human Services (DHHS). (1999). *Mental health: A report of the Surgeon General*. Chapter 6: Mental health. Retrieved from http://www.surgeongeneral.gov/library/mentalhealth/chapter6/sec3.html

Wells, M., Mitchell, K. J., Finkelhor, D., & Becker-Blease, K. A. (2007). Online mental health treatment: Concerns and considerations. *CyberPsychology and Behavior, 10*(3), 453–459. doi:10.1089/cpb.2006.9933

Wilcoxon, S. A., Magnuson, S., & Norem, K. (2008). Institutional values of managed mental health care: Efficiency or oppression? *Journal of Multicultural Counseling and Development, 36,* 143–154.

The Practice of Clinical Mental Health Counseling

5

Professional and Social Advocacy in Clinical Mental Health

Catherine Y. Chang and Maggie E. Walsh

CHAPTER OVERVIEW

In this chapter, we discuss the importance of addressing professional and social advocacy in clinical mental health. We first cover the interrelatedness of professional and social advocacy and then address the importance of professional advocacy as it relates to clinical mental health. Next we explore the importance of social advocacy as a professional imperative. This chapter concludes with recommendations of how mental health counselors can become change agents. Throughout this chapter there are practical activities and exercises designed to promote awareness and knowledge of advocacy issues and to develop advocacy competencies.

LEARNING OBJECTIVES

The learning objectives for this chapter are designed to be consistent with the 2009 Council for Accreditation of Counseling and Related Educational Programs Standards (CACREP, 2009). As such, upon completion of this chapter, the student will have knowledge of the following clinical mental health counseling standards:

1. Understands how living in a multicultural society affects clients who are seeking clinical mental health counseling services. (E.1)
2. Understands the effects of racism, discrimination, sexism, power, privilege, and oppression on one's own life and career and those of the client. (E.2)
3. Understands current literature that outlines theories, approaches, strategies, and techniques shown to be effective when working with specific populations of clients with mental and emotional disorders. (E.3)
4. Understands effective strategies to support client advocacy and influence public policy and government relations on local, state, and national levels to enhance equity, increase funding, and promote programs that affect the practice of clinical mental health counseling. (E.4)

5. Understands the implications of concepts such as internalized oppression and institutional racism, as well as the historical and current political climate regarding immigration, poverty, and welfare. (E.5)

6. Knows public policies on the local, state, and national levels that affect the quality and accessibility of mental health services. (E.6)

Additionally, students will have knowledge of the following core entry-level standards:

1. History and philosophy of the counseling profession. (G.1.a)

2. Professional roles, functions, and relationships with other human service providers. . . . (G.1.b)

3. Professional organizations, including membership benefits, activities, services to members, and current issues. (G.1.f)

4. The role and process of the professional counselor advocating on behalf of the profession. (G.1.h)

5. Advocacy processes needed to address institutional and social barriers that impede access, equity, and success for clients. (G.1.i)

KEY CONSTRUCTS

The following are key constructs necessary for understanding professional and social advocacy:

Advocacy: According to CACREP, advocacy is any "action taken on behalf of clients or the counseling profession to support appropriate policies and standards for the profession; promote individual human worth, dignity, and potential; and oppose or work to change policies and procedures, systemic barriers, long-standing traditions, and preconceived notions that stifle human development" (2009, p. 59). For the purposes of this chapter, any action taken to directly benefit the counseling profession is referred to as *professional advocacy*, and any action taken to directly benefit clients is referred to as *social advocacy*, or *client advocacy*.

Empowerment: Empowerment is the process by which people, organizations, or groups who are powerless and marginalized (a) become aware of the power dynamics at work in their life context, (b) develop the skills and capacity for gaining reasonable control over their lives, (c) which they exercise, (d) without infringing on the rights of others, and (e) which coincides with actively supporting the empowerment of others in their community. (McWhirter, 1994, p. 12)

Oppression: Oppression is a system that allows access to the services, rewards, benefits, and privileges of society based on membership in a particular group. Oppression involves the abuse of power whereby a dominant group engages in unjust, harsh, or cruel activities that perpetuate an attitude or belief which is reinforced by society and maintained by a power imbalance. It involves beliefs and actions that impose undesirable labels, experiences, and conditions on individuals by virtue of their cultural identity. (Ancis & Chang, 2008, p. 1245)

Privilege: Privilege relates to the attitudes and behaviors that perpetuate the belief that one group's beliefs and standards are superior to those of other groups, and it is related to one group having control, power, access, and advantage over another group (Ancis & Chang, 2008; Chang & Gnilka, 2010).

Professional identity: Professional identity relates to one's understanding of the historical foundations of counseling and ethical standards of practice and having a clear definition of counseling and understanding of the counselor role (Chang, 2011).

Social justice: "[S]ocial justice refers to a belief in a just world (i.e., a world with fair treatment and equal distribution of the benefits of society) that respects and protects human rights" (Chang & Gnilka, 2010, p. 53). Thus, the goal of social justice is to ensure that every individual has an opportunity to resources such as health care and employment, and to achieve optimal mental health (Chang, Crethar, & Ratts, 2010).

INTRODUCTION

Advocacy on behalf of the counseling profession and on behalf of its clients is fundamental to the practice of counseling (Chang, 2011; Chang & Gnilka, 2010). Many researchers (e.g., Chang, Hays, & Milliken, 2009; Eriksen, 1997; Myers, Sweeney, & White, 2002) have argued that advocacy is a two-pronged concept that must include both professional advocacy and client/social advocacy. Professional and client advocacy can be viewed as "complementary and intertwined" (Myers et al., 2002, p. 394). Clinical mental health counselors become more effective advocates for their clients if the profession of counseling is recognized and viewed as credible by other mental health professionals and the public at large. Conversely, if clinical mental health counseling is recognized by legislators, employers, third-party payers, as well as the public at large, the profession will have greater resources to promote the optimal psychosocial health and wellness of its clients (Chang et al., 2009; Chi Sigma Iota, 1998; Myers et al., 2002).

Both professional advocacy and client/social advocacy are essential to mental health counseling; as such, this chapter begins by providing an overview of the American Counseling Association Advocacy Competencies. First, however, as you read this chapter, please keep the following case study in mind.

CASE STUDY 5.1

Charlie Stewart is a 10-year-old Hispanic male. He lives with his adoptive parents and three older siblings, one of which is his biological sister. Katherine (23 years old) and Henry (18 years old) attend a local college. Charlie and Caroline (13 years old, biological sister) have lived with the Stewart family since Charlie was three years old following a custody battle with Charlie's biological father, who had been convicted of child abuse and neglect and subsequently sent to prison. While Charlie's father was incarcerated, he relinquished custody of Charlie and Caroline. After being with the Stewarts for 18 months, the Stewarts formally adopted Charlie and Caroline. Arthur and Samantha Stewart have been married for 26 years and are White.

Charlie has been receiving mental health services consistently since the age of four. Charlie's parents noticed Charlie had aggressive tendencies and appeared to be having difficulty coping with anger. His parents describe Charlie as having "huge angry fits" during which Charlie would scream and cry for hours at a time. He has hit family members and thrown objects at them. He has physically hurt family members on several occasions by hitting them with various objects. He has destroyed property both in and out of the home, including smashing dishes and glassware and tearing books. When angry at family members, Charlie has also broken several items that had sentimental value to them. His parents are unable to calm Charlie when he is having one of his "fits" and report that although he can be very loving and caring, they are often fearful of him when he is angry. His parents report that many things can trigger an outburst including not getting what he wants, being told no for any reason, and getting his feelings hurt. Charlie was in play therapy for several years as well as individual counseling.

At the age of eight, Charlie was admitted to an inpatient treatment setting called McAllister Counseling Center after he had made statements that he planned to hurt himself. Charlie told his sister Katherine that he hated himself and that he planned on stabbing himself with "one of dad's building tools." Charlie was in inpatient treatment for four weeks until he was released back into the care of his parents when his insurance ran out and his family was unable to pay the bill themselves.

Charlie came to the community-based counseling agency where you work after having been discharged from the inpatient treatment center. You learn that while he was at McAllister Counseling Center, Charlie was diagnosed with intermittent explosive disorder and depression. In an intake session with his parents, they state one of their goals as "you need to fix him; we've done all we can. It's all up to you." You also learn that the Stewarts are currently in the process of getting divorced, and they are struggling with who will take responsibility for Charlie's care.

In addition to coming to you for individual counseling, Charlie is receiving in-home services from McAllister Counseling Center for skill development. Although Charlie has been homeschooled by his father because of his parents' concerns about his behavior, Charlie has recently been enrolled in a local elementary school. Less than 5% of the students at that school are Hispanic.

Charlie reports that he worries that nobody in his family wants him and that he has "ruined everything." He notes that he has very few friends that he can play with or talk to in his neighborhood and that he hasn't made any new friends at school yet. When asked what he'd like to have different as a result of therapy, he responded, "I just want to be happy and not get in trouble so much because it makes everyone so mad at me."

After three months of meeting with Charlie for individual counseling, you note minimal progress. Several times the family has missed appointments due to a lack of transportation. Although you are aware that Charlie sees team members from McAllister Counseling Center, you are unsure of the progress being made with them or what their treatment goals are.

ACA ADVOCACY COMPETENCIES

In 2000, Jane Goodman, as president of the American Counseling Association (ACA), appointed the Advocacy Competencies Task Force. This task force was charged with developing a set of competencies for counselors working on behalf of their clients to remove the barriers to optimal health and positive growth. A basic assumption behind this charge was that professional counselors can advocate for systemic change by directly and indirectly advocating for their clients (Toporek, Lewis, & Ratts, 2010).

The ACA advocacy competencies center around two intersecting dimensions: the extent of the client's involvement (i.e., acting with and acting on behalf of) and level of intervention (i.e., client/student, school/community, and public arena). Thus, the result is six domains: (a) client/student empowerment, (b) client/student advocacy, (c) community collaboration, (d) systems advocacy, (e) public information, and (f) social/political advocacy. The advocacy competencies assert that advocacy requires social action both in partnership with the client (i.e., empowerment) and on behalf of the client (i.e., advocacy) (Lewis, Arnold, House, & Toporek, 2003). Additionally, the advocacy competencies assume that the needs of the client or the community drive the advocacy actions (Toporek et al., 2010). Although Jane Goodman charged the Advocacy Competencies Task Force with developing competencies to promote client advocacy, the resulting advocacy competencies also address the importance of professional advocacy in the public image and social/political advocacy domains.

Review the ACA advocacy competencies (Lewis et al., 2003). Which activities have you already engaged in? In small groups, develop a plan of action for engaging in some of the other advocacy activities. What resources do you have to help with these activities? What challenges do you face?

PROFESSIONAL ADVOCACY: ADVOCATING FOR CLINICAL MENTAL HEALTH COUNSELING

Professional advocacy refers to actions taken in order to advance the profession of counseling in general and the clinical mental health profession specifically. These actions include but are not limited to the following: (a) promoting standards in counselor training; (b) working toward counselor licensure; (c) advocating for marketplace recognition; (d) developing inter- and intra-professional relationships to promote the counseling profession and the clients that it serves; and (e) collaborating with legislators and policy makers (Chi Sigma Iota, 1998; Myers et al., 2002). Core to all professional advocacy activities is having a strong professional identity as a counselor (Chang, 2011). With the recognition that a unified counselor identity is essential, ACA and the American Association of State Counseling Boards (AASCB) sponsored an initiative called the *20/20: A Vision for the Future of Counseling* (ACA, 2010).

20/20: A Vision for the Future of Counseling

Since 2005, delegates representing 30 (now 31) major, diverse counseling organizations (e.g., ACA, AMHCA, and CACREP) have been collaborating to determine the actions necessary to ensure a healthy and strong future for the counseling profession. The aim of this group was to determine a vision for where the counseling profession should be in the year 2020 and the steps necessary to reach that vision (Rollins, 2010).

The *20/20: A Vision for the Future of Counseling* identified seven principles critical to moving the counseling profession forward:

1. Sharing a common professional identity is critical for counselors.
2. Presenting ourselves as a unified profession has multiple benefits.
3. Working together to improve the public perception of counseling and to advocate for professional issues will strengthen the profession.
4. Creating a portability system for licensure will benefit counselors and strengthen the counseling profession.
5. Expanding and promoting our research base is essential to the efficacy of professional counselors and to the public perception of the profession.
6. Focusing on students and prospective students is necessary to ensure the ongoing health of the counseling profession.
7. Promoting client welfare and advocating for the populations we serve is a primary focus of the counseling profession. (ACA, 2010, para. 3)

In addition to identifying the seven principles, the delegates of the 20/20 Vision agreed for the first time on a common definition of counseling: "Counseling is a professional relationship that empowers diverse individuals, families, and groups to accomplish mental health, wellness, education, and career goals" (ACA, 2010, para. 4). The seven principles have been endorsed by 30 (including AMHCA) of the 31 organizations participating in the 20/20 Vision, and the definition of counseling has been endorsed by 28 (including AMHCA) of the 31 organizations (ACA, 2010).

PROFESSIONAL IDENTITY

The topic of professional identity is not new to the counseling profession, and it is interesting to note that sharing a common professional identity was identified as one of the seven critical principles by the delegates of the *20/20: A Vision for the Future of Counseling*. One of the earlier debates related to the issue of counseling as a profession was deliberated in the 1990s by Ritchie (1990) and Feit and Lloyd (1990). Ritchie asserted that counseling is not a profession because of the lack of professional autonomy and legal recognition. Based on this assessment, he recommended the following: that all counseling programs meet a minimum standard, counselors advocate for licensure across all states, counselors along with insurance companies and regulatory bodies work to establish a balance of professional autonomy and professional accountability, and counselors do a better job of educating the public about the services they can provide. Conversely, Feit and Lloyd contended that counseling is a profession because it meets the main characteristics of a profession such as specialized training, ethical standards, and strong identity with the field.

When Hanna and Bemak (1997) revisited the issue of counselor professional identity, they concluded that counseling had accomplished nearly all of the requisites for status as a profession with the exception of a unique identity. Some researchers have asserted that having a recognizable identity for counselors is essential for the profession's stability, survival, and acknowledgment by courts and legislating bodies (e.g., Altekruse, 1994; Maples, Altekruse, and Testa, 1993). Hanna and Bemak suggested one path toward establishing a unique identity would be for counselors to develop their own knowledge base.

Despite the progress (i.e., professional organization, an ethical code, accrediting body, credentialing and licensure) that the counseling profession has made over the years to establish itself as a profession, some continue to argue that professional counseling has not fully matured and is still struggling to establish a professional identity (Gale & Austin, 2003; Neukrug & Remley, 2009). Myers and Sweeney (2004) reported that participants in their national survey identified a better public image of counseling and counselors as a current advocacy need. The participants stated that they did not believe that the public at large had a clear understanding of who professional mental health counselors are or what their role entails.

This struggle with professional identity is largely due to the fact that counseling is a diverse profession with counselors working in various settings (e.g., schools, community mental health, colleges and universities, private practice, rehabilitation centers, career centers). It has a number of certification bodies, state licensure boards, and counseling organizations that each endorse its own set of ethical codes, thus making the codes difficult to enforce and confusing to both the mental health counseling professionals and their clients (Gale & Austin, 2003; Neukrug & Remley, 2009). For example, the American Mental Health Counselors Association (AMHCA), a division of ACA, states that it is the only group that is dedicated to the work of mental health counselors and has established its own code of ethics (AMHCA, 2010). ACA, the parent organization of AMHCA, states that its mission is "dedicated to the growth and development of the counseling profession and those who are served" (www.counseling.org), and ACA has its own code of ethics (ACA, 2005). Given that as a clinical mental health counselor you may be a member of both AMCHA and ACA, which ethical standards do you use as your guidelines? Additionally, you may have to adhere to the ethical standards of your state licensure board. As a clinical mental health professional, are you a counselor first who happens to work in a clinical mental health setting, or are you a clinical mental health counselor distinct from other counselors in other work settings?

Based on a review of interviews of senior contributors to the counseling profession published in the *Journal of Counseling & Development*, Gale and Austin (2003) provided several recommendations for establishing a unified counseling identity. Their first recommendation was that ACA should initiate a task force to develop a comprehensive strategic plan for the counseling profession's future (see ACA, 2010). Gale and Austin contend that ACA's future plans must benefit all its members rather than focusing only on counseling specialties in a piecemeal fashion. Their second recommendation was that professional associations, accrediting bodies, and credentialing organizations need to work together to promote unity of the profession. Their final recommendation was that clinical mental health counselors should actively continue to discuss their collective identity, the nature of the counseling profession, and the future of counseling.

In a membership bulletin to the members of the Licensed Professional Counselors Association of Georgia (LPCA; state chapter of AMHCA), Don Durkee, its 2010 president, addressed the issue of counselor identity. Durkee (2010) argued that a better approach to the counselor identity debate is to address it from the point of view of the people who least understand the profession—its potential clients. He contended that an effective statement about counselor identity must emphasize the intended benefit for the client; therefore, the goal of counseling is to promote quality of life. As counselors—regardless of whether one is a clinical mental health counselor, professional counselor, school counselor, or rehabilitation counselor—the goal is to help clients heal, grow, develop, and attain optimal health and wellness.

A prerequisite for effective professional advocacy is the development of a solid professional identity as a professional counselor. This is echoed in the 2009 CACREP standards. According to the 2009 CACREP standards, all entry-level programs must meet standard II: Professional Identity, which includes knowledge related to the history and roles and responsibilities of being a counselor. In addition to the common core standard related to professional identity, students who are preparing to work as clinical mental health counselors must have foundational knowledge related to the history and philosophy of clinical mental health counseling as well as an understanding of the roles and functions of a clinical mental health counselor (see CACREP, 2009). Therefore, we believe that clinical mental health counselors must have a firm understanding of what it means to be a professional counselor as well as what it means to be a professional mental health counselor working in a clinical mental health setting (i.e., clinical mental health counselor).

MARKETPLACE RECOGNITION

Related to professional identity and a key component of professional advocacy is marketplace recognition. Once professional mental health counselors have a clear vision of their professional identity, they must be able to articulate it to policy makers and to their potential clients. Additionally, once clinical mental health counselors are recognized by policy makers and the public at large, their public image and credibility can be used to bring attention to mental health issues. Chi Sigma Iota (CSI) (1998), the international honor society for professional counselors, identified marketplace recognition as one of the six key advocacy themes that resulted from its two counselor professional advocacy leadership conferences. The goal of marketplace recognition is "to assure that profes-sional counselors in all settings are suitably compensated for their services and free to provide service to the public within all areas of their competence" (Chi Sigma Iota, 1998, p. 6). The corresponding objective is for mental health counselors to be acknowledged by state and national legislation as service providers. The goal of marketplace recognition complements the ACA Advocacy Competencies (Lewis et al., 2003) domain of public information and social/political advocacy.

Public Information

Professional mental health counselors must be competent in informing the general public about matters that impact the clinical mental health field and issues that affect the optimal health and wellness of the clients that they serve. In order to advocate effectively, clinical mental health counselors must be able to identify both the protective factors and the bar-riers that impact healthy development. Additionally, professional advocacy for clinical mental health counseling needs to include public information efforts that create the social and cultural conditions necessary to eliminate stigma and prejudice against persons with mental disorders (Funk, Minoletti, Drew, Taylor, & Saraceno, 2005). The competencies needed for promoting effective public information include but are not limited to the fol-lowing abilities: (a) to prepare press releases, (b) to write effective letters to editors, (c) to disseminate information through a variety of media, and (d) to identify and collaborate with other professionals.

Social/Political Advocacy

Professional mental health counselors may be called on to serve as change agents in the system by using their advocacy skills to influence public policy. Lewis et al. (2003) assert that the first skill necessary to advocate at the social/political level is to have the ability to distinguish which problems can be best resolved through social/political advocacy. Addi-tional competencies necessary to promote social/political advocacy include (a) an under-standing of various systems, (b) the ability to collaborate with allies, (c) an understanding of the political structure, and (d) the ability to conduct and disseminate research summaries.

SOCIAL ADVOCACY: FOUNDATION TO COUNSELING

As stated previously, professional advocacy and social advocacy are "complementary and intertwined" (Myers et al., 2002, p. 394). Most people enter the mental health profession because they want to help others, and one primary reason they engage in professional advocacy is to provide better care for their clients; thus, client advocacy is central to clinical mental health counselors' efforts as a profession.

In this section, we provide a brief history of the social advocacy movement within the counseling profession. In order to understand social advocacy within the counseling profession, it is important to first understand both the foundation and background of the movement, and how social advocacy and social justice are fundamental to the practice of mental health counseling.

One cannot address social advocacy without first understanding the relationship between social advocacy and social justice. Social justice refers to a belief in a just world, a world that respects and protects human rights (Lee, 2007). Social justice within the mental health context refers to a belief that all clients not only have a right to optimal health and wellness but also have a right to equitable treatment and fair allocation of societal resources. Therefore, social advocacy within the mental health context refers to any action taken on behalf of clients to ensure fair and equitable treatment. Advocacy-oriented clinical mental health counselors who engage in social justice counseling take into consideration the impact of oppression, privilege, and discrimination on the mental health of their clients. Their goal is to ensure that all individuals have an opportunity to resources such as health care and employment, and to achieve optimal mental health (Chang et al., 2010; Chang & Gnilka, 2010; Crethar, Torres Rivera, & Nash, 2008; Ratts, 2009).

Social Justice and Social Advocacy: The Fifth Force

Although social advocacy has gained prominence in recent years due to certain economic and societal issues, it is not new to the counseling profession. Individuals responding to social injustice and advocating for societal change are foundational to the counseling profession (see Hartung & Blustein, 2002; Kiselica & Robinson, 2001). The following time-line demonstrates the important role that social advocacy has played in the development of the counseling profession. Although this list is not exhaustive, it does illustrate how social advocacy has been and continues to be a trend in the maturation of the counseling profession.

1. ***1900s:*** Frank Parsons, a social reformer, established the Vocational Bureau. He believed that power and resources were unequally distributed; thus, he worked toward empowering those in society with the least power and resources, including women, immigrants, and poor children (Hartung & Blustein, 2002). Clifford Beers, committed to bringing public awareness to mental health issues and promoting humane treatment of individuals with mental issues, spearheaded the mental hygiene movement. This movement was the forerunner for some of the most influential mental health advocacy groups, such as the National Mental Health Association (currently Mental Health America) and the National Alliance on Mental Illness (Kiselica, 2004; Kiselica & Robinson, 2001).

2. ***1970s:*** Social and political revolutions were occurring across the United States including in the counseling profession. In 1971, *The Personnel and Guidance Journal* (currently the *Journal of Counseling & Development*) published a special issue on counseling and the social revolution. This issue called for counselors to engage in social change processes by addressing issues related to racism, sexism, destruction of environment, and ending warfare (Chang & Gnilka, 2010). The Association for Non-White Concerns in Personnel and Guidance (ANWC), a division of ACA, was established in 1972 (AMCD, 2010).

3. ***1980s:*** There was a growing movement toward broadening the perspective of multiculturalism to include such cultural variables as gender, sexual orientation, social class, and religion (Ratts, Lewis, & Toporek, 2010). With this in mind, ANWC changed its name to the Association for Multicultural Counseling and Development (AMCD) in 1985. The American Association of Counseling and Development (currently ACA) published a position paper on human rights in 1987 imploring counselors to advocate for social change through personal, professional, and political activities.

4. ***1990s:*** With the growing emphasis on multiculturalism that had developed in the 1980s, Sue, Arredondo, and McDavis (1992) published the multicultural counseling

competencies and standards. After many years of operating informally, the Association for Lesbian, Gay, Bisexual & Transgender Issues in Counseling was formally recognized as a division by ACA in 1997 (Rhode, 2010). Toward the late 1990s, there was an increased focus on social justice issues as a component of multicultural counseling competencies and an increased call for counselors to engage in social action. This culminated in Lee and Walz's (1998) book, *Social Action: A Mandate for Counselors*. In 1999, the *Journal of Counseling & Development* (Robinson and Ginter, editors) published a special issue on racism.

5. **2000s:** The book *Advocacy in Counseling: Counselors, Clients, and Community* (Lewis & Bradley, 2000) was published. Counselors for Social Justice, a division of ACA, was chartered in 2001 and officially recognized by the ACA Governing Council in 2002. The ACA Governing Council adopted the advocacy competencies in 2003 (Lewis et al., 2003). An increased emphasis on multiculturalism and social justice issues within counseling was reflected in the revised ACA Code of Ethics (ACA, 2005). In particular, the new standard E.5.c. directs counselors to "recognize historical and social prejudices in the misdiagnosis and pathologizing of certain individuals and groups and the role of mental health professionals in perpetuating these prejudices through diagnosis and treatment" (p. 12). The Association for Counselor Education and Supervision (ACES) adopted the theme "Vanguards for Change: ACES and Social Justice" and sponsored a Social Justice Summit as a part of the conference (Chang & Gnilka, 2010). There is a special section on advocacy competencies in the summer 2009 issues of the *Journal of Counseling & Development* (Niles, editor).

The growing emphasis on social justice issues in counseling in the early 2000s led Ratts, D'Andrea, and Arredondo (2004) to refer to social justice counseling as the fifth force. Social justice issues and social advocacy continue to serve as a primary force in the maturation of the counseling profession. Clinical mental health counselors operating from a social justice perspective must have the competencies to address the core constructs of social advocacy such as privilege and oppression.

Privilege and Oppression

Hays, Chang, and Dean (2004) described privilege and oppression as having an inverse relationship. Based on a qualitative study, they developed a model of privilege and oppression that described how external and internal factors influence one's awareness of privilege and oppression. Privilege was defined as "having power, access, advantage, and a majority status" (p. 284), whereas oppression was defined as "lacking power, access, and advantage and having a minority status" (p. 284). Oppression is pervasive and exists across multiple groups and at varying levels. A person's awareness of his or her privilege or oppression is cyclical as it develops in response to the internalizing of various external factors such as government, religion, media, family, industry, and education. The internalization process is further influenced by visibility and perception. Visibility relates to visible evidence of a privileged or oppressed status (e.g., skin color), and perception is connected to self-perception and the perception of others based on the visibility of that person's status.

Oppression also has been described as an intersection of two modalities, oppression by force and oppression by deprivation, and three types: primary, secondary, and tertiary. Oppression by force is any act that imposes an unwanted object, label, role, experience, or living condition and leads to physical and psychological pain on an individual or group; whereas oppression by deprivation involves exposing an individual or group to conditions that would hinder their physical and psychological well-being (Hanna, Talley, & Guindon, 2000). Examples of oppression by force include sexual assault and name-calling; and examples of oppression by deprivation include unequal educational opportunities based on socioeconomic status, and unequal pay and promotion based on minority status.

Primary oppression refers to overt acts of oppression including both oppression by force and oppression by deprivation. Secondary oppression occurs when individuals benefit from overt oppressive acts against others. Individuals benefiting from secondary oppression do not necessarily engage directly in the oppressive acts, but they also do not object to others who do directly engage in the oppressive acts and do benefit from such acts. Tertiary oppression, or internalized oppression, occurs when individuals of the minority group identify with the dominant message and seek acceptance by the dominant group. Both secondary and tertiary oppression can be passive (Hanna et al., 2000).

The construct of both privilege and oppression is complex and multidimensional. Privilege and oppression manifest themselves differently based on multiple identities, personal experiences, external factors, and level of self-awareness. One can have privilege and oppressed status concurrently depending on one's race, gender, class, sexual orientation, or religious affiliation (Chang & Gnilka, 2010). Depending on the context, an individual can have multiple intersecting identities; thus, someone can be both an oppressor and oppressed at the same time (Ancis & Chang, 2008).

The CACREP standards (CACREP, 2009) highlight the importance of having awareness of one's privilege or oppressed status. The following activity is designed to personalize privilege and oppression in your own life.

> Construct a table with three (3) columns. In the first column, make a list of privileges that you have personally experienced or witnessed over the past week. In the second column, make a list of oppressive acts that you have experienced or witnessed over the past week. In the third column, indicate whether the acts are examples of power/lack of power, access/lack of access, advantage/lack of advantage, and majority status/minority status. Discuss your listings in a small group. Are there any acts that you did not include in your list that were in others' lists? Are there any acts that others included that you found surprising? (Chang & Gnilka, 2010, p. 55) How did the acts that personally impacted you differ from those that you wrote down about others?

SOCIAL INJUSTICE AND MENTAL HEALTH ISSUES

Social injustice (i.e., discrimination, oppression, and prejudice) has a significant impact on the mental health of members of marginalized groups. Ethnic and cultural minorities experience more social injustices than do members of the majority culture. This high level of exposure to social injustice makes these groups particularly vulnerable to stressors that challenge their mental health and well-being. The relationship between social injustice and the mental health of marginalized groups was highlighted in the US Surgeon General's report, *Mental Health: Culture, Race, and Ethnicity: A Supplement to Mental Health* (DHHS, 2001). Stress is a primary cause of emotional distress, leaving these groups susceptible to depression, suicide, substance abuse, violence, and anxiety. These stressors can also result in physical ailments including hypertension, low birth weight, heart disease, and cancer. Although these groups are at increased risk of mental and medical illness due to social injustice, they are frequently denied mental health and medical services due to socioeconomic and language barriers (DHHS, 2001). This section examines several social injustices and their effect on mental health.

Homelessness

Before examining homelessness and its impact on mental health, it is essential to first discuss the language used in this discussion. Historically, people without a place to live have been labeled "homeless." One way that clinical mental health counselors can advocate for clients is to change this language from "homeless person" to "a person experiencing homelessness." This person-first approach parallels the manner in which a clinician might refer to a person with a diagnosis. For example, instead of the phrase "a schizophrenic," the person-first approach would reframe this descriptor to be "a person with schizophrenia." Person-first language combats stereotypes, frames homelessness as a state rather than a trait, and demonstrates respect for those experiencing homelessness.

Obtaining an accurate number of people experiencing homelessness is difficult given that the primary means for identifying individuals is by counting occupancy in shelters. The significant shortage of shelters nationally therefore makes measuring homelessness problematic. The United States Conference of Mayors (2006) found that 23% of individuals and 29% of families who attempted to go to shelters were denied due to lack of space and resources. An additional hindrance to gaining an accurate estimate is that many people experiencing homelessness are living in places not easily found by researchers; they are referred to as "hidden" or "unsheltered" homeless (National Coalition for the Homeless, 2007). Such places may include living with friends, in vehicles, in tents, or in motels.

Given these barriers to accurate counting of this special population, estimates of how many people are experiencing homelessness in the United States at any given time vary from 600,000 to 2 million (SAMHSA, 2011). Forty percent of those experiencing homelessness are families (Bussuk & Friedman, 2005). At some point within each year, 1.3 million to 1.5 million children in the United States will be homeless; this is approximately 1 in every 50 children (Bussuk & Friedman, 2005; National Center on Family Homelessness [NCFH], 2008).

It is estimated that 20% to 25% of people experiencing homelessness suffer from a severe form of mental illness, whereas 6% of the general population suffers from severe mental illness (National Coalition for the Homeless, 2009; National Institute of Mental Health, 2009). The United States Conference of Mayors (2008) reported that in 23 major cities in the United States 26% of the people experiencing homelessness suffered from a severe mental illness. Mental illness often increases risk for homelessness due to difficulty completing daily life tasks, difficulty making and maintaining relationships, and stresses from living with mental illness.

Children experiencing homelessness undergo significant injustices. They are found to have greater stress and fewer resources than low-income children of similar backgrounds who have housing. Children experiencing homelessness also experience disrupted friendships (Masten, Miloitis, Graham-Bermann, Ramirez, & Neemann, 1993).

These children are also sick four times as often (NCFH, 2008), have four times as many respiratory infections, twice as many ear infections, and five times as many gastrointestinal problems (NCFH, 1999). One in nine children experiencing homelessness has one or more asthma-related health symptoms (NCFH, 2009). Academic performance often suffers, and 36% of children experiencing homelessness repeat a grade (NCFH, 1999). Fewer than one in four children experiencing homelessness will graduate from high school (NCFH, 2009). Delayed development is found in these children at four times the rate of other children, and they are twice as likely to have a learning disability (NCFH, 1999).

Like adults, children experiencing homelessness are at an increased risk for mental illness including anxiety and depression. One in six children experiencing homelessness suffers from emotional disturbances, twice the rate of children from middle-class families (NCFH, 2009). Emotional and behavioral problems are found at three times the rate of non-homeless children, and 20% of children experiencing homelessness will require professional care due to severe emotional difficulties (NCFH, 1999).

Although many people experiencing homelessness are suffering from mental health disorders, they lack the financial and often the community resources necessary to obtain mental health care, resulting in further marginalization. Additionally, a disproportionate percentage of people experiencing homelessness are racial and ethnic minorities, with an estimated 42% of the homeless population being Black, 39% White, 13% Hispanic, 4% Native American, and 2% Asian (The United States Conference of Mayors, 2008).

Although the difficulty in estimation of exact numbers of individuals experiencing homelessness remains, it is crucial that clinical mental health counselors be aware of the magnitude of the homeless crisis, the effect that homelessness has on mental health, and the increased risk of homelessness experienced by racial and ethnic minorities.

Poverty

Poverty rates also illustrate the disparity of resources and living conditions that often exist between Whites and racial and ethnic minorities in the United States. For example, the 2009 poverty rate by race highlights the disparity between cultural groups. The poverty rate for non-Hispanic Whites was 8.6%, whereas the rate for Blacks was 25.8%, for Asian and Pacific Islanders 12.5%, and for Hispanics 25.3% (DeNavas-Walt, Proctor, & Smith, 2010). Black families and female-headed families are at a greater risk for chronic poverty than are White and male-headed families.

Poverty has an effect on mental health, especially for marginalized groups. People living in poverty are more likely to have mental disorders than are those not living in poverty. Children who have experienced poverty in their lives are more prone to lasting deficits in depressive symptoms and antisocial symptoms than are children who have not lived in poverty (McLeod & Shanahan, 1997). Reasons for this increase in risk of mental health disorders may be due in part to stressors experienced by the child and family due to low resources, stress-induced parental discord, exposure to potentially dangerous or unhealthy environments, or limited access to adequate health care (McLeod & Shanahan, 1997). Evans (2004) asserts that children in poverty experience greater family turmoil, less social support, and more violence than do those children who are not in poverty. Children in poverty are more likely to attend lower quality schools and live in crowded, noisy, and dangerous neighborhoods (Albee, 2006).

Adolescents are often more aware than are children of their family's financial struggles, which can result in feelings of shame and inferiority. Poverty increases adolescents' risk of mental illnesses and behavioral risks including depression, anxiety, early sexual activity, criminal activity, and externalizing problem behaviors (for review of literature, see Dashiff, DiMicco, Meyers, & Sheppard, 2009).

Following is a statement regarding poverty presented at the 1993 Biannual World Congress of the World Federation for Mental Health (WFMH):

> Poverty dampens the human spirit creating despair and hopelessness. Poverty underlies multiple problems facing families, infants, children, adolescents, adults, and the elderly. Poverty directly affects infant mortality, mental retardation, learning disabilities, and drug and alcohol abuse. Poverty is the major factor in homelessness. Poverty increases the incidence of racial, ethnic, and religious hatred. Poverty increases abuse against women and children. Poverty results in suicide, depression, and severe mental illness. Poverty is directly linked to violence. (as cited in Albee, 2006, pp. 451–452)

Intimate Partner Violence

Intimate partner violence (IPV) occurs between two people that are current or former spouses or partners. IPV exists on a continuum from a single incident to prolonged violence. IPV includes physical violence, sexual violence, threats, and emotional abuse. Approximately three out of every ten women and one out of every ten men experience IPV in the United States (Centers for Disease Control and Prevention [CDC], 2012). There are 1.5 million female victims and 834,732 male victims annually (Tjaden & Thoennes, 2000). Tjaden and Thoennes (2000) found in a representative sample of 8,000 women and 8,000 men that nearly 25.0% of women and 7.6% of men reported having been raped or physically assaulted by a partner in her or his lifetime. Children often witness IPV between members in their household. More than 15 million children live in homes where IPV has occurred within the past year (Tjaden & Thoennes, 2000).

As was seen with homelessness and poverty, rates of IPV are not consistent across racial, ethnic, and cultural groups. White men and women experience less IPV than do racial and ethnic minorities. Black, American Indian, and Alaska Native men and women report higher rates of IPV than other racial and ethnic groups. Asian and Pacific Islander women and men report lower rates of IPV than other minority groups, although this finding should be interpreted with caution as it may reflect underreporting by this population. IPV affects all socioeconomic groups, but those with an income less than $25,000 per year are three times more likely to experience IPV than those with an income over $50,000 (Catalano, 2007). Being a victim of IPV can have a significant impact on mental health. Women who have experienced IPV are more likely to report needing mental health services than are women who have not been victimized in this way (Lipsky & Caetano, 2007).

Although many survivors of IPV have a need for mental health services, the mental health needs of this population are not being met. This is especially true of minority women (Rodriguez, Valentine, Son, & Muhammad, 2009). El-Khoury, Dutton, Goodman, Engel, Belamaric, and Murphy (2004) found that 48.1% of White women who were referred to mental health services as a result of IPV saw a mental health professional, whereas only 26% of Black women sought out services. There are numerous barriers that keep IPV survivors in racial and ethnic minority groups from mental health services; these include feelings of shame, guilt and fear, partner intrusion, language barriers, culturally related stigmatization of mental health services, lack of financial resources, clinicians' failing to screen for IPV symptoms, perceived discrimination by clinicians, fear of disclosure of immigration status, fear of losing children, and lack of cultural sensitivity within the health care system (Rodriquez et al, 2009).

Clearly, there are multiple opportunities for counselors to be social advocates. The following section presents several advocacy models.

INTEGRATING PROFESSIONAL AND SOCIAL ADVOCACY

Lee (2007) suggests that clinical mental health counselors need to make a paradigm shift in order to engage in social advocacy. He calls for all professional counselors to reject the notion of neutrality and look beyond their traditional roles and scope of practice. By following traditional counseling theories, mental health counselors are at risk of leaving societal issues unaddressed by prescribing interventions that assist clients in adapting to an unjust or inequitable social system (McClure & Russo, 1996). In other words, without advocacy efforts, mental health counselors are at risk for being a part of the problem rather than part of the solution. Social justice–minded clinical mental health counselors need to broaden their scope of practice to intervene not only at the client level but also at the societal level. If clinical mental health counselors want to work for social justice, then they must work for a just and equitable social system. The following advocacy models speak to the importance of addressing both client issues and social issues. Additionally, these models point to the importance of professional advocacy as being a part of client advocacy.

Eriksen Model

Eriksen (1997, 1999) outlined seven steps for counselors engaging in advocacy. Here follows a brief description of each step:

1. ***Professional identity.*** Consistent with others (see Hanna & Bemak, 1997; Myers et al., 2003; Ritchie, 1990), Eriksen (1997, 1999) argued that a strong professional identity is foundational to any advocacy work.
2. ***Problem identification.*** Before engaging in advocacy activities, clinical mental health counselors must be clear about what they are fighting for and be able to articulate it so others will be motivated to take action.
3. ***Assessment of resources.*** Assessment of resources includes both internal (e.g., time, money, personnel, expertise, motivation) and external resources (e.g., individuals outside of the counseling profession, influential community members, stakeholders).
4. ***Strategic planning.*** Develop both short-term and long-term goals and objectives to be disseminated to a wider audience.
5. ***Training advocates.*** In order for advocacy to be effective, advocates must have skills related to public speaking, assertiveness, communication skills, and lobbying. Eriksen (1999) recommends training members to be advocates prior to engaging in advocacy activities.

6. ***Implementing the plan.*** This step includes having a solid strategic plan, having skilled advocates, and then taking action. It also includes continuously evaluating one's progress and making adjustments as needed (Eriksen, 1997, 1999).
7. ***Celebration.*** Celebrate the big and the small accomplishments and take time to share your accomplishments with stakeholders and the public (Eriksen, 1997, 1999).

Three-Tiered Model of Advocacy

Chang, Hays, and Milliken (2009) developed a model of advocacy based on the belief that client/social advocacy and professional advocacy are intertwined. Counselors can be more effective in promoting the optimal health and wellness of their clients if they as a profession are recognized by other mental health professionals, legislators, and policy makers (Myers et al., 2003). According to this model, counselors must advocate on two fronts (i.e., client advocacy and professional advocacy) and across three tiers (i.e., self-awareness, client services, and community collaboration).

Self-awareness is being aware of who we are as cultural beings. What cultural groups do counselors hold membership in, and how does that membership influence their values, beliefs, and their work with their clients (client advocacy)? Additionally, self-awareness includes an understanding of what it means to be a clinical mental health counselor and having pride in the profession. This tier also includes an awareness of what it means to be an advocate both for clients and on behalf of the profession (Chang et al., 2009).

Client services relate to activities that directly impact client issues and client welfare. In working with clients, clinical mental health counselors operating from a social justice perspective understand the interrelatedness and interactions of social, political, and educational systems that directly affect the well-being of their clients (client advocacy). On the professional front, clinical mental health counselors develop their professional identity and professional pride through certification and licensure efforts, understanding that a strong professional identity is directly related to great competence in client work. Community collaboration includes clinical mental health counselors educating the general public about the relationship between oppression and mental health issues as well as collaborating with other mental health professionals and policy makers to promote advocacy matters that benefit their clients, community, society, and profession (Chang et al., 2009).

CSI Advocacy Themes

Chi Sigma Iota (CSI) developed a list of advocacy themes based on the discussions generated at the counselor advocacy leadership conferences. The conferences represented voices from various counseling organizations including the following: the American College Counseling Association (ACCA), the Association for Counselor Education and Supervision (ACES), the Association for Multicultural Counseling and Development (AMCD), the American Mental Health Counselors Association (AMHCA), the American Rehabilitation Counseling Association (ARCA), the American School Counselor Association (ASCA), International Association of Marriage and Family Counseling (IAMFC), the Council for Accreditation of Counseling and Related Educational Programs (CACREP), Chi Sigma Iota (CSI), ERIC-CASS, the National Board for Certified Counselors (NBCC), and the North Carolina Counseling Association (NCCA) (state branch) (Chi Sigma Iota, 1998). Although these themes were not presented as a model, they are included here because their ideas provide a foundation for considering one's advocacy efforts, and the themes are presented with concrete goals, activities, and obstacles.

THEME A: COUNSELOR EDUCATION The goal is for all counselor education students to graduate with a clear professional identity and pride as a professional counselor. Suggested activities to achieve this goal include the following: students and graduates will identify themselves fundamentally as professional counselors and be active members of ACA and its divisions; students and graduates will have knowledge of and respect for counseling specialties; all counselor education programs will incorporate client and professional advocacy training into their curriculum (Chi Sigma Iota, 1998).

THEME B: INTRAPERSONAL RELATIONS The counseling profession will develop and implement a unified, collaborative advocacy plan for the advancement of counselors and the clients they will serve. Activities to promote this goal include the following: professional counseling organizations will build consensus upon a common identity that will be articulated to the public; professional counseling organizations will collaborate on advocacy efforts; and professional counseling organizations will be unified in seeking counselor-related legislation (Chi Sigma Iota, 1998).

THEME C: MARKETPLACE RECOGNITION This goal relates to the assurance that all professional counselors in all settings are compensated appropriately and have the freedom to practice within their scope of competence. Activities related to this goal include the following: professional counseling organizations will work toward state and federal legislative actions that will ensure that professional counselors be service providers in all areas of their competency; professional counselors will be recognized by the media as providing much needed services; and professional counselors will collect data on the employment status of professional counselors, documenting their services and to highlight the benefits of having more counselors to meet the needs of their clients (Chi Sigma Iota, 1998).

THEME D: INTERPROFESSIONAL ISSUES Professional counselors will collaborate with other organizations, groups, and disciplines on matters of professional and client advocacy. Suggested activities within this theme include the following: professional counseling organizations will identify other groups with whom they would like to form a collaborative relationship; strategies will be developed in order to address initiatives by other organizations that have the potential for omitting, limiting, or blocking the employment or practice of professional counseling; and professional counseling organizations are urged to establish and maintain personnel and resources needed to maintain counselor advocacy initiatives (Chi Sigma Iota, 1998).

THEME E: RESEARCH Professional counselors will use data from scientifically sound research to promote their profession and the services they provide. Activities that promote this goal include the following: promotion of research demonstrating the effectiveness of counseling with individuals, children, families, groups, and other systems; encouragement of all practitioners to conduct research; and dissemination of research results to appropriate and relevant populations (Chi Sigma Iota, 1998).

THEME F: PREVENTION AND WELLNESS Professional counselors strive to promote optimal human development through both prevention and wellness across the life span. The following activities are recommended in order to attain this goal: engaging in social action to address human needs; advocating counselor education programs that include wellness and prevention training into the curriculum; and encouraging client wellness through identification and implementation strategies that empower clients to be self-advocates (Chi Sigma Iota, 1998).

MENTAL HEALTH COUNSELORS AS ADVOCATES

The advocacy models previously presented provide a framework for constructing clinical mental health counselors' advocacy efforts. We conclude this section with recommendations for how mental health counselors can become social and professional advocates and become change agents for both their clients and their profession.

VOICE FROM THE FIELD 5.1

To me advocacy has many meanings, the most important of which is helping my clients get the services they need to be healthy both mentally and physically. Here at Positive Impact, Inc. (PI), we see clients who are infected and/or affected by human immunodeficiency virus (HIV). Probably the number-one concern here at Positive Impact is that our clients are receiving treatment by a primary care physician . . . even before we fully begin mental health treatment. I often advocate for my clients by calling AID Atlanta, Fulton County Department of Health and Wellness, or another Ryan White–funded HIV medical care program to help my clients get enrolled into care. I believe the only way a person with HIV can become mentally healthy is by making sure he or she is doing everything possible to stay physically healthy. This act of self-advocacy ultimately influences the client's mental health by increasing both self-efficacy and social engagement.

I advocate for my clients routinely in regard to their housing and substance abuse treatment needs. This is not to say that I perform the duties of a case manager, but I do put clients in touch with in-house services that can help enroll them in substance treatment programs either here at Positive Impact or in other facilities, and I make necessary referrals to housing services like The Living Room or HOPE Atlanta Traveler's Aid. It is often the case that I can personally introduce a client to one of our treatment navigators here at PI, and that personal touch is often therapeutic, especially in the case of a client in crisis.

Another part of my job is to perform HIV testing services and counseling. Often I have clients that disclose during pre- or posttesting interviews that they have been having unprotected sex with multiple partners, or using substances to the point of feeling out of control in their lives. I offer referrals to in-house sexually transmitted infection (STI) testing and medical care, as well as several interventions that work to limit the transmission of HIV by increasing condom use and reducing the number of sexual partners. Often I can perform HIV testing and immediately screen and enroll a client in another of our programs, depending on his or her need. Part of my advocacy for these clients is to know the programs we offer and to be willing to ask the difficult questions about sexual topics to expose high-risk behavior. I think it is beneficial to clients to be offered access to multiple services at one agency and to have a single individual who can guide and refer them through the often convoluted process. Ultimately, my advocacy is aimed at making sure my clients are being provided with the services they need to stay mentally and physically healthy while reducing the transmission of HIV infection and superinfection. At Positive Impact, that's all in a day's work!

MICHAEL MCALLISTER
Clinical Mental Health Counselor, Positive Impact, Inc.

VOICE FROM THE FIELD 5.2

I see advocacy as a crucial piece of the holistic care of my clients. I work primarily with children and adolescents, and there are a lot of important people involved with the care of these clients. I have seen firsthand the importance of getting all those important people on the same page as you in the work you're doing for that child's mental health care. Advocacy for a team model, which is necessary to organize all the aspects of care needed for that child, as well as advocating for any needs not yet met, helps provide for that child as a whole person. Sometimes all this takes is one extra phone call, one extra form filled out, or a trip to the child's school. I think it is also incredibly important to teach our clients to advocate for themselves and their own needs. This can be done using a session to practice with clients how to ask for what they need or what they want. That skill alone will help them their whole lives. I think it is a conversation we cannot afford to miss with our clients.

Furthermore, we also have to advocate for our profession. We need to advocate to governing bodies, so that we are able to continue to provide mental health care to others. We also need to advocate on our own behalf to the general public, so they can be informed of the work we do and see counseling as an option for them, should they need it. This can be as easy as talking to anyone you know about the differences in licensure for mental health care or what counseling hopes to accomplish.

I think it is easy to be overwhelmed by the idea of advocacy. I know I did not initially call a lot of the work I do "advocacy," because I thought advocacy was lobbying the government or organizing mass protests. I know now that is not true. Advocating can be as large as petitioning government bodies, but it can also be an extra phone call, directing clients to community resources, or organizing a team. Everyone can find his or her own comfort zone. The important thing is that we all work together to further our profession and to help our clients. I think you will find doing so as rewarding as I do.

AMANDA WOLFE, MS, LPC, NCC
Kennesaw State University

MENTAL HEALTH COUNSELORS AS CHANGE AGENTS

Given the relationship between social injustice and mental health issues and the connection between privilege and oppression, mental health counselors must be able to identify and understand the complexities of our clients' multiple identities. It is imperative that clinical mental health counselors have the knowledge and skills to address the complex issues related to the various forms of oppression and privilege. In addition, they must understand that clients' expressions of distress are influenced by their culture (e.g., gender, sexual identity, religious affiliation) and context (e.g., region, situation, sociocultural background). For example, mental health counselors are at risk of misdiagnosing individuals from oppressed groups by imposing majority norms as the standard against which all clients are compared, and mental health professionals may mistake trauma-like symptoms of oppressive circumstances for pathology (Ancis, 2004).

Culturally and socially minded mental health counselors must have the awareness, knowledge, and skills to be effective change agents for their clients and the profession. The multicultural counseling competencies and standards outlined by Sue, Arredondo, and McDavis (1992) provide professional counselors with a foundation for culturally appropriate practice. Culturally competent counselors have the attitudes and beliefs, knowledge, and skills to develop self-awareness of their own cultural values and biases; culturally competent counselors have the attitudes and beliefs, knowledge, and skills related to their client's worldview; and culturally competent counselors have the attitudes and beliefs, knowledge, and skills to implement culturally appropriate interventions (Sue, Arredondo, & McDavis, 1992).

In addition to being culturally competent counselors, mental health counselors who are advocates must also be mindful of the greater sociocultural and historical backgrounds of our clients and the historic foundation of our profession. More specifically, researchers (e.g., Hays et al., 2004; Manuppelli, 2000; Reynolds & Pope, 1991; Vodde, 2001) have highlighted the importance of addressing privilege and oppression issues in counseling and counselor training.

The following are recommendations for clinical mental health counselors who want to be culturally competent and effective advocates for their clients and their profession. Consistent with the *three-tiered model of advocacy* (Chang et al., 2009), we recommend that clinical mental health counselors advocate at the client level and the professional level and across the three dimensions of self-awareness, client issues, and community collaboration.

1. Explore your own cultural identities. What are the privileges and challenges of being a member of your various cultural identities?
2. Explore the role privilege and oppression has played in your life.
3. Discuss the reasons that lead you to become a clinical mental health counselor. What does it mean to you to be a clinical mental health counselor?
4. Conduct an inventory of your advocacy skills. What advocacy skills do you have and which ones need further development?
5. What are the most critical social issues in your community? What can you do to help with these social issues? Identify other agencies and organizations that you might network and collaborate with in order to address these social issues.
6. Visit your state legislative Web site. Identify bills that may have a direct or indirect impact on the clinical mental health profession.

Advocacy for Charlie

As we wrap up this chapter, we thought you might like to know a little more about Charlie from Case Study 5.1. Charlie is a real client. Here are the advocacy steps that his mental health counselor generated for working with him. Many of these steps were implemented.

- School
  - Obtain consent from parents and contact school counselor
    - discuss how you can be helpful
    - advocate for what he needs in the classroom to be successful
  - Have sessions in school setting to facilitate effective transition into school environment
- Financially
  - Identify any assistance programs available for financial support through your agency
    - Work with client to help him/family fill out necessary paperwork to acquire funding
    - If unavailable, advocate to your organization or to relevant organizations that support be available

- Identify any assistance available for transportation to and from sessions (Medicaid has program)
  - Go to the client's home if services are unavailable
- Work to coordinate with McAllister Counseling Center
  - Discuss what goals both are focusing on
  - Discuss ways that you can be most effective by working together
  - Coordinate meeting times to space out services as much as possible
  - Coordinate times to make transportation easier for the family
  - Coordinate regular treatment team meetings
- Teach Charlie/family self-advocacy skills
- Help Charlie and family develop a plan to help Charlie develop his ethnic identity

Conclusion

In this chapter, we discussed the importance of professional and social advocacy in clinical mental health counseling. Advocacy is presented as a two-prong concept with both social advocacy and professional advocacy being essential and fundamental to the clinical mental health profession. Clinical mental health counselors are urged to be social change agents by working toward self-awareness, awareness of clients' sociocultural backgrounds, development of culturally appropriate intervention strategies, and development of advocacy skills that promote both client/social advocacy and professional advocacy.

References

Albee, G. W. (2006, September). Historical overview of primary prevention of psychopathology: Address to the 3rd World Conference on the Promotion of Mental Health and Prevention of Mental and Behavioral Disorders, Auckland, New Zealand. *The Journal of Primary Prevention, 27,* 449–456.

Altekruse, M. K. (1994). CACREP doctoral standards and licensed psychologists. *ACES Spectrum, 55*(2), 18.

American Counseling Association (ACA). (2005). *Code of ethics.* Alexandria, VA: Author.

American Counseling Association (ACA). (2010). *20/20: A vision for the future of counseling.* Retrieved from http://www.counseling.org/20-20/index.aspx

American Mental Health Counselors Association (AMHCA). (2010). *2010 AMHCA code of ethics.* Retrieved from https://www.amhca.org/assets/news/AMHCA_Code_of_Ethics_2010_w_pagination_cxd_51110.pdf

Ancis, J. R. (Ed.). (2004). *Culturally responsive interventions: Innovative approaches to working with diverse populations.* New York, NY: Brunner-Routledge.

Ancis, J. R., & Chang, C. Y. (2008). Cross-cultural counseling: Oppression. In F. T. L. Leong (Ed.), *Encyclopedia of counseling* (Vol. 3, pp. 1245–1247). Thousand Oaks, CA: Sage.

Association for Multicultural Counseling and Development (AMCD). (2010). *A historical sketch (1972–2007).* Retrieved from http://www.multiculturalcounseling.org/index.php?option=com_content&view=article&id=93&Itemid=88

Bussuk, E. L., & Friedman, S. M. (2005). *Facts on trauma and homeless children.* Los Angeles, CA: National Child Traumatic Stress Network.

Catalano, S. (2007). *Intimate partner violence in the United States.* Bureau of Justice Statistics: US Department of Justice. Retrieved from http://bjs.ojp.usdoj.gov/content/pub/pdf/ipvus.pdf

Centers for Disease Control and Prevention (CDC). (2012). *Understanding intimate partner violence.* Retrieved from http://www.cdc.gov/violenceprevention/pdf/IPV_factsheet-a.pdf

Chang, C. Y. (2011). Professional advocacy: A professional responsibility. In C. Y. Chang, C. A. B. Minton, A. L. Dixon, J. E. Myers, & T. J. Sweeney (Eds.), *Professional counseling excellence through leadership and advocacy* (pp. 95–108). New York, NY: Routledge.

Chang, C. Y., Crethar, H. C., & Ratts, M. J. (2010). Social justice: A national imperative for counselor education and supervision. *Counselor Education and Supervision, 50*(2), 82–87.

Chang, C. Y., & Gnilka, P. (2010). Social advocacy: The fifth force in counseling. In D. G. Hays & B. T. Erford (Eds.), *Developing multicultural counseling competency: A systems approach* (pp. 53–71). Columbus, OH: Pearson Merrill/Prentice Hall.

Chang, C. Y., Hays, D. G., & Milliken, T. F. (2009). Addressing social justice issues in supervision: A call for client and professional advocacy. *The Clinical Supervisor, 28*(1), 20–35.

Chi Sigma Iota (CSI). (1998). *Counselor professional advocacy leadership conferences May 27–29, 1988 and December 11–12, 1988*. Retrieved from http://csi.affiniscape.com/associations/2151/files/PROADV_AdvocacyLeadershipConferenceReports.cfm

Council for Accreditation of Counseling and Related Educational Programs (CACREP). (2009). *2009 standards*. Retrieved from http://www.cacrep.org/doc/2009%20Standards%20with%20cover.pdf

Crethar, H. C., Torres Rivera, E., & Nash, S. (2008). In search of common threads: Linking multicultural, feminist, and social justice counseling paradigms. *Journal of Counseling & Development, 86*(3), 269–278.

Dashiff, C., DiMicco, W., Meyers, B., & Sheppard, K. (2009). Poverty and adolescent mental health. *Journal of Child and Adolescent Psychiatric Nursing, 22*, 23–32.

DeNavas-Walt, C., Proctor, B. D., & Smith, J. C. (2010, September). US Census Bureau, Current Population Reports, P60-238. *Income, poverty, and health insurance coverage in the United States: 2009.* Washington, DC: US Government Printing Office.

Durkee, D. (2010, October 21). Re: LPCA article on issue of counselor identity [Electronic mailing list message].

El-Khoury, M. Y., Dutton, M. A., Goodman, L. A., Engel, L., Belamaric, R. J., & Murphy, M. (2004). Ethnic differences in battered women's formal help-seeking strategies: A focus on health, mental health, and spirituality. *Cultural Diversity & Ethnic Minority Psychology, 10*, 383–393.

Eriksen, K. (1997). *Making an impact: A handbook on counselor advocacy*. Washington, DC: Accelerated Development.

Eriksen, K. (1999). Counselor advocacy: A qualitative analysis of leaders' perceptions, organizational activities, and advocacy documents. *Journal of Mental Health Counseling, 21*(1), 33–49.

Evans, G. W. (2004). The environment of childhood poverty. *American Psychologist, 59*, 77–92.

Feit, S. S., & Lloyd, A. P. (1990). A profession in search of professionals. *Counselor Education and Supervision, 29*, 216–219.

Funk, M., Minoletti, A., Drew, N., Taylor, J., & Saraceno, B. (2005). Advocacy for mental health: Roles for consumer and family organizations and governments. *Health Promotion International, 21*(1), 70–75. doi:10.1093/heapro/dai031

Gale, A., & Austin, D. (2003). Professionalism's challenges to professional counselors' collective identity. *Journal of Counseling & Development, 81*(1), 3–10.

Hanna, F. J., & Bemak, F. (1997). The quest for identity in the counseling profession. *Counselor Education and Supervision, 36*(3), 194–206.

Hanna, F. J., Talley, W. B., & Guindon, M. H. (2000). The power of perception: Toward a model of cultural oppression and liberation. *Journal of Counseling & Development, 78*, 430–441.

Hartung, P. J., & Blustein, D. L. (2002). Reason, intuition, and social justice: Elaborating on Parsons's career decision-making model. *Journal of Counseling & Development, 80*, 41–47.

Hays, D. G., Chang, C. Y., & Dean, J. K. (2004). White counselors' conceptualization of privilege and oppression: Implications for counselor training. *Counselor Education & Supervision, 43*, 242–257.

Kiselica, M. S. (2004). When duty calls: The implications of social justice work for policy, education, and practice in the mental health professions. *The Counseling Psychologist, 32*, 838–854.

Kiselica, M. S., & Robinson, M. (2001). Bringing advocacy counseling to life: The history, issues, and human dramas of social justice work in counseling. *Journal of Counseling & Development, 79*, 387–397.

Lee, C. C. (2007). *Counseling for social justice* (2nd ed.) Alexandria, VA: American Counseling Association.

Lee, C. C., & Walz, G. R. (Eds.). (1998). *Social action: A mandate for counselors*. Alexandria, VA: American Counseling Association.

Lewis, J. A., Arnold, M. S., House, R., & Toporek, R. (2003). *Advocacy competencies*. Retrieved from http://www.counseling.org/Resources/Competencies/Advocacy_Competencies.pdf

Lewis, J. A., & Bradley, L. (Eds.). (2000). *Advocacy in counseling: Counselors, clients, and community*. Greensboro, NC: ERIC Clearinghouse on Counseling and Student Services.

Lipsky, S., & Caetano, R. (2007). Impact of intimate partner violence on unmet need for mental health care: Results from the NSDUH. *Psychiatric Services, 58,* 822–829.

Manuppelli, L. (2000). *Exploring the therapist's understanding of White privilege: A phenomenological analysis of focus group discussions with culturally diverse therapists* (Unpublished doctoral dissertation). St. Mary's University, San Antonio, TX.

Maples, M. F., Altekruse, M. D., & Testa, A. M. (1993). Counselor education 2000: Extinction or distinction? *Counselor Education and Supervision, 33,* 47–52.

Masten, A. S., Miloitis, D., Graham-Bermann, S. A., Ramirez, M. L., & Neemann, J. (1993). Children in homeless families: Risks to mental health and development. *Journal of Consulting and Clinical Psychology, 61,* 335–343.

McClure, B. A., & Russo, T. R. (1996). The politics of counseling: Looking back and forward. *Counseling and Values, 40,* 162–175.

McLeod, J. D., & Shanahan, M. J. (1997). Trajectories of poverty and children's mental health. *Journal of Health and Social Behavior, 37,* 207–220.

McWhirter, E. H. (1994). *Counseling for empowerment.* Alexandria, VA: American Counseling Association.

Myers, J. E., & Sweeney, T. J. (2004). Advocacy for the counseling profession: Results of a national survey. *Journal of Counseling & Development, 82,* 466–471.

Myers, J. E., Sweeney, T. J., & White, V. E. (2002). Advocacy for counseling and counselors: A professional imperative. *Journal of Counseling & Development, 80,* 394–402.

The National Center on Family Homelessness (NCFH). (1999). *Homeless children: America's new outcasts.* Newton, MA: Author.

The National Center on Family Homelessness (NCFH). (2008). The characteristics and needs of families experiencing homelessness. Retrieved from http://www.familyhomelessness.org/media/147.pdf

The National Center on Family Homelessness. (NCFH) (2009). *America's youngest outcasts: State report card on child homelessness.* Newton, MA: Author.

National Coalition for the Homeless. (2007). *How many people experience homelessness?* Retrieved from http://www.nationalhomeless.org/publications/facts/How_Many.pdf

National Coalition for the Homeless. (2009). *Mental illness and homelessness.* Retrieved from http://www.nationalhomeless.org/factsheets/Mental_Illness.html

National Institute of Mental Health. (2009). *Statistics.* Retrieved from http://www.nimh.nih.gov/health/topics/statistics/index.shtml

Neukrug, E., & Remley, T. P. (2009). Professional identity and ethics: Key historical event. In American Counseling Association (Ed.), *The ACA encyclopedia of counseling* (pp. 411–412). Alexandria, VA: American Counseling Association.

Ratts, M. J. (2009). Social justice counseling—Toward the development of a fifth force among counseling paradigms. *Journal of Humanistic Counseling, Education and Development, 48,* 160–172.

Ratts, M., D'Andrea, M., & Arredondo, P. (2004, July). Social justice counseling: A "fifth force" in the field. *Counseling Today, 47*(1), 28–30.

Ratts, M. J., Lewis, J. A., & Toporek, R. L. (2010). Advocacy and social justice: A helping paradigm for the 21st century. In M. J. Ratts, R. L. Toporek, & J. A. Lewis (Eds.), *ACA Advocacy Competencies: A social justice framework for counselors* (pp. 3–10). Alexandria, VA: American Counseling Association.

Reynolds, A. L., & Pope, R. L. (1991). The complexities of diversity: Exploring multiple oppressions. *Journal of Counseling & Development, 70,* 174–180.

Rhode, B. (2010). *ALGBTIC history.* Retrieved from http://www.algbtic.org/about/history

Ritchie, M. H. (1990). Counseling is not a profession—Yet. *Counselor Education and Supervision, 29*(4), 220–227.

Rodriguez, M., Valentine, J. M., Son, J. B., & Muhammad, M. (2009). Intimate partner violence and barriers to mental health care for ethnically diverse populations of women. *Trauma, Violence, & Abuse, 10,* 358–374.

Rollins, J. (2010, June). Making definitive progress: 20/20 delegates reach consensus on definition of counseling. *Counseling Today,* 36–38.

Substance Abuse and Mental Health Services Administration (SAMHSA). (2011). *Current statistics on the prevalence and characteristics of people experiencing homelessness in the United States.* Retrieved from http://homeless.samhsa.gov/ResourceFiles/hrc_factsheet.pdf

Sue, D. W., Arredondo, P., & McDavis, R. J. (1992). Multicultural counseling competencies and standards: A call to the profession. *Journal of Counseling & Development, 70,* 477–486.

Tjaden, P., & Thoennes, N. (2000). *Extent, nature, and consequences of intimate partner violence: Findings from the National Violence Against Women Survey (NCJ 183781).* Washington, DC: National Institute of Justice and the Centers for Disease Control and Prevention.

Toporek, R. L., Lewis, J. A., & Ratts, M. J. (2010). The ACA advocacy competencies: An overview. In M. J. Ratts, R. L. Toporek, and J. A. Lewis (Eds.), *ACA Advocacy Competencies: A social justice framework for counselors* (pp. 11–20). Alexandria, VA: American Counseling Association.

The United States Conference of Mayors. (2006). *A status report on hunger and homelessness in America's cities: 2006*. Washington, DC: Author.

The United States Conference of Mayors. (2008, December). *Hunger and homelessness survey: A status report on hunger and homelessness in America's cities*. Retrieved from http://usmayors.org/pressreleases /documents/hungerhomelessnessreport_121208.pdf

US Department of Health and Human Services (DHHS). (2001). *Mental health: Culture, race and ethnicity. A supplement to mental health: A report of the Surgeon General*. Rockville, MD: Author.

Vodde, R. (2001). De-centering privilege in social work education: Whose job is it anyway? *Race, Gender & Class, 7,* 139–160.

6

Client Assessment and Diagnosis

CARL J. SHEPERIS, JAYNE SMITH, AND MELANIE BULLOCK

CHAPTER OVERVIEW

This chapter provides an introduction to assessment and diagnosis for clinical mental health counselors. We first discuss the process of assessment and review both formal and informal approaches. Then, we examine the clinical interview process and various assessment instruments, followed by the diagnostic process and the use of the *Diagnostic and Statistical Manual of Mental Disorders* (DSM). This chapter concludes with an overview of the DSM system used for mental health diagnosis. Throughout this chapter, activities and discussion questions are included to promote awareness of and competence in the assessment and diagnosis process.

LEARNING OBJECTIVES

The learning objectives for this chapter are designed to be consistent with the 2009 Council for Accreditation of Counseling and Related Educational Programs Standards (CACREP, 2009). As such, upon completion of this chapter, the student will have knowledge of the following clinical mental health counseling standards:

1. Knows the etiology, the diagnostic process and nomenclature, treatment, referral, and prevention of mental and emotional disorders. (C.2)
2. Knows the principles and models of assessment, case conceptualization, theories of human development, and concepts of normalcy and psychopathology leading to diagnoses and appropriate counseling treatment plans. (G.1)
3. Understands various models and approaches to clinical evaluation and their appropriate uses, including diagnostic interviews, mental status examinations, symptom inventories, and psychoeducational and personality assessments. (G.2)
4. Knows the principles of the diagnostic process, including differential diagnosis, and the use of current diagnostic tools, such as the current edition of the *Diagnostic and Statistical Manual of Mental Disorders (DSM)*. (K.1)

Additionally, students will have knowledge of the following core entry-level standard:

1. Historical perspectives concerning the nature and meaning of assessment. (G.7.a)

INTRODUCTION

Professional clinical mental health counselors have a responsibility to accurately identify issues related to the counseling process and to arrive at an appropriate clinical approach to addressing those issues. As such, assessment and diagnosis are integral parts of all counseling services. The assessment process is used to understand the full scope of issues relevant to the counseling process as well as to measure progress and change during the process. Imagine trying to solve a complex puzzle without some of the key information. Obtaining a correct solution would be difficult, if not impossible. Assessment helps clinical mental health counselors to identify those crucial missing pieces and to determine how they fit into the overall framework (puzzle). Once there is a clear picture of the puzzle, it is possible to arrive at a conclusion about the picture that the puzzle pieces form. Clinical mental health counselors use assessment in every aspect of professional practice. The assessment process can range from a simple informal interview to a complex battery of standardized tests. How counselors use assessment will depend on the setting, the client, and presenting issues. This chapter covers models and types of assessment, with specific attention paid to the principles of clinical diagnosis. It serves as a basic building block for understanding the assessment process. In order to move toward competence in the area of assessment, readers will need to complete additional coursework in the area and conduct supervised practice in assessment.

ASSESSMENT IN CLINICAL MENTAL HEALTH COUNSELING SETTINGS

Assessment provides a foundation from which clinical mental health counselors embark on the counseling journey and continues as a navigational tool throughout each counseling relationship. Assessments offer key information used in goal setting, treatment planning, and counseling outcomes. Thousands of informal and formal assessments exist today, which means clinical mental health counselors must be skilled in identifying and administering appropriate assessments for each client (American Counseling Association (ACA), 2005; Tymofievich & Leroux, 2000). Clinical mental health counselors in training will likely take a course or courses specifically aimed at developing competence in clinical assessment. This chapter is only meant to provide a road map of the assessment and diagnosis process to prepare counseling students to immerse themselves in these topics in a more substantial fashion throughout the remainder of their graduate preparation.

Beginning graduate students may not be clear about what assessment entails. Therefore, it is important to recognize that many definitions of assessment exist. Some leaders in the counseling profession believe assessment involves the use of specific tests to make a diagnosis (Hohenshil, 1996). Critics of this definition of assessment argue that the profession should be rooted in a "developmental, health-focused approach to assessing and counseling clients," and the more traditional focus of diagnosis is rooted in a pathological, deficit model of treating mental disorders (McAuliffe & Eriksen, 1999). The counseling profession has continued to evolve since the 1990s, yet the profession is still divided by the many differences in philosophy among its leaders. In reality, the scope of practice for the field of clinical mental health counseling necessitates an understanding of traditional assessment and diagnosis and an integrated understanding of assessment. Although many definitions of assessment exist, this text adopts the definition put forth in the *Standards for Assessment in Mental Health Counseling* (n.d.), developed in partnership between the

Association for Assessment and Research in Counseling (formerly AACE) and the American Mental Health Counselors Association (AMHCA): "Assessment is the active collection of information about individuals, populations, or treatment programs" (p. 2). This definition incorporates the many different types and uses of assessments that are discussed in the following sections of this chapter.

Why are assessments used? A search for "assessments" in the *Journal of Counseling & Development* from 1984 to the present resulted in 300 articles indicating reasons for using assessments. Topics were related to specific disorders (e.g., ADHD, substance abuse, and eating disorders), client issues (e.g., suicide risk, relationship violence, and career development), various settings (e.g., schools and mental health agencies), and the research offered various models for assessment (see Goldman, 1992; McAuliffe & Eriksen, 1999; Nelson, 2002). The following list of uses for assessment is based on Drummond and Jones's (2003) recommendations:

- To identify clients' assets, interests, achievements, aptitudes, and personality types that may assist in promoting change in the client
- To help clients clarify their study skills, educational and career goals, relationship styles, attitudes, perceptions and knowledge of specific issues, values, problem-solving skills, and leadership styles
- To determine whether the client has a traumatic brain injury
- To help decide the counseling theory, techniques, and treatments to use for each client
- To make an accurate and appropriate diagnosis using the DSM-IV
- To evaluate the effectiveness of counseling interventions, techniques, and treatment plans

McAuliffe and Eriksen (1999) also emphasized the importance of assessing clients' environment, which includes gathering information about their family, neighborhood, school, workplace, peer group, and any other aspect of their social context. Various types of assessments are utilized at different times throughout each counseling relationship to fulfill the different uses described here.

Now that you have a basic understanding that assessment involves gathering information both formally and informally, how have you used assessment in your personal life? What do you think might be different about assessment from a professional perspective? What type of training do you think you might need? How might assessment help you to diagnose a mental disorder?

What Is a Mental Disorder?

The attempt to define and treat mental illness has been an evolving process. What we now call psychopathology was initially believed to be a supernatural possession that resulted from violating taboos or ritual obligations; treatment required releasing the spirits via exorcism and trepanation (LaBruzza, 1994; Millon, 2004). Ancient Egypt is credited with the first psychiatric text and first example of community mental health care (Alexander, Sheldon, & Selesnick, 1966). "Sleep therapy" or dream interpretation was used to discover the source of an individual's mental illness, and treatment included opium, prayers, and magic rituals.

Hippocrates (c. 460–c. 377 B.C.) proposed that mental illness was the result of brain pathology and/or an excess of one or more of the four body humors (Alexander et al., 1966;

LaBruzza, 1994). For example, an excess of phlegm resulted in apathetic behavior, and black bile created melancholia. Treatment included a reduction in fluids, an improved diet, and abstinence from sexual activity. According to Plato (c. 428–348 B.C.), mental health was a reflection of a balanced relationship between the mind, body, and soul. Mental illness was the result of an individual's ignorance of his or her psyche and self-deception. While the scientific community conducted research seeking a clinical explanation for mental illness, the belief in supernatural forces or moral weakness as its cause has continued for centuries.

During the 18th and early 19th centuries, mental illness was increasingly viewed from a biological etiology (LaBruzza, 1994; Millon, 2004). Asylums for the mentally ill provided treatment, but due to lack of understanding, these treatments were often emotionally and physically abusive. The debate regarding the value of treatment continued because many considered mental illness incurable. State hospitals were overcrowded, and there were no standardized criteria for admission, diagnosis, or treatment protocols. As a result, the institutionalized individuals suffered from a complex mix of biological, mental, and socioeconomic issues.

The US government began collecting data concerning the number of individuals identified as suffering from idiocy or insanity using the 1840 census (LaBruzza, 1994). In 1917, the US Census Bureau expanded this process by adopting a plan developed by the National Committee for Mental Hygiene and the Committee on Statistics of the American Medico-Psychological Association to gather statistics about treatment provided in mental hospitals (American Psychiatric Association, 2013; Sanders, 2011).

Researchers explored how various physical diseases impacted mental functioning, and some studied possible connections between psychosocial stressors and mental health. Emil Kraepelin examined statistical data gathered regarding symptoms exhibited during the course of disease to estimate outcomes, which began the process of developing a diagnostic classification system that included behavioral and descriptive information (Alexander et al., 1966; LaBruzza, 1994). In 1928 the American Psychiatric Association set a goal to standardize medical terminology used by psychiatrists. A classification system emerged that included disorders that were severe enough to require hospitalization, and it was expanded after World War II to include disorders experienced by military personnel that were considered less severe.

As history has shown, defining mental illness or mental disorders is a complex issue. In the last century, a concerted effort has been made to provide a clinical definition to eliminate cultural bias (Millon, 2004). Mental health disorders have long been viewed through a narrow lens that reflects the impact of behaviors and associated symptomatology solely upon the individual experiencing distress (American Psychiatric Association, 2000). Today, the definition of a mental disorder has evolved to include a more complex perspective of psychological functioning. Mental health practitioners now consider cultural and environmental issues and how they may impact psychological functioning when considering a diagnosis. They are clear to consider any cultural explanations as well as underlying medical causes for the presentation of psychological symptoms (American Psychiatric Association, 2013).

FORMAL AND INFORMAL ASSESSMENT

Assessment is a complex construct that can involve both formal and informal procedures aimed toward identifying various issues or toward arriving at a mental health diagnosis. One of the best ways to understand a construct is to review it in context. In order to facilitate the understanding of assessment, consider the following counseling scenario: This is your first session with Jamie, who indicated over the phone her feeling unhappy at work and anxious about the possibility of changing careers. Jamie reported feeling uninterested in the current work area. In addition, Jamie was afraid of receiving a poor evaluation and was not able to attend an annual performance review meeting at work due to the anxiety. Considering the initial presenting information, what types of additional information might be important to gather? In other words, what assessments might you use in your work with Jamie?

In working with Jamie, you may decide to use a combination of formal and informal assessments. Typically, formal assessments involve the use of testing instruments that are psychometrically sound—that is, valid and reliable, appropriate for use considering the client's cultural and social groups, and relevant to the client's presenting issue(s). Formal assessments provide information about a focused area of need and generally compare the client's scores to a specific population (Neukrug & Schwitzer, 2005). These assessments tend to be objective. For example, because Jamie indicated a high degree of anxiety, you might decide to include the Beck Anxiety Inventory as part of the initial assessment. Because Jamie discussed concerns about career transition, you might also decide to use the Strong Interest Inventory for career exploration. Each of these instruments is widely used and available for purchase by qualified professionals through their respective test publishers. These instruments have been evaluated for their psychometric properties, and the results of the assessment instruments allow the examiner to compare a client's results to a broad sample of individuals.

If Jamie were presenting with more serious clinical issues, you might consider other formal assessments such as the MMPI-2 used to assess levels of pathology and to assist in diagnosis; projective tests such as the Rorschach Comprehensive System to assess personality; or the Stanford-Binet to assess intelligence, learning disabilities, and brain injury. In specific circumstances, you might administer multiple assessments as part of a comprehensive battery. Specific types of formal assessments are discussed later in this chapter.

Although formal assessments might be useful in your work with Jamie, it would also be important to consider the utility of informal assessments to gather information. Informal assessments have less research support but are often more cost-effective than formal procedures. Examples of informal assessments are the clinical interview, psychosocial and medical history inventories, mental status exam, genogram, counselor observations, client journals, and autobiographies. The information gathered with informal assessments often provides a greater depth of understanding of the client when combined with formal procedures. However, it is important to recognize that informal assessments tend to be more subjective than formal assessments (Neukrug & Schwitzer, 2005). Here follows more detail related to common informal assessments.

Clinical Interview

The clinical interview is one of the essential tools of the clinical mental health counselor. The clinical interview may be structured or unstructured. Imagine that you are a new patient for a physician. What type of questions would you expect when the physician first meets you? Generally, the physician will establish rapport and ask some specific questions about your medical history and reason for the visit. This process is part of a clinical interview. In counseling, the clinical interview may include topics such as the following: reasons for the visit or referral, family background—current and family of origin, cultural and social considerations, medical history including psychopharmacological drug use, substance abuse history, and legal issues. A mental status exam may also be done. What other types of information might be important for clinical mental health counselors to gather in developing a working understanding of their clients' clinical issues?

STRUCTURED CLINICAL INTERVIEWS In structured clinical interviews, each new client is asked specific questions about each of those topics. Intake forms that include basic information related to these topics are often used to supplement the structured clinical interview. As the phrase "intake form" implies, structured clinical interviews generally occur during the initial counseling session. There are benefits of and drawbacks to using a structured interview; advantages include the gathering of consistent, specific information and the need for little training for counselors because a list of questions is available for them to read (Drummond & Jones, 2010). However, structured interviews may create challenges in building rapport, and clinical mental health counselors are limited in that they cannot probe deeper into topics more relevant to the client. In some cases, the intake form may take the place of structured clinical interviews, and clinical mental health counselors may use the information gathered from an intake form to inform the unstructured clinical interview. If you have ever had someone read you a list of questions as he or she wrote down the answers, then you have a general idea of how impersonal a structured interview can be. How could clinical mental health counselors make the process more engaging and more meaningful?

UNSTRUCTURED CLINICAL INTERVIEWS As implied by the name, unstructured clinical interviews do not have a prescribed list of questions that must be asked in the same order. Instead, unstructured interviews allow clinical mental health counselors to determine the topics most relevant to the client in the moment and to use words that are more consistent with the client's epistemology. Advantages of using an unstructured clinical interview include increasing rapport, observing client behavior in an unstructured situation, and exploring topics that may not have been covered in a structured interview (Drummond & Jones, 2010). Every counseling session includes unstructured clinical interviews in that clinical mental health counselors use questions, probes, summaries, reflections of content and feeling, and other micro-skills that aim to gather information relevant to the client's issues and the counseling process (Ivey, Ivey, & Zalaquett, 2009). Oftentimes, the clinical mental health counselor's theoretical orientation and selected counseling techniques guide the information-gathering process. In fact, certain assessments exist to help counselors determine which orientation and techniques may be best suited for different clients, depending on the presenting concern and client background (see Nelson, 2002). In this way, the theoretical orientation and counseling techniques inform the unstructured clinical interviews, and the information gathered through assessment informs the theoretical orientation and counseling techniques used.

As with the structured clinical interview, this type of interview has benefits and drawbacks. Clearly, the unstructured approach allows the clinical mental health counselor the opportunity to be flexible and to adapt to a client's personal framework. However, the flexibility of the approach can result in missing critical information that would have been elicited in a formal interview. For example, if the clinical mental health counselor is not adept at conducting an unstructured interview, he or she may forget to ask questions about substance use. If the client is experiencing hallucinations and the clinical mental health counselor forgets to ask such questions, he or she may end up with a diagnosis of a mental disorder when, in fact, the presenting symptoms are related to the abuse of illicit drugs.

Mental Status Exam

Mental status exams are another form of informal assessment that may occur in each counseling session. The mental status exam is based on clinical mental health counselor observations, assesses the client's level of functioning and self-preservation, and includes the following six main topic areas (Neukrug & Schwitzer, 2005; Polanski & Hinkle, 2000): appearance, behavior and activity level, speech and language, emotional state, thought components, and cognition.

EXAMPLE 6.1

Clinical mental health counselors have to be aware of various facets of client functioning and evaluate the impact of each facet on the client's overall functioning. In general, counselors evaluate whether a client is alert to person, place, time, and situation. In other words, does the client know who he is, where he is, what the general time/day is, and why he is in your office? Imagine a client enters your office and is appropriately dressed for his age. In this case, the client is a 15-year-old male and is wearing jeans, a T-shirt, and tennis shoes. He seems to be well groomed (e.g., his hair is brushed, his clothes are clean, his face and hands are clean), and he has arrived on time for the appointment. In an effort to break the ice, you make a comment about the band pictured on his T-shirt, and he doesn't respond.

As you begin the intake process, you notice that he speaks in a monotone fashion and that there is no change in voice inflection or facial expression. He knows who he is, where he is, and the day. However, when you ask him about why he has come to counseling, he says in the same monotone voice and flat affect that he is extremely popular at school and that all the boys at school are jealous of him. Your first instinct is that the report doesn't seem to fit the client's presenting behavior. According to the client's mother, who referred him for services, the client has no friends and is isolated at school. He has been displaying increasing bizarre behaviors at home.

In this case, the client would be alert and oriented to person, place, time, but not situation. There are some clear problems with perception of reality and certain problems with emotional expression. As a trained clinical mental health counselor, you use your initial mental status exam as a beginning area to target further exploration and to begin the process of clinical diagnosis.

Appearance refers to clients' hygiene, dress, cleanliness, and body posture. Behavior and activity level describe clients' nonverbal cues, activity level during the session, tics, tremors, and mannerisms. Counselors must be comfortable discussing any presenting behavioral issues such as tics. Although it might be impolite in a social situation to call attention to a person's behavioral tic such as an involuntary head movement, it is essential to discuss it in a clinical interview. For example, say that the clinical mental health counselor notices a facial tic during intake and asks the client about the behavior. The client explains that the tics started after his taking an antipsychotic prescription. In this case, the behavior might be a symptom of tardive dyskinesia, which can be a side effect of some psychotropic medications. It would be essential for the clinical mental health counselor to note this issue and to order a medical evaluation based on the client's report and the counselor's observation.

Speech and language includes clients' verbal communication: both content, such as word choice, and expressive style, such as articulation and assembly of words. It is difficult to describe what appears to be within normal limits and what might be considered problematic. One example of a verbal communication issue is anomic aphasia or dysnomia, a disorder characterized by individuals having difficulty recalling words and speaking in circular fashion to describe the construct they are attempting to identify. Although everyone experiences the inability to recall a word or name at some point, the chronic inability to recall could be related to a number of brain-related disorders such as Alzheimer's disease. The issue could also be related to oxygen deprivation in individuals with chronic breathing problems. Being able to differentiate between a common case of forgetfulness and the beginning stages of anomic aphasia takes a trained professional. Even though clinical mental health counselors in training gain a great deal of knowledge about the assessment process from their coursework, additional supervised experience will be critical to truly develop the clinical skills necessary to assess these issues accurately.

The emotional states of clients are evaluated under the categories of affect and mood. Affect is the emotional state observed by the counselor, and mood is the client-reported sustained feeling state. Most people display their emotions spontaneously through facial expressions. You can look at someone smiling and get a feeling about whether he or she is happy, gloating, or flirting. Something as simple as a smile can mean a variety of things. In some cases, such as the example presented above, people have difficulty expressing any emotion. When an individual is void of emotional display, we typically note him or her as having a flat affect. Often, flat affects are tied to mood and psychotic disorders. However, it is important to note that extensive evaluation is needed before arriving at any diagnosis.

Thought components are another aspect of a mental status exam, and these include clinical mental health counselor observations and client reports of hallucinations and delusions. The evaluation also involves assessing the organization, flow, and production of thought. Imagine a client who enters the counselor's office and has difficulty sitting still. He appears agitated and full of energy. As the clinical mental health counselor begins the intake process, the client begins to speak rapidly and his thoughts are jumbled. He jumps from topic to topic, with little connection between them. In this case, it is evident that the client is experiencing some level of mania; however, the reason is not clear. In order to understand the mania, the counselor would need to delve deeper into the assessment process. Mania could be produced by a range of issues including drug use or bipolar disorder. A trained mental health counselor will be able to assess the root causes of the mania and develop a treatment approach based on the assessment.

The final component of a mental status exam is cognition. As part of an assessment of cognition, clinical mental health counselors examine clients' long- and short-term memory, time and place orientation, ability to have insights, and ability to reflect knowledge. Although the areas of observation may appear straightforward, it requires a trained professional to differentiate between various behavioral and verbal nuances. For example, clinical mental health counselors often provide clients with three words (e.g., *apple*, *penny*, and *ball*) and ask them to remember the words after a short period of time. If the client can't recall the words, there may be some problems with short-term memory. As with any other presenting problem, there can be a range of causes. In cases of short-term memory loss, it is always important to request a medical evaluation. Accurate evaluation of mental status is essential for making initial determinations about treatment. For a more detailed description of the components of a mental status exam, see Polanski and Hinkle (2000).

It is recommended that counselors complete at least a short mental status exam at each session. Reporting may be brief, and the information gathered may be used in conjunction with the Global Assessment of Functioning (GAF). The GAF is a numerical score that describes the level of the client's overall functioning and can vary from session to session. Assigning a GAF score related to the mental status exam helps track client function and self-preservation over time, which helps assess client growth and treatment plan effectiveness.

CONSIDERATIONS FOR ASSESSMENT USE

As can be seen from the basic overview presented thus far, the complex process of assessment requires advanced training and skills. In order to regulate the assessment process and to protect the public from poor assessment practice, several organizations have developed standards to guide the assessment process. The *Standards for Assessment in Mental Health Counseling* (n.d.) and *Standards for Multicultural Assessment* (2012) provide crucial guidelines for ethical assessment practice. First, clinical mental health counselors must be trained and have experience in the assessments selected for use. Many advanced-level assessment instruments (e.g., intelligence tests) require additional training beyond what is covered as part of master's-level coursework. Training requirements for administering, scoring, and interpreting instruments may be found in the manuals that accompany the particular assessments and on the assessment developers' Web sites. In general, clinical mental health counselors have the ability to administer and interpret the majority of assessment instruments published as long as they have received appropriate training and supervision. However, state law provides guidelines that stipulate which professionals have the privilege to conduct assessment in each state. Although we believe that counselors should have this privilege based on competency, not all states allow a broad scope of assessment practice.

For example, in Mississippi, licensed professional counselors have a broad scope of practice that allows for the administration, scoring, and interpretation of any assessment procedures for which the clinical mental health counselor has been trained. In contrast, the neighboring state of Louisiana dramatically limits the scope of practice of clinical mental health counselors and limits assessment and diagnosis practices to a small number of presenting issues. Any significant mental health issues must be reviewed by psychologists or psychiatrists in Louisiana. As is evident, the differences in laws across states can be significant. It is imperative that each clinical mental health counselor be very familiar with his or her state law.

Once a clinical mental health counselor determines whether he or she has the right to test, then the next step is selecting the appropriate instruments. There are over 10,000 published assessment instruments available for review. Because of this incredible number, it would be impossible for counseling professionals to be knowledgeable about each one.

Thus, clinical mental health counselors must be able to differentiate qualities of assessment instruments through formal review. Assessments must be selected based on their unique characteristics and the needs of clients. It is important to note that some assessments may further disadvantage clients from diverse backgrounds. Intelligence tests have been hotly debated based upon the potential for cultural bias. In the case of *Larry P. v. Wilson Riles* (1972/1974/1979), a suit was filed against the state of California asserting that discriminatory practices were being used to classify and place students in the special education system. More specifically, the case argued that intelligence tests were culturally biased and that African American children were at a disadvantage when subjected to them. Over the years, the courts have revisited the *Larry P. v. Wilson Riles* case, and the issue remains controversial today.

A related consideration is language proficiency. Assessments must be selected based on clients' English language proficiency and may need to be offered in languages other than English. Formal assessments will include information about appropriate populations for the assessment. Like the *Larry P. v. Wilson Riles* (1972/1974/1979) case, the courts have addressed numerous issues with regard to inappropriate assessment practices related to language proficiency. The most notable case related to language proficiency was *Diana v. State Board of Education* (1970/1973). In the *Diana* case, a student was tested and placed in special education class based on the results. It was later discovered that English was not the student's primary language. When retested in her native language, her intelligence scores were within normal limits. In this case, the court ruled that students must be assessed in the primary language when being considered for special education services.

As can be seen from the court cases cited, assessment, scoring, and interpretation must be conducted in a manner that clients understand. Further, clients must be provided with an informed consent prior to assessment administration. Information in the initial informed consent or disclosure statement may suffice, especially for informal assessments. However, it is essential for clinical mental health counselors to have a conversation with clients about the informed consent process to ensure that clients understand the information in the document. A document by itself does not constitute informed consent. Additional informed consent documents may be needed for formal assessments and other information-gathering tools used later in the counseling process that may not have been included in the initial consent document. These documents must include information about the assessments and the potential uses of the results. Again, any changes in the services should be discussed with the client; and the clinical mental health counselor should make sure that the client understands the rationale for the changes, the potential benefits and challenges, and any potential for a negative impact.

The use of information from assessments for advocacy is another consideration when selecting appropriate assessment tools. Please visit the Association for Assessment and Research in Counseling (AARC) Web site to review the complete *Standards for Assessment of Mental Health Counseling* and *Standards for Multicultural Assessment:* www.theaaceonline.com/resources.htm.

Developmental and holistic approaches to counseling provide a framework for including clients in the assessment process. McAuliffe and Eriksen (1999) described a constructivist framework for counseling that emphasizes that the reality of the client is constructed by the client's experiences, beliefs, values, and perceptions. Tymofievich and Leroux (2000) discussed the concept of edumetrics in assessment, which focuses on the "movement and learning clients are able to achieve" (p. 53). Both pairs of authors emphasized the importance of including the client in assessment selection and use of results, and they promote information gathered through use of assessments as pieces of the overall puzzle being put together to create a picture of the client's world. The clinical mental health counselors' collaboration with clients and not overfocusing on results illustrate ethical assessment practice.

At first glance, the assessment process may not seem complex. Often the word *assessment* is interchanged with *test*. This is partially correct in that tests are the instruments used to gather information—especially during a formal assessment process. Assessment permeates the counseling process in that it encompasses all of the information gathered to inform clinical mental health counselors' work with clients. Counselors must be knowledgeable and trained, culturally alert, and experienced in assessment use. In the rest of this chapter, we describe common areas of assessment used in practice, such as personality, behavior, and cognitive assessments, and the use of assessments in the diagnostic process.

PERSONALITY ASSESSMENT

Personality encompasses all of the unique characteristics that set individuals apart from others. These include feelings, behaviors, thoughts, and interpersonal functioning (Drummond & Jones, 2010; Neukrug & Schwitzer, 2005) and manifest in clients' charm, energy, attitude, temperament, and ways of relating to others.

Returning to the case of Jamie, in the initial session the clinical mental health counselor observes that Jamie is charming, has an easygoing temperament, seems to present a hopeful outlook on life, and reports having a few close, long-term friends. Jamie appears to have low energy and shares that social activities have decreased recently, but in the past she has enjoyed an active social life. From this initial session, the clinical mental health counselor begins to gather information about Jamie's personality and decides to look into formal assessments to help Jamie further clarify personal issues related to anxiety and the change in social functioning. Of the hundreds of personality assessments from which counselors may choose, three of the most popular are described here. It is imperative for counselors in training to become very familiar with each assessment manual prior to use and that they seek supervision during the learning process. We also recommend searching the Mental Measurement Yearbook database to learn about other available personality assessments.

Minnesota Multiphasic Personality Inventory®-2 (MMPI®-2)

The Minnesota Multiphasic Personality Inventory-2 (MMPI-2) is one of the most frequently used personality assessment instruments and measures seven different dimensions of personality—attitudes, adjustment, temperament, values, motivation, moral behavior, and anxiety. The MMPI-2 is a complex instrument and has over 100 scales. However, the primary clinical scales include hypochondriasis, depression, hysteria, psychopathic deviate, paranoia, psychasthenia, schizophrenia, hypomania, and social introversion-extroversion (Drummond & Jones, 2010). Because the names of the scales of the MMPI-2 could have negative connotations, the scales are often referred to by number rather than by name. The MMPI-2 is highly reliable and valid across many settings and populations. Researchers have evaluated the MMPI-2 extensively and have used the instrument in various forms of counseling and psychology research. A general search for the MMPI on the PsychINFO® database resulted in 11,542 results. A search for articles related to the reliability and validity of the MMPI-2 resulted in over 1,000 articles on the same database. In general, researchers have been able to support the application of the MMPI-2 in college counseling, couples counseling, medical problem assessment, military applications, personnel screening programs, counseling with adults 16 and older, forensic applications, and research in psychopathology with adult populations (Butcher & Graham, 1994).

Myers-Briggs Type Indicator® (MBTI®)

The Myers-Briggs Type Indicator (MBTI) is a personality inventory based on Carl Jung's theory of personality (Myers, McCaulley, Quenk, & Hammer, 2003). Personality is described in terms of four dichotomous indexes, and individual preference determines where on the dichotomies an individual falls. The assumption is that type-preference does not change with age. These type-preferences include extraversion-introversion, sensing-intuition, thinking-feeling, and judgment-sensing. The MBTI has been used in counseling couples, families, and individuals in various settings including private practice, college and career counseling centers, substance abuse treatment clinics, and education (Myers et al., 2003). After conducting a study on the longitudinal stability of MBTI types, Cummings (1995) cautioned that type-preference does in fact change with age.

Rorschach: A Visual Projective Test

The Rorschach is a projective test based on the idea that respondents unconsciously project elements of their personality into their descriptions of the various ink blots. Projective tests are not typically used by clinical mental health counselors, but are often part of complete psychological batteries done by psychologists. Because they are used by other professionals, we deemed it essential to discuss them as an aspect of personality assessment. It is important to note that projective tests require specialized training, and the use of these types of instruments is often regulated by state law.

The Rorschach Comprehensive System consists of 10 inkblots that are asymmetrical, part in black and gray, and part in color. Whereas the nonprojective tests described above include rating scales, the Rorschach is a projective test whereby clients are asked to free associate with the inkblots. Counselors probe clients for details about their associations to determine the exact location of the image and which variable, color or inkblot form, was the primary factor in the free association. The information gathered offers insight into the unconscious aspects of personality (Drummond & Jones, 2010). The Rorschach system is quite complex and often requires counselors to take specialized coursework in projective testing before being qualified to use it. Scoring the Rorschach is the most difficult aspect of the projective assessment process. Points are given depending upon the amount of description for each inkblot, the type of image described (e.g., human figure, animal, inanimate), the amount of detail provided, the portion of the inkblot described, and other details. Projective assessment often comes under scrutiny because of the potential for human difference in the evaluation of client responses and the lack of research to fully support the interpretation of the projective scores.

Other personality assessments include sentence completion, story completion, and drawing techniques. Information from personality assessments helps clients understand who they are and increases coping skills, interpersonal skills, and strengths. These assessments also provide evidence needed to make a diagnosis. However, projective assessment is not typically used in isolation. When more standard assessment batteries are used, a projective assessment may add to the interpretation of results related to the other instruments in the battery. Diagnosis is discussed in greater detail at the end of the chapter.

BEHAVIORAL ASSESSMENT

Mental health counselors have often focused on traditional formalized assessment procedures in their assessment process. As discussed earlier, a great deal of attention has been placed on the assessment of personality characteristics and their role in the development of problematic behavior for individual clients rather than on behavioral assessment itself (Sheperis, Doggett, & Henington, 2005). Even though the focus has been more on personality, best practice in assessment requires that clinical mental health counselors evaluate all facets of a presenting problem across multiple settings and via multiple informants. Comprehensive assessment of children, adolescents, and adults requires a behavioral component in order to effectively obtain the requisite information for an accurate picture of client functioning (Doggett, Sheperis, & Butler, 2004).

Behavioral assessment allows clinical mental health counselors to develop a more comprehensive hypothesis about the elements of a client's presenting problems. Comprehensive behavioral assessment provides some essential information that is not gathered during more formal standardized testing. Eaves, Emens, and Sheperis (2008) posited that comprehensive behavioral assessment involves problem identification, problem analysis, problem solution, and problem evaluation. They stated that behavioral assessment can involve both direct (e.g., direct observations) and indirect (e.g., clinical interviews and self-report instruments) procedures.

Direct behavioral assessment methods require the counselor to understand behavioral observation. Indirect methods allow for a less formal process and can occur away from the client. Although not as formal as direct methods, indirect procedures can provide crucial data when used as part of the overall assessment process (Henington, 2004). Clinical mental health counselors often use a combination of direct and indirect methods when conducting behavioral assessment. The combination of such procedures allows clinical mental health counselors to examine behaviors not only from the lens of criteria within the DSM system but also from a statistical evaluation of differences between normal and deviant behavior (Sheperis et al., 2005).

According to Sheperis, Doggett, and Henington (2005), behavioral assessment has direct application to counseling intervention. When clinical mental health counselors observe client behavior directly, they have a much more realistic understanding of that behavior in context and can begin the process of developing interventions to address that behavior. In order to support that understanding of behavior, clinical mental health counselors also employ indirect methods such as (a) clinical interviews, (b) self-report measures, and (c) other report measures.

DIAGNOSIS OF MENTAL DISORDERS

The National Institute of Mental Health (2008) estimates that 58 million Americans live with mental health disorders and only a few of those receive the appropriate treatment. The *Diagnostic and Statistical Manual of Mental Disorders* (DSM) is the diagnostic classification system used in the United States (American Psychiatric Association, 2013; Kupfer, Regier, & Kuhl, 2008). The DSM facilitates communication and data collection among the various mental health, medical, research, and insurance professionals who serve the public in a variety of settings. Clinical mental health counselors will become very familiar with the DSM system.

VOICE FROM THE FIELD 6.1

Assessment became a specialization area for me during my master's degree training. I became especially interested in psychopathology and deviant behavior. As part of one of my first jobs as a professional counselor, I conducted every intake assessment at a counseling clinic over a two-year period. I just about memorized the entire DSM as a result of that experience and gained an even deeper interest in the assessment process. When I pursued my doctoral degree, I decided to specialize in assessment. I was able to take advanced courses in intelligence testing, personality assessment, behavioral assessment, and early childhood assessment. I also completed a 600-hour doctoral internship solely focused on the assessment process.

As a result of my educational preparation, I was able to develop a specialized practice that focused on behavioral assessment with children ages birth to five. Originally, my practice served a single Head Start center in Mississippi. However, over a 10-year period, my practice grew to providing assessment services for over 5,000 children annually. I believe there is a true need for more counselors to specialize in the assessment area. The reason my practice had grown so dramatically was because of a lack of other providers who were able to assess early childhood issues. Assessment can be a viable practice area for all clinical mental health counselors.

CARL SHEPERIS, PhD, LPC, LMHC
Past President, Association for Assessment and Research in Counseling; Chair, Department of Counseling and Special Populations, Lamar University

---

VOICE FROM THE FIELD 6.2

I work as an intake counselor at a mental health facility. My primary job is to conduct assessments and provide a diagnosis for every client who seeks treatment with us. In order to meet client needs, I usually vary my work schedule to allow for at least two evenings a week for intakes. In a typical day, I generally conduct five or six intake assessments. I usually meet my clients in the lobby and try to help them feel comfortable before coming back into my office. I ask whether they had any trouble finding our office and offer them a glass of water or cup of coffee before heading back to my office. Once we get to the office, I start with the informed consent process and make sure I have their signatures before moving forward.

Most of the clients that I see are on Medicaid, and there is a great deal of paperwork associated with the process before I even begin the assessment. In the past, I have asked clients to complete the paperwork prior to coming to the office but found that many of them had difficulty doing so. As a result, my assessments take a bit longer than they normally would. Once the intake paperwork is complete, I begin with a semistructured interview and then, based on the results, determine other types of assessments that may be needed. In some cases, I use rating scales and in others, I use more formal assessments such as the MMPI. I explain the assessment process and each instrument to my clients and help them understand how the results help to guide the treatment process. Usually, clients are happy to have an understanding of the issues that have been giving them trouble. I love the challenge of determining an accurate diagnosis; it is a different job with every client who walks through my office door.

SACKY HOLDINESS, PhD, LPC
The Counselor's Cabin

Relevance to Counselors

Clinical mental health counselor use of the DSM and participation in a formal diagnostic process has been a controversial issue for years (Boylan, Malley, & Reilly, 2001). Some perceive the formal diagnostic process as the domain of psychiatrists, psychologists, medical personnel, and professionals who have earned doctorates specializing in clinical work. Clinical mental health counselors have expressed concern that the diagnostic process itself is incongruent with the guiding principles of counseling (Gladding, 2009). The American Counseling Association's Task Force on the DSM-5 (2011) stated that clinical mental health counselors work from a strength-based approach and resist pathologizing clients and the stigma that is often associated with mental health diagnosis. Additionally, formal diagnosis is incongruent with several counseling theoretical approaches including rational emotive behavior theory, choice theory, and person-centered therapy. There is also the concern that clients may be viewed as their diagnosis (i.e., being an alcoholic instead of John; being bipolar instead of Jane) or that a diagnostic label can become an excuse and interfere with treatment (Seligman, 2009).

Although these concerns may have some validity, the reality is that diagnosis is an inherent element of the counseling process. The current climate requires clinical mental health counselors to be knowledgeable of the diagnostic process regardless of their work setting (Gladding, 2009; Hohenshil, 1996; House, 1999). Understanding the diagnostic process is increasingly required by employers to facilitate treatment accountability, record keeping, research funding, and third-party reimbursement. The DSM multiaxial system creates a common language that strives to provide clarity and credibility when working with other professionals (Seligman, 2009). Although the DSM itself does not include treatment recommendations, it provides clinicians with descriptions and criteria sets for disorders. Clinical mental health counselors are able to research appropriate treatment strategies due to the detailed information regarding the disorders contained in the DSM. Counselors who use the DSM appropriately are operating within the profession's standards of practice, which is believed to increase effectiveness and reduce vulnerability to malpractice (American Psychiatric Association, 2013; Gladding, 2009). Understanding the diagnostic process is also important for clinical mental health counselors who work in school or business settings to aid in the determination of the services required, service availability in that setting, and whether referral is necessary.

(handwritten margin note: Time, frequency, symptoms, duration)

Diagnostic and Statistical Manual of Mental Disorders **(DSM)**

DSM I—1952 The first edition of the DSM evolved from the process of collecting statistical data and from work with psychiatric and neurological conditions conducted by the US Army. Published in 1952, this edition included 106 "reactions" reflecting Adolf Meyer's perspective that "mental disorders represented reactions of the personality to psychological, social, and biological factors" (American Psychiatric Association, 2000, p. xxv).

DSM II—1968 The revisions included in this edition appear to return to Kraepelin's descriptive diagnostic model (LaBruzza, 1994; Sanders, 2011). Although terms that implied causality (i.e., reactions) were removed, the retention of psychoanalytic terminology reflected the theoretical preferences of the time. The number of disorders increased to 182.

DSM III—1980 AND DSM III-R—1987 To address the challenge of psychiatrists making different diagnoses for individuals who exhibited the same symptoms, the DSM III became more medically based and research oriented. In addition, the third edition expanded explicit descriptions of included disorders. There was a shift to include criteria that could be seen and statistically measured (LaBruzza, 1994; Sanders, 2011). Symptom clusters, the multiaxial system, and a decision tree were adopted to aid in the diagnostic process. Identified disorders increased to 265. There was an effort to reduce scientific jargon, and the psychoanalytical terminology and causation (unconscious motives) was removed. Additionally, the term *patient* was changed to *person* or *individual,* and the terms *disease* and *illness* were replaced with *disorder.* These changes improved communication among various mental health professionals and increased the reliability for clinicians and researchers using the DSM.

The DSM III-R was published in 1987 to address system inconsistencies and criteria clarity issues (LaBruzza, 1994; Sanders, 2011). This edition included revisions to older diagnoses, 27 new categories, and an increase to 292 identified disorders. Previous editions used a nomothetic diagnosis system, meaning that an individual had to meet all the symptoms listed for the disorder. To improve diagnostic reliability, the DSM III-R made a transition to a polythetic diagnosis system whereby the individual had to meet only several of the symptoms listed. This edition was the first to allow for dual diagnosis if an individual met the required criteria.

DSM IV—1994 AND DSM IV-TR—2000 This edition reflected a six-year process committed to the goal of establishing a solid empirical basis for revisions (American Psychiatric Association, 2000). The work group for the DSM IV included individuals and professional organizations that conducted extensive review of the literature regarding mental disorders. Previous data were reanalyzed, and field trials were conducted to verify reliability in different settings and types of clinical work. Changes revised criteria sets, descriptive text, and eliminated sexist language. Included disorders now exceed 300.

In the DSM IV-TR in 2000, there were revisions to background information (i.e., family patterns; genetic, gender, and cultural influences) that reflected current research.

Since 1948, the World Health Organization (WHO) has overseen the development and publication of *The International Statistical Classification of Diseases and Related Health Problems* (ICD). Due to concerns expressed regarding the lack of specificity with respect to classification of mental disorders in the ninth edition of the ICD, a revision entitled ICD-9-CM (Clinical Modification) was developed for use in the United States (First & Westen, 2007). The DSM-IV Task Force worked in collaboration with the ICD-10 authors to facilitate compatibility of the classification codes presented in both publications. While continued collaboration between those responsible for revision of both publications is anticipated, there are those who question the "justification for maintaining the DSM as a separate diagnostic system from the ICD" (American Psychological Association, 2009).

MULTIAXIAL SYSTEM This "system involves an assessment on several axes, each of which refers to a different domain of information that may help the clinician plan treatment and predict outcomes" (American Psychiatric Association, 2000, p. 27).

> *Axis I* is for notation of clinical disorders excluding personality disorders and mental retardation. If an individual meets the criteria for multiple disorders, all are included and the primary diagnosis is listed first. If there is no diagnosis, V71.09 No Diagnosis is noted.

Axis II personality disorders or mental retardation are coded on this axis. If an individual meets the criteria for multiple disorders, all are included and the primary diagnosis is listed first. If there is no diagnosis, V71.09 No Diagnosis is noted. The Code 799.9 Deferred indicates that a clinician may suspect a disorder, but requires additional information for a formal diagnosis.

Axis III is for the notation of any medical history that may be relevant to understanding an individual's mental disorder.

Axis IV is used to identify possible psychosocial or environmental issues that may affect an individual's diagnosis or treatment.

Axis V identifies the Global Assessment of Functioning (GAF) score, which indicates the clinician's evaluation of the client's level of functioning.

DSM-5—2013 The DSM-5 is the newest iteration of the *Diagnostic and Statistical Manual of Mental Disorders*. The revision process has exceeded a decade and has involved national and international medical and mental health professionals who work in a wide range of clinical settings (American Psychiatric Association, 2013). Revision guidelines included the support of empirical evidence for all revisions and a commitment to the clinical utility of the manual. The DSM-5 Task Force conducted extensive literature reviews, field trials, and it accepted feedback from practitioners and community members. This revision process was aimed toward ensuring that revisions reflected how gender, race, and ethnicity affect diagnosis (American Psychological Association, 2010). Although the purpose was to develop an empirically based revision, the immediate criticisms of the new manual call its utility into question. There is a strong potential that the Centers for Medicare & Medicaid Services will abandon the new DSM and require all diagnoses to be based on codes from the International Classification of Diseases (ICD) manual. The National Institute of Mental Health (NIMH) is planning to move all future funding away from DSM categories (Insel, 2013). Insel, in his role as director of NIMH, argued that although the DSM has often been seen as the Bible for mental health professionals, its utility is as a dictionary of common terms. This type of criticism at such a high level reflects the lack of support for the current edition.

Although there is ample criticism for the DSM-5, it is still important for clinical mental health counselors to understand the manual and to be able to use it in conjunction with the ICD system. With any change, there are positives and negatives. Insel (2013) did point out that the DSM provides a common language for all mental health professionals to use in communication about psychopathology. Overall, the changes in the new edition, although controversial, are not monumental. An interesting change is that there is a shift from Roman numerals to Arabic numerals for the title and revisions will be identified as DSM 5.1, DSM 5.2, and so on (American Psychiatric Association, 2013). The multiaxial diagnostic system that has been used in previous versions has now been replaced by a dimensional-categorical model. As a result, diagnostic groups have changed and diagnostic codes are now alphanumeric. The dimensional classification model does not include a not otherwise specified (NOS) label, which was used when symptoms did not fit clearly in a diagnostic category. In the new version of the diagnostic manual, there are now 16 diagnostic groups:

1. Neurodevelopmental Disorder
2. Schizophrenia and Primary Psychotic Disorders
3. Bipolar and Related Disorders

4. Mood Disorders
5. Anxiety Disorders
6. Disorders Related to Environmental Stress
7. Obsessive Compulsive Spectrum
8. Somatic Symptom Disorder
9. Feeding and Eating Disorder
10. Sleep Disorders
11. Disorders of Sexual Function
12. Antisocial and Disruptive Disorders
13. Substance Abuse-Related Disorders
14. Neurocognitive Disorders
15. Personality Disorders
16. Paraphilias
17. Other Disorders

The changes in the DSM have been actively debated for several years. Some believe the dimensional classification and other changes contribute to enhancing the clarity of the system (Kupfer et al., 2008; Lopez, Compton, Grant, & Breiling, 2007; Regier, 2007). Others question the transparency and the validation process of proposed changes, as well as the complexity of the change to a dimensional assessment process (American Counseling Association, 2011; Frances, 2011a, 2011b). As counseling students continue their training in clinical mental health counseling, they will develop not only an in-depth knowledge of the new dimensional assessment process but also competence in using the DSM and ICD manuals to arrive at clinical diagnoses.

ADDITIONAL DIAGNOSTIC ASSESSMENTS

It is important that counselors remember that the DSM is a manual used in the diagnostic process but that assessment is needed in order to use the manual accurately. To establish a holistic view of the client, counselors should use other formal and informal assessment tools discussed earlier in the chapter. Assessments such as the Minnesota Multiphasic Personality Inventory-2, the Millon® Clinical Multiaxial Inventory III (MCMI-III™), the Beck Depression Inventory®-II (BDI®-II), the mental status exam, and others assist in gathering information that can lead to understanding presenting symptomology and the fit of that symptomology within the dimensional system of the DSM-5. It is important to note that clinical mental health counselors must be responsible and ethical in their use of assessments and pursue advanced training and supervision. The counseling profession's ethical standards require that clinical mental health counselors remain current in their knowledge of changes in assessment, diagnosis, and treatment protocols.

Conclusion

Assessment and diagnosis are critical aspects of clinical mental health counseling. In this chapter, the various types of assessment and the diagnostic process were introduced. Because these are such in-depth areas of practice, most counselors in training students will have separate courses dedicated to each area. Even with a course in each area, it will be necessary to receive ongoing supervised practice to become competent in assessment and diagnosis. Each of these areas lays the foundation for all work students will do as clinical mental health counselors.

Without accurate assessment and diagnosis, they would be missing the critical pieces of the puzzle that were discussed at the beginning of the chapter.

References

Alexander, F., Sheldon, G., & Selesnick, T. (1966). *The history of psychiatry and evaluation of psychiatric thought and practice from prehistoric times to the present*. New York, NY: Harper and Row.

American Counseling Association (ACA). (2005). *Code of ethics*. Alexandria, VA: Author.

American Counseling Association (ACA). (2011). *ACA expresses DSM-5 concerns to the American Psychiatric Association*. Retrieved from http://www.counseling.org/news/news-release-archives/by-year/2011/2011/11/28/aca-expresses-dsm-5-concerns-to-the-american-psychiatric-association

American Psychiatric Association. (2000). *Diagnostic and statistical manual of mental disorders, fourth edition–text revision* (DSM-IV-TR). Washington, DC: Author.

American Psychiatric Association. (2013). *Diagnostic and statistical manual of mental disorders, fifth edition* (DSM-5). Retrieved from http://www.dsm5.org

American Psychological Association. (2009). ICD vs. DSM. *Monitor on Psychology, 40*(9), 63. Retrieved from http://www.apa.org/monitor/2009/10/icd-dsm.aspx

American Psychological Association. (2010). *DSM-5 development process includes emphasis on gender and cultural sensitivity*. Retrieved from http://www.dsm5.org/Newsroom/Documents/Race-Gender-Ethnicity%20Release%20FINAL%202.05.pdf

Boylan, J. C., Malley, P. B., & Reilly, E. P. (2001). *Practicum and internship: Textbook and resource guide for counseling and psychotherapy*. Bridgeport, NJ: Taylor & Francis.

Butcher, J. N., & Graham, J. R. (1994). The MMPI-2: A new standard for personal assessment and research in counseling settings. *Measurement and Evaluation in Counseling and Development, 27*(3), 130–150.

Council for Accreditation of Counseling and Related Educational Programs (CACREP). (2009). *CACREP accreditation manual: 2009 standards*. Alexandria, VA: Author. Retrieved from http://www.cacrep.org/doc/2009%20Standards%20with%20cover.pdf

Cummings, W. H., III. (1995). Age group differences and estimated frequencies of the Myers-Briggs Type Indicator preferences. *Measurement and Evaluation in Counseling and Development, 28*(2), 69–78.

Diana v. State Board of Education, Civil Action No. C-7037RFP (N. D. Cal. Jan. 7, 1970 and June 18, 1973).

Doggett, R. A., Sheperis, C. J., & Butler, T. (2004). Behavioral interventions for school counselors. In B. T. Erford (Ed.), *The professional school counselor's handbook*. Greensboro, NC: CAPS Press.

Drummond, R. J., & Jones, K. D. (2003). *Assessment procedures for counselors & helping professionals* (7th ed.). Upper Saddle River, NJ: Prentice Hall.

Eaves, S., Emens, R., & Sheperis, C. J. (2008). Training counselors in the managed care era: The efficacy of the data-based problem solver model. *Journal of Professional Counseling: Practice, Theory & Research, 36*(2), 1–12.

First, M. B., & Westen, D. (2007). Classification for clinical practice: How to make ICD and DSM better able to serve clinicians. *International Review of Psychiatry, 19*(5), 473–481.

Frances, A. (2011a, June 3). Who needs DSM-5? *Psychology Today*. Retrieved from http://www.psychologytoday.com/blog/dsm5-in-distress/201106/who-needs-dsm-5

Frances, A. (2011b, November 17). Counselors turn against DSM-5: Can APA ignore 120,000 users? *Psychology Today*. Retrieved from http://www.psychiatrictimes.com/dsm-5-0/counselors-turn-against-dsm-5-can-apa-ignore-120000-users

Gladding, S. T. (2009). *Counseling: A comprehensive profession* (6th ed.). Columbus, OH: Pearson.

Goldman, L. (1992). Qualitative assessment: An approach for counselors. *Journal of Counseling & Development, 70*, 616–621.

Henington, C. (2004). Behavioral assessment. In B. T. Erford (Ed.), *The professional school counselor's handbook*. Greensboro, NC: CAPS Press.

Hohenshil, T. H. (1996). Role of assessment and diagnosis in counseling. *Journal of Counseling & Development, 75*(1), 64–68.

House, A. E. (1999). *DSM-IV diagnosis in the schools.* New York, NY: Guilford Press.

Insel, T. (2013, April 29). *Transforming diagnosis.* Retrieved from http://www.nimh.nih.gov/about /director/2013/transforming-diagnosis.shtml

Ivey, A. E., Ivey, M. B., & Zalaquett, C. P. (2009). *Intentional interviewing and counseling: Facilitating client development in a multicultural society* (7th ed.). Pacific Grove, CA: Brooks Cole.

Kupfer, D. J., Regier, D. A., & Kuhl, E. A. (2008). *On the road to DSM-V and ICD-11.* Retrieved from http:// www.ncbi.nlm.nih.gov/pubmed/18985287

LaBruzza, A. L. (1994). *Using DSM-IV: A clinician's guide to psychiatric diagnosis.* New York, NY: Rowman & Littlefield.

Larry P. v. Wilson Riles, 343 F. Supp. 1306 (N.D. Cal. 1972) (preliminary injunction); affirmed 502 F.2d 963 (9th Cir. 1974); No. C-71-2270 RFP (N.D. Cal 1979).

Lopez, M. L., Compton, W. M., Grant, B. F., & Breiling, J. P. (2007). Dimensional approaches in diagnostic classification: A critical appraisal. *International Journal of Methods in Psychiatric Research, 16*(S1), S6–S7.

McAuliffe, G. J., & Eriksen, K. P. (1999). Toward a constructivist and developmental identity for the counseling profession: The context-phase-stage-style model. *Journal of Counseling & Development, 77,* 267–280.

Millon, T. (2004). *Masters of the mind exploring the story of mental illness from ancient times to the new millennium.* San Francisco, CA: John Wiley.

Myers, I. B., McCaulley, M. H., Quenk, N. L., & Hammer, A. L. (2003). *MBTI manual: A guide to the development and use of the Myers-Briggs Type Indicator* (3rd ed.). Palo Alto, CA: Consulting Psychologists Press.

National Institute of Mental Health (NIMH). (2008). *The numbers count: Mental disorders in America.* Retrieved from http://www.nimh.nih.gov/health /publications/the-numbers-count-mental-disorders- in-america/index.shtml

Nelson, M. L. (2002). An assessment-based model for counseling strategy selection. *Journal of Counseling & Development, 80,* 416–421.

Neukrug, E. S., & Schwitzer, A. M. (2005). *Skills and tools for today's counselors and psychotherapists: From natural helping to professional counseling.* Pacific Grove, CA: Brooks Cole.

Polanski, P. J., & Hinkle, J. S. (2000). The mental status examination: Its use by professional counselors. *Journal of Counseling & Development, 78,* 357–364.

Regier, D. A. (2007). Dimensional approaches to psychiatric classification: Refining the research agenda for DSM-V: An introduction. *International Journal of Methods in Psychiatric Research, 16*(S1), S1–S5.

Sanders, J. L. (2011). A distinct language and a historic pendulum: The evolution of the *Diagnostic and Statistical Manual of Mental Disorders. Archives of Psychiatric Nursing, 25*(6), 1–10.

Seligman, L. (2009). Diagnosis in counseling. In D. Capuzzi & D. R. Gross (Eds.), *Introduction to the counseling profession* (5th ed.). Columbus, OH: Pearson.

Sheperis, C. J., Doggett, R. A., & Henington, C. (2005). Behavioral assessment: Principles and applications. In B. T. Erford (Ed.), *Counselor's guide to clinical, personality, and behavioral assessment* (pp. 105– 123). Boston, MA: Lahaska Press.

Standards for Assessment in Mental Health Counseling. (n.d.). Retrieved from http://aarc-counseling.org /assets/cms/uploads/files/AACE-AMHCA.pdf

Standards for Multicultural Assessment. (2012). Retrieved from http://www.theaaceonline.com /AACE-AMCD.pdf

Tymofievich, M., & Leroux, J. A. (2000). Assessment in action: Counselors' competencies in using assessments. *Measurement and Evaluation in Counseling and Development, 33,* 50–59.

7

Case Conceptualization and Treatment Planning

Monica Leppma and K. Dayle Jones

CHAPTER OVERVIEW

This chapter covers basic models of case conceptualization and treatment planning. We define the essential concepts of case conceptualization and explore its relevance to clinical mental health counseling. Then we delve into the various models of case conceptualization and introduce the treatment planning process. The chapter concludes with an illustrative case study to enhance understanding of the process of case conceptualization and treatment planning.

LEARNING OBJECTIVES

The learning objectives for this chapter are designed to be consistent with the 2009 Council for Accreditation of Counseling and Related Educational Programs Standards (CACREP, 2009). As such, upon completion of this chapter, the student will have knowledge of the following clinical mental health counseling standards:

1. Knows the principles, models, and documentation formats of biopsychosocial case conceptualization and treatment planning. (C.7)
2. Understands how living in a multicultural society affects clients who are seeking clinical mental health counseling services. (E.1)
3. Knows the principles and models of assessment, case conceptualization, theories of human development, and concepts of normalcy and psychopathology leading to diagnoses and appropriate counseling treatment plans. (G.1)
4. Understands ethical and legal considerations specifically related to the practice of clinical mental health counseling. (A.2)
5. Applies multicultural competencies to clinical mental health counseling involving case conceptualization, diagnosis, treatment, referral, and prevention of mental and emotional disorders. (D.2)

INTRODUCTION

Case conceptualization is the name given to the narrative that integrates description and explanation of mental health problems (Vertue & Haig, 2008). Its primary goal is to provide a hypothesis of causal mechanisms, which in turn guides treatment decisions. Conceptualization involves describing clients' problems and diagnoses, as well as understanding the causes of their behaviors. The client's presenting problems are synthesized with theory and research to produce an original and unique explanation of the client's presenting issues (Kuyken, Padesky, & Dudley, 2008). Case conceptualization summarizes the salient features of the case and identifies important issues quickly, particularly for complex cases with multiple problems. The act of writing itself helps clinical mental health counselors organize and integrate important clinical data in order to provide a comprehensive, yet focused, view of the client.

Because case conceptualization helps clinical mental health counselors understand the causes and effects of a client's presenting problems, it thereby facilitates effective treatment planning. It guides therapy by helping identify treatment goals, appropriate interventions, and potential obstacles to therapy (Levenson & Strupp, 1997; Meier, 2003). In fact, preliminary research evidence indicates that treatment guided by case conceptualization improves treatment outcome (Silberschatz, Fretter, & Curtis, 1986).

The purpose of this chapter is to provide an understanding of the essential features of case conceptualization, which is the foundation for effective treatment planning in clinical mental health practice. The first part of the chapter explains case conceptualization and why it is important. Next, the chapter covers various models and outlines the steps of the case conceptualization and treatment planning process. Finally, a case study is included to illustrate the application of case conceptualization leading to the development of an individualized treatment plan. Relevant ethical issues and multicultural considerations are interwoven throughout the chapter.

DEFINITION OF CASE CONCEPTUALIZATION

Case conceptualization is regarded by many to be a core clinical skill for clinical mental health counselors and a fundamental component of providing effective treatment (Eells, 2007b; Kendjelic & Eells, 2007; MacKinnon & Yudofsky, 1991; Scheiber, Kramer, & Adamowski, 2003). No definition of case conceptualization is agreed upon by researchers or practitioners, whether they represent theoretical approaches that are different or the same, or a theory-generic approach. Eells (2007a) defined case conceptualization as a way of viewing the origin of, etiology of, and conditions that sustain a client's presenting problem. Sperry (2010) defined case conceptualization as a "clinical strategy for obtaining and organizing information about a client, explaining the client's situation and maladaptive patterns, guiding and focusing treatment, anticipating challenges and roadblocks, and preparing for successful termination" (p. 110). Both of these definitions are broad, avoiding any theory-specific constructs.

Other definitions of case conceptualization come from the perspective of specific theories. For example, Persons (2008) provided a definition for cognitive-behavior therapy (CBT) case conceptualization, describing it as a "framework for providing CBT therapy that flexibly meets the unique needs of the patient at hand, guides the therapist's decision making, and is evidence based" (p. 1). Similarly, Messer and Wolitzky (2007) offered a psychoanalytic theory–specific definition, denoting psychoanalytic case formulation as a "hierarchically organized set of clinical inferences about the nature of a patient's psychopathology, and, more generally, about his or her personality structure, dynamics, and development" (p. 67).

Eells (2007a) extended her definition of case conceptualization with an emphasis on the format, structure, and organization that the conceptualization process provides. She indicated that case conceptualization allows counselors to structure the information about the person, even when the information is contradictory (e.g., when emotions don't match behavior, such as when someone who is grieving keeps laughing). Case conceptualization allows counselors to understand all of this information and organize it into a design for treatment.

Although these definitions vary somewhat in content, they essentially cover the same scope. This includes describing the client's presenting problems, providing structure to help organize and understand the client's problems, generating hypotheses about the etiology of these problems, and providing a strategy for guiding treatment.

BENEFITS OF CASE CONCEPTUALIZATION

Why is case conceptualization important? At its most basic level, case conceptualization is important because it facilitates effective treatment. This is accomplished in several ways.

Case Conceptualization Can Make Numerous and Complex Problems More Manageable

Counselors working with clients who have numerous and complex difficulties can feel overwhelmed by the sheer number of problems and issues presented (Kuyken, Padesky, & Dudley, 2009). By thinking in terms of conceptualization, counselors can refrain from being bombarded or overloaded with large amounts of unstructured information (Lazare, 1976). A new observation can be viewed in terms of its relevance to a limited number of hypotheses, rather than being one out of thousands of possible facts. Just the act of writing helps to organize and integrate clinical data, allowing counselors to understand and hypothesize the client issues. As one clinical mental health counselor has described it, "Case conceptualization helps put all the pieces of the puzzle together."

Case Conceptualization Helps Counselors Accurately Identify the Causes and Effects Involved in Clients' Presenting Problems

Case conceptualization provides a framework to identify and examine the development, maintenance, and consequences of the client's presenting problems. Counselors are ethically obligated to carefully consider diverse factors when determining clinical diagnoses (ACA, 2005). Moreover, the ethical guidelines of both the American Counseling Association (ACA) and the American Mental Health Counselors Association (AMHCA, 2010) state that counselors must understand and recognize the ways in which cultural and socioeconomic factors affect clients' presenting problems. Thus, case conceptualization helps guide ethical behavior by taking into account a comprehensive picture of a client's particular circumstances and then organizing the pertinent information.

Case Conceptualization Normalizes Clients' Presenting Problems

Many clients worry that their issues are somehow "abnormal" and stigmatizing. They sometimes feel like they're "crazy" or feel ashamed of their problems. Case conceptualization can be an excellent tool to help clients understand their problems and how their problems are maintained (Kuyken et al., 2009). Sharing case conceptualizations with clients can help validate and normalize client experience. It can stop clients from feeling confused, alone, and overwhelmed by the complexity of their problems; as such, they can feel motivated and more hopeful about the therapeutic process.

Case Conceptualization Helps Guide the Selection of Interventions

Arguably the most important function of case conceptualization is to guide therapy. The number of treatment interventions appropriate for various client problems and diagnoses is large and ever expanding. How does a counselor choose the appropriate treatment intervention, especially for clients with several problems or co-occurring disorders that do not fit into one particular model? By providing a working understanding of a client's presenting problems, case conceptualization helps counselors select appropriate interventions, as well as focus and sequence interventions (Kuyken et al., 2009). Furthermore, case conceptualization provides convincing rationales for interventions by showing how each intervention can impact the relevant factors that contribute to the client's problems (Needleman, 1999).

Case Conceptualization Helps Establish a Strong Therapeutic Alliance

The therapeutic relationship is essential in all aspects of counseling, including case conceptualization. Throughout assessment and therapy, the clinical mental health counselor works to build a trusting, collaborative therapeutic relationship. The counselor works collaboratively with the client to develop the case conceptualization, set treatment goals that are meaningful to the client, and clearly tie the interventions to the client's goals (Persons, 2008). Thus, client–counselor agreement on diagnosis, conceptualization, and treatment plan are key elements of a strong therapeutic relationship (Bordin, 1979).

ELEMENTS OF CASE CONCEPTUALIZATION

A case conceptualization provides a plausible explanation for a client's problems or symptoms, based on theories of psychotherapy, which provides a rationale for the interventions and procedures used to resolve them (Frank & Frank, 1991). Based on this, a case conceptualization should include the following elements (Ingram, 2006; Persons, 2008):

- A description of all the client's symptoms, disorders, and problems
- Information about the precipitating, predisposing, perpetuating, and protective factors of the current problems
- A hypothesis based on the above factors and a theoretical framework that provides an explanation
- Decisions about specific treatment interventions

Theoretical Basis

Theories of psychotherapy are an essential component of case conceptualization. The primary function of psychotherapy theories is to infer a mechanism that accounts for the client's symptoms and problems. For example, a conceptualization of depression based on Beck's cognitive theory is that depressive symptoms occur when schemata (i.e., core beliefs) are activated by life events to produce dysfunctional automatic thoughts, maladaptive behaviors, and problematic emotions (Beck, 1976; Beck, Rush, Shaw, & Emery, 1979). Thus, the clinical mental health counselor's task is to apply theory to account for the particular symptoms, schemata, automatic thoughts, maladaptive behaviors, and emotions experienced by the particular client (Persons, 2008). As such, case conceptualization serves as a connection between a client's presenting problems and a theory of psychotherapy (Sim, Gwee, & Bateman, 2005).

One of the strengths of the case conceptualization–driven approach to treatment is that it can be used by clinical mental health counselors of all theoretical orientations. Hence, the nature of case conceptualization, and the hypotheses generated through it, varies depending on the particular theory the clinical mental health counselor uses (Eells, 2007b; Persons, 2006). For example, psychodynamic approaches center on underlying conflicts and traumas, often early in development, and subsequent defenses as causes of the presenting problem. Behavioral approaches focus on learning theory and functional analysis of observable behavior, including their antecedents and/or their consequences. A cognitive therapy orientation emphasizes patterns of faulty thinking, beliefs, and perceptions as explanations for presenting problems. Biological explanations might also be interwoven into a case formulation, which may include genetics, illness or disease, toxins, and disabilities.

Theories help clinical mental health counselors deal with the problem of an ever-increasing number of empirically supported treatments (ESTs) available for psychiatric disorders. An EST is a treatment designed to be applied to a specific population, whose efficacy has been demonstrated through clinical research (Jongsma & Bruce, 2010). The development of new ESTs in the profession is positive—clinical mental health counselors need more effective treatment approaches. However, learning each and every detail of the multitude of EST protocols is overwhelming for counselors. Because most ESTs are based on theories of psychotherapy, clinical mental health counselors can rely more heavily on the basic principles of the specific underlying theory that target problems or disorders the counselor commonly treats (Persons, 2008).

Diagnosis

A diagnosis is considered by many to be the primary basis for treatment decision making. Although diagnoses categorize and classify a client's current symptom presentation, a diagnosis *alone* does not provide enough guidance to clinical mental health counselors in many situations. For example, diagnostic criteria do not necessarily focus on the underlying cause of a client's problem. To select appropriate therapeutic interventions, clinical mental health counselors need information about both symptoms and the various causal explanations of these symptoms (Sturmey, 2009). Furthermore, clients typically have multiple disorders. In this situation, determining the most effective treatment is difficult because most ESTs typically target a single disorder. To treat these clients, the clinical mental health counselor would need to address the following questions (Persons, 2008): Which disorders are most interfering with the client's life? Should I treat the multiple disorders consecutively or concurrently? If I use a consecutive approach, which disorder or problem should I treat first?

Case conceptualization can also help fill the gap between diagnosis and treatment. It is a process that, through narrative form, attempts to link the problems of interest with the various causal explanations involved. In contrast, diagnosis is a descriptive task that results in a "summary term for a particular set of symptoms" (Vertue & Haig, 2008, p. 1049). However, as noted by the American Psychiatric Association (2000), "Making a DSM-IV diagnosis is only the first step in a comprehensive evaluation" (p. xxxiv). The cause of a client's difficulties can include psychological, biological, cognitive, affective, and/or behavioral factors. Hence, an important function of case conceptualization is to integrate all aspects of a case rather than to simply identify the presence of a set of symptoms.

Case conceptualization does not take the place of a diagnosis, and in many ways, diagnoses can aid counselors in developing a case conceptualization and treatment plan. First, because diagnosis provides information about the client's symptoms and problems, Axes I–IV of a DSM diagnosis overlap considerably with the list of problems on a case conceptualization. Second, a diagnosis can provide the clinical mental health counselor with some immediate conceptualization hypotheses (Persons, 2008). For example, a diagnosis of social phobia suggests the conceptualization that anxiety symptoms result when an individual, entering a social or public situation, focuses attention on a negative image of himself or herself as inept, unattractive, or defective (Clark, 2001). Third, because most research on ESTs is organized by diagnosis, counselors would want to know the client's diagnosis to draw on that research in their conceptualization (Persons, 2008).

Ethical and Multicultural Considerations

Although diagnosis is important to case conceptualization and evidence based practice, it should be noted that there are ethical and cultural issues to consider. First, counselors must keep in mind that historical and social prejudices have played a part in pathologizing some individuals and groups (ACA, 2005). It is important to consider such historical influences when working with clients. Furthermore, focusing on diagnosis creates the potential for disregarding individuals' specific context or circumstances, as well as the effects of diversity and cultural issues on problematic behaviors, symptoms, and events. Finally, focusing solely on diagnosis may detract from attention to changes in people's social stressors or relationships as well as to client strengths and abilities (McLaughlin, 2006).

CASE CONCEPTUALIZATION MODELS

Case conceptualization models have proliferated in recent years across multiple theoretical orientations, including psychodynamic, behavioral, cognitive, cognitive-behavioral, and systemic approaches (Kendjelic & Eells, 2007). Similar to having no agreed-upon definition of case conceptualization, there is no single conceptualization model or format. Although most models include descriptive information, they differ in the types of potential components that could be included in a case conceptualization (Eells, 2007b); Meier, 2003) (see Table 7.1).

An example of a psychodynamic case conceptualization model is one proposed by Perry, Cooper, and Michels (1987). This model includes a (a) summarizing statement that describes the client's problems and behaviors and places them in the context of the client's current life situation and developmental history; (b) description of nondynamic factors that may have contributed to the problem, such as genetics, trauma, substance abuse, or physical illness; (c) psychodynamic explanation of the central conflicts and themes, describing their role in the current situation and their genetic origins; and (d) prediction of how these conflicts are likely to affect treatment and the therapeutic relationship.

TABLE 7.1 Components in Case Conceptualization

Source	Theory/Framework	Components

Lazare (1976)	Multidimensional	• Data collection
		• Hypothesis generation and testing
		  • psychologic
		  • social
		  • biologic
		  • behavioral
		• Strategies: Methods (to test hypotheses)

Perry, Cooper, and Michels (1987)	Psychodynamic	• A summarizing statement of the client's problems and behaviors • A description of nondynamic factors • A psychodynamic explanation of the central conflicts and theme • A prediction of how these conflicts may affect treatment and the therapeutic relationship
Persons (1989, 2008)	Cognitive-Behavioral	• The problem list • The mechanism hypothesis that explains the cause of the disorders or problems • The precipitants of current problems • The origins of the mechanism • The case formulation
Wolpe and Turkat (1985)	Behavioral	• The presenting problems • The onset of each problem • The development and maintenance of each problem • The predisposing factors
Weerasekera (1993)	Multiperspective	• Predisposing factors • Precipitating factors • Perpetuating factors • Protective factors
Schwitzer (1996, 1997)	Self-Psychology	• Problem identification • Thematic group • Theoretical inference about client concerns • Narrowed inferences about client difficulties
Kendjelic and Eells (2007)	Generic	• Symptoms/problems • Precipitating stressors • Predisposing events and conditions • Inferred mechanism

Persons' book, *Cognitive Therapy in Practice: A Case Formulation Approach* (1989), provided one of the first guidebooks on case conceptualization. In the second edition of this book, Persons proposed a case conceptualization model for cognitive-behavioral therapy, which has five components: (a) the problem list, (b) the mechanism hypothesis that explains the cause of the disorders or problems; (c) the precipitants of current problems; (d) the origins of the mechanism in the client's early life; and (e) the case formulation (i.e., the written narrative of the components) (Persons, 2008). Central to Persons' case formulation process is developing a hypothesis that underlies the psychological mechanisms that cause the problems and disorders.

Kendjelic and Eells (2007) proposed a generic model of case conceptualization based on previous models from various theoretical perspectives. Their model includes four components: (a) symptoms/problems, which includes diagnostic information, sociocultural issues, financial problems, and client problems that distress others; (b) precipitating stressors that contribute to the onset of the problems or symptoms or have increased their severity; (c) predisposing events in the client's past or other situations that increase the client's vulnerability to symptom development; and (d) the inferred mechanism, which is the clinician's hypothesis (based on the previous components) of the client's current problems.

Ideally, a case conceptualization format contains enough structure to permit the clinical mental health counselor to identify, categorize, and understand important classes of information within a sufficiently encompassing view of the client. Hence, counselors need to strike a balance in how simple or complex they make their case conceptualization. If an overly simplified construction is offered, important dimensions of the client's problems may go unrecognized or misunderstood. If overly complex, the conceptualization may be unwieldy, too time-consuming, and impractical (Eells, 2007b).

Although the models presented in this section vary in organization and interpretation, they share several features. First, they provide descriptive information about the client. Second, they provide a structure in which client information is broken down into separate components and then combined into a narrative summary. Third, most of the models base their conceptualizations about causal explanations on a particular theoretical orientation.

The process of conceptualizing a case based on Beck's cognitive theory (Beck, 1976; Beck et al., 1979) for a client with depressive symptoms was introduced earlier in this chapter. In such a case, the clinical mental health counselor would apply cognitive theory by examining the client's automatic thoughts and schemata to determine how they account for the depressive symptoms and accompanying problems (Persons, 2008). To further apply Persons' cognitive-behavioral model outlined in Table 7.1 in general terms, (a) the problem list would include the client's presenting problem of depression; (b) the mechanism hypothesis is the client's underlying core beliefs that cause the depression; (c) the precipitants are the activating events that brought the client into counseling; (d) the origins of the mechanism (i.e., core beliefs) include incidents the client can recall that support the unhelpful schemata; and (e) the case formulation would follow based on the collected information and hypotheses.

The remainder of this chapter, as well as the case study of Gail, explores these concepts more specifically. Because most case conceptualization models base their causal explanations on a particular theoretical orientation, the case study later in the chapter illustrates how a counselor's cognitive theoretical orientation (Beck, 1976) fits into an

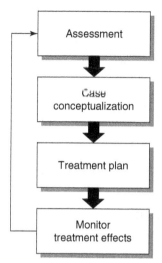

FIGURE 7.1 The relationship among assessment, case conceptualization, and treatment.

atheoretical method for developing a case conceptualization. The five components out-lined in Persons' cognitive-behavioral model (1989; 2008) of case conceptualization are embedded in the details of the case study.

FEEDBACK LOOP

Case conceptualization begins with the assessment. Based on the client data gathered during the assessment process, the clinical mental health counselor can conceptualize the client's presenting problem(s). The counselor then uses the conceptualization to help develop a treatment plan. As treatment progresses, data are collected to monitor the prog-ress of therapy, and treatment is adjusted as needed. All this happens in the context of a collaborative therapeutic relationship (Persons, 2008). Not only is a collaborative thera-peutic relationship essential for effective counseling, but also clinical mental health coun-selors are ethically obligated to work collaboratively with clients on developing their goals and counseling plans (AMHCA, 2010). Assessment, conceptualization, treatment, and treatment monitoring are considered both sequential and as part of a feedback loop (Meier, 1999; Persons, Davidson, & Tompkins, 2001) (see Figure 7.1).

It's important to note that many view the assessment process and conceptualization as closely intertwined (Meier, 1999, 2003). This is due to the fact that case conceptualiza-tion may serve as a guide to the selection of assessment devices for progress monitoring and outcome evaluation (Eells, 2007b).

STEPS IN CASE CONCEPTUALIZATION

This section describes a practical, atheoretical method for developing a case conceptual-ization. It is based on a review of case conceptualization from several different models and theoretical perspectives (Eells, 2007a; Kendjelic & Eells, 2007; Kuyken et al., 2009; Messer & Wolitzky, 2007; Persons, 2008; Sperry, 2010; Wolpe & Turkat, 1985). The goal of this conceptualization approach is to present a comprehensive description of the individual seeking treatment and a concise explanation of the causal factors associated with the individual's presenting problems. We've identified six key questions for clinical mental health counselors to address when conducting a case conceptualization:

1. What are the client's problems?
2. What is the DSM diagnosis?
3. What events or situations precipitated the problems?
4. Why are the problems occurring?
5. What are the client's strengths?
6. What is your overall conceptualization about the client's problem?

What Are the Client's Problems?

Identifying the client's problems is the first step in the case conceptualization process. This is a list of the client's difficulties, including problems that may be apparent to the counselor, but not to the client (Eells, Kendjelic, & Lucas, 1998). The list should be kept to a manageable length, with about five to eight different problems stated in simple, descriptive terms. Items on the problem list come from the following domains: psychiatric symptoms (i.e., DSM diagnosis), family/social, employment/school, medical, financial, housing, and legal (Persons, 2008).

The problem list is more than a list of the client's DSM disorders. It is a place to begin to describe problems in a way that helps the clinical mental health counselor develop a theory-based conceptualization of the case (Persons, 2008). For example, a counselor using a CBT framework would describe problems using cognitive, emotional, and behavioral terms. Thus, instead of placing major depression on the problem list, the clinical mental health counselor would list some key cognitive, emotional, and behavioral aspects of the client's depression.

Ideally, the clinical mental health counselor and the client agree on the problem list. However, complete agreement is not always possible. Common areas of disagreement include substance abuse, suicidality, and self-harm (Persons, 2008). If a client does not agree with the clinical mental health counselor about a particular problem, the counselor still includes the problem on the list, but notes the counselor–client disagreement about the problem.

After identifying the client's presenting problems, the clinical mental health counselor and the client can consider the order in which to address them (Kuyken et al., 2009). Problems can be prioritized in several ways. Typically, problems that may be a threat to the life and well-being of the client are a top-priority treatment goal. For example, suicidal behavior and self-harm are top priorities because of the potential of death and injury to the client. Problems that undermine treatment or prevent treatment from occurring are also placed high on the list (Linehan, 1993). For example, extreme agoraphobia can prevent the client from traveling to the counseling sessions. Similarly, homelessness, unemployment, significant substance abuse, criminal behavior, and living with an abusive partner can undermine therapy or prevent a client from attending therapy sessions. Until these problems are solved, the client is not likely to be able to solve other problems. Decisions about prioritizing can also be based on problems that the client most wants solved, interfere most with functioning, or are most easily solved.

What Is the DSM Diagnosis?

Although some researchers believe a diagnosis is not a necessary component of the case conceptualization, a diagnosis can provide helpful information for the conceptualization in several ways. First, a diagnosis helps inform the case conceptualization by providing information for the list of problems. Second, it provides a link to effective treatment, because most ESTs are organized by diagnosis. Furthermore, a diagnosis helps clinical mental health counselors develop some immediate conceptualization hypotheses about the client (Persons, 2008; Persons & Tompkins, 2007).

What Events or Situations Precipitated the Problems?

Precipitating events or situations, commonly known as *triggers,* are external events or situations that contribute to the onset of the person's current problems or symptoms or have increased their severity. These events may either directly lead to the current problems or worsen the preexisting problems to a level of clinical significance. Most theories account for precipitating events associated with presenting problems. Examples of precipitating factors include a recent divorce or relationship breakup, physical injury, illness, loss of social support, trauma, and/or occupational setback.

To obtain information about precipitating factors, the counselor can ask the client about major life events that immediately preceded the presenting problems. If the client has difficulty identifying situations or events, the clinical mental health counselor can find out about other situations when the client felt or behaved similarly by asking, "Can you think of another time when you felt this way?" or "What were you doing or saying when you had this feeling?" (Persons & Tompkins, 1997, p. 324).

Why Are the Problems Occurring?

This question offers the clinical mental health counselor's hypothesis or explanation of the client's current difficulties. It addresses the factors that caused and/or maintain the client's problems. *Causal factors* or mechanisms are events in the past or other situations that increase the client's vulnerability to experiencing and/or maintaining the current problems (Sperry, 2010). Some authors identify them as *predisposing factors,* which are "any element that makes one person more likely to respond in a particular way to a life circumstance" (Kuyken et al., 2009). Research indicates that a combination of certain environmental (e.g., early abuse, trauma) and genetic or biological factors predisposes people to mental health problems (Rutter, 2005; Rutter, Silberg, O'Connor, & Simonoff, 1999).

Depending on the clinical mental health counselor's theoretical orientation, these causal factors may be expressed as a core or central conflict, a set of dysfunctional thoughts or beliefs, biological predispositions, problematic interpersonal relationship patterns, contingencies of reinforcement, or systemic problems among family members (Kendjelic & Eells, 2007). More specifically, a clinician from a cognitive theory perspective would view a client's problems as the result of the activation of *schemata* (i.e., deep cognitive structures or core beliefs) by stressful life events (Beck, 1976; Beck et al., 1979). Thus, an individual with depressive symptoms might have the schema, "I am worthless unless I'm successful at everything," which remains inactive until a stressful life event (such as being passed over for promotion) triggers or activates the schema. This would result in automatic thoughts, behaviors, and unpleasant emotions that account for symptoms of depression.

Part of case conceptualization from a cognitive framework involves identifying and understanding the origins of the schema, because schemata are learned from early experiences, especially early experiences with significant others. For example, a child who is regularly criticized by a verbally abusive parent may develop schemata of worthlessness or failure, thus leading to later depressive disorders (Persons, 2008).

Behavior theories propose that an individual's behaviors are controlled by their antecedents and/or their consequences. *Antecedents* are events that occur before a behavior or a set of behaviors, and *consequences* are events that follow the behavior or behaviors. Antecedents, behaviors, and consequences can be internal (e.g., thoughts, emotions) or external (e.g., physical). A clinician using behavior theory could conceptualize depressive symptoms as occurring when an individual experiences life events or stressors (antecedent) that cause him or her to lose the ability to obtain positive reinforcers (consequences) (Lewinsohn, 1974; Lewinsohn & Gotlib, 1995). Thus, a depressed individual who was laid off from work (antecedent) might spend more time alone (e.g., staying home and watching television), complain to others, and become self-preoccupied. The continued complaining and preoccupation (behaviors) could contribute to others' rejection of the depressed individual, which would result in a decrease of positive reinforcers (consequences). This negative response by others would further add to the client's depression (Leahy & Holland, 2000).

Psychodynamic case conceptualization focuses on ego functions, drive and defenses, object-related functions, and self-related functions (Messer & Wolitzky, 2007). For example, a conceptualization about an individual with interpersonal relationship difficulties could attend to the person's basic modes of relating to others, such as automatically acquiescing to the partner's demands. In this example, the individual's view of others is that they make demands to fill their own needs but not the needs of others, which was based on the individual's experience of being emotionally abused as a child by a controlling, demanding father. Thus, in relationships with others, the person feels compelled to automatically fulfill others' needs and not ask for his or her own needs to be met.

It is important here to also consider potential multicultural or socioeconomic factors that may be influencing or exacerbating the client's situation. For many clients, societal or institutional discrimination will play a central part in their presenting problems. Many clients may be experiencing unjust circumstances that are out of their personal control. When clinical mental health counselors actively try to comprehend the social and cultural forces affecting clients, they increase their ability to provide ethical and effective treatment. In cases of social injustice, clinical mental health counselors may include advocacy and social justice interventions as part of treatment planning. The ACA Code of Ethics (2005) states, "When appropriate, counselors advocate at individual, group, institutional, and societal levels to examine potential barriers and obstacles that inhibit access and/or the growth and development of clients" (p. 5). Thus, multicultural issues are a critical component of case conceptualization.

In summary, identifying causal factors helps answer "why" a client is having particular problems and symptoms. Ideally, identification of the causal factors helps to organize and guide the choice of treatment interventions. Clinical mental health counselors may identify more than one causal mechanism to account for the client's symptoms or use two different mechanisms at different points in treatment (Persons, 2008). Clinical mental health counselors typically strive to use as few causal factors (if not just one) as possible to keep the conceptualization simple and easy to use in guiding treatment planning. The decision on the number of causal factors to use depends on treatment utility; that is, whether the use of multiple causal mechanisms leads to effective treatment.

What Are the Client's Strengths?

The client's strengths, also called *protective factors*, prevent problems either from developing or from getting worse. This is another area in which it is helpful to consider clients' cultural characteristics, because numerous strengths may exist in their culture that can be drawn upon. Such protective factors promote strength and resilience in clients. For example, for many mental health problems, social support is a protective factor; the greater the support, the lesser the severity of the problems. Social support impacts mental health problems in many ways. It reduces isolation, lessens feelings of stigmatization, and exposes clients to corrective information. Many case conceptualization approaches focus almost exclusively on a client's problems, vulnerabilities, and factors that maintain symptoms. According to Kuyken, Dudley, and Sperry's model of conceptualization (2008), a strengths-focused approach helps harness client resilience in the change process as a way to progress toward lasting recovery. Examples of client strengths include positive social supports, positive behavior patterns, a resilient attitude, a satisfying job, and a positive living situation.

What Is Your Overall Conceptualization About the Client's Problem?

This question ties together each of the previous elements of the case conceptualization. The clinical mental health counselor synthesizes information to create a summary explanation about the client's problems, precipitating factors, causal factors, and strengths. This summary describes the relationships among symptoms, problems, and causal factors. Problems can be related in many ways, and multiple problems can be explained by the same causal factor (Persons, 2008). For example, an individual's schema of being useless if unable to be perfect at work (a cognitive theory mechanism) can lead to anxiety, avoidance behaviors, and procrastination.

This overall conceptualization can be written in paragraph format. Although the case conceptualization attempts to link all the problems and causal factors together, extensive narratives may be too long and complex to be clinically helpful. Thus, clinical mental health counselors need to strive to keep conceptualizations simple and brief.

IDENTIFYING SOURCES OF INFORMATION TO FURTHER UNDERSTANDING OF CLIENT'S ISSUES

Case conceptualization begins with assessment. The purpose of assessment is not only to identify clients' presenting problems but also to understand their concerns within the larger context of the person's current life, as well as to guide treatment planning. Clinical mental health counselors use multiple assessment methods, such as the clinical interview, self-report inventories, and observations, as well as multiple sources of information, including the client's family members and other mental health or medical professionals.

A good general strategy to assessment is the "funnel" approach, in which the counselor begins with a broad-based assessment of all the important domains to determine which areas require more detailed assessment (Mash & Hunsley, 1990). A fairly comprehensive clinical interview can provide much of the information needed in understanding the broader context of clients' issues. Assessment areas in the clinical interview are highlighted in Table 7.2.

TABLE 7.2 Assessment Areas in the Clinical Interview

Identifying Information	• Name, address, phone number, age, gender, date of birth, workplace, relationship status, and referral source
Presenting Problem	• The client's primary problems or symptoms • Onset and course of the problems • Degree of interference with functioning • Precipitating events or situations
Current Life Situation	• Current living situation • Relationship with partner • Work, school • Leisure/relaxation • Social support system • Financial resources/difficulties • Spiritual or religious issues
Social History	• Relationship history, children, social support • Family history (parents, siblings, extended family) • Cultural backgrounds: race/ethnicity, sexual orientation, religion/spirituality, socioeconomic status • School and education • Work history • Major life events or trauma • Past psychological difficulties (including substance abuse)
Developmental History	• Significant developmental events that may influence current problems or circumstances • Current self-view, level of self-esteem, personality style
Medical History	• Previous and current medical conditions or disabilities • Hospitalizations • Medications
Psychiatric History	• Treatment for previous psychological difficulties • Hospitalizations • Previous suicide attempts; suicidal or homicidal thoughts • Psychotropic medications
Mental Status	• Affect, mood, thought content, insight, judgment, speech, attention, concentration, and impulse control

Broadband measures, such as the Symptom Checklist-90-Revised (SCL-90-R®; Derogatis, 2000) and the Brief Symptom Inventory (BSI®; Derogatis, 1993), can be used as a screen to identify specific symptoms or problems for further assessment (Persons, 2008). More narrow-band instruments can then be administered to evaluate specific symptoms. Examples include the following: the Beck Depression Inventory®-II (BDI®-II; Beck, Steer, & Brown, 1996), Beck Hopelessness Scale® (BHS®; Beck & Steer, 1993), Clark-Beck Obsessive-Compulsive Inventory (CBOCI; Clark & Beck, 2002), Hamilton Anxiety Rating Scale (HAM-A; Hamilton, 1959), and Posttraumatic Stress Diagnostic Scale (PDS®; Foa, 1995), to name just a few.

CASE STUDY 7.1

This case study is provided to demonstrate the application of case conceptualization. Client information was collected through the assessment process, which included information from the clinical interview, the Brief Symptom Inventory (BSI), and the Beck Depression Inventory-II (BDI-II).

The client, Gail, was self-referred to individual outpatient counseling. Gail is a 57-year-old divorced White female. For the last three years, she has lived with her adult daughter (who moved in with Gail due to the daughter's being on disability for fibromyalgia and chronic pain) as well as her two teenage granddaughters.

Before her daughter moved in, Gail worked as a church organist, playing for church services on Sunday mornings and for choir practice on Tuesday evenings. She also taught private piano lessons in her home. She reportedly had enjoyed her work, stating that music was always a large part of her life. Gail is currently not working, stating that she has stopped working as both a church organist and a piano teacher to care for her daughter and grandchildren. She maintains that she "doesn't have to work" because she and her daughter live off of Gail's alimony check (from her divorce) and her daughter's disability income. Since living with her daughter, Gail has tended to stay home and isolate herself from others because she is too tired to do anything; "I can't handle working or socializing with everything I have to do at home."

Gail divorced her husband 10 years ago, reportedly due to his anger problems and feeling "controlled" by him. She describes herself as having been the "giver" in the marriage, stating her belief that "women compromise 90% of the time" in a relationship. Gail states that after 25 years of marriage, she'd had enough and wanted to be able to do whatever she wanted, without getting permission or having to please someone else.

Gail is the oldest of five children. Her parents divorced when she was five years old, and they decided that Gail would live with her father, while her younger sister would live with her mother. Gail does not know the reason for this decision. Her father remarried and had three sons. In her family, Gail was required to help raise her three half brothers. She describes her stepmother as an "angry, controlling" woman who "slapped me in the mouth if I said anything she didn't like." Gail reports that she learned to not express her feelings to avoid arguments or confrontations.

Gail was diagnosed with type 2 diabetes one year ago. She appears extremely overweight, and she admits to not eating in a healthy manner or exercising regularly. She reportedly has not tried to lose weight and has, in fact, gained about 20 pounds over the last six months.

Gail sought counseling when she found herself feeling overwhelmed by caring for her daughter and parenting her grandchildren. She reportedly feels tired all the time, sleeps too much, and feels hopeless that her life will ever change. Gail admits feeling very frustrated and angry about her life circumstances and, at times, directs her anger toward her daughter and grandchildren. She wishes her daughter would be more active in trying to get better—her daughter reportedly takes pain medication and sleeps frequently to cope with the pain. Gail feels overwhelmed by being responsible for taking care of her home, daughter, and grandchildren, stating, "It's just too much for one person to do. I can't do everything." When asked about how she copes, she states she has tried to ignore problems and "keep the peace" in her home.

Gail feels guilty about her anger toward her daughter, stating that she needs to be patient, understanding, and giving. From her past experiences in her family of origin and her marriage, Gail feels that she has to put others' needs before her own. She wants to be able to accept her current life situation without feeling depressed and overwhelmed.

CASE CONCEPTUALIZATION

The following case conceptualization of Gail from Case Study 7.1 was based on Beck's cognitive theory, which views problems and symptoms as consisting of linked thoughts, behaviors, and emotions that result from schemata (i.e., core beliefs) that are activated by stressful life events (Beck, 1976; Beck et al., 1979).

WHAT ARE THE CLIENT'S PROBLEMS?

1. **Depressive symptoms:** Gail's score on the BDI was 32, indicating moderate depression. She specifically reported feeling sadness, guilt, and hopelessness. She also was fatigued, slept too much, had significant weight gain, and stopped engaging in activities she used to find enjoyable (e.g., going to church, playing the piano). She disclosed such thoughts as "I will never get my life back" and "there is nothing I can do to change things."

2. ***Anger/frustration:*** Gail scored in the clinical range on the BSI Hostility subscale, which reflects feeling easily annoyed or irritated, having temper outbursts, and getting into frequent arguments. Gail disclosed feeling very frustrated by her current life circumstances, and at times feeling angry and "snapping" at her daughter and grandchildren. She has difficulty coping with her situation, using avoidance and prayer as her primary coping strategies. Gail felt guilty about her anger, stating that she needed to be patient, understanding, and giving.

3. ***No enjoyable work:*** Gail stopped working when her adult daughter and grandchildren moved in with her.

4. ***Medical:*** Gail is clinically obese and has been diagnosed with type 2 diabetes. She was taking prescribed medication for the condition, but she admitted to not eating healthy foods and not exercising regularly to help control her diabetes.

WHAT IS THE DSM DIAGNOSIS?

Axis I	Major depression, moderate
Axis II	No diagnosis
Axis III	Type 2 Diabetes
Axis IV	Inadequate social support
Axis V	55

WHAT EVENTS OR SITUATIONS PRECIPITATED THE PROBLEMS? Disabled adult daughter and grandchildren moving into the home, and Gail taking on a caregiving role.

WHY ARE THE PROBLEMS OCCURRING? The stressful role of caregiving activated a schema of "putting others' needs before her own," which has resulted in depressive symptoms and anger/frustration. Medical condition may also contribute to depressive symptoms.

WHAT ARE THE CLIENT'S STRENGTHS? Musician; previous work experience in teaching piano and being a church organist; strong spiritual faith.

WHAT IS YOUR OVERALL CONCEPTUALIZATION ABOUT THE CLIENT'S PROBLEM? Gail's depressive symptoms resulted when a schema ("I'm unworthy unless I put others' needs before my own") was activated by her daughter and grandchildren moving into her home. The activated schema caused automatic negative thoughts ("I will never get my life back" and "there is nothing I can do to change things"), negative behaviors (avoidance), and negative emotions (anger, resentment). The schema originated during Gail's childhood when she was required to care for her younger brothers, and was maintained during her marriage in which she felt she had to compromise with her husband most of the time. Gail's depressive symptoms may also be associated with her current medical condition, type 2 diabetes.

USING CLIENT CONCEPTUALIZATION TO FORMULATE AN INDIVIDUALIZED TREATMENT PLAN

The treatment plan flows out of the conceptualization of the case. A *treatment plan* can be defined as a process of developing a plan for the progression of counseling. It is a blueprint for the clinical mental health counselor and the client to map how the client's presenting concerns will be addressed and what the likely outcome will be (e.g., decreased depressive symptoms, increased coping skills) (Seligman, 1993). In other words, a treatment plan helps the clinical mental health counselor and the client know where to begin, where they want to go, and the path for getting there.

Treatment plans address the problems identified from assessment and case conceptualization. They are *individualized*, made to "fit" the client based on his or her unique needs, abilities, goals, lifestyle, socioeconomic realities, work history, educational background, and culture (Stilen, Carise, Roget, & Wendler, 2007). Treatment plans include a comprehensive set of tools and strategies that address the client's problems and symptoms, as well as identifiable strengths.

The treatment planning process is cooperative, in which the clinical mental health counselor, client, and other professionals (if relevant) develop a written document that identifies important treatment goals and describes measurable, time-sensitive steps toward achieving those goals. Clients benefit from the treatment plan in that they are aware of what therapy is trying to accomplish. They can channel their efforts into specific changes that help them reach the identified goals and objectives (Jongsma, 2005). Clinical mental health counselors benefit from treatment plans because the plans compel them to think analytically and critically about the treatment interventions they select for the client. Treatment plans also provide practitioners with clear documentation of treatment that becomes part of the client's permanent record.

Treatment plans are developed at the beginning of therapy. Often, a preliminary treatment plan is initially written, followed by a comprehensive treatment plan shortly thereafter. Although developed at the outset of counseling, the treatment plan is continually updated and revised throughout treatment.

VOICE FROM THE FIELD 7.1

My new client, Charlotte, was a 17-year-old girl who was entering counseling for a second time. Her first counseling experience was about 10 years prior, shortly after she was sexually abused by a stranger who broke into her family's home. During her earlier counseling, she also disclosed that she had been sexually abused over the course of two years by a family friend who would occasionally babysit her. Charlotte was asked what she remembered about her earlier counseling experience. She said she had liked her counselor, but since she was doing OK she had stopped sessions after about two months. Now as an adolescent, Charlotte was anything but "OK." Over the last four months, she found herself having nightmares nearly every night, feeling afraid to be alone and easily startled, and was reliving the abuse through vivid flashbacks. Charlotte fit the criteria for posttraumatic stress disorder and desperately wanted the flashbacks, nightmares, and constant feeling of fear to end.

Over several weeks of getting to know Charlotte, it was clear that her guard was up and her trust would not be quickly or easily earned. She wanted the closeness of a relationship, but she was afraid of being vulnerable and letting someone close. Although she had a host of acquaintances, she did not have a single friend. The closest Charlotte would get to anyone was in sexual encounters with partners whom she hardly knew. Several of the situations she described sounded high risk for further victimization. Charlotte also shared that she felt isolated from her parents and resented them for sweeping her abuse under the rug as if it had never happened. Although Charlotte was facing challenges, she entered counseling highly motivated. She also was doing quite well in school and managing a part-time job in an art studio, which was a perfect fit given her natural artist talent.

As Charlotte's clinical mental health counselor, I hypothesized that she had not been able to fully process her childhood traumatic events. I also thought that the emergence of flashbacks and nightmares could be connected to Charlotte's recent sexual experiences. Through the lens of narrative therapy, I knew that Charlotte needed to share her story and process it in a safe, caring environment.

My first challenge would be to establish a strong therapeutic relationship, which I knew could not be rushed. Additionally, I planned to provide psychoeducation about sexual abuse with the goal of helping her realize that she is not alone. I also wanted for her to learn coping skills such as relaxation, guided imagery, and grounding techniques before exploring her trauma. After establishing the counseling relationship, providing psychoeducation, and establishing coping skills, I planned to use expressive arts and a trauma narrative intervention to allow her to tell her story. Although the journey was long and at times difficult, Charlotte was able to process the way her sexual abuse had impacted her world through the various interventions and move toward hope and healing.

JEN FOSTER, PhD, LMHC
Assistant Professor, Western Michigan University

VOICE FROM THE FIELD 7.2

As a former school counselor, a licensed professional counselor, and a current counselor educator, I am often offered wonderful opportunities to work with young clients, teenagers predominantly, that are having difficulties in home and at school. I have found that many colleagues are reluctant to work with teens or, at the very least, find them quite challenging. I have found that if you work with them in a creative, engaging way, they are a real treat in counseling.

When I first met C. J., he was in the midst of his sophomore year in high school, fighting frequently with his parents, specifically his mother, and suffering from school failure. He had recently been discharged from inpatient treatment where he was officially diagnosed with oppositional defiant disorder and attention deficit disorder. He was, however, a willing participant in our outpatient work together, and he responded well to two specific approaches to our work.

I favor active, directive therapy with teens, and my approach is always theory driven. So, in C. J.'s case, I chose to use a combination of reality therapy and transactional analysis (TA), a theory that is often overlooked in the treatment of adolescents. Reality therapy was worthwhile because it helped C. J. understand and take responsibility for the parts of his behavior that were under his control. A treatment plan that included reality therapy exercises and interventions helped C. J. to quickly see that his behavior was directly contributing to his failure to get what he wanted from his parents. Incorporating TA was an effective means for assisting C. J. in understanding how he often communicated with his parents from his "child" ego state. I like to use visual representations in counseling to help explain therapeutic concepts; therefore, I used a small child's chair to represent how C. J. often approached his parents from a "child's seat." This helped C. J. to understand that if he wanted a more positive response from his parents, it would be in his best interest to approach them from his "adult" ego state, or what I often refer to as "your 15-year-old thinking seat."

C. J. responded very well to my approach. If I were to give one piece of advice to new clinical mental health counselors with regard to working with adolescents and younger clients, it would be to always use multisensory techniques to make your work with them interesting and engaging. In my interactions with C. J., it would have been easy for him to see me as an extension of his parents and therefore be resistant to working with me. However, when I was quick to engage in writing exercises and using chairs with him, he was interested and worked hard in our sessions.

CHRISTINE J. SCHIMMEL, EdD, LPC, NCC
School Counseling Program Coordinator, West Virginia University

VOICE FROM THE FIELD 7.3

T. J. was a 27-year-old male who worked as a resident physician in a nearby hospital. His presenting problems stemmed from sustained grief over the breakup of a love relationship. He reported difficulty focusing at work and had started having panic attacks. His problems were compounded by the fact that his ex-girlfriend was a resident at the same hospital. When I saw him, he was having so much difficulty that he had decided to take a month off from work.

From my cognitive-behavioral theoretical standpoint, I conceptualized that T. J.'s problems stemmed in part from normal grieving but were compounded by persistent negative thoughts and the panic attacks. His negative thoughts included such ideas as the following: "I'll never meet someone as good as my ex; I can't stand being alone; I don't know anyone in this town—my ex was the social one and I am bad at making friends. Because I panicked at the hospital, it means I should not be a doctor. Because I couldn't focus, it means I'm losing all that I learned about medicine." Based on my case conceptualization, I believed that T. J. needed to resolve his initial fears and self-doubt. Thus, his treatment plan objectives included providing counseling two times per week, daily telephone check-ins, addressing his irrational beliefs, and educating him on grief, anxiety, and panic attacks. I also emphasized his need to get support from his friends and family, which he did.

T. J.'s strengths included his intelligence and high level of motivation to work on his presenting issues. In addition, T. J. was willing to read, was open to the counseling process, and had strong support from his mother and friends. He responded well to the basic tenet of rational emotive behavior therapy (REBT)—that thoughts cause feelings—and was receptive to challenging his irrational beliefs based on the following: techniques from the REBT literature, impact therapy techniques of writing down his "true" and "not true" thoughts on a whiteboard (Jacobs, 1994), assigned reading homework, talking through the positive and negative aspects of the relationship, and exploring ideas for the future.

T. J. did improve, went back to work, and is now in a new relationship. I think the therapeutic gains can be attributed to the combination of providing a very supportive counseling relationship where he was allowed to grieve and the use of REBT.

ED JACOBS, PHD
Director of Impact Therapy Associates; Coordinator of Master's Program,
West Virginia University

STRUCTURING OBJECTIVE, MEASURABLE TREATMENT PLANS

In general, treatment planning involves individualizing the selection and application of treatment resources to the client's needs. The key to writing effective treatment plans is in using specificity and measurability. Treatment plans must be sufficiently specific so that the clinical mental health counselor and client know what they must do to progress in counseling, and that client progress can be monitored and evaluated. Treatment plans include the following four components: problems, goals, objectives, and interventions.

Problem statements describe specific, observable, and/or measurable client behaviors or circumstances that were identified during assessment and case conceptualization. When developing a treatment plan, clinical mental health counselors first list all the problems. Counselors then prioritize the problem list, understanding that all of the client's problems may not get addressed during the specific treatment period.

Goal statements are global descriptions of what the final outcome will look like (Jongsma, 2005). After identifying the problems that will be addressed in treatment, the clinical mental health counselor and client prepare a goal statement for each of the problem statements. Good treatment goals focus on reducing symptoms and problems, on increasing desired behaviors or outcomes, and on being realistic. Goal statements are written in a manner that is understandable and agreed upon by the client, and their goals are reasonably achievable during the time that the client is in therapy.

Objectives are statements of what the client will do to meet the goals. They can be thought of as a series of steps that, when completed, will result in the achievement of the broader treatment goal (Jongsma, 2005). Typically, there are at least one or two objectives for each goal, but clinical mental health counselors may develop as many as are necessary to achieve the goal. *Interventions* are based on the objectives and are statements of what the counselor will do to assist the client in meeting the goals. These include the theory-based interventions and strategies that counselors employ to help the client complete the objectives. To develop effective objectives and interventions for the treatment plan, counselors may use the M.A.T.R.S. model (Stilen et al., 2007), which is an acronym for the following:

- **M—Measurable.** Objectives and interventions are written in *measurable* terms in order to document change in the client as well as hold the clinical mental health counselor and treatment program accountable. Examples of measurable objectives and interventions in the treatment plan are (a) changes in rating scale scores (e.g., Beck's Depression Scale score drops two points), (b) mental status or behavioral changes (e.g., days of medical problems, number of emergency room visits), and (c) type and frequency of services received (e.g., attend five individual counseling sessions, attend 10 group counseling sessions) (Stilen et al., 2007).
- **A—Attainable.** *Attainable* refers to identifying objectives and interventions that are achievable in the treatment period. Clinical mental health counselors focus on "improved functioning" rather than the "end" or the "cure" of the client's problem ("Treatment Planning—Part 2," 2006, p. 3). For example, an attainable objective might be "fill out job application" rather than "obtain a full-time job."
- **T—Time-limited.** This emphasizes the specific, *time-limited* nature of objectives and interventions. Clinical mental health counselors select objectives and interventions that can be achieved within a specified time period. Completion dates must be realistic to the client, or else the chances of treatment compliance are greatly reduced.
- **R—Realistic.** Clinical mental health counselors set *realistic* expectations for treatment objectives and interventions that are practical and attainable. Thus, the client must have the ability to accomplish objectives and interventions given (a) the client environment, supports, diagnosis, and level of functioning; and (b) the time period of treatment services.
- **S—Specific.** Objectives and interventions are *specific* and stated in behavioral terms, targeting particular symptoms and behaviors that are relevant to the client's presenting problems (e.g., intensity of depressed mood, frequency of night awakenings). This allows both the client and the clinical mental health counselor to monitor progress, allowing both client and counselor to note progress (or lack of progress).

CASE STUDY 7.2

The following case is provided to demonstrate the application of a treatment plan. The treatment plan is based on the previous case study of Gail.

PROBLEM STATEMENT

Gail is experiencing depressive symptoms and anger/frustration associated with her current living situation with her adult daughter with disabilities and two grandchildren.

GOALS

Gail's symptoms of depression will be significantly reduced as measured by a BDI score of less than 13.

OBJECTIVES

1. Gail will learn to identify automatic negative thoughts and how to replace them with more positive, adaptive thoughts, as measured by completion of two homework assignments.
2. Gail will learn effective coping strategies to deal with anger and frustration. This will be measured by her demonstrating these skills in session and by completing homework assignments for two consecutive weeks.
3. Gail will become involved in at least one additional extracurricular activity.
4. Gail will obtain a medical evaluation of her type 2 diabetes by the fourth session.

INTERVENTIONS

1. Counselor will educate Gail about automatic thoughts, feelings, and behaviors in depression, and how to identify and replace negative thoughts with adaptive, positive thoughts.
2. Counselor will teach Gail about effective coping skills to deal with her current life stressors.
3. Counselor will assist Gail in identifying one extracurricular activity and discuss her comfort level in participating in an activity.
4. Counselor will encourage Gail to make an appointment with her medical doctor regarding her diabetes.

Conclusion

Case conceptualization provides the foundation for effective counseling. In general, conceptualization involves describing clients' presenting problems, organizing the problems, generating hypotheses about the causes of the problems, and creating a framework to guide treatment. Utilizing a case conceptualization approach helps clinical mental health counselors to identify treatment goals, counseling interventions, and potential obstacles to success (Levenson & Strupp, 1997). When clinical mental health counselors conceptualize their clients in context, they take into consideration important cultural and social factors that otherwise may be overlooked. Thus, in addition to developing a road map for effective treatment, case conceptualization also helps guide ethical practice.

This chapter introduced the basic principles, models, and formats of case conceptualization and illustrated how this leads to effective treatment planning. In learning about case conceptualization, it becomes clear that multicultural issues significantly affect clients' lives and their course of treatment. The ACA and AMHCA codes of ethics both address the importance of conceptualizing clients in the context of their lives, circumstances, culture, and a diverse society. When clinical mental health counselors take the time to develop and improve their case conceptualization skills, it helps them and their clients in developing meaningful and effective mental health care.

References

American Counseling Association (ACA). (2005). *Code of ethics*. Alexandria, VA: Author.

American Mental Health Counselors Association (AMHCA). (2010). *2010 AMHCA code of ethics*. Retrieved from https://www.amhca.org/assets/news /AMHCA_Code_of_Ethics_2010_w_pagination _cxd_51110.pdf

American Psychiatric Association. (2000). *Diagnostic and statistical manual of mental disorders, fourth edition– text revision* (DSM-IV-TR). Washington, DC: Author.

Beck, A. T. (1976). *Cognitive therapy and the emotional disorders.* New York, NY: International Universities Press.

Beck, A. T., Rush, J. A., Shaw, B. F., & Emery, G. (1979). *Cognitive therapy for depression.* New York, NY: Guilford Press.

Beck, A. T., & Steer, R. (1993). *Manual for the Beck Hopelessness Scale.* San Antonio, TX: Pearson.

Beck, A. T., Steer, R., & Brown, G. K. (1996). *Manual for the Beck Depression Inventory-II.* San Antonio, TX: Pearson.

Bordin, E. (1979). The generalizability of the psychoanalytic concept of the working alliance. *Psychotherapy: Theory, Research, and Practice, 16,* 252–260.

Clark, D. M. (2001). A cognitive perspective on social phobia. In W. R. Crozier & L. E. Alden (Eds.), *International handbook of social anxiety: Concepts, research and interventions relating to the self* (pp. 405–430). Chichester, UK: Wiley.

Clark, D., & Beck, A. T. (2002). *Manual for the Clark-Beck Obsessive-Compulsive Inventory.* San Antonio, TX: Pearson.

Council for Accreditation of Counseling and Related Educational Programs (CACREP). (2009). *CACREP accreditation manual: 2009 standards.* Alexandria, VA: Author. Retrieved from http://www.cacrep.org/doc/2009%20Standards%20with%20cover.pdf

Derogatis, L. R. (1993). *The Brief Symptom Inventory (BSI): Administration, scoring and procedures manual* (3rd ed.). Minneapolis, MN: National Computer Systems.

Derogatis, L. R. (2000). *The Brief Symptom Inventory–18 (BSI-18): Administration, scoring and procedures manual.* Minneapolis, MN: National Computer Systems.

Eells, T. D. (2007a). Comparing the methods: Where is the common ground? In T. D. Eells (Ed.), *Handbook of psychotherapy case formulation* (2nd ed., pp. 412–432). New York, NY: Guilford Press.

Eells, T. D. (2007b). History and current status of psychotherapy case formulation. In T. D. Eells, (Ed.), *Handbook of psychotherapy case formulation* (2nd ed., pp. 3–32). New York, NY: Guilford Press.

Eells, T. D., Kendjelic, E. M., & Lucas, C. P. (1998). What's in a case formulation? Development and use of a content coding manual. *The Journal of Psychotherapy Practice and Research, 7*(2), 144–153.

Foa, E. B. (1995). *Manual for the Posttraumatic Stress Diagnostic Scale.* Minneapolis, MN: Pearson.

Frank, J. D., & Frank, J. B. (1991). *Persuasion and healing: A comparative study of psychotherapy* (3rd ed.). Baltimore, MD: John Hopkins University Press.

Hamilton, M. (1959). The assessment of anxiety states by rating. *British Journal of Medical Psychology, 32,* 50–55.

Ingram, B. L. (2006). *Clinical case formulations: Matching the integrative treatment plan to the client.* Hoboken, NJ: Wiley.

Jacobs, E. E. (1994). *Impact therapy.* Odessa, FL: Psychological Assessment Resources.

Jongsma, A. E., Jr. (2005). Psychotherapy treatment plan writing. In G. P. Koocher, J. C. Norcross, & S. S. Hill, III (Eds.), *Psychologists' desk reference* (2nd ed., pp. 232–236). New York, NY: Oxford University Press.

Jongsma, A. E., & Bruce, T. J. (2010). *Evidence-based psychotherapy treatment planning: DVD facilitator's guide.* Hoboken, NJ: Wiley.

Kendjelic, E. M., & Eells, T. D. (2007). Generic psychotherapy case formulation training improves formulation quality. *Psychotherapy: Theory, Research, Practice, Training, 44,* 67–77.

Kuyken, W., Padesky, C. A., & Dudley, R. (2008). Process issues: The science and practice of case conceptualization. *Behavioural and Cognitive Psychotherapy, 36,* 757–768.

Kuyken, W., Padesky, C. A., & Dudley, R. (2009). *Collaborative case conceptualization: Working effectively with clients in cognitive-behavioral therapy.* New York, NY: Guilford Press.

Lazare, A. (1976). The psychiatric examination in the walk-in clinic: Hypothesis generation and hypothesis testing. *Archives of General Psychiatry, 33,* 96–102.

Leahy, R. L., & Holland, S. J. (2000). *Treatment plans and interventions for depression and anxiety disorders* (Vol. 1). New York, NY: Guilford Press.

Levenson, H., & Strupp, H. H. (1997). Cyclical maladaptive patterns: Case formulation in time-limited dynamic psychotherapy. In T. D. Eells (Ed.), *Handbook of psychotherapy case formulation.* New York, NY: Guilford Press.

Lewinsohn, P. M. (1974). The behavioral study and treatment of depression. In K. Calhoun, H. E. Adams, & K. M. Mitchell (Eds.), *Innovative treatment methods in psychopathology.* New York, NY: Wiley.

Lewinsohn, P. M., & Gotlib, I. H. (1995). Behavioral theory and treatment of depression. In E. E. Beckham & W. R. Leber (Eds.), *Handbook of depression* (2nd ed., pp. 352–375). New York, NY: Guilford Press.

Linehan, M. M. (1993). *Cognitive-behavioral treatment of borderline personality disorder.* New York, NY: Guilford Press.

MacKinnon, R. A., & Yudofsky, S. C. (1991). *The psychiatric evaluation in clinical practice*. Philadelphia, PA: Lippincott.

Mash, E. J., & Hunsley, J. (1990). Behavioral assessment: A contemporary approach. In A. S. Bellack, M. Hersen, & A. E. Kazdin (Eds.), *International handbook of behavior modification and therapy* (2nd ed., pp. 87–106). New York, NY: Plenum Press.

McLaughlin, J. E. (2006). The pros and cons of viewing formal diagnosis from a social constructivist perspective. *Journal of Humanistic Counseling, Education and Development, 45,* 165–172.

Meier, S. T. (1999). Training the practitioner-scientist: Bridging case conceptualization, assessment, and intervention. *The Counseling Psychologist, 27,* 589–613.

Meier, S. T. (2003). *Bridging case conceptualization, assessment, and intervention.* Thousand Oaks, CA: Sage.

Messer, S. B., & Wolitzky, D. L. (2007). The psychoanalytic approach to case formulation. In T. D. Eells, *Handbook of psychotherapy case formulation* (2nd ed., pp. 67–104). New York, NY: Guilford Press.

Needleman, L. D. (1999). *Cognitive case conceptualization: A guidebook for practitioners.* Mahwah, NJ: Erlbaum.

Perry, S., Cooper, A. M., & Michels, R. (1987). The psychodynamic formulation: Its purpose, structure, and clinical application. *American Journal of Psychiatry, 144,* 543–550.

Persons, J. B. (1989). *Cognitive therapy in practice: A case formulation approach.* New York, NY: Norton.

Persons, J. B. (2006). Case formulation–driven psychotherapy. *Clinical Psychology: Science and Practice, 13,* 167–170.

Persons, J. B. (2008). *The case formulation approach to cognitive-behavior therapy.* New York, NY: Guilford Press.

Persons, J. B., Davidson, J., & Tompkins, M. A. (2001). *Essential components of cognitive behavior therapy for depression.* Washington, DC: American Psychological Association.

Persons, J. B., & Tompkins, M. A. (1997). Cognitive-behavioral case formulation. In T. D. Eells (Ed.), *Handbook of psychotherapy case formulation.* New York, NY: Guilford Press.

Rutter, M. (2005). How the environment affects mental health. *The British Journal of Psychiatry, 186,* 4–6.

Rutter, M., Silberg, J., O'Connor, T., & Simonoff, E. (1999). Genetics and child psychiatry: I. Advances in quantitative and molecular genetics. *Journal of Child Psychology and Psychiatry, 40,* 3–18.

Scheiber, S. C., Kramer, T. A. M., & Adamowski, S. E. (Eds.). (2003). *Core competencies for psychiatric practice: What clinicians need to know.* Arlington, VA: American Psychiatric Publishing.

Schwitzer, A. M. (1996). Using the inverted pyramid heuristic in counselor education and supervision. *Counselor Education and Supervision, 35,* 258–267.

Schwitzer, A. M. (1997). The inverted pyramid framework applying self-psychology constructs to conceptualizing college student psychotherapy. *Journal of College Student Psychotherapy, 11*(3), 29–47.

Seligman, L. (1993). Teaching treatment planning. *Counselor Education and Supervision, 32*(4), 287–297.

Silberschatz, G., Fretter, P. B., & Curtis, J. T. (1986). How do interpretations influence the process of therapy? *Journal of Consulting and Clinical Psychology, 54,* 646–652.

Sim, K., Gwee, K. P., & Bateman, A. (2005). Case formulation in psychotherapy: Revitalizing its usefulness as a clinical tool. *Academic Psychiatry, 29,* 289–292.

Sperry, L. (2010). *Highly effective therapy: Developing essential clinical competencies in counseling and psychotherapy.* New York, NY: Routledge.

Stilen, P., Carise, D., Roget, N., & Wendler, A. (2007). *Treatment planning M.A.T.R.S.: Utilizing the Addiction Severity Index (ASI) to make required data collection useful.* Kansas City, MO: Mid-America Addiction Technology Transfer Center in residence at the University of Missouri–Kansas City.

Sturmey, P. (2009). Case formulation: A review and overview of this volume. In P. Sturmey, *Clinical case formulation: Varieties of approaches* (pp. 3–30). West Sussex, UK: Wiley.

Treatment planning—part 2. (2006). *Addiction Messenger, 9*(5), 1–3.

Vertue, F. M., & Haig, B. D. (2008). An abductive perspective on clinical reasoning and case formulation. *Journal of Clinical Psychology, 64,* 1046–1068.

Weerasekera, P. (1993). Formulation: A multiperspective model. *Canadian Journal of Psychiatry, 38*(5), 351–359.

Wolpe, J., & Turkat, I. D. (1985). Behavioral formulation of clinical cases. In I. D. Turkat (Ed.), *Behavioral case formulation* (pp. 5–36). New York, NY: Plenum Press.

8

Working Within the Managed Care System

Laura R. Haddock and Ruth Ouzts Moore

CHAPTER OVERVIEW

In this chapter, we describe the process of working within a managed care system. A rising amount of behavioral health care in the United States is administered through managed care plans. This chapter examines the history of managed care in relation to mental health and explains issues relevant to providers and clients. The discussion includes an in-depth examination of types of managed care plans, concepts and terms related to managed care, and ethical concerns for practitioners and clients. Additionally, an overview of clinical mental health counselor roles when working within a managed care system will be provided including becoming a provider, documentation issues, and common challenges that counselors face.

LEARNING OBJECTIVES

The learning objectives for this chapter are designed to be consistent with the 2009 Council for Accreditation of Counseling and Related Educational Programs Standards (CACREP, 2009). As such, upon completion of this chapter, the student will have knowledge of the following clinical mental health counseling standards:

1. Understands the history, philosophy, and trends in clinical mental health counseling. (A.1)
2. Understands ethical and legal considerations specifically related to the practice of clinical mental health counseling. (A.2)
3. Is aware of professional issues that affect clinical mental health counselors (e.g., core provider status, expert witness status, access to and practice privileges within managed care systems). (A.7)
4. Applies knowledge of public mental health policy, financing, and regulatory processes to improve service delivery opportunities in clinical mental health counseling. (B.2)
5. Understands effective strategies to support client advocacy and influence public policy and government relations on local, state, and national levels to enhance equity, increase funding, and promote programs that affect the practice of clinical mental health counseling. (E.4)

INTRODUCTION

The term *managed care* evokes Intense, often unenthusiastic reactions from clients and counseling professionals. Thus, it is imperative for counseling professionals to have a precise understanding of managed care as they look to provide services in such systems. During the last decade, across the United States, health services have experienced a sudden increase in the expansion of managed mental health care organizations. Although the counseling profession has encountered many challenges over the years, the managed care movement has far-reaching implications for access to service and counselor reimbursement. As managed care continues to evolve, clinical mental health counselors are charged with maintaining awareness and understanding of this ever-changing topic.

THE EMERGENCE OF MANAGED CARE

Subsequent to the Great Depression, a noteworthy amount of people were unable to pay their medical bills. At the beginning of the 1900s, health care delivery routinely involved an uncomplicated payment arrangement between the provider and the client. The bulk of health care costs were paid directly by patients to the medical provider (Harris, 1994). Much like today, insurance plans were available through employers, although at that time the majority of employees bought insurance from the employer as opposed to receiving insurance as a benefit (DeLeon, VandenBos, & Bulatao, 1994). Thus, a large number of people opted simply to pay for medical services out of pocket, making a two-party system between patient and provider.

After an increased incidence of nonpayment of accounts due to the economy, the three-party system was promoted (i.e., provider, recipient of services, and third-party payer), thus improving the health professional's potential of receiving payment for services. Employees were encouraged to purchase insurance plans, and the payment for the cost of medical services was distributed by the insurance provider. Throughout World War II, an era of wage control provoked some employers to offer alternatives to pay increases, such as health insurance coverage. As increasing numbers of employers began to offer this benefit, there was parallel growth in the insurance industry. This trend contributed to the belief still held today that employers ought to offer such benefits to their employees.

WHAT IS MANAGED HEALTH CARE?

You have probably heard the term *managed care* in discussions of mental health services. Or you may have had your own run-ins with managed care. The organization and structure that today is known as managed care originated as a series of health care measures established to assist in meeting the needs of particular groups of individuals. Rural mining and lumber workers would pay a set fee to a physician, who would deliver services according to predetermined arrangements. In metropolitan areas, compassionate social groups often paid fees to physicians to care for vulnerable populations to guarantee that they received medical care. These prepaid group practices created the foundation for the emergence of managed care organizations (MCOs) (Tufts Managed Care Institute, 1998).

Managed care applies to an approach to health care management that is intended to decrease the cost of providing health benefits and advance the value of care for organizations. In general, large health care corporations direct the financing and delivery of health services to members enrolled in a specific type of health care plan. Ultimately, this system is charged with ensuring that providers deliver high-quality care in an environment that manages or controls costs. The process for service delivery includes determination that recommended services are medically essential and suitable for the client's condition, that care is delivered by the most appropriate provider, and that it is conducted in the most suitable and least restrictive environment.

MAJOR TYPES OF MANAGED CARE PLANS

Health Maintenance Organization (HMO)

Health maintenance organizations (HMOs) were the original system of managed care. An HMO establishes contractual agreements with medical providers such as physicians, hospitals, and other health care professionals. The combination of these providers makes up what becomes known as a *network*. In plain terms, a provider is one who administers services to members of specific health plans at economical rates in exchange for patient referrals. Plan subscribers are obligated to see only providers within this system to have their health services covered by the HMO. If the patient receives services from a provider who isn't in that network, the HMO can refuse to pay for the cost of services unless the services were preapproved by the HMO or defined as an emergency.

Clients enrolled in a plan will select a primary care physician (PCP)—often called a "gatekeeper"—who administers, schedules, and approves all aspects of the patient's medical care including mental health care. Members of the HMO can see a specialist only if the PCP approves this action. If the member sees a specialist without a referral, the HMO will not pay for the care. HMOs are the most limiting type of medical care plan because they give patients the smallest number of options in selecting medical providers. However, HMOs routinely offer members an array of health benefits for minimal out-of-pocket expense, such as omitting or minimizing co-payments, which is the quantity of money a patient is obligated to pay the provider in conjunction with what the HMO pays. The co-pay is often required to be paid prior to the patient's receiving the services.

Preferred Provider Organization (PPO)

Preferred provider organizations (PPOs) are similar to HMOs in that they enter into agreements with health care professionals who form a provider network. However, they are different from HMOs in that members do not choose a PCP and they are not required to use in-network providers for the services they seek. Nevertheless, PPOs offer members greater benefits as monetary incentives to use network professionals. The incentives may consist of lesser deductibles, decreased co-payments, and superior reimbursements. For example, if you go to an in-network general practitioner for a routine appointment, you will likely have only a minimal co-payment or deductible. If you receive services from a nonnetwork practitioner, the result could be your having to pay up to 50% of the cost of the services.

PPO members do not routinely need a referral to see a specialist. However, as in the previous example, there could be monetary enticement when using a specialist in the PPO's provider network. PPOs offer fewer restrictions than HMOs, thus giving members greater choices in health care providers. However, members may resultantly have more out-of-pocket expenses in exchange for the freedom to make these choices.

Point of Service (POS) Plan

A point of service (POS) plan is frequently referred to as an HMO/PPO hybrid or an open-ended HMO. The rationale for referring to this plan as point of service is that patients select which plan they prefer—an HMO or a PPO—every time they seek medical services. Similar to an HMO and a PPO, a POS plan has an approved provider system.

POS plans do not require patients to choose a primary care physician, although it is encouraged. As in a conventional HMO, the PCP acts as a gatekeeper when making referrals. Patients who opt not to ask PCPs to make referrals but ultimately receive services from an in-network provider, will still likely have services paid for but will be required to pay larger co-pays and/or deductibles than plan members who have PCPs make a referral. POS members could choose an appointment with an out-of-network provider; however, co-pays and deductibles will likely be significantly increased. POS plans have emerged as a popular trend as they provide members with more flexibility than average HMOs.

Employee Assistance Program (EAP)

Employee assistance programs (EAPs) are offered by employers as a part of their employee benefits package (Gilbert, 2004). The employer typically works directly with an insurance company and pays for a limited number of counseling sessions. Members and their families may seek counseling through their EAP to address mental health issues, wellness, substance abuse, or any difficulties that might affect work performance. Counseling services are provided by an EAP provider at no expense to members. The goal of EAPs is to conduct a thorough assessment and provide brief therapy to members (Gilbert, 2004). If the members need further services outside of the EAP, a referral is given. The members then have the option to seek services that are covered by their health insurance plan.

MANAGED CARE AND MENTAL HEALTH

Prior to the 1950s, mental health care was not routinely included in insurance benefit plans. This was grounded in the prevailing perspective that mental health problems did not occur very often. Mental health treatment was conceptualized as for seriously mentally ill individuals that required institutionalization, and the care and expenses of these clients were provided at the state level. The 1950s saw the emergence of mental health benefits in most insurance plans. Many factors contributed to the inclusion of these services such as studies providing evidence that mental health problems were more common than had been originally believed (Boyle & Callahan, 2005). The 1970s elevated the trend toward outpatient mental health services, because the emphasis on institutionalization decreased and services were provided more frequently on an outpatient basis. Psychiatric units were added to general hospitals, and many psychotropic medications were developed. Simultaneously, the quantity of mental health providers increased, and there was a great expansion in the number of theoretical schools and related interventions. Furthermore, with the Health Maintenance Organization Act of 1973, mental health services were required to be included in federally eligible managed care programs.

MCO Mental Health Concepts and Definitions

It is vital to recognize that managed care is made up of a wide assortment of health care delivery systems and refers to the organization of physical and mental health care services by someone other than the clinical mental health counselor or the client. The managed care movement has resulted in mental health care threading counseling and business into a carefully balanced relationship. The primary goals of HMOs are to (a) limit costs and (b) promote quality care. Quality care is grounded in seeking to offer members assurance that the clinician's work approximates the ideal. HMOs accomplish these goals through dropping the price charged for mental health services, allowing services only in circumstances where treatment is considered medically essential, and evaluating treatment plans and outcomes (DeLeon et al., 1994).

Access to Mental Health Services Provision

Availability of mental health services is a concern; certain studies have indicated that primary care physicians encounter only modest availability of mental health care services for their patients (Cunningham, 2009). Doctors that participate in groups that include a psychiatrist or other counseling professionals reported improved, if not ideal, access to mental health services. Also of concern are researchers who indicate that primary care physicians (PCPs) routinely cannot gain access to outpatient mental health services for patients (Cunningham, 2009). This absence of available services often occurs twice as often as lack of access for other services. Shortages of counseling providers, plan benefit exclusions, and lack of or insufficient coverage have all been cited by PCPs as significant impediments to mental health care access. The likelihood that patients will have challenges accessing mental health care varies by type of medical practice, health networks, and patient insurance policy.

The Mental Health Parity and Addiction Equity Act

The Mental Health Parity and Addiction Equity Act of 2008 (MHPAEA) is a federal law that provides individuals with mental health and substance use coverage parity with benefit limitations under their medical coverage (US Department of Labor, 2010). The Mental Health Parity Act of 1996 (MHPA) states that a collective health plan may not require yearly or lifetime monetary limits for mental health benefits that are different from limits imposed on medical surgical benefits (National Alliance on Mental Illness, 1996). In other words, mental health care is provided at the same level as medical care. You will hear this referred to as parity, which suggests equality of value or being "on par" with other health services (US Department of Labor, 2010).

So how does this work? If an individual develops a disease and requires medical intervention, the law allows treatment according to individualized medical needs and not a predetermined, limited number of health care visits. Because of the MHPAEA and the MHPA, this same parity is now extended to mental health conditions, which allows clinical mental health counselors and other helping professionals to implement interventions according to client need and not a set number of sessions. The Mental Health Parity Act of 1996 and the Mental Health Parity and Addiction Equity Act of 2008 (MHPAEA) require group health plans and health insurance issuers to ensure that financial requirements (such as co-pays, deductibles) and treatment limitations (such as visit limits) applicable to mental health or substance use disorder (MH/SUD) benefits are no more restrictive than the predominant requirements or limitations applied to substantially all medical/surgical benefits.

Although MHPAEA provides significant new protections to participants in group health plans, it is important to note that MHPAEA does not mandate that a plan provide

MH/SUD benefits. Rather, if a plan provides medical/surgical and MH/SUD benefits, it must comply with the MHPAEA's parity provisions. Parity laws for MCOs have been created to guarantee that persons covered by employee benefit plans are permitted access to mental health services. Specifically, legislation was passed that allows individuals who have mental health benefits attached to an MCO medical plan to receive the same mental health coverage as would medical coverage. Therefore, if a consumer's MCO pays 80% of the cost of a medical visit, then the MCO must pay 80% of the cost of a mental health session. Because parity laws vary from state to state and are outlined differently, it is always best for clinical mental health counselors to be familiar with the laws in their state. However, the law provides that employers retain discretion regarding the extent and scope of mental health benefits offered to workers and their families (including cost sharing, limits on numbers of visits or days of coverage, and requirements relating to medical necessity). It is also important to note that there are exemptions in the law that allow for group health plans to exclude this coverage if providing it will result in a significant increase in cost to the employer.

THE HEALTH INSURANCE PORTABILITY AND ACCOUNTABILITY ACT OF 1996 (HIPAA)

If you have visited a medical office in the last 15 years, you have likely heard of and been impacted by the Health Insurance Portability and Accountability Act (HIPAA). HIPAA was enacted by Congress in 1996 to protect the privacy and security of health care information. HIPAA is enforced by the Office for Civil Rights and has had a significant impact on the health care industry (Brendel & Bryan, 2004; DHHS, 2013; Luo, 2007). Health care providers including health insurance companies, HMOs, and government health programs are federally mandated to follow HIPAA regulations (Benefield, Ashkanazi, & Rozensky, 2006; Brendel & Bryan, 2004; DHHS, 2013; Luo, 2007). Most health care providers and health care clearinghouses (e.g., those involved in electronic filing of health insurance claims) are also required to follow HIPAA rules (Benefield et al., 2006; Brendel & Bryan, 2004; DHHS, 2013; Luo, 2007).

The HIPAA Privacy Rule

The HIPAA Privacy Rule is a federal law that protects clients' personal health information and gives them rights concerning the release of such information (DHHS, 2013; Gostin & Nass, 2009). Personal health information in any form (e.g., written, oral, and electronic) cannot be viewed or released unless it is authorized by the client (Brendel & Bryan, 2004; DHHS, 2013; Gostin & Nass, 2009). Thus, clinical mental health counselors must obtain written consent prior to releasing a client's records to a third party to be in accordance with the HIPAA Privacy Rule.

This change to federal law doesn't just affect the transfer of records. Prior to HIPAA, even patient names were not necessarily confidential. One of the authors of this chapter worked in a mental health agency that shared a waiting area with an audiology and speech pathology office. Prior to the protection provided by HIPAA, mental health client names would be called out by the psychiatric nurse, occasionally followed by "Come on; it's time to get your shot!" Now, client names for both offices are protected with consumers being directed to their service provider without such announcements as to who are the mental health patients and who are the audiology and speech pathology patients.

The HIPAA Security Rule

The HIPAA Security Rule is also a federal law outlining national standards regarding the security of electronic protected health care information. The US Department of Health and Human Services states, "The Security Rule specifies a series of administrative, physical, and technical safeguards for covered entities to use to assure the confidentiality, integrity, and availability of electronic protected health information" (DHHS, 2013, para. 1). In other words, clinical mental health counselors who are filing claims or sending client information electronically must be HIPAA compliant. Clients may file a complaint with the Office for Civil Rights if they feel their rights have been violated. Providers may receive civil or criminal penalties if a violation is found (DHHS, 2013; Luo, 2007).

HIPAA regulations concerning privacy and confidentiality are similar to the ethical standards outlined by the American Counseling Association (2005). However, HIPAA rules are federally mandated and carry legal consequences if the rules are not followed. It is important for clinical mental health counselors to make the necessary administrative changes to their business practices to ensure their compliance (Benefield et al., 2006; Brendel & Bryan, 2004; Luo, 2007).

COUNSELING INTERVENTIONS AND MANAGED CARE

Now that we have discussed all of the elements of managed care, let's take a look at how managed care has had an effect on counseling services. The delivery of mental health services is impacted within an MCO because counseling is conceptualized in an MCO as both cost and time efficient. Not surprisingly, brief therapy models are promoted and are characterized by focused and speedy evaluation of the client's presenting problem, concisely defined treatment goals, and the involvement of a directive therapist (Lawless, Ginter, & Kelly, 1999; Williams & Edwardson, 2000).

Although an exact description of this model varies, clinical mental health counselors should consider whether they are skilled in and agreeable to implement a brief therapy approach. For example, if an MCO adopted a crisis management policy that approved treatment for only six sessions without consideration for further treatment, a counselor would have to evaluate whether he or she were knowledgeable and prepared to deliver services within that model. The clinical mental health counselor must determine whether he or she has had sufficient education and preparation in crisis management from a brief perspective. It would be useful for the counselor to explore the MCO's treatment model as thoroughly as possible prior to committing to become a provider. Review of the brief therapy model may help the clinical mental health counselor determine whether he or she is prepared to work within the boundaries of that specific MCO. If a counselor has the necessary preparation and knowledge and is content to work within these boundaries, he or she may elect to follow through with the intervention. Conversely, if a clinical mental health counselor prefers a long-term, insight-oriented theoretical orientation, the counselor should cautiously consider whether it is prudent to work within the managed care framework.

There are a few considerations related to working within a managed care environment. First, of great concern is the clinical mental health counselor's ethical responsibility to have adequate education and skill to deliver services within a brief therapy model. If this skill were lacking, participation in a group that promotes this model would be a misrepresentation of training. Second, the clinical mental health counselor who is not sufficiently qualified to conduct brief therapy approaches may harm clients or may not meet the minimum ethical mandate of nonmaleficence. For example, a 39-year-old female presents with symptoms of an acute depressive episode. During the fourth session, she mentions recurrent flashbacks of a traumatic event that occurred in her childhood. At this stage, the clinical mental health counselor who adheres to the MCO model would proceed in a different way than a counselor practicing from a long-term perspective. To permit the woman to believe that she will have unrestricted opportunity to process this history of trauma and then ultimately have her sessions profoundly restricted could result in harmful consequences. Finally, consenting to work within this model could result in professional impairment if the counselor were to become increasingly frustrated with what might come to be viewed as an insensitive and unsympathetic MCO. Emotional conflict such as this could lead to burnout, which might damage both the counselor and the client.

There are times when a counselor may be providing services within the MCO's treatment model and then the need for additional sessions arises. For example, you may have eight authorized sessions to address anger management issues with a client. During the seventh session, the client discloses for the first time that he was sexually abused as a child. You have only one remaining session and realize that it would be detrimental to the client to terminate counseling without helping the client process this information. You may contact the insurance company and request additional sessions for the client. You will need to provide specifics about the case and justify why additional sessions are needed. It is best to inform the client that you will be sharing clinical information with the MCO to get additional services authorized. The MCO may request an updated treatment plan and session notes before further services are authorized.

When providing services within a managed care system, ongoing information exchange with the primary care physician is routinely required. This is likely to include an initial referral and periodic follow-up (Wilcoxon, Magnunson, & Norem, 2008). Working with HMOs also involves the monitoring of the counseling process by the HMO and typically includes at least documentation of treatment necessity and periodic submission of treatment plans (Harris, 1994; Phillips, 2002). The process of monitoring counseling is called *utilization review* (UR); it refers to the implementation of specified criteria to assess treatment need, suitability of treatment intervention, and treatment effectiveness. UR often occurs before treatment onset, during service delivery, and following termination. Routinely, HMOs employ some form of potential, simultaneous, and retrospective UR. *Potential* UR is utilized to determine treatment necessity and obtain approval to commence treatment. How HMOs establish intervention necessity and technique varies. Within *simultaneous* UR, HMOs review delivered services when professionals request authorization for ongoing treatment. Finally, *retrospective* UR examines treatment outcome and often assesses client satisfaction with services received (Eaves, Emens, & Sheperis, 2008). In some cases, clinical mental health counselors are required to speak to a UR representative and provide a rationale for the treatment they are providing. The representative may offer treatment suggestions to help expedite the treatment process.

There may be times that a client is in need of counseling services, and the MCO will not authorize sessions. The MCO's denial of a request for additional sessions may occur at the beginning of treatment or later in the therapeutic process. An MCO will not authorize sessions when the counselor is not a contracted provider or if the client has a diagnosis that is not eligible for reimbursement. Additional sessions may not be authorized during the course of treatment when a client has used or exceeded the number of authorized sessions, or if the client has exceeded the lifetime maximum amount of coverage. Counselors have an ethical obligation to advocate for appropriate treatment services for their clients. The ACA Code of Ethics (2005) states, "Counselors advocate to promote change at the individual, group, institutional, and societal levels that improve the quality of life for individuals and groups and remove potential barriers to the provision or access of appropriate services being offered" (Section C, Introduction, para. 1). Therefore, the clinical mental health counselor will need to contact the MCO and work diligently to be certain that the client receives the necessary services.

As an example, one of the authors received a referral in private practice on a three-year-old child who had experienced severe abuse and trauma. The author was not a contracted provider with the family's MCO. The parents wanted the child to be seen by the author, because the author was the only provider in the area who specialized in abuse and trauma. There were no providers in the family's network with this specialization. The author contacted the MCO and informed the representative of the child's need for services. After confirming that no other providers in the area worked with young children, the MCO offered an "out-of-network" contract with the author. The MCO authorized 16 sessions for a negotiated rate and agreed to authorize further sessions as needed when sufficient documentation was provided. The documentation included an updated treatment plan and session notes.

Advocating for extended services can be challenging. Because clinical mental health counselors have a therapeutic connection with their clients, they have a greater understanding of their clients' needs. And unfortunately, whereas a counselor may recognize the urgency of a client's receiving further treatment, the MCO representative may not. Therefore, clinical mental health counselors should respond assertively and present pertinent clinical information supporting the medical necessity of further treatment. They should indicate any potential ethical dilemmas that might arise by the client's not receiving further treatment (e.g., the client could harm himself or others if not involved in therapy), as well as present information explaining how additional sessions would allow the client to reach the approved treatment goals.

If the MCO will not authorize additional sessions, it is a good idea for the clinical mental health counselor to review his or her contract and read about the MCO's internal appeal process and grievance policy. It is possible that additional sessions may be authorized when a formal appeal or grievance is submitted (Lammando, 2003). Certain states such as California have passed laws giving consumers the right to request an independent medical review (IMR) if an MCO decides that further treatment is not medically necessary (Jensen, 2004; Lammando, 2003). Lammando (2003) states that over 40 states in the United States have laws recognizing independent review services as the means to appeal health care decisions when there are questions about the treatment's appropriateness or necessity. The IMR is conducted by an independent review organization (IRO), which consists of a team of impartial medical professionals. The IRO reviews the case documentation and determines whether further treatment is medically necessary (Jensen, 2004; Lammando, 2003). If the IRO determines that treatment is medically necessary, a written document will be sent to the MCO recommending the authorization of further sessions (Jensen, 2004). MCOs are legally obligated to authorize further sessions in states where such laws exist (Lammando, 2003). Thus, it is a good idea for clinical mental health counselors to find out whether laws pertaining to IMRs exist in their state and the procedures involved in requesting such a review.

VOICE FROM THE FIELD 8.1

I entered the world of counseling having spent a brief time in business and marketing, first managing a popular ladies' shoe store and then detailing cardiac catheters to cardiologists in major medical centers. You might say my career counseling was by trial and error, but my experience in the business world gave me much needed skills for managing a counseling practice.

I returned to school and received a master's degree in social work with an emphasis in clinical mental health. After passing my licensure exam and completing the required supervisory experience while working for the community mental health center, I began my part-time private practice by renting an office and began counseling individuals, couples, children and groups. That was 30 years ago!

Since that humble beginning, I have closed a full-time private practice in a major urban city, relocated and opened a practice in rural Mississippi, accepted a faculty position to teach bachelor's-level social work, returned to pursue a PhD in counselor education, and today combine a career as a counselor educator with a small private practice.

I began my practice as a sole proprietor business (yes, counseling is a business). Learning to collect fees and manage billing was one of my first lessons. In fact, billing and managing money is such a major part of private practice, and one in which counselors receive little or no training, that I even began a research interest in the role of money in the lives and work of counselors.

In the early years of my practice, there was no managed care. To build my practice, I made marketing calls to physicians, who were generally pleased to have the resource for their patients. Clients usually had private insurance and I provided them a bill with a proper diagnosis. Clients submitted their own forms and were reimbursed with few requests for additional information or treatment planning from me. Ah, the good old days!

For those clients who did not have insurance, I occasionally negotiated the fee with them. If the client was unable to pay close to my fee, I referred the client to the community mental health center, which was able to provide services because the center was subsidized with community funding sources. Matching the client with affordable counseling resources is important for both the client and the counselor. I saw many counselors lose their business perspective, counsel clients at a much reduced fee, and then struggle with their own ambivalence about their lack of income. This soon becomes an obstacle in the therapeutic relationship. I know, because I, too, have made this mistake. I struggled to manage feelings of "giving away my time" with my desire to help the client. The result is added stress to an already demanding profession. This does not mean I did not do my share of pro bono work, but I quickly learned to provide pro bono hours during the slow hours, and not "give away" prime time slots with full-fee clients who provided my income, without which I would not be able to provide pro bono services!

Then came managed mental health care. The rules changed, and so did the collection and billing system. The principal change was that I was no longer solely in charge of what services could be provided to the client. Best practices sometimes meant "fastest" practices, aimed at alleviating symptoms, but not necessarily the chronic underlying patterns that manifested as the presenting problem. Furthermore, confidentiality was no longer limited to counselor and client. The presenting problem, desired outcome, and length of treatment were now a product to be negotiated between a case manager and the counselor. Personal information, with the client's permission, was released to a large corporate industry, whose aim was to reduce costs. My personal protest was about having to provide my clients with a lengthy disclosure statement, which detailed the lack of privacy and potential risks incurred by participation in the managed care system. Many of my clients decided to opt for fee-for-service (sometimes at a reduced fee) in lieu of reimbursement for counseling by their insurance plan. Assisting clients in prioritizing the counseling process and helping them work the fee into their budget when possible can be very empowering for both clients and counselor.

Over time, managed care became the norm and clients did not seem as concerned about the lack of confidentiality. I can only assume this is a paradigm shift that has come with the age of the Internet and the virtual lack of privacy in all areas of our lives.

Counselors today have not known counseling without managed care. Negotiating the paperwork, treatment plans, and progress notes is routine. Ironically, I rarely participated in managed care networks and chose instead to diversify my career, which allowed me the freedom to refer clients who desired to use their managed care plan to counselors who were willing to spend the hours completing paperwork and negotiating sessions. The few times I accepted a managed care client, I failed to submit the right paperwork, procrastinated, and missed the deadline to request additional sessions. This resulted in providing the sessions pro bono. I quickly realized this was not working for me!

Counselors are mandated to be problem solvers and address issues of social justice. To this end, I made a decision to run groups (which I love) that has allowed clients to pay a reduced rate, receive powerful counseling, provide my income, and avoid the paperwork that I dreaded! Everyone wins! This model continued to work for me until I closed my office last year as a part of a move to a new house and new town for the next chapter of my life.

I continue to see a few clients on a fee-for-service basis in my university setting. I am a counselor at heart and I love the profession. I now spend the better part of my time teaching and mentoring the next generation of counselors. I have the perfect niche that works for me. I challenge you to do the same!

JEANNIE FALKNER, PhD
Walden University

CAPITATION

Another concept involved in managed care is capitation. *Capitation* is the process of paying medical professionals a predetermined sum for each client's care in spite of the cost of providing the services to the client. Preferred provider organizations (PPOs) establish arrangements between medical professionals and plan members in which health care providers agree to offer reduced fees from their usual charges in exchange for access to providing services for a group of clients. Capitation is a good example of how managed care practices strive to reduce costs for health care. Many managed care groups also attempt to influence the quality of care. For example, following clinical guidelines that could alter the clinical management of specific diagnoses (e.g., treatment of psychosis) is also a common practice in managed care. This could mean not only limitations to the therapeutic interventions but also limitations to the choices of types of medications that are approved for payment based on expense. This could be especially frustrating because clients might be limited to having plans pay for medications that have undesirable side effects because newer medications with fewer side effects are deemed too expensive.

ETHICAL CONCERNS

Throughout the last decade, the counseling profession has witnessed a sudden increase in the growth of managed mental health care organizations across the nation. Although mental health providers have encountered many challenges over the years, few things have had as great an impact on the profession as the managed care movement. As managed care continues to develop, counseling professionals will likely be faced with many ethical challenges. As a result of these challenges, managed care tends to be quite a dynamic topic among clinical mental health counselors regardless of their area of expertise. This section examines issues that commonly include ethical questions such as diagnosing, confidentiality, and client–counselor relationships.

Efficiency

Managed care is planned around an assortment of incentives intended to promote the practice of cost-effective health care and to decrease disparity in clinical interventions. This is known in managed care language as "efficiency," which means providing quality health care while streamlining resources and cost. Efficiency is heightened by increasing efficiency and reducing cost. Thus, managed care sometimes expects providers to accomplish desired outcomes with minimal time per client, cost-effective medications, and minimal expensive diagnostic tests or interventions.

Financial incentives are frequently employed to entice providers and may include rewarding health care providers that approach treatment frugally by promoting monetary rewards, such as bonuses, for those who offer cost-efficient services. There may be consequences for providers who conduct too many appointments or are deemed to practice in a cost-inefficient manner, such as the withholding of bonuses or portions of income. Nonmonetary expectations to adhere to the limits of care can result in peer pressure or pressure from supervisors that promotes the financial well-being of their employer. These financial and nonmonetary practices invite the ethical question of whether health care providers may negate client care while seeking cost savings.

An additional ethical concern relates to the impact of managed care on counselor–client relationships. Of concern is that managed care undermines counselor–client relationships by threatening clients' trust in their therapist, reducing the amount of time clinical mental health counselors spend with clients, and impacting the availability of counselors.

CASE STUDY 8.1

Elizabeth recently joined a small private counseling practice. She is subleasing office space in an existing practice. After purchasing furniture, testing protocols, and toys for the play therapy room, she is feeling strapped and concerned about meeting her financial obligations. She begins to relax when she has a fairly full appointment book before opening her doors the first day. By the end of the first week, Elizabeth has seen 27 clients and is fully booked for the second week. She feels incredibly grateful for her good fortune. Before heading out for the weekend, she consults with the office manager about her earnings. Much to her dismay, she has generated only $120 of income for the entire week. All of the remaining clients had insurance that will have to be billed. Elizabeth has already completed the application process to be a provider for approximately a dozen insurance companies. Disappointed that she has limited cash flow, but convinced that payment will arrive soon, Elizabeth concludes that she will have to be diligent about paying close attention to diagnostic codes as she learns what is eligible for reimbursement.

Over the next 30 days, Elizabeth receives insurance reimbursement for three clients. All other claims are denied. Elizabeth begins to panic because her rent is due as well as the payment on her small business loan. Examination of the denials reveals that Elizabeth has a tendency to be cautious with diagnosing, which has resulted in nonpayment. The office manager gives Elizabeth a list of codes that are eligible for reimbursement and instructs Elizabeth to use only these codes for all future billing.

1. Is it ethical for Elizabeth to use only a specified set of diagnoses for all clients?
2. What steps should she put in place to make sure she can pay her bills?

Diagnosing

Clinical mental health counselors who elect to participate in insurance plans pay attention to procedures that impact insurance reimbursement for mental health services because these factors have great implications for financial endurance. Researchers have reported that for 21% of LPCs working in private practice or in community mental health centers, managed care represented more than half of their income (Smith, 2003), whereas 85% of private practitioners reported that managed care provided over one third of their income (Murphy, DeBernardo, & Shoemaker, 1998).

When counselors can't get paid for services provided because particular DSM diagnoses are not reimbursed by MCOs, clients may not receive appropriate treatment (Rother, 1996), their treatment may be hastily terminated, or their needs may be neglected (Danzinger & Welfel, 2001). Thus, counselors may feel pressured to choose between a correct diagnosis that may not be reimbursable and an inaccurate diagnosis (e.g., intentional misdiagnosis) that will qualify for payment (Danzinger & Welfel, 2001).

The ACA (2005) and the AMHCA (2010) codes of ethics promote values that guide members' ethical behavior and that create the foundation for ethical complaints. The purposeful misdiagnosis of mental disorders for payment of services violates a variety of parts of the ACA and AMHCA codes of ethics, which include but may not be limited to the following: regarding primary responsibility, the ACA Code of Ethics, Section A: The Counseling Relationship, A.1 Welfare of Those Served by Counselors, Item a (ACA, 2005, p. 4), and the Code of Ethics of the American Mental Health Counselors Association, Principle 1: Commitment to Clients, Item A.1 (AMHCA, 2010, p. 1). Both codes state that counselors are expected to place the client first, work toward the client's benefit, and respect the client throughout the process.

Counselors breach this doctrine when they deliberately misdiagnose mental disorders for insurance compensation and/or ask clients to participate in this conspiracy. For example, in an effort to get a client's insurance to reimburse charges, a clinical mental health counselor suggests to the client that being diagnosed with major depression will secure payment, when a more accurate diagnosis would be one that has a V Code (e.g., a relational problem, employment problem, or religious problem; American Psychiatric Association, 2000). Many clinical mental health counselors convince themselves that they are protecting their clients when they choose to deliberately misrepresent a diagnosis in order to receive insurance reimbursement. However, engaging in premeditated misdiagnosis violates state and federal statutes, and counselors risk ethical reprimands and legal penalty. Clients who do not support the use of inaccurate diagnosis in order to secure payment may question a counselor's ethical principles in general, resulting in the counselor losing integrity, and the counseling profession as a whole losing credibility.

Confidentiality

Many ethical standards address confidentiality. Ethical standard B.1.c. of the American Counseling Association's (2005) ethical principles states the following: "Counselors do not share confidential information without client consent or without sound legal or ethical justification" (p. 7). Ethical standard B.3.d. states that "Counselors disclose information to third-party payers only when clients have authorized such disclosure" (p. 8). Furthermore, ethical standard B.6.f. states that "Unless exceptions to confidentiality exist, counselors obtain written permission from clients to disclose or transfer records to legitimate third parties. Steps are taken to ensure that receivers of counseling records are sensitive to their confidential nature" (p. 8). The counselor–client relationship is vital to the success of mental health interventions. A defining element of the counselor–client relationship is confidentiality. Clients who feel safe within the margins of confidentiality frequently disclose deeply personal information to the counselor. It is important to note that within a managed care context, confidentiality may not be assumed in the counseling relationship. Managed care amends the customary basis for limits of confidentiality to address issues of price suppression. What this means is that customarily confidentiality in the counseling profession is violated only in situations in which a client is a risk to self or others. However, with managed care, the counselor is obligated to reveal sensitive client information to the HMO to determine treatment necessity.

Before managed care became common practice, the counseling ethics codes provided an adequate procedure for counselors to follow in protecting the confidentiality of their clients in a reasonably uncomplicated manner. Because the clinical mental health counselor and the client were the only parties involved, adherence to ethical guidelines was generally maintained without too much difficulty. However in the 1970s, outpatient mental health services began to advocate for third-party reimbursement to obtain parity with organized medicine. This change illuminated concerns for confidentiality, because counselors were required to provide information about their clients to others when they completed insurance forms (Braun & Cox, 2005).

In spite of preliminary concern, anxiety related to the potential compromise of confidentiality did not become a major problem initially, because clinical mental health counselors were rarely asked for information beyond a diagnosis. Most clients agreed because of the costs associated with paying out of pocket. This practice of confidentiality successfully kept information relatively secure, and clients rarely had cause for concern related to their records being compromised. However, since the mid-1980s with the expansion of managed mental health care, the preservation of confidentiality has become a much more multifaceted topic. Today, MCOs often request broad and delicate information about clients, and detailed treatment plans may be required by MCOs at different points during the counseling process. Ideally, treatment plans are securely delivered to the MCO, but time constraints do not always allow sufficient time to do so, and counseling professionals frequently send data electronically to guarantee that sessions will be covered in time for the client's next appointment. Remember that electronic data submission falls under HIPAA. Even if the treatment plan is mailed, the information is then placed into a computer system and could become part of a national database of health records without the client's knowledge. Hence, due to this technology, clinical mental health counselors can no longer pledge confidentiality to their clients at any level, because client information provided to the MCO is no longer under the control of the counselor.

Clients should be plainly and completely informed of the managed care company's role in their treatment, including the possible problems regarding confidentiality. It is advantageous for the clinical mental health counselor to be on the lookout for ethical issues. Thus, the counselor is wise to secure a copy of a managed care company's policy regarding confidentiality. This allows the clinical mental health counselor the opportunity to review the company's policy, anticipate problems, and then, if necessary, make suggestions to the managed care company or the client. In the event that a managed care company's policy for processing confidential information is insufficient and unalterable, the clinical mental health counselor should release only the minimum amount of information needed in order to protect the client's privacy. The counselor should also inform the client of the MCO's policy, and they should discuss the implications of it. It is important for the clinical mental health counselor to remember that the client owns the privilege to release confidential information, and remain mindful that the counselor's primary obligation is to work for the benefit of the client. The managed care company may not have the same priorities. It may be helpful for the clinical mental health counselor to develop professional policy regarding the release of confidential client information. For example, the counselor might have a policy that states treatment summaries will be released rather than case notes or entire records.

In the event that a managed care company requests information about a client that is not compatible with the clinical mental health counselor's policy, the counselor can then discuss this predicament with the client and ask the client to choose whether and how much information should be released to the MCO. In some instances, the clinical mental health counselor may be asked by the managed care company to have general releases of information signed by the client during the first counseling session. In other cases, the client may sign a general release of information before ever seeing the counselor. Clients frequently do not even recall signing such documents. Even if they do, they will not always recall their contents or understand the implications of having signed them. Therefore, in all instances, it is important for clinical mental health counselors to inform clients about the nature of the release form and the implications of their signature. After a client signs a release form, counselors will be periodically required to submit treatment information to the MCO. As a rule, information should not be released without first discussing it with the client, allowing the client time to ask questions and discuss the implications of the release (Pakhomov, Jacobsen, Chute, & Roger, 2008).

Involving clients in all aspects of their care is ethically responsible. Additionally, this process not only is good risk management but also can provide a therapeutic function when done well. In some cases, managed care companies may request case notes from the clinical mental health counselor. Case notes are clinical data, and in some cases it is inappropriate for non–mental health professionals to review them. Counselors should consider submitting an alternative to case notes, such as sending a treatment summary or other documentation that the MCO may approve. Managed care companies usually respect this boundary and are open to this option when they view the counselors as being generally forthcoming.

Technological advances have also resulted in serious challenges to confidentiality. For example, treatment plans sent by fax machines may be sent to the wrong place, conversations over cellular telephones may be overheard by others, and information sent via e-mail may be retrieved from computers without the receivers' knowledge. In light of these advances in technology, it is important for the clinical mental health counselor to take certain precautions. Ideally, the counselor will mail requested paperwork to the MCO whenever it is reasonable to do so. When time does not permit this practice, it is important for the counselor to take precautions such as contacting the managed care company to make certain that the case manager will be the one receiving a fax transmission. Although not foolproof, another precaution is to include a cover sheet with a confidentiality statement written on it. Finally, as with faxes, e-mail messages can be inadvertently sent to the wrong address. As a result, it is recommended that the clinical mental health counselor avoid the use of e-mail communication to discuss confidential client material.

Counselor–Client Relationships

Managed care can impact relationships between clinical mental health counselors and clients in a variety of ways. First, it may change where such relationships form and the way in which such relationships begin and end. Health maintenance organizations, for example, pay only for care delivered by their own providers. If you think about it, preferred provider groups restrict access to care by paying a smaller percentage of the cost of care when clients go outside the network. These restrictions limit clients' ability to establish a relationship with the provider of their choosing. Termination of counselor–client relationships can also occur without clients' choosing. For example, when employers shift health plans, employees may have no economically feasible choice but to sever ties with their clinical mental health counselors.

In addition, some forms of managed care create a financial incentive for counselors to spend less time with each client. For instance, under preferred provider arrangements, clinical mental health counselors may compensate for reduced fees for services by seeing more clients. This reduces the time available to discuss clients' problems, explore treatment options, and maintain a meaningful relationship with clients. As a counseling student, this may be shocking and run counter to what you are learning about ethical treatment provision. However, it is important to remember that MCOs are businesses. When clinical mental health counselors choose to become providers and do business with them, they must continue to hold to the ethical standards of their profession.

Finally, managed care arrangements often control clients' access to medical specialists, thereby restricting clients' freedom to choose providers and obtain the medical services they desire. This occurs, for example, in MCOs where primary care health care providers function as gatekeepers who authorize client referrals to medical specialists. Critics of managed care claim that this will lower the quality of care, whereas supporters believe that gatekeeping functions yield benefits such as promoting rigorous review of standards of care and emphasizing low-technology care-oriented services.

MANAGED CARE AND CULTURAL CONSIDERATIONS

Professional counseling has come to expect multicultural awareness and sensitivity. The Council for Accreditation of Counseling and Related Educational Programs (CACREP) includes multicultural competencies in academic requirements, the American Counseling Association (ACA) created the division of Association for Multicultural Counseling and Development (AMCD), and the profession has established a sociopolitical presence that supports marginalized or oppressed groups. Counseling professionals demonstrate a strong and ongoing commitment to a multicultural perspective in education, supervision, research, and practice. Current ethical counseling practices are grounded in appreciation of and respect for diversity.

Simultaneous to the rising emphasis on multicultural awareness and competencies in counseling practices has been the advancement of the managed mental health care. Efforts to manage escalating costs of insurance and health-related costs have led to an increase of policy restrictions with implications for private and agency practitioners seeking third-party reimbursement for their services to clients. Legislative and business interests have come to dictate decisions in mental health care. HMOs restrict eligibility for services and even stipulate treatment modalities. This practice has limited options for individualized client care, often because of the necessity for reliance on standardized treatment protocols for specific diagnostic categories. For example, Chambliss (2006) noted that for specific diagnoses (e.g., chemical addiction), modern HMOs may require (a) specific treatment modalities (e.g., group counseling), (b) specific treatment settings (e.g., inpatient care), and (c) specific treatment periods (e.g., 28 days), all of which are based on calculated cost–benefit ratios. Similar specifications about intervention protocols exist for other diagnoses (e.g., eating disorders and anxiety disorders). Again, as a counseling student you may find this surprising and counter to counselor autonomy, but these preferred intervention protocols are based on research outcomes, and less standardized approaches are typically disqualified for reimbursement because they are cost prohibitive (Chambliss, 2006; Eaves et al., 2008).

Some HMO procedures have even led to the prevalent practice of utter denial of fee-reimbursement requests for specific diagnostic categories (e.g. adjustment disorders, Axis II diagnoses, and V codes).

Evolution in mental health counseling practices and professional attention to clinical mental health counselors' multicultural competencies are not unrelated historical trends. However, a review of professional counseling literature reveals few discussions concerning the conflicting philosophical paradigms driving these intersecting aspects of current counseling practices. Of particular note in this convergence of paradigms is the nature of time-limited, standardized counseling procedures and the multicultural implications of imposed efficiency and rapidity as a derivative of cost-containment initiatives (Eaves et al., 2008).

To increase access and provide sensitive and appropriate treatment, it is critical that the clinical mental health counselor assess whether he or she is competent to work with the clientele of the MCO. If the MCO's clientele includes persons representing particular socioeconomic groups, ages, levels of education, racial and ethnic groups, and/or sexual orientations, then the counselor should assess whether sufficient education, training, and experience exist for working with these groups. If a clinical mental health counselor is referred to a client and decides that he or she is not competent to work with that particular individual, the counselor is ethically obliged to contact the MCO and obtain an appropriate referral. Unfortunately, things are seldom so simple, because there may be no qualified counselors available within the MCO network. If so, the counselor has a duty to advocate on behalf of the client and should notify the MCO regarding the need to recruit competent providers in the particular area of need. Clinical mental health counselors should be cautious in these situations in spite of being urged to see the client by the MCO, which may prefer not to be inconvenienced by the request. Counselors are charged with remaining self-aware, practicing within the confines of their experience, and practicing ethically.

ELECTING TO BE A PREFERRED PROVIDER

Clinical mental health counselors may likely encounter health plans that employ managed care techniques. They should evaluate the nature of the financial practices that affect their practice and determine whether such mechanisms are consistent with providing competent and ethical care to their clients.

For example, before clinical mental health counselors contract with providers that restrict the amount allowed to be billed for services, they must determine whether this amount will allow them to spend sufficient time with each client. Before becoming employees of a health maintenance organization, counselors need to confirm that the agency practices effective health care services. Prior to accepting clients on a capitated basis, counselors should verify that they will be able to provide competent, high-quality care under such an arrangement. It is important to review contracts with health plans for clauses that limit or restrict counselors' ability to discuss all potentially beneficial health care services with clients, even if they are not covered by the health plan (such clauses are often referred to as "gag" clauses). These kinds of inquiries can help to prevent serious ethical concerns from arising.

Existing arrangements with insurers should also be evaluated on a continuing basis. After contracting with a preferred provider organization, clinical mental health counselors may determine that the financial pressure to minimize costs results in providing less quality care and the contract should not be renewed. They should also make full use of appeal mechanisms that exist for denied coverage. When coverage for a service the counseling professional believes to be effective and clinically indicated is denied, the counselor's role as advocate for the client obligates him or her to take every reasonable avenue to appeal the decision.

In an effort to give counselors in training some insight into the actual process of becoming a provider, we suggest that they look up three insurance companies that are common to their area (e.g., Blue Cross/Blue Shield, United Behavioral Health, and Cigna). Locate the Web site of each one, identify the resources for becoming a provider, and print the application. Compare and contrast the three applications and generate a list of all information that will be necessary to complete the applications (i.e., licensure number, NPI number, liability insurance, vita, etc.). Are there any surprising requests? Do the students know what everything is that they are being asked for? Do they have any questions about what they will need to proceed with the process?

Becoming a Provider

Becoming a provider can be a lengthy process, and it is often difficult to determine how to get started. Clinical mental health counselors should first make sure that they meet the MCO's requirements and possess the necessary credentials before initiating the application process.

LICENSURE In order to become a provider, the counseling professional must be licensed in his or her field. MCOs typically allow medical doctors, licensed clinical psychologists, nurse practitioners, licensed professional counselors (LPCs), licensed mental health counselors (LMHCs), and licensed clinical social workers (LCSWs) to become counseling providers. The requirements for licensure vary from state to state. Thus, to become licensed as a clinical mental health counselor, the professional should be familiar with his or her state's guidelines. MCOs also require that the counselor obtain a certain number of years of clinical experience post licensure before becoming a provider. Such requirements vary according to the plan; therefore, it is critical to read the requirements carefully before submitting the application.

The counseling professional's license must be clear of any open action against him or her. The counselor will not be considered for network participation if there are ethical complaints pending. Any unresolved matters must be resolved before the application will be considered.

LIABILITY INSURANCE   To participate in a provider network, clinical mental health counselors must obtain professional liability insurance with the amount of coverage mandated by the MCO. Professional liability insurance protects counselors in the event that they are faced with a malpractice suit. Most MCOs require counselors to provide a policy with a minimum of $1,000,000 per claim and up to a $1,000,000 aggregate coverage. The American Counseling Association (ACA) endorses the Healthcare Providers Service Organization (HPSO) as the preferred writer for professional liability insurance. Student members of ACA are given liability insurance through HPSO as a benefit of their membership. This is true for student members of the American Mental Health Counselors Association (AMHCA) who receive liability insurance through CPH and Associated. With both organizations, professional members may receive a discount on their liability insurance through these providers. However, there is a range of other insurance companies that provide professional liability insurance to clinical mental health counselors and other health care professionals.

GENERAL PREMISES LIABILITY INSURANCE   Certain MCOs require that counseling professionals' agency or practice carry general premises liability insurance. This protects them from liability if anyone is injured from a fall or accident. It also protects clinical mental health counselors' belongings in the event of a fire or natural disaster. It becomes important for them to evaluate their professional and personal insurance coverage to avoid having their home or other personal belongings involved in litigation. Clinical mental health counselors may obtain general premises liability insurance through their professional liability insurance carrier or from a commercial insurance company.

NATIONAL PROVIDER IDENTIFIER (NPI)   The National Provider Identifier (NPI) is a 10-digit identification number assigned to individuals and organizations providing health care. The number is issued by the National Plan and Provider Enumeration System (NPPES), which was created by the Centers for Medicaid & Medicare Services for those covered entities (e.g., physicians, chiropractors, psychologists, counselors, nurses, etc.) that transmit electronic transactions. The providers are listed in a registry containing identifying information that can be shared with other health care providers. The database is designed to aid in electronic transmission of health-related information as mandated by HIPAA regulations (NPPES, 2010). All health plans and clearinghouses are required by HIPAA to use the NPI when processing electronic health care information (NPPES, 2010). Providers may apply for an NPI at https://nppes.cms.hhs.gov/NPPES/StaticForward .do?forward=static.instructions.

The request for an NPI can be completed online, by mail, or by using an electronic file interchange organization (EFIO). The relatively straightforward online application takes approximately 20 minutes to complete. There is a separate application for organizations wishing to obtain an NPI. The individual provider application requires that counselors provide their name, address, telephone number, date of birth, social security number or Individual Tax Identification Number (ITIN), practice contact number, and their taxonomy (NPPES, 2010). One's taxonomy is one's provider type, and there is a Web site provided to determine the appropriate taxonomy. Counselors typically list "Behavioral Health and Social Service Provider" as their taxonomy.

The application for an organization applying for an NPI is similar to the individual application. However, the application for the organization requires specific information about the practice (NPPES, 2010). A counselor who is starting a counseling center employing a group of professionals will need an individual NPI number as well as an NPI for the organization. The NPI number is issued within 10 days, depending upon the method by which it was submitted (NPPES, 2010).

CURRICULUM VITAE (CV)   Many MCOs will ask for a copy of a clinical mental health counselor's curriculum vitae (CV) as part of the credentialing application. A CV is more than a resume, which the counselor may have created in the past for job searches. Whereas a resume is brief and concise, a CV is a lengthier outline of one's education, licensure and certifications, clinical experience, training, and other related qualifications. Counselors should update their CV regularly to reflect their experience in the field.

EMPLOYER IDENTIFICATION NUMBER (EIN)   MCOs will ask for clinical mental health counselors' social security number or employer identification number (EIN) for income tax purposes. Most profit and nonprofit agencies have an EIN, and some individuals in private practice may opt to apply for an EIN instead of using their social security number. The EIN, also known as the federal Tax Identification Number (TIN), is issued by the Internal Revenue Service (IRS) to help identify the business or organization. EINs are assigned to individuals or businesses that pay withholding taxes to employees. Individuals may also apply for an Individual Tax Identification Number (ITIN) if they do not qualify for an EIN. Counselors in private practice are not required to have an EIN or an ITIN. They may file taxes using their social security number.

A practice may be structured as a sole proprietorship. The provider application will ask for the counselor's name and the name associated with the name of the practice. This is sometimes written as "doing business as" (DBA). Sole proprietors are not required to have an EIN. For more information about EINs or business structure, access the IRS Web site at www.irs.gov. It is best to consult with an accountant or an IRS representative if there are any questions about one's tax identification.

PROVIDER APPLICATION   All potential providers must complete a provider application for each MCO in which they wish to participate. Most applications can be found on the MCO's Web site; however, clinical mental health counselors may also request that an application packet be mailed to them. They will be asked to give basic demographic information, their social security number or employer identification number (EIN), and the contact information for their practice. Potential providers will also need to provide information about their education, licensure and certifications, residencies and internship work, professional memberships, work experience, and personal references.

For each MCO, there is typically a standard provider application that any health care provider requesting to become a part of the network needs to complete. Physicians, nurse practitioners, psychologists, psychiatrists, and counselors all complete the same application. Thus, it should not be surprising that the application includes a significant amount of medical terminology. Certain sections of the provider application will not apply to clinical mental health counselors. For example, many provider applications include sections pertaining to hospital admitting privileges, Drug Enforcement Administration (DEA) certificate and privileges, and laboratory information. Those applying are required to complete only the sections applicable to their profession.

We are living in an era in which there are continuous advancements in technology. Many MCOs require that potential providers have Internet access, a valid e-mail address used for business purposes, and a secure fax line before they submit their provider application. Most MCOs require that applicants use the Internet to complete credentialing and re-credentialing materials, unless prohibited by their state. If potential providers are unable or unwilling to meet these requirements, they should not apply to become a provider.

The provider application contains a section inquiring about applicants' clinical expertise and the populations with whom they are interested in counseling. MCOs have educational and training requirements that clinical mental health counselors must complete in order to be eligible to accept referrals of individuals suffering from various emotional difficulties. This is a means by which MCOs determine competence.

It is also noteworthy that many MCOs will often reject providers if they are not in need of new providers in a particular area of practice. In fact, it is not uncommon for an MCO to accept only those providers who specialize in treating particular disorders. For example, one author once applied for provider status only to be denied due to a lack of need for additional providers within the identified geographic area. After contacting the MCO, the clinician was asked about treatment provision for the lesbian, gay, bisexual, transgender, and questioning (LGBTQ) population. Though the provider confirmed that she was experienced in working with clients on sexual identity issues, the screening interviewer stated that the MCO was specifically seeking providers that self-identified as LGBTQ, as it was the MCO's position that clients related better to treatment providers that shared their sexual identity. Because the author did not self-identify as a sexual minority, she was denied provider status.

When completing the provider application, clinical mental health counselors will likely be asked to list the names of the other networks in which they participate. Once a counselor is a provider in a network, it may be easier to be accepted into other networks. It is a good idea to keep an updated list of all of the networks in which one is a provider.

The provider application also includes an attestation document, which inquires about the potential provider's professional conduct. The document specifically asks about any history of legal difficulties, ethical violations or professional misconduct. Clinical mental health counselors will be asked to complete and sign the document, as well as attest to the truth of the information. In addition, the application packet contains a contract that includes information about fees for service, documentation, handling referrals, submission of claims, and so forth. It is important for applicants to read the contract carefully before signing it to make sure that they are comfortable with the terms of the agreement before entering into the contract.

As previously mentioned, by becoming contracted providers with an MCO, clinical mental health counselors are agreeing to receive an adjusted fee for the counseling services they provide. Fees vary depending on the organization. However, the provider application will provide applicants with a fee schedule listing the fees that are reimbursed for different service codes. The service codes, known as Current Procedural Terminology (CPT®) codes, provide uniform information related to the diagnostic services rendered (American Medical Association, n.d.; Pam Pohly Associates, 2009). The codes are listed in a health care procedure coding system, which is updated annually (American Medical Association, n.d.; Pam Pohly Associates, 2009). CPT is a registered trademark of the American Medical Association. Information about CPT coding can be found at www.ama-assn.org. A CPT coding book is available through the American Medical Association's online bookstore.

TABLE 8.1 Sample Fee Schedule

CPT Code	MD	Licensed Clinical Psychologist	Nurse Practitioner	Other Licensed Mental Health Professionals
90801 Initial Evaluation	$225	$100	$100	$75
90806 Individual Therapy (45–50 minutes)	$150	$ 80	$ 80	$60
90807 Individual Therapy with Med Management	$175		$150	
90808 Individual Therapy (75-80 minutes)				
90846 Family Therapy Without Client	$100	$ 60	$ 60	$50
90847 Family Therapy with Client	$100	$ 60	$ 60	$50
90853 Group Psychotherapy	$ 75	$ 50	$ 40	$25
90857 Interactive Group Psychotherapy	$ 75	$ 50	$ 40	$25

To gain a better understanding of CPT codes, see Table 8.1 for a sample fee schedule. For example, consider that you are going to be reimbursed for an individual therapy session. The CPT code 90806 indicates that an individual therapy session 45 to 50 minutes in duration was conducted. The fee schedule shows that a licensed professional counselor (LPC) would be reimbursed $60. A CPT code of 90847 indicates that family therapy was conducted with the client present. An LPC providing a 90847 CPT code would be reimbursed $50.

Notice that certain cells are blank in Table 8.1. Only MDs and nurse practitioners are reimbursed for individual therapy with medication management. No reimbursement is provided for 90808 individual therapy (75 to 80 minutes).

Fees are reimbursed at a usual and customary rate (UCR). The UCR is a term used by MCOs to indicate the amount of reimbursement allowed for a particular service. The rate is determined by what is considered to be a reasonable charge in the particular service area (Lawless et al., 1999; Pam Pohly Associates, 2009). Fee schedules vary from one MCO to the next. Clinical mental health counselors need to be sure that they are aware of and comfortable with the CPT codes that are eligible for reimbursement, as well as the rate of reimbursement before contracting with the MCO.

Most MCOs require their providers to file claims electronically, whereas a few others accept paper claims filed on HCFA Health Insurance claim forms. Most MCOs are no longer accepting paper claims. Those that are still using paper claims seem to be transitioning into electronic filing; thus it is likely that HCFA forms will no longer be used in the future. If a counselor or his or her agency is filing claims electronically, then that party will be expected to provide information about pertinent billing software and clearinghouse. Counselors will also need to authorize that reimbursement from the MCOs can be done via direct deposit and provide them with their account information. There is a detailed component to the application that addresses electronic claims and disbursement of funds.

It is important to be aware of the MCO's billing requirements before entering into the contract. If electronic billing is required, then clinical mental health counselors must download the billing software from each MCO. They will need a computer with adequate memory and storage space, because billing software files tend to be rather large. Clinical mental health counselors may also opt to purchase their own billing software. However, they will also need to find an electronic data interchange (EDI) to manage the transmission of the claims. Such clearinghouses charge an additional fee but are typically available through billing software companies. It is also recommended that counselors purchase the necessary technical support to help with any software challenges that might occur. Although technical support can be expensive, it is beneficial to have access to computer technicians when needed to avoid any billing delays.

Clinical mental health providers may be surprised to know that some MCOs charge a fee in order to become a provider in the network. One author has paid $250 annually to join and remain a provider in a particular managed care network. Such networks are usually very large and handle the referrals for many insurance companies. Thus, providers will automatically become a provider for numerous plans after completing the application and paying the fee, making the higher fee worthwhile.

As discussed earlier in the chapter, some MCOs authorize out-of-network reimbursement. Therefore, a noncontracted counselor may see a client and receive reimbursement from the MCO, but the member typically has to pay a higher out-of-pocket amount than what she would if she saw an in-network provider. Some MCOs will not reimburse any amount for services provided by out-of-network providers. Thus, it is important to verify that one is an in-network provider before providing service.

Some MCOs use providers that already have approved credentials listed in a provider database. The Council for Affordable Quality Healthcare (CAQH) is a clearinghouse that handles the credentialing of health care providers. Once a counselor completes the online application, the information can be shared with a variety of participating MCOs (CAQH, 2013). If an MCO uses CAQH for its provider credentialing, then there will be a section on the provider application asking for the counselor's CAQH number.

A clinical mental health counselor's contract with each MCO is reviewed annually unless otherwise noted. Counselors will be contacted by the MCO to complete a re-credentialing packet. Re-credentialing can be done online and involves making any changes to the original application. Clinical mental health counselors must also provide the MCO with a current copy of their license and liability insurance. The MCO will also have counselors sign an updated copy of the attestation document stating that they have had no legal or ethical violations. If counselors do not complete the re-credentialing process within the allotted time, they will be dropped from the network and have to repeat the entire credentialing process. Thus, it is best to meet all deadlines mandated by the MCOs.

VOICE FROM THE FIELD 8.2

After working in nonprofit agencies, in community mental health agencies, and for the federal government, I decided to go into private practice. I had no knowledge of managed care; therefore, I had to learn as I went along. My first challenge was becoming a provider for a variety of networks. My practice was in an area with individuals from lower socioeconomic levels; thus the clients were dependent upon insurance reimbursement to pay for their services. I knew that if I did not become a provider, there would be few clients in the area who could afford to pay out-of-pocket fees, even with my sliding scale.

Although I had taken over an existing practice, the process was still exhausting. I had no idea that the application process would be so time-consuming. There were no online applications and only one credentialing database at that time. Paper applications were mailed to the insurance companies, and the process took approximately 90 days.

Once I became a provider, it was hard to keep up with the authorizations for the clients' sessions. I bought billing software to help, but it was difficult to focus on treatment goals while being preoccupied with administrative tasks. Thus, I hired an independent billing consultant. She handled filing the insurance claims and keeping up with the authorizations. I learned the hard way that MCOs will not pay for sessions conducted without an authorization. I once had a client who had had eight sessions authorized. My billing consultant failed to tell me that that client had exceeded his eight sessions. I saw him for four additional sessions before the consultant brought it to my attention. I could not get reimbursed for those four sessions, nor would my contract allow me to bill the client. I lost a considerable amount of money. This happened with multiple clients before we figured out a way to properly track the authorizations. It was an expensive lesson.

I also realized that when you outsource your billing, you are trusting that the individual/company will follow the procedures outlined in your contract. The billing company must be aware of the importance of obtaining the necessary authorizations, as well as of filing claims in a timely manner. On several occasions I lost a considerable amount of money, because the claims were not filed within the designated time frame. Some insurance companies allow one year, and some allow only 60 days. I had assumed all MCOs were the same; however, they were not. That was another expensive lesson.

Another challenge in private practice was keeping up with the changes in technology. I had to update my computer software, increase the amount of technical support I had, and hire an experienced billing company. My practice grew rapidly, and I needed the expertise of a skilled billing company to prevent any further mistakes that would result in financial repercussions.

I remember the days when checks were sent through the mail, and then suddenly most of the payments were directly deposited into my bank account. Direct deposit may sound like an advantage, but providing verification of your bank account to multiple insurance companies is time-consuming. There were also kinks in the system, which resulted in delays with payments. I once encountered problems with incompatibility between my billing company's software and an MCO's software. As a result, I did not receive payments that were owed to me for over six months. This was a large MCO, and I saw approximately 20 patients per week through it. It was stressful trying to stay afloat financially while waiting on reimbursement.

I have now moved on from a billing company to an in-house billing specialist. This not only reduces expenses but also reduces the time it takes to have claims billed and have errant claims corrected. I cannot stress how important it is to be familiar with your managed care contracts. Be familiar with the authorization process, as well as the time limit for filing claims. If you hire a billing representative/company, make sure it is reputable and experienced. As clinical mental health counselors, we can get very busy attending to our clients and forget that we have to manage (or micromanage) the administrative tasks as well.

ANTHONY WOOD, LPC
Owner/Director, Desoto Family Counseling Center, PLLC, Southaven, Mississippi

DOCUMENTATION

In order for MCOs to reimburse for counseling sessions, clinical mental health counselors must first obtain the necessary authorization. Many MCOs and insurance companies require that pre-authorization be obtained before the service can be rendered. If pre-authorization is not obtained, then no reimbursement will be provided. Some MCOs do not require pre-authorization; however, it is best for counselors to verify clients' benefits prior to initiating therapy.

Pre-authorization involves providing the MCO with information about the client's need for treatment. Such information is often provided using an Outpatient Treatment Report (OTR). The OTR is also known as a treatment plan and is also used throughout the course of therapy to request additional sessions. The OTR is a document that gives the client's DSM-IV diagnosis and treatment goals. It outlines measurable goals and the interventions that will be implemented to reach those goals (Phillips, 2002). It is important to consider the client's ideal Global Assessment of Functioning (GAF) when establishing the treatment goals (Phillips, 2002), as well as how the client will be different at the termination of treatment. For example, if a client suffers from major depressive disorder, how would the clinical mental health counselor determine that he would be less depressed based on measurable behaviors? Such questions are likely to be asked by a UR representative and will serve as a basis for determining whether sessions are authorized.

Clinical mental health counselors are required by MCOs to keep a record of their counseling sessions. There must be documentation that a session was conducted, or else the insurance company will not pay for the session (Kettenbach, 2009; Phillips, 2002). A session note, often referred to as a progress note, outlines the basic content and dynamics of each counseling session. It should contain the client's name, the date of the session, and the time of the session. Because MCOs focus on brief, solution-based therapy, the session notes must be concise, behavioral in nature, and reflect specific progress made toward the stated treatment goals (Kettenbach, 2009; Phillips, 2002). The session notes should also contain a significant amount of information reflecting the diagnosis for which the insurance company is paying (Phillips, 2002). Many professionals use the BIRP format or SOAP format for session notes.

BIRP Format

The BIRP format indicates the client's behavior, the intervention used, the client's response to the intervention, and the plan for upcoming sessions. The BIRP format provides concise information about the content of the session.

SOAP Format

The SOAP format is similar to the BIRP format, in that it concisely organizes the content of the session. However, the SOAP format outlines the client's subjective statements, the counselor's objective observations, the counselor's assessment of the client and the nature of his or her difficulties, and the plan for future treatment (Kettenbach, 2009).

There are other similar progress note formats; however, the BIRP and SOAP formats appear to be the most commonly used among counselors. Clinical mental health counselors should review their contract with the MCO to determine whether a particular format for documentation is required.

CASE STUDY 8.2

Jeff graduated from a CACREP-accredited mental health counseling program seven years ago. He has been licensed as a professional counselor (LPC) in the state of Mississippi for five years. Jeff has been working in a mental health agency since he graduated; however, he recently decided to open a private practice. Jeff is trying to become a provider with several managed care organizations. Jeff does not own a computer. He is completing his provider applications at his local public library.

Jeff began applying to become a provider three years ago. However, his application was denied, because he had been licensed for only one year. Many of the MCOs to whom Jeff applied required that he be licensed for two years. Jeff decided to gain additional clinical experience before reapplying.

Jeff has a client suffering from severe depression who was recently referred to his private practice. His client has DoeX insurance. Jeff is not a provider for DoeX; therefore, he has just begun the application process.

Jeff reviewed the basic requirements to become a provider with DoeX. He realized that the claims must be filed electronically; therefore, he had to buy a computer. He also had to decide whether he wanted to use the software provided by DoeX (and any future MCOs he joined), which would require a significant amount of computer memory. Jeff opted to buy a computer billing software program, Counselor-Mate, to do his billing. He paid for one year of technical support and arranged for the claims to be filed electronically through its clearinghouse, MedHelp.

Upon completing the provider application, Jeff became confused by some of the terminology on the application. The application asked for his DEA number. Jeff was not sure what a DEA number was or whether he needed to apply for one. He also was worried that he might not be accepted by the MCO, because one of the sections asked him to identify the hospitals to which he had admitting privileges. Jeff did not have admitting privileges to any hospital.

As Jeff continued to complete the application, he was asked to provide his NPI number. Jeff had not yet applied for an NPI; thus he had to visit the NPPES Web site and apply for one. Although the application process typically takes 20 minutes, Jeff's application took longer to complete. He was not sure how to respond to the section inquiring about his provider taxonomy. After accessing the appropriate Web site, he was able to get the needed information and complete the NPI application. Jeff then had to wait 10 days for his NPI number. He was notified by e-mail when his NPI had been assigned.

Jeff later noticed that DoeX credentials its providers through CAQH. He had not completed an application with CAQH; therefore, he had to access its Web site and complete the application. This application was quite lengthy and asked that he provide detailed information about his education and work experience. Jeff was also asked to name three personal references. Jeff was not sure who to use as references. After much thought, he decided to ask two former supervisors from his work and a former professor from his graduate program. Jeff had not been in touch with any of them in several years. Therefore, he had to locate them and ask their permission to be listed as references. It was two weeks before he was able to locate his references and get their contact information.

Jeff finally completed the CAQH application. He then had to sign and return the required forms along with copies of his license and malpractice insurance. His application with CAQH was approved within seven days, and he was given an identification number.

After Jeff successfully obtained his NPI and CAQH numbers, he was able to finish the provider application. Once he submitted the application online, he was informed by a DoeX representative that the application review process would take 60 days.

Jeff's client will have to pay for his fees, because DoeX does not reimburse for services provided by out-of-network providers. Although Jeff's client needs weekly counseling, she cannot afford to pay for weekly counseling. Thus, she will only have one session per month until Jeff becomes a network provider.

CHALLENGES WITH MANAGED CARE

Clinical mental health counselors are likely to encounter many challenges when functioning as preferred providers. Keeping track of authorizations for treatment can be a tedious process. And, if counselors provide counseling services outside of the umbrella of a current authorization, they will not be reimbursed for those services. Most billing software is able to keep track of managed care authorizations; however, clinical mental health counselors must be sure that they do not provide services once the authorized number of sessions has been used.

It is also important to remember that MCOs have strict policies about the submission of claims. All claims must be filed in a timely manner or payment will be denied. Some MCOs require that claims be filed within 60 days of the date of service, whereas others allow six months to one year for claims to be submitted before they are no longer eligible for payment. Clinical mental health counselors should review the contract carefully to become familiar with the MCO's requirements for the submission of claims.

Another potential challenge for clinical mental health counselors is related to providing services that are not covered by the MCO. For example, most MCOs will not pay for telephone contact with a client. They pay for only face-to-face contact. Thus, if counselors conduct a therapy session via telephone, then they will not be reimbursed. Clinical mental health counselors can bill the client directly for the session; however, many clients are dependent on their insurance for payment of services. Counselors cannot submit a claim for individual therapy if the session was conducted over the phone.

There are also certain CPT codes that are not covered by some MCOs. For example, many MCOs do not reimburse for marriage counseling, couples counseling, family therapy, or play therapy. Many people cannot afford to pay out-of-pocket fees for counseling services; therefore, they rely on their insurance to pay for the sessions. Clinical mental health counselors are ethically obligated to submit for reimbursement only those services that were provided. As a result, a family may not be able to receive the needed interventions due to the regulations of managed care.

MCOs also dictate the length of time that clients may be seen in a counseling session. For example, most MCOs provide reimbursement for a 45- to 50-minute session and will not authorize the provider to offer longer sessions. If the provider spends more time than the allotted amount, he or she will not be paid additional fees. Thus, a counselor who spends two hours with a family in crisis will be reimbursed at the same rate as a counselor who conducts a 45-minute session with a family.

A final challenge for counselors who become MCO providers involves being easily accessible to new referrals. Many MCOs include in the contract that clinical mental health counselors must offer a first appointment for a new client within a given time frame. Such a time frame may be anywhere from three to ten days. Counselors may also be required to provide an immediate appointment for clients with life-threatening emergencies. Some clinical mental health counselors are uncomfortable with a managed care organization dictating when clients must be seen. Counselors who have busy practices may find themselves having to work later hours to accommodate the scheduling requirements of the MCO.

A FINAL NOTE FROM THE AUTHORS

As private practitioners, we would be remiss if we did not pause to talk about clients paying for services. Although the focus of this chapter places great emphasis on becoming an approved provider for insurance companies and being reimbursed for services by HMOs, the reality is that clinical mental health counselors will still have to ask clients for co-pays and unpaid balances. This proves to be a challenge for many counselors. As helping professionals, we are highly motivated to assist people, and particularly in these tough economic times, we often hesitate to ask clients for money. Counselors that serve underprivileged populations have difficulty asking for payment for services when they are face-to-face with individuals and families that struggle to meet basic needs (Falkner, 2006). Counselor education programs often do little to prepare counselors to deal with the anxiety or sometimes even feelings of guilt that result from asking clients for money.

However, let's consider this from another perspective. If you needed eggs, would you walk into the market and take them without paying? No, you would check out and pay for the goods you are purchasing. If you go to a physician to have your tonsils out, you enter into that endeavor knowing you will have to pay for it. You may look at your policy to see who is an approved provider in your area so that out-of-pocket expenses are minimized, but you would not assume that the surgeon would just take out your tonsils out of the goodness of his or her medical heart. No, you would want someone competent and qualified, and you would want to get good service and care for your money. The same is true for counseling professionals. If you are a private practitioner, the sessions you conduct and the payment you receive pay the bills. But if you don't collect, you can't pay the bills. You have invested a considerable amount of time and money in your training as a counselor. You provide a valuable, needed service, and clients value what they pay for. So, if you find yourself struggling to say, "Will that be cash or check today?" then you would be well served to consult with colleagues, seek supervision, or simply role-play with a friend until the new wears off and you can speak the words with certainty.

Conclusion

With the advent of managed care, professional counselors are encountering challenging issues with regard to becoming a provider, ethical issues, and reimbursement concerns. These issues have implications for clinical mental health counselors, researchers, educators, and supervisors.

This chapter examined the evolution of managed care and reviewed basic concepts, attempted to demystify the process of becoming a provider, and took an honest look at the ethical challenges counselors face with diagnosing and documentation.

References

American Counseling Association (ACA). (2005). *Code of ethics*. Alexandria, VA: Author.

American Medical Association (AMA). (n.d.). *About CPT*. Retrieved from http://www.ama-assn.org /ama/pub/physician-resources/solutions-managing -your-practice/coding-billing-insurance/cpt/about -cpt.shtml

American Mental Health Counselors Association (AMHCA). (2010). *2010 AMHCA code of ethics*. Retrieved from https://www.amhca.org/assets/news /AMHCA_Code_of_Ethics_2010_w_pagination _cxd_51110.pdf

American Psychiatric Association. (2000). *Diagnostic and statistical manual of mental disorders, fourth edition–text revision* (DSM-IV-TR). Washington, DC: Author.

Benefield, H., Ashkanazi, G., & Rozensky, R. (2006). Communication and records: HIPAA issues when working in health care settings. *Professional Psychology: Research and Practice, 37*(3), 273–277. doi:10.1037/0735-7028.37.3.273

Boyle, P., & Callahan, D. (1995). Managed care in mental health: The ethical issues. *Health Affairs, 14*(3), 7–22. doi:10.1377/hlthaff.14.3.7

Braun, S., & Cox, J. (2005). Managed mental health care: Intentional misdiagnosis of mental disorders. *Journal of Counseling & Development, 83,* 425–433.

Brendel, R., & Bryan, E. (2004). HIPAA for psychiatrists. *Harvard Review of Psychiatry, 12*(3), 177–183. doi:10.1080/10673220490472436

Chambliss, C. H. (2006). *Psychotherapy and managed care: Reconciling research and reality*. Abbortsford, Canada: Indo American Books.

Council for Accreditation of Counseling & Related Educational Programs (CACREP). (2009). *CACREP accreditation manual: 2009 standards*. Alexandria, VA: Author. Retrieved from http://www.cacrep.org /doc/2009%20Standards%20with%20cover.pdf

Council for Affordable Quality Healthcare (CAQH). (2013). *CAQH*. Retrieved from http://www.caqh.org

Cunningham, P. (2009). Beyond parity: Primary care physicians' perspectives on access to mental health care. *Health Affairs, 28*(3), 490–501.

Danzinger, P. R., & Welfel, E. R. (2001). The impact of managed care on mental health counselors: A survey of perceptions, practices, and compliance with ethical standards [Electronic version]. *Journal of Mental Health Counseling, 23,* 137–151.

DeLeon, P., VandenBos, G., & Bulatao, E. (1994). Managed mental health care: A history of the federal policy initiative. In R. L. Lowman & R. J. Resnick (Eds.), *The mental health professional's guide to managed care* (pp. 19–40). Washington, DC: American Psychological Association.

Eaves, S., Emens, R., & Sheperis, C. J. (2008). Counselors in the managed care era: The efficacy of the data based problem solver model. *Journal of Professional Counseling: Practice, Theory & Research, 36*(2), 1–12.

Falkner, J. (2006). A study to investigate counselor financial wellness as a predictor of counselor money practices among counseling professionals in private practice. *Dissertation Abstracts International: Section A. The Humanities and Social Sciences, 67.*

Gilbert, B. (2004). Employee assistance programs: History and program descriptions. *Journal of the American Association of Occupational Health Nurses, 42*(10), 488–493.

Gostin, L., & Nass, S. (2009). Reforming the HIPAA Privacy Rule: Safeguarding privacy and promoting research. *The Journal of the American Medical Association, 301*(13), 1373–1375.

Harris, J. (1994). *Strategic health management: A guide for employees, employers, and policy makers.* San Francisco, CA: Jossey-Bass.

Jensen, D. G. (2004, July/August). *Independent medical review: A slingshot in your patient's battle with the Goliath of managed care.* California Association for Marriage and Family Counselors. Retrieved from http://www.camft.org/ScriptContent/CAMFTarticles/Misc/IndependentMedicalReview.htm

Kettenbach, G. (2009). *Writing patient/client notes* (4th ed.). Philadelphia, PA: Davis.

Lammando, M. (2003, April). Independent medical reviewer opportunity. *Physician's News Digest.* Retrieved from http://www.physiciansnews.com/2003/04/17/independent-medical-reviewer-opportunity

Lawless, L., Ginter, E., & Kelly, K. (1999). Managed care: What mental health counselors need to know. *Journal of Mental Health Counseling, 21*(1), 50–65.

Luo, J. (2007). HIPAA-proof your practice: From PDA to your office. *Primary Psychiatry, 14*(10), 26–30.

Murphy, M. J., DeBernardo, C. R., & Shoemaker, W. E. (1998). Impact of managed care on independent practice and professional ethics: A survey of independent practitioners. *Professional Psychology: Research and Practice, 29,* 43–51.

National Alliance on Mental Illness. (1996). *The Mental Health Parity Act of 1996.* Retrieved from http://www.nami.org/Content/ContentGroups/E-News/1996/The_Mental_Health_Parity_Act_of_1996.htm

National Plan and Provider Enumeration System (NPPES). (2010). *National Provider Identifier.* Retrieved from https://nppes.cms.hhs.gov/NPPES/StaticForward.do?forward=static.npistart

Pakhomov, S., Jacobsen, S., Chute, C., & Roger, V. (2008). Agreement between client reported symptoms and their documentation in the medical record. *The American Journal of Managed Care, 14*(8), 530–539.

Pam Pohly Associates. (2009). *The glossary of managed care and healthcare terminology.* Hays, KS: Author.

Phillips, J. (2002). Managed care's reconstruction of human existence: The triumph of technical reason. *Theoretical medicine and bioethics, 23*(4–5), 339–358. doi:10.1023/A:1021213807475

Rother, J. (1996). Consumer protection in managed-care: A third generation approach. *Generations, 20,* 42–46.

Smith, D. (2003). 10 ways practitioners can avoid frequent ethical pitfalls. *Monitor on Psychology, 34,* 50–55.

Tufts Managed Care Institute. (1998). *A brief history of managed care.* Retrieved from http://www.thci.org/downloads/briefhist.pdf

US Department of Health and Human Services (DHHS). (2013). *Understanding health information privacy.* Retrieved from http://www.hhs.gov/ocr/privacy/hipaa/understanding

US Department of Labor. (2010). *The Mental Health Parity and Addiction Equity Act of 2008 (MHPAEA).* http://www.dol.gov/ebsa/newsroom/fsmhpaea.html

Wilcoxon, S., Magnunson, S., & Norem, K. (2008). Institutional values of managed mental health care: Efficiency or oppression? *Journal of Multicultural Counseling and Development, 36,* 143–154.

Williams, E., & Edwardson, T. (2000). Managed care and counseling centers: Training issues for the new millennium. *Journal of College Student Psychotherapy, 14*(3), 51–65. doi:10.1300/J035v14n03_07

9

Consultation and Referrals

ROBYN TRIPPANY-SIMMONS, TIFFANY RUSH-WILSON, JASON PATTON, AND MICHELLE PEREPICZKA

CHAPTER OVERVIEW

When high school officials are faced with an epidemic of eating disorders in their student population and are not certain how to develop a program to respond, the administration may consult with a clinical mental health counselor. When a business needs to promote a team approach among its employees, the managers may consult with a clinical mental health counselor. When a clinical mental health counselor needs to understand a client's physical impairment to assist with the mental health treatment, the counselor may consult with a medical professional. These examples are common types of consultation needs.

When a clinical mental health counselor provides a client with contact information for a local public assistance agency, this is referral. When a clinical mental health counselor accepts a job with another agency and provides the client with the name of another counselor, this is referral. When a client seeks services from a clinical mental health counselor who has limited knowledge about that particular issue, and the counselor provides the contact information of a practitioner who has an expertise in dealing with that issue, this is referral.

Consultation and referral are services that clinical mental health counselors regularly provide or engage in. These services are similar in that their purpose is to support work with clients. The goal of this chapter is to provide a contextual understanding of consultation and referral services in the mental health counseling profession.

LEARNING OBJECTIVES

The learning objectives for this chapter are designed to be consistent with the 2009 Council for Accreditation of Counseling and Related Educational Programs Standards (CACREP, 2009). As such, upon completion of this chapter, the student will have knowledge of the following clinical mental health counseling standards:

1. Understands ethical and legal considerations specifically related to the practice of clinical mental health counseling. (A.2)
2. Understands the roles and functions of clinical mental health counselors in various practice settings and the importance of relationships between counselors and other professionals, including interdisciplinary treatment teams. (A.3)

3. Describes the principles of mental health, including prevention, intervention, consultation, education, and advocacy, as well as the operation of programs and networks that promote mental health in a multicultural society. (C.1)

4. Understands the range of mental health service delivery—such as inpatient, outpatient, partial treatment and aftercare—and the clinical mental health counseling services network. (C.5)

5. Recognizes the importance of family, social networks, and community systems in the treatment of mental and emotional disorders. (C.8)

6. Demonstrates appropriate use of culturally responsive individual, couple, family, group, and systems modalities for initiating, maintaining, and terminating counseling. (D.5)

7. Demonstrates the ability to recognize his or her own limitations as a clinical mental health counselor and to seek supervision or refer clients when appropriate. (D.9)

INTRODUCTION

In this chapter, we distinguish consultation as a distinct process from clinical mental health counseling. We first provide a broad overview of consultation and then address the function of consultation for clinical mental health counselors. In addition, there is a discussion of the ways consultation is used to work with other mental health service providers, family members, and community members. This chapter concludes with a discussion of the ethical and legal issues related to consultation.

CONSULTATION: AN OVERVIEW

Consultation is a vehicle for problem solving. It is triadic in nature, involving a consultant, a consultee, and a client(s). The consultant and consultee work together to identify areas of concern and work to support counselor services provided to the client(s). Consultation may be client centered (e.g., clinical mental health counselor needs help conceptualizing a client case) or consultee centered (e.g., clinical mental health counselor needs assistance in gaining skills to work with a specific client issue; Caplan & Caplan, 1993). Consultation may be initiated by the counselor or the consultee; or the clinical mental health counselor's consultative services may be sought by schools, agencies, businesses, organizations, or other counselors. The counselor and consultant will work together to identify the parameters of the consulting relationship and the role of the consultant within the context of the needs of the consultee.

There is often debate about the definition of consultation services and how to distinguish them from other services, such as supervision, counseling, and collaboration (Dougherty, 2005). Essentially, consultation is a form of indirect intervention utilized to help support the services counselors provide to clients. Although it seems that consultation may be very similar to supervision, it is important to note the distinction between the consultation process and supervision (Dougherty, 2005). With the consultation process, the consultant will exit the situation once the purpose of the consultation is resolved. However, supervision is a longer-term, hierarchical relationship between a supervisor and a supervisee that provides developmental support for the clinical mental health counselor. Although the skills used in consultation mirror those used in counseling (i.e., cultural competence, relationship building, problem solving, intervention selection and implementation, and evaluation), consultation is distinguished from counseling by the fact that the focus is on the consultant and consultee working together toward the goal of how to best help the client (Nugent & Jones, 2009). Collaboration, however, is more difficult to differentiate. In fact, collaboration is often an aspect of consultation. The distinction between the two is simple: collaboration involves direct service to clients, whereas consultation does not (Brown & Srebalus, 2003). In collaboration, the services provided to the client are impacted, but with consultation, changes may be made to agency policy or other indirect services that are never noticed by the client.

Why does consultation need to occur? How does a clinical mental health counselor know whether he or she needs to consult? These are great questions to assist in providing foundational understanding of consultation as a role in counseling. Consultation helps a counselor improve the skills needed to perform the work of counseling more effectively, thus enhancing the services provided to clients (Brown, Pryzwansky, & Schulte, 1987). Clinical mental health counselors must continuously self-assess so that they are aware of their limitations, whether with the content of the client issue or their own reaction to the client issue, so they know when to ask for consultation. Caplan (1970) identified four areas of concern for which consultation can support clinical mental health counselors: (a) lack of knowledge (e.g., working with a consultee who has a client with obsessive-compulsive disorder but no clinical expertise with that diagnosis); (b) lack of skill (e.g., when a consultee seeks assistance in developing skills to work with adolescents); (c) lack of confidence (e.g., consultee seeks support with his or her insecurity regarding a presentation that has to be delivered to agency stakeholders, even though the consultee has the necessary knowledge and skill set); and (d) lack of objectivity (e.g., consultant works to assist consultee in maintaining sound judgment with a client similar to the one the consultant has worked with previously).

VOICE FROM THE FIELD 9.1

As much as I love conducting face-to-face therapy with my clients, my personal "style" prefers a variety of activities in work and in play. My doing consulting and nontherapeutic corporate work came into being by default. Early on in my private practice, I began offering free talks to local organizations on topics such as work–life balance, stress management, and other common topics, in which all clinical mental health counselors would be proficient, with the hopes of growing the practice. Sometimes my interactions with the human resource managers of these organizations, who typically arranged these in-service trainings, expanded. I received invitations to assist in conflict resolution situations, time and organization coaching for a particular employee, or team building based on the Myers-Briggs Type Indicator (MBTI) (I was a certified MBTI practitioner) for small departments or the entire workforce of a small company, typically of one hundred or fewer people.

I then met a colleague who was also a therapist; she had been an employment recruiter in the past and was doing some consultation for a few clients. With the combination of our prior individual organizational experiences, her understanding of what employers looked for in employees, and our common expertise in MBTI usage, we created a separate corporate business entity and went to work.

We developed a Web site, a service and fee schedule for some of our activities, and marketing literature. We then joined the local Society for Human Resource Management (SHRM), the local American Society for Training & Development (ASTD), and several area chamber of commerce organizations. All of this was to construct a forum for passing out business cards and even displaying information as a vendor at many of their meetings. We shook hands with and met those people who could hire us or refer us to other companies. Before we knew it, we were taking on bigger projects that moved us further away from the typical skill sets of a therapist. These projects included conducting leadership development classes, confidential employee satisfaction surveys, and 360° manager surveys complete with coaching. A number of these activities required us to put in many hours of research before we felt ethically prepared to offer excellent service; yet we endured and found much variety in our workweek. And it all started with sharing some common counseling knowledge with business groups rather than counseling groups!

GARY WILLIAMS, EdS, LPC
Counseling & Consulting Professionals

Consultant Roles

The role the counselor takes within the consultant relationship is what defines the particular intervention (Wilcoxon, 1989). Some roles of the consultant include (a) trainer/ educator, (b) collaborator, (c) advocate, and (d) expert. Hence, a clinical mental health counselor becomes a consultee in his or her professional relationship with a consultant. If the consultant is hired to assist the consultee with knowledge or skill acquisition, then the consultant will serve in the role of trainer/educator. Acting in this role, the consultant teaches concepts and provides education specific to the consultee's needs. When a clinical mental health counselor lacks the knowledge to fully understand and/or conceptualize a client case, the consultant serves to provide the needed information. If a consultee needs assistance with program development and evaluation, it is likely that the consultant will serve in the role of either collaborator or expert, or both. In these roles, the consultant works with the consultee to identify the program needs and then delivers the consultation within an area of expertise. With some individual system consultation, specifically with regard to public policy, the consultant will serve predominantly in the role of advocate to promote the needs to the consultee. However, the consultant may possibly fluctuate between roles with any given consultation need. To illustrate, let's take a look at a case study.

CASE STUDY 9.1

Sam has been working with his local community mental health agency as a clinical mental health counselor since he graduated with his master's degree in clinical mental health counseling a year and a half ago. He predominantly works with male clients who are referred by their employers after having failed drug and alcohol screenings at work. Sam enjoys his role as a substance abuse counselor and has even submitted a presentation proposal for the state counseling association's yearly conference to discuss the use of narrative therapy with substance abusers. However, recently he has been referred several female clients with addiction issues who have disclosed sexual abuse histories in early childhood. He is not really comfortable working with females and has limited knowledge regarding childhood sexual abuse. He is seeking consultation to assist with gaining knowledge, skill, and confidence in working with these women.

Reflecting on the needs of Sam in this case, identify the roles the consultant would use in supporting Sam as the consultee. How would each role provide distinctly different services? How would the consultant integrate these roles to provide comprehensive services? Finally, consider how you see yourself working with a client like Sam. What are your personal strengths for this type of work? What barriers might you face?

A consultant needs to have an extensive skill set to meet the consultee's multiple needs (Bergan & Kratochwill, 1990; Schroeder, 1996). At the minimum, a consultant would first be required to have expertise in the presenting problem of the consultee. Areas of situational expertise may vary from issues within a school system; child, adolescent, or family community-focused agency; large group–focused organization; or public policy. Second, the consultant would need expertise with regard to the consultation process (Schmidt, 2008). The consultant needs skills to move the consultee through the stages of the consultation from problem identification to final evaluation. As a third skill set category, a consultant would need to be a trainer or educator who could assist the consultee in building the skills needed to implement the newly developed plan.

According to Wilcoxon (1990), certain principles of persuasion are inherent in consultation, and the consultant uses them to influence change. Wilcoxon indicated that consultants use legitimate power (i.e., based in the "hierarchical control" of the consultant; p. 18), expert power (i.e., based in the knowledge and areas of expertise of the consultant), and/or referent power (i.e., based in the consultant having the admiration and respect of the consultee). When consultation is sought to educate or prescribe, the consultant uses expert power. For diagnostic and directive consultation, the consultant utilizes what is known as legitimate power. Consultation that is facilitative or supportive in nature will be based in the referent power of the consultant, or the level of identification with and respect for the consultant.

A Model for Consultation

Perhaps the most recognized model for consultation is Dougherty's (2005) four-stage model. In the first stage, entry, problem identification is the focus. Consultant and consultee work together to identify the purpose of the consultation, along with the needs of the consultant. It is during this stage that a contract is developed to outline the expectations for and understanding of the consultation relationship, including the problem focus, the type of consultation needed, the roles of both the consultant and the consultee, and any compensation or other logistical information. This contract may be verbal or written. In the second stage, diagnosis, problem exploration is the focus. The consultant (with or without the consultee, depending on the mode of functioning) will collect and analyze data/information, set goals, and identify potential courses of action to solve the problem. The third stage, intervention, is when the consultee and consultant select a course of action and implement it, evaluating the outcomes during and after the plan implementation. During the fourth and final stage, disengagement, the consultant begins to turn over the responsibility of the problem solution and continued management of the problem to the consultee. An evaluation of the overall process occurs during this stage and, ultimately, the consultant terminates services.

Types of Consultation

Consultation with mental health providers frequently occurs from either a consultee- or client-centered case perspective. Consultee-centered case consultation (Caplan & Caplan, 1993) occurs when the clinical mental health counselor seeks the services of a consultant to assist in strengthening an area of weakness. For example, a clinical mental health counselor may find that he or she has an influx of clients with a similar issue for which he or she does not have expertise. Rather than refer those clients to other service providers, the clinical mental health counselor may choose to work with a consultant who does have expertise in that area to build his or her own skills and assist with that clinical issue, while concurrently working with these clients. With client-centered case consultation (Caplan & Caplan, 1993), the goal of the consultant is to assist with the treatment planning specific to the client. For example, a clinical mental health counselor works in a nonprofit domestic violence setting. In this setting, the counselor does not provide diagnoses. However, the clinical mental health counselor has a client about whom she is concerned there may be serious mental illness. The counselor may refer the client for testing and then consult with the tester regarding diagnosis and potential treatment needs.

In addition, consultation can occur from a program-centered administrative consultation or consultee-centered administrative consultation (Caplan & Caplan, 1993). With program-centered administrative consultation, the consultant may be tasked to evaluate an existing agency or program and provide feedback about how to improve its functioning. Consultee-centered administrative consultation may involve team building with employees.

Within these types of consultation, the consultant can function under different modes as identified by Schein (1969): (a) expert, (b) prescriber, (c) mediator, and (d) collaborator. Consultants in the expert mode are hired based on their area of expertise, and they can serve to identify solutions, provide training, and/or implement plans themselves. The consultant serving in the prescriber mode provides recommendations for the consultee to follow. The mediator mode allows the consultant to coordinate services of multiple agencies in order to solve a problem. Finally, the collaborative consultant works to facilitate the problem-solving process for the consultee(s).

 ## CONSULTATION WITH OTHER MENTAL HEALTH OR MEDICAL PERSONNEL

Consultation with medical professionals may consist of myriad forms and functions. Doherty (1995) noted that collaboration between mental health professionals and medical professionals could take place by degree, ranging from the most limited sharing of information to shared physical spaces and treatment facilities. When minimal consultation is needed, the clinical mental health counselor may perform one-on-one consultation with a prescribing physician to conceptualize a client's needs and coordinate care, discuss issues related to medication management and adherence, or share information that may have been overlooked or occluded in either of the two settings. In more intensive collaborative efforts, the clinical mental health counselor could be part of a team approach to address a particular client's health care and mental health care needs in a comprehensive, holistic fashion (Yuen, Gerdes, & Waldfogel, 1996). The counselor may be the sole mental health expert in these interactions, or he or she may be collaborating with psychiatrists, psychologists, or other mental health professionals. Alternatively, a clinical mental health counselor who performs work as a consultant-liaison may participate in in-services and training of other mental health professionals or take part in collaborative research efforts (Miller & Swartz, 1990). Although a clinical mental health counselor's specific roles may vary according to circumstance, as with all counseling-related roles, his or her primary obligation and objective remain the same—ethical and competent client care.

Challenges

A number of barriers may impede movement in or through clinical mental health counselors' consulting with physicians. An awareness of the extra time commitment (Edwards,

Patterson, Grauf-Grounds, & Groban, 2001) such consultation requires is frequently an initial concern. Even though clinical mental health counselors may wish to pursue consultation because of its potential benefits to clients or other stakeholders, they may be intimidated by a process for which they have received little training (Dosser, Handron, McCammon, Powell, & Spencer, 2001).

Additionally, an initial contact with and immersion in the biomedical culture could be intimidating or dissuading of continued involvement because of the differences between mental health professionals and physicians (Edwards et al., 2001). Hamberger, Ovide, and Weiner (1999) identified four of these areas of difference: (a) emphasis on different theories, (b) ways of learning information, (c) methods of approaching problems, and (d) professional expectations for collaboration and consultation. These differences in professional culture may be particularly noticeable in situations related to a client's suicidal ideation or extreme risk taking; the intensity of these circumstances may deter future consultation (Gutierrez et al., 2009). Finally, the cacophony of voices can create confusion and dissent, so team consultation efforts may seem to be the most daunting tasks (Edwards et al., 2001).

Another challenge is the gap between the belief that consultation will be helpful and a willingness to actually engage in consultation. Research has consistently found consultation and collaboration to be in the best interest of clients (Dosser et al., 2001; Roesler, Gavin, & Brenner, 1995). Additionally, a majority of practitioners believe in the value of consultation between health and mental health professionals (Brandon & Knapp, 1999; Edwards & Smith, 1998). In a survey of 99 physicians assessing their perceptions of collaboration with mental health professionals, two-thirds expressed satisfaction with consultation with and referral to mental health specialists (Yuen et al., 1996). However, encouraging other health care and mental health professionals to collaborate in the consulting process provides some challenges, despite this evidence that suggests some positive perceptions of consultation. A number of factors may impact physicians' willingness to participate in the process. Kainz (2002) pointed out that one major inhibitor is confusion about or misinterpretation of the profession of mental health professionals. In fact, although perceptions of the work that clinical mental health counselors do have improved within the last decade, many physicians still view counseling as superfluous or unhelpful. When faced with those who hold such viewpoints, the clinical mental health counselor would be forced to justify his or her profession and personal investment prior to any collaboration.

Even upon a physician's agreement to consult, there may be an established power differential that permeates the relationship. McNamara (1981) noted that medical doctors, particularly psychiatrists, are trained to see themselves as experts in all health-related interactions. This viewpoint engenders a belief that others who consult with them are members of a support team—that the work that these individuals do is secondary and in some ways less valuable. Psychiatrists, through a tendency to visually and linguistically set themselves apart from counselors and other mental health professionals, may be particularly complicit in what Miller and Swartz (1990) noted as the biomedical model's domination. This assumed supremacy occurs through a process of either incorporating or marginalizing the biopsychosocial sciences. In other words, medical professionals continue to exert some level of power and privilege over those in the mental health field through a process of assimilation of their information and expertise, or devaluation of the mental health profession's relevance. Counselors should prepare to self-advocate to help ensure that clients are able to access competent, noncompetitive comprehensive care that values the work of all providers.

Treatment Teams and Stakeholders

The decision to pursue consultation for a client's welfare requires careful consideration of who the stakeholders are in the process. A client's wellness is of prime importance to stakeholders. Any health care professional whose work may impact or be impacted by the client's mental health and wellness should be considered a stakeholder. To best benefit the client, the clinical mental health counselor, upon client approval, should consider including all of these professionals in the treatment process. In some cases, the clinical mental health counselor may work with only one person or a very limited number of people. For example, certain stakeholders may not be involved in client treatment if they have little impact on the client's care, if there is a lack of accessibility, or if the stakeholder is simply not interested in participating.

With each additional professional involved in the consulting process comes an increase in the resources required. However, a team approach has been shown to be useful in addressing multiple mental health and health care issues (Edwards et al., 2001). In instances of severe mental illness, significant impairment, or hospitalization with a mental health–related issue, clinical mental health counselors often find that a team approach is useful. The use of these teams is sometimes associated with better health and mental health outcomes and shorter hospital stays. Improved client outcomes and shorter stays may also benefit indirect stakeholders such as family members, health insurance providers, and the like. In other words, the use of treatment teams results in a host of advantages for both clients and their stakeholders.

Treatment teams were designed to provide a complete conceptualization of client issues, which allows for more comprehensive intervention. Treatment teams are utilized with clients who need more intensive services, such as those in partial psychiatric hospitalization programs, inpatient psychiatric programs, and day treatment programs. Typically, treatment team members include a psychiatrist, a psychologist, social workers, counselors, and psychiatric nurses. Treatment teams will meet regularly to staff client cases and develop and review treatment plans. Although all members of the treatment team may provide direct service to a client, treatment teams are consultative by nature in that a variety of mental health professionals work together to explore client issues, determine diagnosis and case conceptualization, and identify treatment plans.

Consultation Process

In order to initiate a consulting relationship, clinical mental health counselors should first be prepared to seek out physicians who are amenable to collaboration (Davis, 2001). Clarity of focus on the needs of the client should be the goal (Patterson, 2001); and a timeline for planning, implementation, and disengagement should be established early in the process (Gutierrez et al., 2009). Additionally, it is important to emphasize that clients should be invited to participate in and be informed about the process (Gutierrez et al., 2009).

Clinical mental health counselors can understand the process of consultation with physicians by applying Dougherty's (1995) generic model of systemic consultation. As previously mentioned, the first stage of consultation involves entry. In this stage, the clinical mental health counselor or physician identifies a consulting need and initiates a working relationship. In the second stage, diagnosis, the clinical mental health counselor and physician work to inform each other in a way that helps them more accurately assess the situation. If, for instance, consultation takes the form of collaboration of care for a

CASE STUDY 9.2

Whereas each consultation with medical professionals has its own specific circumstances and counselor roles, a case study offers insight into how the process might progress. For instance, John, the clinical mental health counselor and consultant, will be working with a general practitioner, Dr. Fargas, to determine the best course of action to meet the mental health and medical needs of John's client Edwino, who has been experiencing what he describes as anxiety. He notes that at times his heart rate races and sometimes he feels tightness in his chest, particularly when he is "keyed up about something." Edwino agrees to allow John to speak with Dr. Fargas to discuss the issue.

John and Dr. Fargas schedule two discussions, during the first of which they share information about Edwino's presenting concerns. John learns that Edwino has had borderline-to-high blood pressure throughout his adult life. Dr. Fargas explains that Edwino has never indicated his experience of anxiety and had merely agreed to reduce his salt intake and exercise more to control his blood pressure. John and Dr. Fargas discuss the possibility that Edwino may be experiencing high blood pressure and/or generalized anxiety disorder (GAD). Dr. Fargas determines that a beta-blocking medication to treat hypertension, also prescribed for anxiety, is in the client's best interest. John indicates his understanding of this and agrees to propose cognitive-behavioral therapeutic interventions to treat Edwino's potential GAD diagnosis. Dr. Fargas and John agree to continue their consultation in six weeks.

During the second discussion between John and Dr. Fargas, they each describe Edwino's marked improvement. Dr. Fargas notes that Edwino's blood pressure is under control, whereas John notes that Edwino indicates lower levels of anxiety symptoms. John's engagement of Dr. Fargas in this example demonstrates competent, effective consultation in order to provide more comprehensive and efficacious treatment of Edwino. Throughout the process, John and Dr. Fargas were open with Edwino about their discussions, and as a result, he felt he was a part of the process and its outcome.

client, then case notes, diagnoses, and the like may be exchanged. The third stage, intervention, results in a plan and implementation. The final stage, disengagement, is the formal end of the consulting relationship. For client-related collaboration, this may result in a commitment to reevaluate the need for further consultation at a later time.

An important consideration is that in order to seek consultation, a clinical mental health counselor must be competent in his or her ability to maintain client confidentiality. When counselors in training begin their first field placement as a clinical mental health counselor, they will likely find that there is an automatic system in place for requesting permission to collaborate. An ethical consultation system will benefit counselors because interdisciplinary medical and mental health consultation, for at least some mental health diagnoses, is associated with more positive mental health outcomes and/or longer lasting effects (Edwards et al., 2001). Additionally, collaboration between primary care physicians and mental health professionals has been associated with decreased costs and fewer hospitalizations (Yuen et al., 1996), as well as timelier patient–client care (Sharfstein & Katz-Levy, 1984). Much like research results related to treatment teams, consultation results in improved outcomes for clients.

CONSULTATION WITH FAMILIES

Another form of consultation involves clinical mental health counselors collaborating with families of clients. Counselors often consult with families in order to promote movement toward clients' mental health and wellness. Research suggests that family consultation is associated with positive client outcomes (Frey & Wendorf, 1984; LeBlanc & Ritchie, 2001;

Van Fleet 2000). A typical family consultation might involve educating the family about a client's needs as these needs were presented in counseling or addressing family dynamics as they apply to a client. Cates, Paone, Packman, and Margolis (2006) identified three primary foci for family consultation: (a) to promote continued treatment, because family members can act as sources of encouragement to and accountability for the client; (b) to promote accurate expectations from family members for a client's mental health prognosis; and (c) to alleviate fears of family members that they are doing something wrong or are somehow to blame for a client's mental health concerns. Additionally, consultation can be tailored to help family members, particularly parents, learn to recognize positive behaviors.

Clinical mental health counselors who consult with the families of severely mentally ill clients have a number of goals. Bernheim (1989) identified seven of these: (a) helping family members find a sense of balance between their needs and the needs of the identified client; (b) facilitating identification of and access to services; (c) bolstering family members' coping strategies so they can thrive in the face of the client's continued manifestations of mental illness; (d) identifying strategies for early recognition of significant episodes or relapse; (e) preparing for inevitable family conflict; (f) establishing strategies of disclosure for acquaintances, family, and friends; and (g) supporting familial efforts to resolve the grief and fear related to the client's illness. Sweeney and Homeyer (1999) added that education and support efforts should include a focus on the family's ability to self-advocate. For example, when consulting with family members of clients with long-term, severe mental illness, community support services and resources may not automatically be awarded to clients and family members of those who need them. Clinical mental health counselors can consult with families to assist them in securing fundamental resources to enhance their ability to weather the stressors and setbacks of coping with mental illness.

Consultation with family members of children who are being counseled often entails many of the same components as consultation with families of the severely mentally ill. Additionally, we know that working to help families not only understand the process of therapy but also have realistic expectations has been associated with more kept counseling appointments (Shuman & Shapiro, 2002). Also, as Cates et al. (2006) have pointed out, family stressors that are impacting the child may not be known to the child, and consultation with family members can illuminate some of these concerns. This consultation can also help the clinical mental health counselor make more informed decisions about how to tailor an intervention with the child, including determining the frequency with which to schedule appointments.

Challenges

Consultation with families carries unique challenges. In order to meet these challenges, Bernheim (1989) suggested approaching these situations with certain key presumptions. First, the clinical mental health counselor should consider the family to be in charge. The consulting counselor may assume the role of a facilitator and advisor, but needs to keep in mind that it is the family that will implement any plans made. Along with this comes the awareness that because the family members have the power and ability to make this choice, their say is final about what is to be implemented. Finally, clinical mental health counselors should approach these interactions with the knowledge and disclosure that

CASE STUDY 9.3

A case presentation may help to clarify the intricacies of the family consultation process. For example, Malachi has been counseling Jonna for six months. Malachi is treating Jonna for a complex form of posttraumatic stress disorder (PTSD) related to a previous intimate partner relationship in which she experienced abuse. Jonna and Malachi decided that the time had come to discuss with her family some aspects of her experience as well as her prognosis for the future. Jonna and Malachi established that they would not disclose actual accounts of the events that had occurred, but would give her family a general sense of the extent of violence she had endured. Jonna plans to involve her parents and brother in this consultation, because they have wondered about her sometimes withdrawn, or "reactive," demeanor over the last several years. Malachi agrees to answer questions that might emerge about PTSD from these family members, but agrees with Jonna that she should be able to tell as much or as little about the actual abuse as she sees fit.

Jonna and Malachi meet with her family, who are relieved to learn that her behavior has not been an indication of her lack of love or appreciation for them. Additionally, her family members express relief that Jonna is receiving support and services in an effort to heal from the effects of intimate partner violence. During the consultation, Malachi learns that Jonna's mother believes herself to be clinically depressed, and he agrees to offer her mother a number of referrals. At the close of the first consultation meeting, Malachi agrees to have two additional meetings (1) to discuss the changes that are being experienced in the household as a result of Jonna's treatment, and (2) to offer support to the family's efforts to create an environment conducive to Jonna's continued movement toward mental health and wellness. Malachi's dedication to ensuring that Jonna had agency in the consultation process, by agreeing to follow her lead, demonstrates a level of competent family consultation.

additional referrals or help in the future may be necessary. This consultation cycle may not be the only interaction a clinical mental health counselor will have with a family.

Clinical mental health counselors preparing to move into a consulting relationship with a client's family will need to consider the power differential inherent in family systems. Through mindful commitment to the client, respect for the system in which the client operates, and a willingness to act as a source of support and facilitation, clinical mental health counselors can optimize client care through incorporating family consultation into their practices.

CONSULTATION WITH COMMUNITY MEMBERS

Consultation within a community setting is a unique process that is very different from other modes of consultation. The core dissimilarity in this approach is its focus on systems and subsystems in relation to problem solving (Dougherty, 2005). Other consultation practices seem to focus more on the individual, a select number of treatment providers, a family, or a group. When consulting within the larger community, however, a much wider perspective is taken into consideration.

Community-based consulting can be framed within the terms of a behavioral systems consultation model (Ikeda, Tilly, Stumme, Volmer, & Allison, 1996). From this perspective, community consultation uses behavioral principles and perspectives to analyze and modify interactions among various parts of the system that exist within a larger community system (Williams, 2000). The focus is on establishing an overall approach that efficiently and effectively reaches set objectives that match the demands of the community (Curtis & Stollar, 2002).

The key participants in the community-based consultation triad are the consultant, client/consultee, and stakeholders (Dougherty, 2005). The consultant is the person who is entering the system to help conduct the analysis of the system, intervention, or assessment. The client or consultee is considered the system or subsystem, including all of those who operate within that realm, that works directly with the consultant to make a change. The stakeholders are those who support the system such as clinicians, those who directly oversee projects or services the system provides, and the larger community served by the system (Maher, 1993).

Levels of Consultation in the Community

The presenting issues and partners in community consultation address a variety of concerns and responsibilities of the specific parties involved. One example of consulting within the community is when consultation occurs within a school system. Consultees may consist of teachers, principals, school counselors, and special education or disability services coordinators (Schmidt, 2008) focused on the issue of establishing or reviewing accommodations for students with disabilities, emotional disturbances, or behavioral disorders (Watson & Sterling-Turner, 2005). Or schools may seek assistance for support programs for parents or programs to help students reenter the school after treatment in a mental health or rehabilitation facility (Murphy, 1999), the criminal justice system (Matvya, Lever, & Boyle, 2006), or a hospital for extended care (Shaw & Woo, 2005; Zins & Erchul, 2002).

As a second example of consulting within the community, consultation may occur with small or large community-based agencies servicing child, adolescent, family, or larger community-focused agencies or programs. Consultants assist these consultees in focusing on assessment of community needs, program evaluation and revision, or new program development. Some types of systems that may seek this type of consultation include the following: intimate partner violence agencies; trauma and disaster mental health teams; parenting programs; child care programs (Center for the Study of Social Policy, 2008); drug prevention and intervention programs; religious programs (McMinn, Chaddock, Edwards, Lim, & Campbell, 1998); youth shelters (Grigsby, 1992); employment agencies; social services such as child, elderly, or disability protective services; medical and nursing care for mentally ill; and HIV/AIDS programs.

A third community consultation opportunity deals with mental health public policy (Hendryx, 2008). Politicians, court systems, and health care administrators are the consultees in this type of public policy consultation. Some of the issues addressed in public policy consultation include planning, design or formulation, and implementation of public policy as well as evaluation of established mental health policies (Townsend et al., 2004). Now that we have addressed the levels of community-based consultation, it is critical to look at the consultation process in community systems.

Process of Community-Based Behavioral Systems Consultation

The process of conducting a community-based behavioral systems consultation is grounded in four steps (Maher, 1981). The initial step in Maher's model, system definition, involves identifying the overall system and subsystems as well as specific behaviors (e.g., tasks, evaluation of particular goals), structures (e.g., policies established in relation to timelines, individuals involved, team process of working toward the goal), and procedures that are in place to reach the intended objectives. At the system definition step, the consultant also works to enter the system in a positive and collaborative manner. If consultation is occurring before the program is developed, this stage would consist of data collection from the larger community system to identify specific needs a future program could serve.

The second step is system assessment. During system assessment, the consultant works with the consultee to gather information about the current behaviors of the members involved in the system that is under examination or that will soon be established related to the presenting outlined goals. In addition, current procedures and structures are reviewed for effectiveness.

Intervention is the third step in Maher's model. The consultant collaborates with the consultee to outline goals for the future and construct an intervention. The intervention would outline the target behaviors of members involved in the system, as well as structured interactions between the members. To implement the plan, the members of the system may receive training in or education about new roles or responsibilities within the new intervention. In a system, each of the individuals, as well as the collective force of the system, is considered a very important component. During this intervention step, evaluative measures for tracking outcomes of the intervention would be created as well. The evaluation plan should be communicated to members so that thorough understanding of the process can be achieved.

During the fourth and final step, evaluation, the consultant collaborates with consultees to collect data regarding the outcomes of the intervention. The collected data is then compared to the outcome goals previously set. At this point, decisions would be made whether to continue the intervention or make additional changes if goals were not reached.

CASE STUDY 9.4

An illustration of the community system consultation process can help bring this process to life. Consider the scenario of a Katie, the director of a domestic violence agency, who seeks your consultation services to help her make counseling services more effective for children who have suffered physical abuse. Your first step as a consultant would be to become familiar with the current program, the clinicians and other workers at the agency, the flow of the system, and the needs of the agency's clients. You would do this by spending a few days observing clinicians as well as digital videos of their counseling sessions, participating in treatment plan meetings, and interviewing parents about the needs of their children. With your understanding of the system, you would then collaborate with the members in the system to establish goals for treatment outcomes. For instance, you may focus on a positive change in the behavior of the clients as measured by the Child Behavior Checklist at baseline and at the end of a three-month treatment time frame and facilitated by cognitive-behavioral play therapy. You may train the clinicians in cognitive-behavioral play therapy as well as use of the Child Behavior Checklist.

Next, the members of the system would complete the pretest, provide the services, and collect the data at the end of the three months. Finally, the data from the two time periods would be compared to see whether there was a statistically and practically significant difference in positive behavioral change. If the goals were met, then the program would continue. If the goals were not met, then adjustments could be made to the children's program. At this point, you as the consultant would terminate the relationship with the consultee and provide support as needed in the future.

CLIENT TRANSITIONS TO ALTERNATIVE LEVELS OF CARE

Consultation often occurs as part of the provision of mental health services. During treatment, clinical mental health counselors make determinations and recommendations about the degree of required treatment intensity based on client presentation (Boisvert & Faust, 2002). Consider the following example: A 16-year-old girl arrives at a clinical mental health counselor's office for treatment related to disturbed eating behaviors. She is 5 foot 3 inches tall and weighs 78 pounds. After an initial assessment, the clinical mental health counselor determines that the outpatient care he or she is able to provide at this outpatient facility is inadequate for this particular client because such treatment would not follow protocols for proper level of care for a client with an eating disorder. The clinical mental health counselor makes a referral to a facility that is better equipped to provide the needed assistance. Why might the counselor have made this referral? Will the client feel abandoned because of the referral?

In the preceding example, the deciding factor for appropriateness of treatment was compliance with *level of care* standards for the client's presenting concerns. When professional counselors describe levels of care, what do they mean? How are these levels of care determined? How are they enforced? Professional mental health counselors work with clients who may present with varying concerns, be assigned the same diagnosis, and yet have different treatment needs. Being able to identify and distinguish between these presentations assists counselors in determining the appropriate level of care, and thus the course of treatment, for the client. In simple terms, level of care is the degree and type of professional support necessary to treat, or remediate, the presenting condition of a person in need. The need for a standardized explanation of care levels led to the creation of the Level of Care Utilization System for Psychiatric and Addiction Services (LOCUS) that was developed to describe adult level of care needs. Further professional collaboration with the American Academy of Child and Adolescent Psychiatry yielded the CALOCUS for children over six years of age (Sowers, Pumariega, Huffine, & Fallon, 2003). Levels of care standards are influenced by ACA ethics (ACA, 2005; Bowers & Pipes, 2000) and the treatment guidelines of professional organizations dedicated to the specific interests of various diagnostic categories (American Psychiatric Association, 2000b) that research and create appropriate standards.

Again, consider the example of working with a client who has an eating disorder. An assessment of the specific symptomatology, or severity of the client's clinical presentation, provides key information needed to determine level of care. If two people, working with the same clinical mental health counselor, meet the criteria for the same diagnosis, the clinical mental health counselor has important, but limited, data to begin core treatment planning. Is it possible that two people with the same diagnosis might need different levels of care? Absolutely. After the severity of the presentation is assessed and clarified, the most appropriate course of action can be determined by the professionals involved and in conjunction with the client. Understandably, a client who presents with a complicated presentation (i.e., medical compromise, multiple mental health concerns, and limited social supports) may have more severe treatment needs. For this reason a clinical assessment, including supporting inventory findings, is needed for each client. Based on findings from clinical assessments and client self-report, it can be determined whether outpatient counseling would be appropriate for one client whereas another may be best served in an inpatient hospital setting. What is clear is that assessment for levels of care is required for work with all mental health diagnoses (American Psychiatric Association, 2000a).

In addition to levels of care, counselors are also concerned with types of client care. There are three types of care with which all counselors need to be familiar. *Primary care* addresses mental health issues before they become problematic. Essentially, this type of care is preventative care (Albee & Ryan-Finn, 1993). For example, a counselor may prescribe, or recommend, primary care (i.e., prevention) for a client who may be at risk for dropping out of school. *Secondary care* addresses client needs and behaviors that are already indicative of substantial risk related to a particular mental health concern or issue (Albee & Ryan-Finn, 1993). A counselor may recommend this type of intervention for a client who is beginning to evidence patterns of truant behavior from school. *Tertiary treatment* addresses behaviors and concerns that are actively a part of a client's life. It is necessary, for instance, if a client has already stopped going to school and is in need of support that may help this client complete his or her education (Albee & Ryan-Finn, 1993). When using any of the levels or types of care described in this section, it is imperative for the clinical mental health counselor to consult with supervisors, other colleagues, and experts to make final decisions about appropriate treatment concerns.

Sometimes a change is necessary in a client's treatment protocol. This change may be reflective of augmentation or reduction of services. A client's current treatment plan may initially support a high level of care. Perhaps this person had to receive medical treatment related to his or her mental health diagnoses (such as what we may see in the case of an eating disorder), might have had injuries sustained in a suicide attempt during a depressive episode or episode of self-injurious behavior, or might present with an injury sustained during an acute psychotic episode. Upon reevaluation and client stabilization, a mental health professional may determine that this degree of care is no longer needed. In such a circumstance, a client may be transferred to a partial hospitalization program, intensive outpatient program, aftercare, or outpatient treatment (Boisvert & Faust, 2002). This change could also happen in the opposite direction, from less restrictive levels of treatment to more restrictive treatment. Someone who has been receiving outpatient care for any given diagnosis may find that he or she needs more intensive support. A shift for a client who has received one level of care may be noteworthy as he or she transitions into a more intensive or less restrictive level of care. What we need to ensure is that clients receive treatment in the least restrictive environment possible.

Other transitions in client care can include situations in which the clients terminate services, temporarily or permanently, with the clinician with whom they have been working throughout their care or when clients need to augment their mental health care by adding other services to their existing treatment. In both of these scenarios, consultation is essential prior to referral. If, for instance, the clinician is referring a client to a new treatment provider for a change in services, clinical mental health counselors must consider the client's feelings about changes. Counselors may need to prepare clients for the feelings they may experience during this transition from a clinician with whom they may have developed a trusting working relationship. Often, these concerns manifest as feelings of abandonment. Whenever a client is referred to a new treatment provider, either as a change of service or for adjunct services, the client will have to make adjustments to the rules and norms of the new provider, which may prove to be psychosocially significant. Referrals and changes to the levels of care could impact the client's motivation level, increase levels of anxiety based on the lack of familiarity with the new settings, or inspire emotional upheaval (Boisvert & Faust, 2002).

Referring Clients for Adjunct Services

The previous section defined the levels of care that clinical mental health counselors consider for their clients and how they are applied. The personal experiences of clients are, of course, important to consider as counselors consider levels of care and their impact (Dougherty, 2005).

Consider the following conversation between Carol and her clinical mental health counselor. Carol is a 36-year-old African American woman who has been in counseling for three months. She is seeking support to deal with feelings of mood disturbance and anxiety she describes as secondary to her brother moving into her home. Carol has been reluctant to consider taking medication, yet her mood and anxiety symptoms have increased as the added stressors of life compound for her. After having had ten sessions, her counselor is speaking with her about possibly adding medication to her treatment regimen.

COUNSELOR:	Hi, Carol. Well, I have been listening to you today and notice that you have shared with me a lot of information about how stressful life has been since your brother moved in with you.
CAROL:	Um hmm . . .
COUNSELOR:	In fact, it seems that in these past three months you have shared quite a bit of information about how unhappy you have been since his arrival. You were excited about his moving in, but since he has been in your house you have had several setbacks in your recovery.
CAROL:	Umm hmm. Yes.
COUNSELOR:	You have been drinking more, sleeping less, having trouble eating, spending less time with your friends, and having some serious problems at work. You even told me that your boss is concerned.
CAROL:	Umm hmm . . .
COUNSELOR:	You have even mentioned that you want to avoid going home and that your brother's being there reminds you of a lot of the "bad things" from your childhood. When I discuss this, how does it feel for you?
CAROL:	I can't think of a particular feeling . . . but listening to it summarized back at me all at once . . . makes me think. I guess it sounds worse than I realized it was.
COUNSELOR:	I notice that your eyes are tearing up as you speak.
CAROL:	Yes . . . again, hearing it all at once makes me realize how unhappy I really have been, and now it seems like you think I am even crazier.
COUNSELOR:	We have been working together for a while. I want to make sure that you have access to *all* [emphasis added] of the best treatment options available to help you. I have brought up the idea of having you speak with a psychiatrist to have you assessed for medications before, but you did not feel comfortable with doing so in the past. I understand your concerns but would like you to speak to Dr. Jackson to see whether medication is appropriate to help you manage

	some of the things you have described to me. We can continue to work together, but I would like you to talk with her to see whether medication might also be helpful. Will you consider speaking with her?
CAROL:	Hmmm. I am not completely comfortable with the idea of medication but am willing to *speak* [emphasis added] with her.
COUNSELOR:	Thank you. I am only asking that you speak with her and learn a little bit about how her services may be able to support what you and I do here in our sessions.
CAROL:	OK. I can do that.
COUNSELOR:	She will be able to answer any questions you have. She has worked with several clients of mine who also were reluctant to consider using medication. I will give you her phone number and also let her know that I am recommending that one of my clients give her a call. May I share your first name with her?
CAROL:	Yes . . . though now I am even more worried. Not only am I unhappy but unhappy enough to need meds.
COUNSELOR:	The unhappiness you mentioned is the same. The medication may be a way for us to help get you back on track sooner. I am no more concerned about you than I was before. Again, I want to make sure that you, however, have access to *all* [emphasis added] of the best treatment options available to help you.
CAROL:	OK. That makes me feel better when you explain it that way.
COUNSELOR:	Great. Will you be able to give her a call this week?
CAROL:	Yes. I will call her, but I still want to come in for my appointment to speak with you next week. We are still on, aren't we?
COUNSELOR:	Yes. We will still meet next Monday at 4:00.

In considering the exchange between Carol and her clinical mental health counselor, what things come to mind? Carol expressed some reluctance about needing medication but was more receptive once she understood the counselor's rationale for making this referral. Carol also expressed fear that her clinical mental health counselor found her *crazy* and that she would no longer be working with her. Because these concerns were clearly and respectfully addressed, Carol was empowered with more information and was thus able to make the decision to meet with the psychiatrist. Her decision to see the psychiatrist for a medication evaluation allowed her to be exposed to more treatment options and ultimately improved the quality of her treatment. The clinical mental health counselor's repeated suggestion that Carol seek an evaluation to understand the appropriateness of medication as an adjunct to the counseling treatment she was receiving places the counselor in compliance with best treatment practices. Additionally, this practice allows the clinical mental health counselor to document these suggestions in Carol's treatment record. Whether or not Carol follows through with the referral for an evaluation from the psychiatrist and/or follows the recommendations made by the psychiatrist, it is important that the clinical mental health counselor document both the suggestion and Carol's response to this suggestion.

Regardless of whether an individual has ever received mental health care services, it is easy to imagine the emotions that may accompany this kind of suggestion or referral. Clients may experience feelings of relief, fear, resistance, anger, or apprehension (Boisvert & Faust, 2002). Best practices in counseling, however, require clinical mental health counselors to check in with their clients to find out initial reactions to a clinician referral for a change in services.

LEGAL, ETHICAL, AND CULTURAL CONSIDERATIONS WITH COMMUNITY CONSULTATION

There are a number of important legal considerations with regard to consultation, primarily when the clinical mental health counselor is serving as a consultant (Wilcoxon, 1989). Entering into a consultation contract that clearly identifies the roles, functions, and guidelines for consultation serves to protect both the consultant and the consultee. Further, this contract can protect either party should there be a breach of contract. An additional legal consideration is that of liability (Wilcoxon, 1989). Because consultation is triadic, there is the possibility that the client may sue the counselor/consultee, who then may sue the consultant. Wilcoxon noted that the consultant's lack of employment status with the consultee's agency does not provide a safety net from a lawsuit. The consultant must always consider his or her vulnerability to liability. Additional legal considerations identified by Wilcoxon are related to courtroom testimony and expert witness status and the extension of privileged communication to consultants.

Comprehensive and principled coordination of care requires clinical mental health counselors to make appropriate and sufficient disclosure (Gutierrez et al., 2009). Clients are ethically and legally entitled to full informed consent. This includes knowledge of a clinical mental health counselor's intent to discuss his or her case with any other medical professionals. In certain instances, counselors have a customary policy of requesting permission to contact any physician who might have a vested interest in a client's mental health and wellness; in particular, when clients are already under some form of psychotropic medication management, these counselors may contact the prescribing psychiatrist or general practitioner to discuss a client's presenting concerns and progression in treatment. Before initiating any such contact, clinical mental health counselors first need to be aware of the most current state and federal requirements, which they must uphold before beginning the process of consulting with other professionals. A foundational piece to this preparation is sound comprehension of HIPAA standards and the standards of the American Counseling Association (Borders & Brown, 2005).

In addition, when a clinical mental health counselor advertises as an expert in a particular area of consultation, the counselor is ethically mandated to appropriately represent the pertinent skill level and credentials (Wilcoxon, 1989). How, then, is expertise acquired? Certainly an understanding of the needs of the consultee must merge with the professional experience of the consultant. Clinical mental health counselors desiring to serve in the consulting role need to disclose to potential consultees evidence of their expertise.

As with any client interaction, familial consultation requires careful attention to informed consent and professional disclosure. Adult clients should have the right to include or exclude family members as they deem necessary; they should also be able to request what kind of information is shared in these consultation interactions. In this vein, to the greatest extent possible, children should be informed of how family members will be included. Proper informed consent and disclosure with the client is made in an effort to address issues of power imbalance between clients and counselors (Bibace, 1993). Comprehensive informed consent further allows for a process of information gathering and sharing in a way that most appropriately meets the needs of the client.

Three common goals should remain in the forefront of a consultant's mind to ensure high ethical practice and cultural competence. The first goal is fostering the independence, self-sufficiency, and autonomy of the consultee (ACA, 2005). The consultee would need to be empowered to set goals and outline interventions under the guidance of the consultant and empirical evidence. In addition, the consultant should train the system members in the interventions. The consultant should avoid prescribing goals or playing a dominant role in the intervention in order to prevent fostering dependence of the consultee (Remley & Herlihy, 2010).

The second goal of the consultant is to have a high level of self-awareness in regard to his or her strengths and competencies as well as limitations (Tannenbaum, 2000). The consultant should be able to communicate clearly the role he or she could fulfill for the consultee. The consultant should avoid taking on roles that he or she does not have the expertise, training, education, or experience to do (ACA, 2005).

The final goal, when working with a large group such as a community, is that the consultant needs to be culturally competent (ACA, 2005). The consultant should work with a global and diverse perspective at all times during the consultation to be respectful of the system members and ensure appropriate services are being provided to the community (Arredondo et al., 1996). As a result, the consultant needs to remain aware of his or her own cultural biases or influence as well as the system's culture to ensure appropriate interventions are utilized and interactions are respectful.

Conclusion

Consultation and referral are indirect services provided for some clients when it is identified that clinical mental health counselors need additional support to deliver effective services. Consultation can occur through counselors seeking or serving to provide consultant services. When clinical mental health counselors identify an area of potential growth with regard to skill level or client need, it is their ethical responsibility to respond to that need. Consultation with other mental health professionals is one way in which clinical mental health counselors can enhance skill and accurately conceptualize client cases. Consultation can also occur with medical personnel, family members, schools, and community agencies and organizations. Referral is an additional service that can be used as an adjunct to counseling. Clients can be provided with resource information that can serve to support their needs. Further, clients may be referred to other agencies or mental health professionals when it is deemed that the counseling professional's current services no longer meet their needs.

References

Albee, G. W., & Ryan-Finn, K. D. (1993). An overview of primary prevention. *Journal of Counseling & Development, 72*(2), 115–123.

American Counseling Association (ACA). (2005). *Code of ethics*. Alexandria, VA: Author.

American Psychiatric Association. (2000a). *Diagnostic and statistical manual of mental disorders, fourth edition–text revision* (DSM-IV-TR). Washington, DC: Author.

American Psychiatric Association. (2000b). Practice guidelines for the treatment of patients with eating disorders (revision). *American Journal of Psychiatry, 157*(1), supplement, 1–39.

Arredondo, P., Toporek, M. S., Brown, S., Jones, J., Locke, D. C., Sanchez, J., & Stadler, H. (1996). *Operationalization of the Multicultural Counseling Competencies.* Alexandria, VA: Association for Multicultural Counseling and Development.

Bergan, J. R., & Kratochwill, T. R. (1990). *Behavioral consultation and therapy.* New York, NY: Plenum.

Bernheim, K. (1989). Psychologists and families of the severely mentally ill: The role of family consultation. *American Psychologist, 44*(3), 561–564. doi:10.1037/0003-066X.44.3.561

Bibace, R. (1993). The family therapist as consultant: Alliances, agency, autonomy. *Family Systems Medicine, 11*(3), 247–249. doi:10.1037/h0089265

Boisvert, C., & Faust, D. (2002). Iatrogenic symptoms in psychotherapy: A theoretical exploration of the potential impact of labels, language, and belief systems. *American Journal of Psychotherapy, 56*(2), 244–259.

Borders, L., & Brown, L. (2005). *The new handbook of counseling supervision.* Mahwah, NJ: Erlbaum.

Bowers, M., & Pipes, R. (2000). Influence of consultation on ethical decision making: An analogue study. *Ethics & Behavior, 10*(1), 65–79.

Brandon, R., & Knapp, M. (1999). Interprofessional education and training: Transforming professional preparation to transform human services. *American Behavioral Scientist, 42*, 876–891.

Brown, D., Pryzwansky, W. B., & Schulte, A. C. (1987). *Psychological consultation: Introduction to theory and practice.* Boston, MA: Allyn & Bacon.

Brown, D., & Srebalus, D. J. (2003). *Introduction to the counseling profession* (3rd ed.). Boston, MA: Allyn & Bacon.

Caplan, G. (1970). *The theory and practice of mental health consultation.* New York, NY: Basic Books.

Caplan, G., & Caplan, R. (1993). Mental health consultation, community mental health, and population oriented psychiatry. In W. P. Erchul (Ed.), *Consultation in community, school, and organizational practice: Gerald Caplan's contributions to professional psychology* (pp. 41–56). Washington, DC: Taylor & Francis.

Cates, J., Paone, T., Packman, J., & Margolis, D. (2006). Effective parent consultation in play therapy. *International Journal of Play Therapy, 15*(1), 87–100. doi:10.1037/h0088909

Center for the Study of Social Policy. (2008). Key program elements: Mental health consultation. In Center for the Study of Social Policy (Ed.), *Strengthening families through early care and education.* Washington, DC: Author.

Council for Accreditation of Counseling and Related Educational Programs (CACREP). (2009). *CACREP accreditation manual: 2009 standards.* Alexandria, VA: Author. Retrieved from http://www.cacrep.org/doc/2009%20Standards%20with%20cover.pdf

Curtis, M. J., & Stollar, S. A. (2002). Best practices in system-level change. In A. Thomas & J. Grimes (Eds.), *Best practices in school psychology* (4th ed., pp. 223–243). Washington, DC: National Association of School Psychologists.

Davis, T. (2001). From pilot to mainstream: Promoting collaboration between mental health and medicine. *Families, Systems, & Health, 19*(1), 37–45. doi:10.1037/h0089460

Doherty, W. (1995). The why's and levels of collaborative family healthcare. *Family Systems Medicine, 13,* 275–281.

Dosser, D., Handron, D., McCammon, S., Powell, J., & Spencer, S. (2001). Challenges and strategies for teaching collaborative interdisciplinary practice in children's mental health care. *Families, Systems & Health, 19*(1), 65–82.

Dougherty, A. (1995). *Consultation: Practice and perspectives in school and community settings* (2nd ed.). Pacific Groves, CA: Thomson Brooks/Cole.

Dougherty, A. M. (2005). *Psychological consultation and collaboration in school and community settings* (4th ed.). Belmont, CA: Thomson Brooks/Cole.

Edwards, J., & Smith, P. (1998). Impact of interdisciplinary education in underserved areas: Health professions collaboration in Tennessee. *Journal of Professional Nursing, 14*(3), 144–149.

Edwards, T., Patterson, J., Grauf-Grounds, C., & Groban, S. (2001). Psychiatry, MFT, & family medicine collaboration: The Sharp Behavioral Health Clinic. *Families, Systems, & Health, 19*(1), 25–35. doi:10.1037/h0089459

Frey, J., & Wendorf, R. (1984). Family therapist and pediatrician: Teaming-up on four common behavioral pediatric problems. *Family Systems Medicine, 2*(3), 290–297. doi:10.1037/h0091665

Grigsby, R. K. (1992). Mental health consultation at a youth shelter: An ethnographic approach. *Child and Youth Care Forum, 21*(4), 347–261.

Gutierrez, P., Brenner, L., Olson-Madden, J., Breshears, R., Homaifar, B., Betthauser, L., . . . Adler, L. E. (2009). Consultation as a means of veteran suicide prevention. *Professional Psychology: Research and Practice, 40*(6), 586–592. doi:10.1037/a0016497

Hamberger, K., Ovide, C., & Weiner, E. (1999). *Making collaborative connections: A guide for mental health providers.* New York, NY: Springer.

Hendryx, M. (2008). State mental health funding and mental health system performance. *The Journal of Mental Health Policy and Economics, 11*(1), 17–25.

Ikeda, M. J., Tilly, W. D., Stumme, J., Volmer, L., & Allison, R. (1996). Agency-wide implementation of problem solving consultation: Foundations, current, implementation, and future directions. *School Psychology Quarterly, 11,* 228–243.

Kainz, K. (2002). Barriers and enhancements to Physician–psychologist collaboration. *Professional Psychology: Research and Practice, 33*(2), 169–175. doi:10.1037/0735-7028.33.2.169

LeBlanc, M., & Ritchie, M. (2001). A meta-analysis of play therapy outcomes. *Counseling Psychology Quarterly, 14*(2), 149–163.

Maher, C. A. (1981). Interventions with school social systems: A behavioral-system approach. *School Psychology Review, 10*(4), 499–510.

Maher, C. A. (1993). Providing consultation services in business settings. In J. E. Zins, T. R. Kratochwill, & S. N. Elliot (Eds.), *Handbook of consultation services for children* (pp. 317–328). San Francisco, CA: Jossey-Bass.

Matvya, J., Lever, N. A., & Boyle, R. (2006, August). *News you can use: School reentry of juvenile offenders.* Baltimore, MD: Center for School Mental Health Analysis and Action.

McMinn, M. R., Chaddock, T. P., Edwards, L. A., Lim, R. K. B., & Campbell, C. D. (1998). Psychologist collaborating with clergy. *Professional Psychology: Research and Practice, 29*(6), 564–570.

McNamara, J. (1981). Some unresolved challenges facing psychology's entrance into the health care field. *Professional Psychology, 12,* 391–399.

Miller, T., & Swartz, L. (1990). Clinical psychology in general hospital settings: Issues in interprofessional relationships. *Professional Psychology: Research and Practice, 21*(1), 48–53. doi:10.1037/0735-7028.21.1.48

Murphy, J. J. (1999). Common factor of school-based change. In B. L. Duncan & S. D. Miller (Eds.), *The heart and soul of change: What works in therapy* (pp. 361–386). Washington, DC: American Psychological Association.

Nugent, F. A., & Jones, K. D. (2009). *Introduction to the profession of counseling.* Upper Saddle River, NJ: Pearson Education.

Patterson, J. (2001). Training: The missing link in creating collaborative care. *Families, Systems, & Health, 19*(1), 53–57. doi:10.1037/h0089462

Remley, T., & Herlihy, B. (2010). *Ethical, legal and professional issues in counseling* (3rd ed.). Upper Saddle River, NJ: Pearson Education.

Roesler, T., Gavin, L., & Brenner, A. (1995). Collaborative treatment in a tertiary care setting. *Family Systems Medicine, 13*(3/4), 313–318.

Schein, R. (1969). *Process consultation: Its role in organization development.* Reading, MA: Addison-Wesley.

Schmidt, J. J. (2008). *Counseling in schools: Comprehensive programs of responsive services for all students* (5th ed.). Boston, MA: Allyn & Bacon.

Schroeder, C. M. (1996). Consultant roles in teaching-family group homes. *Dissertation Abstracts International: Section A. The Humanities and Social Sciences, 57*(06), 2279. (UMI No. AAM9632096)

Sharfstein, S., & Katz-Levy, J. (1984). Implications of cost–benefit research in mental health settings. In *Cost considerations in mental health treatment: Settings, modalities, and providers.* Rockville, MD: Department of Health and Human Services, Public Health Service, National Institute of Mental Health.

Shaw, S. R., & Woo, A. H. (2005). Best practices in collaborating with medical personnel. In A. Thomas & J. Grimes (Eds.), *Best practices in school psychology* (5th ed., pp. 1707–1720). Bethesda, MD: National Association of School Psychologists.

Shuman, A., & Shapiro, J. (2002). The effects of preparing parents for child psychotherapy on accuracy of expectations and treatment attendance. *Community Mental Health Journal, 38*(1), 3–16.

Sowers, W., Pumariega, A., Huffine, C., & Fallon, T. (2003). Level-of-care decision making in behavioral health services: The LOCUS and the CALOCUS. *Psychiatric Services, 54*(11), 1461–1463.

Sweeney, D., & Homeyer, L. (1999). *Handbook of group play therapy: How to do it, how it works, whom it's best for.* San Francisco, CA: Jossey-Bass.

Tannenbaum, R. (2000). Self-awareness: An underlying element underlying consultant effectiveness. In R. Golembiewski (Ed.), *Handbook of organizational consultation* (2nd ed., pp. 945–947). Boca Raton, FL: CRC Press.

Townsend, C., Whiteford, H., Baingana, F., Gulbinat, W., Jenkins, R., Baba, A., . . . Deva, M. (2004). The Mental Health Policy Template: Domains and elements for mental health policy formulation.

International Review of Psychiatry, 16(1/2), 18–23. doi:10.1080/09540260310001635069

Van Fleet, R. (2000). Understanding and overcoming parent resistance to play therapy. *International Journal of Play Therapy, 9*(1), 35–46.

Watson, T. S., & Sterling-Turner, H. (2005). Best practices in direct behavioral consultation. In A. Thomas & J. Grimes (Eds.), *Best practices in school psychology* (5th ed., pp. 1661–1672). Bethesda, MD: National Association of School Psychologists.

Wilcoxon, S. A. (1989). Legal and ethical issues in consultation. *Journal of Independent Social Work, 3,* 47–59.

Wilcoxon, S. A. (1990). Developing consultation contracts: Applying foundational principles to critical issues. *Journal of Independent Social Work, 4,* 17–28.

Williams, W. L. (2000). Behavioral consultation. In J. Austin & J. E. Carr (Eds.), *Handbook of applied behavioral analysis* (pp. 375–397). Reno, NV: Context Press.

Yuen, E., Gerdes, J., & Gonzales, J. (1996). Patterns of rural mental healthcare: An exploratory study. *General Hospital Psychiatry, 18,* 14–21.

Zins, J. E., & Erchul, W. P. (2002). Best practices in school consultation. In A. Thomas & J. Grimes (Eds.), *Best practices in school psychology* (4th ed., pp. 625–643). Bethesda, MD: National Association of School Psychologists.

10

Prevention and Crisis Intervention Services

Mary L. Bartlett, Robyn Trippany-Simmons,
and Stacee Reicherzer

CHAPTER OVERVIEW

Clients may experience negative situations that are unanticipated or that they cannot prevent. Crisis intervention on the part of clinical mental health counselors is useful in reducing the impact of these situations and in helping clients reduce any subsequent degree of debilitation. Clinical mental health counselors who feel equipped to intervene across a wide variety of situations that are defined as crises are better able to render a useful service to the client in an ethical and lasting way. In this chapter, the promotion of mental health through management of clients' crisis experiences is considered by looking at basic crisis intervention models, methods of crisis assessment, crisis intervention strategies, and the increasingly prevalent role of suicide as a response to crisis situations. This chapter also examines concepts related to death, dying, and other trauma; working with populations that are typically underserved by counselors; as well as cultural and ethical considerations in prevention and crisis services.

LEARNING OBJECTIVES

The learning objectives for this chapter are designed to be consistent with the 2009 Council for Accreditation of Counseling and Related Educational Programs Standards (CACREP, 2009). As such, upon completion of this chapter, the student will have knowledge of the following clinical mental health counseling standards:

1. Understands the impact of crises, disasters, and other trauma-causing events on people. (A.9)
2. Demonstrates the ability to apply and adhere to ethical and legal standards in clinical mental health counseling. (B.1)
3. Understands the principles of crisis intervention for people during crises, disasters, and other trauma-causing events. (C.6)
4. Demonstrates the ability to use procedures for assessing and managing suicidal risk. (D.6)
5. Understands how living in a multicultural society affects clients who are seeking clinical mental health counseling services. (E.1)

6. Understands appropriate use of diagnosis during a crisis, disaster, or other trauma-causing event. (K.5)

INTRODUCTION

Crisis is inevitable, and crisis often represents a crossroads in clients' lives. The word for *crisis* in the Chinese language combines the character for *danger* and the character for *opportunity*. Clinical mental health counselors who help clients manage the danger while recognizing and maximizing the opportunity inherent in a crisis can guide them toward personal and mental growth. A key component in work as a clinical mental health counselor is helping clients make sense of various events in their lives, many of which the clients will perceive to be crises. Clinical mental health counselors best prepare for this eventuality by considering the basic crisis intervention models, by becoming more familiar and comfortable with discussing and resolving typical crisis situations that clients often experience in life, and by focusing on trends in crisis such as the increasing prevalence of suicide in our society. Among other commonalities, almost everyone experiences grief and loss at some point in life; counselors who prepare for assisting clients with these eventualities are better able to render services across a range of foreseeable client situations. Although unforeseeable crises cannot, by definition, be anticipated, a solid grounding in crisis management helps clinical mental health counselors be ready to respond to a variety of urgent and emergency client care needs.

PROMOTING MENTAL HEALTH

In the process of becoming counseling professionals, clinical mental health counselors learn about theories, assessment, groups, human growth, diagnosis, and many other subjects. A particular area that warrants discussion is how clinical mental health counselors serve as advocates for promoting mental health and accompanying services. In 1999, the first report issued by a surgeon general on the topic of mental health was published. The report found that, although a lot was known about mental illness, there was still much to learn about promoting good mental health. The report also indicated that even though a range of treatments existed for mental disorders, more than half of all Americans with severe mental illnesses did not seek treatment. Additionally, the report made a clear distinction between mental and physical health, and it recognized the debilitating outcomes of mental illness if it is left untreated (DHHS, 1999).

So why is that important? The findings of the surgeon general's report have been significant in helping to create a new framework for how mental illness is viewed, treated, and researched. The report revolutionized the tone for the next century of progress in the field of mental health, and it inspired the creation of many national organizations to provide assistance to those in need. As a result, not only are issues such as depression, suicide, homelessness, early prevention and intervention, posttraumatic stress, and domestic violence better understood, but their exploration has likely contributed to average Americans talking more about them (Cutler, Bevilacqua, & McFarland, 2003; Levine, Toro, & Perkins, 1993).

The guiding principles of the American Counseling Association (ACA) direct clinical mental health counselors to encourage clients to achieve autonomy in an effort to strive for independence and self-determination. This includes helping clients make their own choices and control their own lives, which by necessity involves promoting clients' positive mental health. Further, the principle of beneficence requires clinical mental health counselors to do good and to promote the welfare, wellness, and mental health of others (ACA, 2005). Certainly that means beneficence with our clients but it also extends to society at large. The ways in which clinical mental health counselors discuss the aims of the counseling profession with others influence perceptions of mental health; and depending on what is said and how it is said, these discussions can promote mental health. The ways counselors conduct themselves both in and out of session can leave an overall impression and thereby influence others about whether to seek mental health services. The ways counselor identity is learned and shaped can dictate whether or not counselors see themselves as advocates of mental health services. In other words, becoming a professional counselor means promoting the profession and mental wellness in all activities.

Clinical mental health counselors have probably embarked on their study of counseling because they care about people and want to make a difference in the lives of others. This is particularly important when joining a profession that involves the protection of clients who are vulnerable, which is the case during crisis events or periods in their lives.

WHAT IS A CRISIS?

Imagine for a moment that you are relaxing in the waters of a calm and crystal-clear tropical paradise. You are listening to the most relaxing playlist you have on your iPod, your eyes are closed, and you are reclining on a sturdy, yet comfortable, float. Then, without any warning, someone flips you over into the water. You weren't prepared! You didn't have time to save your now-ruined iPod! You did not have time to hold your breath and so are coughing out the water you inhaled! You have just experienced, on a small scale, what is known as a critical incident.

One role of clinical mental health counselors is to intervene in the critical incidents that clients experience. Critical incidents may be large-scale events, with significant media attention, including events such as 9/11, the 2004 Indian Ocean tsunami, the Haiti earthquakes, the Virginia Tech massacre, and the Gulf War. However, critical incidents may also include occurrences that do not grab the media spotlight and yet are felt deeply by individuals and their immediate/extended families, such as sexual abuse, terminal illness, divorce, violence in the home, and suicide. Critical incidents can be events that are traumatic or that are marked by threat, fear, and helplessness such as the following: natural disasters such as hurricanes and tornadoes; acts of terror such as the Oklahoma City bombing or the Columbine shooting; accidents such as an airplane crash; and other trauma-causing experiences such as hostage situations or abuse. Another type of critical incident can result in existential crises; that is, a life circumstance that calls into question the meaning of a person's life and the events within it. These incidents might include the death of a loved one or loss of a job (Caviola & Colford, 2006). Psychiatric critical incidents are marked by client situations in which individuals experience intense distress. Examples of these are when a client experiences suicidal ideation, psychotic breaks, or has medication issues.

Although all of these incidents are certainly critical, a *crisis* is more about the response to the incident rather than the actual incident. Not all incidents are necessarily traumatic in nature. There is as much variability in response to critical incidents as there are people who experience them. For example, one client may be in significant crisis as a result of an argument with a loved one, whereas another client who has suffered significant sexual trauma may be stable and able to identify how that experience has brought out her inner survivor. Everly and Lating (2004) indicated that a person's subjective interpretation defines whether the incident is a crisis or traumatic or both. So what makes something a crisis? Crises or traumas result when the subjective interpretation of the critical incident compromises the individual's coping mechanisms, psychological defenses, ego strength, and homeostasis, with resulting distress (Roberts & Ottens, 2005). "Returning to the biological metaphor, a traumatic event is a pathogen that overwhelms one's psychological immune system" (Everly & Lating, 2004, p. 35).

There have been numerous crisis events in recent history of which most Americans are aware. Examples of these human-made and natural disasters that have resulted in serious mental health crises are the Sandy Hook Elementary School shooting in Newtown, Connecticut; the Aurora, Colorado, theater shooting; the Boston Marathon bombing; and Hurricane Sandy. Clearly these traumatic events are of the sort that overwhelm the psyche. No one is prepared for such crises, but clinical mental health counselors may be called upon to respond to them. As they prepare to do so, they must first understand people's reactions to crisis.

Reactions to crisis may best be conceptualized from a continuum perspective. Think of two continuums, one being an immediate reaction and the other being prolonged impact. With the first continuum of crisis reaction, an immediate reaction to a critical incident, it is likely that some disruption in affect and behavior will occur. This impact is in response to the sense of vulnerability attached to a critical incident. Individuals affected by these events may experience what Cannon (1929) identified as the fight-or-flight response. The fight response is based on a conceptualized surge of adrenaline that may be experienced in the face of a crisis. For example, a mother who sees that her child is about to be harmed may develop what feels like super-heroic strength and motivation to rescue her child. Conversely, the flight response is often characterized by a sense of depersonalization or detachment from the event. An example of this response is an individual who indicates that he or she saw a tornado moving closer but felt frozen watching it. It is important to note that some individuals do not experience either the fight or the flight response; rather, they employ other defense mechanisms, which results in their having no response at all (Caviola & Colford, 2006).

The second continuum of crisis reaction is focused on the prolonged impact. Issues that fall on this continuum create some impairment in functioning, are considered maladaptive coping, and would be diagnosable mental health concerns. The *Diagnostic and Statistical Manual of Mental Disorders* (American Psychiatric Association, 2000) describes three disorders that are relevant to individuals experiencing prolonged reactions to crises. First, posttraumatic stress disorder (PTSD) is diagnosable when the client experiences stress-related symptoms, such as reexperiencing of the traumatic event, avoidance of stimuli associated with the traumatic event, numbing of responsiveness, or increased arousal for more than one month (American Psychiatric Association, 2000). Second, acute stress disorder occurs when these symptoms are experienced for more than two days and less than four weeks. Third, an adjustment disorder may be diagnosed when there is a less traumatic critical incident, such as divorce, and is characterized by changes in emotional or behavioral functioning as a result of the incident, but changes that are not representative of grief.

Regardless of the source of the crisis or the reaction associated with the crisis, the fact remains that the experience of crisis changes people. James (2008) suggested that crises are "seeds of growth and change" (p. 4). Although it is possible for clients to independently resolve crisis experiences effectively, the majority of individuals who are faced with critical incidents need some level of professional intervention. Clearly, all critical incidents can have an impact on the emotional health of individuals, families, communities, and also the world. The CACREP standards (2009) identified required competencies for clinical mental health counselors, emphasizing specialized skill sets for responding to critical incidents. These standards mandated that students in clinical mental health counseling programs have academic training with regard to the impact of crises, disasters, and other trauma-causing events on individuals and family systems.

CRISIS INTERVENTION MODELS AND STRATEGIES

When responding to crisis situations, clinical mental health counselors would do well to remember Everly's (2000) crisis intervention principles. They indicate that crisis intervention techniques should be specific to the event itself, to the population that experienced it, and should be implemented only when needed, based on the readiness of the individual to receive intervention rather than there being a strict chronological timeline of treatment. Everly reminds clinicians that not all crisis reactions are pathological, and thus all crisis reactions may not necessarily need crisis intervention. When intervention is warranted, it must be tailored specifically to the client.

With regard to crisis intervention strategies, it is important to understand that the efficacy of these strategies is dependent upon and specific to the type of critical incident, the extent of the crisis response, and the phase of the incident in which the clinical mental health counselor engages. During a disaster, professionals are called to respond at different points. Someone who is an immediate responder will utilize a crisis intervention strategy that is different from that needed by a post-incident responder. To be able to offer effective service delivery in response to crisis, disaster, and other trauma-causing events, clinical mental health counselors must first understand models and theories of how individuals experience and process trauma. For example, being aware of the theoretical conceptualization of childhood sexual abuse accommodation syndrome (Summit, 1983) can help sexual trauma counselors conceptualize the cognitive processing of sexual abuse from the perspective of the child or adult survivor. Knowing that accommodating to the sexual trauma also means the child accommodates to consistent chaos and absence of boundaries, which can result in repeated psychiatric crises as an adult, helps clinical mental health counselors to understand and respond to the underlying issue for adult survivors of childhood sexual trauma. Having knowledge of these theories and models in regard to crisis intervention allows for necessary foundational knowledge that informs effective service delivery.

Models for general crisis intervention abound, and no single model has been endorsed in the counseling profession. This section, which explores various theories and models, begins with an overview of the basic skills relevant to all types of crisis intervention.

VOICE FROM THE FIELD 10.1

J. P. had been through every other counselor on staff at the hospital, and many staff members and nurses found her difficult to work with, maintaining that she was a "raging borderline." Because I was the only counselor who had not had direct experience with J.P., she became part of my caseload.

I found J. P. to be immersed in suicidal ideation. She stated that she had nothing to live for and life is worthless. She disclosed a history of rape and abuse throughout her childhood and adolescence. J. P. reported that her brother had killed himself a year ago, which "made suicide a real for me."

Over time, J. P. began trusting me, asking for my services daily instead of my asking to see her. She asked why I cared so much whether she lived or died if she herself did not care. This is a good question for emerging clinical mental health counselors to consider, and a simple "I think you are a good person" may not do the trick. I sat quietly for a moment while I formulated my answer: "You deserve an ally sometimes when you can't be your own. It is my job to help you to be able to help yourself, and I care simply because you are here."

As a therapist, working with J. P. was like being on a roller coaster. After gaining an understanding of her history with the staff, I maintained consistency in mood, mannerisms, and in providing her with support. There were times when I felt frustrated because I could see that she was protecting her depression, and I knew no further work could be done until she realized that. I was also frustrated because I did not like hearing other staff characterizing J.P. as a raging borderline. I didn't buy into that label, but rather saw J. P. as an individual who was reacting to unresolved trauma, although overidentifying with her depressed suicidal mood, which was a part of her life. J. P.'s healing began when she realized she was protecting her depression; then she was ready to work on dealing with the trauma.

BILLIE GILLIAM-FRIERSON
Doctoral Student, Counselor Education and Supervision, Walden University

Basic Skills

The skills that clinical mental health counselors need for crisis intervention include the following: one-on-one crisis intervention skills, small group crisis intervention skills, large group crisis intervention skills, and the ability to work within the treatment team framework with other professionals in a crisis response system (Kaminsky, McCabe, Langlieb, & Everly, 2006). Most important, however, are assessment skills (Everly, 2000; Kaminsky et al., 2006; Roberts & Ottens, 2005). Through making a comprehensive assessment, the clinical mental health counselor can identify where the client may be on the continuum of emotional response to a critical incident. Once an assessment has been made, the clinical mental health counselor can accurately identify appropriate treatment interventions.

With any crisis response—be it traumatic, existential, or psychiatric—intervention must match the needs and experiences of the individual client. Thus, clinical mental health counselors need to have a solid understanding of the effects, impact, and dynamics associated with crisis, disaster, and other trauma-causing events on individuals, families, and communities. In addition, an understanding of emotional and cognitive developmental models is essential to accurate client conceptualization. A five-year-old child's understanding and experience of a tornado is much different from that of a 50-year-old adult. Evidence based interventions inform clinical mental health counselors about effective approaches to working with clients specific to the critical incident that was experienced. These interventions may look different dependent on the type of crisis and the type of intervention. For some crisis interventions, clinical mental health counselors may need to be aware of referral resources and legal concerns.

For many clients, reestablishing a sense of control is one of the more crucial therapeutic needs following a critical incident (Kaminsky et al., 2006). Most critical incidents are unexpected by clients, thus leaving them feeling powerless. In some cases, proactive

CASE STUDY 10.1

Tracy was a 24-year-old African American graduate student working on her doctorate in higher education administration. Tracy was living in graduate student housing on campus when, in the middle of the night, her apartment complex caught on fire. She rushed outside in her pajamas after hearing the alarm sound. She watched with others from the complex as everything they owned—all of their textbooks, computers, and schoolwork—were consumed by flames. As a new graduate student, she had not made any significant friendships, and her closest relative was 600 miles away.

interventions can be implemented that prepare clients for critical incidents (Kaminsky et al., 2006). For example, a school or agency may have drills for natural disasters, which give students and employees a sense of what they would do if an actual emergency occurred. Being prepared allows for identification of appropriate expectations with regard to response to the crisis and development of effective coping skills. Further, clients will benefit through fostering a social network to aid in their support, because social support has been shown to be critical in helping clients experience fewer significant reactions to a number of crisis situations (Littleton, Axsom, & Grills-Taquechel, 2009; Rosenthal, Wilson, & Futch, 2009). Additionally, clinical mental health counselors will want to help clients decondition fear responses related to the incident and assist in helping clients to make sense of the traumatic experience. Victor Frankl (1984) stated, "Suffering ceases to be suffering at the moment it finds meaning" (p. 135). Finding meaning allows clients to reestablish a sense of hope and an opportunity to use their difficult experiences to help others.

With the immediate processing of crisis situations, Ruzek et al. (2007) cautioned clinical mental health counselors not to take emotion-processing approaches in a short-term crisis intervention approach. Doing so would be counterproductive, given the heightened emotions and limited opportunity for follow-up and deeper processing. In other words, clinical mental health counselors should not draw out emotions that there will not be sufficient time to address in the immediate aftermath of the crisis. Additionally, the researchers cautioned against cognitive approaches, because the chaos inherent in the immediate postdisaster experiences does not allow for the mental energy needed to cognitively process through the tasks associated with these approaches. Clients have difficulty thinking in the aftermath of such experiences; therefore, clinical mental health counselors need to help clients keep it simple.

Models of Crisis Intervention

Models and theories that assist clinical mental health professionals in understanding how clients process through traumatic experiences are beneficial in case conceptualization and treatment planning. There are multiple models of crisis intervention described in the professional literature (Everly, 2000; Kanel, 1999; Slaikeu, 1990; Wainrib & Bloch, 1998). The majority of these models have similar concepts; some include more steps or stages than others. Essentially, however, these models have the following components in common: stabilization, assessment, exploration of feelings, identification of effective coping, and referral or follow-up or both. The models presented in recent counseling literature are explained in more detail in this section.

CRISIS IN CONTEXT THEORY Myer and Moore (2006) offer the crisis in context theory (CCT) to describe how individuals and communities experience critical events. This theory, founded in Bronfenbrenner's (1986) ecological approach, is based on three premises. The first premise suggests there are layers of crisis that influence the impact of the event. In essence, the closer an individual or community is to a critical event, the more significant the effect of that event will be. It is understandable that the reactions to the event are influenced by the meaning assigned to the event by the people who are impacted by it. The second premise is that a critical event has a reciprocal effect; the crisis impacts the community, and the community response impacts those directly affected by the crisis. The third premise is that time mediates the first two premises by following the common adage that time heals wounds. The amount of time since the event has occurred has a direct impact on the severity of the response, with more time leading to less impact. As you can imagine, however, anniversaries and significant holidays related to the event can trigger emotional responses.

PSYCHOLOGICAL FIRST AID The Psychological First Aid (Ruzek et al., 2007) model is based on these eight core actions: contact/engagement, safety/comfort, stabilization, information gathering, practical assistance, connection with social support, information on coping support, and linkage to collaborative services. This approach is based on the philosophy that when these core actions are provided, clients will be able to return to their normal functioning (unless there are other mental health issues that complicate the process). The Psychological First Aid model is designed to be applicable to a variety of critical events, including traumatic crises, existential crises, and psychiatric crises.

PREPARATION, ACTION, RECOVERY FRAMEWORK McAdams and Keener (2008) formulated a crisis response model that begins at a precrisis stage and carries individuals through a postcrisis stage. There are application and reflection components in each stage of this model. The authors suggest that assessment and preparedness can minimize the significance of crisis response for those experiencing the critical incidents. Further, this framework focuses on the readiness of clinical mental health counselors to respond to crisis situations and the importance of their being adequately trained. While responding to clients' needs during the crisis, clinical mental health counselors need to use many of the same principles identified in other models, including assessing for safety and being mindful of their own experiences as crisis response counselors. In the postcrisis stage, counselors conduct triage, process through grief responses, and promote change while maintaining an awareness of self-care needs.

RESISTANCE, RESILIENCE, AND RECOVERY MODEL The resistance, resilience, and recovery model proposed by Kaminsky, McCabe, Langlieb, and Everly (2006) offers a proactive approach to crisis intervention. In this model, resistance is positively conceptualized as how the client develops emotional immunity to the negative impact of critical incidents. Resilience develops as individuals use their resistance to recover from the crisis event. Both resistance and resilience can be fostered through the following: the provision of a realistic understanding of natural responses and method of coping, identification and creation of support systems, development of positive cognitions and reframes, and enhancement of feelings of self-efficacy and hardiness. Recovery involves both behavioral and psychological recovery from the actual crisis. This approach is most relevant to responding to traumatic crises.

ROBERTS' SEVEN-STAGE CRISIS INTERVENTION MODEL   The model proposed by Roberts (2005) is appropriate for responding to traumatic, existential, and psychiatric crises. The seven stages are assessing of the individual, establishing rapport, defining the problem, exploring emotions, identifying coping mechanisms, implementing an action plan, and conducting follow-up. Roberts and Ottens (2005) referred to this model as a road map to guide clients as they recover from a critical incident.

Students learning about crisis counseling sometimes wonder how they will manage this intense work environment. One way to prepare yourself for crisis counseling is to do some introspection into your reactions to crises you have experienced. For example, consider a time when something unpleasant happened to you. Specifically, select something that you were unprepared to deal with. You may even want to journal your responses with regard to vulnerability, safety, emotional reaction, meaning, and sense of support. By understanding your challenges and strengths when faced with your own crises, you will better prepare yourself to work with others in crisis.

Cultural Considerations of Crisis Intervention Models and Strategies

In describing her experiences in responding to Hurricane Katrina survivors, Dass-Brailsford (2008) provided some considerations for cultural competencies within a crisis situation. She indicated that during critical situations, clients' cultural values become more salient as the familiarity inherent in these values and norms play an increasingly critical role in recovery. It is best to have diversity within the crisis response team, so that members of various cultural groups can feel connected to mental health professionals. When there is not an opportunity for diverse representation, an open and accepting approach should help minimize potential barriers. Stone and Conley (2004) indicated that for clinical mental health counselors to effectively deliver crisis intervention to culturally different clients, counselors must be culturally self-aware, sensitive to cultural differences in worldview, and able to provide culturally and contextually responsive interventions. Each of these elements must be applied to the crisis intervention model from which a counselor operates.

Ethical and Legal Considerations of Crisis Models and Interventions

Many of the ethical and legal considerations that counselors must be aware of were previously discussed in Chapter 2 of this text. You may remember Kitchener's (1984) foundational ethical principles of fidelity, beneficence, nonmaleficence, autonomy, and justice. Using these principles as a foundation, Sommers-Flanagan (2007) described ethical considerations for clinical mental health counselors who engage in crisis response work. With regard to fidelity, clinical mental health counselors must take care in their approach toward clients, because opportunities for informed consent, confidentiality, and record keeping in a field-based response situation may be lacking. As in any counseling situation, clinical mental health counselors must assess their motivation with regard to helping others in crisis situations. The need to play the role of a superhero, the need for attention for heroic efforts, and curiosity and voyeurism do not promote beneficence for the client. Further, clinical mental health counselors can engage in non-maleficence if they are not adequately trained to respond to crisis situations or if they pathologize what are normal responses to an abnormal situation. Because crisis situations frequently leave clients feeling powerless, clinical mental health counselors must work to help clients reestablish a sense of autonomy by providing them with opportunities to make choices. Finally, justice is achieved when counselors appropriately advocate for clients with regard to procuring resources that will assist them in their recovery process. In addition to these considerations, competence, boundary issues, abandonment, and counselor impairment are all components of the ACA Code of Ethics (2005) that may be compromised when clinical mental health counselors are not proactive in protecting their crisis intervention practice.

CRISIS ASSESSMENT

Crisis assessment requires a highly developed and diverse skill set (Macy, Giattina, Parish, & Crosby, 2010) that is uniquely tailored to the counseling environments and client communities served. Strategies for assisting clients can differ greatly between telephone and in-person assessments, as well as the settings in which those services are provided. However, crisis counselors share a basic assessment goal of comprehensively addressing safety and mental well-being for clients and working to ensure clients' commitment to a plan of change.

Identifying and ameliorating a client's level of present danger involves a stepwise process, such as the problem, options, plan (POP) model used by the Girls and Boys Town National Hotline (Ingram et al., 2008). Another such option is James's (2008) crisis assessment model that summarizes this counseling function in six clear steps: identifying and clarifying the problem, ensuring that the client is safe, supporting the client throughout the assessment process, identifying different possible alternatives, making a plan for safety, and gaining the client's commitment to a plan for safety. In this section, James's model in both telephone and in-person crisis settings is discussed.

Telephone Assessment

In order to accurately assess the problem for the client so that client safety is ensured, a clinical mental health counselor must rely on listening skills while asking targeted questions that will help quickly determine the risk to which the client is currently exposed. It is essential to create a sense of engagement and partnership (Smith et al., 2010) for the client so that trust in the clinical mental health counselor's ability to provide support is established. For telephone crisis assessment, an important consideration is whether the client's physical safety may be in great jeopardy. Specific, targeted questions, such as, "Are you alone in the house?" "Do you have a weapon?" and "Can you lock your door?" can gather the types of information that crisis counselors need in order to assess the level of danger to a caller and whether there is an immediate need for the police or an ambulance.

Clients who are in immediate danger, as well as those who have just experienced a traumatic event, often have great difficulty in organizing their responses (Ko et al., 2008).

It is up to the crisis counselor to clarify confusing or ambiguous data that the client is presenting while providing verbal encouragement to let the client know that he or she is not alone (McLeod, Hays, & Chang, 2010). In practice, what has been found useful is to keep an agency-approved list of questions specific to the function of the agency to ask clients, which then can be quickly checked off based on the information a client provides. This allows clinical mental health counselors to maintain the structure of the assessment while making sure that vital questions are answered to ensure the client's safety. Also, a client's responses to a standardized agency-approved question list are a helpful means of recalling important material when the counselor later needs to develop more extensive case notes about the client's crisis.

When sufficient details about the case have been obtained in order to understand the present level of danger and the client's needs respective to this, the clinical mental health counselor is able to help the client identify alternatives to meet needs for safety and shelter. At this point in the assessment, the counselor should focus attention on learning information about the client's resources, and his or her ability to use them. Questions remain targeted, such as "Is there a place where you can stay tonight and be safe?" "What essentials do you need to take with you?" "How will you get to your sister's house?" "Will your boyfriend look for your car at your sister's house?" In some cases, it is necessary to help clients examine the feasibility of using resources with a question such as, "You said that your sister lives 15 miles away and doesn't have a phone, and that you need to take two buses to get there. What will you do if she's not home when you arrive?"

When the client's plan for safety is determined, clarify the details with the client, specifying actions for both the client and the clinical mental health counselor: "I will now call the taxi and send them to your address at _____. The taxi driver is instructed to bring you to our shelter. When you arrive, come in through the red gate. We will let our security guard know to expect you. Once you're inside, one of our office staff will take a voucher out to the taxi driver to cover the fare." To ensure the client's commitment, it is helpful to ask the client to repeat back the steps to follow for the safety plan, which include "I" statements that specify the actions the person will take (Kalafat, Gould, Munfakh, & Kleinman, 2007). Even in less urgent cases in which there is not a concern for emergency shelter, the

CASE STUDY 10.2

While working the night shift on a domestic violence hotline, one of the authors got a call from a man named Gary, who indicated he was lonely and needed someone to talk to. He seemed to be whispering on the phone, and the hotline counselor commented that it sounded as though Gary had had a pretty rough day. From there, Gary began to cry, sharing that he was in a wheelchair and homebound. He continued, explaining that he and his wife, Sharon, had gotten into an argument over the cost of Gary's medical bills, and that Sharon had hit him over the head with a dinner plate, shoved him out of his wheelchair, and taken the wheelchair upstairs with her, leaving Gary downstairs. Sharon had then left for work, leaving Gary alone in the house. Gary began sharing a number of unrelated details and had to be worked with to slow down. The hotline counselor asked Gary for his address and told him that an ambulance would be coming. He was reluctant to provide his location information, stating that there would be "hell to pay." The hotline counselors assured him that they would work together to be sure that he'd be safe, and that Sharon would not be able to hurt him anymore, once he was transported to a place of safety. After several minutes, Gary agreed and provided the necessary information. 911 was dialed on a second line, and Gary was kept on the phone until the police and ambulance arrived.

client's safety plan may involve activities to be carried out over the next day or several days such as attending counseling, contacting the police, or ensuring adequate transportation to social agencies.

In-Person Assessment

In-person crisis assessment is similar to telephone assessment in that client safety is the primary goal (James, 2008). Although the risk to the client is generally much easier to manage inside a crisis counseling agency than it is over the telephone, prevention of client harm in face-to-face assessment presents its own challenges. Clients who are in crisis may be volatile and even violent. Agencies who welcome walk-in clients must take reasonable precautions to ensure the safety of crisis counselors and other agency staff.

Just as with telephone-based crisis assessment, in-person crisis assessments begin by defining the problem. In interpersonal violence (IPV) or rape crisis centers, the challenges for clients in disclosing details about violent encounters can be extreme, and so can be the challenge to ensure client safety and privacy once security matters have been addressed. Clinical mental health counselors can help organize the client's presentation of information and clarify details to support the client's need. In many cases, a client is brought into an agency by a friend or relative, who may also help determine the scope of the problem by providing context for the client's presentation. Whereas immediate safety is easier to manage when the client is seen in an agency, it must also be remembered that clients may arrive with urgent needs for medical attention or for help from police. Opening questions that are used with these client crises should first address the issues of greatest concern for safety.

Clients in crisis may be easily overwhelmed by the volume of questions asked by law enforcement officers, medical examiners, and other human service workers. Care should be taken to ensure that only necessary questions are asked, and that clients are not expected to provide more details than they are ready to discuss (Smith et al., 2010). For example, having a rape survivor provide details about injuries before a therapeutic alliance of trust has been established may be particularly re-traumatizing. Alternatively, empowering clients to share details of a rape when they are ready is particularly supportive of their needs, and provides an immediate focus for longer-term counseling (Chaudoir & Fisher, 2010).

During screening of client safety issues, it is also helpful to observe the client's presentation of details. Clients who have been recently traumatized may dissociate, particularly if they are survivors of long-term or severe forms of child abuse (Chu, 2010). It is recommended that clinical mental health counselors who perform crisis assessments be skilled in the use of grounding techniques that can assist clients in responding to their immediate surroundings, in the event that clients are having difficulty remaining focused in the sessions. Such grounding techniques may include having clients wiggle fingers and toes, noticing the "feel" of their legs and back in the chair in which they are sitting, and recite events of the day such as what clients had for breakfast. Engaging in these activities helps center clients, allowing for a more cohesive presentation of information when the more difficult questions are asked of them.

Exploring alternatives with clients may include helping them identify support from other agencies. For example, many intimate partner violence shelters do not provide housing for abused men or transsexual women (Hamel, 2008). Shelters may also have limited numbers of beds or not be wheelchair accessible, which may be a particular problem in rural areas with fewer services (Kulkarni, Bell, & Wylie, 2010). Just as it is important to identify a client's resources, counselors also must work to understand services available in the community (Rolling & Brosi, 2010); these may include hotel voucher systems or other alternative living arrangement that address client safety.

In the final stages of crisis assessment (James, 2008), it is important to ensure that the client has the ability to carry out the safety plan. If this involves the client leaving the agency, the counselor needs to ensure that the client can do so safely. Even if the client initially drove himself or herself to the agency, the assessment process may have been emotionally triggering or even disorienting to the point that the client cannot safely drive home immediately after the session.

Additional Considerations

A 1995–1996 survey of 16,000 women and men (Tjaden & Thoennes, 2000a) for the US Department of Justice found that nearly 25.0% of women and 7.6% of men in the United States had been physically assaulted or raped by a present or former partner. Of these participants, 41.5% of women and 19.9% of men had been physically injured as a result. Of people who reported rape in a national violence survey (Tjaden & Thoennes, 2000b), 64% of women and 16% of men reported that they had been stalked, physically assaulted, or raped by a current or former partner. Even in view of these statistics, many cases of intimate partner violence and rape go unreported, particularly by men (Cheung, Leung, & Tsui, 2009; Pantalone, Hessler, & Simoni, 2010), lesbian women (Hester, Donovan, & Fahmy, 2010), and women of color (Coker, 2005). Women with disabilities may be especially vulnerable to unreported domestic violence (Robinson-Whelen et al., 2010), particularly when mobility is controlled by the abuser.

Crisis assessment engages a specific skill set in which clinical mental health counselors demonstrate empathy for the client while asking direct questions to determine immediate needs. Knowledge of community resources and an ability to consider multiple alternatives are equally valuable skills.

Cultural Considerations of Crisis Assessment

A final consideration is the need for cultural competence in both providing services to the spectrum of crisis clients and advocating for a better continuum of care, to include improved access to shelter services and other provisions for clients in need.

Ethical and Legal Considerations in Crisis Assessment

In most crisis assessments, it is important to consider that adult clients, unless they are suicidal or homicidal, have autonomy in choosing whether they will seek services or not; additional exceptions to this occur when children, elderly adults, or persons with disabilities are involved in the decision. All states maintain child abuse reporting laws, although variations exist on what constitutes abuse (Green & Roberts, 2008). Clinical mental health counselors who work in agencies that serve rape or IPV survivors are likely to encounter client cases that involve members of protected classes. This may be directly, when the client is a member of a protected class, or indirectly, when the client is not of a protected class, but it is indicated that abuse may be occurring to one of these persons. It is important to review agency procedures for reporting abuse before beginning crisis work in order to be prepared to address emergencies within assessments. If in doubt about whether a case is reportable, always check with the state agency that investigates abuse of children, older adults, or persons with disabilities.

THE SUICIDE CRISIS

It is not a matter of *if* a counselor will work with a suicidal client, but rather a matter of *when*. No other patient behavior generates more stress and fear among mental health professionals than suicidal behavior, and it continues to be the most frequently encountered mental health emergency. Studies show that one in five psychologists and clinical mental health counselors lose a patient to suicide in the course of their careers (Bersoff, 1999; McAdams & Foster, 2000; McIntosh, 2003). Yet many mental health professionals are under-trained on the assessment, treatment, and management of this crisis, which results in a lack of understanding and preparedness. There is a variety of materials available to help counselors approach the issue of under-training, but these materials are generally neither widespread nor available in clinical training programs. Consequently, there have been exponential increases in suicide-related malpractice liability lawsuits against clinical mental health counselors (Granello & Granello, 2007; Jobes & Berman, 1993; Neimeyer, 2000; Peterson, Luoma, & Dunne, 2002; Reid, 2004). Responding to the difficult issue of suicide and suicidal ideation is inevitable for clinical mental health counselors practicing today; and so the material in the next section, focusing on the suicidal crisis and on a general overview of theories related to suicide and how counselors can work effectively with clients during this crucial psychiatric emergency, is of particular importance.

History

In 1999, US Surgeon General David Satcher indicated that society as a whole does not like to talk about suicide. His *Call to Action to Prevent Suicide* report was key in the development of suicide prevention, intervention, and postvention programs across the nation because it identified suicide as a public health problem and called for implementation of a national suicide prevention strategy (US Public Health Service, 1999). In 2005, the Substance Abuse and Mental Health Services Administration (SAMHSA), the US Department of Health and Human Services (DHHS), and other key federal agencies completed a *Federal Mental Health Action Agenda*. These organizations made an unprecedented commitment to collaborate on behalf of adults and children with mental health illnesses. Among the goals for these organizations was to "act immediately to reduce the number of suicides in the nation through full implementation of the National Strategy for Suicide Prevention" (SAMHSA, 2005, p. 6). The national strategy is designed to transform attitudes, policies, and services, and represents the combined work of advocates, clinicians, researchers, and survivors by declaring suicide a public health problem. Further, the strategy outlines a framework for action that provides direction to modify the current social infrastructure in hopes of changing basic attitudes about suicide and changing the judicial, educational, social service, and health care systems (DHHS, 2001).

Prevalence

Deaths by suicide have increased 60% in the past 45 years worldwide, and suicide rates in the United States continue to rise (US Department of Defense [DOD], 2010b;

World Health Organization [WHO], 2010). In 2007, there were 34,598 suicides in the United States, at least 800,000 attempts, and it is estimated that from 1982 to 2007 there were 4.6 million survivors who had lost a loved one to suicide. More people in the United States die by suicide each year than by homicide; suicide is ranked as the eleventh most frequent cause of death among Americans, whereas homicide is ranked fifteenth. Although rates of suicide for adolescents have declined over the past decade, in the 14 years prior to 1990, the adolescent suicide rate increased by 300% (Centers for Disease Control and Prevention [CDC], 2010). Presently, suicide significantly impacts youth in this country, is the third leading cause of death for young adults between the ages of 15 and 24, and is the second leading cause of death for American college-aged students. Suicide rates increase with age and are the highest among White elderly men over the age of 60. Ninety percent of the individuals who die by suicide had a diagnosable psychiatric disorder at the time of their death (American Association of Suicidology [AAS], 2010b; CDC, 2010).

Whereas depression, bipolar disorder, and substance abuse disorders are the leading contributors to suicide, anorexia nervosa has the highest mortality rate of any psychiatric disorder, with death rates estimated as high as 17% (Favaro & Santonastasco, 1997; Franko & Keel, 2006; Harris & Barraclough, 1998; Keel et al., 2003; Pompili, Girardi, Tatarelli, Roberto, & Tatarelli, 2006). The US Department of Defense (DOD) is experiencing record numbers of suicide among all of its branches. In fact, from 2007 to 2009, more deaths of army personnel in the US National Guard were attributed to suicide than to combat. For male veterans, the rates of suicide increased by 25% between 2005 and 2007 (Defense Manpower Data Center, 2011; Department of Veterans Affairs, 2010); DOD, 2010a).

Based on this information, it is imperative that counselors understand how to work effectively with suicidal clients. Understanding basic theories related to how and why people may become suicidal helps to give the topic context. In understanding how the suicidal mind works, a clinical mental health counselor may more fully comprehend the experience of a suicidal person and therefore be better able to prevent and intervene during a suicidal crisis.

VOICE FROM THE FIELD 10.2

What is alarming is that about half of those who die by suicide are or were in treatment, which points to not only the need for more effective treatments but also the importance of compliance with treatment. Equally alarming is the fact that the other half have not received any treatment for these underlying illnesses.

Misinformation about suicide and why it occurs perpetuates the stigma that surrounds suicide and the mental disorders associated with it. The lack of accurate information also serves as a barrier to seeking treatment and to staying in treatment. Clinicians must play a vital role in educating patients and their families about the risk for suicide and protective factors.

As a clinician, you will treat a suicidal patient at some point in your career. The best advice is to be prepared by knowing what to look for, what to say, to repeatedly inquire about thoughts of suicide, and most important to be up-to-date on the latest advances in treatment.

ROBERT GEBBIA
Executive Director, American Foundation for Suicide Prevention

Theories About Suicide

Suicide typically does not have a simple cause; it has a complex developmental history. Suicide is not a specific disorder; rather, it is a painful process impacted by biological, psychological, social, and cultural factors (see Figure 10.1). Understanding the phenomenology of suicide enables a clinical mental health counselor to assist a client who wants to die and to relieve the psychological pain the client may be experiencing (Suicide Prevention Resource Center [SPRC], 2008). No one theory fully explains suicide risk, but each model contributes to a better understanding of it.

According to Joiner (2005), the last theoretical statement about suicide appeared in the literature in 1990. The first was presented in 1897 by French sociologist Emile Durkheim, who "attempted a systematic, comprehensive, coherent, and testable theory of suicide" (1897, p. 35). Accordingly, Durkeim theorized that collective social forces were predominant factors in the reasons people die by suicide more than individual factors. When a person becomes a burden to the larger society, suicide can seem to be a reasonable option.

Edwin Shneidman, founder of the American Association of Suicidology (AAS), theorized that suicide results from thwarted psychological needs. Shneidman (1993) coined the term *psychache*, which he explained to be the psychological pain that reaches intolerable intensity and predisposes a person to suicidality. Shneidman (1996) also purported that lethality and thwarted needs were key elements in a person's decision to die by suicide.

Aaron Beck (1986) concluded that hopelessness was a primary factor in a person's decision for suicide. He explained that hopelessness can be reduced fairly rapidly using cognitive therapy interventions, and the assessment of hopelessness could improve the prevention and the prediction of suicide. Baumeister (1990) contended that suicide is an attempt to escape aversive self-awareness. In essence, when a person experiences events in life that fall short of his or her expectations, the failures are attributed internally, which makes self-awareness painful. Self-examination is avoided, which fosters irrational thinking, making drastic measures seem acceptable; suicide becomes the ultimate step in escaping the self and world.

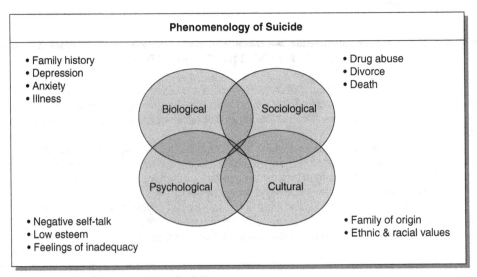

FIGURE 10.1 The phenomenology of suicide.

Marsha Linehan (1993) initially developed dialectical behavioral therapy (DBT) in the 1970s to treat suicidal individuals. She contended that people who want to be dead lack basic skills to build a life worth living; she claimed that biological deficits, exposure to trauma, and an inability to tolerate negative emotion contribute to suicidal behavior. Although Linehan may be predominantly known for her work in using DBT with borderline personality disorder, her earliest work on emotional dysregulation provides an understanding of how self-harm and suicide ideation correlate and potentially lead to suicide.

More recently, Joiner (2005), a prominent leader in the field of suicide research, proposed the interpersonal-psychological theory of suicide (IPTS). Joiner explained that suicide can be understood in the context of three dimensions: perceived ineffectiveness and resultant burdensomeness on others, thwarted belongingness, and an acquired capability for suicide. Joiner offered the IPTS as a comprehensive theory of suicide that addresses limitations of previous theories by integrating empirically supported aspects of those models. A review of previous models is important because once clinical mental health counselors understand fundamental theories related to why a person may become suicidal, it is more likely they will relate to the suicidal desire rather than fear, deny, and avoid it. Consequently, this leads to more effective work in the prevention, intervention, and postvention of the suicidal crisis.

We contend that it is important for clinical mental health counselors and students to better understand and speak the language of suicide. Does a person commit suicide or die by suicide? For the loved one of a person who was in severe psychological distress and ended that pain through the process of suicide, wording makes a difference. Historically, the word *commit* has negative connotations. Suicide is not the same as a person who commits a crime or commits a felony. A person who has no more emotional strength to live and who suicides is not believed to have committed anything, but simply is one who succumbed to his or her extreme internal pain (Joiner, 2005; T. Joiner, personal communication, April 21, 2010; SPRC, 2008). Working toward a universal scientific understanding of the terminology surrounding suicide not only leads to the development of treatment modalities that are more reliable and valid, but also is useful in reducing patient distress and enhancing therapeutic alliance (Moscicki, 1995; Rudd et al., 2006; Silverman, 1997, 2006; Silverman, Berman, Sanddal, O'Carroll, & Joiner, 2007).

Suicide Assessment and Intervention

Clinical mental health counselors often indicate that they feel unprepared to assess and intervene during a suicide crisis, and yet it is precisely during such a crisis that they need to be most secure and prepared in their training. Completing a comprehensive assessment is imperative, because if this aspect is not done well, a clinical mental health counselor will not know which interventions are most appropriate for the situation. This can lead to devastating outcomes up to and including suicide. And while understanding how to prevent and intervene during a suicide crisis is important, a third component is gaining recognition, which completes the prevention cycle: postvention (or follow-up). Research continues to support the contention that by allowing a person who is having initial thoughts of suicide to discuss and process the thoughts in a safe, low-threatening environment, the suicidal thinking may be remediated (Jobes, 2006; Shea, 2002; SPRC, 2008). It is the process of being connected to another human being that likely helps to reduce

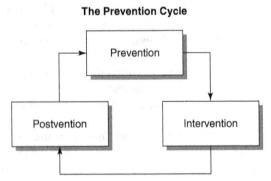

FIGURE 10.2 The prevention cycle.

the feelings of burdensomeness and thwarted belongingness that Joiner (2005) describes. This connectedness can lead to more effective work in the prevention, intervention, and postvention of the suicidal crisis (see Figure 10.2). All three aspects are described in greater detail to provide context.

The Prevention Cycle

PREVENTION Sources (Gladding & Newsome, 2010; Mann et al., 2005; SPAN USA, 2001; SPRC, 2008) indicate that as it relates to suicide, *prevention* is a term used to describe efforts taken to stop a suicide from happening. The three kinds of suicide prevention are primary, secondary, and tertiary.

Primary prevention is effort taken before suicide crisis events erupt, with the goal of reducing the number of suicide occurrences. Primary prevention largely includes mental health efforts to build self-esteem, resiliency, problem resolution, and coping skills in hopes that by doing so, a person will be less likely to reach the point of feeling suicidal. Primary prevention can include developing programs for issues such as bullying, increasing access to services, and reducing access to lethal means.

Secondary prevention is effort directed toward people who may be at risk for becoming suicidal or who may already be evidencing suicidal signs and symptoms. The objective is to help such a person choose an alternative solution or to ameliorate the problem through appropriate referral and treatment for the suicide risk.

Tertiary prevention is effort following self-injury or to reduce the likelihood of the injury occurring again. This includes a direct intervention during the suicidal crisis and therapeutic treatment following an attempt or to prevent future attempts.

There is an emphasis on increasing primary prevention for suicide rather than using tertiary methods because primary prevention is time and cost efficient; however, it is difficult to quantify primary efforts or assess which prevention efforts are making a difference in reducing the number of suicides through a direct correlation. A term often heard in reference to prevention is *epidemiology*, the study of factors relating to the health of large populations. In studying the epidemiology of suicide, experts examine causal relationships between risk factors (exposures) and disease outcomes. In doing so, decisions can be made about what programs, interventions, and treatment modalities are most effective in preventing suicide. However, limited empirical data are available about the assessment process, and there are vast discrepancies in how programs are implemented and assessed, which makes the assessment and treatment of suicide ambiguous and particularly challenging (Jobes, Wong, Conrad, Drozd, & Neal-Walden, 2005; Mann et al., 2005; Moscicki, 1995; Neimeyer, Fortner, & Melby, 2001). This sort of tracking is complicated by the fact that managed care companies are increasingly making reimbursement decisions for services based on efficacy. Accordingly, clinical mental health counselors are pressured to use empirically based approaches, but because the data are limited, the assessment and treatment of suicide are precarious (Jobes, 1995).

PROGRAMS   Nonetheless, there has been some success in the area of suicide assessment. Evidence-based suicide prevention and interventions are programs that have demonstrated successful outcomes (reductions in suicidal behaviors or risks) based on well-designed research studies. In 2007, the Suicide Prevention Research Center (SPRC) and the American Foundation for Suicide Prevention (AFSP) created a registry of evidence-based suicide prevention practices. For five years, experts reviewed submitted practices and 12 were selected for inclusion on the registry. Among them were the United States Air Force Suicide Prevention Program and the Reduced Analgesic Packaging; for primary care settings, the Prevention of Suicide in Primary Care Elderly was selected; and among school-based programs were Lifelines, and SOS Signs of Suicide. A comprehensive list of the programs for review can be located at www.sprc.org/whatweoffer/ebp.asp.

Assessment Process

Although there is much variation in how assessments are conducted, an appropriate assessment of suicidality includes but is not limited to the following: assessing for and ruling out emergency risk, integrating risk assessment early and often in the counseling relationship, eliciting factors that put a person at risk for suicide as well as factors that seem to protect the person, eliciting suicide ideation, behaviors and plans, eliciting warning signs of imminent risk, assessing access to means, obtaining records from collateral sources, and conducting multiple assessments throughout the counseling relationship (SPRC, 2008; Wingate, Joiner, Walker, Rudd, & Jobes, 2004).

LEVELS OF RISK   It is necessary to complete an appropriate and comprehensive assessment on a client's status with regard to suicidality because clinical mental health counselors must make decisions about risk (or lethality) based on the information obtained, which then dictates treatment and intervention decisions. Without understanding the context and degree of suicidality a client is experiencing, the clinical mental health counselor is unable to formulate risk level and make necessary decisions to best protect the client.

Joiner, Walker, Rudd, and Jobes (1999) made the following recommendations for risk severity ratings: nonexistent, mild, moderate, severe, and extreme. Whatever levels a clinical mental health counselor uses, they should be defined in a standardized manner and used consistently. Determining risk level for a client is largely a subjective process, but if completed by engaging the client in a thoughtful and meaningful discussion that includes the aforementioned components, the process will be less daunting. Clinical mental health counselors should base decisions about risk levels on clinical and collaborative evidence and prioritize the information, gauge intent and lethality, evaluate predisposing conditions and precipitating factors, consider a person's psychopathology and compliance with counselor recommendations, be able to justify the decision made, and carefully document observations of all these aspects, including specific risk and protective factors and warning signs that were indicated in the process (Jobes, 2006; Jobes et al., 2005; SPRC, 2008).

RISK FACTORS AND PROTECTIVE FACTORS   Risk factors are well-defined constructs that are empirically derived and population dependent such as age, sex, and psychiatric diagnosis. Risk factors for suicide also include the following: mental and physical illness, relationship instability, family history, previous exposure to suicide, the client's perceptions about suicide, previous suicide attempts, history of substance abuse, experiences of loss, childhood trauma, and access to weapons. It is important to note that just because a person presents with risk factors doesn't mean he or she is suicidal. Additionally, a person doesn't have to have many risk factors to be at risk for suicide; a person may have a single one, such as loss, but the intensity of that loss can put that person at a higher risk (AAS, 2010b; Rudd et al., 2006; SPRC, 2008).

Protective factors are constructs that influence a person's desire to live and include family cohesion, pets, extended supports, access to care, restricted access to means, spirituality, good problem-solving and conflict resolution skills, resilience, and a connection to community (AAS, 2010b; SPRC, 2008).

WARNING SIGNS   Warning signs are not the same as risk factors. According to Rudd et al. (2006), warning signs have yet to be effectively defined. "Warning signs are specific to the current state of a person and are distinct from risk factors. Risk factors are static and enduring (such as lifetime psychiatric diagnosis), whereas warning signs (such as behaviors preparing for suicide) are episodic and variable" (p. 257). Risk factors are better understood and assessed by clinical mental health counselors, whereas laypeople are typically taught and asked to look for, observe, and perhaps record warning signs. Warning signs are more subjective and may include mood changes, acts of recklessness, withdrawal from social activities, increased anger, and feelings of hopelessness. When warning signs are present, specific and immediate intervention is warranted by whoever observes them, whereas risk factors are considered as part of the whole context of the client's presentation (AAS, 2010b; Rudd et al., 2006; SPRC, 2008).

ASSESSMENT APPROACHES   To solicit the risk and protective factors, various assessment approaches can be utilized, including the Collaborative Assessment and Management of Suicidality (CAMS) approach (Jobes, 2006), the Chronological Assessment of Suicide Events (CASE) approach (Shea, 2002), and the Question, Persuade, and Refer (QPR) process (Quinnett & Stover, 2007). These are just a few for consideration, but whichever approach is utilized, it is important to select one based on its empirical value, clinical setting, and professional comfort.

ASSESSMENT INSTRUMENTS   Additionally, in an effort to demonstrate that multiple assessments were included, it is recommended that clinical mental health counselors utilize empirically based instruments. Examples for adult clients include the following: the Suicide Ideation Questionnaire (SIQ), Suicide Potential Rating Scale, Beck Scale for Suicide Ideation® (BSS®), Self-Monitoring Suicide Ideation Scale (SMSI), and Suicide Ideation Scale. For children and teens, the following may be useful: Brief Reasons for Living Inventory for Adolescents, Columbia Teen Screen, and the Reasons for Living Inventory for

Adolescents. Recommended measures for children may include the Child Suicide Potential Scale; Expendable Child Measure; Reynolds Child Depression Scale™; Challenges and Coping Survey for Lesbian, Gay, and Bisexual Youth; Child-Adolescent Suicidal Potential Index (CASPI); and Juvenile Suicide Assessment (Granello & Granello, 2007; SPRC, 2008). There are many instruments that can be considered, and clinical mental health counselors can select them based on cost, availability, and setting.

According to Jobes (1995), because scant data exist about what actually works in assessing suicidal clients, clinical mental health counselors often rely on their clinical experience. This is precarious for the novice counselor, who likely lacks adequate training and experience from which to draw. Given the apparent lack of training that most mental health providers receive in working with suicidal clients, most fail to inquire about suicide risk. When clinical mental health counselors do address suicide with a client, they often avoid exploring the client's suicidal thinking; this typically is likely due to both the lack of training and their own discomfort with the topic. By the same token, Jobes (1995) also pointed out that effective treatment of the suicidal condition requires sensitivity to fundamental human considerations. He purported that counselors are charged with helping a "struggling person find an alternative to the finality of suicide, provide an empathic ear to those who speak of their suicidal pain, and ensure that suicidal people with personal and interpersonal problems receive appropriate and effective care" (p. 448). Whether a clinical mental health counselor agrees morally, spiritually, or philosophically with the notion of suicide as an option, there is no doubt that working with a suicidal person will evoke strong emotions in the provider. Clinical mental health counselors are strongly urged to assess their own perspectives on suicide, so that they can come to terms with the gamut of emotions they may experience in the process of helping a person who is experiencing suicidal thinking. In the absence of their own intrapersonal examination of feelings, clinical mental health counselors may not perform a competent assessment during this highly interpersonal process.

Intervention

The SPRC defines intervention as actions designed to change the thoughts, behavior, mood, environment, or biology of individuals as well as to help them satisfy their needs without using self-destructive behaviors (2008). Neimeyer, Fortner, and Melby's (2001) research resulted in the identification of a variety of factors, such as experience with suicidal clients and capacity to contend with death, as being indicators of competency in suicide intervention. Effective treatment strategies are those in which the model is clearly articulated with suicidality as the target; skills deficiencies, self-reliance, self-awareness, and individual control are addressed; access to crisis management and emergency services are provided; and access to lethal means is limited (Rudd & Joiner, 1998).

TREATMENT MODALITIES Empirical evidence for treatments that effectively prevent suicide attempts is limited. Psychosocial interventions that target problem solving have been shown to reduce suicidal behaviors. Specific psychotherapeutic approaches that are of benefit include dialectical behavior therapy, interpersonal psychotherapy, cognitive-behavioral therapy, psychodynamic therapy, and multisystem therapy with psychiatric supports (American Psychiatric Association, 2003; Brown et al., 2005; Jobes, 2000; SPRC, 2008). In the process of cognitive restructuring, clinical mental health counselors are asked to listen to and explore the client's narrative about his or her suicidal thinking, identify and explore thought distortions, explore the client's suicidal belief system, emphasize suicide ideation events or attempt events, and use Socratic questioning to lead a client to find understanding of the suicidal wish (Jobes, 2006; Shea, 2002; SPRC, 2008).

QUESTIONS   Counselors often struggle when deciding what kind of questions to ask. The SPRC (2008) and APA (2003) suggest that, when a clinical mental health counselor begins to suspect a client may be having suicidal ideation, he or she should start with questions such as, "Have you ever felt that life was not worth living?" or "Did you ever wish you could just go to sleep and not wake up?" Follow up with questions like, "Is death something you've thought about recently?" or "Have things ever reached the point that you've thought of harming or killing yourself?" Additionally, a clinical mental health counselor will want to formulate and ask questions of individuals who have thoughts of self-harm or suicide, of individuals who have attempted suicide or engaged in self-damaging action(s), and of individuals with psychosis (which requires specific inquiry about hallucinations and delusions). The counselor will want to use follow-up questions for when a client returns after a suicide attempt, such as these: "Have your thoughts about suicide increased, decreased, or remained the same since we last met?" "Since I last saw you, what suicidal thoughts have you had?" "What have you done to deal with the thoughts more effectively?" and "Do you feel more in control of your thoughts since the last time we met?"

TREATMENT SETTINGS   Once questions are asked and answered, and suicide risk level is determined, clinical mental health counselors must then decide in which setting the client can best be treated. Options include outpatient, partial hospitalization, intensive outpatient, and inpatient settings. The setting for treatment is largely determined by the risk level. In considering an appropriate setting, clinical mental health counselors should not automatically assume that inpatient care is in the patient's best interest. Some counselors tend to err on the side of caution and prefer to admit clients to the hospital if they present with suicidal thinking. This option should be used carefully and not without first considering other less restrictive treatment options. Because it is likely that clinical mental health counselors will treat many clients who have suicidal thinking, most of whom never reach the level requiring hospitalization, it is efficacious for counselors to learn how to treat the suicidal thinking in a manner that best fosters therapeutic alliance and is appropriate to the situation (Granello & Granello, 2007; Jobes, 2000; SPRC, 2008). When clients are treated on an outpatient basis, in addition to utilizing the aforementioned interventions, the National Suicide Prevention Lifeline (1-800-273-TALK) is a resource that coordinates a network of 140 crisis centers across the United States and provides suicide prevention and crisis intervention services to individuals seeking help at any time, day or night (SAMHSA, 2012).

DOCUMENTATION   The importance of documenting suicidal crises cannot be stressed enough. The process begins during the assessment phase and continues through treatment and follow-up once the crisis has passed. If a malpractice claim is brought against a provider, documentation assists courts in determining the quality of the assessment, intervention, and follow-up care of the client. In the absence of careful documentation, a court can only conclude that the required care for this psychological crisis is in question (American Psychiatric Association, 2003). It takes skill to know what to document, and clinical mental health counselors are not encouraged to write just for the sake of writing. What is documented should be strategic and supportive to the work. Both the AAS and SPRC (2008) indicate that documentation on suicidal clients should include the following: informed consent; information from biological, psychological, and social perspectives; a formulation of risk and rationale; treatment and service plans; explanations of treatment management throughout the crisis and in follow-up; progress and outcomes; and interactions the provider had with professional colleagues to demonstrate collaboration and consultation. Additionally, VandeCreek, Knapp, and Herzog (1987) suggested that when working with a client who is experiencing a suicidal crisis, a model-risk-benefit note should include the following: a description of the comprehensive assessment of suicide risk, specific information obtained that alerted the counselor of risk, indication of which high- and low-risk factors were present, what questions were asked to elicit the information to make a determination of risk and protective factors and what responses were given, how the information directed the action of the counselor, and why other actions were rejected. Clinical mental health counselors are wise to follow this or a similar format first and foremost to best protect the client as well as their practice.

NO-SUICIDE CONTRACTS   In the past, some clinical mental health counselors have been inclined to use a no-suicide contract with clients who present as suicidal. Although there may be some possible therapeutic use if they integrated into comprehensive treatment, there continue to be questions about the efficacy of no-suicide contracts. Additionally, no-suicide contracts have not been demonstrated to reduce suicide, have no legal standing, provide no protection against litigation (and in some instances can prove to be harmful to a counselor's case, if litigated), are reliable only to the extent of the therapeutic alliance, and are not recommended with various populations. Instead, clinical mental health counselors are encouraged to establish what clients will do within the next 12 to 24 hours, have them create a list of soothing alternatives, make a list of helpful people and phone numbers, and create a crisis response plan. A crisis response plan is fundamentally different from a no-suicide contract, because it shifts the focus from what the client won't do to what the client will do to remain alive and safe. Nonetheless, there continue to be organizations that use no-suicide contracts, and each clinical mental health counselor will have to make a professional decision for himself or herself regarding the use of the no-suicide contract (American Psychiatric Association, 2003; Bongar, 2002; Bongar et al., 1998; Jobes, 2006; Jobes & Berman, 1993).

Postvention

Support service actions that are taken after a suicide has occurred to help family, friends, coworkers, or others cope with the loss is postvention. This work is an integral part of the suicide prevention cycle, as it addresses the needs of those affected by a suicide. Suicide attempt survivors are those who have survived a suicide attempt, whereas survivors of suicide are those who are affected by a completed suicide (AAS, 2010a; SPRC, 2008). According to Cain (1972), Edwin Shneidman stated that survivors make up the largest suicide casualty in the suicide arena. It is estimated that there are nearly 200,000 people per year left behind to deal with the aftermath of a suicide (AAS, 2010b).

  The suicide, or attempted suicide, of a person upsets the equilibrium of any community. Even when people were not directly involved or did not know the person who died by suicide directly, once a suicide occurs, it sends a ripple effect through a group like a pebble in a pond (Granello & Granello, 2007; Kaslow & Aronson, 2004). If people are already vulnerable and contemplating suicide, the completed suicide of another may increase their determination to die as well (AAS, 2010b; Joiner, 2010; SPRC, 2008). Further, the effect that suicide has on survivors cannot be overestimated. Likewise, for a person who attempted, obtained treatment, and returns to the various communities he or she is a part of, the stigma associated with the experience; the reaction of family, friends, and peers; and the degree to which the attempt affects him or her should be monitored and addressed. This may help to promote smooth reintegration back into home, work, and social communities, and can be an opportunity to rebuild resiliency for the returning attempter and affected peers and family members. Prevention and intervention without postvention supports fail to complete the cycle of full prevention and potentially undermine the work of the former two efforts (DOD, 2010a; Granello & Granello, 2007; Kaslow & Aronson, 2004; King, 1999; Motto & Bostrom, 2001; Parrish & Tunkle, 2005; SPRC, 2008).

Responses to Suicide Loss

When working with a survivor of suicide, counselors should be familiar with Elizabeth Kübler-Ross's typical grief stages mentioned previously. Clinical mental health counselors also need to understand that initially survivors experience myriad feelings including shock, shame, guilt, confusion, and sometimes relief. Later in their grief process, survivors of suicide may experience feelings of rejection, disconnection, stigma, and isolation. Isolation is a particular challenge given that many people are uncomfortable discussing death to begin with; when the death is a result of suicide, people are even more uncomfortable given the stigma surrounding the topic in society. This compounds, complicates, and prolongs the grief of surviving friends and family members (AFSP, 2010; Bartlett & Daughhetee, 2010; Jordan, 2001; Jordan & Harpel, 2007).

The responses of parents, spouses, and siblings may vary, with parents often experiencing guilt, spouses suffering the accusation of others, and siblings not receiving adequate support. Clinical mental health counselors are advised to be familiar with how suicide impacts clients at all different ages and stages of life. When providing initial assistance to survivors of suicide, counselors should be aware of their own reactions to suicide, be familiar with community and national survivor support resources, prepare to give the client uncomplicated literature, let the survivor talk at his or her own pace, and refer to the decedent by his or her name rather than saying "your son" or "your husband." Losing someone to suicide is highly personal, and survivors indicate finding comfort when another person refers to their loved one lost to suicide by name. Long-term goals include helping survivors to reconcile feelings of anger, to forgive the decedent and others they may perceive to have been involved in the suicide death, to reduce isolation and increase engagements in social networks, to accept the mysteries of the unknown factors surrounding the suicide loss, and to increase survivors' sharing of the grieving process with others (AAS, 2010a; AFSP, 2010; Jordan, 2001; Jordan & Harpel, 2007; Klott & Jongsma, 2004).

Clinician Loss to Suicide

Another consideration for clinical mental health counselors occurs when they lose a client to suicide. The experience impacts counselors on both a personal and professional level and is likely to make a counselor question his or her own competence and self-esteem and lead to thoughts about leaving the profession. Client suicide may impact relationships

CASE STUDY 10.3

A young woman, Becky, was being treated for issues related to chronic mental illness. She reported that she had been thinking about death and killing herself since the age of 10 and planned to die when she turned 24. Becky attempted suicide twice before turning 24 and had been parasuicidal for as long as she could remember. It was not uncommon for her to present for a session with a new cut, bruise, or burn on her body. She explained that she felt guilty if she did anything rewarding for herself, and so she punished herself whenever she did something enjoyable. She was 25 when she started treatment with her seventh counselor and expressed feeling overwhelmed and tired by her continued fight to stay alive. However, she wasn't actively suicidal every day and so didn't meet criteria to be hospitalized. Yet her suicidality remained consistent and persistent. Her mood was labile from session to session and within each session. Her parents were supportive of her treatment, but refused to believe that Becky had been thinking about suicide since such an early age or that she had attempted suicide twice (although Becky consistently told them so). Becky was highly intelligent and articulate and she journaled her emotions daily, but continued to self-harm regularly with these punishments becoming more severe each time because she felt guilty for relying on her parents financially.

a clinical mental health counselor has with his or her friends and family. Aside from feelings of guilt, a counselor may realistically wonder about the potential for litigation (Farberow, 2005; McAdams & Foster, 2000). It is not uncommon for clinical mental health counselors to experience discomfort around and isolation from other mental health colleagues, staff, and supervisors. The isolation can result in counselors becoming ambivalent about disclosing their own feelings and reactions to the loss of a client to suicide. However, because this kind of loss may impact the counselor's continued clinical work, it is important to seek close supervision, individual counseling, and the support of other clinical mental health counselors who have experienced a similar loss. It may also be helpful to know that many clinical mental health counselors report increased compassion and understanding about the suicidal crisis and report becoming better educated about suicide following their loss of a client to suicide (Gutin & McGann, 2010). The AAS now has a clinician survivor task force that provides consultation, support, and education to assist in understanding and responding to loss resulting from the suicide death of a client or family member (AAS, 2010a).

Special Populations

There are many populations that warrant special attention and require clinical mental health counselors to have specific training in order to respond appropriately to a suicidal crisis. These include children, teens, college students, the elderly, those with mental and emotional disorders, people with physical illnesses, and other high-risk populations such as those who are LGBT, incarcerated populations, those in law enforcement, and health care professionals. Examining these populations in depth is beyond the scope of this chapter; however, counselors should be aware that the assessment, intervention, and postvention process with these and other populations are different. A review of specific assessment and intervention protocols is essential. Clinical mental health counselors should seek additional training to ensure they are adequately prepared to meet the special needs of various populations such as those mentioned.

Recently, an increased emphasis on cyberbullying and bullycide has emerged as a growing issue of concern for children and youth. According to Fryer (n.d.), the National

Crime Prevention Council defines *cyberbullying* as using the Internet, cell phone, or other devices used to send and post text or images, to hurt or embarrass another person. Fifty-eight percent of kids surveyed indicated that someone had said hurtful things to them online, and 53% admit to having done so (i-SAFE, 2004). This is particularly significant because it is increasingly believed that bullying may lead to *bullycide*—which is described as suicide influenced by bullying and depression (Field, 1996; Leff, Power, Costigan, & Manz, 2003). It is important to note, however, that only a small number of studies have used an experimental design with a control group, evaluated long-term effects using longitudinal designs, or used environmental change strategies. There is limited research about effective interventions to prevent or reduce the impact of bullying and victimization, and the efficacy of the discrete components of comprehensive, universal primary bullying prevention programs (Houry, 2010). Although research is being conducted to assess a connection between bullying and suicide, at present little conclusive data exist to link the two—but experience commonly suggests otherwise. Therefore, while school counselors are increasingly being trained on these two concepts and their specific intervention and treatment considerations, clinical mental health counselors should also be aware of how these concepts impact the clients and families with whom they work.

One population that has received increased attention and warrants deliberate consideration is the military. The Department of Defense (DOD) is experiencing record numbers of suicide within all of its branches. As indicated previously, from 2007 to 2009, army personnel in the US National Guard had more deaths attributed to suicide than to combat, and the numbers continue to increase (Defense Manpower Data Center, 2011; DOD, 2010a). Appropriately, the DOD responded by immediately focusing on exploring, creating, and adopting intervention programs with strategies to ensure that when a service member presents as suicidal, leadership and first-line supervisors have basic knowledge about and skills in supporting and referring the member for necessary services. In July 2010, the DOD Task Force on the Prevention of Suicide by Members of the Armed Forces released a year-long study of trends, causal factors, and programs, with 49 findings and 76 recommendations to prevent suicide by members of the armed forces and to provide DOD leadership with actionable and measurable recommendations for policy and programs.

Gebbia (2010) explained that talking about suicide with family or friends is rarely done; so, discussing it with platoon leaders and generals is a huge step toward prevention among the armed services and veteran populations. Additionally, a main focus has been placed on building resilience among service members and their family members through prevention programs and increasing direct mental health services and personnel available within units of all military branches, and for the National Guard at state levels. Further, expanding and securing collaborative partnerships among community-based providers will not only improve resiliency but also go a long way toward enhancing civilian providers' understanding of military culture and the unique stressors and needs of all military members and their families (Hall, 2008). Educating civilian providers is crucial as the numbers of military members returning from overseas combat and support postings and reintegrating into communities increases monthly.

Cultural Considerations When Working With Suicidal Clients

As previously mentioned, there are nearly a million deaths by suicide around the world every year. In both developed and developing countries, rates of suicide dominate among elderly men and youth suicide continues to increase, with young adults at the highest risk in all third world countries. Comparatively, mental disorders are associated with over 90% of all suicides across the world (WHO, 2010). Psychological theories of suicide have led professionals to believe that the inner dynamics of the suicidal mind are similar in people around the world despite variations of external problems; likewise, sociological perspectives contend that social organizations and characteristics of a society shape suicidal behaviors in particular societies (Mishara, 2006).

In exploring assessment tools used within the United States, none were identified that had empirically assessed cultural appropriateness for use with various multicultural populations. Rather, leaders in suicide research seem to be in agreement that culturally sensitive assessment of suicidal behavior has more to do with the actual assessment process as opposed to a specific instrument (Alan L. Berman, personal communication, August 20, 2007). Effective and culturally sensitive assessment procedures, regardless of culture, appear to include the following elements: phrasing questions well to elicit the most information about suicidal thoughts; specific sequencing or structure for asking questions about suicide; sequencing questions for inquiring about specific aspects of suicidal thoughts, plans, and behaviors; and collecting collateral sources of information to best determine how to proceed (American Psychiatric Association, 2003; International Association for Suicide Prevention [IASP], 2000; Shea, 2002).

In the United States, White men continue to lead in the phenomenon of suicide; however, an examination across and within other ethnic groups is critical for clinical mental health counselors practicing in the United States. Ethnic groups such as Hispanic, Asian, Native American, and African American persons have distinguishable family values and correlates that should be considered when directing suicide prevention and treatment programs among these group members. However, there is a plethora of other cultural groups that must be understood, including LGBT, military, school, those with disabilities, and elderly populations. Each of these groups present with specific and unique considerations that clinical mental health counselors must be aware of in order to assess and treat suicidality factors within them in a culturally appropriate manner (Granello & Granello, 2007; Leenars, 2008; Leong & Leach, 2008).

Despite increased research and growing literature over the past decade, there continues to be a paucity of information related to suicide and multicultural factors. Suicidology research either ignores cultural differences or focuses on specific cultures without examining commonalities across cultures. Although gaining momentum in the United States, likely due to increased government involvement, the prevention of suicide worldwide has not been adequately addressed and continues to remain largely a taboo topic. Future research needs to explore and understand all that exists between universal aspects and cultural specificity of suicidal behavior (Granello & Granello, 2007; Mishara, 2006; WHO, 2010).

Ethical and Legal Considerations When Working With Suicidal Clients

Given that we live in a highly litigious society in which bereaved survivors seek compensation for perceived negligence of care, clinical mental health counselors are advised to ensure they are well trained in the assessment and treatment of suicidality. Each case must be developed and the plan executed in a way that meets the specified needs of the client at risk. Because standards of care are constantly changing, and there is no one agreed-upon way to act in every situation, potential risks and benefits exist for each decision, particularly when working with the suicidal crisis (Bongar, 2002; Bongar et al., 1998; Jobes & Berman, 1993; Simon, 2004).

The ACA Code of Ethics does not give much guidance on the handling of suicidal clients. The code simply indicates that confidentiality does not apply "when disclosure is required to protect clients or identified others from serious and foreseeable harm" (ACA, 2005, B.2.a., p. 7). Foreseeable harm does not mean the clinical mental health counselor is expected to predict or prevent suicide, but rather he or she is expected to provide a reasonable and comprehensive assessment so that if suicidality exists, appropriate interventions can be implemented. In this single guideline, there seems to be an implicit expectation that clinical mental health counselors know how to complete an appropriate assessment to provide competent and safe practice for all clients, but particularly for those who may be suicidal. These decisions are best determined by the information that clinical mental health counselors gather, and failure to obtain as much data as possible through a variety of means would likely fall below the standard of care counselors are expected to provide.

As research on suicide progresses and prevention, intervention, and postvention programs change, it is incumbent on clinical mental health counselors to implement periodic evaluations of their services to ensure that evidence-based best practices are in place, that lessons learned are incorporated into practices, and that practices and programs are restructured when necessary (DOD, 2010a). Adapting existing suicide prevention and intervention practices and integrating postvention practices and models to the specific needs of individual clients will help ensure programs are reasonably replicated without compromising their effect, and will best fit the needs of clients and their families. For more information on legal and ethical responsibilities of clinical mental health counselors, see Chapter 2.

DEATH, DYING, AND OTHER TRAUMA

Just as it is highly probable that all clinical mental health counselors at some point in their career will encounter a suicidal client, it is also likely that they will work with clients who experience the loss of someone by death; struggle with dying, grief, and loss; and face other complicated traumas. This section introduces dominant theories about grief and loss; the role of religion, spirituality, and culture in conceptualizing death and dying; and the role of the clinical mental health counselor in addressing death and dying within a multicultural client population that uses client belief systems in healing work. It concludes with a discussion of the continuing support needs that clients experience as their relationships to a loss change.

Understanding Death and Dying

The loss of loved ones in our lives is perhaps one of the hardest inevitabilities in life. Experiences of death and dying are mitigated by the cultures in which one lives (Cimete & Kuguoglu, 2006; Van der Heijden & Swartz, 2010), religiosity and spirituality or lack thereof (Kaslow, Ivey, Berry-Mitchell, Franklin, & Bethea, 2009), and most specifically, the role and relationship the deceased played in the person's life (Worden, 2008). The experience of dying is itself a journey of an evolving grief experience (Kübler-Ross, 2000).

Grief Models

In her work with terminally ill patients, Elizabeth Kübler-Ross (1970) theorized one of the earliest models for understanding grief as a series of five stages: denial, anger, bargaining, depression, and acceptance. Kübler-Ross, whose model continues to be widely used in counseling practices today, observed that the grief process was similar both for people who were dying and for those around them who experienced the loss, and that the stages of grief were not necessarily sequential. Similarly, Parker's (1972) model of the phases of bereavement identifies stages of alarm, searching, mitigation, anger and guilt, and gaining a new identity. Parker observed these stages in working with multiple groups of people in the United States who had experienced the death of a loved one. William Worden (2008) identified the following tasks of bereavement, which he viewed as integral to the process of grief counseling: acceptance of loss, processing the pain of grief, adjusting to a world without the deceased, and finding an enduring relationship with the deceased in the midst of embarking on a new life.

Whereas models of grief present similar concepts in the journeys through which clients move as they integrate the experiences of death, great variations in the grief experience can exist depending on the circumstances surrounding the loss. Prolonged illness, for example, allows family members to begin their anticipatory grieving process (Rolland, 2006) as the person's health declines (Worden, 2008). Alternatively, sudden deaths such as can occur in traffic accidents, particularly when they involve young people, can create prolonged grief that involves complex feelings of guilt and responsibility (Breen & O'Connor, 2010). Grief can also vary depending on social stigma surrounding a person's death. Houck (2007) surveyed 150 survivors who had lost a loved one to HIV/AIDS, cancer, or suicide. Houck identified that stigmatization was a significantly higher concern for people who had lost someone to HIV/AIDS than it was for cancer or suicide, but that suicide survivors faced unique questions and challenges related to the person's choice to die that were not experienced by the other groups.

For people who are dying, depression is a common development as abilities begin to lessen and health decreases (Olden, Rosenfeld, Pessin, & Breitbert, 2009). Depression can be exacerbated by increasing and often intense physical pain in continuing to carry out bodily functions, such as the extreme discomfort and difficulty of breathing with cancer pathologies in the lungs (Das, Chauhan, Gupta, Mishra, & Bhatnagar, 2008). However, in a longitudinal study of late-stage cancer patients, Rabkin, McElhiney, Moran, Acree, and Folkman (2009) found that only 10 of 54 patients not diagnosed with depression at the start of the study experienced depression as they neared their deaths, with some patients reporting positive moods at the last interview with the researchers prior to death. Rabkin et al. (2009) identified that spirituality was correlated with a positive mood and overall quality of life, even as the patients were within days of their deaths. Similarly, Daaleman and Dobbs (2010), in a regression analysis, identified that religiosity and closeness to a personally accepted deity figure, in addition to self-efficacy, were associated with accepting attitudes about death. These studies would suggest that despite the common feature of depression for people who are dying, a belief in a spiritual purpose provides comfort and peace even in the last moments of life.

Crisis Intervention Models and Strategies for Death, Dying, and Other Trauma

Religio-cultural rituals for celebrating the dead are significant for clinical mental health counselors to understand the context in which the client conceptualizes the experience of death. However, death rituals may not adequately provide a system for processing the complex emotions and experience of loss that a client faces (Cimete & Kuguoglu, 2006; Van der Heijden & Swartz, 2010). The clinical mental health counselor may be supporting a client through denial (Kübler-Ross, 1970) or what Parker (1972) referred to as alarm at the initial stages of understanding loss. It has been found that clients who are newly experiencing grief are often more in need of a space that allows them to feel supported or heard than they are in need of any specific form of intervention. Indeed, counseling may be the only experience in a client's life in which he or she is not actively trying to pretend to be okay for the sake of others or not feeling so overwhelmed with emotion that others in the client's relational network do not know how to provide real support (Worden, 2008). Clients may need to acknowledge difficult emotions, such as anger at the deceased for their feeling left behind.

As central as a supportive environment is, therapeutic interventions that engage the grief process more actively may derive additional benefits. In an experimental study that tested cognitive-behavioral therapy (CBT) against a non-technique-oriented support form of counseling, Boelen, de Keijser, van den Hout, and van den Bout (2007) found that the group that experienced CBT had greater treatment results in confronting loss. In addition to the practice of CBT, the empty-chair Gestalt technique and other experiential activities have also proved successful in helping clients recognize disowned or displaced anger and other complex emotions. These counseling techniques are aimed at encouraging the client to fully acknowledge the pain of the loss; by providing this experience, the stage is set for a consideration of how to use the intensity of love for the deceased to carry out actions that the deceased would wish for the client. Thus, clinical mental health counselors help the client move into Worden's (2008) third phase: adjusting to life without the person and supporting the client in new action steps that acknowledge and honor the person who has died. This is often marked by symbolic acts that reflect the client's making an important change: going back to school to finish a degree, embarking on a vacation the client has always wanted to take, or simply getting out of the house and meeting new friends.

In Worden's (2008) final task of bereavement, the client is supported in finding a new relationship with the deceased. Clinical mental health counselors work with clients to consider the value of ritual in grief support, and may invite the client to consider designating a special place in the home for a small shrine or altar commemorating the deceased that is brought out during the year at certain times or that remains visible throughout the year. Some clients plant a memorial tree or other symbolic reminder of the ongoing bond with the deceased. Others may choose to celebrate the person through a yearly ritual of some sort that involves engaging active memories of the deceased person's life. However the client chooses to represent the ongoing relationship with the deceased, the clinical mental health counselor supports the client in carrying out this commemoration while continuing to actively engage in life.

Grief models (Kübler-Ross, 1970; Parker, 1972; Worden, 2008) have been used to address many forms of trauma related to loss, such as grief related to divorce and job loss (Tunajek, 2009) or significant financial losses and changes in lifestyle. Clients may process these losses in a manner that is not dissimilar to death bereavement. It is important to consider that trauma is subjectively defined. What may be processed with a less severe reaction for one client may be deeply traumatic for others. Clinical mental health counselors must be clear in examining the developmental impact of trauma on the client's life, regardless of the type of loss that's been experienced.

CASE STUDY 10.4

Sherilyn presented for counseling to learn how to cope with long-term grief. By the age of seven, Sherilyn had lost her mother and been raised by her father, with the help of her older sister, who was 13 at the time. Two years before presenting for counseling, Sherilyn lost her best friend in a car accident. Now as a 22-year-old woman, Sherilyn explained that she felt sad much of the time, and that while everyone had been supportive at first when she lost her friend, people now expected her to "get over it, already." She recounted that she had moved through life coping with her mother's loss by not ever talking about it, but she noticed herself feeling the intense emotional pain of the loss of her mother now that she had also lost her best friend. Together, goals were identified for counseling, including coping strategies for managing bouts of crying that seemed to occur in the middle of the workday and determining how means could be found for Sherilyn to create a "living presence" of both of these women in her present life. To achieve these goals, the following ground rules were set: all emotions were permitted in the counseling room, and neither the client nor the counselor would judge an emotion that she experienced; she would practice at least one new self-care strategy per week, which would be identified before each session ended; she would let people close to her know that she was doing hard "work" on herself; and she needed those close to her to understand and respect that she might need quiet time alone alternated with social engagement.

Cultural and Spiritual Considerations of Death, Dying, and Other Trauma

Rich moral traditions seek to explain the world and the place of humans in it, particularly with regard to the experience of death. Spirituality plays such a significant role in counseling that it is the entire focus of the Association for Spiritual, Ethical, and Religious Values in Counseling (ASERVIC), a division of ACA. ASERVIC has defined a series of spirituality competencies that both clarify the clinical mental health counselor's own belief system with regard to religion and spirituality and provide clear support of the client from the counselor's own worldview (2009). Engaging client belief systems is a significant part of the counseling process, particularly in addressing existential matters of death and dying. In working with grieving clients, as the client's belief system becomes understood, it may be a valuable practice for the clinical mental health counselor to ask where the client believes the deceased person is now. Particularly for cases in which the client believes the person is in a "better place," it may be helpful to incorporate this belief into a strength-based approach. Guided meditation exercises that allow clients to visualize the person in the after-death experience can be part of particularly healing work.

Engaging spirituality can be of particular value for survivors of traumatic loss. Kaslow, Ivey, Berry-Mitchell, Franklin, and Bethea (2009) developed a culturally oriented group counseling model, called Healing and Understanding Grieving Suicide Survivors (HUGSS), to address the needs of Black families who had survived a suicide. In addition to supporting clients as they share their suicide stories, these authors identified the significant role that reflecting on cultural history and religious engagement within their group has on client improvement. Thus, the emphasis on spirituality was a valuable means of support and healing. Equally important was drawing from the rich heritage of Black cultural identity.

Religiosity, spirituality, and culture provide context for the traditions that surround death rituals across a range of cultures. Extending far beyond funeral rites, many rituals are carried out for as long as the person is in memory, such as the Mexican indigenous tradition of el Día de los Muertos (the Day of the Dead), in which the spirits of the deceased are invited back each year on November 1 and 2 to join their families and friends in enjoying their favorite foods, games, music, and other experiences that were important in their lives.

Equally important to consider is long-term trauma that may be related to histories of social mistreatment (Reicherzer, Patton, & Pisano, 2009) that occur for non–sociopolitically dominant communities in a culture of heterosexism: White supremacy and sizeism, for example. Long-term chronic histories of social abuse often reflect as trauma responses for survivors. Treatment planning in the context of social trauma when working with clients who have histories that include marginalization is often useful in such cases.

Ethical and Legal Considerations of Death, Dying, and Other Trauma

The ACA Code of Ethics (2005) provides ethical guidelines for counselors in work with clients with terminal illnesses (A.9.) who are making end-of-life decisions. In supporting client efficacy for end-of-life decisions, counselors must operate within the laws of the state in which they practice for reporting client risk for hastening their own deaths (A.9.c.). It is recommended that clinical mental health counselors seek legal aid to clarify the scope of practice in addressing end-of-life concerns, as well as clearly communicate to the client how state law informs his or her role for the work. Additionally, the reader is referred to Chapter 2 in this text.

VOICE FROM THE FIELD 10.3

As a grief counselor, I counseled individual clients and facilitated a group called Growing Through Grief. This group was held once a month for those new to the grief experience. One week, 13 people were in attendance, including those who had already suffered loss of a parent, men who had suffered the recent loss of their wives, widows and widowers with sudden loss, a sister whose brother was murdered, and two supportive friends. One member knew that her mother's death was imminent and was in a great deal of pain because that weekend would be Mother's Day. Every person in the room was anticipating Mother's Day and how difficult it was going to be without their loved parent, spouse, or brother.

Trauma in the loss of a loved one can be a very lonely experience because each griever's journey is a very individual one. Death, the feelings when loss happens, and the void afterward can create a shock in mind, spirit, and body. Most people, unless they have experienced and have been in similar circumstances as a griever, cannot really relate, do not know what to say, and, although they try to empathize, cannot fathom the amount of pain someone may be in. The benefit of the Growing Through Grief group is that it provides a safe place to express the level of pain, shock, guilt, anger, and myriad other emotions that may come up at this time, including from any prior losses experienced. First, the courage to walk in the door to a grief group is acknowledged. Next, people are encouraged, but not forced, to tell their story. The commonality of not being alone, that other people can relate because of a similar experience, and having a safe place to talk can have a very healing effect. One who believes bringing in hospice care for her loved one was justified may nevertheless feel guilty. A father of four adult daughters may want to hear from his children because he is missing his wife, and at the same time, may become irritated by their phone calls. A friend may come to the group to support someone whose sibling was murdered, but the supportive friend does not know what to say or do for the friend who remains traumatized long after the event. No one can work through another person's grief—the griever must do his or her own work. But sometimes just being with someone is the most important help a friend can give.

My Saturday client who lost her husband and her mother is still struggling to understand why she is here and her husband is not. One of her two sons is getting married in September, and she is dreading attending without her husband beside her. However, this client, who seemed to lose herself in taking care of her husband prior to his death, has managed to survive, be with friends, take several trips, and she is starting to get a sense of herself. She is no longer shocked by acquaintances who ask, "How is it for you?" She has reached acceptance that her life has changed and that this change may be an opportunity to grow. Surviving the trauma of a death can be a real chance to form a new identity. The problem is that we do not make the choice. Death occurs without one's permission. As a counselor, I find that the most important part of working with grief and trauma is the validation given to people in acknowledging the depth of the pain of loss. Dr. Wolfelt, director of the Center for Loss & Life Transition in Fort Collins, Colorado, says, "You have to say hello to pain before you can say goodbye to it; and darkness is the chair upon which light sits."

HELEN PHELPS

Doctoral Student, Counselor Education and Supervision, Walden University

WORKING WITH UNDERSERVED POPULATIONS

It is important for counselors to recognize that the counseling profession has significantly evolved to address the needs of underserved communities. Efforts to this end include the following: the Association for Multicultural Counseling and Development's (AMCD) Multicultural Counseling Competencies (Arredondo et al., 1996); the American Counseling Association's (ACA) Advocacy Competencies (Lewis, Arnold, House, & Toporek, 2003); and the Association for Lesbian, Gay, Bisexual & Transgender Issues in Counseling's *ALGBTIC Competencies for Counseling with Transgender Clients* (ALGBTIC, 2009). Despite such efforts, clinical mental health counselors must still recognize that many racial and ethnic communities (Kaslow et al., 2009; Ramirez-Valles, Garcia, Campbell, Diaz, & Heckathorn, 2008), the LGBT community (Kenagy, 2005; Ramirez-Valles et al., 2008; Reicherzer et al., 2009), and persons who have disabilities and for whom mobility is limited (Robinson-Whelen et al., 2010) continue to be underserved by mental health professionals.

Many underserved communities have histories that may include disparity of treatment when seeking medical care or police protection. As such, these communities often turn inward to find support and resources from family or others in the group. This has had the effect of strengthening communities in addressing perceptions of social disgrace through advocacy (Cheung et al., 2009; Hester et al., 2010) while also maintaining a situation in which many members of a marginalized community do not seek services, thus denying them advances taking place in the medical and mental health professions (Hill, 2005). Thus, the system of mistrust that pervades and keeps persons from marginalized communities from seeking needed services can best be addressed by targeted efforts in which evidence-based practices are married with cultural knowledge and practice for these communities, such as the HUGSS project that Kaslow et al. (2009) developed in counseling African American families who had lost loved ones to suicide. Efforts such as this serve to heal communities and ensure that mental health is a universally accessible service.

Conclusion

In this chapter, the role of crisis intervention and management was examined, starting with the general promotion of good mental health in typical client populations and working through crisis as a theoretical construct, basic crisis intervention models, assessment of crisis, and crisis intervention strategies including appropriate uses of diagnosis during a crisis, disaster, or other trauma-causing event. The assessment of suicide, as well as intervention methods used with suicidal clients, was examined, and issues related to common client trauma such as death and dying were discussed. Finally, the chapter considered working with typically underserved populations in the mental health arena, and presented ethical, legal, and multicultural issues that affect clients during various crisis situations. These issues related to the prevention of crisis and management of client crisis situations when they occur can be expected to be common mechanisms used by the typical clinical mental health counselor in practically any setting of modern practice.

References

American Association of Suicidology (AAS). (2010a). *Clinician survivor task force.* Retrieved from http://mypage.iusb.edu/~jmcintos/therapists_mainpg.htm

American Association of Suicidology (AAS). (2010b). *Fact sheets: Reliable information about suicide.* Retrieved from http://www.suicidology.org/resources/facts-statistics-current-research/fact-sheets

American Counseling Association (ACA). (2005). *Code of ethics.* Alexandria, VA: Author.

American Foundation for Suicide Prevention (AFSP). (2010). *Surviving a suicide loss: A resource and healing guide.* New York, NY: Author.

American Psychiatric Association. (2000). *Diagnostic and statistical manual of mental disorders, fourth edition–text revision* (DSM-IV-TR). Washington, DC: Author.

American Psychiatric Association. (2003). *Practice guideline for the assessment and treatment of patients with suicidal behaviors.* Retrieved from http://www.vbh-pa.com/provider/info/qual_mgt/APA_Suicide_Guidelines.pdf

Arredondo, P., Toporek, M. S., Brown, S., Jones, J., Locke, D. C., Sanchez, J., & Stadler, H. (1996). *Operationalization of the Multicultural Counseling Competencies.* Alexandria, VA: Association for Multicultural Counseling and Development.

Association for Lesbian, Gay, Bisexual & Transgender Issues in Counseling (ALGBTIC). (2009). *ALGBTIC competencies for counseling with transgender clients.* Alexandria, VA: Author.

Association for Spiritual, Ethical, and Religious Values in Counseling (ASERVIC). (2009). *Spiritual competencies.* Retrieved from http://www.aservic.org/resources/spiritual-competencies/

Bartlett, M. L., & Daughhetee, C. (2010). Risk assessment. In B. Erford & L. Jackson-Cherry (Eds.), *Crisis: Intervention and prevention.* Upper Saddle River, NJ: Pearson Education.

Baumeister, R. F. (1990). Suicide as escape from self. *Psychological Review, 97*(1), 90–113.

Beck, A. T. (1986). Hopelessness as a predictor of eventual suicide. In J. J. Mann & M. Stanley (Eds.), *Psychobiology of suicidal behavior* (pp. 90–96). New York, NY: Academy of Sciences.

Bersoff, D. N. (1999). *Ethical conflicts in psychology* (2nd ed.). Washington DC: American Psychological Association.

Black, H. C. (1979). *Black's law dictionary.* St. Paul, MN: West.

Boelen, P., de Keijser, J., van den Hout, M., & van den Bout, J. (2007). Treatment of complicated grief: A comparison between cognitive behavioral therapy and supportive counseling. *Journal of Consulting and Clinical Psychology, 75*(2), 277–284. doi:10.1037/0022-006X.75.2.277

Bongar, B. (2002). *The suicidal patient: Clinical and legal standards of care* (2nd ed.). Washington, DC: American Psychological Association.

Bongar, B., Berman, A. L., Maris, R. W., Silverman, M. M., Harris, E. A., & Packman, W. L. (1998). *Risk management with suicidal patients.* New York, NY: Guilford Press.

Breen, L. J., & O'Connor, M. (2010). Acts of resistance: Breaking the silence of grief following traffic crash fatalities. *Death Studies, 34*(1), 30–53. doi:10.1080/07481180903372384

Bronfenbrenner, U. (1986). Ecology of the family as a context for human development: Research perspectives. *Developmental Psychology, 22,* 723–742.

Brown, G. K., Ten Have, T., Henriques, G. R., Xie, S. X., Hollander, J. E., & Beck, A. T. (2005). Cognitive therapy for the prevention of suicide attempts: A randomized controlled trial. *The Journal of the American Medical Association, 294*(5), 563–570.

Cain, A. C. (1972). *Survivors of suicide.* Springfield, IL: Thomas.

Cannon, W. (1929). The sympathetic division of the autonomic system in relation to homeostasis. *Archives of Neurology and Psychology, 22,* 282–294.

Caviola, A. A., & Colford, J. E. (2006). *A practical guide to crisis intervention.* Boston, MA: Houghton Mifflin.

Centers for Disease Control and Prevention (CDC). (2010). *Injury prevention & control: Suicide prevention.* Retrieved from http://www.cdc.gov/violenceprevention/suicide/index.html

Chaudoir, S., & Fisher, J. (2010). The disclosure process model: Understanding disclosure decision-making and postdisclosure outcomes among people with a concealable stigmatized identity. *Psychological Bulletin, 136*(2), 236–256. doi:10.1037/a0018193

Cheung, M., Leung, P., & Tsui, V. (2009). Asian male domestic violence victims: Services exclusive for men. *Journal of Family Violence, 24,* 447–462. doi:10.1007/s10896-009-9240-9

Chu, J. A. (2010). Posttraumatic stress disorder: Beyond DSM-IV. *American Journal of Psychiatry, 167,* 617–617. doi:10.1176/appi.ajp.2010.10030310

Cimete, G., & Kuguoglu, S. (2006). Grief responses of Turkish families after the death of their children from cancer. *Journal of Loss and Trauma, 11,* 31–51. doi:10.1080/15325020500194455

Coker, D. (2005). Shifting power for battered women: Law, material resources, and poor women of color. In N. J. Sokoloff & C. Pratt (Eds.), *Domestic violence at the margins: Readings on race, class, gender, and culture* (pp. 369–388). New Brunswick, NJ: Rutgers University Press.

Council for Accreditation of Counseling and Related Educational Programs (CACREP). (2009). *CACREP accreditation manual: 2009 standards.* Alexandria, VA: Author. Retrieved from http://www.cacrep.org/doc/2009%20Standards%20with%20cover.pdf

Cutler, D. L., Bevilacqua, J., & McFarland, B. H. (2003). Four decades of community mental health: A symphony in four movements. *Community Mental Health Journal, 39*(5), 381–398.

Daaleman, T., & Dobbs, D. (2010). Religiosity, spirituality, and death attitudes in chronically ill older adults. *Research on Aging, 32*(2), 224–243. doi:10.1177/0164027509351476

Das, S. C., Chauhan, H., Gupta, D., Mishra, S., & Bhatnagar, S. (2008). Peaceful surrender to death without futile bargaining to live relieves terminal air hunger and anguish. *American Journal of Hospice and Palliative Medicine, 25,* 496–499. doi:10.1177/1049909108322286

Dass-Brailford, P. (2008). After the storm: Recognition, recovery, and reconstruction. *Professional Psychology: Research and Practice, 39,* 24–30.

Defense Manpower Data Center. (2011). *U.S. active duty military deaths—1980 through 2011 (as of November 2, 2011).* Retrieved from http://siadapp.dmdc.osd.mil/personnel/CASUALTY/death_Rates.pdf

Department of Veterans Affairs. (2010). *US: Suicide rate surged among veterans.* Retrieved from http://www.ipsnews.net/2010/01/us-suicide-rate-surged-among-veterans/

Durkheim, E. (1987). *Le suicide. Etude de sociologie.* Paris, France: F. Alcan.

Everly, G. S. (2000). Five principles of crisis intervention: Reducing the risk of premature crisis intervention. *International Journal of Emergency Mental Health, 2,* 1–4.

Everly, G. S., & Lating, J. M. (2004). The defining moment of psychological trauma: What makes a traumatic event traumatic? In G. Everly & J. M. Lating (Eds.), *Personality-guided therapy for posttraumatic stress disorder.* Washington, DC: American Psychological Association.

Farberow, N. L. (2005, February). The mental health professional as suicide survivor. *Clinical Neuropsychiatry: Journal of Treatment Evaluation, 2*(1), 13–20.

Favaro, A., & Santonastasco, P. (1997). Suicidality in eating disorders: Clinical and psychological correlates. *Acta Psychiatrica Scandanivicia, 95*(6), 769–782.

Field, T. (1996). *Bully in sight.* London, England: Success Unlimited.

Frankl, V. (1984). *Man's search for meaning.* New York, NY: Simon & Schuster.

Franko, D. L., & Keel, P. K. (2006). Suicidality in eating disorders: Occurrence, correlates, and clinical implications. *Clinical Psychology Review, 26*(6), 769–782.

Fryer, L. (n.d.). *What is the definition of cyberbullying?* Retrieved from http://www.ehow.com/about_5052683_definition-cyberbullying.html?ref=Track2&utm_source=ask

Gebbia, R. (2010). *Military suicide—The war within our ranks.* Retrieved from http://thehill.com/opinion/op-ed/106033-military-suicide-the-war-within-our-ranks

Gladding, S. T., & Newsome, D. W. (2010). *Clinical mental health counseling in community and agency settings* (3rd ed.). Upper Saddle River, NJ: Pearson Education.

Granello, D. H., & Granello, P. F. (2007). *Suicide: An essential guide for helping professionals and educators*. Boston, MA: Pearson Education.

Green, D. L., & Roberts, A. R. (2008). *Helping victims of violent crime: Assessment, treatment, and evidence-based practice*. New York, NY: Springer.

Gutin, N. J., & McGann, V. (2010). *Clinicians and suicide loss*. Retrieved from http://app.e2ma.net/app2/campaigns/archived/25465/11e2327ff56588fb1303b45d2c2f3e9b/

Hall, L. (2008). *Counseling military families: What mental health professionals need to know*. New York, NY: Taylor & Francis.

Hamel, J. (Ed.). (2008). *Intimate partner and family abuse: A casebook of gender inclusive therapy*. New York, NY: Springer.

Harris, E. C., & Barraclough, B. (1998). Excess mortality of mental disorders. *The British Journal of Psychiatry, 173*, 11–53.

Hester, M., Donovan, C., & Fahmy, E. (2010). Feminist epistemology and the politics of method: Surveying same sex domestic violence. *International Journal of Social Research Methodology, 13*(3), 251–263. doi:10.1080/13645579.2010.482260

Hill, D. B. (2005). Trans/gender/sexuality: A research agenda. *Journal of Gay & Lesbian Social Services, 18*(2), 101–109.

Houck, J. (2007). A comparison of grief reactions in cancer, HIV/AIDS, and suicide bereavement. *Journal of HIV/AIDS & Social Services, 6*(3). doi:10.1300/J187v06n03_07

Houry, D. (2010). *Project Title: CE 09 001 Emory Center for Injury Control*. Retrieved from http://www.cdc.gov/injury/erpo/icrc/emory.html

Ingram, S., Hallstrom, K., Gohr, V. M., Ringle, J. L., Schill, D. E., & Thompson, R. W. (2008). Coping with a crisis across the lifespan: The role of a telephone hotline. *Journal of Child and Family Studies, 17*, 663–674. doi:10.1007/s10826-007-9180-z

International Association for Suicide Prevention (IASP). (2000). *IASP guidelines for suicide prevention*. Retrieved from http://www.iasp.info/suicide_guidelines.php

i-SAFE. (2004). *Cyberbullying: Statistics and tips*. Retrieved from http://www.isafe.org/outreach/media/media_cyber_bullying

James, R. K. (2008). *Crisis intervention strategies* (6th ed.). Belmont, CA: Brooks/Cole.

Jobes, D. A. (1995). The challenge and the promise of clinical suicidology. *Suicide and Life-Threatening Behavior, 25*(4), 437–449.

Jobes, D. A. (2000). Collaborating to prevent suicide: A clinical-research perspective. *Suicide and Life-Threatening Behavior, 30*(1), 8–17.

Jobes, D. A. (2006). *Managing suicidal risk: A collaborative approach*. New York, NY: Guilford Press.

Jobes, D. A., & Berman, A. L. (1993). Suicide and malpractice liability assessing and revising policies, procedures, and practice in outpatient settings. *Professional Psychology: Research and Practice, 24*(1), 91–99.

Jobes, D. A., Wong, S. A., Conrad, A. K., Drozd, J. F., & Neal-Walden, T. (2005). The collaborative assessment and management of suicidality versus treatment as usual: A retrospective study with suicidal outpatients. *Suicide and Life-Threatening Behavior, 35*(5), 483–497.

Joiner, T. (2005). *Why people die by suicide*. Cambridge, MA: Harvard University Press.

Joiner, T. (2010). *Myths about suicide*. Cambridge, MA: Harvard University Press.

Joiner, T. E., Walker, R. L., Rudd, D. M., & Jobes, D. A. (1999). Scientizing and routinizing the assessment of suicidality in outpatient practice. *Professional Psychology: Research and Practice, 30*(5), 447–453.

Jordan, J. R. (2001). Is suicide bereavement different? A reassessment of the literature. *Suicide and Life-Threatening Behavior, 31*(1), 91–102.

Jordan, J. R., & Harpel, J. L. (2007). *Facilitating suicide bereavement support groups: A self-study manual*. New York, NY: American Foundation for Suicide Prevention.

Kalafat, J., Gould, M. S., Munfakh, J. L. H., & Kleinman, M. (2007). An evaluation of crisis hotline outcomes part 1: Nonsuicidal crisis callers. *Suicide and Life-Threatening Behaviors, 37*(3), 322–337.

Kaminsky, M., McCabe, O. L, Langlieb, A. M., & Everly, G. S. (2006). An evidence-informed model of human resistance, resilience, and recovery. The Johns Hopkins' outcome-driven paradigm for disaster mental health services. *Brief Treatment and Crisis Intervention, 7*, 1–11.

Kanel, K. (1999). *A guide to crisis intervention*. Pacific Grove, CA: Brooks/Cole.

Kaslow, N. J., & Aronson, S. G. (2004). Recommendations for family interventions following a suicide. *Professional Psychology: Research and Practice, 35*(3), 240–247.

Kaslow, N. J., Ivey, A. Z., Berry-Mitchell, F., Franklin, K., & Bethea, K. (2009). Postvention for African American families following a loved one's suicide. *Professional Psychology: Research and Practice, 40*(2), 165–171. doi:10.1037/a0014023

Keel, P. K., Dorer, D. J., Eddy, K. T., Franko, D., Charatan, D. L., & Herzog, D. B. (2003). Predictors of mortality in eating disorders. *Archives of General Psychiatry, 60,* 170–183.

Kenagy, G. P. (2005, February 1). Transgender health: Findings from two needs assessment studies in Philadelphia. *Health & Social Work, 30*(1), 19–26.

King, K. A. (1999). High school suicide postvention: Recommendations for an effective program. *American Journal of Health Studies, 15*(4), 217–222.

Kitchener, K. S. (1984). Intuition, critical evaluation and ethical principles: The foundation for ethical decisions in counseling psychology. *Counseling Psychologist, 12,* 43–55.

Klott, J., & Jongsma, A. E. (2004). *The suicide and homicide risk assessment & prevention treatment planner.* Hoboken, NJ: Wiley.

Ko, S. J., Ford, J. D., Kassam-Adams, N., Berkowitz, S. J., Wilson, C., Wong, M., ... Layne, C. L. (2008). Creating trauma-informed systems: Child welfare, education, first responders, health care, juvenile justice. *Professional Psychology: Research and Practice, 39*(4), 396–404. doi:10.1037/0735-7028.39.4.396

Kübler-Ross, E. (1970). *On death and dying.* New York, NY: Macmillan.

Kübler-Ross, E. (2000). What is it like to be dying? *American Journal of Nursing, 100*(10), 96–101.

Kulkarni, S., Bell, H., & Wylie, L. (2010). Why don't they follow through? Intimate partner survivors' challenges in accessing health and social services. *Family & Community Health, 33*(2), 94–105. doi:10.1097/FCH.0b013e3181d59316

Leenars, D. (2008). Theories of suicide. In F. T. Leong & M. M. Leach (Eds.), *Suicide among racial and ethnic minority groups: Theory, research, and practice.* New York, NY: Taylor & Francis.

Leff, S. S., Power, T. J., Costigan, T. E., & Manz, P. H. (2003). Assessing the climate of the playground and lunchroom: Implications for bullying prevention programming. *School Psychology Review, 32*(3), 418–430.

Leong, F. T., & Leach, M. M. (2008). Suicide among racial and ethnic minority groups: An introduction. In F. T. Leong & M. M. Leach (Eds.), *Suicide among racial and ethnic minority groups: Theory, research, and practice.* New York, NY: Taylor & Francis.

Levine, M., Toro, P. A., & Perkins, D. V. (1993). Social and community interventions. *Annual Review of Psychology, 44,* 525–558.

Lewis, J., Arnold, M., House, R., & Toporek, R. (2003). *Advocacy competencies.* Retrieved from http://www.counseling.org/Resources/Competencies/Advocacy_Competencies.pdf

Linehan, M. M. (1993). *Cognitive-behavioral treatment of borderline personality disorder.* New York, NY: Guilford Press.

Littleton, H. L., Axsom, D., & Grills-Taquechel, A. E. (2009). Adjustment following the mass shooting at Virginia Tech: The roles of resource loss and gain. *Psychological Trauma: Theory, Research, Practice, and Policy, 1,* 206–219.

Macy, R. J., Giattina, M. C., Parish, S. L., & Crosby, C. (2010). Domestic violence and sexual assault services: Historical concerns and contemporary challenges. *Journal of Interpersonal Violence, 25,* 3–32. doi:10.1177/0886260508329128

Mann, J. J., Apter, A., Bertolote, J., Beautrais, A., Currier, D., Haas, A., . . . Hendin, H. (2005). Suicide prevention strategies: A systemic review. *The Journal of the American Medical Association, 294*(16), 2064–2074. doi:10.1001/jama.294.16.2064

McAdams, C. R., & Foster, V. A. (2000). Client suicide: Its frequency and impact on counselors. *Journal of Mental Health Counseling, 22,* 107–121.

McAdams, C. R., & Keener, H. J. (2008). Preparation, action, recovery: A conceptual framework for counselor preparation and response in client crises. *Journal of Counseling & Development, 86,* 388–398.

McIntosh, J. L. (2003). Control group studies of suicide survivors: A review and critique. *Suicide and Life-Threatening Behavior, 23,* 146–161.

McLeod, A. L., Hays, D., & Chang, C. Y. (2010). Female intimate partner violence survivors' experiences with accessing resources. *Journal of Counseling & Development, 88*(3), 303–310.

Mishara, B. L. (2006). Cultural specificity and universality of suicide: Challenges for the International Association for Suicide Prevention. *Crisis, 27*(1), 1–3.

Moscicki, E. K. (1995). Epidemiology of suicidal behavior. *Suicide and Life-Threatening Behavior, 25*(1), 22–36.

Motto, J. A., & Bostrom, A. G. (2001). A randomized controlled trial of postcrisis suicide prevention. *Psychiatric Services, 52*(6), 828–833.

Myer, R. A., & Moore, H. B. (2006). Crisis in context theory: An ecological model. *Journal of Counseling & Development, 84,* 139–147.

Neimeyer, R. A. (2000). Suicide and hastened death: Toward a training agenda for counseling psychology. *The Counseling Psychologist, 28,* 551–560.

Neimeyer, R. A., Fortner, B., & Melby, D. (2001). Personal and professional factors and suicide intervention skills. *Suicide and Life-Threatening Behavior, 31*(1), 71–82.

Olden, M., Rosenfeld, B., Pessin, H., & Breitbart, W. (2009). Measuring depression at the end of life: Is the Hamilton Depression Rating Scale a valid instrument? *Assessments, 16*(1), 43–54.

Pantalone, D. W., Hessler, D. M., & Simoni, J. M. (2010). Mental health pathways from interpersonal violence to health-related outcomes in HIV-positive sexual minority men. *Journal of Consulting and Clinical Psychology, 78*(3), 387–397. doi:10.1037/a0019307

Parker, C. M. (1972). *Bereavement: Studies of grief in adult life.* New York, NY: International Universities.

Parrish, M., & Tunkle, J. (2005). Clinical challenges following an adolescent's death by suicide: Bereavement issues faced by family, friends, schools, and clinicians. *Clinical Social Work Journal, 33*(1), 81–102.

Peterson, E. M., Luoma, J. B., & Dunne, E. (2002). Suicide survivors' perceptions of the treating clinician. *Suicide and Life-Threatening Behavior, 32,* 158–166.

Pompili, M., Girardi, P., Tatarelli, G., Roberto, A., & Tatarelli, R. (2006). Suicide and attempted suicide in eating disorders, obesity, and weight-image concern. *Eating Behaviors, 7*(4), 384–394.

Quinnett, P., & Stover, C. (2007). Suicide prevention training now available online. *Student Affairs Leader, 35*(23), 4–5.

Rabkin, J. G., McElhiney, M., Moran, P., Acree, M., & Folkman, S. (2009). Depression, distress and positive mood in late-stage cancer: A longitudinal study. *Psycho-Oncology, 18,* 79–86. doi:10.1002/pon.1386

Ramirez-Valles, J., Garcia, D., Campbell, R. T., Diaz, R. M., & Heckathorn, D. D. (2008). HIV infection, sexual risk behavior, and substance use among Latino gay and bisexual men and transgender persons. *American Journal of Public Health, 98*(6), 1036–1042.

Reicherzer, S. L., Patton, J. L., & Pisano, A. (2009, March). *The boy code betrays me: Addressing societal and sex-based trauma in the lives of gay and bisexual men.* Paper based on a program presented at the American Counseling Association Annual Conference and Exposition, Charlotte, NC.

Reid, W. H. (2004). Avoiding the malpractice snare: Documenting suicide risk management. *Journal of Psychiatric Practice, 10*(3), 1–5.

Roberts, A. R. (2005). The ACT Model: Assessment, crisis intervention, and trauma treatment in the aftermath of community trauma and terrorism attacks. In A. R. Roberts (Ed.), *Crisis intervention handbook:*

Assessment, treatment, and research (3rd ed.). New York, NY: Oxford University Press.

Roberts, A. R., & Ottens, A. J. (2005). The seven-stage crisis intervention model: A road map to goal attainment, problem solving, and crisis resolution. *Brief Treatment and Crisis Intervention, 5,* 329–339.

Robinson-Whelen, S., Hughes, R. B., Powers, L. E., Oschwald, M., Renker, P., Swank, P. R., & Curry, M. A. (2010). Efficacy of a computerized abuse and safety assessment intervention for women with disabilities: A randomized controlled trial. *Rehabilitation Psychology, 55*(2), 97–107. doi:10.1037/a0019422

Rolland, J. S. (2006). Genetics, family systems, and multicultural influences. *Families, Systems, & Health, 24*(4), 425–441.

Rolling, E. S., & Brosi, M. W. (2010). A multilevel and integrated approach to assessment and intervention in intimate partner violence. *Journal of Family Violence, 25,* 229–236. doi:10.1007/s10896-009-9286-8

Rosenthal, B., Wilson, W. C., & Futch, V. A. (2009). Trauma, protection, and distress in late adolescence: A multideterminant approach. *Adolescence, 44,* 693–703.

Rudd, M. D., Berman, A. L., Joiner, T. E., Nock, M. K., Silverman, M. M., Mandrusiak, M., . . . Witte, T. (2006). Warning signs for suicide. Theory, research, and clinical applications. *Suicide and Life-Threatening Behavior, 36*(3), 255–262.

Rudd, M. D., & Joiner, T. (1998). The assessment, management, and treatment of suicidality: Toward clinically informed and balanced standards of care. *American Psychological Association, 5*(2), 135–150.

Ruzek, J. I., Brymer, M. J., Jacobs, A. K., Layne, C. M., Vernberg, E. M., & Watson, P. J. (2007). Psychological first aid. *Journal of Mental Health Counseling, 29,* 17–49.

Shea, S. (2002). *The practical art of suicidal assessment: A guide for mental health professionals and substance abuse counselors.* Hoboken, NJ: Wiley.

Shneidman, E. (1993). *Suicide as psychache.* Northvale, NJ: Aronson.

Shneidman, E. (1996). *The suicidal mind.* New York, NY: Oxford University Press.

Silverman, M. M. (1997). Current controversies in suicidology. In R. W. Maris, M. M. Silverman, & S. S. Canetto (Eds.), *Review of suicidology* (pp. 1–21). New York, NY: Guilford Press.

Silverman, M. M. (2006). The language of suicidology. *Suicide and Life-Threatening Behavior, 36,* 519–532.

Silverman, M. M., Berman, A. L., Sanddal, N. D., O'Carroll, P. W., & Joiner, T. E. (2007). Rebuilding the tower of

Babel: A revised nomenclature for the study of suicide and suicidal behaviors: Part 2. Suicide-related ideations, communications, and behaviors. *Suicide and Life-Threatening Behavior, 37*(3), 264–277.

Simon, R. I. (2004). *Suicide risk: Guidelines for clinically based risk management.* Washington, DC: American Psychiatric Association.

Slaikeu, H. (1990). *Crisis intervention: A handbook for practice and research* (2nd ed.). Needham Heights, MA: Allyn & Bacon.

Smith, T. E., Burgos, J., Dexter, V., Norcott, J., Pappas, S. V., Shuman, E., . . . Essock, S. M. (2010). Best practices for improving engagement of clients in clinic care. *Psychiatric Services, 61*(4), 343–345.

Sommers-Flanagan, R. (2007). Ethical considerations in crisis and humanitarian interventions. *Ethics and Behavior, 17,* 187–202.

Stone, D. A., & Conley, J. A. (2004). A partnership between Roberts' crisis intervention model and the multicultural competencies. *Brief Treatment and Crisis Intervention, 4,* 367–375.

Substance Abuse and Mental Health Services Administration (SAMHSA). (2005). *Transforming mental health care in America: The federal action agenda: First steps.* Rockville, MD: Author.

Substance Abuse and Mental Health Services Administration (SAMHSA). (2012). *Suicide prevention.* Retrieved from http://www.samhsa.gov/prevention /suicide.aspx

Suicide Prevention Action Network USA (SPAN USA). (2001). *Suicide prevention: Effectiveness and evaluation.* Washington, DC: Author.

Suicide Prevention Resource Center (SPRC), in collaboration with the American Association of Suicidology. (2008). *Assessing and managing suicide risk: Core competencies for mental health professionals.* Washington, DC: Education Development Center.

Summit, R. C. (1983). The child sexual abuse accommodation syndrome. *Child Abuse Neglect, 7,* 177–193.

Tjaden, P., & Thoennes, N. (2000a). *Extent, nature, and consequences of intimate partner violence: Findings from the National Violence Against Women Survey.* Report for the National Center for Justice (NCJ 181867). Retrieved from http:// www.ojp.usdoj.gov/nij/pubs-sum/181867.htm

Tjaden, P., & Thoennes, N. (2000b). *Full report of the prevalence, incidences, and consequences of violence against women: Findings from the National Violence Against Women Survey.* Report for the National Center for Justice (NCJ 183781). Retrieved from https://www.ncjrs.gov/pdffiles1/nij/183781.pdf

Tunajek, S. K. (2009). Change, grief, and healing. *American Association of Nurse Aesthetics Journal, 63*(10), 24–26.

US Department of Defense (DOD). (2010a). *The challenge and the promise: Strengthening the force, preventing suicide and saving lives: Final report of the Department of Defense Task Force on the prevention of suicide by members of the armed forces.* Washington, DC: Author.

US Department of Defense (DOD). (2010b). *DOD establishes suicide prevention task force.* Retrieved from http://www.defense.gov/releases/release .aspx?releaseid=12941

US Department of Health and Human Services (DHHS). (1999). *Mental health: A report of the Surgeon General.* Rockville, MD: US Department of Health and Human Services, Substance Abuse and Mental Health Services Administration, Center for Mental Health Services, National Institutes of Health, National Institute of Mental Health.

US Department of Health and Human Services (DHHS). (2001). *National strategy for suicide prevention: Goals and objectives for action.* Rockville, MD: Author.

US Public Health Service. (1999). *The Surgeon General's call to action to prevent suicide.* Washington, DC: Author.

VandeCreek, L., Knapp, S., & Herzog, C. (1987). Malpractice risks in the treatment of dangerous patients. *Psychotherapy: Theory, Research, and Practice, 24,* 145–153.

Van der Heijden, I., & Swartz, S. (2010). Bereavement, silence and culture within a peer-led HIV/AIDS-prevention strategy for vulnerable children in South Africa. *African Journal of AIDS Research, 9*(1), 41–50. doi:10.2989/16085906.2010.484563

Wainrib, B. R., & Bloch, E. L. (1998). *Crisis intervention and trauma response: Theory and practice.* New York, NY: Springer.

Wingate, L. R., Joiner, T. E., Walker, R. L., Rudd, M. D., & Jobes, D. A. (2004). Empirically informed approaches to topics in suicide risk assessment. *Behavioral Sciences & the Law, 22,* 651–665. doi:10.1002. /bsl.612

Worden, W. (2008). *Grief counseling and grief therapy: A handbook for the mental health practitioner.* New York, NY: Springer.

World Health Organization (WHO). (2010). *World report on violence and health.* Retrieved from http://www.who.int/violence_injury_prevention /violence/world_report/en/

PART 3

Contemporary Trends in Clinical Mental Health Counseling

11

Psychopharmacology

Donna S. Sheperis

CHAPTER OVERVIEW

Psychopharmacology is a central topic to the provision of clinical mental health counseling. Regardless of whether counselors personally agree with the use of medication, their clients will take medication, have symptom relief, and experience side effects. The role of clinical mental health counselors, as the providers who likely spend more time with their clients than the professionals providing the medication, is to help inform their clients. Toward that end, this chapter covers the basics of neuroanatomy and pharmacodynamics, major classes of mental health concerns and their corresponding medication options, and the use of psychotropic medications with special populations.

LEARNING OBJECTIVES

The learning objectives for this chapter are designed to be consistent with the 2009 Council for Accreditation of Counseling and Related Educational Programs Standards (CACREP, 2009). As such, upon completion of this chapter, the students will have knowledge of the following clinical mental health counseling standards:

1. Knows the principles, models, and documentation formats of biopsychosocial case conceptualization and treatment planning. (C.7)
2. Understands professional issues relevant to the practice of clinical mental health counseling. (C.9)
3. Understands current literature that outlines theories, approaches, strategies, and techniques shown to be effective when working with specific populations of clients with mental and emotional disorders. (E.3)
4. Understands basic classifications, indications, and contraindications of commonly prescribed psychopharmacological medications so that appropriate referrals can be made for medication evaluations and so that the side effects of such medications can be identified. (G.3)

INTRODUCTION

Clinical mental health counselors are in a unique position to spend more time with their clients than are many other helping professionals. As a result, they are often the first to assess a need for medication. Through the therapeutic relationship, they gain the trust of their clients and can assist them in determining the benefits of initiating medication as well as the possible side effects. Finally, clinical mental health counselors are often called upon to educate clients about medication. Although they neither prescribe medications nor recommend specific types of psychopharmacological interventions, it is ethically responsible for clinical mental health counselors to be well versed in the use of pharmacotherapy as a potential treatment for many types of disorders with which their clients present.

To best understand the role of the clinical mental health counselor in medication use and management, we must first look at how medications work from a mental health perspective. Then, we survey the various mental health concerns often treated with either medication or a combination of medication and counseling. Finally, the chapter explores how to best integrate psychopharmacological interventions into a client's treatment, including the necessity for referrals and relationships with medical professionals.

PSYCHOPHARMACOLOGY AND CLINICAL MENTAL HEALTH COUNSELING

It is not possible to provide all you would need to know about the physiology of psychopharmacology in a single chapter. Many graduate-level courses are dedicated to the study of neuroanatomy, the anatomy of the brain and nervous system; pharmacodynamics, how drugs affect the body; and psychopharmacology, the medications used to treat various mental disorders. What is important to know is that clinical mental health counselors do not have prescribing privileges. All specializations of doctors of medicine (MD), physician's assistants (PA), family nurse practitioners (FNP), and some clinical psychologists (PhD or PsyD) have prescription privileges. Because this ability varies by profession and by state, clinical mental health counselors will have to research their state regulations to find out who has prescribing privileges in their area. This chapter offers a brief survey of the basic concepts of psychopharmacology that clinical mental health counselors need to know.

Neuroanatomy

Neuroanatomy is basically the anatomy of the brain and nervous system. The brain impacts human functioning (which includes mental health) and is central to the delivery of psychotropic medications. It relays messages and manages physical functions. In addition, human thoughts and even feelings are housed in the brain. Thus, it is important for clinical mental health counselors to have a working knowledge of how the brain works.

There are a few important elements of neuroanatomy to consider as we begin the discussion of psychopharmacology. The messages that the brain sends and receives pass from neuron to neuron through synapses. Synapses are basically gaps between the neurons, which are nerve cells. You might think of a series of buildings on a street. Between each building there is a space. As you walk from building to building, you exit one building and move through this open space before entering the next building. In this analogy, the buildings are neurons and the spaces are synapses.

Messages that are sent through this process fall into two classes: they are either excitatory or inhibitory. Excitatory messages are transmitted further, and inhibitory messages are slowed down or stopped (Gray & Robinson, 2009). The neuron determines the type of message it has received and then responds accordingly.

Messages are transmitted through the synapse via neurotransmitters. Several neurotransmitters that are often involved in the transmission of psychotropic medications are acetylcholine, dopamine, norepinephrine, epinephrine, and serotonin. The neurotransmitters are sent into the synaptic gap (the space between) by the neuron (a building in the analogy). They then enter the next neuron via a process known as reuptake.

What does this have to do with mental health? Two things, actually. The first reason is that a failure in the sending of messages from neuron to neuron can impact a person's mental health. Problems arise when the initial neuron malfunctions and doesn't send the message to the next neuron. Problems also arise when the message gets sent but there aren't enough ways for it to get into the receiving neuron. In the analogy of the series of buildings on a street, this would mean you leave one building and walk through the open area but cannot find a door to the next building. The final form of malfunction that causes problems is when some of the message gets left in the synaptic gap (Czerner, 2001).

The second reason this discussion relates to mental health is that the same neuroanatomy that causes mental health concerns when it malfunctions is used by psychotropic medications to transmit chemicals to address the symptoms. Let's take a look at how medications can impact this process and influence the body.

Pharmacodynamics

Pharmacodynamics refers to how medications affect the body. Specifically, it relates to how the medications impact the various neurotransmitters previously discussed. When considering medication, clinical mental health counselors first want to determine the role of the particular drug. In other words, what is its intended effect? Does it enhance, replace, or suppress something? Psychotropic medications are either agonist or antagonists. If a medication is classified as an agonist, its role is to increase the body's response or natural state. If a drug is classified as an antagonist, it serves to block these normal responses (Czerner, 2001).

Clinical mental health counselors not only must be aware of the role of the medication but also must understand the duration of its effect. This is particularly important when helping a client determine whether a physical reaction is a side effect or something else entirely. What is important to realize, and to convey to their clients, is that while medications have some generally expected effects, they affect individuals in different ways. Although clinical mental health counselors are not expected to know every type of medication available—even pharmacists can't keep up with that—they should be familiar with general classes of medications and how they work. Clients will likely take a number of medications, some psychotropic and some not, and will have myriad questions. It will therefore be important for clinical mental health counselors to adhere to their limits of competence and refer clients back to their medical professionals for answers.

OVERVIEW OF COMMON MENTAL HEALTH DISORDERS AND PSYCHOPHARMACOLOGICAL INTERVENTIONS

Anxiety and Panic

Anxiety disorders are some of the most common mental health issues. In fact, some theories view anxiety as a central dilemma of social existence. Panic is defined as an attack of symptoms that occurs suddenly, lasts a short amount of time, but can be quite intense. The familiar term *panic attack* is used to describe a discrete episode of panic. Anxiety, on the other hand, is of a lesser intensity than panic, gradually builds up, and can last over a prolonged period of time. Think of anxiety and panic as being on a continuum from mild to severe. Anxiety occurs in the mild to moderate range and has a longer period of duration, whereas panic is a brief, more intense burst of that same feeling and so is at the severe end of the continuum. Anxiety and panic can be viewed as having either endogenous (internal) or exogenous (external) origins. Specific symptoms found in anxiety and panic disorders include motor tension, autonomic hyperactivity, vigilance or feeling "on guard," and scanning for threats. Restlessness, insomnia, dizziness, poor concentration, trembling, shortness of breath, and even heart palpitations are also commonly found in these disorders.

ANXIETY DIAGNOSES   The *Diagnostic and Statistical Manual of Mental Disorders* (DSM) lists a number of anxiety disorders that are often treated with psychopharmacological interventions. These diagnoses range in severity from a generalized feeling of anxiety to an intense experience of panic. It is important for clinical mental health counselors to recognize that anxiety disorders are distinguished from one another based on prevailing symptoms, etiology, duration, and intensity.

Understanding anxiety disorders is critical for practitioners. With an overall lifetime prevalence rate of 25% in the United States, it is expected that helping professionals will work with sufferers of anxiety on a routine basis. An estimated 37 million people each year deal with anxiety problems, with women outnumbering men by 2 to 1. Specific challenges exist in the treatment of anxiety disorders. Clients with panic disorder are 18 times more likely to attempt suicide, making this a critical treatment concern. Medications used to treat panic and anxiety are very effective; however, they are also some of the most abused medications on the market today (American Psychiatric Association, 2000).

MEDICATIONS USED TO TREAT ANXIETY   Antianxiety agents work by increasing the inhibitor effect of gamma-aminobutyric acid (GABA). GABA is considered the "brakes" of the brain and can calm down excessive brain activity such as anxiety. In other words, antianxiety medications decrease neural activity and thereby provide a mild to extreme numbing of the feeling. Because this fairly immediate relief makes such medications so attractive to clients, they can become dependent on their use as a sole coping mechanism for dealing with anxiety. Descriptions of the most effective antianxiety agents follow.

Barbiturates   Barbiturates were first developed in the 1860s by chemist Adolph Bayer, of Bayer® Aspirin fame. Prior to this discovery, physicians had few resources available for calming down patients or for prescribing a sleep aid. The arrival of barbiturates was viewed as a blessing because they were fast acting. Initially, this class of medication was used for the treatment of anxiety, depression, grief, and seizures.

Barbiturates became widely used by the early 1900s, and by 1950 over 50 brands were marketed and available. However, several problems emerged with the use of barbiturates in the treatment of anxiety. First, the nonselective effect of barbiturates means they are not limited to one area of the body and therefore have effects across the board. Physicians discovered that even limited use of these medications could lead to depression, sleep disruptions, and inhibition of motor and cognitive abilities. Second, persons using barbiturates showed a rapid development of tolerance of them, and so they needed progressively more and more of the drugs in higher doses to reach the same effect. Third, upon discontinuing barbiturates, there is a complicated withdrawal process that often requires medically supervised detoxification and stabilization. As an added concern, barbiturates—because of their ability to inhibit breathing—were found to be easy to overdose on and so have become a drug of choice for assisted suicides.

By the 1960s, barbiturates had been largely replaced by a class of drugs known as benzodiazepines, but the barbiturates became an illicit drug of abuse known as "downers." Health professionals today seldom use barbiturates in standard treatment protocols for anxiety. Instead, this class of medication is used for seizure control, as an IV anesthetic, as a way to reduce brain activity post head trauma, and as a means of assisted suicide. A few barbiturates you may encounter include thiopental, secobarbital, pentobarbital, and phenobarbital.

Benzodiazepines   Benzodiazepines are hands down the most common drug type prescribed for anxiety today. The first benzodiazepine, Librium, was synthesized in 1959 and marketed in 1960. The three types of benzodiazepines are 2-Keto, 3-Hydroxy, and Triazolo. 2-Keto benzodiazepines are metabolized in the liver, have a long half-life, and persons who use them are prone to tolerance and dependence. Examples of these include Librium, Valium, and Klonopin. The 3-Hydroxy benzodiazepines are also metabolized in the liver, have a shorter half-life, and result in persons using them to have some dependence and withdrawal issues if used for an extended time. These medications include Ativan, Restoril, and Serax. Finally, the Triazolo benzodiazepines have the least impact on the liver and are quicker to metabolize. They have the briefest half-life of the benzodiazepines and include the popular drug Xanax.

Hypnotics   Hypnotics are not very common in the United States although the term may be familiar. A form of substance abuse or dependence is termed sedative, hypnotic, or anxiolytic abuse or dependence. A hypnotic under development for the treatment of anxiety is Ambien, which is currently approved only for use as a sleep aid.

Nonbenzodiazepines   Other antianxiety medications that are useful, if not generally as immediately potent, are the nonbenzodiazepines. These include antihistamines such as Benadryl and Vistaril, beta-blockers such as Inderal, and azapirones such as Buspar. A safer choice due to their lowered chance of addiction and lack of withdrawal symptoms, these medications are routinely used to treat the symptoms of anxiety. Although nonbenzodiazepines are the weakest anxiolytics, they have very little, if any, physiological dependence.

PATIENT EDUCATION   With all psychopharmacological interventions, patient education is key. As previously mentioned, antianxiety medications can be highly addictive. Therefore, patient education must include information about becoming dependent on them. Because symptoms of anxiety can be very severe, and because antianxiety medications can provide immediate relief, it is no wonder that clients turn to them time and again for symptom management. It is common for clients to wonder why therapy should be the only answer when clearly the benefits from these substances is substantial. As the treating clinicians, it will be up to clinical mental health counselors to talk about dependency risk, short-term versus long-term symptom management, and the role of concomitant medication and psychotherapies.

Clients who are prescribed antianxiety medications will need to avoid alcohol use. The side effects of these medications include drowsiness, impaired coordination, and dulled thinking, which are worsened by the addition of alcohol. Additionally, clients will require information on possible withdrawal effects and the need to follow doctor's instructions when increasing or decreasing dosages or ceasing use of the medication. Clinical mental health counselors are the professionals that will ultimately monitor this type of patient education.

Depression and Antidepressants

Depressive disorders join anxiety disorders as part of a larger group called mood disorders. Mood disorders are the most commonly diagnosed psychiatric conditions. Although anxiety diagnoses occur more frequently, depressive diagnoses follow close behind. It is estimated that a minimum of 3% of adults suffer some form of ongoing depression with many sufferers not seeking treatment (NIMH, 2013). Depressive disorders carry the added distinction of accounting for approximately 75% of all psychiatric hospitalizations, making them one of the more expensive disorders to treat. Further complicating the treatment of this class of disorder, 80% of all suicidal individuals have a depressive disorder of some kind (NIMH, 2013).

Everyone has experienced feelings of sadness or being "blue" on occasion. However, the depressive disorders represent diagnoses that move beyond fleeting, yet tolerable, feelings related to circumstances that ultimately resolve themselves. In fact, depressive disorders pose treatment challenges to helping professionals across disciplines specifically due to their severity and potential consequences. Prevalence rates are high and causes of depression include both biological and environmental reasons. Many patients are not able to be properly diagnosed as clinicians attempt to sort out the impact of life stressors, physical symptoms, and genetic influences on each individual. Unfortunately, many symptoms of depression are often misattributed to other health problems, and therefore the depressive disorders go largely undiagnosed.

An understanding of the criteria for diagnosing depressive disorders as well as an overview of the prevalence and expected course of these disorders is critical to providing effective treatment. Medications compose a portion of that treatment and must be evaluated in the context of the many other factors that contribute to making an accurate diagnosis.

DSM CRITERIA, PREVALENCE, AND ETIOLOGY

Depressive Disorder Diagnoses Depressive disorders are often referred to as unipolar depression. This label helps distinguish the disorders with only depressive symptoms from the bipolar disorders, which contain depression along with symptoms of mania. We begin with a discussion of the diagnoses referred to as unipolar in nature and then move to the bipolar disorders.

General symptoms of depression include feelings of prolonged sadness, hopelessness, guilt, loss of pleasure, poor concentration, decreased energy, and sleep or appetite disturbances. To meet the criteria for depression in the DSM (American Psychiatric Association, 2000), a person must have a feeling of depressed mood or loss of pleasure in almost all activities that lasts for at least two weeks. These feelings interfere with activities of daily living such as working or even eating and sleeping. In addition, there is usually an inability to cope, feelings of guilt and shame, and less of a need for social activity. Depressed individuals tend to feel helpless and hopeless and to blame themselves for having these feelings. Some may have thoughts of death or suicide (American Psychiatric Association, 2000).

It is important to consider both the lifetime prevalence and the base prevalence rates of depression. Lifetime prevalence rates refer to the number of people at a given time who have a depressive diagnosis in the total population. For major depressive disorder, those rates are 5% to 12% among males and 10% to 25% among females (American Psychiatric Association, 2000). Base rates, on the other hand, represent the number of newly diagnosed cases in a given year within the population.

The DSM (American Psychiatric Association, 2000) lists several diagnoses of unipolar depression that are often treated with psychopharmacological interventions. It is important for counselors to recognize that, similar to anxiety disorders, depressive disorders are distinguished from one another based on prevailing symptoms, etiology, duration, and intensity.

What Is the Cause of Depression? Depression is often viewed as a biochemical imbalance that may have genetic origins. Endogenous depression refers to depression that comes from within the individual and is impacted by genetics, physical health, and certain substances. Exogenous factors, on the other hand, are situations or life stressors (e.g., grief) impacting the person who subsequently suffers from depression.

Medical conditions may cause someone to present with symptoms of depression. These medical conditions are often very common and can cause or worsen symptoms of depression. Some examples include lupus, hepatitis, stroke, forms of cancer, brain tumor, chronic fatigue, and HIV/AIDS (Sinacola & Peters-Strickland, 2006).

You or someone you care about has likely suffered from one or more of these medical conditions but may not have been aware of its link to depressive symptoms. Clearly, clinicians need to be well informed of the patient's medical history and recent medical changes to fully diagnose any of the depressive disorders.

In addition, the ingestion of substances, whether prescribed medications or other substances, can create or worsen depressive symptoms. Sinacola and Peters-Strickland (2006) provide examples of such substances, some of which are familiar medications used to treat other psychiatric disorders discussed in this chapter. For example, antianxiety medications may worsen depressive symptoms but so can over-the-counter medications such as antihistamines. Alcohol, a depressant itself, can also exacerbate the symptoms.

It is certainly challenging to diagnose depression because it may occur genetically, because of an outside event, or because of a general medical condition. Then the medications used to treat depression can be compromised by medications used to treat other medical or psychiatric conditions. It does not fall on clinical mental health counselors to make these determinations, but they may find it necessary to consult with all of a client's primary health care providers in order to offer the best treatment option to the client.

TREATING DEPRESSION Both counseling and medication are effective interventions in the treatment of depression. Although studies have shown that both the medical approach and the counseling approach are individually equally effective, it is also clear in the research that a combined approach works better than counseling by itself (Segal, Kennedy, Cohen, & Group CDW, 2000). Individuals suffering from dysthymia are better candidates for counseling alone, whereas those who have what are referred to as the "vegetative symptoms" of depressive disorders are better suited to an approach that includes medication. Vegetative symptoms are simply factors such as sleep and appetite disturbance, fatigue, impaired attention, and anhedonia (loss of interest in previously enjoyable activities).

MEDICATIONS USED TO TREAT DEPRESSION   Depression was historically viewed as a natural emotional experience that sufferers could simply get over by pulling up their bootstraps and making some behavioral change (e.g., eating more or less, sleeping more or less, or getting involved in former activities). However, the need for pharmacological intervention grew as these efforts were unsuccessful in treatment of depression. The first antidepressants, developed in the 1950s, included the use of iproniazid, a monoamine oxidase inhibitor (MAOI) that was originally prescribed for the treatment of tuberculosis. During its use for tuberculosis, significant improvements in the patients' moods were evident. These mood changes were found to be unrelated to the relief of tuberculosis symptoms, and hence iproniazid was regularly prescribed for treatment of depression. Complications and flaws in research related to liver damage and effectiveness caused ipronazid to be taken off the market shortly after it was released (McKim, 2003). However, modern MAOIs are quite effective and are discussed later in this section.

Another early entry into the medical management of depression included the use of imipramine, an antipsychotic medication that successfully addressed depressive symptoms. Changes to the molecular structure of these drugs resulted into a category known as tricyclic antidepressants, which were subsequently proven to be safer than MAOIs. However, the safety of the tricyclics was also questioned, and a new class of second-generation medications evolved to address side effects of earlier medical alternatives. This new wave of medications was spearheaded in the 1980s by the arrival of a selective serotonin reuptake inhibitor (SSRI), fluoxetine, more commonly known by its brand name Prozac (McKim, 2003).

Given the variety of drug classifications previously mentioned, it is easy to see that multiple theories exist to substantiate the need for and effectiveness of particular types of drugs used to treat depression. The amine theory posits that depression is related to decreased levels of amines, specifically norepinephrine, in the synapse. The reuptake inhibition theory espouses that depression is not due to decreased levels of norepinephrine but rather to the rate at which it is recycled back into the system. This theory indicates that the levels are not necessarily insufficient, but the amount of time the neurotransmitters are left in the synapse to actually provide benefit is cut short by the brain's reuptake process; allowing the neurotransmitters to stay in the synapse longer will improve symptoms of depression. Thus, medications created in support of this hypothesis serve as artificial blocks to the reuptake system, thereby allowing the desired neurotransmitters to remain in the synapse and provide the needed effect in the brain.

Another popular hypothesis related to brain chemistry and depression is the down-regulation theory, which focuses on the desensitization of the postsynaptic receptor sites. It posits that the postsynaptic receptor is "starved" for the amine so it increases the number of receptor cells to ensure it gets what it needs. These added receptor cells begin to take too much norepinephrine (NE), which depletes the brain's ability to receive the benefit of the neurotransmitter. Finally, the cellular/molecular theory focuses on changes that occur within the cell itself. The use of antidepressants appears to increase the production of another member of the brain's messenger system, cyclic adenosine monophosphate or cyclic AMP, which is disturbed in cases of depression.

CLASSES OF ANTIDEPRESSANTS We will explore the commonly prescribed medications for the treatment of depression in terms of four classes: MAOIs, tricyclic antidepressants, SSRIs, and the newer class commonly known as heterocyclic antidepressants.

Monoamine Oxidase Inhibitors (MAOIs) MAOIs were developed to address the amine theory and inhibit the enzyme responsible for breaking down the neurotransmitters that aid in the improvement of depressive symptoms. In lay terms, this MAO enzyme disintegrates the neurotransmitters necessary to feel good, or not be depressed. Because the goal is to maintain the functioning of these neurotransmitters as long as possible, the MAOIs attack the enzyme and prevent it from doing its job, leaving the neurotransmitters untouched and free to perform the "feel good" function for the brain. Think of them as the special forces unit assigned to take out a particular threat to our well-being.

Specific MAOIs include Nardil (phenelzine) and Parnate (tranylcypromine). Because of some serious side effects and other restrictions, these medications are now used only when patients suffer from atypical depression and fail to respond to some of the other classes of medications. Side effects include changes in blood pressure, sleep disturbance, headache, muscle cramps, weight gain, difficulty urinating, hives, and the potential to induce a manic episode. Despite this list of side effects, the most commonly cited problems with MAOIs are the dietary restrictions imposed on patients. Patients are cautioned to avoid a variety of foods such as cheese (particularly aged cheese), wine, beer, some liquor, chocolate, caffeine, yogurt, and some pickled items. MAOIs are not advisable for use with patients who have a history of hypertension, liver disease, congestive heart failure, or drug use.

Tricyclic Antidepressants As previously indicated, tricyclics were created in response to the need for drugs with fewer side effects than the ones present in MAOI use. Their primary purpose is to block or prevent the reuptake of neurotransmitters back into the presynaptic cell. Tricyclics simply function as blockers, and because they do not discriminate in which neurotransmitters they block, side effects occur. Blockage of other neurotransmitters allows the additional transmitters to stay in the synapse longer, which is not always desirable. Failure to reuptake acetylcholine, for example, results in what are known as anticholinergic side effects. Side effects generated by the presence of these other neurotransmitters include sedation, weight gain, difficulty urinating, dizziness, blurred vision, and sexual dysfunction.

Common tricyclics include Anafranil (clomipramine), Asendin (amoxapine), Elavil (amitrityline), Pamelor (nortriptyline), Sinequan (doxepin), and the original tricyclic, Tofranil (imipramine). Tricyclics are well studied, and so there is a wealth of empirical evidence substantiating their effectiveness. They are easily available and generally quite inexpensive, making them attractive to individuals without insurance and institutions treating a number of patients. Unfortunately, effectiveness and side effects of tricyclics can be unpredictable and vary from client to client. Additionally, these medications are extremely toxic and thus pose a strong overdose potential, particularly in an outpatient or other setting where clients can horde medications or obtain access to them in large amounts.

Selective Serotonin Reuptake Inhibitors (SSRIs) As mentioned in the section on the history of medications used to treat depression, SSRIs are part of the second generation of antidepressants and arrived in the 1980s as a new approach to treatment. Also included in this group are the serotonin and norepinephrine reuptake inhibitors (SNRIs) and the NE uptake inhibitors to be discussed later. SSRIs inhibit the reuptake or "recycling" of the serotonin amines. The brain has a series of synapses that exists between receptor sites and helps move neurotransmitters from receptor to receptor as they make their way through the brain. Each receptor has essentially an inflow and an outflow side. The neurotransmitter is expelled into the synapse via the outflow side, remains in the synapse for a period of time, and then is recycled via the inflow side of the next receptor. This inflow side has receptor sites that function like little vacuum cleaners and "suck" the neurotransmitter into the receptor. These openings are sized specific to the neurotransmitters they receive. SSRIs work by imitating the neurotransmitter serotonin and blocking the uptake sites on the inflow side. By blocking some of the receptor sites with, essentially, fake serotonin, the real serotonin remains in the synapse and can be utilized more effectively by the brain. Thus, SSRIs do not generate more serotonin; they simply make it easier for the brain to use what is already available.

Side effects common to SSRIs include headaches, nausea, dizziness, diarrhea, dry mouth, weight loss or gain, restlessness, tremors, insomnia, sweating, and inhibited sexual desire or response. It is not uncommon for clients to report that after taking an SSRI for a period of time, they are more interested in sex but physically unable to achieve orgasm. Side effects of SSRIs may be temporary or longer lasting. The initial two-week period of introducing an SSRI may result in what is known as a serotonergic surge during which the body has excessive use of serotonin, which ultimately balances out. Specifically, clients may report feeling jittery, sleeplessness, and muscle tension. Clinicians familiar with this surge of serotonin can educate clients on the predicted course of this medical intervention.

Specific SSRIs include Celexa (citalopram), Lexapro (escitalopram), Luvox (fluvoxamine), Paxil/Paxil CR (paroxetine), Prozac/Sarafem (fluoxetine), and Zoloft (sertraline). These medications may be familiar largely due to their manufacturers' enormous amounts of marketing to increase consumers' knowledge base of the products. The hope is that clients will then specifically ask for one of these medications when meeting with a physician or psychiatrist. SSRIs are also popular because they interact with very few medications, are not considered to be addictive, have low potential for overdose, and have become the preferred method for the treatment of depression. Although the drugs themselves are not highly toxic, we would be remiss not to mention the potential for an increase in suicidal thinking and behavior. In 2004, the US Food and Drug Administration (FDA) reported such thinking and behavior in 2% to 3% of children and adolescents who are prescribed SSRIs. That research has been cited as highly controversial and is currently under debate, causing practitioners to evaluate whether the treatment does truly cause the increase in suicidal thoughts and behavior (Sinkman, 2008).

Heterocyclic Antidepressants　A fourth class of antidepressants is the heterocyclics. Unlike SSRIs, which impact the neurotransmitter serotonin, heterocyclics impact multiple neurotransmitters. Medications that fall in this category tend to have less likelihood of sexual side effects, making them a popular choice for consumers. Heterocyclics include SNRIs, noradrenaline reuptake inhibitors (NRIs), and others.

Serotonin norepinephrine reuptake inhibitors, SNRIs, block the reuptake of both serotonin and norepinephrine. They provide the client with the combination of effects experienced from using tricyclics and SSRIs. Effexor/Effexor XR (venlafaxine) is an example of an SNRI; it has been shown to be useful with generalized anxiety as well as depression. Effexor has also been found effective for treatment of postpartum depression (Cohen et al., 2001). Additionally, SNRIs are indicated in cases in which the depression is combined with neuropathic pain. Another example of an SNRI is the heavily marketed Cymbalta (duloxetine), which entered the market in 2004.

NRIs block the reuptake of noradrenaline (norepinephrine). These drugs are unusual in that they were initially developed to address attention deficit disorder (ADD) and attention deficit hyperactivity disorder (ADHD). Having been found to improve the symptoms of depression, NRIs are often prescribed for what is considered an off-label use. The most common NRI is Strattera (atomoxetine). The primary difference between a drug such as Strattera and some of the other common ADHD medications such as Ritalin is that Strattera is not a stimulant. Such considerations become important given that drug-seeking adults may present with false symptoms to obtain stimulant medication. Drug-seeking behavior is something all clinicians must be attuned to and familiar with.

Other atypical antidepressants to consider in this category may also be familiar to the general public. Wellbutrin (bupropion) and BuSpar (buspirone) are two such atypical antidepressants. These medications operate on a different mechanism than SSRIs, SNRIs, or NRIs. The pharmaceutical community knows that these drugs do not influence the reuptake process, but it is still unclear exactly how they work. What is known is that they are effective with mediating the symptoms of depression and are also typically effective with anxiety. Ironically, some common side effects of these medications include nausea, lightheadedness, excitement, and rapid heart rate—symptoms that mirror the indicators of anxiety.

ALTERNATIVE THERAPIES   This discussion would be incomplete without considering another common class of medication used in the treatment of depression: the herbal or homeopathic remedies. Due to increased consumer information, the advent of the Internet, and some measures of effectiveness, these available, cost-effective options are often the first line of attack for sufferers of depression. The fact that most anyone can walk into a local drugstore, discount chain, or supermarket and purchase St. John's wort or S-adenosyl-L-methionine (SAMe) right off the shelf without a prescription or a valid diagnosis of depression makes these products attractive to consumers. Clients without medical insurance in particular may turn to self-diagnosing and homeopathic remedies as means of managing the financial burden of nonemergency health concerns. Due to the potential for interaction with other prescribed medications, clients must be encouraged to share any over-the-counter or homeopathic regimens with their physician. Some commonly purchased alternatives to prescribed antidepressants include St. John's wort, SAMe, and omega-3 fatty acids.

St. John's wort is derived from a flowering plant that blooms around the time of the feast of St. John the Baptist in late June. It is often taken by consumers to combat symptoms of depression. Sources vary regarding the evidence that St. John's wort is useful for treating mild to moderate depression. However, a large study sponsored by the National Institutes of Health showed that it was effective only as a placebo when used to treat major depression (2013). St. John's wort can produce a number of unpleasant side effects such as increased sensitivity to the sun, nausea, and fatigue; and it interacts with other common drugs such as birth control pills and prescribed antidepressants.

The theory behind the use of SAMe, or S-adenosyl-L-methionine, is that the brain of a healthy person manufactures all the SAMe compound it needs, but production is impaired in people who are depressed. This compound supposedly increases levels of certain neurotransmitters and improves the binding of serotonin and dopamine to their receptor sites, where the effects of these neurotransmitters are experienced. Results of the efficacy of SAMe in the treatment of depression are mixed. Although there is some promising evidence of its helpfulness in improving symptoms of depression, no conclusion of efficacy has been made by the mainstream medical community (Agency for Healthcare Research and Quality, 2002). A better understanding of how SAMe works and its risks to the user is warranted to be able to fully back the use of this homeopathic option.

Omega-3 fatty acids are essential to health but are not produced by the body. They must be ingested through food intake (e.g., fish) or the use of supplements. Because a deficiency in omega-3 fatty acids has been linked to depression, consumers may take the supplement to counteract this fact. Omega-3 fatty acids are essential to helping nerve cells communicate with each other, which improves the pathway for neurotransmitters related to depression. Omega-3 fatty acids have been found effective in the treatment or mediation of depression as well as other health concerns including high blood pressure and arthritis (University of Maryland Medical Center, 2008).

FINAL CONSIDERATIONS Given the overwhelming amount of information available to consumers of antidepressants, clinical mental health counselors have an ethical obligation to help their clients make informed choices regarding treatment of depression. Clients need to know that, for the most part, antidepressants are not fast acting. In fact, taking one for several weeks or months is needed to determine its full therapeutic effect on a given patient. Information about side effects must also be provided. Because sexual dysfunction is a common side effect, clinical mental health counselors will need to be comfortable talking with their clients about clients' sexual activity, interest in sex, and ability to achieve erection and/or orgasm.

Bipolar Disorder and Mood Stabilizers

Having previously discussed anxiety and depression, two of the most common mood disorders, this section covers another type of mood disorder: bipolar disorder, an often diagnosed and yet misunderstood mental health problem. The DSM (American Psychiatric Association, 2000) recognizes two variations of bipolar disorder: bipolar I and bipolar II. Foundational to both types is the presence of a depressive disorder. What differentiates the two is the type of manic episodes also present. Bipolar I contains full manic episodes, whereas bipolar II is characterized by the presence of less severe hypomanic episodes.

DSM CRITERIA, PREVALENCE, AND ETIOLOGY Formerly known as manic-depressive illness, bipolar disorder is a brain disorder that causes unusual shifts in a person's mood, energy, and ability to function. Bipolar episodes are periods of highs and lows that are more severe than they should typically be. Everyone experiences low mood, feelings of sadness, or the blues from time to time. In depressive and bipolar disorders, however, these lows are lower than expected, given the circumstances. They may be unrelated to any life stressors the client is experiencing. Conversely, most people have had days when they felt really good, confident, and on top of their game. Manic episodes are much more severe than that; they involve intense feelings of euphoria or grandiosity as well as chaotic behaviors such as reckless spending or sexual activity. Again, these are not simply hours or even a day or two at a time but persistent states of depression and mania.

The estimated lifetime prevalence in adults falls between 0.4% and 1.6% of t' population. At any point in a given year, bipolar disorder affects about 5.7 million in viduals in the United States. Bipolar disorder is most commonly diagnosed in late ado... cence or early adulthood, although signs and symptoms may have been previously present. The mean age of first diagnosis is 18 (American Psychiatric Association, 2000).

Symptoms of bipolar disorder include, first of all, symptoms of depression. As discussed previously, these symptoms include prolonged sadness, hopelessness, guilt, loss of pleasure, poor concentration, decreased energy, and sleep or appetite disturbances. What separates depression from a bipolar disorder is the presence of mania or hypomania.

Manic symptoms can be some of the most difficult for clinical mental health counselors to help clients manage. They include increased energy and a highly euphoric mood. Such states of being are not ones we tend to want to get rid of—they feel great! Who doesn't enjoy a day of feeling more capable and happy with high motivation? Unfortunately, manic episodes push the upper limits of euphoria, and these feelings come paired with extreme irritability, racing thoughts, poor concentration, a decreased need for sleep, poor judgment, and increased sex drive. Typical manic episodes cause clients to feel as though thoughts are coming faster than they can control or understand them, result in days without any sleep, and are full of reckless choices and behaviors. It is often hard to tell the difference between true mania and the type of high received from an amphetamine such as what is commonly called crystal meth. As you can imagine, use of such a substance must first be ruled out before treating the symptoms of bipolar disorder.

Unfortunately, there is no cure for bipolar disorder; the episodes of mania and depression are lifelong. Cycles or patterns of episodes differ from person to person and can even change for one person over the course of the disorder (i.e., occurring more or less frequently). Characteristic of bipolar disorder is the fact that depressive episodes last longer than manic episodes. Depressive episodes average about six months, whereas manic episodes average about one to two months.

In a particular type of bipolar disorder known as rapid cycling, the client experiences four or more depressive and/or manic episodes in a 12-month period. Rapid cycling occurs in only 10% to 20% of those diagnosed with bipolar disorder, and nearly 90% of those suffering from rapid cycling type are women. These clients have a poorer prognosis for recovery than those with traditional bipolar disorder. It is important to note that the episodes in rapid cycling still occur over periods of weeks or months. Thus, the client's mood will not change within hours or even a day in bipolar disorder. If mood swings are that pronounced, the client needs to be treated for another disorder.

Bipolar disorder presents with a host of clinical concerns that impact treatment. It is clear that diagnosed bipolar clients are at a greater risk for suicide with approximately 19% of them being successful. Given the desire to self-medicate the lows and highs, or to re-create the highs when they are gone, over 50% of those diagnosed have a comorbid substance abuse or dependence issue. Medication can help address the symptoms but is not a perfect remedy. Even with successful treatment and medication adherence, 35% to 50% of those with bipolar disorder will experience the symptoms of mania or depression during ongoing episodes (American Psychiatric Association, 2000).

Where does bipolar disorder come from? Current research suggests that the onset of bipolar disorder is caused by collection of issues. Genetic influences, environmental factors, and chemical aspects of individual brain functioning all play a role in this disorder. There is a clear genetic link with bipolar disorder. Identical twin studies show up to an

80% rate of bipolar in both if one has the disorder (American Psychiatric Association, 2000). Other theories include deficits of or imbalances in neurotransmitters in the brain. Stress plays a role as well, with onset of symptoms often precipitated by an identifiable stressor. All of these factors influence the presence of bipolar disorder and must be further studied before conclusions about cause and effect can be discussed. But how should it be treated?

MEDICATIONS USED TO TREAT BIPOLAR DISORDER Bipolar disorder is a serious mental health concern that can be debilitating and life threatening if left untreated. However, as previously mentioned, clients tend to enjoy the manic or hypomanic states, at least in the beginning, and so do not seek treatment. Once treatment is initiated, medication is by far the most common approach used to treat this disorder. Clients diagnosed with bipolar disorder are often treated with mood stabilizers; however, anticonvulsants and atypical antipsychotics have also provided promising results.

The most common mood stabilizer is lithium, which has been used medicinally for centuries. In the 19th century, lithium was employed as a treatment for anxiety, gout, and seizures. Then its antimanic properties were discovered in 1949 after a series of animal studies. Because of its toxicity with cardiac patients, lithium was not widely prescribed until the 1970s. Although researchers are still not sure exactly how lithium works, it is currently used to treat acute manic episodes and to prevent manic-depressive episodes. Lithium is considered an extremely successful treatment because 60% to 80% of patients who take it experience symptom relief (American Psychiatric Association, 2000). A caution with lithium: this medication has a very narrow therapeutic window. This means that the level needed to benefit the client is also close to the level that would prove toxic to the client. As such, lithium must be regularly monitored, and clients must have their lithium levels checked on a routine basis. Prescriptions are adjusted based on the stage of symptoms being experienced and the blood concentration levels. Lithium doses range from 600 mg for maintenance of mood up to 2,400 mg for treatment of acute mania.

Lithium is not a very fat-soluble substance, meaning it has a more difficult time breaking through the blood–brain barrier. Higher levels of lithium are needed in the bloodstream for it to work properly in changing the client's current mood state. However, excess lithium in the blood can cause a toxic reaction that overstimulates the brain and leads to an increase in calcium production and free radicals. This leads to problems such as confusion, slurred speech, loss of balance, tremors, gastrointestinal disturbances, coma, and possibly death. Consequently, as previously mentioned, careful monitoring of lithium levels is needed to achieve maximum benefit.

One of the editors of this text once worked with a client diagnosed with bipolar I disorder, meaning he experienced both depressive and manic episodes. A middle-aged male with a master's degree in business, this client was able to monitor his episodes and report fairly accurately on changes to mood, thoughts, and behavior. He began to notice a pattern of manic episodes that occurred during allergy season. A number of precipitating causes were considered before discovering that the injection he received periodically to combat the severe symptoms of his allergies resulted in a decrease in his blood concentration of lithium. This decrease subsequently resulted in the onset of mania and created a number of problems related to spending sprees and sexual acting out before the discovery was made. Now, the client knows to have his psychiatrist increase his lithium dosage and frequency of blood level monitoring when the client needs to take any other medications.

Another popular choice for the treatment of bipolar disorder is one of the anticonvulsants. These meds are used because some feel that the presentation of manic episodes closely resembles seizure-like behaviors. The three main anticonvulsants used are carbamazepine (Tegretol), valproic acid (Depakote), and lamotrigine (Lamictal). Tegretol is commonly used to treat mania or mixed episodes, whereas Depakote is generally used to treat mixed episodes. Lamictal is commonly prescribed for bipolar depression, maintenance, and rapid cycles.

Carbamazepine (Tegretol) was first synthesized in the 1950s as a treatment for epilepsy. It affects ion channels by inhibiting neuron production and works in the synaptic gap to inhibit message transmission. In other words, carbamazepine works to slow down the brain, which ultimately calms the symptoms of mania. Valproic acid (Depakote) was synthesized in the 1880s as a solvent and then used as a psychotropic by accident. Approved for use in the United States in the 1990s, valproic acid quickly became a popular alternative to lithium. Valproic acid increases GABA by increasing its production, decreasing metabolism, and increasing receptor sensitivity. Lamotrigine (Lamictal), approved for use by the FDA in 1994, is more effective in treating the depressive symptoms associated with bipolar disorder. Lamotrigine inhibits the production of glutamate, which then causes portions of the brain to slow down.

Finally, there are the atypical antipsychotics. Some limited research currently exists supporting the efficacy of atypical antipsychotics in treating bipolar disorder (Gao, Muzina, Gajwani, & Calabrese, 2006). Typically used as a second-line agent, atypical antipsychotics include trade names such as Zyprexa, Risperdal, Seroquel, Symbyax, Geodon, and Abilify. Clients often take several medications to treat their bipolar disorder and, for some, the addition of an atypical antipsychotic allows for greater symptom relief and/or increased time between episodes.

In general, clients with bipolar disorder will take lithium as a long-term maintenance medication. These clients are typically on some dosage of lithium for their entire lives. During acute phases, and for short intervals, antidepressants and anxiolytics can also be prescribed. Like other mental health disorders, bipolar I and bipolar II disorders present uniquely in each individual, and so each medication regimen must be tailored to meet the client's specific needs. As the treating clinician, the clinical mental health counselor may be one of the primary points of information both to the client about the role of these medications in the treatment of bipolar disorder and to the psychiatrist about the changes in symptoms evident in the client.

Psychosis and Antipsychotics

An often frightening and debilitating group of disorders are the psychotic disorders. Let's start with a broad definition of psychosis. Initially *psychosis* was the term used to describe any and all mental illness. However, psychosis is really a collection of mental disorders manifested by three distinct symptoms:

- Inability to perceive and test reality
- Difficulty communicating clearly
- Trouble managing everyday living

Clients with psychotic disorders are unable to differentiate between what is real and what is imagined, which results in greater difficulty interacting with others. This impairment interferes with the client's capacity to meet the ordinary demands of life.

Psychotic symptoms include those categorized as positive symptoms and negative symptoms. Positive symptoms indicate an addition to the thinking, feeling, or behaving of the client (e.g., delusions and hallucinations), whereas negative symptoms indicate an absence (e.g., lack of speech). Delusions represent a false belief or incorrect interpretation of reality that defies credibility. Delusional beliefs are firmly held despite obvious evidence to the contrary. These beliefs are more firmly held than ideas that are merely unreasonable; in fact, they are unshakable. Types of delusions follow.

Bizarre—A belief that is completely mistaken and impossible within the person's culture. For example, the belief that the FBI has removed the brain of the person is bizarre. Conversely, a nonbizarre delusion is one whose content is definitely mistaken, but is at least possible; an example may be that the affected person mistakenly believes the FBI is watching the him or her constantly.

Delusional jealousy—A belief that a spouse or partner is unfaithful despite evidence to the contrary. This belief remains consistent for the client in all romantic relationships.

Erotomanic—A belief that another person, usually someone of higher status, is in love with him or her. For example, the author of this chapter has had multiple clients believe that Michael Jackson was their boyfriend and one client who believed she was married to then-president Bill Clinton.

Grandiose—A belief system in which clients exaggerate their sense of self-importance and are convinced that they have special powers, talents, or abilities. Sometimes, clients may actually believe that they are a particular famous person or deity.

Of being controlled—A belief that the client's thoughts, feelings, or behavior are being controlled by someone or something else. Often, clients will believe their thoughts are controlled by aliens or the government.

Of reference—A belief that insignificant remarks, events, or even objects have personal meaning or significance. For example, clients may believe that the person on television or on the radio is speaking personally and directly to them.

Persecutory—Perhaps the most common type of delusion, this involves themes of harassment such as being followed, cheated, drugged, or spied on. This delusional system may be used as a means to explain behaviors or changes in thoughts: "I started hearing voices after someone put something in my drink."

Somatic—A belief related to bodily functioning, sensations, or appearance. This type of delusion often manifests in the false belief that the body is somehow diseased, abnormal, or changed. An example of a somatic delusion would be a belief that the body is infested or carries a particular odor, which is untrue.

Thought broadcasting—A belief that the person's thoughts are being broadcasted so that others can hear them. An example occurred recently when a professor colleague was accused by a student of hearing what he was thinking and writing it on the board.

Thought insertion—A belief that thoughts have been placed in one's brain by an external force and are not the thoughts of the client.

Another type of positive symptom of psychosis is the existence of hallucinations. Hallucinations are sensory perceptions accompanied by a compelling sense that they are true despite possible insight that they are not. Simply put, a hallucination is a sensory experience in which a person can see, hear, smell, taste, or feel something that is not there. These perceptions occur without the necessary external stimulus. Some common types of hallucinations follow.

Auditory—Involves a perception of hearing something that is not there. Sometimes this is as simple as hearing one's name called from another room. Auditory hallucinations most commonly manifest as voices that may be perceived as talking to the client or simply talking nearby.

Gustatory—Involves the sense of taste and alters the real taste of food or other substances for the client.

Olfactory—Affects the sense of smell and occurs when the client smells something that is not present. Typically, these are foul smells that interfere with the client's well-being.

Somatic or tactile—Involves the body and experiences of touch. Clients may report feeling spiders crawling on their arms or even under their skin.

Visual—False perceptions involving sight. Clients may see colors, objects, animals, or people that are not truly there.

DSM CRITERIA, PREVALENCE, AND ETIOLOGY   Using the symptoms of psychosis as building blocks for diagnosis, the DSM (American Psychiatric Association, 2000) offers a number of types of psychotic disorders. These include organic brain syndrome, affective disorder, schizoaffective disorder, and schizophrenia. The discussion here focuses on schizophrenia because the medications used to treat it are used with all of the psychotic disorders. Schizophrenia is a developmental brain disorder with typical onset of illness occurring in the mid- to late twenties. This chronic, incapacitating disease affects approximately 1.0% to 1.5% of the adult population. Sadly, schizophrenia can be quite debilitating. Approximately 20.0% of clients do not respond to any medication, and up to half are noncompliant with taking meds. It is difficult to maintain clients' medication regimens because of the significant number (up to 40.0%) that experiences side effects (American Psychiatric Association, 2000).

Schizophrenia is broken down into the following subtypes: catatonic, disorganized, paranoid, residual, and undifferentiated. Each subtype presents its own set of treatment challenges. Catatonic schizophrenia is characterized by extreme inactivity or engaging in purposeless activity (i.e., repetitive motor movements). Disorganized schizophrenia sufferers display disturbed and disorganized thoughts and behaviors. Critical to the definition of paranoid schizophrenia is the presence of auditory or visual hallucinations. Residual schizophrenia can be diagnosed when positive symptoms disappear and this absence may last a year or more. Finally, the diagnosis of undifferentiated schizophrenia is made when the symptoms are not sufficiently formed or specific enough to permit classification of the illness into one of the other subtypes.

What causes schizophrenia? The answer is unclear, but several factors have been found to influence the disease. Although stress may speed up or exacerbate the onset of the disease (the stress-diathesis model), it is a misconception that stressors or substances cause schizophrenia. As evidence that schizophrenia is a biological disease, first-degree relatives of schizophrenics are at 10 times the risk of developing the disease. Another common explanation for schizophrenia is the dopamine hypothesis; this posits that the problems within the dopamine system in the brain result in the positive or negative symptoms of schizophrenia (Lopez, Kreider, & Caspe, 2004).

MEDICATIONS USED TO TREAT PSYCHOTIC DISORDERS   Treatment of schizophrenia can be challenging and virtually always involves medication. Because there is no cure, the primary goal of treatment is to reduce symptoms so that the person can function better and benefit more from other forms of treatment. A combination of psychotropic meds and psychotherapy/counseling is the preferred treatment regimen. It is quite common for medication to be initiated first in order to stabilize the client so that therapy can be effective.

Antipsychotic medications are introduced to regulate dopamine (the dopamine hypothesis, as mentioned previously). These may be referred to as antipsychotics, major tranquilizers, or neuroleptics. Antipsychotic medications fall into one of two categories: typical and atypical. Typical antipsychotics are considered neuroleptics and are usually effective in treating the positive symptoms associated with the disorder. However, they also bring about an increase in the negative symptoms due to their side effect profiles. Typical antipsychotics, or neuroleptics, will produce either extrapyramidal symptoms (EPS) or anticholinergic and sedative side effects. These side effects include the following: movement disorders (rigidity, tremor, or tardive dyskinesia), tachycardia, hypotension, impotence, blurred vision, dry mouth, constipation, urinary retention, light-headedness (dizziness), sunlight sensitivity, weight gain, lethargy, nightmares, and seizures. As a result, the addition of anticholinergic meds is necessary. Anticholinergic medications used to treat side effects include Cogentin (benztropine in pill or injectable form), benapryzine, benzhexol, orphenadrine, and bornaprine.

A commonly recognized class of medication used to treat psychotic disorders includes those drugs referred to as first-generation antipsychotics. Often referred to in this fashion because they were the first types of medications used to combat psychosis, first-generation antipsychotics include such medications as the following: haloperidol (Haldol), chlorpromazine (Thorazine), fluphenazine (Prolixin), perphenazine (Trilafon), prochlorperazine (Compazine), thioridazine (Mellaril), and trifluoperazine (Stelazine). An advantage of some of these medications—Prolixin, for example—is that they can be administered in a long-acting form via injection. This allows the client to receive a monthly or bimonthly shot in lieu of oral medications. As you can imagine, injectable antipsychotics are especially useful in cases in which compliance with taking meds is an issue. Unfortunately, these first-generation medications cause some of the most severe side effects discussed previously and are rarely prescribed without a complementary anticholinergic medication.

The second-generation antipsychotics, or atypical antipsychotics, were developed to improve the client's quality of life by diminishing these horrible side effects. Unfortunately, these medications come with a price—literally—because they are significantly more expensive than the first-generation medications. However, for clients who are not experiencing symptom relief or who are facing debilitating side effects, these antipsychotics are a good choice. Clozapine (Clozaril), a popular medication, requires weekly to biweekly blood panels due to the potential of a severe decline in white blood cell count. Olanzapine (Zyprexa) has been found effective with both psychotic disorders such as schizophrenia as well as acute manic episodes, which often present with psychotic features. Side effects include increase in appetite, weight gain, and altered glucose metabolism, which leads to an increased risk of diabetes. Risperidone (Risperdal) can be taken once daily or is available in a long-acting form (Risperdal Consta) that is administered every two weeks. Both Risperdal and Zyprexa come in a form that quickly dissolves in the mouth. Quetiapine (Seroquel) is actually a sedative that can also be used to treat sleep disorders but is effective as an antipsychotic. Typically, clients taking Seroquel take a smaller dose during the day and a larger dose at night due to the high sedative effect. New on the scene and considered a third-generation antipsychotic is aripiprazole (Abilify). This medication has been shown to reduce side effects experienced by the second-generation drugs. Currently under development as an antipsychotic medication is the use of cannabidiol, which is actually a component of cannabis (marijuana).

Clients beginning treatment on antipsychotics will generally be prescribed an atypical antipsychotic medication first (e.g., Risperdal). If symptoms persist or there are too many side effects, the next treatment option is generally another atypical medication (e.g., Geodon, Abilify, or Zyprexa). If symptoms still continue, a typical antipsychotic medication may be prescribed, with Clozaril and Haldol being the most common. Clients may also be placed on a regimen of three atypicals to improve symptoms with the fewest side effects possible. The treatment goal is to provide symptom relief while maintaining the client's quality of life.

As clinicians, clinical mental health counselors will be in the position to educate clients on the importance of compliance in taking prescribed medications to provide the greatest symptom relief and to prevent relapse. Given the host of side effects associated with even the best, most progressive antipsychotics, educating the client on side effects and aiding in the development of an action plan for managing these effects is critical. Prodromal symptoms, or warning signs of psychosis, are commonplace for clients suffering from these disorders. Teaching clients how to self-monitor for these prodromal symptoms serves as a form of secondary prevention.

INTEGRATING DRUG THERAPY INTO THE THERAPEUTIC PROCESS

As helping professionals, clinical mental health counselors should have a broad understanding of the role of drug therapy and how it can complement all therapies available to the client. Because clinical mental health counselors are not in a position to prescribe or adjust medications, defining the role of the therapist with the client as well as the rest of the treatment team is critical. From an ethical perspective, counselors have an obligation to practice from both a nonmalficence perspective (to do no harm) and a beneficence perspective (to do good). Mental health professionals are faced with a challenging array of client concerns in a variety of settings. A comprehensive understanding of the role of psychopharmacology with the client populations served is foundational to ethical practice.

Many helping professionals do not receive substantive education in psychopharmacology in their training programs. This lack of education combined with limited experience can cause practitioners to question the use of medication in the treatment of mental health disorders. Sometimes, helping professionals believe that medication should be the option of last resort, that psychiatric drugs are no different than drugs of abuse, that medication is ineffective and working with the medical community is impossible, or that learning about brain chemistry and medication is too difficult to pursue (Buelow, Hebert, & Buelow, 2000). The reality is that these medications are effective when used appropriately and, as treating professionals, clinical mental health counselors have an ethical obligation to operate from a best-practice perspective. This best-practice model includes an understanding of psychopharmacology.

Professional clinical mental health counselors are expected to know when a referral for medication intervention is warranted. Additionally, they are expected to understand how and why various medications work in treating mental health disorders. They must be knowledgeable of side effects and be able to effectively educate their clients. Clinical mental health counselors are in a position to encourage and monitor drug compliance. They are responsible to a comprehensive treatment plan that addresses client mental health concerns from multiple perspectives.

Clinical mental health counselors typically serve as part of formal or informal treatment teams. In hospital, agency, or other multidisciplinary settings involving wraparound services, many professionals serve the greater good of the client. It is the obligation of clinical mental health counselors to provide informed consent to their clients and get permission to consult with other professionals involved in their treatment. Having done so, counselors can then interact with the treatment team for the client's benefit. An example of this would be having the ethical and legal authority to consult with a client's psychiatrist about side effects the counselor is seeing; this helps provide not only the best picture of medication effectiveness to the medical professional but also the best education to the client.

Diagnosis, Referral, and Consultation Issues

Diagnosis, as discussed in Chapter 6, and case conceptualization, as discussed in Chapter 7, are integral to the overall treatment process. This process then impacts the type of medications considered most effective for the client. Of course, of concern are clients whose onset of psychiatric symptoms comes out of the blue with no predisposing events or precipitating factors and/or those with no personal or family history of any psychiatric condition. Additionally, clients over the age of 55 or those taking multiple medications require special attention. If the client appears physically ill, has abnormal vital signs, or has had any form of recent head trauma, medical conditions must be ruled out before a mental health diagnosis can be acknowledged as the primary cause of psychiatric symptoms.

When working with a client, the need to rule out a medical condition is one instance that warrants a referral. Because psychiatric symptoms closely resemble symptoms caused by medical disorders, it is imperative to involve the medical community in the diagnostic and treatment process. Another time that a referral is needed is when a client has made no progress under the current course of counseling treatment. Or perhaps the clinical mental health counselor believes that progress could be enhanced with the addition of medication, as in the case of a client who is too anxious or psychotic to benefit from talk therapy without psychiatric intervention. Instability in mood or symptoms would need to be investigated medically as well. Realistically, whenever clinical mental health counselors question the current diagnosis or suspect medical conditions are the cause of psychiatric symptoms, a referral is warranted. Finally, any time a patient requests a referral or a second opinion is advisable, it is the ethical responsibility of the helping professional to facilitate such a referral.

From a practical perspective, what happens when the clinical mental health counselor suspects a client needs psychiatric medication? Whether this is a new client or someone the counselor has worked with for a period of time, some common client reactions are likely to occur. These include statements such as "Even my counselor thinks I'm crazy!" or fears that the counselor is abandoning the client and passing him or her off to another professional. Clients may believe that clinical mental health counselors view them as too weak to handle the problem and that they need medication to cope with things that a stronger person could manage quite well (it is no surprise that this belief about the counselor is often a projection of the client's own belief system). Another fear is that the referral is an indication that the client's condition is worse than previously suspected, meaning that the client is somehow a worse person than expected.

After having tackled the customary concerns of a psychiatric referral, the clinical mental health counselor must consider how the client will manage the referral. Specifically, what are the limits of the client's health care coverage? Does the client have the financial means to pay for psychiatric evaluation and medication? Given the extraordinary costs associated with health care in our culture, finding measures that are both helpful to the client and affordable to accomplish is key to compliance and effective treatment strategies.

Realistically, psychiatrists are not the only doctors who prescribe medications. Although they are certainly the most well-trained MDs for the treatment of mental health concerns, private practice physicians, certain psychologists, physician assistants, family nurse practitioners, and other primary care physicians (e.g., pediatricians, internists, general practitioners) are also eligible to provide psychiatric medication to clients.

As the referral source, clinical mental health counselors will be in a position to help their clients make the best decision about psychiatric care. It will be the counselor's responsibility to create positive referral relationships in their community, establish clear communication patterns with physicians and others, clarify boundaries as therapists, and avoid triangulation between himself or herself, the medical professional, and the client ("But my doctor said . . ." versus "But my therapist said . . .").

When the clinical mental health counselor does decide to make a referral, what will the recipient of the referral need from the counselor? First off, he or she will need documentation of proper release of information and consent to share. Once established, the medical professional will need a detailed client history including specific reasons for the referral. Although the medical professional will want to know the counselor's expectations (e.g., what does the counselor want the medical professional to do?), it is not the time to play amateur psychiatrist. The clinical mental health counselor must refrain from "practicing medicine," but instead guide the medical professional by offering his or her knowledge of the problem. The following are basic elements to include in a referral:

- Chief complaint
- History of the illness
- Past psychiatric history
- Past medical history
- Current medications
- Known allergies
- Substance use
- Family history
- Social history
- Review of systems
- Mental status exam
- DSM diagnosis

Sometimes, referrals will be made using written referral letters. This is helpful, because such a letter clearly documents the need for the referral and provides a point of documentation for later, so it is important to follow basic ethical considerations when preparing a written referral. Just as with progress notes, a clinical mental health counselor must write the letter with the assumption that the client will read it or that it may be read in court. The counselor must be professional and respectful when discussing the client and keep a professional tone throughout all correspondence. One of the editors of this text experienced quite the opposite when receiving correspondence from a treating psychiatrist. The case note regarding a mutual client's most recent medication check appointment began with the words "I hate to see this woman coming." Obviously, this is not something that a professional should document in a client's chart.

Experience working with the medical community will teach clinical mental health counselors to become more succinct when communicating with medical professionals. Their time is limited and their patient base large. The better that clinical mental health counselors communicate, the better their relationship with medical professionals will be. Counselors should respond quickly to requests from the medical community and accept all referrals from these professionals, at least for an initial consultation. They should align themselves with the clients' strengths and serve as an advocate for their care. Clinical mental health counselors need to recognize the financial and administrative concerns inherent in providing mental health treatment and be respectful of the liability and risk assumed by medical professionals in mental health care.

Finally, a word of caution is in order. Clinical mental health counselors will encounter clients whose primary motive is seeking drugs. Medical professionals are often attuned to this behavior and may question the counselor's referral. Counselors need to be clear with their information and be willing to hear medical professionals' perspective about whether drug seeking is a possibility for particular clients. By being informed, professional, and working as an advocate for their clients, never an adversary against medical professionals, clinical mental health counselors are in a unique position to provide maximum benefit to their clients from a multidisciplinary perspective.

VOICE FROM THE FIELD 11.1

When I have a client who is under the care of a psychiatrist or primary care physician for psych med management, I ask the client for written consent to consult with the prescribing practitioner, and most clients happily agree because they know that collaborative care is better care. Believe me, most of the doctors prescribing psych meds are grateful for the information I provide them about treatment goals, med compliance, and other related "your-doctor-should-know-this-about-you" information.

I once had a client who was diagnosed as bipolar by her doctor and prescribed a mood stabilizer as well as an antidepressant. I just happened to ask the client about caffeine intake, and she admitted to drinking an astonishing three Venti size Pike Place® Roast coffees daily, which is about quadruple the amount it takes to reach caffeine intoxication. (Go ahead . . . look it up in the DSM and compare it to the criteria for manic episode.) One quick phone call to the prescriber with this very easily missed little nugget of information completely changed the course of the client's treatment—for the better, of course!

BETH WOMBOUGH, MS, LMHC
Private practice, Jacksonville, Florida

WORKING WITH SPECIAL POPULATIONS

As helping professionals, clinical mental health counselors operate from a multicultural perspective, taking a client's culture, norms, and experiences into account when developing treatment interventions. Just as groups differ in their attitudes toward mental health treatment, some cultural groups are comfortable with pharmacological interventions whereas others are not. It is important to take this into account when discussing treatment options with clients. Mental health treatment carries an inherent stigma. Many clients prefer to discuss medications with their primary care physician: a "keep it in the family" approach to treatment. Conversely, others will want a referral outside of their typical medical community due to perceptions that they will be judged or criticized for seeking medical help for a psychological problem.

Children and Adolescents

For many years, children were diagnosed and treated the same way as adult clients. However, the medical community now knows that treating children and adolescents, because of their minor status and due to differences in physiology, requires additional attention from the treatment team. Medication developed to work on adults may prove beneficial to children, if properly studied and prescribed with the correct dosage. Simply prescribing antidepressants that were tested on adults will not be effective with—and could be quite harmful to—children and adolescents. Although medical professionals will make the ultimate decision, clinical mental health counselors can work effectively with minor clients for whom medication is an option.

Realistically, many mental illnesses begin in childhood (e.g., early onset dysthymia begins before age 21). There may be an inadequate number of medical professionals that are trained and willing to work with mental health concerns in children. It is expected that the need for mental health care among children will double by the year 2020. Although a number of children suffer from a mental health disorder (up to 10%), few of them actually receive help (as little as 20%) (Buck, 2000). Why the challenge? For starters, unlike adults, children have no ability to enter into care for themselves; they require a parent or guardian to get involved in the treatment process. Parents may be willing to bring children to therapy but not be willing to look at larger, systemic issues or to participate in the process themselves. Additionally, media horror stories about medication and mental health concerns in children have many parents suspicious of psychopharmacological intervention. Finally, given that there is no "magic pill" for mood, disposition, and behavioral control of children, parents may simply give up on this treatment approach.

A primary concern in the use of medication in children is metabolism. Young children have high rates of metabolism, which require them to receive larger dosages of medication. This can cause concern among parents. Subsequently, metabolism changes as the child ages, which then requires ongoing medication adjustments particularly around puberty. Combined with the fact that most psychotropic drugs are not approved for use with children by the Food and Drug Administration (FDA), psychopharmacology with children is difficult business. The FDA Modernization Act of 1997 was enacted to improve pediatric labeling of drugs, keeping medical professionals from relying on off-label prescribing for children (Buck, 2000). This act requires that thousands of drugs be evaluated annually for pediatric use. Some may wonder whether the medical community is going too far in medicating children because of the increase in preschool-aged children being prescribed psychotropic medications. Two common medications for attention deficit hyperactivity disorder, Ritalin and Adderall, as well as the antipsychotic medications Haldol and Thorazine, are all approved drugs for use in this preschool population. Understanding the challenges of medicating children and adolescents and staying abreast of current trends in medical intervention will allow clinical mental health counselors to serve clients from a best-practice approach to mental health care.

Geriatrics

Another population receiving psychopharmacological intervention is the elderly or geriatric population. Treatment of older adults is fraught with some of the same concerns as treatment of children: changes in metabolism due to aging and health concerns, and potential cognitive decline resulting in inability to consent for their treatment. The complex physiological changes inherent in the aging process result in changes that vary from person to person. Adding to the challenge of treating this population is older adults' high rate of medical comorbidity (the amount of additional medical concerns present at the time of psychological treatment) and the number of medications they are already prescribed. Prescription drug use increases with age, with persons over age 65 filling approximately 13 prescriptions annually in the United States. This population averages six active medical disorders at a given time in addition to any mental health conditions (Zubenko & Sunderland, 2000).

Realistically, the geriatric population has a less predictable response to medication, and older adults' use of multiple prescription and nonprescription medications contributes to this unpredictability. Symptom relief and side effects must be closely monitored. Weakening physical health presents potential for toxicity. Changes to neurochemistry as well as the presence of comorbid physical ailments combine to make medication intervention for mental health concerns risky and unpredictable (Zubenko & Sunderland, 2000).

Because all aspects of drug treatment may be affected by aging, physicians must take into account multiple process points of drug therapy; these include absorption, distribution, metabolism, and elimination of medications. Certain medications may have a delayed onset of action or their clinical effect may be diminished due to aging. Changes in muscle mass and an increased body fat ratio impact the drug's efficacy. Of greatest concern are malnourished elderly patients. Because of decreased liver functioning, dosages may need to be lessened in elderly patients. The medical guideline is to "go low and go slow" when prescribing psychopharmaceuticals for older adults. Essentially, drug sensitivity increases as systems decline due to aging. Clinical mental health counselors will need to watch for adverse reactions whenever new medications are added.

Adverse drug reactions in the elderly can be deadly. It is estimated that up to 8% of hospital admissions are related to such occurrences and are one of the top six causes of death in the United States (Nova Scotia Mental Health Services, 2008). Elderly patients are often misdiagnosed and receive inappropriate medication. For example, older adult patients presenting with anxiety, which is often a symptom of depression in this population, are more likely to be prescribed an anxiolytic than an antidepressant (Nova Scotia Mental Health Services, 2008). It is generally recommended that elderly clients who are depressed should try other therapy options prior to the use of medication.

Patient compliance is a concern in this population as well. Estimates of noncompliance in elderly medication use range from 40% to 75% (Zubenko & Sunderland, 2000). Clients living alone may miss dosages or have an erratic use pattern. Such complications worsen with cognitive decline. As with any client, the clinical mental health counselor is often in the position of assessing for medication compliance, educating the client on the reasons for such compliance, and communicating with the medical community about the client's compliance. A solid therapeutic relationship combined with an understanding of how medications impact the elderly differently from other populations is key to facilitating the most effective treatment plan for the clients served.

VOICE FROM THE FIELD 11.2

Pharmacotherapy can be an important element of successful treatment. In my practice, most clients are referred to me by psychiatrists or general practitioners, and already have medication support in place. My role as a clinician often includes educating the client about the medications and their side effects. I also need to monitor the effectiveness of the medications for the client, and the adherence to the protocol outlined by the medical doctor. I confer with the prescribing physician about these observations, progress in therapy, and ongoing treatment focus. It is vital that the medical doctor be kept up-to-date on the client's progress, as such can have significant influence on medication decisions.

Not all clients choose to include pharmacotherapy in their treatment for a variety of reasons, and some may become noncompliant with the prescriptions they have been given. Even though I support an individual's right to make decisions about medical care, I also believe it is important for clients to understand the impact of such decisions. In some cases—such as with mild depression or anxiety—medication may not be required but does have the potential for a very positive effect on treatment. In other cases—such as with severe bipolar disorder or psychosis—medication is generally necessary for the most basic functioning, and therefore is an essential component of successful treatment. It is important for clients to understand this and to be empowered to make proactive decisions regarding their health.

In my experience, most clients do not like the idea of taking medication. There remains a stigma in society about mental health treatment, and acceptance of the role of medication in psychological functioning can be difficult for people to accept. However, with proper education and support, I do find that most clients make good decisions in this area. Working closely with the medical doctors is an important aspect of this as well, as is being able to answer client questions about the purpose and effects of medications. Guiding clients through the unknown is a fundamental aspect of psychotherapy, and the subject of medication is no different.

STEPHANIE K. SCOTT, PHD, LMHC
Core Faculty, School of Counseling and Social Service,
College of Social and Behavioral Sciences, Walden University

Conclusion

Clinical mental health counselors have the unique privilege of spending more time with clients than many of their other service providers do. As a result, it is critical for counselors to have some familiarity with basic neuroanatomy and psychotropic medications. Medications serve an important role in the treatment of many symptoms and mental health conditions. An understanding of the general classes of medications, the potential benefits and side effects, as well as how and when to refer for medication is necessary to best serve clients. Although most mental health medications are developed for and initially tested on physically healthy adults, it is our responsibility to understand potential uses in the different populations served. As ethical providers of mental health counseling services, clinical mental health counselors maintain their knowledge of all treatment modalities including psychopharmacology so that they may provide the best possible outcome for their clients.

References

Agency for Healthcare Research and Quality. (2002). *S-adenosyl-L-methionine for treatment of depression, osteoarthritis, and liver disease.* Summary, Evidence Report/Technology Assessment: Number 64. AHRQ Publication No. 02-E033, August 2002. Retrieved from http://archive.ahrq.gov/clinic/epcsums/samesum.htm

American Psychiatric Association. (2000). *Diagnostic and statistical manual of mental disorders, fourth edition–text revision* (DSM-IV-TR). Washington, DC: Author.

Buck, M. L. (2000). The FDA Modernization Act of 1997: Impact on pediatric medicine. *Pediatric Pharmacotherapy: A Monthly Newsletter for Health Care Professionals, 6*(12), 1–5. Retrieved from http://www.medicine.virginia.edu/clinical/departments/pediatrics/education/pharm-news/1995-2000/200012.pdf

Cohen, L. S., Viguera, A. C., Bouffard, S. M., Nonacs, R. M., Morabito, C., Collins, M. H., & Ablon, J. S. (2001). Venlafaxine in the treatment of postpartum depression. *Journal of Clinical Psychiatry, 62*(8), 592–596.

Council for Accreditation of Counseling and Related Educational Programs (CACREP). (2009). *CACREP accreditation manual: 2009 standards.* Alexandria, VA: Author. Retrieved from http://www.cacrep.org/doc/2009%20Standards%20with%20cover.pdf

Czerner, T. B. (2001). *What makes you tick? The brain in plain English.* New York, NY: Wiley.

Gao, K., Muzina, D., Gajwani, P., & Calabrese, J. R. (2006). Efficacy of typical and atypical antipsychotics for primary and comorbid anxiety symptoms or disorders: A review. *The Journal of Clinical Psychiatry, 67*(9), 1327–1340.

Gray, R. T., & Robinson, P. A. (2009). Stability and structural constraints of random brain networks with excitatory and inhibitory neural populations. *Journal of Computational Neuroscience, 27*(1), 81–101.

Lopez, M. E., Kreider, H., & Caspe, M. (2004). Co-constructing family involvement. *The Evaluation Exchange, X*(4), 2–3.

McKim, W. A. (2003). *Drugs and behavior: An introduction to behavioral pharmacology* (5th ed.). Upper Saddle River, NJ: Pearson Education.

National Institute of Mental Health (NIMH). (2013). *The numbers count: Mental disorders in America.* Retrieved from http://www.nimh.nih.gov/health/publications/the-numbers-count-mental-disorders-in-america/index.shtml

National Institutes of Health (NIH). (2013). *St. John's wort.* National Center for Complementary and Alternative Medicine (NCCAM). Retrieved from http://nccam.nih.gov/health/stjohnswort/

Nova Scotia Mental Health Services. (2008, October 1). *Geriatric psychopharmacology: Seniors' mental health tele-education session.* Retrieved from http://novascotia.ca/dhw/mental-health/documents/seniors/depression_seniors_Geriatric_Psychopharmacology.pdf

Segal, Z., Kennedy, S., Cohen, N., & Group CDW. (2000). Combining psychotherapy and pharmacotherapy. *Canadian Journal of Psychiatry, 46*(Supp. 1), 59S–62S.

Sinacola, R. S., & Peters-Strickland, T. (2006). *Basic psychopharmacology for counselors and psychotherapists.* Boston, MA: Pearson/Allyn & Bacon.

Sinkman, A. (2008, January 25). SSRIs: Do they increase rates of suicide? *Clinical Correlations: The NYU Langone Online Journal of Medicine.* Retrieved from http://www.clinicalcorrelations.org/?s=SSRIs%3A+Do+they+increase+rates+of+suicide%3F+

University of Maryland Medical Center. (2008). *Omega-3 fatty acids.* Retrieved from http://www.umm.edu/altmed/articles/omega-3-000316.htm

Zubenko, G. S., & Sunderland, T. (2000). Geriatric psychopharmacology: Why does age matter? *Harvard Review of Psychiatry, 7*(6), 311–333.

12

Forensic Mental Health Counseling

CARL J. SHEPERIS, L. MARINN PIERCE, AND R. J. DAVIS

CHAPTER OVERVIEW

Forensic mental health counseling is a growing specialization area for professional counselors. Clinical mental health counselors with forensic training can provide a range of services related to the legal system, ranging from child custody evaluations to evaluations of competency to stand trial. Of course, general counseling services are equally important for the criminal justice system. According to a 2006 US Department of Justice report (James & Glaze, 2006), about 25% of the prison population has a mental illness, yet only one in three inmates receives mental health services. As a forensic mental health counselor, you might be offering an individual his or her first opportunity for appropriate treatment. The purpose of this chapter is to provide a basic understanding of the forensic mental health process and the various types of forensic mental health services that clinical mental health counselors might provide.

LEARNING OBJECTIVES

The learning objectives for this chapter are designed to be consistent with the 2009 Council for Accreditation of Counseling and Related Educational Programs Standards (CACREP, 2009). As such, upon completion of this chapter, the student will have knowledge of the following clinical mental health counseling standards:

1. Is aware of professional issues that affect clinical mental health counselors (e.g., core provider status, expert witness status, access to and practice privileges within managed care systems). (A.7)
2. Demonstrates the ability to apply and adhere to ethical and legal standards in clinical mental health counseling. (B.1)
3. Understands the range of mental health service delivery—such as inpatient, outpatient, partial treatment and aftercare—and the clinical mental health counseling services network. (C.5)
4. Understands professional issues relevant to the practice of forensic mental health counseling. (C.9)
5. Understands current literature that outlines theories, approaches, strategies, and techniques shown to be effective when working with specific populations of clients with mental and emotional disorders. (E.3)

INTRODUCTION

Forensic mental health counseling is an area of specialization that involves a range of counseling services related to the justice system. Clinical mental health counselors who pursue this type of specialization will develop an in-depth understanding of the law and the role of various entities within the justice system. There are many subspecialization areas within the justice system, and forensic mental health counselors are likely to focus on a small number of these. For example, forensic mental health counselors might develop an expertise in child custody evaluation and serve as expert witnesses in court. Those counselors pursuing this subspecialty would develop a considered knowledge base in family law.

Regardless of the subspecialization area, forensic mental health counselors will need to understand legal terminology and be able to effectively communicate with other professionals in the justice system. Clearly, becoming a forensic mental health counselor is a complex process. To best understand the role of the forensic mental health counselor, we must first look at the basic principles of forensic mental health counseling. Then, we review ethical considerations for the practice of forensic mental health counseling. Finally, we explore the practice of clinical mental health counseling, including the various subspecialization areas.

WHAT IS FORENSIC MENTAL HEALTH?

To understand forensic mental health practice, we must first differentiate it from other forms of clinical mental health counseling. Although the word *forensic* is often used to define methods used in criminal investigations, it also refers to anything related to court or legal matters (Oxford Dictionaries, 2012).

The American Counseling Association (ACA) defined *forensic evaluation* as any time a counselor or other mental health professional conducts an assessment expressly for use within a court or other legal matter (ACA, 2005). ACA (2005) further noted that when conducting forensic assessment, clinical mental health counselors are charged with providing objective, valid, and reliable findings that are evidence based. Forensic mental health, however, is broader than assessment and now includes research, assessment, treatment, and consultation with those interacting with courts of law as offenders, those at risk of offending, and at times the victims of offenders. This work includes the assessment and evaluation of juvenile and adult offenders, child custody evaluations, expert witness testimony, and evaluations of competency (Springer & Roberts, 2007).

Historically, psychologists were the only mental health professionals who worked in the forensic arena. However, due to the increased need for professional service providers, the field of forensic mental health has widened, and so forensic mental health counseling has emerged as a relatively new profession and a viable career option for counselors. Much of the work that forensic mental health counselors do is within the realm of the criminal justice system.

Crime has been a significant issue in the United States throughout history. Fortunately, over the last five years, violent crimes have been declining. Yet even though there are fewer violent crimes committed per year, the number of violent crimes is still staggering. Each year the Federal Bureau of Investigation (FBI) compiles a Uniform Crime Report (UCR) that details statistics related to violent crimes and property crimes. In 2011, violent crimes were once again lower than the previous year, yet there were still 1,203,564 violent crimes reported to law enforcement personnel in the United States (Federal Bureau of Investigation [FBI], 2011). Violent crimes include acts such as murder, forcible rape, robbery, and aggravated assault.

It is often difficult to look at such a large number as the 1.2 million violent crimes reported in 2011 and understand what that means at the local level. The FBI (2011) estimates that the violent crime rate for 2011 was 386.3 offenses per 100,000 inhabitants. Breaking down the crime rate in this manner makes it clear that communities with large populations are likely to experience a considerable number of violent crimes.

For every crime committed, a large amount of human resources is used to respond, starting with conducting the preliminary investigation and continuing through the incarceration of someone convicted of the crime. Forensic mental health counselors can play a role in every stage of the process. Although not all forensic mental health counselors work within the criminal justice system, there are certainly a large number of potential opportunities for them to specialize in the criminal justice sector.

History and Development of Forensic Mental Health Counseling

As previously mentioned, forensic mental health counseling is a relatively new specialization. Although crime rates correlate with the need for forensic professionals, the initial development of forensic mental health as a professional practice area grew out of the need for out-of-home placement for individuals deemed not competent to stand trial or those found not guilty of an offense by reason of insanity. During the initial development of the professional practice area, there was little scientific evidence to support the work of forensic mental health professionals. Because the initial practice field was relatively small, individuals waiting for a competency evaluation often spent considerable time in maximum-security facilities, including prisons and state-run mental hospitals (Petrila, 2004). Unfortunately, the waiting periods for forensic evaluations have remained long. In the 1990s and 2000s, court-ordered pretrial evaluations for competency increased. Each state designates the time frame in which a pretrial evaluation must be completed; this ranges from seven days to one year (Washington State Department of Social & Health Services, 2006).

Although it is clear that delays in evaluation negatively impact the individuals being served by the system, it is also important to note that the professionals providing forensic services have historically been separated from the rest of the mental health community. Mullen (2000) described forensic mental health services as "marred by isolation: geographical isolation in the insane asylums and prisons; professional isolation . . . and institutional isolation, with forensic services all too often organizationally fragmented and isolated from general mental health services" (p. 308). He went on to note that this isolation resulted in a specialization that has lagged behind the progress made in the provision of other mental health services (Mullen, 2000).

Fortunately, within the last two decades, forensic mental health services have changed significantly. The deinstitutionalization of intense psychiatric services began in the 1970s and has continued to this day. With the increased loss of state-run mental institutions, more and more forensic services are being offered in community settings and prisons (Petrila, 2004). Today, forensic mental health services are provided in inpatient facilities, community agencies, client homes, state and federal prisons, and mental health and drug courts. The presence of forensic services outside institutionalized settings has increased offenders' access to mental health services. The greater availability of these services in a variety of settings has allowed for expanded forensic services in community settings.

In addition to providing service to offenders placed in secure facilities, forensic mental health counselors now offer expert witness testimony for victims of offenders as well as risk assessments for those potentially at risk of offending. Also, forensic mental health services now include substance abuse assessments; child custody and domestic violence evaluations; and consultation with businesses regarding decreasing offending risk among employees (Mullen 2000; Petrila, 2004). The American Mental Health Counselors Association (AMHCA, 2010) included the following activities as potential forensic services: assessment, interviews, consultations, report writing, responding to subpoenas, and offering expert witness testimony. Because most of these services are either assessment or consultation based, eligibility for third-party reimbursement by insurance companies is limited (Hayes, 2004). Thus, forensic mental health counselors typically work on a contractual basis rather than with insurance companies.

Increased awareness of the importance of forensic mental health and a greater need for services have led to increased information and research relating to the practice of forensic mental health. Although courts of law in the past did value the input of mental health service providers, there still was a lack of standardized assessments and evaluation measures to support their work. Those assessing individuals for competence, custody, and other matters now have access to standardized assessments and procedures. In addition, increased research regarding psychopathology and offending behavior has supported the development of standards of training and practice (Mullen, 2000; Petrila, 2004). These standards include certifications and credentialing opportunities for forensic mental health counselors, discussed later in the chapter. One recent expansion of forensic mental health services includes consultation related to preventing workplace violence. Such services might include preemployment screenings, psychological fitness evaluations, threat assessments, and trainings and workshops related to violence prevention (Fletcher, Brakel, & Cavanaugh, 2000).

Professional associations have been developed to support those practicing in the forensic arena. Some examples are the following: the International Association of Forensic Mental Health Services (IAFMHS), the National Board of Forensic Evaluators (NBFE), the National Association of Forensic Counselors (NAFC), the International Association of Addictions & Offender Counselors (IAAOC), the Forensic Counseling Interest Network of the American Counseling Association, and the American Psychology-Law Society (Division 41 of the American Psychological Association). Ethical and best-practice standards also have been developed with the increase in professional organizations and recognition. The American Counseling Association (2005) and the American Mental Health Counselors Association (AMHCA, 2010) have designated sections for forensic activity within their respective ethical codes.

In 2006, Sestoft identified three key issues for the future of forensic services. The first, diversion, involves the development and implementation of programs and services to accurately and efficiently identify those individuals within the criminal justice system whose criminal acts may be the result of untreated mental health disorders. Once identified, these individuals should be referred to appropriate programs that provide proper treatment and/or rehabilitation services in lieu of criminalization (Sestoft, 2006). As previously noted, the rise of community-based forensic mental health services is related to the deinstitutionalization of intense psychiatric services. Even though decriminalization of mental health–related issues makes sense and has been a goal of the criminal justice system, The Sentencing Project (2002) noted that the limited availability of services for forensic clients, due to a lack of physical or financial resources, has impacted the development and implementation of these programs.

The second key issue as noted by Sestoft (2006) is that the field of forensic mental health will need to continue to develop evidenced-based assessment and treatment protocols for supporting change in offending populations. The development of standardized assessment and treatment protocols has been one of the greatest advances in forensic mental health in recent years. Even though some progress has been made in these areas, more is needed. For example, further research is necessary on the practice of forensic consultation, particularly related to preventing workplace violence (Fletcher et al., 2000). Also, although there have been advancements in the development of assessment instruments and treatment protocols for adult offenders, there remains a need for valid and reliable assessment instruments for the adolescent offender population. Given increased rates of offending during adolescence and young adulthood, developmentally appropriate assessment and treatment for offenders across the life span is warranted (Wiesner, Kim, & Capaldi, 2005).

The third key issue according to Sestoft (2006) is that ongoing research regarding forensic mental health is critical. Soothill and Francis (2010) noted a dearth of literature regarding forensic mental health services outside the fields of psychiatry and psychology. Of the literature that is available within the psychology-related journals, little is research based. Also, while a handful of articles on forensic counseling have been published in the rehabilitation counseling literature, very few articles related to forensics have been published in the mainstream counseling journals. As previously stated, the emergence of forensic mental health counseling as a viable field is relatively new. As such, little research specific to forensic mental health has been done. Because evidence-based practice is essential, counseling research is warranted. This research and literature might include the continued evaluation of standardized assessment protocols as well as increased understanding of evidenced-based interventions with individuals with a variety of diagnoses and in a range of settings. Additionally, much of the research regarding offending behavior and mental illness has been conducted solely with prisoners (Mullen, 2000). Given the continued expansion of forensic services to community settings, forensic mental health counselors would benefit from research regarding the provision of services in the community.

Ethical Considerations in Forensic Mental Health

Given that the features of forensic mental health differ from the features of traditional clinical mental health counseling, there are specific ethical considerations for those working in this specialization. Much of the ethical emphasis is related to establishing boundaries between the three parties involved: the client, the counselor, and the court system. Although informed consent has long been a requirement for traditional counseling services, there have been few regulations to guide special conditions such as working with individuals that are under the care of the state. In its 2005 Code of Ethics, ACA mandated professional counselors to obtain written consent for forensic evaluation, which includes information regarding the nature of evaluation, the limits of confidentiality related to the forensic counseling relationship, and who will receive the evaluation report. Additionally, it is expected that counselors will not provide forensic services for those to whom they previously have provided counseling services and vice versa, and that they will avoid professional and personal relationships with individuals close to those for whom they provide forensic services (ACA, 2005).

As previously noted, the American Mental Health Counselors Association (2010) also addressed forensic mental health services in the "Assessment and Diagnosis" section of its code of ethics. AMHCA (2010) was even more explicit in describing the role of forensic mental health counselors. First, these counselors should be free from bias or "personal investment" (p. 12) in the assessment outcome. In fact, forensic mental health counselors serve in an evaluative role and are expected to avoid advocating for offenders, victims, or courts of law. In addition to addressing the limits of confidentiality within the forensic mental health relationship, counselors should inform clients of the potential for negative outcomes from forensic evaluation. Forensic mental health counselors provide information regarding their training and credentials during informed consent as well as during any expert witness testimony. Finally, they provide only those services for which they are trained and qualified (AMHCA, 2010).

As is the case in all forms of counseling, there are potentials for differences between ethical guidelines for practice and the legal scope of practice. Although counselors may be ethical in determining that they have the requisite training and experience to provide a forensic evaluation, state law may not allow professional counselors to deliver that service. It is essential that forensic mental health counselors review their state practice laws and determine what services they are allowed to offer under the scope of the law. When the law and the ethical codes conflict, the clinical mental health counselor should always obey the law and seek consultation and supervision before taking any further action.

TRAINING AND CREDENTIALING

Currently, no definitive training standards exist for forensic mental health counselors; however, some counselor education programs are beginning to offer specializations in forensic mental health. Additionally, organizations such as the National Board of Forensic Evaluators and the National Association of Forensic Counselors, offer a variety of postlicensure professional credentials in forensic mental health services. In addition to the core clinical mental health curriculum, those seeking specialization in forensic mental health should expect, at a minimum, to complete additional coursework or training in forensic assessment, clinical interventions with offending populations, and mental health law. Other advanced coursework or postgraduate training might include child custody assessment, addictions and substance abuse counseling, domestic violence intervention, sexual offender assessment and treatment, juvenile justice, assessment of competency, and divorce/family mediation and family law. Although forensic mental health counselors are eligible to obtain national certification, the scope of practice to provide forensic services varies by state, so individuals should determine the eligibility requirements for the state in which they are working.

National Association of Forensic Counselors

A variety of advanced national credentials are available for forensic mental health counselors. The National Association of Forensic Counselors (NAFC) offers the Master

Addictions Counselor (MAC) and Certified Forensic Addictions Specialist (CFAS) as well as the following clinical certifications: Clinically Certified Forensic Counselor (CCFC), Clinically Certified Criminal Justice Specialist (CCCJS), Clinically Certified Domestic Violence Counselor (CCDVC), Clinically Certified Sex Offender Treatment Specialist (CCSOTS), and Clinically Certified Juvenile Sex Offender Treatment Specialist (CCJSOTS). These clinical certifications require a minimum of a master's degree, licensure as a professional counselor in good standing, and a minimum of three years and 6,000 hours of experience in the area in which certification is being sought. Following the assessment of eligibility, individuals must pass a certification examination covering the following domains: Clinical Assessment and Treatment Planning; Counseling and Case Management; Psychosocial Dynamics of Criminal Behavior and Substance Abuse; Criminal Justice Process; and Legal, Ethical, and Professional Responsibility (American College of Certified Forensic Counselors Certification Commission, n.d.). A second credential in forensic mental health is available through the National Board of Forensic Evaluators.

National Board of Forensic Evaluators

Established in 2003, the National Board of Forensic Evaluators (NBFE) aims to serve licensed master's-level clinicians in training and recognition as forensic evaluators. It is the only forensic credentialing body recognized by the American Mental Health Counselors Association as well as being endorsed by the American Counseling Association. The board originally was formed by licensed clinical mental health professionals, physicians, and family attorneys to establish a forensic certification. In addition to its work supporting the continued education and credentialing of professional counselors, NBFE also supports treatment of adolescents and their families through assessment and treatment planning (Hayes, 2004; NBFE, n.d.a).

In order to obtain NBFE board certification, individuals must meet several requirements and complete an extensive postlicensure evaluation process. Candidates must be licensed mental health clinicians with three years postlicensure experience. They also must provide documentation for a minimum of 40 hours of training via classes, workshops, supervision, or publication related to the following topics: forensic mental health assessment, sexual offending, domestic violence, expert witness testimony, child custody evaluations, competency evaluations, malingering, civil commitment, juvenile justice, and substance abuse. Upon completion of the requirements, candidates submit their applications, which include three professional references addressing the candidates' ethical conduct and abilities for forensic practice, and fees. They are then eligible to sit for a written exam, which is followed by a review of candidates' practice and an oral examination. Upon successful completion of these requirements, candidates are granted Diplomate status and are board certified by NBFE (NBFE, n.d.b).

Although advanced credentialing is not required for the general practice of clinical mental health counseling, it is essential that counselors interested in forensic work seek additional training and supervision. Counselors working in the forensic area must have mastery of mental health treatment approaches and understand the implications of their work within the context of the legal system. This complex combination of requisite skills and knowledge necessitates further training. Training in forensic mental health counseling may be gained through certification programs or through traditional graduate study.

MENTAL DISORDERS AND OFFENDING

Although forensic mental health services are improving, criminalization of the mentally ill is still a major issue in the United States. In 1999, more people with mental disorders were housed in the Los Angeles County Jail and Rikers Island than in the largest inpatient facilities in the United States (Torrey, 1999). Since that study was conducted, the problem has become worse rather than better. Multiple studies have demonstrated that the presence of mental disorders is significantly higher in the incarcerated population than the general population (Ditton, 1999; National GAINS Center for People with Co-Occurring Disorders in the Justice System, 2004). According to a study commissioned by the Treatment Advocacy Center and the National Sheriffs' Association (Torrey, Kennard, Eslinger, Lamb, & Pavle, 2010), the average number of persons with serious mental illness in prisons and jails was three times greater than the number in hospitals. Torrey et al. (2010) also discovered that Arizona and Nevada had an almost 10 times greater number of persons with serious mental illness in prisons and jails. Clearly the mental health needs of those in the prison system are immense.

Although the need for forensic mental health services in the criminal justice system is clear, it is important to note that community psychiatric facilities also serve individuals for the criminal justice system. In 2002, approximately 30% of those admitted to public psychiatric facilities were court-mandated forensic patients (The Sentencing Project, 2002). Because community psychiatric facilities are a likely workplace for clinical mental health counselors, it is essential for all clinical mental health counselors to have some understanding of forensics.

It is also important to state that mental illness does not equate with criminal behavior, and there is no evidence that mental disorders cause offending behavior. Yet, because of the prevalence of mental health issues within the offender population, the dynamics of mental health within the offender population needs to be understood. Unfortunately, there have been some problems with research methodology and data analysis for many of the prevalence studies already conducted. As a result, the prevalence rates for mental health concerns among offender populations have varied from study to study. One study that has been repeatedly cited is by James and Glaze (2006). They reported that in 2005 more than 50% of all inmates in local jails and state and federal prisons demonstrated identifiable symptomology of mental health problems. James and Glaze further found that inmates with mental health problems were significantly more likely to have had multiple incarcerations and that jail inmates were the most likely to display the highest rate of symptomology. The common symptomology displayed by inmates included mania, depression, and psychosis. It is also important to note that the James and Glaze study (2006) found that mental disorders were more common in female inmates than in their male counterparts.

In addition to the prevalence data, James and Glaze (2006) found several common factors among inmates with mental disorders. Those with mental health problems were more likely to have been homeless prior to incarceration and to have lived for a period of time in a foster home. Rates of childhood physical and sexual abuse also were higher for inmates with mental health concerns than those without. Mental illness was correlated with lower rates of employment and increased likelihood to rely on other sources of income, including illegal sources (James & Glaze, 2006).

One of the greatest concerns regarding offenders with mental health concerns is the potential for violence. James and Glaze (2006) found that the most serious offenses of inmates with mental illness were violent offenses, although there was no difference between those with and without mental health problems regarding the use of a weapon in violent crimes. Additionally, inmates with mental illness were more likely to have rule violations or have sustained injuries from fighting while incarcerated. At the same time, it also should be noted that inmates with mental disorders were incarcerated in state institutions longer than those without mental disorders who were incarcerated for the same offense (James & Glaze, 2006).

For the most part, the primary diagnoses of inmates are the same as typical outpatient mental health center clients. Several specific disorders, however, are correlated with higher rates of offending behavior. In an assessment of male inmates in Quebec, Canada, Côté and Hodgins (1990) found that the rate of depression was twice as high for those incarcerated than in the general population. These findings are supported by the work of Wiesner, Kim, and Capaldi (2005), who found that increased rates of criminal behavior in adolescence were positively correlated with increased rates of depression and substance use in early adulthood. In addition, prevalence rates for the diagnosis of bipolar disorder in the prison population were six times higher than those in the general population, and prevalence rates for the diagnosis of schizophrenia were seven times higher. Wallace, Mullen, and Burgess (2004) found that individuals with schizophrenia were more likely to be convicted of violent crimes than the general population; however, The Sentencing Project (2002) noted that violent behavior often occurs when psychotic symptoms are present. James and Glaze (2006) reported rates of delusions and hallucinations as high as 24% for jail inmates.

Although the diagnoses of inmates and outpatient clients may be similar, Stone and Taylor (2000) reported that forensic mental health practitioners should expect to see more clients with treatment-resistant schizophrenia and personality disorders. Multiple researchers have reported significant correlations between personality disorders, particularly Cluster B disorders such as borderline personality disorder, and violent behavior (Coccaro, Berman, & Kavoussi, 1997; Widiger & Trull, 1994; Windle & Windle, 1995). Co-occurring substance use disorders appear to increase offending behavior in those with mental illness. Rates of co-occurring disorders are higher for those with mental disorders than for those without mental health concerns (James & Glaze, 2006). Forensic mental health counselors working in the juvenile justice system will likely be faced with presenting issues that are precursors to some of the adult diagnoses and more severe problem behavior. For example, Johnson et al. (2000) found that adolescent offenders with Cluster A (such as paranoid personality disorder) and Cluster B personality disorders demonstrated a greater risk for violence later in life.

Although mental health disorders such as depression and bipolar disorder are common among the prison population, forensic mental health counselors must also be able to address substance abuse and substance dependence. Co-occurring substance use disorders appear to increase offending behavior in those inmates with mental disorders (The Sentencing Project, 2002; Wallace et al., 2004). James and Glaze (2006) found substance use rates were higher for inmates with mental disorders than those without mental health problems. Thus, treatment for these individuals with co-occurring disorders is more complex than for those with either a mental health disorder or a substance-related issue.

The prevalence of substance abuse, mental disorders, and co-occurring disorders varies by the level of incarceration. Rates of alcohol or other substance abuse or dependence were lowest among those inmates housed in federal prisons (49.5% without mental health problems and 63.6% with mental health problems). Inmates in state prisons who did not have a mental health diagnosis had the highest rates of substance abuse or dependence (55.6%). Inmates in local jails had the highest rates of co-occurring disorders at 76.4%. Overall, more inmates suffered from co-occurring disorders than from only mental health problems or substance use disorders or from no mental health problems at all (James & Glaze, 2006).

As previously noted, forensic mental health counselors provide an array of assessment and treatment services for offenders and those at risk of offending. Given that offending behavior, especially among adolescents and young adults, is correlated with presenting mental health issues and that forensic mental health services are increasingly being deinstitutionalized, it might be difficult for counselors to determine when mental health counseling has become forensic mental health counseling. Because the issues can be complex and it may be difficult to separate forensic issues from mental health issues, forensic mental health counselors specialize in assessing and managing the risks of offending as well as understanding the relationships between and among the client, the counseling professional, and the courts of law (Stone & Taylor, 2000).

 ## WHO ARE FORENSIC MENTAL HEALTH CLIENTS?

We have given a great deal of attention to the issues of mental health among the offender population. Although there is clearly a need for forensic mental health services among this population, clients of forensic mental health services can come from a broad spectrum of society. For the purposes of this discussion, potential consumers of these services are separated into professional and private groups.

First, a number of professional groups may utilize forensic mental health services. These include but are not limited to those that operate within the legal system and in courts of criminal and civil law. The courts may utilize forensic services in cases that range from child custody to crimes of violence (Wrightsman & Fulero, 2005). Increasingly, forensic mental health counselors are asked to conduct psychological evaluations of individuals involved in criminal or civil court cases. Requests for such evaluations from judges or attorneys are commonplace in modern courts of law. In addition, forensic mental health counselors with the appropriate training and background may serve as expert witnesses in legal proceedings. Expert witnesses possess additional or special knowledge in subject areas such as mental competence, negligence, malpractice, societal issues, mental disorders, and child custody, among many others. Attorneys also utilize forensic professionals as consultants during jury selection or actual trials. Often, judges send cases to mediation in an attempt to resolve disputes so as to avoid going to trial. Some forensic mental health counselors are qualified to fulfill this role as well. Typically, forensic mental health counselors who serve as mediators have received additional certification to work in this area.

Next, law enforcement utilizes forensic mental health counselors as well. For example, police departments may work with forensic professionals to construct psychological profiles or assess risk in specific settings such as prisons or schools. In addition, forensic professionals may be asked to work with law enforcement to identify potential candidates for officer training or assess the fitness for duty of existing personnel. Undoubtedly, the legal system will find additional ways to utilize the services of forensic mental health counselors. This system remains the largest consumer of forensic mental health services.

Last, private groups such as businesses, nonprofits, and private citizens also utilize the services of forensic professionals. Companies or foundations may hire forensic mental health counselors to act as mediators, consultants, or researchers. Possible tasks include creating protocols for crisis management or designing campaigns to influence public policy. Private citizens, including the victims of offenders, may engage the services of forensic mental health counselors as well.

ASSESSMENT AND EVALUATION

Assessment and evaluation are primary functions of many forensic mental health counselors. Chief among these functions is assessing competency to stand trial (Robbins, Waters, & Herbert, 1997). Forensic professionals are routinely called to assess the mental competency of individuals to stand trial, although this practice has been criticized by some as lacking relevance and exceeding role boundaries (Robbins et al., 1997). Despite such criticisms, the practice of using forensic mental health counselors to provide evaluations and expert testimony continues. Each state now licenses professional counselors and defines the scope of practice for counselors according to the specific licensure law. According to Watson and Sheperis (2010), there are considerable debates from state to state over the qualifications to administer, score, and interpret psychological tests. We recommend that forensic mental health counselors consult state laws before conducting any formal assessment procedures. The American Counseling Association publishes a list of state counseling boards and links to state laws (www.counseling.org).

One type of information included in forensic evaluations—called collateral information—comes from third parties. Collateral information is considered essential in forensic evaluations because the client often cannot be considered reliable as the only source of information (Heilbrun, 2001). Evaluations of this type are used in legal proceedings such as child custody cases, among others. The American Counseling Association's Code of Ethics (2005) addresses this common practice. The code admonishes counselors to provide objective findings and to support their conclusions. It also addresses informed consent, which is required unless otherwise ordered by a court of law. In addition, the code restricts counselors from conducting forensic evaluations of past or current clients and calls for counselors to avoid potentially harmful or dual relationships with individuals being evaluated.

In general, forensic evaluators use two types of assessments. The first type is referred to as forensic assessment instruments (Grisso, 1986). Instruments of this sort are designed to measure or assess specific legal concepts such as capacity, ability, or competence. An instrument designed to measure competency to stand trial is an example of a forensic assessment instrument. The second type of assessment used is referred to as forensically relevant instruments, which are designed to measure clinical or psychological concepts (Otto & Heilbrun, 2002). For example, the Minnesota Multiphasic Personality Inventory-2 (MMPI-2), an instrument used in all facets of mental health counseling assessment, is also employed for forensic purposes, ranging from detecting malingering to being part of a competency evaluation.

Over the past three decades, the number of instruments developed in both categories of forensic assessment has increased sharply (Jeglic, Maile, & Calkins-Mercado, 2011). Many of the instruments used today are developed in accordance with accepted procedures and are well validated. However, forensic mental health counselors should approach the assessment process with a careful eye because some forensic instruments lack appropriate validation or have been used in ways that were not intended by the instrument developers. Because forensic mental health counseling is a new specialization area, any practices that lack scientific evidence or any improper practices bring scrutiny to the field of forensic evaluation.

Child Custody

One area outside of the criminal justice system in which forensic mental health counselors are playing an increasing role is in child custody proceedings. As mentioned previously, appropriately credentialed forensic professionals may act as mediators in the court system. Mediation is a very different process than typical mental health counseling, but some of the same facilitative skills are used. In child custody cases, a mediator works with the couple to reach an agreement on parenting and custody issues (Wrightsman & Fulero, 2005). The forensic mental health counselor acting as mediator is objective, maintains confidentiality, and creates an environment in which communication can flow freely between both sides. Issues resolved in mediation may include important considerations such as division of assets, provisions for education of children, and living accommodations. The agreements reached in mediation are part of the legal process and are enforceable by the court. The need or demand for mediation by trained forensic mental health counselors in child custody cases will likely increase as their services reduce the burdens on the courts. As such, becoming a credentialed court mediator could be a beneficial career opportunity for forensic mental health counselors. It is important to remember that forensic mental health counselors involved in custody mediation or disputes do NOT act as counselors to the children involved. The role of the mediator is to serve as a neutral party, helping the parents to come to an acceptable agreement in relation to custody. Recall that the ACA Code of Ethics (2005) instructs counselors to avoid dual or potentially harmful relationships.

Mediator is not the only role played by forensic mental health counselors with regard to child custody. In many cases, the court may require that a custody evaluation be conducted, and appropriately trained forensic mental health counselors may be called upon to provide this service. The evaluation may consist of interviews, administration of assessment instruments, and direct observations. In this situation, the forensic professional acts as an agent of the courts. He or she will gather relevant information from a number of sources and share that information with the judge, often in a written report. Forensic evaluators operating in this capacity must be objective and fair, not favoring one side or the other. In addition, their reports should be easily understood, clear, and focused on behavior. Of course, any forensic counselors acting in this capacity must consult their state laws to determine the legal ability of counselors to provide assessment services. Whereas the international testing standards are based on competency, some US states have opted to enact laws that limit the scope of practice for counselors regardless of competency.

Today, the standard guideline for custody issues is the best interests of the child. From a legal standpoint, both sides in the dispute are considered appropriate placements until proven otherwise in court.

Expert Witness

Another role for forensic mental health counselors is that of expert witness. In addition to providing evaluations of several types, the forensic professional may be called upon to provide his or her expertise in court. The forensic professional may be appointed by the court or hired by one of the parties involved. Under no circumstances should the forensic mental health counselor be engaged by the court and a particular litigant at the same time. Attorneys on both sides of the dispute will have the opportunity to examine the testimony of a forensic mental health counselor acting as an expert witness.

Forensic mental health counselors may also act as researchers for the court. In this capacity, instead of evaluating a family system in a custody case, the forensic professional may be asked to provide the court with the current understanding of custody issues and any relevant research about the effects of custody on a child. The recommendations made to the court based on said research may then be used to decide the issue of custody.

Courts and evaluators appointed by them usually operate by guidelines established by the US Congress in 1970. Generally speaking, these guidelines include consideration of the following: the mental and physical health of all parties involved, adjustment issues including school and community adjustment, the ability to provide for the material needs of the child or children, the social environment, and the wishes of both the parents and the child or children (Sales, Manber, & Rohman, 1992). Having a forensic counselor serve as researcher can be informative to the overall legal process.

Competency

A critical role for forensic evaluators is the determination of competency. In the US legal system, an individual can be guilty of an illegal act only if there was free will and an understanding of right and wrong. The concept of *mens rea* means the presence of a guilty mind. This legal standard emanated from the case of *Durham v. United States* (1954). Mens rea is also related to the legal concept of insanity, which is quite complex and can vary across court jurisdictions. Regardless of the jurisdictional differences in the definition of insanity, if there is a potential that an individual's acts could have been the result of a mental health issue, an assessment of competency is required. This is when forensic counselors may become involved. Each state determines the qualifications for professionals to conduct competency evaluations, so it is necessary to check state laws.

Although the *Durham* case served as the initial standard for determining competence, it is now used only by New Hampshire. Currently referred to as the Durham rule, the notion is that a defendant is not "criminally responsible if his unlawful act is the product of a mental disease or defect" (Simon & Gold, 2004, p. 349). However, the ambiguity of the Durham rule has led to the adoption of varying standards across the United States.

Competency evaluation, as with other forensic assessments, has come under greater scrutiny because of issues with reliability and validity of assessment instruments (Jeglic et al., 2011). There certainly is cause to be skeptical of the assessment process when it comes to the evaluation of juvenile offenders. There is a paucity of legal guidance for the process of forensic evaluation of juvenile offenders, which results in great variation in procedures from region to region.

A limited number of models are generally used for conducting pretrial evaluations for both adults and juvenile offenders (Macfarlane, Lurie, Bettridge, & Barbaree, 2004; Poythress, Otto, & Heilbrun, 1991). These models have been in place for some time, yet they remain the most common today. First, the most extensive evaluation is conducted through the inpatient hospital model. In this process, individuals being evaluated can be observed for 24 hours per day and may be assessed by numerous hospital personnel. In addition, these individuals may receive an array of psychological and medical assessments during their hospitalization (Poythress et al., 1991). The inpatient hospital model is generally well accepted by the court system, because of its thoroughness and opportunity for standardization of procedures. However, this model is also the most expensive and so is usually reserved for the most serious cases. There are a limited number of psychiatric beds available nationwide and, as a result, this model would not be viable unless it were part of a stepwise system of evaluation.

Hospital-based outpatient evaluation is the second model commonly used for pretrial evaluation (Poythress et al., 1991). These evaluations are usually conducted at state hospitals or centralized hospitals that serve a broad catchment area (Washington State Department of Social & Health Services, 2006). This model is less expensive than the inpatient counterpart and allows for a less restrictive evaluation environment, which may be applicable to protecting an individual's civil rights. Because the process is centralized, the standardization of the assessment process may be similar to that within an inpatient evaluation. Although it is less expensive than the inpatient model, the outpatient hospital evaluation is still costly. Also, the evaluation process lacks the thoroughness of the inpatient assessment.

Community-based outpatient evaluation is the third model commonly used for pretrial evaluation (Poythress et al., 1991). These evaluations typically occur in community mental health centers and are conducted by the mental health staff employed by those centers (Washington State Department of Social & Health Services, 2006). Although this model is the least restrictive, it allows for extensive evaluation because the center is located in the individual's community. However, because forensic mental health counseling is a relatively new specialization, community mental health centers do not always have appropriately trained personnel available to conduct these types of evaluations. The human resources available to conduct community-based outpatient evaluations become even scarcer in rural areas throughout the United States. Further, the lack of standardization from center to center may call the evaluation process into question by the court system.

The court clinic is the fourth model used for pretrial evaluation; however, this model is more common in urban areas (Poythress et al., 1991). The court clinic model is somewhat experimental and was designed to fill a gap in needed services. In this model, a range of mental health services pre- and posttrial are provided in or near a court building (Washington State Department of Social & Health Services, 2006). The court clinic typically assigns a case coordinator to arrange and supervise the range of services needed. Similar to the outpatient model, the court clinic is community based and allows for ease of access by the individual in need of evaluation. Although this model may help to divert some individuals from state hospital inpatient and outpatient evaluations, the cost structure is born by the court system and, as such, may be prohibitive. As is the case with community mental health assessment, the lack of trained professionals may also be an issue in the development of a court clinic.

The private practitioner model is the fifth option used for pretrial evaluation (Poythress et al., 1991). The private practitioner model is a fee-for-service contractual system in which forensic mental health professionals conduct evaluations in their office or in the jail system (Washington State Department of Social & Health Services, 2006). There are numerous concerns with this model. Although the private practitioner may be able to provide assessment in a least restrictive environment, there is less structure and control over the type of evaluation conducted. Further, there is some potential for changes in the quality of evaluation based on fees available.

A mixed model is the sixth option used by some jurisdictions (Poythress et al., 1991). In this model, there is a balance between inpatient and outpatient evaluations. This model allows for professional judgment about the type of evaluation needed and may result in some cost savings by diverting less serious cases to the outpatient option (Washington State Department of Social & Health Services, 2006). Overall, the mixed model is beneficial because it not only allows varied approaches based on need but also allows for least restrictive assessment when possible.

Regardless of the model implemented by a jurisdiction, the need for pretrial evaluations is increasing. Therefore, appropriately trained and credentialed forensic mental health counselors who can provide these services are clearly needed. Unfortunately, the financial resources necessary to provide quality pretrial assessment do not always match the need. It is imperative that communities adopt cost-effective yet quality models for competency evaluation and that appropriate financial resources be allocated to implement these models.

Competency Restoration

When an individual is found incompetent to stand trial, then an order may be issued from the court to provide competency restoration services. A competency restoration order means that treatment is required to bring the individual back to a state of competency so that a trial may proceed. Of course, in certain cases, the individual may never become competent. According to *Jackson v. Indiana* (1972), competency restoration services may not extend past a reasonable amount of time to establish whether returning to competency is probable. According to The National Judicial College (2012), best practice is that the competency restoration services should not last longer than a typical sentence for the criminal act and should be concluded within one year maximum. In many competency restoration cases, only the provision of psychoeducational services is needed to help an individual prepare to stand trial or plead (The National Judicial College, 2012). Individuals who receive competency restoration orders may have either mental health disorders or developmental disorders.

When an order for competency restoration is issued, then a model of treatment must be selected that meets the least restrictive requirement. The models of competency restoration are similar to the models of competency assessment and range from community-based services to inpatient hospitalization. The National Judicial College developed a best-practice model of competency evaluation and competency restoration. In its model, The National Judicial College (2012) identified the following six conditions necessary for the most restrictive competency restoration (inpatient hospitalization):

> (a) imminent threat to self or others; (b) potential for substantial self-neglect; (c) concern that the treatment of the client cannot be determined due to unclear pathology and need for observation; (d) observation to determine whether the client is presenting verifiable or false symptoms (e.g., malingering); (e) the client cannot consent to or voluntarily ingest necessary medications for a return to mental competence; or (f) emergency treatment is needed.

In many cases, competency restoration occurs within the jail system. In these instances, there is a potential for the jail system to become a pseudo-treatment facility. As you might conclude, there are numerous issues related to restoration services within the jail system. Housing individuals who are mentally incompetent in a jail system may result in even further difficulties. Of those individuals with developmental disabilities, only 18% to 30% are ever restored to competency (Washington State Institute for Public Policy, 2013).

Competency restoration services are a viable specialization area for forensic mental health counselors. Some prison systems create mental health units that allow for the provision of competency restoration services. These types of units require appropriately trained professionals to make them run effectively. In addition to working within the jail system, forensic mental health counselors can provide competency restoration services in other agencies, hospitals, and institutions.

Civil Commitment

Involuntary civil commitment is a process by which individuals are admitted to psychological/psychiatric treatment against their will. The legal process for civil commitment varies from state to state. However, the general reasons for involuntary commitment are mental illness, developmental disability, and substance dependence (Reisner, Slobogin, & Rai, 2009). In each of these cases, the general standard across states is that an individual must be an imminent danger to self or others in order to be committed to a facility. Emergency commitment is for the purpose of completing a thorough evaluation and to stabilize the individual.

According to the Treatment Advocacy Center (2013), 44 states and the District of Columbia have enacted laws that provide for assisted outpatient treatment (AOT). In these types of cases, an individual can be ordered to seek outpatient treatment in order to stabilize presenting concerns. In an AOT commitment, the individual must not be an imminent danger to him- or herself or others but must be in a state of crisis.

The Treatment Advocacy Center (2013) published a state-by-state guide for civil commitment that includes a summary of each state law and the qualifications for a professional to initiate a civil commitment. Mental health counselors are not eligible to initiate civil commitment in every state, so it is imperative to consult either the Treatment Advocacy Center guide or one's state law for information about qualifications.

Florida is one state where mental health counselors have the legal right to initiate civil commitment. According to the Florida Mental Health Act (2011), also known as the Baker Act:

> a physician, clinical psychologist, psychiatric nurse, mental health counselor, marriage and family therapist, or clinical social worker may execute a certificate stating that he or she has examined a person within the preceding 48 hours and finds that the person appears to meet the criteria for involuntary examination and stating the observations upon which that conclusion is based.

In Florida, there is a provision that requires that danger to self or others be unavoidable even with the help of willing family members or friends. Each state's civil commitment procedure is multifaceted, and forensic mental health counselors should be thoroughly familiar with their state statutes. Like Florida, most states have time limits in place for the maximum length of commitment prior to additional court action.

Interpretation and Report Writing

Forensic mental health counselors spend a great deal of time conducting assessments for a variety of court-related issues. Administering assessment instruments certainly requires training and supervision, yet the more difficult process occurs after the administration. The interpretation of assessment data and conveyance of that information through a professional report are complex activities that have high-stakes implications within the court system. Because forensic assessment can literally impact life and death, forensic mental health counselors must make every effort to attain and maintain professional competency in the administration and interpretation of assessment instruments. They must also use best practices in the development of professional forensic reports.

In many cases, assessment instruments can be administered by psychological technicians who have received appropriate training and supervision. However, scoring and interpretation of the data from these instruments are reserved for appropriately credentialed professionals. For example, intelligence tests such as the Wechsler series can be administered by a forensic assistant who has received appropriate training and supervision. However, the scoring and interpretation of the Wechsler series is reserved for mental health professionals. One of the things that make the scoring difficult is that in a number of the scales for the Wechsler series, the scorer must determine whether a response is worth 0, 1, or 2 points based on examples provided in the scoring manual. Differentiating the points would be quite difficult without extended training and supervision.

Although it might be possible to train someone without a professional degree to score an intelligence test correctly, the implications of an incorrect intelligence score are too immense to leave the process to a paraprofessional. In school systems, intelligence tests are considered high stakes because they can be a part of the determination for special education or gifted education services. In the criminal justice system, an intelligence test can determine whether someone has the mental capacity to be sentenced to death. Even a single scoring error has the potential to make a change in overall IQ score and as such can mean the difference between life and death.

Clearly, the scoring of an assessment instrument is complex, yet understanding the scores of an assessment requires even more training. For example, imagine that a student from a local college is referred to a forensic mental health counselor working in the local community for a risk assessment. The student made a threat against one of her professors, and the school declared that she could not return to campus until cleared by a mental health counselor. As part of the risk assessment, the counselor decides to administer the MMPI-2, which has 567 items and over 100 scales.

The MMPI-2 is one of the most complex instruments because of the number of scales and the implications for scores across a combination of scales. Even though there are scoring programs available for the MMPI-2, it takes a trained professional to dissect the scores and understand their implications for human behavior. Imagine that in this case the client has a high 4-9 profile on the primary scales. This means that the individual has high scores on scale 4 (psychopathic deviate [PD]) and scale 9 (mania). A high 4-9 profile is common not only for individuals in the criminal justice system but also for high-profile political leaders and CEOs. The level of elevation and combinations of subscores differentiates the individual in the criminal justice system from a president of the United States.

In this case, the client also scores high on the bizarre mentation subscale and the explosive anger subscale. High scores on these scales add a great deal of information about the high 4-9 profile. This individual has reported a high degree of antisocial thoughts and behaviors (PD), high degree of anxious energy (mania), abnormal bizarre thoughts, and the potential for explosive anger. The individual made a threat against her professor. Based on these MMPI-2 scores, there is a potential for the individual to be dangerous, and it would be important to conduct further evaluation and potentially take action for civil commitment.

Once the assessment process is complete, forensic mental health counselors typically develop a forensic report that conveys all of the information about the assessment process and recommendations. The types of recommendations provided depend upon the rationale for the evaluation. In today's world of technology, numerous report writer software programs are available. However, the best practice for report writing is that a report should be individualized.

Because a report conveys information that can impact the sentencing of a criminal, the custody of a child, or the commitment of a mentally ill individual, forensic mental health counselors should invest considerable effort into the development of each report. When constructing a forensic report, the information should be communicated clearly and in language that is understandable to the recipient of the report. In other words, if the report is meant for the court, a judge must be able to understand the elements of the report and the recommendations. Report writing is a skill that requires practice and supervision, just like counseling.

Testifying in Court and Depositions

Forensic mental health counselors are called as expert witnesses in the court system for a variety of issues. Although in many cases the forensic mental health counselors provide testimony about assessment, they may also offer professional opinions on issues such as child custody, divorce, child abuse, workers' compensation, and vocational issues (la Forge & Henderson, 1990). Moore and Simpson (2012) caution that the role of expert witness requires careful consideration of legal and ethical boundaries of practice and that failure to understand these boundaries could result in legal sanctions.

It is important to recognize that an expert witness is different from a witness of fact. In cases in which a counselor has had a professional relationship with one of the parties in court, then that counselor can be called as a witness of fact and testify as to his or her role and the facts of the case. The counselor is not able to draw conclusions. In contrast, expert witnesses rarely have a relationship with the parties involved in a court case. The counselor who acts as an expert witness is asked to render professional opinions and to inform or teach the court about particular issues. In order to be an expert witness, the court must accept the counselor's qualifications. These qualifications can come under the scrutiny of the attorneys in the case, and the counselor may be required to validate his or her expertise through a cross-examination process.

Stacy Notaras Murray (2011) wrote an article for *Counseling Today* that examined the role of counselor as expert witness. In her article, Murray interviewed several counselors who had provided expert testimony and highlighted some of the strategies they used in preparation. One of the key points was that counselors need to have appropriate credentialing to establish credibility in the court system. Many of the counselors interviewed were certified forensic counselors through NBFE. Another point of preparation was that counselors should work with the attorney calling them as witnesses prior to the trial. In other words, it is important to prepare for the testimony and to get a feel for the type of cross-examination questions that might be posed. Once a counselor takes the stand, then it is important to be honest and to offer opinion only within the scope of expertise. It is recommended that counselors who are interested in becoming expert witnesses spend time in the court system and observe what other witnesses do on the stand.

Nelson and Kaushall (1996) provided a guide for attorneys to depose mental health providers prior to testimony in a case. Counselors should be prepared to answer the following common questions:

1. What are your general qualifications as a therapist?
2. What is your educational background?
3. What are your specialization areas, and what special knowledge base do you possess?
4. Can you provide a timeline of your involvement in the case? Discuss how the client was referred and any prior knowledge of the case that you possess.
5. Is there anything to your knowledge that would cause a conflict of interest in this case?
6. Can you provide an in-depth explanation of work with the client from intake to completion?
7. What methods or approaches did you use to establish your opinion?
8. Discuss your training and knowledge related to experimental research.
9. What is your understanding of your professional responsibilities in regard to this case?

Of course, these questions are only examples of what might be asked as part of a forensic mental health counselor's testimony in court. There are many different types of questions that may be asked of an expert witness. As previously suggested, it would be beneficial to observe expert witness testimony before deciding to enter this type of forensic practice.

In many cases, clinical mental health counselors are called to testify in cases related to their clients. Even though this is not typical forensic mental health work, it is important to briefly discuss this type of testimony. All counselors have the potential to be called as witnesses in court. Thus, it is important that they understand the issues related to confidentiality of information.

Release of information to a court can be a somewhat complex issue. For example, in some jurisdictions, the counselor–client relationship is considered privileged communication and is protected by law. However, in jurisdictions that do not allow for privileged communication, a judge can order a clinical mental health counselor to provide records (Remley & Herlihy, 2010). In such a situation, the counselor can ask the court to allow him or her either not to disclose information or to provide a summary of information. If the request is denied and the judge in the case orders disclosure, then the counselor must comply. Although it is important to comply in this instance, a counselor should provide copies of records rather than the original documents (Remley & Herlihy, 2010). In any case in which a clinical mental health counselor is subpoenaed to appear in court, it is important to seek supervision. It may also be important to consult an attorney.

In addition to testifying in court, clinical mental health counselors may also be asked to provide a deposition related to a case. Remley and Herlihy (2010) recommended that counselors who provide depositions have an attorney present during the process. In a deposition, a judge is not present to preside over the process and to manage any controversies. Thus, the counselor will likely need an attorney to consult with during the process and to protect him or her from attorney pressure. Typically, the opposing attorneys, a court reporter, and witnesses are the only individuals present for a deposition.

VOICE FROM THE FIELD 12.1

"So, Dr. Hamza, are you 100% sure you have the knowledge, experience, training, and proper education to evaluate clients with TBI (traumatic brain injury)?" the prosecutor asked in an adamant and less than kind way.

"Yes, I do," Dr. Hamza responded.

"So, what makes you 100% sure and not 90% or 95% sure?"

"I am 100% sure with no doubts because I have had the proper training, education, experience, and knowledge necessary as required by the state rules and regulations, board of examiners rules and regulations, and the APA rules and regulations to evaluate patients or clients with TBI."

"So, how sure are you when you diagnose someone with TBI, Doctor?"

"Well, once the testing has been compl . . . ."

"You are not answering my question, Doctor! Just answer the question."

"Well, when you evaluate a person for T . . . ."

"Once again, Doctor, how sure are you? Give the jury a percentage."

"I cannot. This is not chemistry or math to tell you one plus one is equal to two. We are dealing w . . . ."

"So, you are telling me that what you do is soft science. Not real science."

This is an example of the type of cross-examination I have experienced in my work as a forensic professional. As clinical mental health counselors, you should be prepared for this type of experience when a court orders you to appear and testify. Cross-examination aims to influence the jury opinion; discredit or credit an expert's credentials and testimony; belittle the statements or the opinion of the expert; or reverse or impact the mental health counselor's testimony in a negative way. Usually and more likely than not, the mental health counselor will feel anxious, humiliated, agitated, and at times angry. Following is an example of some tactics that I have seen attorneys use to demolish a professional's opinion in front of the jury and judge.

"So, Dr. Hamza, what we learned from you here [the prosecutor is looking at the jury with a disingenuous smile and a few glances at the expert witness] is that you are not sure of your expertise, your evaluations, and the science of your profession you are depending on in evaluating this man! Correct, yes or no, please!" the prosecutor demanded.

"With all due respect, no. Not cor . . . .! If I may explain, it i . . . ."

"No, you may not." The prosecutor responded with mild, harsh tone and a stare at the expert, who smiled back calmly and with genuine kindness. "Well, Doctor, your expertise and knowledge is really about trying to understand human behaviors, which can be complex and difficult to understand. Correct?"

"Yes, correct."

"So, isn't it true to say as a psychologist, you predict things, you are not sure of things, like research? You do not really know whether something is 100% the case or not; and you psychologists have much to learn about prior to making a definite decision regarding a diagnosis?"

"No, not true. First, I came here to provide my expertise not only as a psychologist but also as a neuropsychologist due the evaluation I have conducted. Also . . . ."

"OK, whatever the title is, you are not a chemist with hard science background, or an oncologist to be precise and accurate and tell whether a person has cancer or not!"

"Sorry, that is not true. Many medical professionals are not sure when diagnosing an illness. Medicine was never like math, one plus one is equal to two. Misdiagnosis or not being able to find a d . . . ."

The prosecutor interrupted Dr. Hamza to tell the court that he had no further questions.

As you may have observed, the prosecutor attempted to get the expert to admit a lack of confidence in the assessment and attempted to discredit the witness. The expert, on the other hand, remained calm and was in control of his emotions. A key point to note is that the expert did not make the exchange personal, or let the information he was attempting to present become lost by defending his process. Had he gotten upset, angry, or defensive, it would have negatively impacted his testimony and cross-examination. The expert realized the tactics of the process and responded with total calmness, confidence, and professionalism.

M. K. Hamza, PhD, LP
Clinical, Forensic, & Neuropsychology Professor,
Clinical Mental Health Counseling, Lamar University

Conclusion

In this chapter, we introduced the elementary aspects of forensic mental health counseling. As was noted, forensic involves anything related to the court system. We reviewed some of the basic concepts related to forensics and some of the areas of practice within the world of forensics. Although all counselors receive some basic training in legal and ethical issues, forensic mental health counselors must have advanced knowledge of legal concepts and be familiar with court proceedings.

Because courts have been overburdened, forensic mental health counseling has become a growing profession. There are many opportunities for mental health counselors to practice within the realm of the court system. Forensic mental health counselors can conduct custody evaluations, serve as court-appointed mediators, serve as expert witnesses, provide competency evaluations, consult with law enforcement, and exercise a range of other specialized activities. Counselors interested in this area of practice should seek additional courses and certification before engaging in professional practice.

References

American College of Certified Forensic Counselors Certification Commission. (n.d.). *National Association of Forensic Counselors, Inc.: Candidate handbook*. Fort Wayne, IN: Author.

American Counseling Association (ACA). (2005). *Code of ethics*. Alexandria, VA: Author.

American Mental Health Counselors Association (AMHCA). (2010). *Principles for AMHCA code of ethics*. Retrieved from http://www.amhca.org/assets/news/AMHCA_Code_of_Ethics_2010_w_pagination_cxd_51110.pdf

Coccaro, E. F., Berman, M. E., & Kavoussi, R. J. (1997). Assessment of life history of aggression: Development and psychometric characteristics. *Psychiatry Research, 73*, 147–157.

Côté, G., & Hodgins, S. (1990). Co-occurring mental disorders among criminal offenders. *Bulletin of the American Academy of Psychiatry and the Law, 18*(3), 271–281.

Council for Accreditation of Counseling and Related Educational Programs (CACREP). (2009). *CACREP accreditation manual: 2009 standards*. Alexandria,

VA: Author. Retrieved from http://www.cacrep.org/doc/2009%20Standards%20with%20cover.pdf

Ditton, P. M. (1999). *Special report: Mental health and treatment of inmates and probationers*. Washington, DC: US Department of Justice.

Durham v. United States, 214 F.2d 862 (1954).

Federal Bureau of Investigation (FBI). (2011). *Crime in the United States 2011*. Retrieved from http://www.fbi.gov/about-us/cjis/ucr/crime-in-the-u.s/2011/crime-in-the-u.s.-2011/fbi-releases-2011-crime-statistics

Fletcher, T. A., Brakel, S. J., & Cavanaugh, J. L. (2000). Violence in the workplace: New perspectives in forensic mental health services in the USA. *The British Journal of Psychiatry, 176*, 339–344.

Florida Mental Health Act, § 394.463(2)(a)(3) (2011).

Grisso, T. (1986). *Evaluating competencies*. New York, NY: Plenum Press.

Hayes, L. L. (2004, September). New credential to open (courtroom) doors for counselors. *Counseling Today*. Retrieved from http://www.nbfe.net/nbfe/aca_article.php

Heilbrun, K. (2001). *Principles of forensic mental health assessment*. New York, NY: Kluwer.

Jackson v. Indiana, 406 U.S. 715 (1972).

James, D. J., & Glaze, L. E. (2006, September). *Bureau of Justice Statistics special report: Mental health problems of prison and jail inmates*. Washington, DC: US Department of Justice.

Jeglic, E. L., Maile, C., & Calkins-Mercado, C. (2011). Treatment of offender populations: Implications for risk management and community reintegration. In L. Gideon & H. Sung (Eds.), *Rethinking corrections: Rehabilitation, reentry, and reintegration* (pp. 37–71). Thousand Oaks, CA: Sage. doi:10.4135/9781452230474.n3

Johnson, J. G., Cohen, P., Smailes, E., Kasen, S., Oldham, J. M., Skodol, A. E., & Brook, J. S. (2000). Adolescent personality disorders associated with violence and criminal behavior during adolescence and early adulthood. *American Journal of Psychiatry, 157*, 1406–1412.

la Forge, J., & Henderson, P. (1990). Counselor competency in the courtroom. *Journal of Counseling & Development, 68*(4), 456–459. doi:10.1002/j.1556-6676.1990.tb02530.x

Macfarlane D., Lurie S., Bettridge, S., & Barbaree H. (2004). Mental health services in the courts: A program review. *Health Law in Canada, 25*(2), 21–28.

Moore, R. O., & Simpson, L. R. (2012). *Counselors in the courtroom: Implications for counselor supervisors*. (ACAPCD-83). Alexandria, VA: American Counseling Association.

Mullen, P. E. (2000). Forensic mental health. *The British Journal of Psychiatry, 176*, 307–311.

Murray, S. N. (2011, February). Your witness. *Counseling Today*. Retrieved from http://ct.counseling.org/2011/02/your-witness/

National Board of Forensic Evaluators (NBFE). (n.d.a). National Board of Forensic Evaluators, Inc. home page. Retrieved from http://www.nbfe.net/

National Board of Forensic Evaluators (NBFE). (n.d.b). *Professional recognition: Requirements*. Retrieved from http://www.nbfe.net/requirements.php

National GAINS Center for People with Co-Occurring Disorders in the Justice System. (2004). *The prevalence of co-occurring mental illness and substance use disorders in jails*. Retrieved from http://gainscenter.samhsa.gov/pdfs/disorders/gainsjailprev.pdf

The National Judicial College. (2012). *Mental competency: Best practices model*. Retrieved from http://www.mentalcompetency.org/model/model-sec-VI.html

Nelson, E. L., & Kaushall, P. I. (1996). Deposing a mental health provider in civil lawsuits involving sexual abuse allegations. *Issues in Child Abuse Accusations, 8*(2). Retrieved from http://www.ipt-forensics.com/journal/volume8/j8_2_6.htm

Otto, R. K., & Heilbrun, K. (2002). The practice of forensic psychology: A look toward the future in light of the past. *American Psychologist, 1*, 5–18.

Oxford Dictionaries. (2012). *Forensic*. Retrieved from http://oxforddictionaries.com/definition/forensic

Petrila, J. (2004). Emerging issues in forensic mental health. *Psychiatric Quarterly, 75*, 3–19.

Poythress, N. G., Otto, R. K., & Heilbrun, K. (1991). Pretrial evaluations for criminal courts: Contemporary models of service delivery. *Journal of Mental Health Administration, 18*(3), 198–208.

Reisner, R., Slobogin, C., & Rai, A. (2009). *Law and the mental health system: Civil and criminal aspects* (5th ed.). Eagan, MN: West.

Remley, T. P., & Herlihy, B. (2010). *Ethical, legal, and professional issues in counseling* (3rd ed.). Upper Saddle River, NJ: Pearson Education.

Robbins, E., Waters, J., & Herbert, P. (1997). Competency to stand trial evaluations: A study of actual practice in two states. *Journal of the American Academy of Psychiatry and the Law, 25*(4), 469–483.

Sales, B., Manber, R., & Rohman, L. (1992). Social science research and child-custody decision making. *Applied and Preventative Psychology, 1*, 23–40.

The Sentencing Project. (2002, January). *Mentally ill offenders in the criminal justice system: An analysis and prescription*. Washington, DC: Author.

Sestoft, D. (2006). Crime and mental illness: It is time to take action. *World Psychiatry, 5*(2), 95.

Simon, R. I., & Gold, L. H. (2004). *The American Psychiatric Publishing textbook of forensic psychiatry*. Washington, DC: American Psychiatric Association.

Soothill, K., & Francis, B. (2010). The debate rumbles on: The measurement tail is now wagging the dog. *New Law Journal, 7401*, 94–95.

Springer, D. W., & Roberts, A. R. (2007). Forensic social work in the 21st century. In D. W. Springer (Ed.), *Handbook of forensic mental health with victims and offenders: Assessment, treatment, and research* (pp. 3–22). New York, NY: Springer.

Stone, H., & Taylor, A. (2000). Forensic psychiatry services. In A. Gregoire (Ed.), *Adult severe mental illness* (pp. 257–282). London, England: Greenwich Medical.

Torrey, E. F. (1999). Reinventing mental health care. *City Journal, 9*. Retrieved from http://www.city-journal.org/html/9_4_a5.html

Torrey, E. F., Kennard, A. D., Eslinger, D., Lamb, R., & Pavle, J. (2010, May). *More mentally ill persons are in jails and prisons than hospitals: A survey of the states.* Report of the Treatment Advocacy Center and National Sheriffs' Association. Retrieved from http://www.treatmentadvocacycenter.org/storage /documents/final_jails_v_hospitals_study.pdf

Treatment Advocacy Center. (2013). *State standards for assisted treatment: Civil commitment procedure for inpatient or outpatient psychiatric treatment.* Retrieved from http://www.treatmentadvocacycenter .org/storage/documents/Standards_-_The_Text -_June_2011.pdf

Wallace, C., Mullen, P. E., & Burgess, P. (2004). Criminal offending in schizophrenia over a 25-year period marked by deinstitutionalization and increasing prevalence of comorbid substance use disorders. *American Journal of Psychiatry, 161,* 716–727.

Washington State Department of Social & Health Services. (2006, June). *Forensic competency evaluation and restoration—Strategies to minimize waiting periods.* Retrieved from http://www.dshs.wa.gov /pdf/main/legrep/Leg1006/Forensic0606.pdf

Washington State Institute for Public Policy. (2013, January). *Standardizing protocols for treatment to restore competency to stand trial: Interventions and clinically appropriate time periods.* Retrieved from http://www.wsipp.wa.gov/ReportFile/1121/Wsipp _Standardizing-Protocols-for-Treatment-to-Restore -Competency-to-Stand-Trial-Interventions-and -Clinically-Appropriate-Time-Periods_Full-Report.pdf

Watson, J. C., & Sheperis, C. J. (2010). *Counselors and the right to test: Working toward professional parity.* (ACAPCD-31). Alexandria, VA: American Counseling Association.

Widiger, T. A., & Trull, T. J. (1994). Personality disorders and violence. In J. Monahan & H. J. Steadman (Eds.), *Violence and mental disorder: Developments in risk assessment* (pp. 203–226). Chicago, IL: University of Chicago.

Wiesner, M., Kim, H. K., & Capaldi, D. M. (2005). Developmental trajectories of offending: Validation and prediction to young adult alcohol use, drug use, and depressive symptoms. *Developmental Psychopathology, 17,* 251–270.

Windle, R. C., & Windle, M. (1995). Longitudinal patterns of physical aggression: Associations with adult social, psychiatric, and personality functioning and testosterone levels. *Developmental Psychopathology, 7,* 563–585.

Wrightsman, L. S., & Fulero, S. M. (2005). *Forensic psychology.* Belmont, CA: Thomson Wadsworth.

13

Addictions Counseling

TODD F. LEWIS

CHAPTER OVERVIEW

This chapter provides a broad overview of addictions counseling. The aim is to summarize theoretical, clinical, and research perspectives in the treatment of substance abuse problems from a practitioner's point of view. First, the scope of the problem, definition of key terms, and phases of addiction are discussed. Next, the theoretical models of addiction, which serve as philosophical foundations for any addictions counseling practice, are covered. The focus then turns to the important topic of screening, assessment, and diagnosis of substance use problems. Individual treatment considerations, including relapse prevention and strategies, are discussed next. The chapter concludes with a checklist of key questions and considerations when counseling someone struggling with substance-related problems.

LEARNING OBJECTIVES

The learning objectives for this chapter are designed to be consistent with the 2009 Council for Accreditation of Counseling and Related Educational Programs Standards (CACREP, 2009). As such, upon completion of this chapter, the student will have knowledge of the following clinical mental health counseling standards:

1. Knows the models of treatment, prevention, recovery, relapse prevention, and continuing care for addictive disorders and related problems. (C.2)
2. Understands the principles and philosophies of addiction-related self-help programs. (C.6)
3. Provides appropriate counseling strategies when working with clients with addiction and co-occurring disorders. (D.3)
4. Identifies standard screening and assessment instruments for substance use disorders and process addictions. (G.4)
5. Knows the impact of co-occurring addictive disorders on medical and psychological disorders. (K.2)

INTRODUCTION

Substance abuse and addiction have become serious problems facing our society, exacting a toll that manifests as individual, family, community, occupational, and financial consequences. Indeed, substance abuse and addiction capture the daily attention of media outlets, law enforcement, and government agencies. Despite significant empirical research on, and awareness of, the substance abuse and addiction problems in the United States, prevalence rates have not declined in a number of years. As such, a significant reality that clinical mental health counselors are beginning to face in their mental health practice is the relatively large number of clients who present with substance abuse and/or addiction issues. These issues may not surface at the start of counseling, but over time the metaphorical "elephant in the living room" emerges. What do clinical mental health counselors need to know in order to work with clients presenting with substance abuse issues? How do they go about counseling those struggling with substance abuse and addiction issues?

SUBSTANCE ABUSE AND ADDICTION

The scope of substance use and abuse in the United States is difficult to pin down, with estimates varying across studies. However, a relatively reliable means of assessing the extent of substance abuse and addiction has been through the annual National Survey on Drug Use and Health (NSDUH), engineered by the Substance Abuse and Mental Health Services Administration (SAMHSA). The most recent results (2011) from the NSDUH paint a bleak picture. In 2011, an estimated 8.7% (approximately 22.5 million people age 12 and older) of the US population had consumed an illegal substance or abused a medication within the past 30 days (National Institute on Drug Abuse [NIDA], 2012). The overall trend in illicit substance use rose from 2002 to 2010 (NIDA, 2012). Statistics on alcohol use also are alarming. In 2011, 30.0% of men and 13.9% of women age 12 and older reported engaging in heavy, episodic drinking (five or more drinks on one occasion) within the past 30 days (NIDA, 2012). One can only conclude that the prevalence of illicit drug and alcohol use and abuse poses significant challenges in our society.

Aside from the alarming prevalence rates, substance abuse and addiction exact a colossal toll on our society, in both financial and personal terms. Although statistics vary depending on the study (Doweiko, 2011), it has been estimated that the annual cost of substance-related disorders in the United States is $375 *billion* (Falco, 2005, as cited in Doweiko, 2011). Damaged relationships, domestic violence, medical problems, work problems, psychological problems, intoxicated driving, and increased risk of suicide are but a handful of the personal problems that are often associated with abuse and addiction.

Clearly, the extent of substance use is a cause for concern, and the search for understanding causes, prevention, and treatment continues (Miller, 2005). In recent years, mental health trainers have emphasized addictions training either in their graduate programs or as continuing education. The 2009 Council for the Accreditation of Counseling and Related Educational Programs (CACREP) curriculum standards now include addiction as an important component throughout programs of study. CACREP has a separate accreditation for an addictions track within counselor education and related programs.

Some Key Terminology

There is definitely a common vernacular related to the addictions field. According to Miller (2005), grasping this language helps substance abuse counselors communicate effectively with clients and other helping professionals. The following list, though by no means exhaustive, gives a general idea of the major substance abuse terms, most of which are used throughout the chapter.

1. ***Substance misuse***—Using a drug in greater quantities or for reasons other than those prescribed by a doctor; experiencing negative consequences as a result of using substances inappropriately.
2. ***Abuse***—Continued use of a substance in a manner, amount, or situation despite problems or negative consequences of such use; using a drug in excess of accepted social standards.
3. ***Dependence***—Compulsive substance use despite negative consequences. There are generally two types of dependence. Physiological dependence is when the brain and body react to substance use by developing a physical need for the drug to function normally. Psychological dependence is developing an intense psychological need and/or craving for the drug, often times to deal with stress or some problem. Individuals can have either form of dependence or both.
4. ***Tolerance***—Results from physical and psychological adaptations of the individual. Individuals are tolerant if they need increasing quantities of the drug in order to create the same effects as the original dose.
5. ***Withdrawal***—Physiological and psychological symptoms when a dependent person ceases drug use. As a general rule, withdrawal symptoms and experiences are the opposite of the drug's effect.
6. ***Addiction***—Analogous to substance dependence. Addiction refers to the out-of-control use of substances that results in numerous personal, social, occupational, and familial consequences. Addiction is the layperson's term for those who have hit "rock bottom" related to their substance use. It connotes a serious, progressive, and dangerous problem with substances. Dependence, on the other hand, is the *clinical* term that addiction specialists use when communicating with each other and/or diagnosing the client's symptoms. However, in my opinion, the terms *addiction* and *dependence* can essentially be used interchangeably.

The vernacular of addictions counseling is important to grasp when working with those struggling with substance-related problems. Clarifying the extent of their substance use can provide valuable feedback to clients who may in fact be surprised that their behavior meets criteria for a substance use disorder when they thought they were just casual users.

Phases of Addiction

Addiction is often perceived as an insidious, progressive process that gradually breaks down the individual, and without intervention, the person is likely to suffer serious injury or worse. Nakken (1996) generated a model of how addiction progresses. According to Nakken, the addictive process is an aimless, out-of-control searching for wholeness, happiness, and peace through a relationship with an object or event. Nakken highlighted three phases of addiction.

PHASE 1 (INTERNAL CHANGE)   Phase 1 begins when the first high from the substance is experienced. Relationships with drugs replace natural relationships (family/friends, higher power, self, community). An addictive personality emerges from the addictive process; it is not necessarily present before the addiction begins. According to Nakken (1996), the addictive personality splits into two parts—the self side and the addict side—which propels one into an addictive cycle. The addictive cycle is a continuous sequence in which the person (a) experiences pain (either physical or psychological), (b) which is followed by a need to use, (c) which is then followed by using the substance, (d) which leads to more pain from acting out, (b) which is followed by a need to use and so on as the cycle repeats itself.

PHASE 2 (LIFESTYLE CHANGE)   Phase 2 is when individuals are out of control internally and behaviorally. They have developed a deep, totally consuming dependency. They may develop addictive rituals, and their personal relationships with others worsen (Nakken, 1996).

PHASE 3 (LIFE BREAKDOWN)   Phase 3 is marked by stress caused by ever-increasing pain, anger, and fear from acting out. All normal forms of coping (from self) break down. Resolving emotional issues works *against* the addictive process. The addict side of the self wants to be alone; the self side craves emotional connection with others. Physical signs of breaking down begin to emerge (Nakken, 1996).

Nakken's (1996) model is an example of the seemingly progressive nature of addiction. An interesting component of this model is how the addicted person abandons relationships with others in favor of a relationship with the substance. A key implication for counseling is that the counselor will need to work to help clients reestablish relationships with others (as opposed to the chemical) in order to heal. Indeed, this may be a reason why many people addicted to alcohol commit to Alcoholics Anonymous (AA). AA is, among other things, a venue where individuals can reestablish relationships with human beings who care for their survival and happiness. In addition, a significant component of substance abuse counseling programs is group counseling, another setting in which positive relationships are established.

MODELS OF ADDICTION

Models of addiction are explanatory mechanisms that can help practitioners conceptualize addictive behavior. Proponents of each model hold differing assumptions as to the causes and best treatment options for addictive behavior. As such, the models give practitioners an underlying philosophy from which to guide clinical intervention. Here follows a review of the major models of addiction, including their advantages and disadvantages.

Disease (or Medical) Model

Adherents of the disease, or medical, model suggest that addiction is a progressive, deteriorating disease that proceeds through a series of stages, from slow deterioration to, if left untreated, death (Thombs, 2006). From this perspective, addiction is conceptualized as a long-term condition that can be managed but not cured. Individuals who become addicted experience a loss of control related to their drug use. Addiction is a primary disease in that it does not result from some underlying psychological, sociological, familial, or moral mechanism (although these may be results of the addiction). The only acceptable treatment goal in this model is complete abstinence; harm reduction or other "controlled use" treatment approaches are seen as setting the client up for failure.

ADVANTAGES AND DISADVANTAGES OF THE DISEASE MODEL Conceptualizing substance addiction as a deteriorating, progressive disease has done much to remove the societal and moral stigma of substance abuse and dependence. The result has been less shame and guilt associated with substance abuse, resulting in more individuals getting help or treatment (Thombs, 2006). From a counseling perspective, the disease model is attractive in that there is no ambiguity about counseling goals; a clear, straightforward treatment goal is abstinence. A final advantage is that the disease model has associated language (i.e., brain disease, 12 steps, AA, recovery, etc.) that allows for communality and communication among clinicians and clients. This shared vernacular promotes ease of understanding among all parties involved.

Unfortunately, the disease model is not without its disadvantages. Those who do not subscribe to the disease model concept, or who do not find a fit with its assumptions, may feel excluded. Fisher and Harrison (2012) argued that the disease model pardons individuals from taking personal responsibility for their substance problems and leads them to make excuses for deviant behavior ("it's not me; it's my disease"). In addition, the disease model appears to ignore other variables that play a role in addictive behavior, such as psychological, sociological, and environmental factors. From a counseling perspective, the disease model does not offer much in terms of counseling interventions, leading to treatment that is too simplistic. Key concepts of the disease model (e.g., it is a progressive disease; use leads to loss of control) are not supported by empirical evidence, especially related to alcoholism (Pattison, Sobell, & Sobell, 1977; Thombs, 2006). Finally, one may reasonably ask where to draw the line in terms of the disease concept. In other words, what will be called a disease next? Gambling? Internet use? Shopping?

ABSTINENCE CONTRACT Most people do not realize how difficult it is to give something up that they know is not good for them, but at the same time provides comfort and security. This has certainly been true for students I teach in my substance abuse counseling class. To foster greater appreciation for how difficult remaining drug free can be, I require that my students pick something that they know is not very good for them (e.g., a food, drink, behavior, or habit) and discontinue this behavior for the length of the semester. They sign an "abstinence contract" that specifies exactly what they will give up. I ask students to list what positive behavior they will engage in to replace the bad behavior (e.g., exercise). Common items that students give up include nail biting, swearing, diet soda, candy, sugar, Facebook, and so forth. Students really get a feel for how difficult it is to give up something they have relied on, and they are sometimes surprised by the feelings and emotions that surface when they can no longer self-soothe. They experience episodes of indifference, anger, sadness, relapse, and recommitment. Throughout the semester, students journal their experiences, process their feelings in small groups, and create an end-of-semester creative project in which they share their journey with the class. The abstinence contract is an excellent way for students to feel a little more compassion toward the clients they will serve.

Moral Model

Proponents of the moral model believe that substance addiction is a matter of moral weakness, flawed character, and poor decision making (Fisher & Harrison, 2012). Indeed, addiction is viewed as sinful, and thus the addicted person should be punished or is in need of spiritual intervention. The general philosophy of the moral modal is that because of a bankrupt spiritual life, the individual uses drugs in search of a higher power. The societal perspective that poor choice must be punished is why the moral model has served as the underpinning of our present legal system.

ADVANTAGES AND DISADVANTAGES OF THE MORAL MODEL The advantages of the moral model appear to address some of the disadvantages of the disease model. Indeed, the moral model places choice back into the equation, which can help promote personal responsibility. It empowers people to make better choices about their lives. The moral model may appeal to individuals or even a society that holds strong positions on what behavior is good or bad, just or unjust.

The moral model is not without its critics, and many of its disadvantages have helped the disease model gain notoriety. As you might imagine, critics of the moral model point out that it is too judgmental and tends to minimize the complexity of substance addiction (Fisher & Harrison, 2012). If addiction is as simple as making choices, then why do so many individuals have trouble stopping unhealthy behavior and making better choices? Another concern with the moral model is that it has perpetuated the negative stigma related to substance addiction. As a result, the belief that addicts are somehow unworthy, flawed, or have some inherent weakness can foster a sense of shame, culpability, and fault (Thombs, 2006). Instead of encouraging those struggling with addiction to seek help, proponents of the moral model may inadvertently engender resistance to treatment by those who need it because of their hidden guilt and their shame from feeling judged.

Psychological Model

The psychological model holds that addiction is driven by psychological stress. As such, substance addiction is viewed as a form of coping with negative affective states and other behavioral and psychological issues. Addiction from this perspective is not considered to be primary; rather it is the result of, or secondary to, psychological stress. Proponents of the psychological model argue that an addictive personality exists, even though research has been equivocal on this matter (Hart & Ksir, 2012).

The psychological model has intuitive appeal and, in my experience, clients readily see the connection between their addiction problems and psychological struggles in their lives (e.g., depression, anxiety). Prentiss (2007) put forth the notion that all substance addiction results from internal psychological pain that must be addressed if any lasting change is to occur. This basic underlying philosophy has served as the foundation for Prentiss's well-known Passages Addiction Treatment Center in California. Unfortunately, however, mental health problems have sometimes gotten "lost in the shuffle" in terms of professionals' understanding their potential influence on addictive behavior.

ADVANTAGES AND DISADVANTAGES OF THE PSYCHOLOGICAL MODEL As with the disease model, the psychological model helps to assuage the guilt and shame connected to drug use. In essence, the addicted individual might say, "I am using as a way to medicate my underlying depression," rather than admit having a character flaw. This model helps individuals conceptualize the underlying causes of substance use. Rollo May (1981) likened problems in living to physical symptoms such as a fever. When one has a fever, there is an underlying infection that needs to be rooted out. Once the infection is gone, the fever (or symptom) disappears. Similarly, according to the psychological model, substance abuse and addiction can be seen as symptoms of an underlying "infection." This infection can be past trauma or abuse, underlying death anxiety, or deep feelings of guilt and shame. Once these issues are addressed, individuals will no longer feel compelled to engage in deleterious substance use as a way to medicate their emotional lives.

A key advantage of the psychological model over the disease model and the moral model is the greater range of interventions and strategies used to help clients address underlying psychological issues. Counselors can better fit treatment protocols that fit the client's situation. An underlying assumption of the disease model is that abstinence is the only alternative; and the best ways to achieve this are 12-step group attendance, medical management (if available), and talking to a counselor every now and then. Proponents of the psychological model also may encourage abstinence (and any other goal that best fits the client's circumstances), but the way to achieve this may be through cognitive, behavioral, gestalt, motivational interviewing, or eclectic methods. Counseling takes greater priority, with 12-step groups and medication management serving as useful adjuncts.

A final advantage of the psychological model is that by addressing the underlying psychological causes of addiction, the risk of relapse is lessened, thereby offering optimism for a sustained recovery. Proponents of the psychological model, such as Prentiss (2007), argue that alcoholism and addiction can be cured, primarily because the emotional and psychological baggage has been healed.

As with the disease model, a disadvantage of adhering to the psychological model is that it may encourage clients to blame their addiction on some underlying psychological problem rather than taking responsibility for their behavior. A related (and unintentional) consequence of the psychological model is that it may promote "problem generation" as a way to continue substance abuse. For example, a client might exaggerate his or her anxiety as a way to justify using drugs. An additional disadvantage is the model's constricted focus; sociocultural, biological, and spiritual aspects of addiction are not emphasized or given appropriate attention.

Sociocultural Model

Proponents of the sociocultural model suggest that familial, peer, and cultural influences play a large and primary role in the development of substance addiction. Certainly, it would be difficult to argue that sociocultural factors do not have at least some influence on the development of addiction (Thombs, 2006). As such, for any intervention to be effective, one must examine the individual in relation to his or her surrounding environment.

Thombs (2006) discussed four primary sociological functions of substance use. The first function is that drugs *facilitate social interaction*. An example of this is the role that alcohol plays in our society. In American culture, alcohol is seen as a way to enhance one's social life and pleasure, especially after a difficult day or week of work. Beer advertisers often depict employees blowing off steam after a tough week of work, watching a game, and having a beer. The second function is taking a *timeout from social obligations*. The pressure to succeed, especially in US society, can bring about unwanted stress; substances are seen as a way of letting go of these responsibilities, at least temporarily. In the case of extreme substance use, such as abuse and dependence, individuals may use substances as a backlash against society's mandate to achieve, get ahead, and produce. Addiction is a demonstration of freedom from conforming to society's definition of success (Thombs, 2006).

The third function is *promoting group solidarity*. Here, individuals use substances as a way to bond with other members of their peer, ethnic, or racial group. I recently counseled a young teenager who had ingested an entire bottle of cough medicine. Upon inquiry, it was revealed that he was involved in a group of peers that valued experimentation and risk taking. Using substances was a way to promote cohesion among this group of friends. Many cultural groups have strict rules regarding consumption, such as it is OK to drink in moderation but intoxication is not allowed. Other groups may view drinking or drug use as acceptable in that it is a way to cope with a personal history of oppression, violence, and uncertainty (Thombs, 2006).

The final function of substance abuse is *repudiation of middle-class values via drug subcultures*. Drug subcultures are a means for individuals to reject and "flip off" middle- or upper-class, White, American values. Each subculture has its own values, norms, social situations, and roles for its members. For example, in the cocaine subculture, there is a clear line of authority, from the kingpin to the runners who are responsible for selling and delivering the product. As Levitt and Dubner (2005), coauthors of the best-selling book *Freakonomics,* pointed out, drug subcultures in large cities often have elaborate authority structures, rules of operations, and norms. And, despite their illegal and underground operations, these subcultures are remarkably effective, efficient, and successful, thereby rivaling many top government and private corporations.

ADVANTAGES AND DISADVANTAGES OF THE SOCIOCULTURAL MODEL The main advantage of the sociocultural model is that it offers a systemic look at substance abuse and addiction. Through this systemic perspective, community leaders are encouraged to promote norms that do not include substance use. From a counseling perspective, the sociocultural model encourages practitioners to understand the value structure of their clients based on the culture in which they live. If clinical mental health counselors fail to understand their clients' values, which may be quite different from their own, resistance is sure to ensue. There is benefit to value exploration. Values play a large role in motivations, hopes, desires, and fears. Potential conflicts between counselor and client value systems can be avoided if clinicians take an open stance toward exploring these differences (Thombs, 2006). It may be worthwhile to conduct an honest, genuine, nonjudgmental exploration of the consequences of value priorities the client holds.

As with other models discussed, a disadvantage of the sociocultural model is that responsibility for one's substance addiction may be placed on peers, the family, or the larger culture instead of self. Critics argue that whereas these environmental factors most likely play a role in addictive behavior, the individual still must assume responsibility for making the choice to use substances. Overreliance on the sociocultural model also may typecast certain cultures or subcultures as "drug abusers." Such stereotypes may negatively impact the type and quality of care afforded to those addicted to substances. Finally, counseling may become overly complex, with more and more systems and individuals involved. The risk here is that what a client accomplishes in counseling may inadvertently be undermined by sociological forces outside of the counseling setting. To combat this, clinical mental health counselors need to be aware of the plethora of services a client may be able to access in the community and then attempt to work collaboratively with these resources.

Biopsychosocial Model

As one may suspect, the biopsychosocial model incorporates many factors—including biological, psychological, and sociological elements—that, in combination, lead to addiction. This model is composed of elements from each of the individual models and is built on the assumption that addiction most likely has a numerous causes, each contributing to the final common pathway called addiction. By implication, addiction treatment needs to be holistic and address the biological, psychological, and cultural elements that underlie addictive behavior.

ADVANTAGES AND DISADVANTAGES OF THE BIOPSYCHOSOCIAL MODEL   An advantage of the biopsychosocial model is that all potential causes are "captured" in one model. Treatment, although complex, addresses the bevy of influences that uniquely contribute to addiction. The biopsychosocial model allows for flexibility in addiction care, as any one factor can be a focus for treatment, depending on client circumstances. Unfortunately, what is considered an advantage of this model may also be a disadvantage: treatment can get bogged down and overly complicated with many different facets working at the same time. Regrettably, this can create inefficiency and bewilderment for both the client and treatment providers.

Counseling Interventions Based on the Models of Addiction

Why is it important for clinical mental health counselors to have a working knowledge of the models of addiction? The various models of addiction help counselors conceptualize the etiology, or how substance-related problems develop, and also provide direction for counseling interventions. Specific interventions depend largely on what philosophy of addiction clinical mental health counselors adopt as their modus operandi. For example, counselors who subscribe to the disease model will most likely establish abstinence as the only goal, encourage 12-step attendance, and perhaps conduct group and individual counseling, as needed. For those who adopt the psychological model, any theoretical approach may be used to help clients resolve underlying issues that are believed to be the root cause of addiction. It is important that clinical mental health counselors take some time to consider the model or models that resonate most with their understanding of addiction.

The reality of addictions counseling suggests that many counselors will take an eclectic approach, adopting elements of each model in their work with clients. For example, a clinical mental health counselor may stress that abstinence is the only goal (disease model) with a client who has been drinking for 20 years and has significant physiological damage. The counselor believes that the best way to help the client reach this goal is cognitive therapy methods (psychological model). Over time, the counselor also stresses the client's choice in whether to remain alcohol dependent or not (moral model). Environmental factors, such as the client's peer network and familial atmosphere, are addressed throughout the counseling sessions (sociocultural model). As one can see, elements of each model can be made to work synergistically to help clients in recovery.

12-STEP GROUP ATTENDANCE One of the goals I have for the substance abuse counseling class I teach every fall is to help students become more empathetic toward those struggling with substance abuse and addiction. Many students enter class with preconceived notions of the typical addict, who might be of a different race than their own, who is of a lower social class, and who has hit rock bottom. An assignment that I have used for several years to help generate empathy is to mandate that students attend four open 12-step group meetings in the community, spaced throughout the semester (one of the groups can be online). After the students' expressions of considerable protest and anxiety, I ask whether clients might feel the same way when they are encouraged to attend Alcoholics Anonymous (AA) or Narcotics Anonymous (NA). I provide guidelines for how to act (e.g., don't go as a large group; go only to open meetings), but it is up to individual students which meetings they choose and with whom they go. I also encourage attendance at multiple home fellowships, which provide students the opportunity to observe that people struggling with addiction are from all walks of life. I have been amazed at how much students gain from these experiences. Although they are quite anxious at the start, they then realize that their psychological defenses and anxiety might be exactly what is going on with clients who attend their first meeting.

ASSESSMENT AND DIAGNOSIS OF SUBSTANCE ADDICTION

The assessment and diagnostic process plays a critical first step in helping clients who are in the throes of an addiction. According to Juhnke (2002), assessment serves as the foundation of the recovery process. It can help identify clients who fail to see their addiction as a problem, yet clearly are in need of clinical attention. A well-executed, thorough assessment helps clinicians conceptualize client problems, clarifies the diagnostic picture, and provides a possible road map for treatment planning. Inquiry into substance use and abuse problems should, at the very least, be a part of every intake assessment. The process includes observation, intent listening, as well as more standardized questionnaires.

One should not think the assessment process has a definite beginning and ending, perhaps after the first session, and then is over. In fact, clinical assessment is a complicated, ongoing process in which the clinical picture becomes clearer over time (Doweiko, 2011). The term *assessment* actually entails three primary components: screening, assessment, and diagnosis (Doweiko, 2011). Screening for alcohol and other drug problems is a brief assessment procedure that is *not* designed to provide a definitive diagnosis. Rather, screening allows clinical mental health counselors to determine whether further assessment is needed through more formal means.

A common screening device for alcohol problems is the CAGE questionnaire (Ewing, 1984). CAGE—which stands for cut down, annoyed, guilty, and eye-opener—and is reflected in four questions: (a) Have you ever felt that you needed to **C**ut down on your drinking? (b) Have you ever been **A**nnoyed by others who have commented that you drink too much? (c) Have you ever felt bad or **G**uilty about your drinking? (d) Have you ever had a drink first thing in the morning to steady your nerves and get rid of a hangover (**E**ye-opener)? An affirmative response to one of these questions suggests further assessment for alcohol problems; an affirmative response to two or more suggests serious alcohol problems.

The Substance Abuse Subtle Screening Inventory (SASSI-3), and its adolescent version (SASSI-A2), is a 10-minute screening device designed to determine whether one is at "high probability" of substance dependence. The SASSI instruments have become increasingly popular as screening tools for substance abuse and dependence problems (Juhnke, 2002). In addition to direct questions about alcohol and drug use, the subtle part of the SASSI includes questions that are not obviously tied to substance use, but rather indirectly predict substance use behavior. For example, questions about negative emotions, poor relationships, or family problems are not directly related to drug use but can be associated with these behaviors. One strength of the SASSI is its ability to determine levels of defensive responding, an important gauge when screening for substance abuse problems.

Screening for alcohol and other drugs can be performed effectively without the use of formal instruments. Many screening devices are in the public domain, available free of charge, and quite effective in teasing out drug use problems (Miller, Forcehimes, & Zweben, 2011). Even simple questions that directly ask about alcohol and drug use, which can easily be incorporated into any intake evaluation, can be a good starting point. Brown, Leonard, Saunders, and Papasoulioutis (1997) created two questions to detect problems with substance use: (a) In the last year, have you ever drunk or used drugs more than you meant to? and (b) Have you felt you wanted or needed to cut down on your drinking or drug use in the last year? Brown et al. (1997) noted that when a respondent answers at least one question in the affirmative, this response can effectively (but not perfectly) discriminate between those with a substance use disorder and those without one. As such, further follow-up would be warranted.

If, through the screening process, a client indicates possible substance use problems, more formal means of assessment and evaluation are warranted. One useful follow-up procedure is the clinical interview (Doweiko, 2011), which may take a session or two, but the extra time can be well worth it. An effective clinical interview addresses the extent of substance use, substance use history, possible causes, antecedents, motivations, and other important factors that provide context and direction for treatment planning. Although the components of a clinical interview vary, its major parts might look like the following:

1. *Referral source.* Who referred the client? With client permission, it might be important to get his or her perspective on the client's substance abuse issues.
2. *History of substance use behavior.* History can include when substance use began as well as periods or times when the client was abstinent from drugs.
3. *Prior treatment history.* Understanding prior treatment history can help the clinician determine what has worked and not worked as well as the extent of the substance use problem (whether the client has been in and out of treatment, which suggests a more severe problem with drug use).
4. *Current life functioning.* This section of the interview generally entails the health of one's emotional state. Although it is a broad category, problems in many areas of one's emotional life many indirectly suggest a substance use issue.
5. *Family history of substance abuse.* Family history of abuse can be an important indicator of substance use problems. For example, if the client reports growing up in a home in which both parents used drugs, the probability increases that the client struggles with the same issues.
6. *General personal history.* This section entails questions about work, legal problems, relationships, and so forth. The clinician has much flexibility here; in essence, he or she is gauging how the client has functioned up to this point.

These six generic components of a clinical interview are based on my clinical experiences and training, but are certainly not the only way to go about conducting the interview. Other topics, such as client motivation and religious/spiritual development, also may be important components. The substance abuse clinician should exercise a degree of flexibility and tailor his or her assessment and treatment procedures based on client needs. I agree with Juhnke (2002) in that the clinical interview allows the clinician to get to know the client and build rapport, which is more difficult with the exclusive use of formal assessment instruments. An effective assessment process, then, would seem to occur with a combination of the clinical interview and assessment tools, if necessary. A quality assessment helps clinical mental health counselors determine a diagnosis. The next section briefly covers how substance disorders are diagnosed.

DSM-5: Addiction and Related Disorders

The American Psychiatric Association recently updated its *Diagnostic and Statistical Manual of Mental Disorders* (DSM) to the fifth edition. Perhaps the most notable change related to substance disorders in the DSM-5 is that the section where they can be found is now titled "Addiction and Related Disorders," rather than "Substance Related Disorders." Addiction, which is considered more of a layperson's term related to severe substance use, is used in the DSM-5 to reflect non-substance-related addiction problems, such as gambling (www.dsm5.org). However, the word *addiction* is used as a description rather than a diagnosis.

In addition to changing the section title, the DSM-5 did away with the terms *abuse* and *dependence* when making a diagnosis and replaced them with a single diagnosis: *substance use disorder* (APA, 2013). For example, in previous editions of the DSM, a client would have been diagnosed with alcohol abuse or alcohol dependence. In the DSM-5, however, the client would be diagnosed with alcohol use disorder. The substance use disorder can range from mild (client meets two to three specified criteria) to severe (client meets six or more of these criteria). In this manner, substance use is truly viewed on a continuum. Criteria are clustered into four groups: impaired control over the substance (e.g., taking the substance in larger quantities than intended); social impairment (e.g., difficulty managing daily tasks because of use); risky use (e.g., continuing to use despite adverse health effects); and a fourth group that contains tolerance and withdrawal (APA, 2013).

Finally, the DSM-5 allows for diagnosis of a client based on the type of substance. For example, the client may have a cannabis use disorder, an alcohol use disorder, or a tobacco use disorder (APA, 2013). In addition, intoxication on a substance and withdrawal from a substance are diagnoses. As you can imagine, intoxication and withdrawal are relatively short-term diagnoses.

The removal of abuse and dependence from the substance-related diagnoses—and the movement to diagnosing across a band or spectrum of abuse—is probably a good thing. In my opinion, substance use *is* most likely on a continuum of use, from less severe to more severe. Technically, a client could meet two criteria for dependence, but no criteria for abuse. In the past, this client would have slipped through the cracks and not received a diagnosis (called a "diagnostic orphan"), despite having obvious problems with substance use. The use of a continuum in the DSM-5 should help clinical mental health counselors best treat clients with substance use issues.

TREATING COMORBIDITY

It is rare that clients attend counseling with only one presenting problem. In addition to substance abuse or addiction, many struggle with concomitant anxiety, depression, eating disorders, and relationship problems. The term *comorbidity* (also known as dual diagnosis and co-occurring disorders) refers to clients who have one or more disorders related to drug and alcohol use and one or more mental health disorders (Center for Substance Abuse Treatment, 2005). In other words, clients diagnosed with multiple disorders are experiencing significant life problems. This creates more complexity in the assessment and diagnostic process. Evans (1998) noted the importance of accurately assessing substance use disorders and mental health disorders, and knowing what symptoms are attributable to each. It also is important to get a sense of what came first, the mental health problem or the addiction problem. Such information helps to determine the focus for treatment planning.

Miller (2005) suggested that paying attention to the client's recovery process is an effective way to clarify whether a co-occurring disorder is present. For example, if a client does not feel any better after a period of abstinence from drugs, an underlying psychological disorder might be present. If a client fails to respond to any counseling or treatment approach for a mental health problem, a substance use issue may be the reason. As an additional concern, combining psychopharmacological interventions with drugs of abuse can have disastrous effects for the client. A solid assessment can help formulate the most appropriate treatment. Closely observing the client's response to treatment and recovery can inform the treatment plan.

Because of the greater complexity surrounding co-occurring disorders, counselors are encouraged to contact all parties who have involvement with the client's well-being and care. This might include family members, past treatment providers, physicians, and friends (Center for Substance Abuse Treatment, 2005). Securing information from important others in the client's life can add essential components to aid in client conceptualization and diagnosis. Counselors also are encouraged to become familiar with the criteria related to mental health disorders (Center for Substance Abuse Treatment, 2005), including the most common associated with substance abuse: personality disorders, anxiety disorders, and mood disorders. Much of the evaluation process related to co-occurring disorders follows traditional assessment methods. However, clinicians are encouraged to be flexible with their assessment tools and approaches as new information emerges throughout the process. According to Thombs (2006), comorbidity is one of the least understood problems in medicine. However, as research continues to develop in this area, some preliminary findings are encouraging.

Traditional treatment approaches to comorbidity were based on the idea that substance abuse and mental health problems should be treated separately by different specialists (Thombs, 2006). As such, clients would see one specialist for addiction problems and another for mental health issues. Although intuitively this separation of treatment is appealing, it has proven unsuccessful and inefficient, leading to an integrated treatment model (Drake, Mercer-McFadden, Mueser, McHugo, & Bond, 1998).

Research has shown that the most effective integrated treatment for comorbidity is long term, stage based, and motivational, whereby clinicians are trained in the treatment of both substance use and mental health (Drake et al., 1998). Long term is a critical aspect of integrated care because of the additional time needed for clients who have multiple problems in living (Thombs, 2006). Stability in their environment over a long period of time promotes a sense of safety and a chance to establish recovery. The motivational element of integrated care allows for the development of a strong alliance between client and counselor. Client input is valued, and choice is respected and honored. Clients are not mandated or forced to do anything that goes against their core values. The National Institute on Drug Abuse (2009) has provided support for the integrated treatment model.

Miller (2005) noted that clients with co-occurring disorders may be at greater risk for relapse due to their multiple, complex problems. Indeed, a common risk factor for relapse is negative emotional states that can accompany a psychiatric diagnosis. Thus, relapse prevention strategies should be infused within the counseling process. For a more extensive review of treatment for co-occurring disorders, see Center for Substance Abuse Treatment (2005). Miller (2005) provided online resources that clients with co-occurring disorders can consult for education, skill development, and support: Double Trouble in Recovery (www.doubletroubleinrecovery.org) and Dual Recovery Anonymous (www.draonline.org).

TREATMENT METHODS AND INTERVENTIONS

This section covers several counseling methods and interventions to use when working with clients struggling with substance abuse and addiction. The intention is to provide an overview of these common approaches, as well as guidelines that emanate from empirical research. First, however, we turn briefly to two special considerations in substance abuse counseling: ethical and multicultural issues.

Ethical and Legal Issues

Ethical and legal issues are a critical part of any counselor training program. Probably all counseling students are familiar with the general guidelines for confidentiality from their courses, workshops, and the ACA ethical code. In the substance abuse and addiction field, however, the Code of Federal Regulations (CFR), published annually by the US Government Printing Office (2014), places specific mandates on confidentiality when working with clients struggling with substance addiction. These regulations were created because individuals with substance use problems were reluctant to seek help if confidentiality could not be guaranteed (Fisher & Harrison, 2012). Consider the resistance a client addicted to an illegal substance might feel when calling a treatment facility. Without federal protection of confidentiality, acknowledgment of addiction to an illegal substance is essentially an admission of guilt (Fisher & Harrison, 2012). The specific code of federal regulations for alcohol and other drug services is 42 CFR, Public Health.

According to Fisher and Harrison (2012), 42 CFR addresses releasing of records and other information about clients who abuse substances and is a *very* strict legislation. At its core, any mental health professionals who work for a program or agency that provides any substance abuse counseling or treatment services, *and receives federal funding*, must comply with 42 CFR. Legally, clinicians cannot provide any identifying information about clients who receive addiction services from programs that fall under the regulation (i.e., those that receive federal funding). Despite the strict nature of this federal law, there are some exceptions, such as client written consent and medical emergencies (Fisher & Harrison, 2012).

A complete exploration of ethical and legal considerations related to substance abuse counseling is beyond the scope of this chapter. Certainly, however, 42 CFR is a major law, and clinical mental health counselors, *even if they do not specifically counsel substance abuse clients yet are employed in an agency that provides these services,* need to be aware of this legislation. For an excellent review of the ethical and legal issues facing addiction counselors, see Fisher and Harrison (2012).

Multicultural Issues in Substance Abuse Counseling

As US society becomes more multifarious, the need for multiculturally competent, effective mental health and addictions counselors is more critical than ever. In addictions counseling, understanding a client's sociocultural background not only shows respect, sensitivity, and awareness, but also enhances treatment outcomes. As previously discussed in the "Sociocultural Model" section, substance abuse and addiction do not occur in a vacuum. Cultural norms, values, and perspectives on drug use can have a profound influence on drug-using behaviors. Failure to account for these influences does the client a great disservice.

According to Miller (2005), multicultural counseling takes into account differences and developing the ability to competently work with these differences. In actuality, of course, every human being is unique, with differing values, roles, perspectives, motivations, tendencies, personalities, and so forth. Indeed, working with differences occurs with every client that walks through the consulting room door. Some differences are more pronounced, whereas others are more subtle. The bottom line is that addictions counselors must take a stance in which these differences, however small, are honored and incorporated into any treatment plan. Counselors must be aware of how their own culture impacts them; of how some groups have endured great hardship, oppression, and discrimination throughout history; and of how to communicate effectively across cultural lines (Miller, 2005).

An example may clarify these guidelines. Assume a White counselor is working with a Hispanic American client of a low socioeconomic status (SES) who is struggling with cocaine dependence. From a multicultural perspective, a competent clinical mental health counselor would be aware of and sensitive to the economic oppression and discriminatory struggles many Hispanic American individuals have faced in the United States. A disproportionate number of Hispanic Americans may not be able to pursue opportunities for education and economic success due to institutional racism or poorly funded social services. With this background information in mind, the clinical mental health counselor can avoid mistakenly applying counseling theory and technique as though the client might not have had such disadvantages. Cultural sensitivity places the counselor in a better position to appreciate cultural differences, explore the client's take on the substance use problem, explore potential barriers to employment and other social services, and devise an appropriate treatment plan that takes cultural issues into account.

Substance abuse and addiction do not discriminate; people from all walks of life are affected and experience both misery and celebrations of success. Alcoholics Anonymous is one organization that appears to espouse the philosophy that, no matter what one's background or history, alcoholism creates struggle and suffering for all who come under its influence. Addictions counselors, then, need to strike a balance between understanding the ubiquitous nature of addiction, and at the same time being sensitive to how cultural differences influence and shape unique behavior patterns. For a broader overview of multicultural issues in addictions counseling, see Fisher and Harrison (2012) and Miller (2005).

Counseling Methods

Counseling methods and interventions for substance abuse and addiction occur in different formats: individual therapy, group therapy, and family therapy. As previously noted, the models of addiction provide a philosophical basis for intervention. For example, counselors who believe strongly in the medical, or disease, model of addiction will most likely focus on 12-step support, abstinence as the only treatment goal, and psychoeducation on the disease process of addiction. If counselors work primarily from the psychological model of addiction, they focus on helping clients resolve underlying emotions, modify negative thought patterns, or address other fundamental psychological reasons believed to "cause" addiction. Of course, counselors also may work in an integrative fashion, drawing from two or more models to help clients on their recovery journey.

Specific counseling strategies for clients struggling with addiction can generally be divided into two types: atheoretical and theoretical. Atheoretical considerations include strategies that do not rely on a particular theory but are nonetheless essential in any comprehensive work with substance addiction. Examples of atheoretical strategies include ensuring client safety, encouraging 12-step attendance, strengthening support systems, and providing educational material.

Theoretical strategies have their foundation in counseling theory; many counseling techniques that derive from theory are quite useful in working with clients struggling with addiction. One theory that has provided a significant contribution to the addiction field is cognitive theory. In their landmark book on treating substance abuse, Beck et al. (1993) outlined a comprehensive guide to working with those struggling with substance addiction through a cognitive lens. Their emphasis was on identifying cognitive distortions about substance use, providing corrective rational thoughts in their place, and identifying and working through concomitant mood/personal problems that may thwart progress in therapy. Cognitive therapy also is the foundation of empirically supported relapse prevention methods (see Marlatt & Gordon, 1985).

Another approach that has amassed an impressive amount of empirical support in the treatment of substance abuse and addiction is motivational interviewing (MI; Miller & Rollnick, 2002). Although it is not a theory per se, MI draws from many theoretical approaches, including person-centered counseling, motivational psychology, the theory of cognitive dissonance, and the stages of change model (Miller & Rollnick, 2002). The definition of MI has evolved over the years since the first book on the topic hit the market in 1991 (Miller & Rollnick, 1991). The most recent definition appeared in 2009: motivational interviewing is a collaborative, person-centered form of guiding to elicit and strengthen motivation to change (Stephen Rollnick, personal communication, 2010).

MI was born out of the substance addictions field in the early to mid-1980s, primarily as a response to the more traditional, confrontational approaches that were popular at the time. Traditional substance abuse counseling operated from a deficit model, in that clients were seen as lacking the skill, motivation, and honesty to address their substance use problem. Ambivalence to give up a problem was seen as pathological, and denial needed to be broken down before any change would occur. Clients needed fixing from the outside and did not have anything useful to add to their own treatment. Not surprisingly, this approach had limited success and engendered a major stumbling block to behavioral change in the form of resistance. MI represents an alternative approach whereby counselors avoid argumentation, show great respect and empathy for clients, support client strengths, and "roll" with resistance. MI practitioners are mildly confrontational by pointing out discrepancies between what clients value (e.g., work, family) and their behavior (e.g., substance abuse).

The goals of MI include helping the client to increase intrinsic motivation to change, lowering levels of resistance, and resolving the client's ambivalence about change. Helping to increase intrinsic motivation to change rests on the finding that internal motivation has a greater impact on behavior change than does external motivation (Plotnik & Kouyoumdjian, 2013). Lowering resistance creates space in counseling sessions in which clients are more willing to consider change and entertain ideas about change. Too much resistance precludes discussions about change and keeps the client in a defensive mode. Client arguing, interrupting, avoiding, or ignoring the clinician are all forms of client resistance (Center for Substance Abuse Treatment, 1999). Resolving ambivalence is a critical goal in MI. Ambivalence, or feeling two ways about something, is a major reason why those struggling with addiction often feel stuck (Miller & Rollnick, 2002). On the one hand, drug use makes clients feel good, and on the other hand it has caused numerous problems in their lives. Clients feel "pulled in two directions." In MI, clients are invited to explore ambivalence by examining values and goals and how their substance abuse behavior conflicts with these.

I predict that MI will become a cornerstone of most addiction training programs. It can be used as a stand-alone approach. It is a highly effective way of starting off with clients, especially those who are precontemplative (i.e., characterized by low motivation, high resistance, and not seeing a problem or need for change) about their substance use. MI also can be used on an as needed basis; throughout counseling, client motivation is likely to ebb and flow, and MI can be used to bolster motivation should it start to lag.

EMPIRICALLY SUPPORTED TREATMENTS AND GUIDELINES In 2009, the National Institute on Drug Abuse (NIDA) published the second edition of its popular *Principles of Drug Addiction Treatment: A Research-Based Guide*. This booklet outlines 13 principles of effective treatment for substance abuse and addiction, which are grounded in the empirical outcome literature. These principles are listed in Table 13.1.

An examination of these principles suggests that counseling plays a critical role in any treatment program for those struggling with substance abuse or addiction. In addition, medication for some addictive problems has proven helpful and complements behavioral counseling. I currently work at an agency that is certified to prescribe buprenorphine (marketed as Suboxone) for opiate addiction. Much of my work at this agency entails counseling individuals in conjunction with their buprenorphine medication protocol. In my experience, medications such as buprenorphine help clients by easing physiological craving and creating enough stability in their lives to hold a job, repair relationships, and enter and engage in successful counseling.

Relapse Prevention: Concepts and Strategies

Unfortunately, relapse is often the rule rather than the exception. In fact, clients may relapse *several times* before maintaining sobriety and treatment gains. In many ways, much of substance abuse counseling is helping clients prevent or manage relapse. By the time clients are ready for outpatient counseling, they are most likely beginning the long, arduous journey of recovery. It is important to note that being in recovery does not

---

TABLE 13.1 Principles of Drug Addiction and Treatment

1. Addiction is a complex but treatable disease that affects brain function and behavior.
2. No single treatment is appropriate for everyone.
3. Treatment needs to be readily available.
4. Effective treatment attends to multiple needs of the individual, not just his or her drug abuse.
5. Remaining in treatment for an adequate period of time is critical.
6. Counseling—individual and/or group—and other behavioral therapies are the most commonly used forms of drug abuse treatment.
7. Medications are an important element of treatment for many patients, especially when combined with counseling and other behavioral therapies.
8. An individual's treatment and services plan must be assessed continually and modified as necessary to ensure that it meets his or her changing needs.
9. Many drug-addicted individuals also have other mental disorders.
10. Medically assisted detoxification is only the first stage of addiction treatment and by itself does little to change long-term drug abuse.
11. Treatment does not need to be voluntary to be effective.
12. Drug use during treatment must be monitored continuously, because lapses during treatment do occur.
13. Treatment programs should assess patients for the presence of HIV/AIDS, hepatitis B and C, tuberculosis, and other infectious diseases as well as provide targeted risk-reduction counseling to help patients modify or change behaviors that place them at risk of contracting or spreading infectious diseases.

Source: National Institute on Drug Abuse (NIDA). (2009). *Principles of drug addiction treatment: A research-based guide* (2nd ed.). NIH Publication No. 09-4180. Rockville, MD: US Department of Health and Human Services.

simply mean abstaining from a substance, although that is certainly part of it. Recovery is defined as intentionally stopping substance use *and* expanding one's life beyond the narrow confines of addictive behavior; positive behaviors and habits are formed and built upon (C. Osborn, personal communication, 2000). Recovery includes the presence of new life goals and behaviors, not just the absence of substance use. It is a difficult, lifelong process that has a definite beginning point but no guaranteed end point; constant ups and downs are the norm until eventual stabilization is achieved. Relapse is a constant danger.

Relapse is defined as losing control of one's substance use after a period of no use (Fisher & Harrison, 2012) or a return to pretreatment levels of use. This is in contrast to a *lapse,* whereby a person slips after a period of abstinence. An example of a lapse might be an alcoholic who has a sip of beer at a school reunion without any other drinking. The person "slipped" in the sense that he or she did not return to uncontrolled drinking. The concept of a lapse is seen as a myth in some AA and traditional treatment circles; that is, any return to alcohol, even if it is a small sip, is the progressive disease taking over and the person will inevitably lose control.

Part of preventing and managing relapse is to help clients avoid the abstinence violation effect (AVE; Marlatt, 1985). The AVE is the internal experience of intense shame, guilt, and embarrassment that follows a slip or lapse. The client who experiences an AVE might have the following internal dialogue after a slip: "I can't believe I took a drink. I am such a loser. All the people in my life have helped for nothing. I am a no-good drunk. I don't deserve anything. What the hell, I might as well go all the way." The AVE increases the likelihood that a lapse will turn into a relapse. An important part of early counseling with clients is to educate them on the differences between lapse and relapse, and help them understand that either does not mean personal failure (Thombs, 2006). Clients are taught to restructure their thought processes and interpret slips as simply mistakes, not evidence of total failure. The client is human and all humans make mistakes. Attribution of slips should be appropriately placed on environmental cues (i.e., driving by my old neighborhood). Doing so frees the client from devastating emotions that can lead to a relapse and allows them to better handle and manage high-risk situations.

THE PROCESS OF RELAPSE The study of relapse is probably best known through the work of G. Alan Marlatt (1985), who proposed a popular relapse model that draws heavily from cognitive-behavioral ideas. In Marlatt's model, relapse begins when individuals find themselves in stressful situations. When this happens, they can cope with the situation either effectively or ineffectively. Effective coping increases self-efficacy, whereas ineffective coping decreases self-efficacy. Coping ineffectively also is combined with positive outcome expectancies, which are beliefs that substances will have a generally positive effect on mood, feelings, and behavior. The lower self-efficacy combined with positive outcome expectancies then leads to initiation of use, followed by the AVE, which then greatly increases the likelihood of have a full-blown relapse. A partial diagram of Marlatt's model, also called the cognitive-behavioral model of relapse, is provided in Figure 13.1.

As one can see, the cognitive-behavioral model of relapse allows for several potential points of intervention that the clinical mental health counselor can use to help the client prevent or manage a relapse. First, exploring with clients what situations and environmental cues are high risk may help them avoid potential problems. If clients find themselves in a tempting situation, teaching them coping skills may help interrupt the relapse process. If clients have positive expectancies of drug use, clinical mental health counselors can intervene to help them see the other, more negative side of use. Counselors can help prepare clients for the AVE by encouraging them to write down realistic appraisals of a slip on three by five note cards that they can carry with them. Examples might include "It's only a slip. It doesn't mean I am a complete failure," and "A slip is not a relapse. I just simply made a mistake and will get right back on track."

RELAPSE PREVENTION AND MANAGEMENT STRATEGIES Relapse prevention refers to strategies and skills one can use to prevent a return to uncontrolled use. Relapse management refers to strategies and skills used when one returns to use, either through a slip or a return to pretreatment levels of use. Strategies for relapse prevention can be drawn from Marlatt's (1985) model previously discussed: identifying high-risk situations, developing coping skills, balancing positive expectancies with negative expectancies, and coping with the AVE.

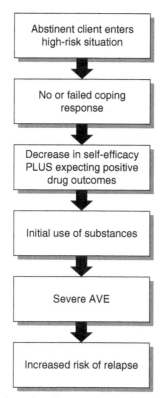

FIGURE 13.1 The path to relapse based on the cognitive-behavioral model of relapse.

Based on Larimer, M. E., Palmer, R. S., & Marlatt, G. A. (1999). Relapse prevention: An overview of Marlatt's cognitive-behavioral model. *Alcohol Research and Health, 23,* 151–160.

The goal for relapse management is to minimize the degree of setback and help clients take steps in the right direction (Weingardt & Marlatt, 1998). The focus of relapse management strategies is to help clients cope with the AVE. Specific strategies to this end (Weingardt & Marlatt, 1998) follow:

1. ***Stop, look, listen.*** This strategy encourages the client to become aware of the particular surroundings when he or she slips. Stopping includes removing oneself from a tight situation, such as going to the bathroom, going for a walk, and so forth.
2. ***Stay calm.*** Anxiety is impossible when one is relaxed. Being more relaxed lowers risk for overreacting to a slip.
3. ***Renew commitment.*** Help the client repeat positive self-statements and create a brief ritual that renews commitment to abstinence.
4. ***Review high-risk situation.*** Break down the situation that got the client into trouble. Who, what, when, where, and why are good questions to explore.
5. ***Make an appropriate plan for recovery.*** The plan may need to be tweaked or updated.
6. ***Use social support.*** Find out who is in the client's corner, and help the client elicit this support.

Fostering Family and Community Support

Clinical mental health counselors are in a unique position to help families struggling with addiction problems. Often, families develop rules for interaction that preclude a genuine, honest assessment of how substance use may be destroying them from the inside (Fisher & Harrison, 2012). Counselors are encouraged to educate and support families in their struggle to cope with and understand a family member's addiction. Counselors also are in a position to explore what support is available in their communities for individuals and families struggling with substance abuse and addiction. Such resources can address issues that are outside of the counseling realm, such as transitional living problems, transportation, halfway house placement, financial planning, job training, education, and general personal care. Clinical mental health counselors can provide education and information on these services; access to a number of community resources, such as Alcoholics Anonymous, can be a powerful adjunct to counseling.

PUTTING IT ALL TOGETHER

Substance abuse counseling can be a challenging endeavor for addictions counselors. The relatively high rate of relapse, combined with slow progress, can set the stage for therapeutic burnout. On the other hand, substance abuse counseling can be quite rewarding when clients who have struggled with addiction for years discover the happiness and freedom that comes from a sober and clean life. Addictions counselors should keep in mind that many resources, both within and outside of mental health agencies, are available to them; they do not have to carry the burden of care by themselves. Considering all the treatment options may initially seem overwhelming, yet it need not be. Based on my clinical experiences and teaching graduate students in substance abuse counseling, I have developed a list of key questions and considerations when counseling clients struggling with substance-related problems. This list is sequential in that it starts with assessment and includes considerations through aftercare. Although comprehensive, the following list is not exhaustive; there may be other considerations to investigate.

Checklist of Key Questions and Considerations

1. *Assessment, diagnosis, and evaluation.* A thorough assessment and evaluation can go a long way to help conceptualize the extent and intensity of the client's substance abuse problem. It is important to include (a) medical evaluation, (b) psychological evaluation, (c) social evaluation, (d) recreational evaluation, and (e) spiritual evaluation.

Questions to consider include the following:
1. What assessment instruments/procedures will you use?
2. How severe is the client's substance use?
3. How severe is interference in social, occupational, family, and personal functioning?
4. What is the client's Global Assessment of Functioning (GAF)?
5. Based on assessment and evaluations, does the client meet criteria for substance dependence or substance abuse?

2. *Determine proper needs and treatment format: Least restrictive environment.* The client should be placed in the least restrictive environment possible. To help determine appropriate placement, the American Society of Addiction Medicine listed several considerations (Doweiko, 2011): (a) acute intoxication/withdrawal potential, (b) biomedical conditions or complications, (c) emotional/behavioral conditions or complications, (f) treatment acceptance and resistance, (g) relapse potential, and (h) recovery environment.

The options for treatment generally fall into four categories: (a) intervention, (b) inpatient treatment, (c) partial hospitalization/intensive, and (d) outpatient treatment. General issues in determining inpatient versus outpatient placement include the following:

1. Whether the client's condition is associated with significant medical or psychiatric conditions or complications
2. The severity of actual or anticipated withdrawal from drug(s) being used
3. Whether multiple failed attempts at outpatient treatment have occurred
4. The strength of the client's support systems
5. The severity of client's addiction and possibility of polysubstance abuse/dependence

3. Client motivation—How motivated is the client? What is the level of resistance? As previously noted, client motivation is a significant, yet often overlooked, variable in substance abuse counseling. If motivation is low, then it is doubtful that other interventions will be useful. If client motivation is high, then the chances of achieving and maintaining counseling goals are enhanced. Consider the following general guidelines:

1. For lower motivation, high resistance, and early stages of change: use MI.
2. For high motivation, low resistance, and later stages of change: use MI and/or other theoretical models.
3. Remember the different ways to utilize MI: (a) as an approach in and of itself, (b) as a way to begin counseling designed to increase motivation to change followed by incorporation of psychological theory, and (c) on an as needed basis; that is, use MI as the client's motivation level naturally rises and falls throughout the duration of counseling.

4. What philosophy or model of addiction do you adhere to (may depend on agency philosophy and client needs/issues)? If the disease model is the main philosophical perspective, consider using the Minnesota Model (Doweiko, 2011). Components of the Minnesota Model follow:

1. Evaluation by treatment team
2. Goal setting by treatment team
3. Development of a formal treatment plan with client and case manager
4. Abstinence as ONLY goal
5. Social support
6. Must encourage 12-step attendance

If the psychological model is the counselor's main philosophical perspective, consider the following components:

1. Use MI to build motivation.
2. Controlled use/harm reduction may be an acceptable goal.
3. Twelve-step approaches may be encouraged but not enforced.

4. Decide which counseling theoretical model(s) will best address psychological aspects of addiction. Some possibilities include psychoanalysis/ego-psychology, cognitive and cognitive-behavioral therapy, behavioral therapy, motivational interviewing, family systems approaches, reality therapy, solution-focused counseling, or eclectic/integrative approaches.

5. *"Blending" of models may be appropriate and useful.* For example, cognitive-behavioral counseling may work for clients who manifest irrational beliefs related to remaining abstinent. In this instance, the goal of abstinence suggests operating from the disease model, yet a psychological intervention is utilized to help the client remain alcohol free.

6. *Consider an appropriate aftercare program.* In general, an aftercare program includes 12-step groups, continued outpatient treatment, relapse prevention/management strategies, transitional living issues, family issues, and an emphasis that the recovery is more than remaining substance free; it is incorporating a positive lifestyle in place of substance use.

CASE STUDY 13.1

I am currently counseling Stan, a 42-year-old accountant who has been struggling with alcohol problems for quite some time. He was required to see me for an assessment based on a mandate from the court due to his third DUI. By using the CAGE questionnaire and clinical interview outlined earlier, it was clear that Stan began using alcohol at an early age, was neglected and verbally abused as a child, and felt empty and spiritually bankrupt. He met criteria for alcohol dependence, and my recommendation was for him to enter a detoxification program followed by intensive outpatient counseling. Stan complied, albeit reluctantly. His full axis I diagnosis was alcohol dependence, with physiological dependence.

When Stan began outpatient counseling, there was a high level of resistance about having to attend twice a week. Further, Stan was ambivalent about his alcohol use. On the one hand, he knew how alcohol had created problems in his life, yet on the other hand, he enjoyed having a few drinks with his buddies; the thought of stopping completely scared him. Based on this initial assessment, I decided to use MI to help Stan clarify his goals, reduce resistance, and resolve ambivalence about using. We worked on increasing the importance he gives to addressing his alcohol use, as well as increasing his confidence about making a sustained change. Adjunct services, such as AA, were encouraged.

After a few sessions using MI, Stan acknowledged a need for change and agreed that, despite being a difficult choice, abstinence was the best option. Operating from the psychological model as my philosophical base, I moved from an MI focus to a more therapeutic focus, emphasizing both cognitive and gestalt models of counseling. Shifting Stan's tendency to think irrationally about a sober life took priority. Gestalt methods were used to explore early messages that Stan had received when growing up in a chaotic home. Resolving these psychological problems was considered essential to helping Stan in the recovery process.

Through six months of weekly counseling and consistent AA attendance, Stan was feeling better about his ability to maintain sobriety. He reported having better communications with his wife and son, and overall felt healthier. However, he was constantly aware of the possibility of relapse. Every now and then, he would run into an old buddy, or drive by the old "stomping ground," and experience latent cravings for alcohol. We developed a relapse prevention plan that included preparing for a "slip" should it occur. I helped Stan write down sobriety affirming statements on three by five note cards to carry with him, so that he could read them out loud should he experience a craving.

Stan's counseling is currently down to about a session every three weeks, and he has reported no slips since he received his DUI almost eight months ago. He continues to struggle with cravings every now and then; however, he is beginning to see the benefits of a sober life and how he used alcohol to cover up feelings of inadequacy and pain. Relapse prevention and relapse management are the topics of our sessions at this time. Continued attendance at AA also has helped Stan be accountable to the goals he has set for himself.

This case study represents work from both the disease and psychological models of addiction. There was not much "wiggle room" regarding Stan's goal for drinking; he needed to abstain, given his obvious legal and family difficulties. Had Stan been younger, not involved with the law, and experienced relatively minor problems, controlled drinking may have been an option for him. The approach to counseling was to use MI to start things off, move into cognitive and psychological explorations, and then develop a solid relapse prevention/management plan. In this case, AA was an essential component as well.

VOICE FROM THE FIELD 13.1

I specialize in addiction medicine and have been in practice for several years. Recently, I became one of the few psychiatrists in the Greensboro area to prescribe buprenorphine (marketed as Suboxone) to patients struggling with opiate addiction. Suboxone has great promise for helping opioid-dependent individuals because it assists in reducing opioid use, helps patients to stay in treatment, helps to reduce withdrawal symptoms, and decreases cravings. Although I have seen good success with buprenorphine therapy, it is definitely not enough to help clients turn their lives around.

Counseling is a critical and important component in patients' overall care. In fact, as medical director of the Presbyterian Counseling Center (PCC), in collaboration with the rest of the treatment staff, I have made counseling a mandatory part of the Subuxone treatment program. Not all Suboxone treatment programs do this. Unfortunately, all too often counseling is either viewed as optional or not discussed at all. Suboxone will help take the edge off in terms of withdrawal and cravings, but patients' lives are often in disarray. Counseling can help them get back on track by developing coping skills and setting/achieving goals. As research builds in supporting the use of counseling in addition to medication for addiction, many more programs–if they have not already done so–will likely adopt our treatment model and philosophy.

MASOUD HAJAZI, MD
Medical Director, Presbyterian Counseling Center (PCC),
Greensboro, North Carolina

Conclusion

Substance abuse and addiction can exact an enormous toll on society. Substance abuse and addiction account for not only billions lost in annual worker productivity in the United States (Hoffman & Froemke, 2007) but also an untold number of personal, financial, and relationship problems. In the coming years, clinical mental health counselors will observe that substance abuse and addiction compose a substantial part of client care in agencies across the country. Several models of addiction have been proposed in the literature to help conceptualize how addiction begins and how it is maintained. Addictions counselors should have knowledge of how to screen, assess, and diagnose substance-related problems when they arise, and how to counsel those struggling with addiction using accepted models and empirical research. The greater focus on addictions counseling, instigated by the 2009 CACREP standards, will put mental health counselors at the forefront of substance abuse and addictions counseling.

References

American Psychiatric Association. (2013). *Diagnostic and statistical manual of mental disorders, fifth edition* (DSM-5). Washington, DC: Author.

Beck, A. T., Wright, F. D., Newman, C. F., & Liese, B. S. (1993). *Cognitive therapy of substance abuse*. New York, NY: Guilford Press.

Brown, R. L., Leonard, T., Saunders, L. A., & Papasoulioutis, O. (1997). A two-item screening test for alcohol and other drug problems. *Journal of Family Practice, 44*, 151–160.

Center for Substance Abuse Treatment. (1999). *Enhancing motivation for change in substance abuse treatment*. Treatment Improvement Protocol (TIP) Series 35. DHHS Publication No. (SMA) 99-3354. Rockville, MD: Substance Abuse and Mental Health Services Administration.

Center for Substance Abuse Treatment. (2005). *Substance abuse treatment for person with co-occurring disorders*. Treatment Improvement Protocol (TIP) Series 42. DHHS Publication No. (SMA) 05-3992. Rockville, MD: Substance Abuse and Mental Health Services Administration.

Council for Accreditation of Counseling and Related Educational Programs (CACREP). (2009). *CACREP accreditation manual: 2009 standards*. Alexandria, VA: Author. Retrieved from http://www.cacrep.org/doc/2009%20Standards%20with%20cover.pdf

Doweiko, H. E. (2011). *Concepts of chemical dependency* (8th ed.). Independence, KY: Cengage Learning.

Drake, R. E., Mercer-McFadden, C., Mueser, K. T., McHugo, G. J., & Bond, G. R. (1998). Review of integrated mental health and substance abuse treatment for patients with dual disorders. *Schizophrenia Bulletin, 24*, 589–608.

Evans, W. N. (1998). Assessment and diagnosis of the substance use disorders (SUDs). *Journal of Counseling & Development, 76*, 325–332.

Ewing, J. A. (1984). Detecting alcoholism: The CAGE questionnaire. *The Journal of the American Medical Association, 252*, 1905–1907.

Falco, M. (2005). US federal drug policy. In J. H. Lowinson, P. Ruiz, R. B. Millman, & J. G. Langrod (Eds.), *Substance abuse: A comprehensive textbook* (4th ed.). New York, NY: Lippincott Williams & Wilkins.

Fisher, G. L., & Harrison, T. C. (2012). *Substance abuse: Information for school counselors, social workers, therapists, and counselors* (5th ed.). New York, NY: Pearson.

Hart, C., & Ksir, C. (2012). *Drugs, society, and human behavior* (15th ed.). New York, NY: McGraw-Hill.

Hazelden Foundation. (2007). *The twelve steps of Alcoholics Anonymous*. Center City, MN: Author.

Hoffman, J., & Froemke, S. (Eds.). (2007). *Addiction: Why can't they just stop? New knowledge. New treatments. New hope*. New York, NY: Rodale Press.

Juhnke, G. A. (2002). *Substance abuse assessment and diagnosis*. New York, NY: Brunner-Routledge.

Larimer, M. E., Palmer, R. S., & Marlatt, G. A. (1999). Relapse prevention: An overview of Marlatt's cognitive-behavioral model. *Alcohol Research and Health, 23*, 151–160.

Levitt, S. D., & Dubner, S. J. (2005). *Freakonomics: A rogue economist explores the hidden side of everything*. New York, NY: HarperCollins.

Marlatt, G. A. (1985). Relapse prevention: Theoretical rationale and overview of the model. In G. A. Marlatt & G. Gordon (Eds.), *Relapse prevention. A self-control strategy for the maintenance of behavior change* (pp. 3–70). New York, NY: Guilford Press.

Marlatt, G. A., & Gordon, G. (Eds.). (1985). *Relapse prevention. A self-control strategy for the maintenance of behavior change*. New York, NY: Guilford Press.

May, R. (1981). *Man's search for himself*. New York, NY: Norton.

Miller, G. (2005). *Learning the language of addiction counseling* (2nd ed.). Hoboken, NJ: Wiley.

Miller, W. R., Forcehimes, A. A., & Zweben, A. (2011). *Treating addiction: A guide for professionals*. New York, NY: Guilford Press.

Miller, W. R., & Rollnick, S. (1991). *Motivational interviewing: Preparing people to change addictive behavior*. New York, NY: Guilford Press.

Miller, W. R., & Rollnick, S. (2002). *Motivational interviewing: Preparing people for change* (2nd rev. ed.). New York, NY: Guilford Press.

Nakken, C. (1996). *The addictive personality: Understanding the addictive process and compulsive behavior* (2nd ed.). Center City, MN: Hazelden.

National Institute on Drug Abuse (NIDA). (2009). *Principles of drug addiction treatment: A research-based guide* (2nd ed.). NIH Publication No. 09-4180. Rockville, MD: US Department of Health and Human Services.

National Institute on Drug Abuse (NIDA). (2012). *DrugFacts: Nationwide trends*. Retrieved from http://www.drugabuse.gov/publications/drugfacts/nationwide-trends

Pattison, E. M., Sobell, M. B., & Sobell, L. C. (1977). *Emerging concepts of alcohol dependence*. New York, NY: Springer.

Plotnik, R., & Kouyoumdjian, H. (2013). *Introduction to psychology* (10th ed.). Independence, KY: Cengage Learning.

Prentiss, C. (2007). *The alcoholism and addiction cure: A holistic approach to total recovery*. Los Angeles, CA: Power Press.

Thombs, D. L. (2006). *Introduction to addictive behaviors* (3rd ed.). New York, NY: Guilford Press.

US Government Printing Office. (2014). *Electronic Code of Federal Regulations—Title 42: Public health*. Retrieved from http://www.ecfr.gov/cgi-bin/text-idx?c=ecfr&rgn=div5&view=text&node=42:1.0.1.1.2&idno=42

Weingardt, K. R., & Marlatt, G. A. (1998). Sustaining change: Helping those who are still using. In W. R. Miller & N. Heather (Eds.), *Treating addictive behaviors* (2nd ed.). New York, NY: Plenum Press.

14

Clinical Supervision

HEATHER C. TREPAL AND IOANA BOIE

CHAPTER OVERVIEW

This chapter presents an overview of clinical supervision. As new counselors, counselors in training will be introduced to supervision throughout their graduate training as well as their postdegree clinical work. The discussion here defines clinical supervision, provides an overview of the supervision process and modalities, and helps counselors in training prepare for their role as supervisees.

LEARNING OBJECTIVES

The learning objectives for this chapter are designed to be consistent with the 2009 Council for Accreditation of Counseling and Related Educational Programs Standards (CACREP, 2009). As such, upon completion of this chapter, the student will have knowledge of the following clinical mental health counseling standards:

1. Understands a variety of models and theories related to clinical mental health counseling, including the methods, models, and principles of clinical supervision. (A.5)
2. Demonstrates the ability to recognize his or her own limitations as a clinical mental health counselor and to seek supervision or refer clients when appropriate. (D.9)

Additionally, students will have knowledge of the following core entry-level standard:

1. Counseling supervision models, practices, and processes. (G.1.e)

INTRODUCTION

The field of counseling relies on both formal and informal training to facilitate the growth of future counselors. Most of the formal training occurs throughout graduate coursework, including practicum and internship experiences. Informal training occurs after graduates pursue clinical experience toward state or national licensure requirements. Both formal and informal training and clinical growth are enhanced and facilitated through the process of clinical supervision.

In order to help you better understand the role of supervision, both as a beginning counseling student and future intern, and potentially as a future supervisor, it is important to describe the different roles and responsibilities of supervisors. The following working definition of supervision has been offered by Bernard and Goodyear (2013) in their text *Fundamentals of Clinical Supervision:*

> Supervision is an intervention provided by a more senior member of the profession to a more junior member or members of the same profession. This relationship is evaluative and hierarchical, extends over time, has the simultaneous purposes of enhancing the professional functioning of the more junior person(s); monitoring the quality of professional services offered to the clients that she, he or they see; and serving as a gatekeeper for those who are to enter the particular profession. (p. 7)

In the process of supervision, the supervisor often takes on multiple roles, such as advisor, teacher, mentor, coach, evaluator, or consultant (Remley & Herlihy, 2010). In these roles, the supervisor maintains responsibility for both the welfare of the supervisee(s) as well as the welfare of the clients the supervisee(s) counsel (ACA Code of Ethics, 2005, Standard F.1.a.). However, it is important to remember that although there are several similarities and overlaps between supervision and teaching, counseling and consultation, there are also clear distinctions.

Supervision also plays an important role in the training of counselors. For example, according to the CACREP 2009 standards, supervision is defined as "a tutorial and mentoring form of instruction in which a supervisor monitors the student's activities in practicum and internship, and facilitates the associated learning and skill development experiences. The supervisor monitors and evaluates the clinical work of the student while monitoring the quality of services offered to clients" (2009, p. 63). The CACREP 2009 standards mandate practicum and internship supervision, including an average of one hour of individual supervision per week and 1.5 hours of group supervision for practicum, and an average of one hour per week of onsite individual supervision and an average of 1.5 hours per week of group supervision for internship (CACREP, 2009, Section III, F, G.).

After reading this chapter, counselors in training will have learned about the differences between clinical and administrative supervision, the scope and function of supervisors, supervision requirements according to the CACREP standards; and they will have an understanding regarding how supervision works and know what to expect from supervision according to the supervisee and supervisor roles in the supervision process.

WHO ARE SUPERVISORS?

Supervisors are mental health professionals who have the training and experience necessary to supervise clinical mental health counselors. Similar to the licensure process for mental health professionals, the requirements to become a recognized supervisor vary by state. Although a national supervision license does not exist, there is a voluntary national supervision credential offered by the National Board for Certified Counselors (that of Approved Clinical Supervisor [ACS]) (www.cce-global.org/credentials-offered/acs). Supervisors typically work with a supervisee for a defined time period to offer supervision needed for licensure in a particular state.

For training purposes, the CACREP 2009 standards mandate that practicum supervisors have at least two years post-master's degree experience in counseling or a related field. Preferably, they are licensed or credentialed as supervisors (CACREP, 2009, Section III, C). Further, the standards also mandate specific training in supervision for both program faculty and students who serve as individual or group practicum or internship supervisors (CACREP, 2009, Section III, A, B.).

There is no national standard for clinical supervision licensure or credentialing, and every state has different requirements (i.e., training in supervision, experience) for counselors to meet in order to become eligible to supervise. The National Board for Certified Counselors (NBCC) provides a directory of each state counseling licensure board (2010), including more specific information about supervisors, such as length of training, length of clinical practice, and other specific requirements. As counselors in training prepare for their own licensure, they will need to fully understand the laws in the state or states where they intend to be licensed.

Counselors in training who seek supervision must be sure that the supervisor meets the minimum requirements to supervise in the particular state. Typically, a roster of current and approved supervisors is available through the state licensure board Web site. Checking the current status of a supervisor through the official state licensure board is important because practicum or internship hours accrued under the supervision of an unlicensed supervisor could result in the annulment of those hours. Depending on the state, the supervisor's license could be either suspended as a result of an ethical violation or not renewed. Aside from the minimum requirements, this chapter highlights other important aspects of clinical supervision, including factors that may contribute to a positive and growth-oriented supervision experience.

Another role in supervision is the administrative supervisor, who ensures that in the workplace supervisees complete their job responsibilities; these supervisors typically have direct managing control and authority over the counselors they are supervising (Remley & Herlihy, 2010). The Association for Counselor Education and Supervision's publication *Ethical Guidelines for Counseling Supervisors* (ACES, 1993) differentiates between clinical and administrative supervision:

> Administrative supervision refers to those supervisory activities which increase the efficiency of the delivery of counseling services; whereas, clinical supervision includes the supportive and educative activities of the supervisor designed to improve the application of counseling theory and technique directly to clients. (p. 1)

Further, administrative supervisors are charged with helping to create satisfying and productive work environments, managing counseling departments' policies, and designing and maintaining effective service delivery systems (Henderson, 2009, p. 8). For further reading on the topic of administrative supervision, see *The New Handbook of Administrative Supervision in Counseling* (Henderson, 2009).

VOICE FROM THE FIELD 14.1

A primary responsibility of administrative supervisors is to help professional counselors perform at their best. Effectively organized counseling departments use a performance management system. The systematic approach helps professional counselors know what is expected of them and helps administrative supervisors know what they expect for themselves. A performance management system links an annually established job description for each counselor with supervision, performance evaluation, and goal setting for ongoing professional development. It is best carried out in a collaborative relationship; counselors and supervisors share responsibility for the quality of the counselor's performance.

The job description specifies each clinical mental health counselor's roles and responsibilities, not in a vacuum, but in light of the individual's training and competence, and the department's annual service delivery plan. An effective and efficient service delivery plan for the counseling department is developed in the context of the agency's mission and with regard to what the funding sources pay for. This approach allows counselors to be very clear about what services their clients will benefit from.

Administrative supervisors lead the dialogues that define a specific counselor's job, but it is key that supervisees are comfortable enough to be candid about their strengths and areas that need improvement. A good way to begin the conversation is to discuss what the counselor is licensed to do; for example, in Texas, licensed professional counselors are authorized to use "counseling treatment interventions that include: (A) counseling; (B) assessment; (C) consulting; and (D) referral" (Texas Occupations Code, 1999; Chapter 503, §503.003, (a), (4)). Further, "The use of specific methods, techniques, or modalities within the practice of professional counseling is limited to professional counselors appropriately trained in the use of those methods, techniques, or modalities" (§503.003, (c)).

An approach that works well for administrative supervisors is to ask open-ended questions, listen carefully to nuances in the supervisees' answers, and follow up from there. Different from using questions that can be answered in a word or two, open-ended questioning leaves room for dialogue as led by the supervisee, while at the same time helping keep the conversation on track. What supervisors want to know is what theoretical bases counselors adhere to, and how and when they apply them. They want to know how competent/incompetent and comfortable/uncomfortable counselors think they are in using each of the four intervention skill sets—counseling, assessment, consulting, and referral. This will help counselors perform as well as possible. Seeking vivid anecdotal examples of successes and setbacks for each provides word pictures of counselors' performance. In order to help counselors find satisfaction in their jobs, supervisors also attend to ensuring that counselors get to use the skill set they enjoy the most.

PATRICIA G. HENDERSON, EdD

However, the focal point of this chapter is clinical supervision, not administrative supervision. In order to understand who the clinical supervisor is and what are the different responsibilities inherent in being a supervisor, several organizations with authority in the field of supervision have been consulted, such as the Association for Counselor Education and Supervision (ACES), CACREP (2009) standards, and the ACA Code of Ethics (2005). According to ACES (1993), supervisors are

> counselors who have been designated within their university or agency to directly oversee the professional clinical work of counselors. Supervisors also may be persons who offer supervision to counselors seeking state licensure and so provide supervision outside of the administrative aegis of an applied counseling setting. (p. 2)

Additionally, the supervisor's responsibilities follow: to monitor the client's welfare; to encourage and monitor compliance with the legal, ethical, and professional standards for practice; to monitor clinical performance and professional development; as well as to evaluate and certify current performance of the supervisees for academic, screening, selection, placement, employment, and credentialing purposes.

THE SUPERVISION PROCESS

Supervision involves several important processes: informed consent, supervision agreements, fair evaluation, supervisor competence, confidentiality and limits to confidentiality, ways to maintain accountability and responsibility, and vicarious liability concerns (Remley & Herlihy, 2010).

The informed consent in supervision concerns both the supervisee (ACA Code of Ethics, 2005, Standard F.4.a) as well as the supervisee's client. The client has to be aware that the supervisee is offering counseling under supervision, what the implications and confidentiality limitations are, and also what the supervisee's qualifications are (ACA

Code of Ethics, 2005, Standard F.1.b). Along with the informed consent, some of the recommended topics to discuss before the sessions begin are related to the purpose of supervision, the logistics (i.e., frequency, length, emergency contact, agreement for state licensure), the supervisor's professional disclosure (i.e., credentials, theoretical orientation, and style), expectations, roles and responsibilities, the evaluation process, as well as components of legal and ethical professional practice (Remley & Herlihy, 2010).

What to Expect From the Supervision Process in General

Counselors in training might ask themselves what occurs in clinical supervision for a minimum of one hour every week. Neufeldt (1999) identified some of the most common strategies used to facilitate growth during the supervision process. These include evaluating the counselors in training's counseling session interactions, asking counselors to provide a hypothesis about the client, and identifying appropriate interventions. The supervisor may encourage the counselors in training to explore alternative ways of conceptualizing their clients, brainstorming techniques and interventions, as well as to consider the client's motivation. In some situations, the supervisor may teach or model intervention techniques while explaining the rationale behind them. The supervisor may ask the supervisee to identify significant events that occurred in the counseling session and explore the supervisee's feelings vis-à-vis the counseling session, the supervision session, or the specific techniques suggested. Most supervisors encourage an open exploration of the counselors in training's self-confidence, affect, defenses, biases, and may help them define areas of strength and of future growth. Additionally, most supervisors will disclose what their preferred theoretical orientation is and will expect supervisees to have chosen their own preferred theory. Some authors suggest exploring the counselors in training's theory of change in their lives and how it applies to their clients' concerns and progress in the counseling sessions (Neufeldt, 1999).

While counselors in training progress through practicum and internships, some of the most common strategies used in supervision might change to accommodate more advanced client conceptualization strategies. These may include exploring the supervisee's feelings to facilitate an understanding of the client. The counselor may identify and use various cues during the counseling session to facilitate the process. At a more advanced level, the supervisor will explore the counselor's intentions in the session, and whether the supervisee's behaviors in the counseling session are consistent with the theory of change. Oftentimes, supervision may address counselor–client boundaries and may use a parallel process to illustrate approaches for counseling sessions. Hopefully, the supervisor will also help the trainee reframe situations and thoughts, and build on his or her strengths. This may all sound intense, and it can be. But when good supervisees have good supervisors, the process is beneficial to the supervisee, the client, and even to the supervisor.

CASE STUDY 14.1

Mai is a master's student in a CACREP-accredited clinical mental health counseling program. She is about to begin her practicum at the university counseling clinic. Mai is nervous, but excited as she begins to schedule her first clients. Luis is Mai's assigned practicum supervisor. He contacts Mai during her first week and invites her to look at her schedule and coordinate a weekly individual supervision session with him throughout the semester. Mai is a bit overwhelmed by this news and many questions run through her mind: What will she talk with him about for an hour each week? Will these be like personal counseling sessions? How will Luis evaluate her, and will this supervision impact her grade in the course?

Luis begins the first supervision session by showing Mai a supervision contract and having a discussion regarding informed consent (see Box 14.1 for an example of a supervision contract). He describes himself and his background as a counselor and supervisor and invites Mai to do the same. Together, they go over the contract and discuss the particulars of their supervision agreement, including the format for their sessions, the evaluation process, as well as emergency procedures (i.e., suicidal clients, crisis situations) at the center. Finally, Luis asks Mai to tell him how she is feeling about starting practicum and beginning to see clients for the first time. They also discuss some of the paperwork procedures at the counseling center. Luis asks Mai to be prepared to talk about her initial client sessions in supervision the following week and to bring her files with her so that he can review her case notes. When the session ends, Mai takes a deep breath. Luis has been clear and structured in his approach to supervision, and she feels prepared and confident that their relationship and her practicum are off to a good start.

Supervision Contracts

The supervision agreement, sometimes called a supervision contract, is a document that outlines the relationship and work between the supervisor and supervisee. The CACREP 2009 standards dictate that "supervision contracts for each student are developed to define the roles and responsibilities of the faculty supervisor, site supervisor, and student during practicum and internship" (2009, III, E, p. 16). Supervision contracts can also be used for postgraduate supervision and can detail the same arrangements. This agreement mirrors a legal arrangement and provides a plan outlining the responsibilities of both the supervisor and the supervisee, as well as the parameters of the supervision process. It has been recommended that supervision contracts include the following elements: purpose, goals and objectives; context of services; method of evaluation; duties and responsibilities of supervisors and supervisees; procedural considerations; supervisor's scope of practice (Osborn & Davis, 1996); and agency conformity (i.e., specifics about work elements in the practice setting) (Munson, 2002). See Box 14.1 for an example.

BOX 14.1   Sample Supervision Contract

This serves as a supervision contract between <u>Luis Sanchez</u> (supervisor) and <u>Mai Chan</u> (supervisee/practicum student) for <u>the Fall Semester 2014</u> at the Campus Community Family Counseling Clinic (CCFCC).

Supervisor: Luis Sanchez

Credentials and Background: Luis Sanchez, MS, LPC, received his graduate degree in clinical mental health counseling, and is currently licensed in the state of Texas as a Licensed Professional Counselor and Board Approved Supervisor. He is the clinical director of the Campus Community Family Counseling Clinic (CCFCC). He also maintains a private practice specializing in working with clients with eating disorders.

Supervisor Responsibilities:

Monitor the welfare of the supervisee's clients.

Facilitate the supervisee's professional growth through various supervision methods including live observation, self-report, and the use of digitally recorded review of sessions.

Facilitate the supervisee's professional growth through a developmental perspective.

Evaluate the supervisee in accordance with practicum requirements at both midterm and final intervals. Provide both the supervisee and the practicum instructor with a copy of the evaluation.

Adhere to the CCFCC documentation requirements regarding supervision sessions.

Follow the ACA 2005 Code of Ethics.

Supervisee: Mai Chan

Credentials and Background: Mai Chan, BA, received her undergraduate degree in psychology and is currently enrolled in a master's degree program in clinical mental health counseling.

Supervisee Responsibilities:

Follow the ACA 2005 Code of Ethics.

Follow and adhere to CCFCC policies and procedures.

Adhere to the CCFCC documentation requirements regarding counseling sessions.

Demonstrate and document informed consent procedures with all clients, including the supervisee's status as a trainee as well as the supervisor's role and contact information.

Supervision Setting:

Campus Community Family Counseling Clinic (CCFCC)

Supervision Times:

Individual supervision will take place for one hour per week, while the supervisee is enrolled in practicum, for the Fall Semester 2014.

In the case of an emergency when the supervisor is not available, the supervisee is instructed to call Dr. Boie, Assistant Director, CCFCC (210-458-2900).

Signature/Supervisor: _____ Date: _____

Signature/Supervisee: _____ Date: _____

Signature/Practicum Faculty: _____ Date: _____

Adapted from Munson, 2002; Osborn & Davis, 1996; Sutter, McPherson, & Geeseman, 2002

TYPES OF SUPERVISION

Typically, supervision sessions occur in either individual, triadic, or group formats. Each of these modalities is described in detail here. Before you begin supervision, you and your supervisor will clarify the types of supervision to be used.

Individual Supervision

Individual supervision sessions occur between one supervisor and one supervisee. Bernard and Goodyear (2013) state that individual supervision seems to be the cornerstone of the counselors' professional growth, and it also appears that it is the most preferred method when compared to other types of supervision (Prieto, 1998; Ray & Altekruse, 2000).

Triadic Supervision

CACREP 2009 standards delineate the role of triadic supervision, or one supervisor and two supervisees in the session, as being comparable to individual supervision. CACREP (2009) defines triadic supervision as one supervisor and two counseling students who work for a minimum of one hour via a teaching and consultative relationship. This model of supervision has been used across disciplines under a variety of names. For example, the American Association for Marriage and Family Therapy (2007) includes triadic supervision as an acceptable form of individual supervision, defined as "face-to-face contact between a supervisor and a maximum of two [marriage and family therapists]/trainees" (p. 17).

Lawson, Hein, and Getz (2009) state that the main advantage of triadic supervision is its time-saving aspect. Another advantage of triadic supervision is the opportunity it affords for vicarious learning and observing multiple perspectives on counseling. Because both the supervisor and the peer will offer feedback, the counselor receiving supervision benefits from a richer supervision process (Lawson et al., 2009; Stinchfield, Hill, & Kleist, 2007). The most commonly used forms of triadic supervision are the *split-focus form,* in which each supervisee has half of the allotted supervision time, and the *single-focus form,* in which supervisees take turns in receiving the entire supervision session time (Lawson et al., 2009).

In triadic supervision, both the supervisor and the supervision peer take on active roles, thus resembling individual supervision and peer supervision processes. Observations offered by the peer in triadic supervision are beneficial because peers find it easier to communicate and model new concepts among themselves, under supervision, rather than directly with a supervisor (Hillerbrand, 1989; Lawson et al., 2009). Supervisees may also be less dependent on their supervisors in this process. Additionally, triadic supervision appears to be a favorable context for using active supervision techniques, such as tracking nonverbal responses and counseling skills as well as role plays.

Certain challenges may arise if the supervisee pairing is not effective. Some of these challenges may result in negative peer-to-peer dynamics, loss of trust, unwillingness to provide critical feedback, and an overall lack of effectiveness in the supervision process (Lawson et al., 2009).

Group Supervision

Group supervision usually involves one supervisor and a small group of six to eight supervisees. One of the many advantages of this format is time efficiency (Bernard & Goodyear, 2013; Hawkins & Shohet, 2000; Proctor, 2000; Riva & Cornish, 1995; Werstlein & Borders, 1997). This benefit has been instrumental especially in academic environments, where practicum courses typically involve a maximum of 10 students, as recommended by CACREP (2009). As counselors in training progress in their degree program, they will likely engage in this type of supervision. Additional benefits of group supervision consist of each supervisee having an opportunity to test the reality of self-perception in the context of a group of peers, where distorted perceptions about self and clients can be challenged. Consistent feedback can improve the supervisee's accuracy in perception and communication with clients and other professionals. The group format also provides a safe and supportive environment for the following: eliminating self-defeating behaviors and practicing skills such as self-disclosure, feedback, developing an appreciation of group dynamics, empathy, and social interest.

Group supervision also facilitates the learning process by offering alternative modes of helping and appreciation of different counseling styles, as well as a forum to practice perspective-taking skills with other group members. Overall, the supervisees also have an opportunity to appreciate the universality of their experiences in the practicum or internship, as well as some of their personal concerns. This facilitates the understanding of each other's cognitive processes, thus fostering less dependency on the supervisor (Hayes & Stefurak, 2010). Some other noted perceived benefits are peer support and noncompetitive feedback on evaluation of skills, as well as receiving helpful resources, which in turn increase the degree of confidence and camaraderie between supervisees (Hilber, 1999).

SUPERVISION METHODS

Aside from frequent sessions, supervisors gather information from supervisees in a number of ways. Common methods include self-report, digital or audio recordings, interpersonal process recall (IPR), reflective process, live observation, and live supervision. A description of each method follows.

Self-Report

The most common method of supervision is called self-report. It is as simple as it sounds; supervisees report to supervisors what happened in their counseling sessions, client issues as they see them, and their own issues and topics of concern. It is the least preferred method of supervision for beginning students, and it is more appropriate for postgraduate supervision (Goodyear & Nelson, 1997), mainly because it is only as effective as the counselor in training's level of experience and competence. Self-report can be subjective, thereby intentionally or unintentionally distorting the facts. Oftentimes, self-report is accompanied by the presentation of digital recordings, which can complement the supervisee's perspective. Advantages of self-report are that it can foster an intense tutorial relationship, in which the counselor in training has an opportunity to practice his or her case conceptualization skills as well as personal knowledge pertinent to both the counseling and the supervisory relationships (Noelle, 2002).

Digital or Audio Recordings

Sometimes, supervisors are able to view digital recordings or listen to audio recordings of their supervisees working with clients. Technology offers a complex tool for examining counseling skills and processes, and it gives supervisors direct access to the work of the supervisees (Bernard & Goodyear, 2013). It provides an opportunity to receive feedback on areas of concern or the entire session, but it can also offer the supervisor an occasion to identify strengths and to help the supervisee build upon them. Bernard and Goodyear (2013) also emphasized that digitally recording counseling sessions has many advantages, including the ability to see and hear the complexity of the interaction between counselor and client, and the ability to notice congruency between verbal and nonverbal communication. Another advantage listed by Bernard and Goodyear is that counselors in training can literally see themselves in the role of helper. Transcripts are oftentimes a useful tool to accompany an audio or digital recording of a counseling session, especially for novice supervisees (Arthur & Gfoerer, 2002). Based on their study, Arthur and Gfoerer mentioned that the advantages of transcribing the sessions were the ability to review the whole counseling session rather than just a snapshot of it, and the review gave both concrete examples of what the supervisees needed to work on as well as a visual or audio reminder of the sessions. On the other hand, one disadvantage of digital or audio recordings of counseling sessions is the associated cost, which includes the medium and the recording device.

VOICE FROM THE FIELD 14.2

A key component of counselor growth and development is the ability to generate multiple perspectives of clients and their clinical issues (e.g., Blocher, 1983). Achieving multiple perspectives is a primary goal of Borders' (1991) structured approach for peer supervision groups. Participants' perspectives are broadened and deepened by peers' feedback in the voice of the client, family members, and others connected to the client.

Katie was very concerned about the welfare of her client, a young married mother of two small children working in a minimum wage job. The client reported her marital relationship was an unhappy one due to financial challenges and general boredom. She said she wanted to improve her marriage while at the same time she was involved in an affair. Katie feared the client would end up in even more dire straits if the husband discovered the affair and left her. Determined to "save" the client from this outcome, she repeatedly brought the focus of counseling sessions back to the positive aspects of the marital relationship.

After watching a digitally recorded segment of a counseling session of Katie and her client, peers were asked to speak from the voice of the client. One peer responded, "I wish you would notice when I tear up and ask me about that. Look at my body, how hunched over and small I look." Another said, "I'm really scared and see no good way out of this situation. You make it sound so easy to decide, but it's not." A third peer reported, "I feel like you are lecturing me rather than listening to me." The last peer said, "I know you are trying, but it's not just my marriage. I really don't have any hope about anything." This critical feedback, delivered indirectly through the voice of the client, helped Katie back off her own solutions for the client, broadened her focus of the presenting and underlying issues, and reminded her to use counseling skills that helped her achieve needed depth with the client.

L. DiAnne Borders
Burlington Industries Excellence Professor,
Department of Counseling and Educational Development,
The University of North Carolina at Greensboro

Interpersonal Process Recall (IPR)

Interpersonal process recall (IPR) entails the supervisor and supervisee watching a digital recording or listening to an audio recording of a counseling session together. Either one of them can stop the recording at any point when something significant is observed, especially if the issue is not addressed in the counseling session. This process calls for the supervisor to allow for a safe haven for internal reactions (Kagan, 1980) and for investigating unstated agendas, affective explorations, cognitive examination, and expectations (Bernard & Goodyear, 2013). IPR does have disadvantages, one of which is that the process is slow because it can focus on only one portion of the digital or audio recording. As a result, it is helpful for the supervisee to choose a section that might be significant and to allow for the psychological space to investigate the processes. Another disadvantage is that, because of this focus, certain interpersonal dynamics might be magnified to the point of potential distortion. At this point, the clinical skill of the supervisor may help decide which interactions deserve further investigation (Bernard & Goodyear, 2013).

Reflective Process

Oftentimes, the supervisor may create a context for reflection, whereby the supervisee has an opportunity to reflect upon a "problem or a dilemma—something about which the learner feels confusion or dissonance and intends to search for a solution. The problem should revolve around an issue of consequence, one that is important to good practice" (Nelson & Neufeldt, 1998, pp. 81–82). This method is accompanied by Socratic questioning, whereby the supervisor is the source of important questions, rather than the source of all answers (Bernard & Goodyear, 2013, p. 232).

Live Observation

Although challenging because of scheduling and structural difficulties, live observation entails supervisors observing supervisees during their actual counseling sessions, without intervening. The advantages of live observation highlighted by Bernard and Goodyear (2013) include timeliness of the counseling session, with the opportunity for immediate supervision, which maximizes the supervisee's time to prepare for subsequent counseling sessions. Other advantages consist of providing the best safeguard for the client's welfare, due to the opportunity to intervene in case of emergency, and obtaining a more complete picture of the counseling session, more so than with audio or digital recordings.

Live Supervision

Live supervision is used mostly in training programs in which the context and availability of technology support this method (Bernard & Goodyear, 2013; Carlozzi, Romans, Boswell, Ferguson, & Whisenhunt, 1997). In the context of live supervision, the differences between counseling and supervision are less obvious, and the supervisor's role becomes more focused on coaching the supervisee. Live supervision relies on observation and interactive methods that enable the supervisor to guide the supervisee's decisions and work. Some of the methods used in live supervision are bug in the ear, monitoring, in vivo, phone-in, consultation, and interactive television (Bubenzer, Mahrle, & West, 1987). The bug in the ear (BITE) is a wireless earphone through which the supervisor can communicate with the supervisee throughout the counseling session. Its advantages are that the supervisee can make minor adjustments, as the supervisor supports and encourages the supervisee without interrupting the session. Because the client is unaware of this intervention, the counseling relationship is protected. Because of its being unobtrusive, BITE may be overused and thus may be distracting to the supervisee, as well as influencing the supervisee's level of independence in the counseling interactions (Bernard & Goodyear, 2013).

Another form of live supervision is monitoring via closed-circuit camera, which entails the supervisor observing the live sessions and intervening when the counselor experiences any difficulty (Minuchin & Fishman, 1981). Its advantages are that it protects the clients' welfare, the supervisor can directly observe session dynamics, and the supervisor can model counseling interactions within the context of the session. However, it can be disruptive to the dynamic between the counselor and the client (Bernard & Goodyear, 2013). Similar to monitoring is in vivo supervision, whereby instead of the supervisor taking over the session, the supervisor will consult on the intervention with the supervisees while the clients are present. Although in vivo is more of an intervention meant to redirect the counselor and the process of counseling, it still may be intrusive to the overall process (Bernard & Goodyear, 2013).

The last three methods of live supervision are perhaps the least invasive: phone-ins, consultation breaks, and using computers and interactive television for live supervision. The phone-ins and consultation breaks both entail stopping the session so that feedback can be provided to the supervisee or counselor in training. During the phone-ins, an intercom system is used for the purpose of consultation, whereas during consultation breaks, the supervisee physically exits the room and meets with the supervisor. In the latter situation, the supervisee has an increased opportunity to ask for clarification than in the phone-ins. The disadvantage of both is that they are still fairly interruptive of the counseling session (Bernard & Goodyear, 2013).

The interactive television in live supervision consists of the supervisor typing messages, which will appear on a screen behind the supervisee's client. This method is similar to BITE; however, it is less intrusive, because the supervisee can control when he or she wants to look at the screen and does not have to interrupt the client's story. Additionally, the messages written on the computer screen can also be saved and provided as feedback to the supervisee. Similar to the disadvantages of using the BITE method, the interactive television may overwhelm or distract the supervisee with the information. In an attempt to correct these drawbacks, a couple of alternatives have been developed. One of them, for example, used a monitor and a 14-icon system to provide simple feedback to the supervisee while in the counseling session (Tracey et al., 1995).

Some of the drawbacks of live supervision include the following: the high costs associated with the necessary facilities and equipment; the logistics of coordinating supervisee's and supervisor's schedules; the clients' reactions to this form of supervision; and the potential for decreased supervisee independence, self-confidence, and creativity within the counseling sessions (Bernard & Goodyear, 2013). Overall, there are many benefits of live supervision; for example, the ability to coach the supervisee, which increases the quality of the outcome of the counseling session, therefore providing a built-in system for protecting the client's welfare. Lee and Everett (2004) also state that the methods of live supervision may have a positive influence on the supervisory relationship, increasing the supervisee–supervisor alliance. The supervisee is more likely to try out interventions knowing that the supervisor has shared responsibility for the session and that the supervisor can also intervene, if needed. Based on the supervisor's conceptualizations and interventions, the supervisee has the opportunity to experience the predictability of the client's patterns in sessions, which increases confidence both in the supervisor's competence level and also in oneself as a counselor.

THE SUPERVISEE'S ROLE

An equally important role in supervision is that of the supervisee. Supervisees are either counselors in training in university programs at any level that are working with clients in applied settings as part of their university training program, or pre–independently licensed counselors or counselor interns who have completed their formal education and are employed in applied counseling settings.

Supervisees play a paramount role in the direction of supervision and heavily influence the supervision agenda. Pearson (2004) has suggested that "self-assessment of one's interest in and motivation for receiving supervision is a logical first step in preparing for the supervision experience" (p. 362). When it comes to supervision, it is recommended that counselors in training and postdegree counselors become informed consumers (Magnuson, Norem, & Wilcoxon, 2002). Although students do not often have the choice of practicum and internship supervisors, postdegree/prelicensed counselors usually have more options. When supervisees have the option of choosing a supervisor, they need to make a careful and deliberate consideration of a number of practical factors (see Box 14.2). They also need to take into account the personal and contextual factors that contribute to positive supervision outcomes. For example, Norem, Magnuson, Wilcoxon, and Arbel (2006) found that maturity, autonomy, perspicacity, motivation, self-awareness, and openness to experience were key attributes of "stellar supervisees" (p. 40). Conversely, supervisee factors associated with unresolved inter- and intrapersonal development, as well as limited cognitive and counselor development, were found to contribute to "lousy supervision outcomes" (Wilcoxon, Norem, & Magnuson, 2005, p. 39). See Box 14.3 for journal questions related to preparation to be a stellar supervisee.

BOX 14.2   Factors to Consider When Choosing a Supervisor

1. Self-assessment of interest and motivation in receiving supervision
2. Review relevant professional ethical codes related to supervision
3. Consult with others and interview potential supervisors (prepare to be interviewed as well)
4. Cost (typical fee per hour)
5. Location and frequency of meetings (at your work site, private practice, logistics)
6. Fit (personality and theory, style of working)
7. Affirm that potential supervisors maintain current state certification/license to supervise interns
8. Match with the supervisor's specialty area (e.g., addictions, eating disorders, children, etc.)

(Adapted from Magnuson et al., 2002; Pearson, 2004)

It is vital for supervisees to be proactive and assertive because the actual time spent in supervision sessions is usually limited. Therefore, preparation for supervision is important, and supervisees need to be ready to discuss their most urgent concerns. Depending on how structured both the supervisee and the supervisor are, a typical supervision session agenda may focus on the following issues: new clients, follow-up on current clients, available resources, administrative issues, evaluation, crisis, personal feelings and awareness, legal and ethical issues, and professional development (Somody, Padilla, & Lebron-Striker, 2008).

BOX 14.3 Journal Questions to Prepare to Be a Stellar Supervisee

(Maturity)

When have I opened myself up to a diverse idea in order to acquire a better understanding of it?

(Autonomy)

How do I react to negative feedback?

(Perspicacity)

How absolute am I in my thinking?

(Motivation)

What do I do to increase my skills and knowledge outside of class?

(Self-Awareness)

How vulnerable can I allow myself to be in order to gain insight into my personality and actions?

(Openness to Experience)

How often do I try something new in my life?

Questions from Somody, Padilla, and Lebron-Striker (2008)

In sum, Pearson (2004) recommends the following strategies to mental health counseling students for taking a proactive approach to supervision: be flexible, ask for (not demand) what is needed, take responsibility for learning in supervision, utilize self-assessment and reflection, avoid blaming and focus on solutions, and concentrate on what the supervisor can teach you instead of what he or she cannot provide (pp. 371–372).

THE SUPERVISORY RELATIONSHIP

The relationship between the supervisor and supervisee, whether in the context of a dyad or a triad, is a working alliance meant to provide support and feedback, which help the counselor in training define his or her new role. Mirroring other types of relationships (i.e., the counseling relationship), it is not static, but rather fluid and multidimensional. As mentioned previously, it is important to remember that the supervisory relationship not only is influenced by but also has an impact on the supervisee, the supervisor, and also the client.

The supervisory relationship is built on premises similar to the therapeutic relationship. For this relationship to foster growth in the supervisee, it has to be based on empathy, positive regard, genuineness, and concreteness. Other authors suggest that supervision is a working alliance (Bordin, 1983) founded on mutual agreement on goals, agreement on tasks, and bonds. In order to encourage the most growth in a supervisory relationship, it is important that these goals and tasks are based on a congruence of expectations (Ellis et al., 1994); this happens when participants communicate expectations and collaborate on developing common goals, which can be part of the supervision contract.

Research has shown that several factors may impact the effectiveness of supervisory alliances: the supervision style, based on the supervisor's attractiveness and interpersonal sensitivity; the extent to which the supervisor uses expert and referent power in the relationship; the extent to which the supervisor uses self-disclosure; both the supervisor's and the supervisee's attachment styles, because the ability to form healthy attachments predicts a successful alliance; and the supervisor's evaluative practices and adherence to the ethical codes of the profession. Additionally, the supervisee's previous negative experiences with supervision may also impact and weaken the supervisory alliance. In an examination of critical incidents in practicum supervision, Trepal, Bailie, and Leeth (2010) found that supervisees valued and found feedback, observational learning, and normalizing to be important aspects of practicum supervision. In addition, they found that practicum students saw a lack of support and unprofessionalism as negative incidents or harmful to their growth.

VOICE FROM THE FIELD 14.3

I make sure that I explain the importance of supervision to the counseling interns, and I work very hard on establishing their trust. Of course, this can only be done by treating the new counselors with respect, not ridiculing or admonishing them, yet letting them know when things are not going quite right. I have found it is very important to have written guidelines on how to handle critical situations, such as clients sharing that they are suicidal, hearing voices, or being abused. Procedures must be established and discussed in advance, particularly on reporting critical information to the supervisor (on site and at the university) and handling scary situations to the best of the counselor's ability based on experience and competence.

When I take on new interns, I feel that it is my job to reinforce the basics, yet add different points of view as well. I want the new counselors to become comfortable in their role as a counselor and a professional. In supervision, we discuss not only how things went with clients but also where the counselors in training are going as professionals. We explore what populations are most suitable for them, what settings they would like to work in, and, most important, how their counseling approach fits their personality and their personal preferences. We talk about training opportunities, conference/workshop attendance, alternative/complementary approaches to counseling, future sites, and even spirituality.

The most difficult part when I started doing supervision was to criticize or correct a beginning counselor. I then found that if I asked questions, just like I did with my clients, it became much easier for me. For example, I would ask for students to show me how they sat when they were with their clients (at the edge of the chair or in a relaxed position), and then I would demonstrate different positions and when to use each. I had student counselors check in on their own emotions, learn to feel with their gut, and respond to clients from more of an emotional rather than cranial point of view. I focused on teaching basic tools that the counselors could send home with their clients, particularly for stress reduction and relaxation. We used assigned reading to learn about the different forms and meanings of anger and what to do with them. I introduced tarot cards, play dough, balloons, and toys to see how they could be used even with adult clients in therapy. It is important to me that the new counselors learn that there is so much more than what they get in the classroom—that earning a master's degree is only the beginning. There are so many different ways of "doing counseling," and still, the bottom line is not what we do that is important but rather the relationship between the client and the counselor.

Having said that, my philosophy is that if it is the relationship that is the most important part of counseling, why can't I have some fun with what I'm (we're) doing? So, I attend workshops, read about different techniques, buy all sorts of gadgets, and give my clients the option to choose. The same goes for supervision. I value each and every intern and respect them all as professionals who are willing to help people get to a better place. I want to offer them a good experience with their initial site, so they can be happy with the choice of becoming a counselor, while teaching them what it takes to do well, including self-care. I don't believe that supervisors should look down on the graduate students, considering that we all had to start somewhere. Coming to a supervision experience should not be seen as a rite of passage, but instead as an opportunity to learn from someone who has been doing the work for quite some time.

Having said that, I would like the interns to be willing to learn *all* of the business, including paperwork, filing, answering phones, scheduling appointments, creating treatment goals, planning groups, and more. I want the new counselors to take their time in learning the new material, and not just go through the paces, filling in all the squares. I would like to see our counselors be committed, creative, involved, and proud—proud to be professional counselors and participants in another person's life, with all that it brings. It is an honor to be with a client, just as it is an honor to be part of this profession.

SONJA B. MONTGOMERY, PHD, LPC-S
Edelweiss Counseling Center,
San Antonio, Texas

LEGAL AND ETHICAL ISSUES IN SUPERVISION

Similar to counseling, there are numerous legal and ethical issues involved in supervision. Although many are beyond the scope of this chapter, some of the most relevant issues at this point for counselors in training include supervisor training, evaluation, and vicarious liability. The first ethical and legal responsibility is that supervisors have the necessary foundation to perform their role. According to the American Counseling Association (ACA) Code of Ethics (2005), "prior to offering clinical supervision, counselors are trained in supervision methods and techniques" (p. 14). This is an important responsibility for two reasons: supervisors not only serve as the gatekeepers of the profession but also are responsible for the professional growth of new counselors and counselors in training.

As stated earlier, the requirements to become a supervisor are similar to those for mental health professionals and vary by state. Supervisors generally agree to supervise prelicensed counselors for a specified time period and then are required to make a recommendation toward licensure. Typical requirements include postlicense experience and a specific number of clock hours of training in supervision models, methods, and techniques. For training purposes, the CACREP 2009 standards mandate that practicum and internship supervisors have experience and training in supervision and at least two years post-master's-degree experience in counseling or a related field (2009, Section III, F, G). Counselors who do not meet the requirements to supervise should not be performing this role.

Because supervisors are charged with the important task of monitoring and facilitating the work of their supervisees, it is paramount that supervisors explain to them the parameters of the supervisory relationship and all that it entails. According to Haynes, Corey, and Moulton (2003), in order "to make optimal use of supervision, supervisees need to clearly understand what their responsibilities are, what the supervisor's responsibilities are, and how they will be assessed" (p. 153). By clearly explaining the supervision process, the responsibilities of both parties, and the procedures for evaluation, supervisors are able to communicate their expectations to their supervisees. Supervisors can accomplish this by providing several documents including the following: an informed consent for supervision, a supervision contract/agreement, and a professional disclosure statement that outlines their supervision experience, philosophy, and approach. At some point, supervisors also need to address the issue of evaluation. Ideally, this will be done when they outline the process of supervision and evaluation, and this information will be presented in writing in the supervision contract. Research has suggested that although evaluation can be anxiety provoking, supervisees desire regular and ongoing feedback that is both positive and negative (Heckman-Stone, 2003).

An important ethical issue involving evaluation is called due process. Due process occurs when an individual has the right, time, and opportunity to respond to a negative evaluation or assessment. Because one of the supervisor's main responsibilities is to assess supervisees' competence, both for training programs and for licensure boards, evaluation is a paramount ethical issue in supervision. Ideally, supervisees should be told when and how both formative (along the way) and summative (final) evaluations will occur, as well as the process involved for improving and remediating their performance. As Remley and Herlihy (2010) explain, "the most blatant violations of supervisees' fair evaluation rights occur when a supervisee is given a negative final evaluation or is dismissed from an internship or job without having been given warning that performance was inadequate along with reasonable opportunity to improve" (p. 338). Because supervisors' evaluations weigh heavily in supervisees' professional outcomes, supervisors need to be particularly cautious and thorough in executing them. These evaluations are very important, so supervisees are also advised to respond to them in a timely manner.

Supervisees practice under their supervisor's license; thus, supervisors are legally and ethically responsible for ensuring client care. In addition, supervisors are held accountable for monitoring supervisees' development as well as their actions and interventions. Remley and Herlihy (2010) describe this as, "the legal principle that holds individuals who have control and authority over others will be held accountable for their negligence" (p. 345). This is called vicarious liability; it means that even though supervisors aren't actually counseling their supervisees' clients, they are responsible for their supervisees' actions. Supervisors must say, do, and document various directives in order to protect clients, agencies, and themselves from potential legal malpractice actions.

Finally, students and future supervisees are cautioned that not all supervisors are ethical. They need to be aware of the following standards for supervisors in the supervisory relationship: supervisors must have the appropriate training and credentials to perform their role, they should follow through on agreements to meet with their supervisees as required by their training program or licensure board, evaluations must be fair and supervisees afforded the due process to respond to negative assessments, and supervisors should respond to concerns and complaints in a timely and professionally appropriate manner.

MULTICULTURAL AND DIVERSITY ISSUES IN SUPERVISION

Issues of multiculturalism and diversity impact supervision in many ways. One aspect that supervisors focus on is helping their supervisees to examine and develop their multicultural competence. Aside from helping supervisees evaluate and refine their own multicultural knowledge, attitudes, and skills with clients, multicultural and diversity issues also exist in and impact the supervisory relationship. According to Estrada, Wiggins Frame, and Williams (2004), "Cross-cultural supervision, on the other hand, refers to the analysis of contents, processes, and outcomes in supervision in which racial, ethnic, and/or cultural differences exist between at least two members of the client-counselor-supervisor triad" (p. 310).

As a counselor, multicultural awareness is not only an asset but also a critical part of being a competent and ethical professional (ACA, 2005; Arredondo et al., 1996). Most programs require a course focusing on counseling diverse populations, yet some may infuse this focus throughout the entire program coursework. However, many times actual direct counseling work with the clients does not begin until practicum and internship. Much of the multicultural skill and competence building does not start until then; therefore, the impact of multiculturally aware supervision is tremendous.

Two dimensions of the supervision process are impacted by the way in which multicultural issues are addressed. First is the supervisory relationship itself, in which the supervisor and supervisee may share different backgrounds. This can result in many differences, ranging from dissimilar worldviews to different theoretical approaches to counseling. Second is the relationship between the supervisee or counselor, and the client. They too may share the same cultural background, or these may be different. Multiculturally competent supervision seems to influence both aspects of the supervision process in a positive manner.

Toporek, Ortega-Villalobos, and Pope-Davis (2004) found that counselors reported a higher satisfaction with the supervisory relationship if multicultural issues are attended to. Additionally, the counselors' perceived multicultural awareness increased as a result of their supervisor's multicultural competence. This translated into how the counselors incorporated the feedback into their counseling sessions with their clients (Dickson & Jepsen, 2007; Pope-Davis, Liu, Toporek, & Brittan-Powell, 2001). As a result of multicultural supervision in response to various critical incidents, specific areas of growth were identified in supervisees, including the following: awareness of how culture affected the counselor, clients, and supervisor; skills to effectively address individual differences; increased knowledge in terms of the multicultural competency in counseling as well as supervision; exposure to situations that highlighted the need for multicultural counseling and supervision; increased confidence in one's own ability to address matters effectively; and recognition of need for more training (Toporek, Ortega-Villalobos, & Pope-Davis, 2004).

As a counselor or a supervisee, multiculturalism may be addressed differently, depending on the supervisor, the supervisory relationship, and the clients' concerns. For example, the supervisor may address the strengths and limitations of his or her cultural knowledge, and may proactively introduce multicultural issues in the supervision sessions. Additionally, the supervisor may disclose some of his or her cultural biases, background, values, and experiences. Last, the supervisor would likely demonstrate the clinical significance of racism and oppression in counseling and supervision (Ancis & Marshall, 2010). Some ways in which the supervisor may encourage growth in the counseling relationship are by promoting discussions of the ways the counselors' cultural background may impact their clients, exploring a situation from the client's perspective, increasing awareness through experiential exercises, and considering cultural assumptions and stereotyping (Ancis & Marshall, 2010).

CASE STUDY 14.2

As a supervisor, Luis wanted to openly address the cultural differences between him and Mai by learning more about Mai's background and some of her cultural traditions and beliefs. He expressed genuine interest and enthusiasm in doing so. He stated that Mai's having experienced two cultural perspectives and her awareness of her own cultural worldview will be an asset to understanding her clients' worldviews. Luis invited her to share some of her insights and what she thought of working with clients of ethnicities different from her own. He listened to her intently and shared his growth-oriented perspective in working with clients in general. He offered some information about his background, having grown up in Mexico and lived in California for most of his life. He was eager to share certain similarities between his background and that of his supervisee. Luis encouraged Mai to openly address any differences that might arise, whether between her and her counseling clients, or between the two of them in the supervisory process. He emphasized his belief that using respect, awareness, and competence in addressing any multicultural issues is a cornerstone in professional counseling.

Based on an adaptation of Aten, Madson, and Kruse's (2008) supervision genogram, Luis also asked Mai to complete a genogram (see Figure 14.1) in which she would include some of her previous work supervisors and mentors. This was accomplished by drawing a horizontal timeline across the page, and would include various symbols to describe the quality of each relationship or alliance. The setting of the supervision or mentoring was included as well to differentiate between types of work-related supervision. Mai added the supervisor's race or ethnicity. In facilitating the process, Luis asked questions such as the following: What characteristics of the supervisor did you like and would you want to emulate? What were some characteristics you disliked? How were differences in opinions or potential conflicts taken care of? How did culture (including age, sexual orientation, religion, and socioeconomic background) impact the relationship? Luis was open to Mai's descriptions, and together they were able to reflect on ways that cultural differences may have impacted these relationships. As a result of this activity, Mai left the session with an increased sense of confidence in Luis's genuineness and openness to discussing multicultural issues.

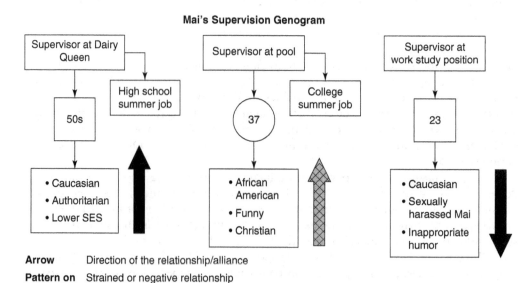

Mai's Supervision Genogram

FIGURE 14.1   Mai's supervision genogram.

As a result of Luis's openness to discussing multicultural and diversity-related issues, halfway through her semester, Mai shared with him her struggles about dealing with one of her client's religious affiliation and strong religious beliefs. She shared feeling stuck, sometimes resentful and unsure about how to address the client's long and "preachy" tirades. She said she felt ineffective and frustrated about the lack of progress with her client. Luis encouraged Mai to explore her own religious beliefs and consider ways in which her beliefs might differ and influence her perception of the client's religious beliefs. Once Mai acknowledged that her family did not emphasize any religious affiliation and that she was not familiar with Christian values, she was able to step back and look at her concerns from a slightly different perspective. Luis also invited Mai to explore what role she believed religion played in her client's life, from the client's perspective.

Conclusion

This chapter examined clinical supervision through diverse aspects including the following: the differences between clinical and administrative supervision, the scope and function of supervisors, training and supervision issues according to the CACREP standards, various methods and modes of supervision delivery, and supervisee and supervisor factors in the supervision process. It also highlighted the special role of the supervisee in order to better prepare counseling students to enter the supervisory relationship.

References

American Association for Marriage and Family Therapy. (2007). *Approved supervisor designation standards and responsibilities handbook.* Alexandria, VA: Author.

American Counseling Association (ACA). (2005). *Code of ethics.* Alexandria, VA: Author.

Ancis, J., & Marshall, D. (2010). Using a multicultural framework to assess supervisees' perceptions of culturally competent supervision. *Journal of Counseling & Development, 88*(3), 277–284.

Arredondo, P., Toporek, M. S., Brown, S., Jones, J., Locke, D. C., Sanchez, J., & Stadler, H. (1996). *Operationalization of the Multicultural Counseling Competencies.* Alexandria, VA: Association for Multicultural Counseling and Development.

Arthur, G. L., & Gfoerer, K. P. (2002). Training and supervision through the written word: A description and intern feedback. *The Family Journal: Counseling and Therapy for Couples and Families, 10,* 213–219.

Association for Counselor Education and Supervision (ACES). (1993). *Ethical guidelines for counseling supervisors.* Retrieved from http://files.acesonline.net/doc/ethical_guidelines.htm

Aten, J. D., Madson, M. B., & Kruse, S. J. (2008). The supervision genogram: A tool for preparing supervisors-in-training. *Psychotherapy: Theory, Research, Practice, Training, 45*(1), 111–116. doi:10.1037/0033-3204.45.1.111

Bernard, J. M., & Goodyear, R. K. (2013). *Fundamentals of clinical supervision* (5th ed.). New York, NY: Pearson.

Blocher, D. H. (1983). Toward a cognitive developmental approach to counseling supervision. *The Counseling Psychologist, 11*(1), 27–34. doi:10.1177/0011000083111006

Borders, L. D. (1991). A systematic approach to peer group supervision. *Journal of Counseling & Development, 69,* 248–252.

Bordin, E. S. (1983). A working alliance model of supervision. *The Counseling Psychologist, 11*(1), 35–42. doi:10.1177/0011000083111007

Bubenzer, D. L., Mahrle, C., & West, J. D. (1987). *Live counselor supervision: Trainee acculturation and supervisor interventions.* Paper presented at the American Association for Counseling and Development Annual Convention, New Orleans.

Carlozzi, A. F., Romans, J. S. C., Boswell, D. L., Ferguson, D. B., & Whisenhunt, B. J. (1997). Training and supervision practices in counseling and marriage and family therapy programs. *The Clinical Supervisor, 15*(1), 51–60. doi:10.1300/J001v15n01_04

Council for Accreditation of Counseling and Related Educational Programs (CACREP). (2009). *CACREP accreditation manual: 2009 standards*. Alexandria, VA: Author. Retrieved from http://www.cacrep.org/doc/2009%20Standards%20with%20cover.pdf

Dickson, G., & Jepsen, D. A. (2007). Multicultural training experiences as predictors of multicultural competencies: Students' perspectives. *Counselor Education and Supervision, 47*(2), 76–95.

Ellis, M. V., Anderson-Hanley, C. M., Dennin, M. K., Anderson, J. J., Chapin, J. L., & Polstri, S. M. (1994, August). *Congruence of expectations in clinical supervision: Scale development and validity data*. Paper presented at the annual meeting of the American Psychological Association, Los Angeles.

Estrada, D., Wiggins Frame, M., & Williams, C. B. (2004). Cross-cultural supervision: Guiding the conversation toward race and ethnicity. *Journal of Multicultural Counseling and Development, 32,* 307–319.

Goodyear, R. K., & Nelson, M. L. (1997). The major supervision formats. In C. E. Watkins (Ed.), *Handbook of psychotherapy supervision* (pp. 328–344). New York, NY: Wiley.

Hawkins, P., & Shohet, R. (2000). *Supervision in the helping professions* (2nd ed.). Philadelphia, PA: Open University Press.

Hayes, R. L., & Stefurak, J. T. (2010). Group supervision. In N. Ladany & L. J. Bradley (Eds.), *Counselor supervision: Principles, process, and practice* (4th ed., pp. 215–232). New York, NY: Routledge.

Haynes, R., Corey, G., & Moulton, P. (2003). *Clinical supervision in the helping professions: A practical guide*. Pacific Grove, CA: Brooks/Cole–Thompson Learning.

Heckman-Stone, C. (2003). Trainee preferences for feedback and evaluation in clinical supervision. *The Clinical Supervisor, 22*(1), 21–33. doi:10.1300/J001v22n01_03

Henderson, P. A. (2009). *The new handbook of administrative supervision in counseling*. New York, NY: Routledge.

Hilber, P. R. (1999). *Group supervision: A qualitative examination* (Unpublished doctoral dissertation). University of North Dakota, Grand Forks, ND.

Hillerbrand, E. (1989). Cognitive differences between experts and novices: Implications for group supervision. *Journal of Counseling & Development, 67,* 293–296.

Kagan, N. (1980). Influencing human interaction— Eighteen years with IPR. In A. K. Hess (Ed.), *Psychotherapy supervision: Theory, research, and practice* (pp. 262–286). New York, NY: Wiley.

Lawson, G., Hein, S., & Getz, H. (2009). A model for using triadic supervision in counselor preparation programs. *Counselor Education and Supervision, 48,* 257–270.

Lee, R. E., & Everett, C. A. (2004). *The integrative family therapy supervisor: A primer*. New York, NY: Brunner-Routledge.

Magnuson, S., Norem, K., & Wilcoxon, S. A. (2002). Clinical supervision for licensure: A consumer's guide. *Journal of Humanistic Counseling, Education and Development, 41*(1), 52–60.

Minuchin, S., & Fishman, C. (1981). *Family therapy techniques*. Cambridge, MA: Harvard University Press.

Munson, C. E. (2002). *Handbook of clinical social work supervision* (3rd ed.). Binghamton, NY: Haworth Press.

National Board for Certified Counselors. (2010). *State board directory*. Retrieved from http://www.nbcc.org/directory/

Nelson, M. L., & Neufeldt, S. A. (1998). The pedagogy of counseling: A critical examination. *Counselor Education and Supervision, 38,* 70–88.

Neufeldt, S. A. (1999). Training in reflective processes in supervision. In M. Carroll & E. L. Holloway (Eds.), *Training counselling supervisors: Strategies, methods and techniques* (pp. 92–106). London, England: Sage.

Noelle, M. (2002). Self-report in supervision: Positive and negative slants. *The Clinical Supervisor, 21,* 125–134.

Norem, K., Magnuson, S., Wilcoxon, S. A., & Arbel, O. (2006). Supervisees' contributions to stellar supervision outcomes. *Journal of Professional Counseling: Practice, Theory & Research, 43*(1/2), 33–48.

Osborn, C. J., & Davis, T. E. (1996). The supervision contract: Making it perfectly clear. *The Clinical Supervisor, 14*(2), 121–134.

Pearson, Q. M. (2004). Getting the most out of clinical supervision: Strategies for mental health counseling students. *Journal of Mental Health Counseling, 26*(4), 361–373.

Pope-Davis, D. B., Liu, W. M., Toporek, R., & Brittan-Powell, C. (2001). What's missing from multicultural competency research: Review, introspection and recommendations. *Cultural Diversity and Ethnic Minority, 7,* 121–138.

Prieto, L. R. (1998). Practicum class supervision in CACREP-accredited counselor training programs: A national survey. *Counselor Education and Supervision, 38,* 113–124.

Proctor, B. (2000). *Group supervision: A guide to creative practice*. London, England: Sage.

Ray, D. C., & Altekruse, M. (2000). Effectiveness of group supervision versus combined group and individual supervision. *Counselor Education and Supervision, 40*(1), 119–130.

Remley, T., & Herlihy, B. (2010). *Ethical, legal, and professional issues in counseling* (3rd ed.). Upper Saddle River, NJ: Pearson Education.

Riva, M. T., & Cornish, J. A. (1995). Group supervision practices at a psychology predoctoral internship program: A national survey. *Professional Psychology: Research and Practice, 26,* 523–525. doi:10.1037/0735-7028.26.5.523

Somody, C., Padilla, E., & Lebron-Striker, M. (2008). *Reflections of a stellar supervisee.* Unpublished manuscript.

Stinchfield, T. A., Hill, N. R., & Kleist, D. M. (2007). The reflective model of triadic supervision: Defining an emerging modality. *Counselor Education and Supervision, 46,* 172–183.

Sutter, E., McPherson, R. H., & Geeseman, R. (2002). Contracting for supervision. *Professional Psychology: Research and Practice, 33*(5), 495–498. doi:10.1037/0735-7028.33.5.495

Texas Occupations Code. (1999). *Licensed Professional Counselor Act.* Retrieved from http://www.statutes.legis.state.tx.us/Docs/OC/htm/OC.503.htm

Toporek, R. L., Ortega-Villalobos, L., & Pope-Davis, D. B. (2004). Critical incidents in multicultural supervision: Exploring supervisees' and supervisors' experiences. *Journal of Multicultural Counseling and Development, 32,* 66–83.

Tracey, M., Forechle, T., Kelbley, T., Chilton, T., Sandhofer, R., Woodward, D., . . . Benkert, R. (1995, April). *Data centric counseling: The development of a computer-assisted observation system for use in process studies in counseling, supervision and counselor training.* Paper presented at the annual meeting of the American Educational Research Association, San Francisco.

Trepal, H., Bailie, J., & Leeth, C. (2010). Critical incidents in practicum supervision: Supervisees' perspectives. *Journal of Professional Counseling: Practice, Theory, and Research, 38*(1), 28–38.

Werstlein, P. O., & Borders, L. D. (1997). Group process variables in group supervision. *The Journal for Specialists in Group Work, 22*(2), 120–136. doi:10.1080/01933929708414374

Wilcoxon, S. A., Norem, K., & Magnuson, S. (2005). Supervisees' contributions to lousy supervision outcomes. *Journal of Professional Counseling: Practice, Theory and Research, 33*(2), 31–49.

15

Internet-Based Counseling

Caroline S. Booth

CHAPTER OVERVIEW

Almost every industry has seen significant changes brought about by technology, and counseling is no different. Once thought to be only a face-to-face (FTF) paradigm, it is now understood that Internet-based counseling affords clinical mental health counseling practitioners extended opportunities to serve clients. Along with these opportunities come potential risks and unique considerations that must be discussed to maintain best practices. This chapter provides an overview of Internet-based counseling.

Beginning with a discussion on the evolution of technology and the Internet, the chapter highlights important considerations for the clinical mental health practitioner considering Internet-based work. Included are a thorough discussion of Internet counseling modalities, online counseling considerations, ethical and legal issues, professional standards and accreditation, informed consent, online counseling skills, client assessment, and multicultural considerations. Interspersed within this content are pedagogical exercises and other activities designed to facilitate understanding of the topics and stimulate meaningful dialogue.

LEARNING OBJECTIVES

The learning objectives for this chapter are designed to be consistent with the 2009 Council for Accreditation of Counseling and Related Educational Programs Standards (CACREP, 2009). As such, upon completion of this chapter, the student will have knowledge of the following clinical mental health counseling standards:

1. Understands the history, philosophy, and trends in clinical mental health counseling. (A.1)
2. Understands ethical and legal considerations specifically related to the practice of clinical mental health counseling. (A.2)
3. Knows the professional organizations, preparation standards, and credentials relevant to the practice of clinical mental health counseling. (A.4)
4. Is aware of professional issues that affect clinical mental health counselors (e.g., core provider status, expert witness status, access to and practice privileges within managed care systems). (A.7)

5. Understands the management of mental health services and programs, including areas such as administration, finance, and accountability. (A.8)

6. Understands the impact of crises, disasters, and other trauma-causing events on people. (A.9)

7. Understands the range of mental health service delivery—such as inpatient, outpatient, partial treatment and aftercare—and the clinical mental health counseling services network. (C.5)

8. Understands how living in a multicultural society affects clients who are seeking clinical mental health counseling services. (E.1)

9. Understands how to critically evaluate research relevant to the practice of clinical mental health counseling. (I.1)

INTRODUCTION

Over the last several decades, the world has been in the midst of a global revolution. Although a peaceful process, this revolution has been brought about by technological advances that have changed the way people work, socialize, and live. Thomas Friedman (2005) famously coined the phrase "the world is flat" to describe how technology has made the 21st century one of unprecedented connection, which has, in effect, leveled the globe. We now live in a world where communication in written, spoken, or digital form can be instantaneous and acquired seamlessly from just about any location on Earth.

According to the US Census Bureau (2009), 68.7% of households in the United States used the Internet at home in 2009, up from 18% in 1997. This means that in just over one decade, homes with computer and Internet access have increased almost *four*fold. Such an increase has created an American populace that is more technologically savvy and con-nected than ever before. No longer limited to face-to-face communication, people not only have a choice to communicate through audio, text, pictures, or video but also have a fur-ther choice to do so at home, at work, in a wireless coffee shop, or even on a plane. In addition, the advent of devices such as smartphones, laptops, and tablets has made it pos-sible to take this technology along wherever we go.

The Internet, which began as a US–government-sponsored academic project, has liter-ally transformed the world. As Bill Gates predicted in 2000, the Internet has become one of the key cultural and commercial forces of this century by making the world "smaller" (Gates, 2000). Evidence of this can be seen through the transformation of both industry and society. It is now possible to buy, sell, and trade goods ranging from simple household items and food to lavish cars, vacations, and homes with a few simple clicks of a computer mouse (Booth & Watson, 2009). What is most fascinating about this is that most of these Internet-based commercial transactions do not require ever speaking to a live person or even leaving the comfort of one's home. More and more services once delivered primarily face-to-face, such as education, are rapidly moving into the online realm. It is now possible to receive an education, locate employment, and pursue a career without ever having entered a brick and mortar building. Or perhaps a more relevant example is how graduate students no longer need to enter a library to conduct research because online databases, journals, and e-books are at the touch of a fingertip.

In addition to the commercial changes created by the Internet, a tremendous social transformation has occurred. Whereas the Internet provided digital access to commerce and paperless information initially, more recent applications have allowed the Internet to become a more social place. These Web 2.0 software applications, so-called because of the shared construction of data, allow users to share information, photos, music, videos, and anything else with other users from around the planet (O'Reilly, 2005). In effect, the users of the Internet are creating the content with management and mediation by the host application. You probably use some of the more popular Web 2.0 technologies such as Facebook, YouTube, Wikipedia, Skype, and Twitter. These platforms allow users to upload or live stream their media and share content with a select person, group, or the entire online community. Through these shareware applications, social networks are created and managed as information enters the public domain and others comment on it, post about it, and interact with it. There is growing anecdotal evidence that these "virtual world" relationships are increasingly influencing and even supplanting face-to-face ones. Whereas online dating was once an anomaly, it is now commonplace and has advanced to the point that avatars (virtual representations of self) are now marrying in online communities. Indeed, one only has to view the documentary *Google Baby* (2010), which illustrates how a person with a computer can create a child using online donors and surrogates that are continents apart, to witness the power of the Internet.

Although many do not agree with or approve the changes that have been brought about by the Internet age, it is clear that the World Wide Web has become a powerful force. Interestingly, counseling and other human services occupations are at the crossroads of the commercial and social realms of the Internet, although these professions have been slower than others to embrace the Internet and its many applications. Whereas once it might have been possible for professional counselors to ignore this paradigm, it is increasingly obvious that doing so may place the 21st-century counselor at economic risk. Providing services online might not be a good fit for all clinical mental health practitioners, yet it is important for everyone to understand the parameters of Internet-based counseling.

REFLECTIVE EXERCISE: THE POWER OF THE INTERNET ILLUSTRATED

Nineteen-year-old Abraham Biggs was a Florida college student who, like many young people today, was very active online. He was interested in *lifecasting*, whereby users have their own Internet-based video channel that broadcasts 24 hours a day via webcam. Because Abraham was interested in bodybuilding, he became active on a bodybuilding Web site, where he noted that this online community had "become like a family" to him. He said he preferred discussing his troubles online, because he did not feel comfortable speaking to anyone in person about them.

In mid-November 2008, Abraham posted messages describing his intention to kill himself and directing others to his lifecasting Web site. He reported that overwhelming sadness and disappointment had led him to make this decision. The online bodybuilding community later reported that this was not the first time he had threatened suicide, and his posting was met with discussion ranging from disbelief to users who encouraged him to follow through with his intent. Over the course of the subsequent 12 to 13 hours, Abraham listed the drugs he was going to take and also posted a suicide note. Followers of his lifecast encouraged him to commit suicide and joked as Abraham overdosed on medication, some of which was originally prescribed for his bipolar disorder. Some viewers continued to watch as Abraham lapsed into unconsciousness. Ultimately, several viewers, including a person in India, summoned police who arrived at Abraham's home, which was also captured on streaming video. Later, it was noted that 181 people were watching as Abraham killed himself (Stelter, 2008).

Abraham's story highlights the power of the Internet. What are your thoughts on how the Internet played a role in his death? What ethical and moral values were involved? How could the outcome have been different?

TECHNOLOGY OF ONLINE COUNSELING

Before beginning a comprehensive discussion of online counseling, it is important to understand that multiple terms exist in the literature to describe the practice. Among the more common names are e-counseling, e-therapy, e-psychotherapy, Internet counseling, Web counseling, cybercounseling, Internet psychotherapy, and online counseling or psychotherapy (Germain, Marchand, Bouchard, Drouin, & Guay, 2009; Patrick, 2006). All refer to the practice of providing counseling using computer technology. Patrick (2006) believes this multitude of terms illustrates a lack of clarity with regard to technologically assisted counseling. Although this may be true, it is perhaps reflective of the evolution of a practice still in its early stages; online counseling is a recent phenomenon (Patrick, 2006).

Internet Counseling Defined

Internet counseling may be relatively new, but many counselors have always used technology in counseling, although they may not have recognized it as such. The National Board for Certified Counselors (NBCC; 2012b) provided a useful taxonomy in its document, *Policy Regarding the Provision of Distance Professional Services*. In the NBCC's classification system, counseling is described as being deliverable in a variety of forms, but it separates it into two broad modalities. Face-to-face counseling is the practice of counseling using a strictly in-person format, whereas technology-assisted counseling is the use of either a telephone (telecounseling) *or* computer (Internet counseling) in counseling. Many may not recognize the telephone as a technological device, but clinical mental health counselors have been using telecounseling for years as a modality to, among other things, conduct preliminary intakes, brief counseling interventions, follow-ups, and crisis assessments.

While telecounseling continues as a popular mental health practice, Internet counseling has grown along with the expansion of the Internet. When discussing Internet counseling, it is useful to revisit the NBCC (2012b) classification system, which recognizes the broad scope of counseling services delivered via computer. It separates Internet counseling into two broad categories defined as *asynchronous* counseling, which is characterized by a time gap between communications, and *synchronous* counseling, which does not have a time gap between interactions. Asynchronous forms of Internet counseling include such modalities as e-mail and bulletin board counseling, whereas synchronous forms include chat-based and video-based communications. NBCC recommends selecting the modality of counseling based on the preference of the client. Internet counseling may be indicated out of necessity or convenience, or it may be chosen as a supplement to face-to-face counseling. NBCC also acknowledges that Internet-based counseling can be done both individually and in multiple client formats such as couple and group counseling. A more thorough discussion of the major modalities of Internet counseling follows. For ease of discussion, only individual counseling modalities will be reviewed.

E-mail-Based Internet Counseling

One of the most popular features of the Internet has become electronic mail. The ability to send correspondence instantly has shaped the way society communicates. In fact, many mental health providers are already using e-mail to communicate with clients even if they do not offer e-mail therapy (Welfel & Heinlen, 2009). This has become the preferred communication mode for many, and e-mail-based treatment is one of the most popular applications of Internet-based practice (Bloom & Waltz, 2005). The practice involves a client sending an e-mail that describes a personal issue or concern to a counselor and the counselor responding via the same modality. Both client and counselor have time to reflect on their writings before submitting, which is one of the most frequently cited benefits of the practice (Centore & Milacci, 2008). However, Maples and Han (2008) noted that this feature can come at the price of spontaneity.

Although e-mail has been revolutionary, privacy concerns may limit therapeutic uses of this resource for some. Frequently cited concerns include misdirecting an e-mail to an unintended sender, difficulty establishing the identity of the sender, truthfulness of information provided, e-mails being logged and stored on provider or employer servers, failures in technology, unprotected e-mail accounts, and misunderstanding the intent of communications (Grohol, 1999; Mallen, Vogel, & Rochlen, 2005; Welfel & Heinlen, 2009). Concerns have also been voiced about duty-to-warn issues associated with e-mail transactions, because some believe clients to be more likely to verbalize self-harm via e-mail versus calling or making an appointment (Welfel & Heinlen, 2009). Despite these concerns, it appears that use of e-mail by practitioners is on the rise, at least partly driven by consumer demand (Welfel & Heinlen, 2009).

Several e-mail counseling services have been established, and more are sure to come. Some provider Web sites use their own secure e-mail server to maintain confidentiality; clients are given an e-mail address, and all communication takes place via this platform (Murphy, MacFadden, & Mitchell, 2008). Other e-mail-based practitioners direct clients to free shareware that encrypts and protects e-mail beyond the services provided by most providers. Clients need to understand that all e-mails are logged and stored on provider servers in digital format. Even though it might be highly unlikely that any service provider would seek to access this information, it is, at least in theory, an option. Encryption provides additional protection, but confidentiality can never be wholly guaranteed, so clients need to understand the technology behind e-mail enough to provide adequate consent to engage in the practice. In addition to service provider access, clients need to be aware that employer-based e-mail accounts can be considered to be the property of the employer.

Research has suggested that e-mail therapy may be effective if practitioners have sufficient experience in counseling and can tolerate the abrupt and brief exchanges that frequently characterize e-mail work (Stummer, 2009). However, even though the exchanges may be brief, the asynchronous nature of the exchange can ensure that counselors have ample time to compose their responses in thoughtful and intentional ways (Tate & Zabinski, 2004). Various issues that have been found to be effective with e-mail counseling range from smoking cessation (Abroms, Gill, Windsor, & Simons-Morton, 2009) to male sexual dysfunction (Van Diest, Van Lankveld, Leusink, Slob, & Gijs, 2007). E-mail can also provide a safe way for clients, particularly clients who are underserved by other modalities—such as male clients—to seek help using a familiar medium (Lester, 2008/2009).

Bulletin Board or Listserv Counseling

A more recent type of counseling, bulletin board counseling, has become increasingly popular on the Internet. This practice involves a client posting a concern on a public forum anonymously and a counselor responding with a posting (Maples & Han, 2008). Because this work is anonymous and public, acceptable topics may include those of a less sensitive nature, and clients may frequently use pseudonyms or avatar names (Haley & Vasquez, 2009). You may have seen some professional association Web sites that offer this service to members, who get to ask a professional a question. These discussion boards can be moderated by a practitioner and offer a convenient way to communicate useful information to multiple individuals (Tate & Zabinski, 2004). Listservs function in a similar way, except that postings are e-mailed to all subscribers of the list.

Chat-Based Internet Counseling

Chat-based Internet counseling consists of counseling that occurs via text in a synchronous environment. Using readily available chat or text messaging software, clients engage in real-time discussions with counselors. Initially bound by a desktop computer, the rise of laptops, smartphones, and wireless Internet has now expanded this practice to any remote location. Clients and counselors can set up prearranged times to chat, and the popularity of mobile phones enables this technology to be handheld (Preziosa, Grassi, Gaggioli, & Riva, 2009).

Centore and Milacci (2008) have examined the research and identified several advantages of this type of text-based counseling practice. A primary advantage is that these text-based interactions allow both the counselor and the client to attend *exclusively* to the dialogue of the interaction. Writing versus speaking can also invoke a greater level of reflection in clients and a lesser degree of social restriction or apprehension. The process of writing one's story can also facilitate new associations or help to recapture older memories and observations. Clients also have the opportunity to set the pace of the counseling by choosing when and how they respond. Both counselor and client are more accountable by virtue of having all communication written and saved. This also can be beneficial for both as interactions can be printed and stored for both counselor records and client reviewing.

Although there are multiple types of chat and messaging software available, it is important to ensure that the program selected for counseling has complete and extensive encryption capabilities. Much of this encryption software is available for free and can easily be located on the Web. The Electronic Privacy Information Center (www.epic.org) offers a comprehensive listing of software that can be used to protect chat programs. Counselors should not attempt to use chat-based treatment without taking the necessary steps to ensure not only that they have the appropriate encryption software but that their client does as well.

Video-Based Internet Counseling

Video-based counseling is a newer modality that has arisen from increased availability and affordability of Web cameras, integrated webcams, and videoconferencing equipment. This type of counseling is believed to be most like face-to-face counseling, because it involves a visual and auditory presence by both the counselor and the client (Germain et al.., 2009; Murphy et al., 2008; Tsan & Day, 2007). This allows for counselors to fully appreciate visual cues and nuances not available to the text-based practitioner.

Video counseling is often accomplished using videoconferencing technology whereby the client and the counselor see and hear each other in synchronous or real-time fashion (Germain et al., 2009). This videoconferencing can be accomplished by using specialized conferencing hardware and software in conjunction with either a video camera or web camera. Much of the videoconference technology in use today involves clients accessing the service by traveling to a location such as a provider office, but technology experts predict this will change. Although not yet widely available, it is expected that clients will be able to receive videoconference services from locations such as home, the workplace, retail locations, or via personal smartphone in the very near future (Earnhardt, 2010). This telehealth technology is being widely explored in the medical health professions as a way to increase access to treatment and expand the continuum of care (Brennan, Holtz, Chumbler, Kobb, & Rabinowitz, 2008; Earnhardt, 2010).

Another type of video-based health service that counselors use is web-based video software. This free meeting software (i.e., Skype) enables encrypted video chatting or audio chatting using VoIP, or voice over Internet protocol. This service, along with others, offers no-cost secure video and audio chat software to anyone that has Internet access (Berson, 2005). Users only need to establish an account with the chosen software provider. Similar to other social sharing applications, users must request and be accepted as a contact prior to any video chatting. Other providers, such as Learn-Central at www.learncentral.com, have expanded video capabilities to include file sharing, web browsing, and a whiteboard as additional means of communication. Although all of these sites were designed primarily for meetings, collaborations, and social networking, it is expected that sites designed specifically for counseling and mental health service delivery will become available in the near future.

Virtual Reality Counseling

A final synchronous counseling modality that is beginning to emerge is virtual reality counseling. Virtual reality involves participating and interacting in a three-dimensional world through an individual avatar. Currently, virtual reality in clinical mental health counseling is most commonly used to provide client simulations whereby clients get the opportunity to practice new behaviors and decision making in an immersive and realistic environment (Tate & Zabinski, 2004). Many virtual simulations can be purchased as software packages, and now there is even open source software such as NeuroVR (www.neurovr.org) that mental health practitioners can download to offer customizable simulations for their clients (Riva, 2009). Although these simulations do not provide synchronous counseling, they offer behavioral rehearsal and other therapeutic benefits.

Other open source virtual reality software goes beyond the asynchronous experience of the virtual simulations to the creation of virtual communities, such as Second Life (www.secondlife.com). In this application, a user-designed and password-protected avatar enters one of many virtual worlds where he or she freely interacts with other avatars using messaging and microphones to communicate. In addition, avatars are able to move and gesture to increase expressiveness. Users join public spheres or purchase customized worlds where only invited users are permitted entry. Although these platforms provide a viable social space, they do not seem to be entirely appropriate for counseling at this time. This type of software does have the potential to greatly expand counseling service delivery options in the near future.

Other Uses of Technology in Mental Health Practice

Although online counseling is often thought of as a stand-alone paradigm, many practitioners are using technology as an adjunct to their practice. Ninety percent of counselors reported using at least some aspect of technology in their practice, from client spreadsheets and practice management systems to publishing and billing software (Haley & Vasquez, 2009). These organizational and marketing tools can enhance professional practice through saving both time and money. In fact, it would be unusual to find a "paper only" practice, because more and more mental health agencies are moving toward electronic systems. As in other areas, going paperless is not only more cost effective and "green," but data are much easier to access, manage, and analyze in digital or electronic form.

In addition to the practical applications of technology for clinical mental health counselors, there are also multiple beneficial uses for clients. Technology has provided new applications for several cognitive-behavioral techniques. Practitioners have the option to supplement their FTF work with computer technologies. Some of the ways in which clinical mental health counselors are doing this are through the use of computer-assisted techniques, web-based programs, e-mail supplemental counseling, and online self-help groups. Meta-analytic analysis has found these computer-assisted techniques to be as effective as FTF work (Cuijpers et al., 2009).

One of the most common computer-assisted techniques is the creation of unique virtual realities, described earlier (Tate & Zabinski, 2004). Consider, for example, how valuable this format could be for the practice of effective systematic desensitization. With computer application, the work can be standardized, conducted safely in the counselor's office, and has been shown to be highly effective (Tate & Zabinski, 2004). The process involves exposing clients to increasing levels of anxiety-provoking stimuli and has been used successfully with a variety of client phobias. It has been shown to be more effective for clients than merely imagining the stimuli, and it can induce more profound emotional responses. In addition, it is cost effective for the counselor, because it can be used as a substitute for in vivo treatments.

There is also some evidence of handheld computers and mobile phones being used to supplement cognitive-behavioral treatments (Preziosa et al., 2009). The computer can stimulate self-monitoring through preprogrammed reminders or to record and analyze such data to help facilitate client change. Modules walking clients through certain techniques such as relaxation exercises can also be accessed from these handheld computers and can provide a sense of security, as if the counselor is present in the client's hand (Anderson, Jacobs, & Rothbaum, 2004; Tate & Zabinski, 2004). These methods offer a way to expand treatment yet shorten in-person counseling time. An added benefit is that they extend counseling outside the session, which is the ultimate goal of cognitive-behavioral therapy (Anderson, Jacobs, & Rothbaum, 2004).

There are also increasing numbers of mental health–related software programs available. These allow practitioners to expand access to educational and self-help modalities that serve to supplement or sustain treatment. Some, such as FearFighter (www .fearfighter.com), attempt to guide clients through an interactive experience that helps them identify fear triggers, teach goal setting and anxiety management, and promote relapse prevention (Anderson, Jacobs, & Rothbaum, 2004).

There are, of course, ethical considerations. Computer applications are not intended to be a substitute for treatment and can be practitioner or corporate created and managed. If the practitioner is not the owner of the program or Web site, then he or she will need to thoroughly evaluate any program prior to encouraging client participation (Tate & Zabinski, 2004). These psychoeducational counseling modules can address issues ranging from weight loss to smoking cessation (Tate & Zabinski, 2004). Client participation can be in the form of learning units, viewing videos, blogging, online journaling, chatting with the counselor, corresponding with others participating in the unit, or any combination of the above. One example of a successful web-based program is substance abuse counseling. Clients participate in a preset program following individualized treatment that expands the continuum of care through participation in online groups and learning modules (King et al., 2009).

Another application of technology involves using the computer and Internet as an adjunct to treatment. One of the most frequently cited adjuncts to treatment is online support groups available to deal with a variety of topics from self-injury to grief (Lester, 2008/2009; Tate & Zabinski, 2004). Not only are these groups convenient, but they have also been found to be very effective, even if clients remain anonymous (Tate & Zabinski, 2004). Supplementing clinical work with clinician e-mails has also been reported as a helpful way to increase client accountability and client perception of clinician access. Counselors would need to be mindful of the parameters of e-mail-based counseling discussed in this chapter prior to engaging in this practice.

Perhaps the most promising area of technology related to mental health concerns the topic of gaming. Once thought to be purely a recreational activity, video games have seen new applications in both educational, fitness, and mental health arenas. In a literature review of video gaming in psychotherapy, Ceranoglu (2010) found increasing use of video games by practitioners. You are probably familiar with the use of board games such as checkers, backgammon, or the Ungame in counseling. In a similar fashion, video games can be used to teach social skills, improve problem solving, enhance rapport building, raise emotional awareness, assess cognitive processing, and achieve other psychosocial goals. Video games can also enhance cooperation and enthusiasm related to the therapeutic process and can be particularly effective with younger clients. Researchers are beginning to study games designed to provide or reinforce aspects of cognitive-behavioral treatment. These games usually involve a client-operated avatar navigating through decision-making and behavioral rehearsal type exercises. Although this technology is relatively new, it is expected that game developers will join with the social sciences to create more therapeutic games in the future.

In summary, technology has already affected most counselors in one way or another, and that trend is only expected to continue. Counselors are using the existing modalities previously mentioned and are also exploring new avenues such as e-coaching and radio and television counseling (Haley & Vasquez, 2009). The intersection of mental health practice and technology is one of the most exciting growth areas for this profession, and it is clear that this will only continue to influence the way counseling is practiced.

ESTABLISHING AN ONLINE COUNSELING PRACTICE

Given the popularity of the Internet and Web 2.0 technologies, clinical mental health counselors now find themselves competing with both professionals and laypersons that have a presence on the Internet. For example, one has merely to search for a mental health concern using a search engine to find not only legitimate sites sponsored by professional associations, organizations, or hospitals but also a slew of other "hits" leading to individual blogs, discussion boards, videos, and chat groups (Lester, 2008/2009). The author has found that sites produced by laypersons dispense untrained information, assessment, and advice quite freely, and their popularity is astounding. In addition, professional online counseling practices have grown from 11 in the 1990s to estimates of hundreds, or more, in existence today (Ainsworth, 2002).

What this means for the professional counselor is that people are already seeking help using the Internet, and clients will expect both their counselor and their counseling to be in line with what they see online (Green, Lawson, & Getz, 2005). Therefore, the first thing to consider when establishing an online counseling practice is to create a presence on the Web.

Web Page

One of the most common tools used by clinical mental health counselors to create a Web presence is a Web page (Haley & Vasquez, 2009). This is an effective way for counselors to advertise, and a simple search for counselors on the Internet will highlight multiple mental health practitioners that have taken advantage of the marketing potential offered by the Internet. Clinicians frequently post their counseling specialty, practice location, operating hours, directions, professional disclosure statements, pricing structure, licensure and certification information, and photos. Some practitioners have also elected to include intake and other forms online to lessen client paperwork time (Haley & Vasquez, 2009). Clinical mental health counselors may also choose to link their Web sites to other sites that offer mental health services or information. If counselors elect to do this, the ACA Code of Ethics (2005) stipulates that these links, as well as all other posted information, be frequently checked to ensure accuracy. Clinical mental health counselors should also consider ensuring their sites comply with the standards set forth by the Americans with Disabilities Act (US Department of Justice, 2007). It is imperative that counselors represent themselves accurately and adhere to all copyright and intellectual property laws (Zack, 2008). For example, counselors must be careful when adding images or documents to their Web sites, making sure to obtain proper permission for such works before using. Simply because something is available online doesn't mean it can be used on a professional Web site.

Social Networking Media

With the prevalence of online applications changing the way that people socialize, it is reasonable that clients will search for and expect to find their counselors on the popular social networking sites such as Facebook, Twitter, and LinkedIn. Recent research examining users of these social networking sites illustrates that these individuals are often seeking information, connection, and/or friendship online (Bonds-Raacke & Raacke, 2010). Self-expression and emotional expression have also been found to be motivators for users who blog extensive personal information on these sites (Fullwood, Sheehan, & Nicholls,

2009). Even though privacy issues abound with such practices, it is clear that most users still perceive that the benefits outweigh the risks; many users fail to realize that their information is realistically a public diary, which is routinely archived by the application host (Barnes, 2006). Social networking privacy has been called an illusion, and there are often stories in the news about jobs being lost when content from these sites is revealed to parties for whom it was not intended.

Although this information may or may not impact the average user of social networking sites, it is important for professional counselors to realize that these platforms are a primary way that people establish connections (Bonds-Raacke & Raacke, 2010). There has been no clear policy from counseling oversight bodies on counselor participation in social networking sites, yet evidence suggests that clinical mental health practitioners are using these sites as a way to market their practices and send traffic to their Web sites (Scarton, 2010). For those who believe these sites to be beneficial, it has been recommended that clinical mental health counselors participating in such sites disclose minimal personal information and develop a *social media policy* that restricts client "connecting" and "befriending" online (Grohol, 2010; Scarton, 2010). Keep in mind that maintaining therapeutic boundaries and preserving the therapeutic relationship should be used as guides when developing such a policy. Other social media use considerations for clinical mental health counselors include only publishing information to these sites that one would feel comfortable sharing with the general public and paying close attention to account settings that manage access to profiles (Grohol, 2010). It is generally agreed that no direct counseling services would ever be provided using these forums, given the aforementioned privacy issues.

CASE STUDY 15.1

Alicia is just beginning her counseling practice and decides that a great way to recruit clients is to use a video sharing site, such as YouTube, to upload videos related to common mental health concerns. She decides to film herself discussing common diagnoses (such as attachment disorder and childhood depression) as well as brief self-help tips related to her areas of expertise: play therapy and counseling adolescents. She believes this should be a great way to create a web presence for her counseling practice, and she looks forward to an increase in client referrals.

After uploading multiple videos, Alicia tracks the number of views and also monitors the comments viewers frequently leave her. Most are positive and thank her for the useful information. However, after a few weeks, Alicia notices some comments of a negative nature (cyberbullying) attacking her credibility and criticizing components of her videos, including her style of dress, speech pattern, and office setting. Other users post comments describing their personal situations that relate to the video topics, and these receive quick responses from other viewers. One or two individuals even describe current crises that they are experiencing.

Alicia is distressed, and somewhat hurt, by some of the negative comments. She is also disturbed by some of the personal situations that people are posting anonymously as well as the amateur advice that other users are giving viewers of her videos. She wonders whether she bears any professional responsibility and ponders several courses of action:

1. Keep the videos posted but disable and delete all comments.
2. Remove the videos, thereby deleting all comments.
3. Respond to the comments that she feels warrant professional attention.
4. Do nothing because she is not responsible for anonymous postings.

Discuss the pros and cons of each course of action. What should Alicia do?

Web-Based Practice Management Systems

There is another option for counselors considering online practice: to become a part of a web-based practice management system (e.g., counsol.com/site, www.theravive.com /therapists/e-counseling.aspx). These services match clients with counselors, who in turn conduct services using instant messaging or e-mail technology (Lester, 2008/2009). Such services are similar to practice management systems often used in FTF counseling practice to store and manage client data, organize appointments, house insurance information, and process client credit card payments, but they contain an added chat or e-mail component. The hallmark of these systems is an extensive encryption system for all data transmissions and storage.

Other web-based practice management systems take a different approach by providing counseling services to clients who remain anonymous. Client session rates for these Internet counseling services range from hourly rates of $1.60 per minute to flat rates of $1,200 for three months (LaVallee, 2006). Similar to other online communities, some of these Web sites even allow clients to select a clinical mental health counselor and then review and rate their counselor at the end of their sessions. Although it is clear that many are using these anonymous services, it is less clear whether this is counseling (as it is advertised) or simply information giving, similar to what one would find by accessing an anonymous help line.

Mental health counselors who consider joining a web-based counseling service will need to research their options thoroughly to ensure that professional, ethical, and legal standards of practice have been upheld (Zack, 2008). Many of these services appear to disown any liability and place all responsibilities on the client and counselor. Also, identity verification of clients appears to be problematic, given the anonymous or semi-anonymous nature of the work (Zack, 2008). What is perhaps most compelling about these Web sites is the idea of charging for counseling by the minute, which is most certainly a new commercial paradigm for clinical mental health service delivery.

Technological Competencies and Skills

Clinical mental health counselors considering web-based work will need to continue moving forward with their technological competencies (Green et al., 2005). Not only are technical skills needed to provide service on the Internet, but it is expected that counselors working on the Web should be able to assist clients with technological issues that may occur during the course of treatment (Murphy et al., 2008). The Association for Counselor Education and Supervision (ACES, 2007) has established a list of technological competencies that counseling students should possess upon graduation. Although these may not be comprehensive enough for entry into a web-based practice, they provide a definitive starting point. At the very least, clinical mental health counselors would need to have a complete working knowledge of any technological element that they hoped to incorporate into their practice prior to attempting usage.

Currently, clinical mental health practitioners hoping to establish an online practice can either create their own online presence or join an existing corporate managed service. Practitioners should consider cost, technological knowledge, and client needs prior to beginning any web-based work. Of paramount importance are the ethical and legal issues inherent in web-based work that must be considered prior to any online practice work. A complete discussion of these issues follows.

ETHICAL AND LEGAL ISSUES PERTINENT TO ONLINE PRACTICE

Currently, no one oversight organization for Internet-based counseling exists. As such, online counseling practice must adhere to all standards of care outlined by professional counseling associations, boards, and related organizations (Shaw & Shaw, 2006), as well as all federal, state, and local laws (Zack, 2008). Although the International Society for Mental Health Online (2000) has established some suggested principles for the practice of online mental health treatment, these have yet to become ethical guidelines (Shaw & Shaw, 2006). Many state counseling boards and other governing bodies have also been reluctant to address the issue of Internet-based counseling (Shaw & Shaw, 2006). Therefore, for practicing counselors, the most important documents related to ethical online counseling have been established by the professional counseling organizations. These guidelines not only require adherence to the full codes of ethics of the respective organizations but also give special consideration to Internet practices.

There are numerous risks accompanying online counseling practice. Although these risks may be inherent in the medium, it is the counselor's responsibility to maintain ethical practice (Shaw & Shaw, 2006). Multiple areas have been identified in the literature as posing ethical complications: (a) confidentiality and privacy issues, (b) misinterpretations arising from lack of nonverbal cues, (c) complications managing client crises, (d) difficulties verifying counselor and client identity, (e) complications with the therapeutic relationship, (f) state jurisdiction issues, and (g) lack of empirically validated techniques (Finn & Banach, 2000; King, Engi, & Poulous, 1998; McClure, Livingston, Livingston, & Gage, 2005; Shaw & Shaw, 2006).

Confidentiality and Privacy Issues

Confidentiality is a frequently cited concern with Internet-based work (Zack, 2008). Counselors need to have a strong working knowledge of the ethical guidelines on confidentiality with Internet-based transmissions (see the codes of ethics of the major professional organizations: ACA, 2005; AMCHA, 2010; NBCC, 2012a). Mental health counselors must also familiarize themselves with federal HIPAA regulations concerning the transmission and storage of confidential health information (Zack, 2008). To be able to comply with these regulations, clinical mental health counselors need a rudimentary understanding of Internet data transmission and storage.

Sophisticated encryption is now available for everything from e-mail and Internet chatting to video communication. Some software has encryption as a standard feature, whereas other programs may require an add-on to achieve the necessary security. Encryption involves instantaneous coding of information and data (Cobb, 2004). The "keys" to unlock this data are housed with the counselor and the client. There are multiple levels of encryption currently available. These encryption technologies are frequently used in online purchases, banking transactions, and other sensitive data transmissions. Although a thorough understanding of encryption and ciphering technologies is beyond the scope of this chapter, any practitioner considering Internet-based work would need to have a working knowledge of applicable software or hardware used in professional counseling practice.

Encryption protects data traveling on the Internet, yet other steps can be taken to further enhance privacy and confidentiality. Not only can any computer or user account be configured with password protection, but users can also install fingerprint identification technology to limit computer access with biometric technology. It is also recommended that all data, such as client information, be stored on an external hard drive to limit the possibility of computer virus access to sensitive information. Likewise, passwords should not be stored on computer hard drives; this is tantamount to leaving the keys in the ignition of an unlocked car.

Prior to commencing any treatment, clients need to understand not only the boundaries of confidentiality inherent in the use of technology but also the traditional limitations on confidentiality. This is a fundamental component of any informed consent and is further discussed later. Clients need to understand that even though Internet counseling may be more convenient for them, it may also mean greater threats to confidentiality.

INTERNET PRIVACY   The first step toward understanding the security limitations of Internet-based work is gaining a rudimentary knowledge of common Internet Web site practices. Internet privacy is a relevant concern for all consumers; take a few minutes and surf the Web. Visit a few Web sites, including at least one social networking site and a retail Web site. Familiarize yourself with their policies and procedures, particularly as they relate to privacy. Conduct additional Internet research if needed, and consider the following questions:

1. What does Internet privacy mean, and what should consumers reasonably expect when navigating the Web or visiting a Web site?
2. Threats to privacy abound from cookies to Trojans. What are these and what do they do?
3. Is Internet privacy the same as confidentiality? Describe how they are similar or different.
4. Did you discover anything that surprised you?

Misinterpretations Arising From Lack of Nonverbal Cues

Although misinterpretations may be part of the process in any counseling practice, some believe that these misinterpretations are more likely in an online environment due to the lack of nonverbal interaction. This might not be an issue in certain instances, such as with video-based treatment, yet some still believe that there is no substitute for being in the same room with a client. Currently, all clinical mental health counselors are trained to interpret and assess facial and visual cues, and this information can be vital to treatment (Maples & Han, 2008). For instance, a counselor doing Internet-based counseling might not notice whether a client is crying during a session and could miss other therapeutic red flags (Recupero & Rainey, 2005). To minimize this problem, counselors and clients can use certain techniques, discussed later, such as the addition of emoticons to provide emotional presence to text. Practitioners can also educate clients about the possibility of misinterpretation arising from lacking nonverbal signals and frame this as a pitfall of text-based Internet counseling. Clients would need to understand, prior to treatment, that this could be a possible limitation of the service.

Complications Managing Client Crises

It is known that clinical mental health counselors will likely encounter numerous client crises in their professional work (Newsome & Gladding, 2013). Such crises range from personal difficulties that interrupt functioning to more extreme suicidality or psychosis. Counseling with technology can potentially complicate the counselor's ability to provide effective crisis intervention and has frequently been cited as one of the greatest ethical concerns with the practice (Centore & Milacci, 2008; Zack, 2008). Some believe that those in crisis are not appropriate clients for web-based treatment, but others consider video-conferencing (and other distance modalities) an excellent way to provide much needed emergency or disaster response services (Simmons et al., 2008). Regardless, clients using Internet-based counseling need to be made aware of the parameters of the counseling relationship, including the potential impaired abilities of the counselor to respond in emergency situations and exercise duty-to-warn responsibilities (Zack, 2008).

Many counselor Web sites provide disclaimers for clients advising clients in emergency situations to seek help through a hospital emergency room or another face-to-face provider (Murphy et al., 2008; Welfel & Heinlen, 2009). Other considerations include making clients aware of time zone differences (Welfel & Heinlen, 2009) and providing them with alternative counselor contact information. At least one counseling web-based management system provides training to help clinical mental health counselors learn how to conduct appropriate crisis assessments, including gathering all client data that may be needed to report where the client resides (Murphy et al., 2008). Such assessments may require phone conversations or the addition of other service modalities to best acquire the necessary information. Interestingly, Murphy, MacFadden, and Mitchell (2008) state that reports have been made by counselors about potential child abuse only to be informed that the particular practice does not constitute abuse in the client's country. Counselors also need to familiarize themselves with state laws in the client's home state that mandate disclosure parameters. This highlights another potential complication for providing services in a virtual world.

Difficulties Verifying Counselor and Client Identity

Counselors often report discomfort with being able to verify a client's identity online. At the onset of the counseling relationship, counselors should engage in an intake process comparable to an in-person experience. This includes consent to treatment with special consideration that the client is over the age of 18 and legally able to give consent. The counselor should not proceed with counseling unless he or she is satisfied that the individual is presenting his or her identity accurately. Online identity theft is a growing concern; new viruses and e-mail scams emerge daily that threaten to steal passwords, account numbers, and other personal information. However, the presence of these threats has helped propel the computer protection industry forward. Numerous software programs have been developed to safeguard identity and protect computers from cyberattacks. Although nothing is fail-safe (either in person or online), considerable progress has been made in securing personal information, from biometric computer passwords to complex encryption software. The use of multiple passwords and encryption helps to guarantee client identity, and proponents point out that few people would be willing to pay for a service when one is pretending to be another (Murphy et al., 2008). These authors understand that this does not mean that untruths are not sometimes shared with the counselor, but they see no distinction between FTF and Internet-based work in this respect. In fact, some research has suggested that clients may disclose more honestly over the Internet because the social desirability factor is reduced when face-to-face contact is removed (Tate & Zabinski, 2004).

Complications With the Therapeutic Relationship

Both practitioners and clients have questioned the quality of the therapeutic relationship in Internet-based counseling work (Swinton, Robinson, & Bischoff, 2009). The loss of the face-to-face experience has been hypothesized to impact the core counseling relationship negatively, which then impacts treatment negatively. Although the counseling relationship may be vastly different based on the communication medium used, there is growing evidence to suggest that a sufficient relationship can be created in Internet-based counseling (Hanley & Reynolds, 2009). Researchers have also discovered that comfort and disclosure levels of clients do not appear to be affected negatively by the online relationship. In fact, there is a noted increase in disclosure and honesty among clients who seek services via the Internet (Joinson, 2001), perhaps indicating comfort with both the counseling relationship and the technology.

Jurisdiction Issues

National certifications for clinical mental health counselors are available, and all states also require licensure or the like to regulate professional counseling services. However, these mental health counselor credentials can greatly vary from state to state (Zack, 2008). Even though Internet counseling occurs in a "virtual" location suspended in time and space in certain respects, the counselor and the client are geographically located. The physical location of both counselor and counselee can create difficulties with practice compliance, particularly when the counselor and counselee reside in different states. The question arises as to where the actual counseling is occurring and therefore which state regulations have legal jurisdiction. Zack (2008) believes this to be the largest impediment to Internet-based practice.

While it appears there is no clear philosophical answer to where the counseling is occurring, there has been a slow response to this issue from counseling boards and associations (Kraus, 2004). Some current counseling providers espouse the belief that the counseling is theoretically and legally occurring where the counselor is located because that is the site of the mental health expertise (Murphy et al., 2008). A simple search quickly locates other providers who adhere to this belief, with multiple practitioners expanding their state-licensed practices to clients from varying national and international locations. Still other practitioners seem to be trying to sidestep this issue by providing anonymous service or service without any type of counseling licensure, both of which can be ethically risky practices. It has been suggested that the absence of a unifying Internet practitioner regulatory body may be partially to blame for the wide discrepancy in jurisdictional parameters among service providers (Maples & Han, 2008).

According to Shaw and Shaw (2006), professional counselors are not only bound to national standards dictated by professional associations (e.g., ACA) but also *ethically* required to comply with practice laws in their home state *as well as* the client's home state. Maheu (2009) reports that counselors and other mental health providers are also *legally* responsible to obey laws that govern all health care providers, which clearly state the practitioner must be licensed in the state in which the client resides. Many state counseling laws stipulate that practitioners providing mental health services to state residents must hold the required state credentials (e.g., New York), although exemptions may be applicable in cases of temporary practice (Zack, 2008). Counseling boards (e.g., Louisiana) are beginning to reiterate these legal positions in their licensure laws by stating that services rendered occur where the client is situated, thus making licensure in the client's state a necessity (Louisiana LPC Board of Examiners, 2012). This issue will, no doubt, become clearer in the coming years, particularly as it highlights the need for licensure reciprocity (Zack, 2008). In the meantime, clinical mental health counselors will need to ensure their conformity with all federal and state jurisdictional and practice laws governing their Internet-based practice in accordance with professional ethical standards (ACA, 2005; AMCHA, 2010; NBCC, 2012b).

Lack of Empirically Validated Techniques

Currently, there is insufficient evidence on the efficacy of Internet-based counseling (Maples & Han, 2008; Recupero & Rainey, 2005). Treatment techniques and models designed exclusively for Internet-based work are just beginning to emerge (Graff & Hecker, 2010). This lack of evidence-based practices is an issue because it could be in direct opposition to ethical standards requiring best practice. More research is clearly needed in this area, although all mental health professions have been slower to respond to this call. At present, some consider Internet-based counseling to be an experimental type of treatment due to this lack of evidence-based efficacy (Graff & Hecker, 2010). Other researchers have examined Internet counseling studies and report favorable outcomes, but recognize that the number of studies is limited (Hanley & Reynolds, 2009).

Barak, Hen, Boniel-Nissim, and Shapira (2008) conducted an extensive meta-analysis of the literature on the effectiveness of Internet-based psychotherapeutic interventions. They analyzed both web-based therapy and e-therapy studies. According to their definitions, the former involves a client entering and navigating a preprogrammed Web site for activities such as self-help, whereas the latter is more individualized and personalized treatment. Although the treatment goals and modalities of the two therapies differ, the findings indicate that web-based therapy is on average as effective as e-therapy. In addition, Barak et al.'s (2008) examination of 14 studies that compared FTF and Internet interventions in e-therapy found, on average, no difference in effectiveness. Cognitive-behavioral techniques using these methods were also found to be more effective than other theoretical approaches. These findings are very encouraging and seem to provide a preliminary empirical foundation for Internet-based work as a valid therapeutic modality.

Although the ethical requirements of counseling with technology clearly place additional responsibility on the clinical mental health counselor, standards of practice remain paramount. Unfortunately, at least one study has highlighted that few counselors are managing their online practices in such a way as to maintain compliance with one standard, the ACA Code of Ethics (Shaw & Shaw, 2006). Frequent violations found in a study of 88 counseling Web sites were related to inappropriate informed consent, frequent client abandonment, poorly stated or unstated emergency procedures, incomplete client intake information, and failure to supply alternative counselor contact information. These findings highlight the importance of maintaining ethical practice to safeguard both the welfare of clients and the integrity of the profession.

Maheu (2009) recommended several steps toward establishing an ethical Internet counseling practice. First, research and gain a firm understanding of relevant codes of ethics that establish standards of care for clinical mental health counselors, such as the AMHCA Code of Ethics (2010), which specifically addresses counseling that is assisted by technology. Second, research and verify the licensure laws in the counselor's home state as well as states of potential clients for reciprocity agreements and statutes related to required credentials. Third, contact the counselor's malpractice insurer to learn the parameters of the policy and whether or not Internet-based counseling is covered.

In summary, it is important to be mindful of the counselor's responsibility to ensure ethical and legal compliance (Shaw & Shaw, 2006). Although the risks associated with Internet-based practices may seem substantial, it does not mean that good counseling practice cannot be provided in an online environment. It is hoped that, with its increased popularity, additional guidelines and laws will be established to facilitate and regulate Internet-based counseling.

PROFESSIONAL STANDARDS AND ACCREDITATION

As previously discussed, there is no singular training or accrediting body for Internet-based counseling. However, clinical mental health counselors are expected to abide by all standards of practice outlined by the American Mental Health Counselors Association, the American Counseling Association, and other professional organizations that pertain to a counselor's professional affiliations and credentials. It has been suggested that face-to-face training is not sufficient to establish competence in an online realm (Zack, 2008). Therefore, it is highly recommended that counselors interested in web-based practice receive specialized training. Training programs that address this need are just beginning to emerge.

Perhaps the best-known one is offered through the Center for Credentialing & Education (n.d.), which offers a new credential—the Distance Credentialed Counselor (DCC)—for practitioners interested in Internet-based work. This credential can be earned with an approved master's degree in counseling, state licensure or national certification, and a 15-hour educational course. This course offers comprehensive ethical and legal information, as well as a thorough examination of best practices related to Internet counseling. This credential does not take the place of state licensure, but it does indicate that the clinical mental health counselor has received additional training in Internet-based counseling. This credential is based on NBCC's *Policy Regarding the Provision of Distance Professional Services* (2012b). It is strongly recommended that any clinical mental health counselors considering distance counseling become familiar with these policies prior to engaging in such practice.

It is expected that additional training and credentialing for Internet-based counseling will materialize in the future. Practitioners are encouraged to stay up to date through memberships in professional organizations and by familiarizing themselves with current and emerging research. A good source for recent research activity related to Internet-based counseling is the e-publication *Journal of Technology in Counseling*. Another useful way to obtain Internet counseling research and training is through professional conference attendance and online training modules.

INFORMED CONSENT AND CLIENT CONTRACTS

A key part of the therapeutic process for clinical mental health counselors is ensuring the informed consent of their clients. With Internet-based counseling, the informed consent process becomes even more paramount because clients must understand both the parameters of counseling and the further dimensions that technology adds. Clients must be able to make an educated choice about entering into an Internet-based paradigm, and this involves a thorough understanding of the risks and benefits of the process (Recupero & Rainey, 2005; Zack 2008). Practitioners should understand that counselor liability is the same for both FTF and Internet-based practice (Zack, 2008).

Recupero and Rainey (2005) describe the informed consent process as being composed of three parts: information is conveyed by the counselor, the client interprets and understands the information, and the client consents to treatment. Clinical mental health counselors must not only present the relevant information but also ensure that the client understands it. Practitioners may do this by posting informed consent documentation for clients to download and then engaging in synchronous discussions with clients to answer questions and ensure their adequate comprehension of the process. Recupero and Rainey (2005) believe this discussion element is a key component because the information concerning risks and benefits may vary from client to client depending on the presenting issue. Although some practitioners may use generic "click-wrap" technology, whereby a box is checked to indicate agreement with the process, the authors believe this is not sufficient and that clients must be able to demonstrate understanding (Recupero & Rainey, 2005). Adding a discussion element to the informed consent also helps to return it to a process-oriented practice. Having transcripts or other records of these discussions may also be beneficial for the practitioner as well as the client.

It is imperative that informed consent documentation be clear with easy-to-understand language (Recupero & Rainey, 2005). Of particular importance is client understanding of the risks unique to Internet-based practice. Zack (2008) compiled a comprehensive listing of these risks, including the following: the accidental disclosure of confidential information, technical difficulties, misunderstandings stemming from text-only interactions, and the risk that counselors might not be able to adequately intervene in the cases of emergency. He further recommended that counselors disclose that Internet-based counseling is an emerging or experimental treatment based on the limited empirical evidence. Clients need to be fully aware of these limitations and should be able to demonstrate adequate understanding of these concepts. Clients must also understand the difference between psychoeducation, a support group, and individualized counseling treatment (Recupero & Rainey, 2005). It is also possible that consent may need to be verified more than once as the treatment process unfolds and additional client information arises (Recupero & Rainey, 2005).

The required elements of informed consent for Internet practice are equivalent to FTF consent, although multiple areas must be addressed more in depth in accordance with the additional element that technology brings to the process. The most significant consideration concerns the confidentiality of information, including who may have access to counseling sessions, what encryption processes are being used, the use of session recording, and data storage parameters (ACA, 2005). Other considerations concern the possibility of technological failure, procedures to verify client identity, access issues, and emergency procedures. For a more complete listing of required informed consent elements, see Section A.12.g of the ACA Code of Ethics (2005).

VOICE FROM THE FIELD 15.1

Technology tools can be helpful additions to a clinical mental health counseling practice. In my own clinical work, I have used Skype video calls on several occasions to provide continuity of treatment with clients who were temporarily unable to attend sessions in person. Before using technology, however, it is important to consider whether the tools will best serve the client's needs and provide a high standard of care.

For example, a client with whom I had worked for several months had taken a temporary position in Europe. She was going to be living there for six months and did not want to find a new counselor for such a brief period. We agreed to use Skype for her counseling sessions on the same schedule—once per week—as we had arranged for her in-person sessions in the states. At her location, the client used her personal laptop computer with video camera and made sure she was at home alone for the duration of her 50-minute session. I conducted my session from my counseling office to better maintain privacy and confidentiality for the client. The session progressed much like our in-person sessions had, although we did periodically experience interruption due to connectivity challenges. This is one of the unpredictable aspects of using the Internet as an access point; and on more than one occasion we needed to resort to a phone call as a backup, which was a much more expensive option.

As another example, I used Skype calls to augment the termination process with a client. I had worked with an adolescent weekly for over a year, and she had stepped down to sessions only once or twice a month. At that point, I was also relocating more than two hours away. Though I did return to see her in person several times, we used Skype for the in-between sessions that were part of her continued step-down and termination process. This worked very well for this client, who had a history of trauma and very high anxiety. Using Skype allowed her to feel more connected while she was simultaneously letting go.

Skype and other videoconferencing services can be viable alternatives in the short term for counseling, but there are certainly drawbacks. Though the counselor and client do have the benefit of being able to see each other, as a general rule, the eye contact is not direct due to the offset placement of cameras and screens. Also, clinical mental health counselors cannot view other body language and movement that is often essential to fully understanding and processing topics at hand. In addition, regardless of the previous client–counselor relationship, there is an inherent disconnect that results from the use of technology. Because of these considerations, video calls and other technology-based tools should be used on a time-limited basis and only when necessary.

STEPHANIE K. SCOTT, PHD, LMHC
Core Faculty, School of Counseling and Social Service,
College of Social and Behavioral Sciences,
Walden University

ONLINE COUNSELING SKILLS

Standards of care for online counseling work are not established at this point in time (Welfel & Heinlen, 2009). This means that practitioners may be altering the modalities they use for in-person counseling for use on the Internet. This may be appropriate practice in certain cases; for example, it has been suggested that video-based counseling may not differ substantially from face-to-face counseling, so alternative techniques may not be required (Murphy et al., 2008). However, in other instances, such as text-only practice, counseling techniques developed solely for this modality are very limited, but some have been designed to facilitate rapport building and establish a stronger counselor presence.

Whereas some believe that establishing rapport and providing sound treatment are not as effective online, others have found that providing efficacious treatment is possible (Centore & Milacci, 2008). Perhaps in response to critics that believe emotional expression and therapeutic work cannot be conveyed using text alone, several techniques have been developed and reported by Murphy, MacFadden, and Mitchell (2008). These authors have created an online training program for clinical mental health counselors, and their techniques of bracketing, descriptive intimacy, and spacing and pacing are briefly described next.

Bracketing

The bracketing technique involves inserting the counselor's thoughts, feelings, and observations into text to help establish warmth and connection in the relationship. These comments are placed in brackets after text, and this technique is primarily used in e-mail counseling. Similar to the use of emoticons in e-mails, bracketing simply spells out emotional immediacy. It is obvious from the following training example that this technique requires great self-awareness and intentionality on the part of the counselor.

> The work that you have done thus far is remarkable [big smile]! It is a pleasure to work with you. I have seen so much growth on your part and have great hopes for you. So [suddenly serious], let's work harder [playful smile]—I'm counting on you!

Descriptive Immediacy

This technique is also used to establish a counselor presence. Descriptive immediacy involves the counselor describing himself or herself as well as the setting. This could include describing an office space, the weather, the counselor's reflections and observations, or other aspects that a face-to-face client might observe when entering the counselor's work space. The goal of these descriptions is to facilitate rapport building and connection between the counselor and the client. For example:

> I'm here in my office waiting for you this afternoon. The warm Texas sun shines in through the leaded glass windows. My office is just off the foyer of the building, and if you were here with me, you would be sitting comfortably in one of the two big, comfy chairs I have or perhaps on the loveseat with cushions across the back. My office is in an old home, and I suspect this room was a parlor or reading room back in the day. It has hardwood floors and a small gas fireplace for when it gets chilly.

Spacing and Pacing

In response to concerns about the flow of counseling sessions that occur via text, the technique of spacing is used to establish pace in a counseling session. As counselors typically control the counseling session's movement and direction, doing so in a virtual environment can be more challenging. Spacing and pacing involves spacing text as a way to slow down the client to ensure that material is consumed in a therapeutic way (Murphy et al., 2008, p. 455). For example, rather than simply typing to a client to slow down and review the material, a counselor can convey that message in the following way.

> Okay.
>
> Let's see.
>
> Why don't we take a moment.
>
> And look at this again?

The goal is to slow down the reader and make the information more manageable to the client.

Although Murphy et al. (2008) state that these techniques can be used with a variety of theoretical orientations, it is unclear what empirical validation, if any, has been done on each. However, at the very least, bracketing, descriptive intimacy, and spacing and pacing provide illustrations of text-based work. Practitioners should be cautioned that the enhanced disclosure that characterizes text-based work, coined "swift trust" (MacFadden, 2005), can also affect practitioners. Counselors need to be mindful of professional boundaries and be sure that self-disclosure is of an appropriate and professional nature (Gutheil & Simon, 2005).

CLIENT ASSESSMENT AND EVALUATION

Assessment has moved more readily to the online realm than have other areas of counseling. Many assessments once thought appropriate only as in-person activities have now moved online. The career counseling realm is an excellent example of this. Many career and educational assessments are now primarily computer based, and mental health assessment techniques are also beginning to migrate more and more to the computer. At the very least, most practitioners currently use the Internet for assessment by facilitating diagnosis through online searches for diagnostic information and relevant literature (Cummings, 2009). New assessment methodologies are also emerging. The two main types of online appraisal activities are clinical assessment and diagnosis and psychological testing.

Clinical Assessment and Diagnosis

Assessing clients without any FTF contact may feel like a daunting task for any practitioner. After all, practitioners rely on their clinical judgment, and not being present with a client may cause clinical mental health counselors to feel impaired and worried about missing vital diagnostic elements, leading to misdiagnosis and inaccurate assessment. This concern may be more founded with text-based interaction and much less so with synchronous audio- or video-based assessments. Although research in this area is somewhat limited, some studies have found online assessment to be equivalent to in-person clinical assessments (Emmelkamp, 2005). One example of this research was the study by Cicmins, Holloway, Coon, McClosky-Armstrong, and Min (2009) that reported the successful adaptation of the Mini-Mental State Examination using video technology. Using clients in an office, an in-person practitioner and a web-based practitioner assessed the same clients. They found agreement on 80% of assessment items and suggested these results indicated the efficacy of conducting cognitive assessments using a distance modality.

Some believe that severe pathologies (suicidal and risky behavior clients) may not be appropriate for online work. However, many mental health practitioners, particularly in psychiatry, are now routinely diagnosing via the telehealth modalities of videoconferencing and home-based video (Godleski, Nieves, Darkins, & Lehmann, 2008). Assessments, including suicide assessments and other emergency psychiatric assessments, are so frequently conducted that online protocols are being developed to ensure accuracy.

Godleski, Nieves, Darkins, and Lehmann (2008) discuss one such protocol, using extensive decision trees, that has been developed at the Veterans Health Administration hospitals. Their research also outlines multiple studies that have substantiated the efficacy of online mental health assessment as well as multiple court rulings that have upheld the legality and authenticity of the practice, even in cases where involuntary commitment was necessary. Godleski et al. (2008) note that any assessment conducted online would need to be of the same comprehensive nature as an in-person assessment. Other issues to keep in mind include having a backup means of communication (e.g., phone) should there be an Internet technical issue, particularly in cases of emergency.

One concern frequently raised by practitioners concerns the accuracy of client self-report, particularly in the absence of visual and verbal cues when conducting a text-based treatment. Although these fears are understandable, evidence suggests that clients may be more likely to self-disclose and disclose more honestly because the social desirability factor is lessened in Internet-based work (Tate & Zabinski, 2004). This can actually lead to more accurate assessment as clients more truthfully report symptomatology markers such as frequency and duration. The pressures of an FTF interaction are removed, thereby enabling the client to be more honest with himself or herself and the practitioner. Given this scenario, the question arises as to the cultural competence of the online assessment. Is it possible to provide a culturally competent clinical assessment in an online environment? Again, although research is limited in this area, at least one study found that Native American men were accurately assessed in a culturally sensitive way using videoconferencing technology, and these individuals also reported satisfaction with the online assessment process (Shore et al., 2008). Although further research needs to be conducted in this area, practitioners must always be aware of client cultural issues that may impact assessment and diagnosis, even if these dimensions are not readily apparent due to limited visual or auditory cues.

Psychological Testing

Computers have been used since the 1950s for psychological assessment, most often for scoring, interpreting, and analyzing data (Butcher, Perry, & Hahn, 2004). Test developers have expanded this range of activities to include computer-administered testing to multiple counseling realms, including clinical and diagnostic work. Perhaps the best example of this is the MMPI-2; it can be computer administered and the results used as the foundation for a DSM diagnosis with great correlation to face-to-face diagnosis (Butcher et al., 2004). In this instance, meta-analytic research has revealed that administration format had little impact on scale scores for this instrument. However, these computer-assisted tests are not Internet based but are conducted in a clinician's office using purchased testing software.

Internet-based testing is a newer paradigm, and there is considerable interest in developing this practice. Butcher, Perry, and Hahn (2004) discovered an abundance of Internet-based psychological tests but found that few adhered to professional testing guidelines or ethics. This means that much of the appraisal material readily available on the Internet has *not* been created by professional researchers or test developers but perhaps by laypersons and corporations. Clinical mental health counselors should be extremely cautious about these instruments because they have not been validated by research. Counselors also need to be warned against attempting to modify or accessing unsanctioned modifications of existing instruments for Internet application.

Butcher, Perry, and Hahn (2004) outlined several concerns inherent in Internet-based testing that need to be addressed, including test taker attitudes, the need for Internet testing norms, test validity, and test security. These issues stem from the differences between a computer-assisted, office-based administration and a home administration, specifically procedural variations and changes in testing environment. These variances threaten the validity of the instrument, although additional test development and pilot testing should be able to address these concerns. It is anticipated that clinical testing will continue to migrate into the online realm with test publishers currently researching and developing procedures to make Internet administration feasible.

There has been significant research to suggest that Internet-based psychological tests can effectively measure the same constructs as FTF assessments (Buchanan et al., 2005). For example, research has proven the efficacy of Internet-based questionnaires to screen for depression (Donker, van Straten, Marks, & Cuijpers, 2010), postpartum depression (Le, Perry, & Sheng, 2009), obsessive-compulsive symptoms (Coles, Cook, & Blake, 2007), and other psychological disorders. This research, combined with the immediacy and convenience of Internet-administered testing, ensures that this paradigm will continue to expand. The challenge continues to be the need for all Internet-based testing to adhere to established psychometric standards (Naglieri et al., 2008). This means clinical mental health counselors need to remain responsible for evaluating any appraisal instrument located on the Internet and ensuring its individual appropriateness for a client. The standards are exactly the same as if the assessment were to be conducted in person.

While there is growing evidence of the effectiveness of computer-administered psychological testing, it should be remembered that testing alone does not constitute an accurate clinical assessment (Butcher et al., 2004). Clinical mental health counselors need to use all assessment avenues available to ensure that clients receive accurate diagnosis and treatment (for a more complete discussion of best practices, please see Chapter 6). The optimum Internet-based appraisal paradigm might be a combination of synchronous discussion, via phone or Web, combined with psychological testing, such as online screening questionnaires (Donker, van Straten, Marks, & Cuijpers, 2009). Counselors considering online assessment techniques are encouraged to use multiple tools to ensure accuracy, including a synchronous element. In the future, the development of online assessment protocols would be of great benefit to counselors. Further research is also needed on culturally competent online clinical assessment as well as the development of psychometrically sound online psychological instrumentation.

Consider this vignette: you are a clinical mental health counselor in private practice in a small rural community. One of your clients is a middle-aged Asian American female client experiencing grief and loss issues surrounding her recent divorce and ongoing custody battle for her two preschool-aged children. A personal associate informs you that her friend (who happens to be your client) has voiced suicidal intent on her social networking page. Although your associate does not realize that you are her friend's counselor, she is seeking your professional advice about how to help her friend. What are you going to do? You would want to consider the following: Do you give professional advice to the friend? Do you ask to view the social networking page of your client? Do you contact your client? As you can see, there are numerous ethical considerations in this simple vignette. Ethical dilemmas do not have to be complex, but they are almost always challenging.

MULTICULTURAL IMPLICATIONS

Numerous researchers have identified certain common characteristics of online counseling consumers. For instance, younger generations of individuals (e.g., the Millennial Generation, Generation Y, and Generation Z) that have grown up in a time of expansive technology are very comfortable with services provided in this way (Delmonico & Griffin, 2008; Maples & Han, 2008). This also means that older clients from nontech generations may find Internet counseling threatening and be less likely to use this modality to seek help. In addition, at least one study discovered that men were less likely than women to seek help, either in person or online, perhaps indicating that women might be more comfortable than men with online counseling (Tsan & Day, 2007).

It has also been reported that many clients seeking Internet help possess greater access to and comfort with technology (Patrick, 2006). However, it is important for counselors to remember that not all cultures have equal access to technology (Jencius, 2003). Although a majority of US households do have broadband Internet service at home (US Census Bureau, 2009), one-third of households do not have *any* access. This means that one-third of the populace is not served effectively by this medium, and these households are likely to fall into one of several categories. First, these homes without access are more likely to have household members that are older and have a high school education or less. Also, certain cultural groups account disproportionately for homes without Internet access, including Hispanic and African American homes; almost one-half of these households do not have Internet capabilities (US Census Bureau, 2009). Even in those homes with the Internet, lack of comfort with technology and technological literacy is also a potential issue (Maples & Han, 2008; Patrick, 2006). Other individuals may need to employ modifications in order to access Internet-based care. These clients may have a disability or language barrier that prevents them from utilizing technology without modification or additional software, which can be expensive (US Department of Justice, 2007). Along those same lines, computer hardware and software, smartphones, and Internet or mobile phone access are also costly.

Internet-based counseling is subject to technological limitations because technology is prone to disruption, user error, and other complicating factors that can be extremely frustrating for both client and counselor (Maples & Han, 2008). Some clients may not be at ease communicating in this medium, and many practitioners also express discomfort with the practice (Centore & Milacci, 2008). Ethically, counselors should provide Internet-based service only if it suits the needs of the client (ACA, 2005).

Conclusion

One of the greatest qualities of the Internet is that it is never closed. Providing counseling using this medium means not only service delivery outside of traditional business hours but also greatly increased access to services (Maples & Han, 2008; McClure et al., 2005; Patrick, 2006; Shaw & Shaw, 2006). Face-to-face counseling limitations such as location, time zones, and weather constraints are suspended in the virtual world. Advocates of Internet counseling frequently cite numerous advantages of engaging in the practice.

However, the challenge cited most frequently when discussing Internet counseling is the efficacy of the practice, particularly since counseling has historically been a qualitative and face-to-face experience (Maples & Han, 2008;

Patrick, 2006). There are also multiple ethical and clinical concerns related to the ability to provide sound practice using the Internet (Centore & Milacci, 2008). Whether these concerns stem from reality or from a lack of viable research on these subjects remains a question for researchers to solve.

Although additional research is needed, it appears that Internet-based counseling practice is rapidly becoming a viable 21st-century counseling service delivery option. Mental health practitioners interested in working in this milieu are encouraged to seek additional training related to providing ethical and evidence-based treatment. Advocacy is needed on the part of counselors toward the establishment of licensure reciprocity to alleviate legal issues currently affecting Internet-based work. It is estimated these issues will be completely resolved in the next decade as the clinical mental health counseling profession more successfully integrates technology and best practices.

References

Abroms, L. C., Gill, J., Windsor, R., & Simons-Morton, B. (2009). A process evaluation of e-mail counseling for smoking cessation in college students: Feasibility, acceptability, and cost. *Journal of Smoking Cessation, 4*(1), 26–33.

Ainsworth, M. (2002). *ABC's of "Internet therapy": E-therapy history and survey.* Retrieved from http://www.metanoia.org/imhs/history.htm

American Counseling Association (ACA). (2005). *Code of ethics.* Alexandria, VA: Author.

American Mental Health Counselors Association (AMHCA). (2010). *2010 AMHCA code of ethics.* Retrieved from https://www.amhca.org/assets/news/AMHCA_Code_of_Ethics_2010_w_pagination_cxd_51110.pdf

Anderson, P., Jacobs, C., & Rothbaum, B. O. (2004). Computer-supported cognitive behavioral treatment of anxiety disorders. *Journal of Clinical Psychology, 60*(3), 253–267. doi:10.1002/jclp.10262

Association for Counselor Education and Supervision (ACES). (2007). *Technical competencies for counselor education: Recommended guidelines for program development.* Retrieved from http://files.acesonline.net/doc/2007_aces_technology_competencies.pdf

Barak, A., Hen, L., Boniel-Nissim, M., & Shapira, N. (2008). A comprehensive review and a meta-analysis of the effectiveness of Internet-based psychotherapeutic interventions. *Journal of Technology in Human Services, 26*(2/4), 109–160. doi:10.1080/15228830802094429

Barnes, S. (2006). A privacy paradox: Social networking in the United States. *First Monday.* Retrieved from http://firstmonday.org/htbin/cgiwrap/bin/ojs/index.php/fm/article/viewArticle/1394/1312

Berson, T. (2005, October 18). Skype security evaluation. *Anagram Laboratories.* Retrieved from http://www.anagram.com/berson/skyeval.pdf

Bloom, J. W., & Waltz, G. R. (2005). *Cybercounseling and cyberlearning: Strategies and resources for the millennium.* Alexandria, VA: American Counseling Association.

Bonds-Raacke, J., & Raacke, J. (2010). MySpace and Facebook: Identifying dimensions of uses and gratifications for friend networking sites. *Individual Differences Research, 8*(1), 27–33.

Booth, C. S., & Watson, J. C. (2009). Technology in counseling: Global implications for the 21st century. *North Carolina Perspectives: Journal of the North Carolina Counseling Association, 3,* 38–43.

Brennan, D. M., Holtz, B. E., Chumbler, N. R., Kobb, R., & Rabinowitz, T. (2008). Visioning technology for the future of telehealth. *Telemedicine and e-Health, 14*(9), 982–985. doi:10.1089/tmj.2008.0116

Buchanan, T., Ali, T., Heffernan, T. M., Ling, J., Parrott, A. C., Rodgers, J., & Scholey, A. B. (2005). Nonequivalence of on-line and paper-and-pencil psychological tests: The case of the prospective memory questionnaire. *Behavior Research Methods, 37*(1), 148–154.

Butcher, J. N., Perry, J., & Hahn, J. (2004). Computers in clinical assessment: Historical developments, present status, and future challenges. *Journal of Clinical Psychology, 60*(3), 331–345. doi:10.1002/jclp.10267

Center for Credentialing & Education (CCE). (n.d.). *Distance credentialed counselor.* Retrieved from http://www.cce-global.org/DCC

Centore, A. J., & Milacci, F. (2008). A study of mental health counselors' use of and perceptions of distance counseling. *Journal of Mental Health Counseling, 30*(3), 267–282.

Ceranoglu, T. A. (2010). Video games in psychotherapy. *Review of General Psychology, 14*(2), 141–146. doi:10.1037/a0019439

Ciemins, E. L., Holloway, B., Coon, P. J., McClosky-Armstrong, T., & Min, S. (2009). Telemedicine and the Mini-Mental State Examination: Assessment from a distance. *Telemedicine and e-Health, 15*(5), 476–478. doi:10.1089/tmj.2008.0144

Cobb, C. (2004). *Cryptography for dummies*. Indianapolis, IN: Wiley.

Coles, M. E., Cook, L. M., & Blake, T. R. (2007). Assessing obsessive compulsive symptoms and cognitions on the Internet: Evidence for the comparability of paper and Internet administration. *Behaviour Research and Therapy, 45*(9), 2232–2240. doi:10.1016/j.brat.2006.12.009

Council for Accreditation of Counseling and Related Educational Programs (CACREP). (2009). *CACREP accreditation manual: 2009 standards*. Alexandria, VA: Author. Retrieved from http://www.cacrep.org/doc/2009%20Standards%20with%20cover.pdf

Cuijpers, P., Marks, I. M., van Straten, A., Cavanagh, K., Gega, L., & Andersson, G. (2009). Computer-aided psychotherapy for anxiety disorders: A meta-analytic review. *Cognitive Behaviour Therapy, 38*(2), 66–82. doi:10.1080/16506070802694776

Cummings, E. J. (2009). Trends in mental health googling. *The Psychiatrist, 33*(11), 437. doi:10.1192/pb.33.11.437

Delmonico, D. L., & Griffin, E. J. (2008). Cybersex and the e-teen: What marriage and family therapists should know. *Journal of Marital & Family Therapy, 34*(4), 431–444. doi:10.1111/j.1752-0606.2008.00086.x

Donker, T., van Straten, A., Marks, I., & Cuijpers, P. (2009). A brief web-based screening questionnaire for common mental disorders: Development and validation. *Journal of Medical Internet Research, 11*(3), 1–12. doi:10.2196/jmir.1134

Donker, T., van Straten, A., Marks, I., & Cuijpers, P. (2010). Brief self-rated screening for depression on the Internet. *Journal of Affective Disorders, 122*(3), 253–259. doi:10.1016/j.jad.2009.07.013

Earnhardt, J. (2010, January 20). Chambers and Schwarzenegger announce telemedicine pilot program for California. *Cisco*. Retrieved from http://blogs.cisco.com/tag/telehealth

Emmelkamp, P. M. G. (2005). Technological innovations in clinical assessment and psychotherapy. *Psychotherapy and Psychosomatics, 74*, 336–343. doi:10.1159/000087780

Finn, J., & Banach, M. (2000). Victimization online: The down side of seeking human services for women on the Internet. *CyberPsychology & Behavior, 3*(2), 243–254. doi:10.1089/109493100316102

Frank, Z. B. (Producer & Director). (2010). *Google baby*. Tel Aviv, Israel: Home Box Office.

Friedman, T. (2005). *The world is flat: A brief history of the twenty-first century*. New York, NY: Farrar, Straus and Giroux.

Fullwood, C., Sheehan, N., & Nicholls, W. (2009). Blog function revisited: A content analysis of MySpace blogs. *CyberPsychology & Behavior, 12*(6), 685–689. doi:10.1089/cpb.2009.0138

Gates, B. (2000, December 1). Shaping the Internet age: An essay by Bill Gates. *Internet Policy Institute*. Retrieved from http://www.microsoft.com/presspass/exec/billg/writing/shapingtheinternet.mspx

Germain, V., Marchand, A., Bouchard, S., Drouin, M., & Guay, S. (2009). Effectiveness of cognitive behavioural therapy administered by videoconference for posttraumatic stress disorder. *Cognitive Behaviour Therapy, 38*(1), 42–53. doi:10.1080/16506070802473494

Godleski, L., Nieves, J. E., Darkins, A., & Lehmann, L. (2008). VA telemental health: Suicide assessment. *Behavioral Sciences & the Law, 26*(3), 271–286. doi:10.1002/bsl.811

Graff, C. A., & Hecker, L. L. (2010). Ethics and professional issues in couple and family therapy. E-therapy: Developing an ethical online practice. In L. Hecker (Ed.), *Ethics and professional issues in couple and family therapy* (pp. 243–255). New York, NY: Routledge/Taylor & Francis.

Green, R. T., Lawson, G., & Getz, H. (2005). The impact of the Internet: Implications for mental health counselors. *Journal of Technology in Counseling, 4*(1). Retrieved from http://jtc.columbusstate.edu/Vol4_1/Lawson/Lawson.htm

Grohol, J. M. (1999, April 8, rev. 3). Best practices in eTherapy: Confidentiality and privacy. *PsychCentral*. Retrieved from http://psychcentral.com/best/best2.htm

Grohol, J. (2010). Google and Facebook, therapists and clients. *PsychCentral*. Retrieved from http://psychcentral.com/blog/archives/2010/03/31/google-and-facebook-therapists-and-clients/

Gutheil, T. G., & Simon, R. I. (2005). E-mails, extra-therapeutic contact, and early boundary problems: The Internet as a "slippery slope." *Psychiatric Annals, 35*(12), 952–960.

Haley, M., & Vasquez, J. (2009). Technology and counseling. In D. Capuzzi & D. R. Gross (Eds.), *Introduction to the counseling profession* (5th ed., pp. 156–186). Upper Saddle River, NJ: Pearson Education.

Hanley, T., & Reynolds, D. (2009). Counselling psychology and the Internet: A review of the quantitative research into online outcomes and alliances within text-based therapy. *Counselling Psychology Review, 24*(2), 4–13.

International Society for Mental Health Online (ISMHO). (2000, January 9). *Suggested principles for the online provision of mental health services.* Retrieved from https://ismho.org/suggestions.asp

Jencius, M. (2003). Applications of technological advances for multicultural counseling professionals. In F. D. Harper & J. McFadden (Eds.), *Culture and counseling: New approaches* (pp. 350–362). Boston, MA: Allyn & Bacon.

Joinson, A. N. (2001). Self-disclosure in computer-mediated communication: The role of self-awareness and visual anonymity. *European Journal of Social Psychology, 31*(2), 177–192. doi:10.1002/ejsp.36

King, S., Engi, S., & Poulos, S. (1998). Using the Internet to assist family therapy. *British Journal of Guidance and Counseling, 26*(1), 43–53. doi:10.1080/03069889800760051

King, V. L., Stoller, K. B., Kidorf, M., Kindbom, K., Hursh, S., Brady, T., & Brooner, R. K. (2009). Assessing the effectiveness of an Internet-based videoconferencing platform for delivering intensified substance abuse counseling. *Journal of Substance Abuse Treatment, 36*(3), 331–338. doi:10.1016/j.jsat.2008.06.011

Kraus, R. (2004). Ethical and legal considerations for providers of mental health services online. In R. Kraus, J. Zack, & G. Strickler (Eds.), *Online counseling: A handbook for mental health professionals.* New York, NY: Elsevier Academic Press.

LaVallee, A. (2006, March 28). Chat therapy: Patients seek help via instant messaging. *The Wall Street Journal,* p. D1.

Le, H., Perry, D. F., & Sheng, X. (2009). Using the Internet to screen for postpartum depression. *Maternal and Child Health Journal, 13*(2), 213–221. doi:10.1007/s10995-008-0322-8

Lester, D. (2008/2009). The use of the Internet for counseling the suicidal individual: Possibilities and drawbacks. *Omega: Journal of Death and Dying, 58*(3), 233250. doi:10.2190/OM.58.3.e

Louisiana LPC Board of Examiners. (2012). *Louisiana's position on Internet counseling.* Retrieved from http://www.lpcboard.org/position_statements_Internet_Counseling.htm

MacFadden, R. (2005). Souls on ice: Incorporating emotion in web-based education. In R. MacFadden, B. Moore, M. Herie, & D. Schoech (Eds.), *Web-based education in the human services: Models, methods, and best practices* (pp. 79–98). Binghamton, NY: Haworth Press.

Maheu, M. M. (2009, July 7). Online counseling and professional licensure? *Telehealth.* Retrieved from http://telehealth.org/blog/online-counseling-and-professional-licensure/

Mallen, M. J., Vogel, D. L., & Rochlen, A. B. (2005). The practical aspects of online counseling: Ethics, training, technology, and competency. *The Counseling Psychologist, 33*, 776–818. doi:10.1177/0011000005278625

Maples, M. F., & Han, S. (2008). Cybercounseling in the United States and South Korea: Implications for counseling college students of the millennial generation and the networked generation. *Journal of Counseling & Development, 86*(2), 178–183.

McClure, R. F., Livingston, R. B., Livingston, K. H., & Gage, R. (2005). A survey of practicing psychotherapists. *Journal of Professional Counseling: Practice, Theory & Research, 33*(1), 35–46.

Murphy, L., MacFadden, R., & Mitchell, D. (2008). Cybercounseling online: The development of a university-based training program for e-mail counseling. *Journal of Technology in Human Services, 26*(2/4), 447–469. doi:10.1080/15228830802102081

Naglieri, J. A., Drasgow, F., Schmit, M., Handler, L., Prifitera, A., Margolis, A., & Velasquez, R. (2008). Psychological testing on the Internet: New problems, old issues. In D. N. Bersoff (Ed.), *Ethical conflicts in psychology* (pp. 306–312). Washington, DC: American Psychological Association.

National Board for Certified Counselors (NBCC). (2012a). *National Board for Certified Counselors (NBCC) code of ethics.* Retrieved from http://www.nbcc.org/Assets/Ethics/NBCCCodeofEthics.pdf

National Board for Certified Counselors (NBCC). (2012b). *Policy regarding the provision of distance professional services.* Retrieved from http://www.nbcc.org/Assets/Ethics/NBCCPolicyRegardingPracticeofDistanceCounselingBoard.pdf

Newsome, D. W., & Gladding, S. T. (2013). *Clinical mental health counseling in community and agency settings* (4th ed.). Upper Saddle River, NJ: Pearson Education.

O'Reilly, T. (2005, September 30). What is Web 2.0: Design patterns and business models for the next generation of software. *O'Reilly.* Retrieved from http://oreilly.com/web2/archive/what-is-web-20.html

Patrick, P. K. S. (2006). Providing counseling online: Because we "can," should we? *VISTAS 2006 Online.* Retrieved from http://counselingoutfitters.com /Patrick2.htm

Preziosa, A., Grassi, A., Gaggioli, A., & Riva, G. (2009). Therapeutic applications of the mobile phone. *British Journal of Guidance & Counselling, 37*(3), 313–325. doi:10.1080/03069880902957031

Recupero, P. R., & Rainey, S. E. (2005). Informed consent to e-therapy. *American Journal of Psychotherapy, 59*(4), 319–331.

Riva, G. (2009). Virtual reality: An experiential tool for clinical psychology. *British Journal of Guidance & Counselling, 37*(3), 337–345. doi:10.1080 /03069880902957056

Scarton, D. (2010, March 20). Google and Facebook raise new issues for therapists and their clients. *Special to The Washington Post.* Retrieved from http:// www.sponsoravillage.ca/just-citizens/controversial -issues/google-and-facebook-raise-new-issues-for -therapists-and-their-clients/

Shaw, H. E., & Shaw, S. F. (2006). Critical ethical issues in online counseling: Assessing current practices with an ethical intent checklist. *Journal of Counseling & Development, 84*, 41–53.

Shernoff, M. (2000). Cyber counseling for queer clients and clinicians. *Journal of Gay & Lesbian Social Services, 11*(4), 105–111. doi:10.1300/J041v11n04_06

Shore, J. H., Brooks, E., Savin, D., Orton, H., Grigsby, J., & Manson, S. M. (2008). Acceptability of telepsychiatry in American Indians. *Telemedicine and e-Health, 14*(5), 461–466. doi:10.1089/tmj.2007.0077

Simmons, S., Alverson, D., Poropatich, R., D'Iorio, J., DeVany, M., & Doarn, C. (2008). Applying telehealth in natural and anthropogenic disasters. *Telemedicine and e-Health, 14*(9), 968–971. doi:10.1089 /tmj.2008.0117

Stelter, B. (2008, November 24). Web suicide viewed live and reaction spur a debate. *The New York Times.* Retrieved from http://www.nytimes .com/2008/11/25/us/25suicides.html

Stummer, G. (2009). Client contact styles in online therapeutic work via e-mail. *Counseling Psychology Review, 24*(2), 14–23.

Swinton, J. J., Robinson, W. D., & Bischoff, R. J. (2009). Telehealth and rural depression: Physician and patient perspectives. *Families, Systems, & Health, 27*(2), 172–182. doi:10.1037/a0016014

Tate, D. F., & Zabinski, M. F. (2004). Computer and Internet applications for psychological treatment: Update for clinicians. *Journal of Clinical Psychology, 60*(2), 209–220. doi:10.1002/jclp.10247

Tsan, J. Y., & Day, S. X. (2007). Personality and gender as predictors of online counseling use. *Journal of Technology in Human Services, 25*(3), 39–55. doi:10.1300/J017v25n03_03

US Census Bureau. (2009). *Households with a computer and Internet use: 1984 to 2009.* Retrieved from http://www.census.gov/population/www /socdemo/computer/2009.html

US Department of Justice. (2007). *Website accessibility under Title II of the ADA.* Retrieved from http:// www.ada.gov/pcatoolkit/chap5toolkit.htm

Van Diest, S. L., Van Lankveld, J. J. D. M., Leusink, P. M., Slob, A. K., & Gijs, L. (2007). Sex therapy through the Internet for men with sexual dysfunctions: A pilot study. *Journal of Sex & Marital Therapy, 33*(2), 115–133.

Welfel, E. R., & Heinlen, K. T. (2009). Ethics in technology and mental health. In M. A. Cucciare & K. R. Weingardt (Eds.), *Using technology to support evidence-based behavioral health practices: A clinician's guide* (pp. 267–290). New York, NY: Routledge.

Young, K. S. (2005). An empirical examination of client attitudes towards online counseling. *CyberPsychology & Behavior, 8*(2), 172–177. doi:10.1089/cpb .2005.8.172

Zack, J. S. (2008). How sturdy is that digital couch? Legal considerations for mental health professionals who deliver clinical services via the Internet. *Journal of Technology in Human Services, 26*(2/4), 333–359. doi:10.1080/15228830802097083

INDEX